THE LAW OF DEVELOPMENT COOPERATION

Development interventions are agreed by states and international organizations which administer public development funds of huge proportions. They have done so with debatable success, but, unlike the good governance of recipients, the rules applying to donors have hitherto received little scrutiny. This analysis of the normative structures and conceptual riddles of development cooperation argues that development cooperation is increasingly structured by legal rules and is therefore no longer merely a matter of politics, economics or ethics. By focusing on the rules of development cooperation, it puts forward a new perspective on the institutional law dealing with the process, instruments and organization of this cooperation. Placing the law in its theoretical and political context, it provides the first comparative study on the laws of foreign aid as a central field of global public policy and asks how accountability, autonomy and human rights can be preserved while combating poverty.

PHILIPP DANN is a professor at the Justus Liebig University Giessen, Germany, where he holds the Chair for Public and Comparative Law.

CAMBRIDGE INTERNATIONAL TRADE AND ECONOMIC LAW

As the processes of regionalization and globalization have intensified, there have been accompanying increases in the regulations of international trade and economic law at the levels of international, regional and national laws.

The subject matter of this series is international economic law. Its core is the regulation of international trade, investment and cognate areas such as intellectual property and competition policy. The series publishes books on related regulatory areas, in particular human rights, labor, environment and culture, as well as sustainable development. These areas are vertically linked at the international, regional and national level, and the series extends to the implementation of these rules at these different levels. The series also includes works on governance, dealing with the structure and operation of related international organizations in the field of international economic law, and the way they interact with other subjects of international and national law.

Series Editors

Dr Lorand Bartels, *University of Cambridge*
Professor Thomas Cottier, *University of Berne*
Professor William Davey, *University of Illinois*

Books in the series

Trade Policy Flexibility and Enforcement in the WTO: A Law and Economics Analysis
Simon A.B. Schropp

The Multilaterization of International Investment Law
Stephan W. Schill

The Law, Economics and Politics of Retaliation in WTO Dispute Settlement
Edited by Chad P. Bown and Joost Pauwelyn

Non-Discrimination in International Trade in Services: "Likeness" in WTO/GATS
Nicolas Diebold

Processes and Production Methods (PPMs) in WTO Law: Interfacing Trade and Social Goals
Christiane R. Conrad

African Regional Trade Agreements as Legal Regimes
James Thuo Gathii

The Law and Politics of WTO Waivers: Stability and Flexibility in Public International Law
Isabel Feichtner

Public Services and International Trade Liberalization: Human Rights and Gender Implications
Barnali Choudhury

International Organizations in WTO Dispute Settlement: How Much Institutional Sensitivity?
Marina Foltea

Domestic Judicial Review of Trade Remedies: Experiences of the Most Active WTO Members
Müslüm Yilmaz

WTO Disciplines on Subsidies and Countervailing Measures: Balancing Policy Space and Legal Constraints
Dominic Coppens

The Law of Development Cooperation: A Comparative Analysis of the World Bank, the EU and Germany
Philipp Dann

THE LAW OF DEVELOPMENT COOPERATION

A Comparative Analysis of the World Bank, the EU and Germany

PHILIPP DANN

CAMBRIDGE
UNIVERSITY PRESS

CAMBRIDGE
UNIVERSITY PRESS

University Printing House, Cambridge CB2 8BS, United Kingdom

One Liberty Plaza, 20th Floor, New York, NY 10006, USA

477 Williamstown Road, Port Melbourne, VIC 3207, Australia

314-321, 3rd Floor, Plot 3, Splendor Forum, Jasola District Centre, New Delhi - 110025, India

79 Anson Road, #06-04/06, Singapore 079906

Cambridge University Press is part of the University of Cambridge.

It furthers the University's mission by disseminating knowledge in the pursuit of education, learning and research at the highest international levels of excellence.

www.cambridge.org
Information on this title: www.cambridge.org/9781107020290

First published in German by Mohr Siebeck 2012

First published in English by Cambridge University Press 2013

A catalogue record for this publication is available from the British Library

Library of Congress Cataloging in Publication data
Dann, Philipp.
[Entwicklungsverwaltungsrecht. English.]
The law of development cooperation : a comparative analysis of the world bank, the EU and Germany / Philipp Dann ; translated from the German by Andrew Hammel.
pages cm
Includes bibliographical references and index.
ISBN 978-1-107-02029-0 (hardback)
1. Administrative law. 2. Economic development–International cooperation. 3. Economic development projects. 4. International organization. I. Title.
K3400.D3613 2013
343.07′4–dc23
2013015862

ISBN 978-1-107-02029-0 Hardback

CONTENTS

ACKNOWLEDGMENTS

This book has evolved in two stages. It was written first in German and served as my Habilitationsschrift, i.e. the study qualifying to teach law in Germany, submitted at the Goethe University in Frankfurt and published in German.[1] It was then substantially revised, updated and translated into English. During both stages I benefited greatly from a wide range of support and encouragement - financially, intellectually, and personally, for which I am immensely grateful.

My studies were sponsored by a research fellowship from the German Research Council as well as a Schumpeter Fellowship from the Volkswagen Foundation. This helped finance my research at the Georgetown University Law Center in Washington D.C. and the Max Planck Institute for Comparative Public Law and International Law in Heidelberg where most of the book was written.

While these scholarships allowed me to visit and work at various places, it is the people I met there who helped sharpen the focus of my inquiries, enabling them to deepen and finally be completed. I am greatly indebted to a variety of interlocutors, first of all, at the institutions that I am writing about, in particular to Evarist Baimu, Soe Lin, Galina Mikhlin, Rudy Van Puymbroek, Maurizio Ragazzi, Vikram Raghavan, Andrės Rigo Surreda, Martin Serrano (all World Bank), Sandra Bartelt, Bernd Martenczuk, Frank Hoffmeister (all EU) as well as Susanne Dorasil, Julia Lehmann, Anja Pauls and Albrecht Stockmayer (German Ministry of Economic Cooperation and Development as well as Deutsche Gesellschaft für internationale Zusammenarbeit / GIZ). I benefited immensely from their profound knowledge as well as from their openness towards my questions and patience with my slow grasp.

While understanding the institutions is one thing, moulding this information into a book is quite another. For this, I was helped through

[1] Entwicklungsverwaltungsrecht. Theorie und Dogmatik des Rechts der Entwicklungszusammenarbeit, Mohr Siebeck, Tuebingen 2012.

encouragement and critical reflection at various stages, in particular from Jürgen Bast, Jochen von Bernstorff, Francesca Bignami, Armin von Bogdandy, Dany Bradlow, Gabriele Britz, Edith Brown Weiss, Brun-Otto Bryde, Kevin Davis, Christoph Engel, Matthias Goldmann, Leonie Guder, Stefan Kadelbach, Markus Kaltenborn, Benedict Kingsbury, Nico Krisch, Thilo Marauhn, Christoph Möllers, Niels Petersen, Rainer Pitschas, Kirsten Schmalenbach, Eberhard Schmidt-Aßmann, Christoph Schönberger, Richard Stewart and Ingo Venzke. I am deeply indebted to all of them. The study was presented at various workshops and conferences and I thank the participants for their reactions including those at the Center of Advanced Studies Berlin (Wissenschaftskolleg), the Collaborative Research Center on 'Governance in Areas of Limited Statehood', the Max Planck Institute for Comparative Public Law and International Law in Heidelberg, the Max Planck Institute for Research on Collective Goods in Bonn, the New York University School of Law, the Viterbo Global Administrative Law Seminar and the Research Training Group 'Constitutionalism beyond the State' in Berlin.

I wish to extend special thanks to my collaborators in the Schumpeter Research Group: Marie von Engelhardt, Michael Riegner, Julia Sattelberger, Leonie Vierck and Martin Wortmann. First in Heidelberg and then in Giessen they inspired and encouraged, corrected and complemented my work in a unique and truly marvellous way.

With the translation into English, a second birth of this book took place. This was made possible by generous funding again from the Volkswagen Foundation. Andrew Hammel took upon himself the surely arduous task of transferring German legalese into readable English - and I am very grateful for the wonderful job he did. I also want to thank Gwyneth Schulz, Jasmin Schnitzer and Jan Martin Vogel at my chair in Giessen for their very valuable research assistance and ready support in finalizing the manuscript, as well as Kim Hughes, Richard Woodham, Sue Browning and Jenny Slater for organizing a smooth production at and with Cambridge University Press.

Finally and most of all, I want to thank Sheetal Asrani. Her intellectual and emotional support, patience, encouragement and love despite the hardships that this endeavour also entailed have been the lifeline for this undertaking. It is quite simple: this book would in many ways have been inconceivable without her.

TRANSLATORS' ACKNOWLEDGMENTS

I would like to thank my research assistant Laura Jael Schweitzer for her help locating sources and researching potential approaches to some of the challenging translation tasks this book presented. I would also like to thank the faculty and staff of the Law Faculty at Heinrich-Heine University Düsseldorf for helpful suggestions and support.

Andrew Hammel

Introduction

A Concept and context of development cooperation law

Development cooperation contains a promise. It is the promise of a global community, based on solidarity and built in fairness. But the reality of development cooperation often looks different. It poses seemingly insolvable problems of global governance in a postcolonial world. This book analyzes the normative structures and conceptual riddles of development cooperation. Yet, it is not a book about ethics or politics, but about law.

The book argues that development cooperation is increasingly structured by legal rules and hence no longer merely a matter of politics, economics or ethics. In focusing on the rules of development cooperation, it puts forward a specific and still rather unusual perspective. It is less concerned with good governance or the rule of law, which have become key words in development policy and legal approaches to the field. Instead, it focuses on the institutional law of development cooperation and hence on the rules dealing with the process, instruments and organization of this cooperation. The present study points out that development interventions are agreed upon by states and international organizations, which administer public development funds of huge proportions – with debatable success. But the rules applying to these organizations have hardly been a matter of interest. While good governance of recipients is discussed intensively, the good governance of donors is not. This book is intended to help close that gap.

Charting the law of development cooperation faces specific challenges. More than in almost any other field, it involves international actors (like the World Bank or the European Union) as much as national donors and recipients. The relevant laws organize an inherently inter- and trans national cooperation and are set simultaneously though separately on an international and national level. The law of development cooperation is therefore fundamentally an area of international or even global (administrative) law.

It requires vertical comparison of national, supranational and international legal regimes to understand it. To this end, this study will focus on the relevant laws of the World Bank, the EU and Germany. It contends that beyond the obvious differences in the nature of these actors, there is convergence in the general structures of their laws organizing and structuring development cooperation. To understand converging as well as divergent elements and to analyze them critically is the aim of this book.

How to approach this task? As mentioned, the law of development cooperation is still a rather unusual topic. Section A of this introductory chapter will therefore first provide the context. In fact, it will describe three layers of context: it will briefly describe the history of development cooperation to understand where theory and policy debate stand today (I.1), it will introduce alternative legal approaches to explain what lawyers have focused on so far (I.2) and it will end by recognizing an institutional turn in development studies that supports the thesis and approach of this study (I.3). In a second step, the chapter will sketch the central thesis of this book: the proposal to focus on the *transfer* of official development assistance (ODA) as the abstract link between actors, procedures and instruments in order to develop a more systematic and transparent understanding of the normative standards of development cooperation (II.1). It will explain in more detail the definition of ODA in order to sketch the scope of inquiry (II.2) and, equally fundamental, explain the focus on ODA through the basic and political understanding of the development process (II.3). Finally, remarks on the approach and structure of the study (III) and on the language of development (IV) will complete this first main section.[1] The second main section will then examine some of the challenges and chances of studying the law of development cooperation, seeking first to explain why this area has been somewhat neglected (B.I), and then to propose that the inquiry into the law of development cooperation could bring positive benefits (B.II).

I. Development cooperation and the law: three layers of context

1. A (very) brief history of development cooperation

It is not by coincidence that development cooperation as a policy field and as organizational structure emerged at the beginning of the Cold

[1] A terminological remark at the very outset: there is no set notion for development cooperation itself. Instead, *foreign aid*, *foreign assistance*, *development aid*, *development assistance* and *development cooperation* are often used interchangeably among English-speaking writers. See *infra* A.IV. This study prefers the notion of development cooperation but will also use the other terms.

War. The two central powers of the time, the USA and the USSR, were keen to bind potential allies to their ideological camps. The USA as an imperial power without a colonial past was especially eager to create a new system of cooperation between richer and poorer nations, not least to advertise its own approach (and business) to the world.[2] Soon, new institutional structures emerged. The International Bank of Reconstruction and Development, created in 1945 and quickly baptized as "World Bank," began to provide funds not just to the war-torn states of Europe, but also to newly independent developing countries; the European Economic Community, created in 1958, immediately established a development fund; and also states created new institutions to deal with the field (the USA in 1960, Germany in 1961), if they did not have existing colonial structures (such as the UK and France). Altogether the new policy field was greeted with great optimism. The process of decolonization produced a large number of states which were eager to shed their colonial structures and reform their economic and political systems. The UN, which soon had a majority of new states, declared the 1960s as the "development decade." Last but not least, the financial dimension of the new field grew dramatically. By the early 1970s, public donors invested almost US$10 billion per year.[3]

And yet, early on, development cooperation met with criticism. Soon the organizational structures were considered too complex and often prone to disguised pressures and illegitimate influence.[4] Doubts were also raised on the effects that aid flows would have. Against the eager optimism of the modernization theory, though often without larger empirical data, critics questioned the overall and the long-term effect of aid. Before long, development cooperation was perceived by some as the "aid business" that rather served advisors and industries in the North instead of people in the South.[5] After the political momentum of the independent

[2] On the continuities between development and previous colonial policies, see G. Rist, *The History of Development: From Western Origins to Global Faith*, 3rd edn (London: Zed Books, 2008).

[3] The history of development policy, development theory and their connection to the institutional structures of development cooperation will be analyzed in detail in Part I below. On the great optimism of the early phase, see *infra* Ch 1.A. The numbers are based on OECD data, see http://stats.oecd.org/ (last visited July 2013).

[4] L. Pearson, *Partners in Development: Report of the Commission on International Development* (New York: Praeger, 1969); H. Morgenthau, "A Political Theory of Foreign Aid," *The American Political Science Review*, 56 (1962), 301–9 at 301, 302.

[5] E.g. G. Hancock, *Lords of Poverty: The Power, Prestige, and Corruption of the International Aid Business* (London: Macmillan, 1989); W. Easterly, *The White Man's Burden: Why the West's Efforts to Aid the Rest Have Done So Much Ill and So Little Good* (New York: Penguin Press, 2006).

Third World movement broke in the mid to late 1970s, the dynamism of donors also waned. The 1980s are often considered a lost decade for development efforts. When the Cold War ended and the ideological confrontation disappeared, the development system plunged into a deep crisis. Its legitimacy and purpose were at stake.

With the late 1990s, however, a renaissance and a rethinking began. The increasingly perceived globalization created a new sense for the possibility of inter- and transnational interaction, soon epitomized in the notion of global governance. A re-energized political will to engage with the problem of poverty manifested itself in the Millennium Development Goals (MDG) of 2000; the 2005 G-8 Summit at Gleneagles made development the main topic at this forum for the first time ever. There was also a renewed interest in theories of justice which became a much more widely discussed topic of social theory, philosophy and international relations.[6]

Parts of this renewed theoretical interest were deeply critical. The notion of development was profoundly questioned, not least by authors from the Global South. Inspired by postcolonial studies, a new school of post-development thinkers emerged. They laid bare the terminological violence that the language of development (and underdevelopment) can contain and rejected fundamentally the concept of development and its idea that the Global South should copy Northern paths.[7] Politically, however, foreign aid proved to be a promising tool for rising powers. New donors like China and Brazil emerged, using aid to build new alliances and offering new forms of aid.[8] Moreover, a variety of new flexible

[6] J. Rawls, *A Theory of Justice* (Harvard University Press, 1971); J. Rawls, *Justice as Fairness: A Restatement*, edited by Erin Kelly (Harvard University Press, 2001); J. Rawls, *The Law of Peoples* (Cambridge: Harvard University Press, 1999); T. Franck, *Fairness in International Law and Institutions* (Oxford University Press, 1995); M. Walzer, *Spheres of Justice: A Defense of Pluralism and Equality* (New York: Basic Books, 1983); C. Beitz, *Political Theory and International Relations* (Princeton University Press, 1979); M. Walzer (ed.), *Toward a Global Civil Society* (New York, Oxford: Berghahn Books, 1995); A. Sen, *Development as Freedom* (New York: Knopf, 1999); C. Barry and T. Pogge (eds.), *Global Institutions and Responsibilities: Achieving Global Justice* (Malden: Blackwell, 2005).

[7] A. Escobar, *Encountering Development: The Making and Unmaking of the Third World* (Princeton University Press, 1995); W. Sachs (ed.), *The Development Dictionary: A Guide to Knowledge as Power* (London: Zed Books, 1992); S. Pahuja, *Decolonising International Law: Development, Economic Growth, and the Politics of Universality* (Cambridge, New York: Cambridge University Press, 2011). For more on this, see *infra* Ch 2.B.IV.

[8] L. Song and J. Golley (eds.), *Rising China: Global Challenges and Opportunities* (Acton: ANU E Press, 2011); S.-L. de John Sousa, *Brazil as an Emerging Actor in International Development Cooperation: a Good Partner for European Donors?*, German Development Institute – Briefing Paper 5/2010 (2010). Available at www.die-gdi.de (under Publications – Briefing papers) (last visited July 2013).

instruments and private channels for aid emerged, which provided alternatives to the aid by Northern states and international financial institutions that had dominated the development system. One result of these new dynamics was a sharpened sense of self-critique among the "traditional" donors, which increasingly recognized the necessity of reforming the system, indicated by an intense discussion on "aid effectiveness."

2. Alternative approaches to law and development

A central element of this renaissance and reform was the law. Since the 1990s, law has been (again) ascribed a central role in development processes. The discussion returned to approaches that had already shaped the early, optimistic phase of development in the 1950s and 1960s. At that time, two schools had emerged that understood the role of law in the development process in very different yet complementary and telling ways: the francophone (and rather visionary) school of *international development law* (or *droit international du développement*) and the *law and development* movement, led by anglophone (and rather pragmatic) scholars.[9]

The (francophone) international development law sought to rewrite the principles of public international law in a way that would strengthen the idea of substantive justice and benefit developing countries. This rather deductive and teleological approach originated with the French scholar Michel Virally, who, in the context of decolonization in 1965, criticized the inadequacy of the principle of sovereign equality in light of the immense economic and social inequalities between developing and industrialized nations.[10] Virally and soon others proposed a broad review of the principles, institutions and rules of interstate relations which affected developing nations in order to reinterpret them toward the overall goal of fostering development and a more just world order.[11] This goal and the final aim of international law should become the dominant maxim of interpretation.

[9] An unusual collection of essays of both approaches can be found in P. Slinn and F. Snyder (eds.), *International Development Law* (Abingdon: Professional Books, 1987).

[10] M. Virally, "Vers un droit international du développement," *Annuaires français de droit international*, 11 (1965), 3–12 at 3, 4.

[11] G. Abi-Saab, "The Third World and the Future of the International Legal Order," *Revue égyptienne de droit international*, 29 (1973), 27–66; M. Flory, *Droit international du développement* (Paris: Presses universitaires de France, 1977); K. Hossain, *Legal Aspects of the New International Economic Order* (London, New York: Frances Pinter, 1980); A. Pellet, *Le droit international du développement*, 2nd edn (Paris: Presses universitaires de France, 1987); G. Feuer and H. Cassan, *Droit international du développement*, 2nd edn (Paris: Dalloz, 1991); M. Bedjaoui (ed.), *International Law: Achievements and Prospects*

A principal instrument of this approach is the idea of a duality of norms, in which, depending on context, industrialized and developing countries are not treated identically, but rather according to specific rules which do justice to their respective positions.[12] Another important tool soon became the right to development that was first formulated in the 1970s.

The more anglophone school of law and development, by contrast, pursued a more pragmatic or perhaps bottom-up approach and concentrated primarily on the role of *municipal* law as an instrument of development. Scholars here asked how domestic law rather than international law could foster development. They concentrated on the analysis of the laws of developing countries, often using comparative law or legal-transfer approaches to reform indigenous legal orders.[13] The central question of this approach, that is, how (domestic) law influences development processes, is also studied in other areas of legal study, particularly legal anthropology and sociology. They are a central part of a broader approach to law and development.[14]

While both schools lost momentum in the late 1970s and 1980s, probably because the grand visions and high hopes proved somewhat naïve,[15]

(Paris, Dordrecht: Martinus Nijhoff Publishers, 1991) (presenting many of the relevant scholars); a precursor to this approach is W. Friedmann, "The Changing Dimensions of International Law," *Columbia Law Review*, 62 (1962), 1147–65 at 1147; M. Bulajic, *Principles of International Development Law*, 2nd edn (Dordrecht: Martinus Nijhoff, 1993).

[12] For overviews see M. Kaltenborn, "Entwicklungs- und Schwellenländer in der Völkerrechtsgemeinschaft: Zum Stand und zu den Perspektiven des Entwicklungsvölkerrechts," *Archiv des Völkerrechts*, 46 (2008), 205–32 at 228, 229; A. Mahiou, "International Law of Development," in R. Wolfrum (ed.), *Max Planck Encyclopedia of Public International Law* [online edition] (Oxford University Press, 2008–) at margin no. 1.

[13] D. Trubek, "Toward a Social Theory of Law: An Essay on the Study of Law and Development," *Yale Law Journal*, 82 (1972), 1–50 at 1; M. Galanter, "The Modernization of Law," in M. E. Weiner (ed.), *Modernization: The Dynamics of Growth* (New York: Basic Books, 1966), pp. 153–65 at p. 153; also A. Seidman (ed.), *Making Development Work: Legislative Reform for Institutional Transformation and Good Governance* (The Hague: Kluwer Law International, 1999). For a retrospective see D. Trubek, "The 'Rule of Law' in Development Assistance: Past, Present and Future," in D. Trubek and A. Santos (eds.), *The New Law and Economic Development: A Critical Appraisal* (Cambridge, New York: Cambridge University Press, 2006), pp. 74–94 at p. 74.

[14] F. von Benda-Beckmann, "'Recht und Entwicklung' im Wandel," *Verfassung und Recht in Übersee*, 41 (2008), 295–308; F. von Benda-Beckmann, K. von Benda-Beckmann and M. Wiber, *Changing Properties of Property* (New York: Berghahn Books, 2006); M. Hobart (ed.), *An Anthropological Critique of Development: The Growth of Ignorance* (London: Routledge, 1993).

[15] D. Trubek and M. Galanter, "Scholars in Self-Estrangement: Some Reflections on the Crisis in Law and Development Studies in the United States," *Wisconsin Law Review*, 55

they both are enjoying a renaissance today. An offspring of the international development law school (though without the overall teleology and without the francophone dominance) can be seen in the variety of studies that address the position of developing countries in various fields of international law. They describe an established practice of dual norms, particularly in international economic,[16] environmental[17] and intellectual property law.[18] Law reform in developing countries, the hallmark of the law and development movement, was rediscovered by development agencies in the 1990s, first and especially by the World Bank as the largest and often agenda-setting donor organization. A political system based on the rule of law was now considered a necessary precondition for successful development. Broader still, responsive or good governance, human rights and the rule of law became key words in development policy. Though there is a sharp ideological divide between today's approach to law reform (by the World Bank and other donors) and the early activists in the 1960s,[19] these issues have become a prime area of legal research.[20]

One perspective, however, has hardly been analyzed – and that is the law governing the institutions and processes of development cooperation, and hence the object of the present study. There are only a few studies on

(1974), 1062–101 at 1062; J. Gardner, *Legal Imperialism: American Lawyers and Foreign Aid in Latin America* (Madison: University of Wisconsin Press, 1980); resumptive B.-O. Bryde and F. Kübler (eds.), *Die Rolle des Rechts im Entwicklungsprozess* (Frankfurt am Main: Metzner, 1986) (therein, cf. especially the correspondent article by Bryde, pp. 9–36).

16 J. Faundez and C. Tan (eds.), *International Economic Law, Globalization and Developing Countries* (Cheltenham: Edward Elgar, 2010); M. Krajewski, *Wirtschaftsvölkerrecht* (Heidelberg: C.F. Müller, 2009), p. 264; C. Thomas and J. P. Trachtman (eds.), *Developing Countries in the WTO Legal System* (Oxford University Press, 2009).

17 M. Bothe, "Environment, Development, Resources," *Recueil des Cours*, 318 (2005), 323–516 at 337; P. Cullet, *Differential Treatment in International Environmental Law* (Aldershot: Ashgate, 2003).

18 K. C. Shadlen, S. Guennif, A. Guzmán and N. Lalitha (eds.), *Intellectual Property, Pharmaceuticals, and Public Health: Access to Drugs in Developing Countries* (Cheltenham: Edward Elgar, 2011); H. Hestermeyer, *Human Rights and the WTO: The Case of Patents and Access to Medicines* (Oxford University Press, 2007); J. Watal, *Intellectual Property Rights in the WTO and Developing Countries* (London, The Hague, Boston: Kluwer Law International, 2001).

19 D. Trubek and A. Santos (eds.), *The New Law and Economic Development: A Critical Appraisal* (Cambridge University Press, 2006); especially D. Kennedy, "The 'Rule of Law,' Political Choices and Development Common Sense," pp. 95–173 at p. 95.

20 See the recently founded *The Hague Journal on the Rule of Law*; J. Gillespie and P. Nicholson, *Law and Development and the Global Discourses of Legal Transfers* (Cambridge University Press, 2012); M. Riegner and T. Wischmeyer, "'Rechtliche Zusammenarbeit' mit Transformations- und Entwicklungsländern als Gegenstand öffentlich-rechtlicher

the law of the World Bank – often by staff lawyers, only recently also by external observers.[21] The legal regime of the EU's development cooperation has been examined only from time to time.[22] Lately, the role of human rights has caught lawyers' attention.[23] The legal aspects of German development cooperation or that of other national donors, on the other side, have only rarely been addressed,[24] and there are almost no comparative studies of the field.[25]

Forschung," *Der Staat*, 50 (2011), 436–68 at 436; Y. Dezalay and B. Garth (eds.), *Lawyers and the Rule of Law in an Era of Globalization*, Law, Development and Globalization (Oxon, New York: Routledge, 2011); M. J. Trebilcock and R. J. Daniels, *Rule of Law Reform and Development: Charting the Fragile Path of Progress* (Cheltenham: Edward Elgar, 2008); K. Dam, *The Law-Growth-Nexus: The Rule of Law and Economic Development* (Washington, DC: Brookings Institution Press, 2006); T. Carothers (ed.), *Promoting the Rule of Law Abroad: In Search of Knowledge* (Washington, DC: Carnegie Endowment for International Peace, 2006).

21 See especially the writings of *general counsels* such as Aron Broches, Ibrahim Shihata and Andres Rigo Sureda. Among the more regularly writing external observers of the Bank are Daniel Bradlow, John Head, David Hunter or Sabine Schlemmer-Schulte. For an up-to-date overview of the law of the World Bank, see D. Bradlow and D. B. Hunter (eds.), *International Financial Institutions and International Law* (Alphen aan den Rijn: Kluwer Law International, 2010); also H. Cissé, D. Bradlow and B. Kingsbury (eds.), *International Financial Institutions and Global Legal Governance*, The World Bank Legal Review (Washington, DC: World Bank Publications, 2012), vol. III.

22 J. Becker, *Die Partnerschaft von Lomé: Eine neue zwischenstaatliche Kooperationsform des Entwicklungsvölkerrechts* (Baden-Baden: Nomos, 1979); K. R. Simmonds, "The Fourth Lomé Convention," *Common Market Law Review*, 28 (1991), 521–47 at 521; B. Martenczuk, "From Lomé to Cotonou: The ACP-EC Partnership Agreement in a Legal Perspective," *European Foreign Affairs Review*, 5 (2000), 461–87 at 461. For a recent overview see S. Bartelt and P. Dann (eds.), *Entwicklungszusammenarbeit im Recht der Europäischen Union – The Law of EU Development Cooperation: Europarecht-Beiheft Nr. 2* (Baden-Baden: Nomos, 2008).

23 F. Hoffmeister, *Menschenrechts- und Demokratieklauseln in den vertraglichen Außenbeziehungen der Europäischen Gemeinschaft*, Beiträge zum ausländischen öffentlichen Recht und Völkerrecht (Berlin/ New York: Springer, 1998), vol. CXXXII; C. Pippan, *Die Förderung der Menschenrechte und der Demokratie als Aufgabe der Entwicklungszusammenarbeit der Europäischen Gemeinschaft*, Europäische Hochschulschriften (Frankfurt: Peter Lang Verlag, 2002), vol. MMMCDLX; L. Bartels, *Human Rights Conditionality in the EU's International Agreements* (Oxford University Press, 2005); S. Skogly, *The Human Rights Obligations of the World Bank and the International Monetary Fund* (London: Cavendish, 2001); M. Darrow, *Between Light and Shadow: The World Bank, the International Monetary Fund and International Human Rights Law* (Oxford: Hart Publishing, 2003).

24 For more information see P. Dann, *Entwicklungsverwaltungsrecht* (Tübingen: Mohr Siebeck, 2011); S. Burall, J. M. White and A. Blick, *The Impact of U.S. and U.K. Legislatures on Aid Delivery*, Economic Policy Paper Series 09. Available at www.odi.org.uk/resources/docs/4652.pdf (last visited July 2013); and *infra* Ch 3.A.II.

25 The few exceptions are S. Rubin (ed.), *Foreign Development Lending – Legal Aspects: The Papers and Proceedings of a Conference of Legal Advisors of National and International Development Lending and Assistance Agencies* (Leiden: Sijthoff, 1971); M. Pellens,

What is missing, then, is both a more general understanding of the legal field and a more detailed (and critical) analysis of the intricacies of their legal regimes. We know fairly little about how development interventions are legally agreed upon or whether and which legal criteria govern the distribution of funds. While there are studies on the human rights obligations of donors, there is precious little analysis on the accountability of development organizations (or recipients) or on the legal nature of conditionality. Development cooperation is fundamentally a political process of choice and contestation and yet we know little of the legal rules governing the participation in development processes or whether and how the autonomy and sovereignty of recipients and donors are brought into a balance. As put earlier: while the good governance of aid recipients is a major topic of legal research, the good governance of donors is not.

The present study will try to help close this gap by providing a comparative analysis of the institutional law of the World Bank, the EU and Germany and by proposing general principles for critically comparing and analyzing these laws. In this approach the study profits from the more general institutional turn in development studies – and the discussion on global governance.

3. The institutional turn in development studies

A third layer of context that is important for this study is what I would call "the institutional turn" in development studies. This turn has been taken first by economists as well as political scientists. In economics, development studies used to be a field for development economists studying the economic causes of poverty and ways to overcome them.[26] Since the 1990s, however, scholars of institutional economics have discovered the field too. Some of them pick up on the law reform idea, follow the World Bank's lead and study the economic effects of good governance and rule of law in developing countries.[27] Others, however, are more directly relevant to this study, focus their attention on the structures of the delivery of

Entwicklungshilfe Deutschlands und der Europäischen Union: Rechtsgrundlagen und Verfahren bei der finanziellen und technischen Zusammenarbeit, Berliner Europa-Studien (Berlin: Verlag Dr. Köster, 1996), vol. IV; A. Rigo Sureda, "The Law Applicable to the Activities of International Development Banks," *Recueil des Cours*, 308 (2004), 13–249 at 13; Skogly, Human Rights Obligations; early, and compiling rather than arranging: W. Friedmann, G. Kalmanoff and R. F. Meagher, *International Financial Aid* (New York: Columbia University Press, 1966).

26 M. P. Todaro and S. C. Smith, *Economic Development*, 10th edn (Harlow: Addison Wesley, 2009); P. Collier, *The Bottom Billion: Why the Poorest Countries Are Failing and What Can Be Done About It* (Oxford University Press, 2007).

27 S. Voigt, *Institutionenökonomik* (Munich: W. Fink Verlag, 2002).

aid – and hence on the development administrations themselves. A number of thoughtful studies now analyze the incentive structures within development organizations, examine the strategic interplay of donors and recipients in aid relationships, or present experimental approaches to a marketplace for the delivery of aid.[28]

The same new interest in the institutional structures of development cooperation can be observed in the political sciences. Scholars here too have discovered the role of institutions and procedures in the delivery of aid. These scholars are more inclined to produce qualitative studies that take into account more of the concrete political, social and ideological circumstances of individual actors as well as being shaped by history and culture.[29] Political scientists are often also more attentive to the power structures that underlie development policy and global governance structures in general.[30]

This institutional turn is not just a matter of academic discourse, but has also shaped the policy discussions. Since the 2000s, the idea of "aid effectiveness" has been predominant here. In particular, the Organisation for Economic Co-operation and Development (OECD), supported by the World Bank, has driven a process to establish common standards that would reform how donors deliver aid and cooperate with recipients – strengthening a focus on results, demanding alignment with recipient country systems of accounting and administration and calling for more mutual accountability.[31]

Lawyers are only slowly taking the institutional turn. They do so generally on the coat tails of the larger discussion on global governance.[32] A

[28] T. Killick, *Aid and the Political Economy of Policy Change* (London: Routledge, 1998); C. C. Gibson, A. Krister, E. Ostrom and S. Shivakumar, *The Samaritan's Dilemma: The Political Economy of Development Aid* (Oxford University Press, 2005); B. Martens, U. Mummert and P. Murrell (eds.), *The Institutional Economics of Foreign Aid* (Cambridge University Press, 2002); W. Easterly (ed.), *Reinventing Foreign Aid* (Cambridge: MIT Press, 2008); E. Duflo and A. Banerjee, *Poor Economics: A Radical Rethinking of the Way to Fight Global Poverty* (New York: PublicAffairs, 2011).

[29] C. Lancaster, *Foreign Aid: Diplomacy, Development, Domestic Politics* (University of Chicago Press, 2007); L. Whitfield (ed.), *The Politics of Aid: African Strategies for Dealing with Donors* (Oxford University Press, 2009); N. van de Walle, *African Economies and the Politics of Permanent Crisis* (Cambridge University Press, 2001).

[30] A. Leftwich, *States of Development: On the Primacy of Politics in Development* (Cambridge: Polity Press, 2000); C. J. Bickerton, P. Cunliffe and A. Gourevitch (eds.), *Politics Without Sovereignty: A Critique of Contemporary International Relations* (University College London Press, 2007); G. Hyden, "After the Paris Declaration: Taking on the Issue of Power," *Development Policy Review*, 26 (2008), 259–74.

[31] On this discussion and process, see *infra* Ch 2.C.III.1.

[32] The origins of the term global governance can be traced back to J. N. Rosenau, "Governance, Order, and Change in World Politics," in J. N. Rosenau and E.-O. Czempiel (eds.), *Governance Without Government: Order and Change in World Politics*

signature article by Benedict Kingsbury, Nico Krisch and Richard Stewart proposed to understand the emerging structures as a global administration that should be studied with recourse to the tools and sensitivities of (domestic) administrative law.[33] This implies a fundamentally different perception of international institutions not only as forums of states but as actors in themselves and affecting life and liberties of individuals. This approach was reinforced by others who stressed the public character of global governance and the ensuing need for accountability.[34] At the same time, the study of international organizations and international institutional law generally surged – analyzing the law-making powers of international institutions,[35] explaining the historical shifts in powers and procedures,[36] scrutinizing human rights,[37] conceptualizing the legal

(Cambridge University Press, 1992), pp. 1–29, at p. 1; J. Kooiman, "Findings, Speculations and Recommendations," in J. Kooiman (ed.), *Modern Governance: New Government-Society Interactions* (Thousand Oaks, CA: Sage Publications, 1993), pp. 249–62, at p. 249. The concept of "governance" was borrowed from economics, see O. E. Williamson, "The Economics of Governance: Framework and Implications," *Zeitschrift für die gesamte Staatswissenschaft*, 140 (1984), 195–223, at 195. Global governance is marked by four elements. First, it recognizes the importance of international institutions, but highlights the relevance of actors and instruments that are of a private or hybrid nature, as well as of individuals; governance is not only an affair of public actors. Second, global governance marks the emergence of an increased recourse to informality: many institutions, procedures and instruments escape the grasp of established legal concepts. Third, thinking in terms of global governance means putting as much emphasis on actors as on structures and procedures. Last, but not least, as is obvious from the use of the term "global" rather than "international," global governance emphasizes the multi-level character of governance activities: it tends to overcome the division between international, supranational and national phenomena.

33 B. Kingsbury, N. Krisch and R. Stewart, "The Emergence of Global Administrative Law," *Law and Contemporary Problems*, 68 (2005), 15–62, at 15.

34 A. von Bogdandy, P. Dann and M. Goldmann, "Developing the Publicness of Public International Law: Towards a Legal Framework for Global Governance Activities," *German Law Journal*, 9 (2008), 1375–400; see also P. Dann and M. von Engelhardt, "Legal Approaches to Global Governance and Accountability: Informal Lawmaking, International Public Authority, and Global Administrative Law Compared," in J. Pauwelyn, R. Wessel and J. Wouters (eds.), *Informal International Lawmaking* (Oxford University Press, 2012).

35 J. Pauwelyn, "Informal International Lawmaking: Framing the Concept and Research Questions," in Pauwelyn, Wessel and Wouters, *Informal International Lawmaking*; A. von Bogdandy, P. Dann and M. Goldmann, "Developing the Publicness of Public International Law," in A. von Bogdandy, R. Wolfrum, J. von Bernstorff, P. Dann and M. Goldmann (eds.), *The Exercise of Public Authority by International Institutions: Advancing International Institutional Law* (Heidelberg: Springer, 2010), pp. 3–32; J. E. Alvarez, *International Organizations as Law-Makers* (Oxford University Press, 2005).

36 J. von Bernstorff, "Procedures of Decision-Making and the Role of Law in International Organizations," *German Law Journal*, 9 (2008), 1939–64.

37 M. Koskenniemi, "Human Rights Mainstreaming as a Strategy for Institutional Power," *Humanity*, 1 (2010), 47–58; G. A. Sarfaty, "Why Culture Matters in International

contours of indicators and evaluations as new instruments of global governance[38] and generally providing a much more contextualized and critical understanding of these actors.[39]

Global governance studies signify the institutional turn. They signal that institutions matter. They are driven – beyond their curiosity about new phenomena – by a double impulse. On one side, they have a neo-functionalist or managerial streak. They perceive the ordering of the emerging world society as a big puzzle that is challenging but can be managed by well-thought-out technocratic processes. On the other side, they are driven by a concern about legitimacy and accountability.[40] New actors come with new powers that are so far hardly matched by the structures to hold them accountable. This may refer to human rights concerns with regard to the actions of the Security Council, to the power to influence public policy debates through OECD studies, or – closer to home – to the pressuring of developing states by the International Monetary Fund or the World Bank.

This leads back to development cooperation and its law. Lawyers and legal analysis are slowly taking note of this field. The present study makes a conceptual proposal on how to approach and study the relevant laws – in order to make the exercise of public authority more transparent and ultimately more effective and accountable.

II. *The law of development cooperation: a conceptual proposal*

1. The law of development cooperation as the law of ODA transfer

Development cooperation is a central field of global public policy. The abject poverty of millions of people is an inacceptable stain on human

Institutions: The Marginality of Human Rights at the World Bank," *American Journal of International Law*, 103 (2009), 647–83.

[38] B. Kingsbury, K. Davis and S. E. Merry, "Indicators as a Technology of Global Governance," *Law and Society Review*, 46 (2012), 71–104; A. von Bogdandy and M. Goldmann, "Die Ausübung internationaler öffentlicher Gewalt durch Politikbewertung: Die PISA-Studie als Muster einer neuen völkerrechtlichen Handlungsform," *Heidelberg Journal of International Law*, 69 (2009), 51–102.

[39] See, for example, J. Klabbers, *An Introduction to International Institutional Law*, 2nd edn (Cambridge University Press, 2009); P. Sands and P. Klein, *Bowett's Law of International Institutions*, 6th edn (London: Sweet & Maxwell, 2009); B. Chimni, "International Institutions: An Imperial Global State in the Making," *European Journal of International Law*, 15 (2004), 1–37. A good indicator for the popularity of a research field is also the existence of specialized journals. Since 2004, there has been for the first time a journal dedicated only to this field, the *International Organizations Law Review*.

[40] A. Reinisch, "Securing the Accountability of International Organizations," *Global Governance*, 7 (2001), 131–49; R. W. Grant and R. O. Keohane, "Accountability and

society. There is no doubt that cooperation is an important path to change it. Such cooperation normally takes place through institutions – of different size and nature, of different vision and approach, but through institutionalized action. As just described, economists and political scientists have started to provide a fuller understanding of the structures and impact of such institutions.

The expertise of lawyers should be an important complement to studies of other disciplines. Lawyers are the technicians of power. They are especially qualified to dissect and explain the competences, decision-making procedures and substantive standards that apply here – and hence to provide transparency and a more systematic understanding. Law is naturally counterfactual but is the only accepted way to lay down the ideals and normative standards that everybody should comply with. Legal knowledge is therefore also central to ensure the accountability and legitimacy of development-aid institutions.

The study of the law of development cooperation faces hurdles, though. There is no lack of relevant legal rules, but a more systematic approach faces a challenge in the immense diversity of actors, instruments and themes in the field. There is bilateral and multilateral cooperation, financial and technical assistance, project aid and budget support – not to mention the various fields like health policies or governance reform.[41] Can such a diverse field really be analyzed from *one* angle and be thought of as one field of inquiry?

The present study indeed proposes to think of the law of development cooperation as *one* field. It suggests understanding it in reference to one shared element. This element is the transfer of development funds. The present study focuses on public funds and hence the category of ODA, as it is defined by the OECD. Development cooperation law can thus be described as the *law of ODA transfers*. It regulates the procedures, instruments and criteria by which ODA is awarded. This transfer normally takes place in four stages: first, the general budget decision to reserve a certain amount for ODA expenses; second, the multi-year planning for one country or one sector; third, the negotiation and agreement on a concrete development intervention (project or program); and fourth, the implementation of such intervention. Accompanying this process or

Abuses of Power in World Politics," *American Political Science Review*, 99 (2005), 29–43.

[41] For an overview see P. Haslam, J. Schafer and P. Beaudet (eds.), *Introduction to International Development: Approaches, Actors, and Issues* (Oxford University Press, 2009); T. Rauch, *Entwicklungspolitik* (Braunschweig: Westermann, 2009).

retrospectively checking, there are also rules on oversight and accountability. The law of development cooperation concerns and covers all of these phases and angles – alongside laws on the basic institutional set-up of donors, recipients and rule-making in this area. In that sense, one could say there is a "constitutional law" of development cooperation, covering the mandates, competences, institutional structures and rule-making powers of the relevant institutions, and an "administrative law" of development cooperation, covering the process described above with all its procedures, instruments and criteria of ODA transfer.[42]

There are two more elements to the conceptual proposal. These concern less the scope of inquiry than the approach to how to study it. First, given the immense variety and the need for transparency to better understand the field, it is necessary to study the relevant laws in a comparative perspective. Such an approach seems somewhat evident, though (of course) hardly mandatory to develop a more systematic overview and understanding of the field.[43] And second, this study proposes to use general principles as normative yardsticks and comparative guideposts for the study of development cooperation law. It argues that we can formulate such sector-specific principles on the basis of general international law and the concrete provisions in the field. Such an approach, however, also assumes that there is a certain autonomy of the law and legal standards of development cooperation.

The following sections will explain the concrete meaning of ODA, clarify further the scope of inquiry, and explain its focus on public institutions.

2. The definition of ODA and the scope of inquiry

Like any definition, this focus on the transfer of ODA has an excluding as well as an including function. In order to understand its scope better, one has to take a closer look at its characteristics.

The category of ODA was introduced in 1969 by the OECD and is recognized today as the central definition of what is accepted as publicly funded development aid.[44] Its definition is based on a guideline which is

[42] On the constitutional law of development cooperation, see *infra* Chs 3 and 4 and on the administrative law of development cooperation, see *infra* Chs 5–9.

[43] For a more extensive explanation of the specific approach of this study, see *infra* Intro.A.III.

[44] For more information on ODA in general, cf. OECD webpage www.oecd.org/dac/stats/; R. C. Riddell, *Does Foreign Aid Really Work?* (Oxford University Press, 2007), pp. 18–21. As early as 1970, the UN General Assembly used the category of ODA to put the claim for

adopted and routinely updated by the OECD's Development Co-operation Directorate.[45] It is addressed primarily to those ministers of OECD member states who report to the OECD on their countries' financial engagement in development. The guideline defines what expenditures can be registered as ODA as opposed to other international financial transfers.[46] The guideline and its ODA category aim to establish an objective and transparent standard for defining what activities will count as development aid and are thus "praiseworthy." Given its wide currency, the definition is central to creating a mutual understanding of the scope and financial volumes of development aid.

ODA is defined as "flows of official financing administered with the promotion of the economic development and welfare of developing countries as the main objective, and which are concessional in character with a grant element of at least 25 per cent."[47] The definition is built on three elements. First, it relates to the transfer of *public* funds. This excludes all development financing based on private donations or investments. ODA also includes only transfers by government entities, although these can include all kinds of local or central governments or agencies. Donor institutions fit this definition in all cases. Recipients and cooperation partners are generally developing countries, but may also be private organizations in these countries.[48]

The second component of the definition of ODA relates to the instrument, which is "assistance." This comprises all financial or monetary assistance, loans or grants that have at least a 25 percent grant character. This component highlights the financial basis of all development cooperation programs: a rather banal, yet nevertheless crucial component of development cooperation. The grant element can be present in all the various formats and structures that development aid can be delivered in (which are meticulously listed in the guideline). ODA as cooperation

financial support for developing countries into more precise terms. In Resolution 2626 (XXV), October 24, 1970, the GA for the first time called for economically advanced countries to progressively increase the "official development assistance to the developing countries" and to exert their "best efforts to reach a minimum net amount of 0.7 per cent of its gross national product at market prices by the middle of the Decade" (marginal number 43). This claim has remained unchanged until today.

45 OECD, *DAC Statistical Reporting Directives*, DCD/DAC(2010)40/REV1 of November 12, 2010 (2010). Available at www.oecd.org/investment/aidstatistics/38429349.pdf (last visited September 2012). On the OECD as an institution, see *infra* Ch 3.C.I.

46 These transactions fall into the category "Other Official Flows" (OOF), cf. ibid., margin no. 38.

47 Ibid., margin no. 35.

48 Ibid., margin no. 33. For more on the selection of countries, see *infra* Ch 3.B.

can take the form of project assistance or program assistance.[49] It can fund both technical and financial cooperation.[50] It can also be used for humanitarian or disaster relief, or to reduce indebtedness.[51] Finally, the category includes the entire spectrum of development activities, as long as they require financing and contain a grant element. Thus, although the province of development cooperation law is broad, the ODA definition can be used to separate it from other development-related instruments that are not based on financial transfers. Examples of the latter include, for instance, market-access regulations or patent law regimes. The ODA definition is, therefore, critically important, since it distinguishes the law of development cooperation from other legal fields involved with support for developing countries – such as trade law, patent law, the law of migration, or environmental law.

Finally, the category of ODA includes the "D" for development and thus specifies the goal which a payment must serve. The definition covers only those payments which serve the principal goal, in the words of the ODA Guideline, of the "economic development and welfare of developing countries." Clearly, this is the soft underbelly of the definition, so to speak, since the concept of development is malleable, somewhat holistic and not very precise.[52] The purpose of the definition is primarily to exclude payments which are clearly aimed at purposes unrelated to development: in particular, military assistance or purely private profit-oriented activities. Export credits and other investment-related support payments, thus, do not fall under the definition of ODA.[53]

The ODA category has been discussed intensely in past years. One notable recent discussion revolved around whether security is a precondition

[49] "Project aid" refers to activities that are temporally, spatially and functionally limited and aimed at achieving concrete outputs; "program aid," on the other hand, means either the pooling of different projects in a sector-wide approach (so-called SWAp) or a grant to a state's general budget (called budget support). For more information, see Riddell, *Does Foreign Aid Really Work?*, pp. 18, 195; F. Nuscheler, *Entwicklungspolitik: Lern- und Arbeitsbuch*, 5th edn (Bonn: Dietz, 2004), p. 472; more on these instrument and their legal structures, *infra* Part III, Chs 6 and 7.

[50] For technical cooperation, see OECD, *DAC Statistical Reporting Directives*, Line I.A.1.2.

[51] On debt relief: ibid., Line I.A.1.6; on humanitarian aid or civil protection: ibid., Line I.A.1.5. Even though humanitarian aid and debt relief can, at least in part, be encompassed by the ODA definition and are therefore the subject matter of the law of development cooperation, the present analysis will not cover these topics. However, one could define humanitarian aid, in principle, as a special area of the law of development cooperation containing specific provisions (regarding EU law, cf. Art. 214 TFEU).

[52] On the concept of development in this study, see *infra* Intro.A.III. On different concepts of development, see *infra* Ch 1.A.IV, B.I.2, Ch 2.A.I.2 and specifically Ch 2.B.I–IV.

[53] See OECD, *DAC Statistical Reporting Directives*, Line II. and margin no. 39.

for development, which would argue in favor of classifying security-related measures as ODA. These are indeed now recognized as ODA, albeit in a limited fashion.[54] There is also the discussion of whether ODA as a category might become irrelevant because of new donors that do not report to the OECD or are members of it (such as China) and a generally changed landscape of development financing, in which ODA captures only a very limited extent of aid flows.[55]

Despite these important discussions, this study chose to focus on the transfer of ODA. It did so for a variety of reasons that will be explained now.

3. The political nature of development as reason for the ODA focus

By concentrating on the transfer of ODA, this study chooses a particular focus. It concentrates on *public* actors and *public* funds. This focus grows out of an understanding of the development process as inherently contested and political in nature – and the recognition of the qualitative difference between private and public actors and their respective responsibilities in such a political process. This nutshell-credo has to be explained.

In the past sixty years, various concepts of development have been formulated. Many of them understand "development" primarily as an economic process and economic goal that is better achieved by technical experts than by (corrupt/short-sighted/ …) politicians.[56] The underlying understanding here is different. The present study understands development as an ongoing process of taking decisions about public choices

[54] Cf. ibid., margin no. 39. On this discussion, including the recommendation to create an additional reporting category for "Official Security Assistance" M. Brzoska, "Extending ODA or Creating a New Reporting Instrument for Security-related Expenditures for Development?" *Development Policy Review*, 26 (2008), 131–50, at 131; on the role of security issues in the context of development cooperation more generally N. Woods, "The Shifting Politics of Foreign Aid," *International Affairs*, 81 (2005), 393–409, at 393; see also ECJ, Case-91/05 (ECOWAS), Judgment May 20, 2008.

[55] J.-M. Severino and O. Ray, *The End of ODA: Death and Rebirth of a Global Public Policy*, Working Paper Number 167 (2009). Available at www.cgdev.org/files/1421419_file_End_of_ODA_FINAL.pdf (last visited September 2012); T. Chahoud, *Southern Non-DAC Actors in Development Cooperation*, German Development Insitute – Briefing Paper 13/2008 (2008). Available at www.die-gdi.de (last visited July 2013); making a similar argument, C. Zilla and C. Harig, *Brasilien als "Emerging Donor": Politische Distanz und operative Nähe zu den traditionallen Gebern*, German Institute for International and Security Affairs – SWP-Studie S 07/2012 (2012), pp. 9; 19. Available at www.swp-berlin.org/fileadmin/contents/products/studien/2012_S07_zll_harig.pdf (last visited July 2013). On the changing landscape, *infra* at Ch 2.C.III.

[56] On these and other concepts of development, see *infra* Ch 1, and Ch 2.A.

to better the lives of those affected by poverty. It assumes that any decision about development interventions involves a wide variety of interests which – naturally – conflict. These may be the interests of political parties in the developing country, of the government of this country, of the citizens concretely affected by the interventions or the societal process generally – and also interests of donors, to name just a few, very generic groups. "Development" is not, as postcolonial writers have rightfully stressed, a universal value. It involves a constant grappling with options that have profound implications for the people involved. It is about public choices and about the power to decide. It is about using and creating freedoms. It is political.[57]

Such a political concept of development is ultimately also a procedural concept of development. People concerned have to decide what option should be taken. A specific characteristic of development cooperation is, however, that such decisions take place in the context of often sharp imbalances of power. Recipients are normally economically and often politically weaker than donors. Affected citizens are often less influential than politicians, if not wholly excluded. Decision-making in development cooperation is therefore frequently in danger of undermining the autonomy and free will of the participants. They can be pressurized, they can lack information or the resources to fully explore the implications. It is therefore of central concern how the procedures of participation are designed. Formally structured and transparent procedures are necessary to mitigate imbalances; fair procedural rights are essential.[58]

Besides this political and procedural understanding of development, this study is based on recognition of the qualitative difference between private and public actors and their respective responsibilities. It assumes that public actors spending public funds are ultimately faced with different and higher standards of accountability and legitimacy than private donors or corporate actors – for good reasons: only public actors have the authority to unilaterally determine the fate of citizens. It is the special feature of public authority that comes with special obligations.[59] Also, public authorities act in the name of the public and the society that has constituted them. They do not serve a corporate goal or private

[57] The postcolonial perspective was recently laid out by Pahuja, *Decolonising International Law*; also A. Anghie, "Time Present and Time Past," *New York University Journal of International Law and Politics*, 32 (2000), 243–90. The participatory, political and liberal understanding of the process draws on Sen, *Development as Freedom*.

[58] M. Koskenniemi, "Constitutionalism as Mindset: Reflections on Kantian Themes About International Law and Globalization," *Theoretical Inquiries in Law*, 8 (2007), 9–36.

[59] Bogdandy, Dann and Goldmann, "Developing the Publicness of Public."

foundation's charter but have to be guided by the common interest of the public.[60] Public authorities spending public funds are therefore accountable to their societies and their collective understanding of how and on what to spend funds. This involves a broad variety of viewpoints. And this normally differs from, for example, a shareholder's logic. Finally, public actors are also accountable to different legal standards from private actors. Human rights, the rule of law and democracy are standards that apply first of all to public actors who normally (and not just traditionally) have much more power than private ones.

Some might argue that the difference between public and private actors has little meaning in a policy field that is more about spending money and creating opportunities than curbing freedoms. Public power, so they could argue, has to be tamed and limited only where individuals' freedom is at stake. However, it would be misconceived to flatten the difference between public and private-law standards in development assistance out of such thought. First of all, as will become apparent throughout this study, development cooperation does not just create opportunities but can also threaten individual freedom and collective autonomy. Involuntary resettlements or environmental risks are often part of development projects; not every developing country that needs funds agrees with, for example, the EU development policies that it is still pressed to implement. But, in any case, it would be too narrow to apply public law only in those constellations in which freedoms are curbed. There is also a public responsibility for enabling freedom that has to comply with general standards of law. Public power and authority have to be held in check in curbing as well as enabling settings.

The public law approach taken here might also be questioned from the perspective of global governance studies. For many, the structures of global governance merely show that it does not make sense any more to distinguish between private and public, since they cooperate and merge in many instances. The insights of the global governance debate are certainly not lost on this study.[61] But these insights do not erase the differences just mentioned between public and private. On the contrary, an

[60] M. Loughlin, *Foundations of Public Law* (New York: Oxford University Press, 2010), p. 10; M. Loughlin, "Reflections on 'the Idea of Public Law'," in E. Christodoulidis and S. Tierney (eds.), *Public Law and Politics: The Scope and Limits of Constitutionalism* (Aldershot: Ashgate, 2008), pp. 47–68 at p. 49; C. J. Friedrich, *Constitutional Government and Democracy* (Boston: Ginn, 1950), p. 247; K. Loewenstein, *Political Power and the Government Process* (University of Chicago Press, 1957).

[61] It responds, actually, to all four characteristics of global governance mentioned above (fn. 32), as it considers more informal norms of interaction (including soft law and internal laws of international organizations), pays attention to procedural structures

approach that too easily equates private and public structures of cooperation runs the risk, as do many global governance approaches, of favoring a managerial approach to global affairs, promoting a rather technocratic understanding of structures and processes. In choosing a focus on public actors and public funds, this approach wants to avoid the dangers of such an understanding.

All of this is not to say that deepened legal analysis of other, private forms of development finance is not necessary. On the contrary, it would certainly also benefit the understanding and further reform of ODA transfer if we knew more about private forms of development cooperation and other forms of development finance. In that sense, I see great value in the recent proposal to study *all* legal rules concerning the financing of development, as put forward by Kevin Davis.[62] Such a law of development finances would analyze ODA transfers, but also private flows (such as remittances), commercial flows (such as loans offered at market rates) as well as the rules pertaining to foreign direct investment or sovereign debt – and hence would stress the immense variety of forms, actors and terms of financing.[63]

This proposal finds especially strong justification in view of the immense increase in instruments and actors that have provided financing for development purposes since the late 1990s. While public donors like the Western states or the World Bank clearly dominated the field until then, ever since we can observe the emergence of new donors not subscribing to the ODA definition (like China), private or hybrid public-private actors, or simply an abundance of new modes and instruments of financing such as micro-finance or climate-change financing.[64]

of rule-making and to the (global) multi-level interplay between donors, recipients and others, and considers the role of individuals and non-governmental organizations in these processes.

62 K. E. Davis, *"Financing Development" as a Field of Practice, Study and Innovation*, New York University Institute for International Law and Justice Working Paper 2008/10 (New York, 2008), p. 174. Available at http://papers.ssrn.com/sol3/papers.cfm?abstract_id=1341291 (last visited July 2013); Cissé, Bradlow and Kingsbury, *International Financial Institutions*.

63 C. G. Paulus, "What Constitutes a Debt in the Sovereign Debt Restructuring Context?" in A. Ligustro and G. Sacerdoti (eds.), *Problemi e tendenze del diritto internazionale dell'economia: Liber amicorum in onore die Paolo Picone* (Naples: Editoriale Scientifica, 2011), pp. 231–48 at p. 231; K. E. Davis and A. Gelpern, "Peer-to-Peer Financing for Development: Regulating the Intermediaries," *New York University Journal of International Law and Politics*, 42 (2010), 1209–68 at 1209.

64 Easterly, *Reinventing Foreign Aid*; Duflo and Banerjee, *Poor Economics*.

At the end of the day, however, it seems premature (but greatly thought-provoking and hence enriching) to declare "the end of ODA," given the substantive amount of funds and institutional powers that still comes with ODA transfer.[65] There is clearly a need to be attentive to the concrete contexts and draw conclusions first within those. In this sense, development finance and the law of development cooperation are complementary not exclusive approaches.[66] This study just focuses on one important part of a broader field.

III. *Structure and approaches of this study*

The concrete structure and approach of the present study rests on three elements that also foreshadow the structure of the study: a contextualization (provided in Part I), the formulation of general principles (undertaken in Part II), and the comparative analysis of the legal regimes of the World Bank, European Union and Germany (in Part III).

1. Contextualization

The first step to understanding the law of development cooperation is to understand the history and political economy of aid. Part I of this study will recount the origins of development cooperation and detail the genesis of its most important institutions and ideas. It seems especially important to understand the administrations which the law is supposed to govern, in particular the supranational and international administrations, which may be less familiar than regular national ones. Parallel to the political history of development cooperation, Part I will trace the history of ideas and of development policies. More than in other policy areas, development policy has seen a constant shifting in leading paradigms and ideas. Tracing the gradual changes in the concept as it slowly evolved into its present form is central also to understanding its legal regulation. Finally, the study will aim at understanding the practical problems of development cooperation, and will therefore survey the contemporary state of discussion in political science and economics, with a particular focus on institutional economics.[67]

[65] Severino and Ray, *The End of ODA*.

[66] Kevin Davis, too, underlines that despite them all furthering development processes, different instruments and actors have to be analyzed in their own context, for example, with reference to the commitments that they demand from the contracting parties, the standards which they uphold or the rules on liability that they involve. See Davis, *Financing Development*, p. 174, pp. 5–6.

[67] See in particular Ch 2.C.II, Ch 5.A and Ch 6.A.

2. Principles

Part II of this study will lay out what could be called the constitutional foundations of the law of development cooperation. It will describe the relevant institutions and the legal sources and frameworks within which these institutions operate.[68] But it goes beyond this analytical and descriptive presentation. The present study does not deny its roots in a continental European tradition of legal scholarship.[69] It attempts to provide a systematic understanding of the law of development cooperation and its doctrines. Part of this is its attention to basic notions, recurrent structures and potential tensions among concrete rules.[70] A classic element of such a systematic approach is to formulate general principles of the field at hand, here *sectoral* principles for the law of development cooperation.[71] While principles of public international law in general are helpful in this endeavor, they might be too broadly formulated to capture specific aspects of development cooperation. Therefore, the focus will be on determining *specific principles* of development cooperation law, namely development, collective autonomy and sovereignty, individual autonomy and human rights, and finally coherence and efficiency.[72]

Just a brief explanation of the functions of these principles: they mainly serve three purposes. First, they assist in systematization. By defining four principles (development, collective autonomy, human rights and efficiency), one can better understand which functions the concrete rules

[68] See Ch 3.

[69] For a critical introduction, see A. Somek, "The Indelible Science of Law," *International Journal of Constitutional Law*, 7 (2009), 424–41; J. E. K. Murkens, "The Future of Staatsrecht: Dominance, Demise or Demystification?" *Modern Law Review*, 70 (2007), 731–58.

[70] From the German scholarship cf. E. Schmidt-Aßmann, *Das allgemeine Verwaltungsrecht als Ordnungsidee: Grundlagen und Aufgaben der verwaltungsrechtlichen Systembildung*, 2nd edn (Berlin: Springer, 2004), p. 2; C. Möllers, "§3 Methoden," in W. Hoffmann-Riem, E. Schmidt-Aßmann and A. Voßkuhle (eds.), *Methoden, Maßstäbe, Aufgaben, Organisation*, 3 vols. (Munich: C.H. Beck, 2006), vol. I, pp. 121–76 at margin nos. 35–9; M. Eifert, "Das Verwaltungsrecht zwischen 'klassischer' Dogmatik und steuerungswissenschaftlichem Anspruch," in C. Hillgruber, U. Volkmann, G. Nolte and R. Poscher (eds.), *Die Leistungsfähigkeit der Wissenschaft des Öffentlichen Rechts: Berichte und Diskussionen auf der Tagung der Vereinigung der Deutschen Staatsrechtslehrer in Freiburg im. Breisgau vom 3. bis 6. Oktober 2007* (Berlin: de Gruyter, 2008), vol. LXVII, pp. 286–333 at pp. 286, 302–7.

[71] On the content, function and meaning of sectoral principles for the concept of international administrative law see M. Koskenniemi (ed.), *Sources of International Law* (Burlington: Ashgate, 2000); also A. von Bogdandy, "General Principles of International Public Authority: Sketching a Research Field," *German Law Journal*, 9 (2008), 1909–38.

[72] See *infra* Ch 4.B–E.

serve, how they relate to each other and the principles, and where clusters (or gaps) of regulation are. Second, principles help evaluate the relevant rules. Although this is not about a sharp verdict on the legality or illegality of rules, principles help to normatively evaluate whether rules help implement or contradict relevant principles. This function is particularly relevant where it helps in comparing the normative preferences of different legal regimes of cooperation, and in this study especially of the World Bank, the EU and Germany. This leads to the third function fulfilled by the principles: they create transparency, especially in understanding tensions and trade-offs between values. This aspect is especially important in the area of development cooperation. Social science discussions of development cooperation frequently address these value conflicts, but tend toward staking out an absolute position based on one or another fundamental premise. To put it crudely, one is either for the protection of the sovereignty of recipient countries *or* for the right of donors to attach precise conditionalities to allocation of aid, either for human rights in development *or* for the more efficient and less participatory use of funds. But such either–or approaches are generally unsuited to a proper appreciation of the (often conflicting) normative situation. The better approach is to determine the points of conflict between simultaneously valid basic norms, and hence to furnish a practical basis for balancing them.

3. Comparison

The third method deployed in this study is its comparative approach. Since this study searches for *general* legal structures that apply to many different organizations, a comparative approach seems almost necessary. Only such an approach can bring to light divergences in the particular legal regimes of the various actors and thus allow us to "decode" the general structures of development cooperation law. This study uses two dimensions of comparison: vertical and intra-disciplinary.

The vertical comparison means that the study will not focus on the law at one level (for instance, national law), but include supranational and international law.[73] It is hence a multi-level comparison. More specifically, the study focuses on the development cooperation law of the World Bank, the European Union and Germany. A vertical perspective seems

[73] Methodological reflections on this type of vertical comparison are rare but likely to gain more importance in the context of global problems, especially due to a rising interest of legal scholarship in issues of global governance. So far see H. F. Zacher, "Horizontaler und vertikaler Sozialrechtsvergleich," in B. von Baron Maydell and E. Eichenhofer (eds.), *Abhandlungen zum Sozialrecht* (Heidelberg: C.F. Müller, 1993), pp. 377–430 at pp. 422–4;

particularly appropriate for the context of development cooperation, since it involves not only cooperation between states, but also, characteristically, between international organizations (such as the World Bank or EU) and developing countries. The analysis of the law of these organizations may therefore furnish important insights.

If appropriate, the study will also engage in "intra-disciplinary" comparison, asking, for instance, whether categories and notions of administrative law can also be applied to international law. The reasons for this are simple. Development law deals with the transfer of public funds for common purposes and hence raises issues which are well investigated in national but hardly studied in international law. Domestic administrative law suggests promising comparative avenues of inquiry and terminology. This book will thus apply one of the central ideas that has shaped the discussion about global or international administrative law.[74]

IV. A word of caution on the language of development

There is another aspect that merits attention: the language of development cooperation. It is a political language. Theoreticians of social constructivism[75] (and fiction writers[76]) have shown how language affects our perceptions of reality. The terminology of development cooperation, in particular, has shown itself an exceptionally fruitful field for unmasking the politically laden connotations. Even the notion of *development* itself is highly contentious.[77] While it is obviously not a new

also C. Schönberger, "§71 Verwaltungsrechtsvergleichung: Eigenheiten, Methoden und Geschichte," in A. von Bogdandy, S. Cassese and P. M. Huber (eds.), *Verwaltungsrecht in Europa: Wissenschaft* (Heidelberg: C.F. Müller, 2011), vol. IV, pp. 493–540 at p. 513.

[74] See Kingsbury, Krisch and Stewart, "Emergence of Global Administrative Law"; E. Schmidt-Aßmann, "Die Herausforderung der Verwaltungsrechtswissenschaft durch die Internationalisierung der Verwaltungsbeziehungen," *Der Staat*, 45 (2006), 315–38; Bogdandy, Dann and Goldmann, *Developing*; M. Ruffert, "Perspektiven des Internationalen Verwaltungsrechts," in C. Möllers, A. Vosskuhle and C. Walter (eds.), *Internationales Verwaltungsrecht: Eine Analyse anhand von Referenzgebieten.* (Tübingen: Mohr Siebeck, 2007), vol. XVI, pp. 395–419; C. Tietje, *Internationalisiertes Verwaltungshandeln* (Berlin: Duncker & Humblot, 2001).

[75] P. L. Berger and T. Luckmann, *The Social Construction of Reality* (New York: Anchor Books, 1966).

[76] G. Orwell, *1984* (London: Secker and Warburg, 1949).

[77] Escobar, Encountering Development, p. 30; P. L. Berger, "Speaking to the Third World," in P. L. Berger and M. Novak (eds.), *Speaking to the Third World: Essays on Development and Democracy: Studies in Religion, Philosophy, & Public Policy* (Washington, DC: Aei Press, 1985), pp. 4–20 at p. 20.

term, it has gained a new meaning and has become an almost inescapable notion since the post-World-War-II and decolonization era. In contrast to the notion of "civilizing," which had dominated the previous discourse, the highly suggestive term "development" was supposed to describe the humanitarian and (ideally) egalitarian endeavor of cooperation without the paternalistic (and Eurocentric) touch of the past, or at least fading, colonial age. Nonetheless, it continued to distinguish and discriminate. The term is therefore seen to suggest that non-developed countries are "backward," "infantile," or "retarded," and thus need the help of advanced or "developed" states to "grow" and "develop." It is therefore criticized for implying a certain set standard that has to be achieved, a certain goal to be considered as better and to be deserved, and thus masking an imperial or colonial project, since the set standard is that of the West.

The present study nevertheless uses the (almost inescapable) term but will not subscribe to any substantive meaning of it. As explained above,[78] it deploys a *procedural notion of development*. It understands development primarily as the political process in which the relevant participants decide on their understanding of development. It therefore stresses the inherently political nature of development cooperation. Its core lies in negotiation and decision-making.

The terminological pitfalls continue with the fact that there is no set notion for *development cooperation* itself. Instead, "foreign aid," "foreign assistance," "development aid," "development assistance" and "development cooperation" are often used interchangeably. In Germany, by contrast, the 1990s saw a consensus emerge behind the term "development cooperation" instead of "development aid," since cooperation better suggested the element of an equal partnership.[79] One can ponder whether this has only been the stale success of political correctness or even the evil intent to cover up persisting inequalities. This study rather sides with those who understand language indeed as an important instrument in the construction of perception. Even though it might have an idealistic overtone, it is therefore justified to call the interaction what it should be: a cooperation among equal partners.[80]

[78] See *infra* Intro.A.II.3. [79] Rauch, *Entwicklungspolitik*, p. 12.

[80] On the term of "developing countries" and their categorization, see *infra* Ch 3.B and A. Greig, D. Hulme and M. Turner, *Challenging Global Inequality: Development Theory and Practice in the 21st Century* (Basingstoke: Palgrave Macmillan, 2007), pp. 48–52.

A notion that also changed connotations but should not be forgotten is that of the *Third World*. Today, this notion has a more negative tone, understood as cementing a hierarchical reading in which the Third World is behind or below the first (Western capitalist) and second (former Eastern communist) worlds. Used less and less, it is often replaced by the notion of the Global South. However, such a negative reading obscures the progressive and self-confident roots of the term. It was first coined by the French demographer and anthropologist Alfred Sauvy and popularized around the Bandung Conference 1955 of those states that did not want to play along the lines of the Cold War and constituted an alternative, free and non-ideological third way.[81] Dipping into the history of political ideas, the notion was introduced to be evocative of Abbé Sieyès's notion of the "third estate." In his famous pamphlet "*Qu'est-ce que le tiers-état?*" published just months before the outbreak of the French Revolution, Sieyès describes what the non-aristocratic and non-clerical majority meant by the notion of the third estate as the actual and complete French nation and calls for its self-constitution and fair representation as the broad democratic majority. In so calling the group of newly independent countries of the south (and east), which easily form the majority of countries in the world, thinkers and politicians demanded just that: the fair and equal representation and treatment in world affairs. With this emancipatory meaning in mind, this study will use the notion too.

And there is another, final, aspect to the treatment of terminology and language here: international organizations and especially development organizations like the World Bank, OECD or UN also create their own languages.[82] They have the power to shape notions and coin phrases, such as "structural adjustment," "governance," "ownership" or "aid effectiveness." Often these notions conceal more than they reveal and hide the intentions of the instruments behind them. To shield itself, this study tries to preserve a somewhat *autonomous language of scholarship*. As far as possible, it will not take cues from organizations and political declarations but rather from scholarly practice – and, of course, the law.

[81] Alfred Sauvy, *L'Observateur* August 14, 1952; on the history of the term, see also Pahuja, *Decolonising International Law*.

[82] W. Easterly, *The Cartel of Good Intentions: Center for Global Development Working Paper No. 4*. Available at www.cgdev.org/content/publications/detail/2786/ (last visited July 2013).

B On studying the law of development cooperation: challenges and chances

I. Challenges: reasons for the reluctance of lawyers

If the law of development cooperation is an important field of law but has so far only rarely been studied by lawyers, the reasons for such reluctance should be considered. They could well indicate general doubts about the interplay of law and development cooperation – and could therefore help us to understand its challenges and tasks. Among the reasons, five stand out.

The most obvious objection against even the ability to legally regulate development aid might lie in its manifestly *political nature*. Development aid is traditionally awarded in a manner that serves the political goals of donors in their foreign policy. It is considered a tool of donors to shore up support, ensure economic benefits or quell opposition, but not as one used because of legal considerations.[83] On the contrary, the conduct of foreign policy is seen as a sovereign prerogative of every state. Strict duties to cooperate and especially to financially support have only found very limited application. Put more abstractly, one could say that development cooperation is guided by other rationalities than obedience to the law.[84]

Another aspect complements this first objection: the *inequality* between the participants. Law and especially public international law is based on the assumption of equality. This entails that legal persons meet, negotiate and bind each other as equals and, more specifically, as *free* equals. Equality in this sense contains the idea that equals do not and cannot coerce each other.[85] They are free to agree or disagree. In the context of development cooperation, it is exactly this that is in doubt. The factual inequality, especially in terms of economic strength, is an inherent part

[83] Most eloquently argued by Morgenthau, "Political Theory of Foreign Aid."

[84] These are not just political; especially in the case of development cooperation one could easily refer to economic rationalities; but also other sectors can "develop" their own rationalities, such as science, technology, morality – or, as in our case, law. Among the more recent literature, see G. Teubner, "Altera Pars Audiatur: Law in the Collision of Discourses," in R. Rawlings (ed.), *Law, Society, and Economy: Centenary Essays for the London School of Economics and Political Science, 1895-1995* (Oxford University Press, 1997), pp. 149–76, especially p. 150; A. Fischer-Lescano and G. Teubner, "Regime-Collisions: The Vain Search for Legal Unity in the Fragmentation of Global Law," *Michigan Journal of International Law*, 25 (2004), 999–1046.

[85] But on the dubious grounds of this claim in general, see B. Kingsbury, "Sovereignty and Inequality," *European Journal of International Law*, 9 (1998), 599–625.

of the constellation. From inequality follows bondage. Recipients are often economically dependent on the donor's contribution and not free to decide and choose.[86] Hence, even the core constellation of development cooperation seems to militate against its adequate and legitimate regulation in law.

Development cooperation and law could, secondly, be considered a difficult combination because of the type of activity and *mode of operation* in question. Development cooperation is about spending money and (ideally) creating opportunities; it is not about curbing freedom. Law and especially public law, however, are (at least traditionally) thought of as limiting unchecked powers. It is most needed where liberties are under threat, not where opportunities are created. Of course, the way public authorities spend money is also to be regulated in law. Particularly in the welfare states of continental Europe this has been an important topic for lawyers. But it concerns a very specific understanding of the role of state and law in their protective capacity.[87] It is unusual and can therefore easily fall outside the scope of attention. This might explain why lawyers first picked up on the issue of development cooperation when the rights of affected people were at stake.[88] Here, the traditional threat of public power and modus of law can be found – and law can be applied.

A third reason could have contributed to the neglect. This could be called the *structural disconnect in transnational decision-making*. Law is best developed where those whose interests are at stake can raise their voices and inject their concerns in the law- and decision-making process, be it through legislatures or courts. This is not the case in the area of development cooperation.[89] There is a structural disconnect between those who might be adversely affected by development interventions and those who set the rules. In fact, there is a double disconnect: one is based on the internationality in the structure of foreign aid. If, for example, the

[86] For an empirical studies on this, see Whitfield, *The Politics of Aid*.

[87] See L. F. M. Besselink, F. Pennings and S. Prechal (eds.), *The Eclipse of the Legality Principle in the European Union* (Alphen aan den Rijn: Kluwer Law International, 2011), p. 40; G. Haverkate, *Rechtsfragen des Leistungsstaats: Verhältnismässigkeitsgebot und Freiheitsschutz im leistenden Staatshandeln* (Tübingen: Mohr Siebeck, 1983); more generally on different modes of operation H. Schulze-Fielitz, "§12 Grundmodi der Aufgabenwahrnehmung," in Hoffmann-Riem, Schmidt-Aßmann and Voßkuhle, *Methoden, Maßstäbe, Aufgaben, Organisation*, vol. I, pp. 761–838 at margin no. 39.

[88] Human rights in development cooperation is probably the only aspect that has found wider attention among lawyers, see Bartels, *Human Rights Conditionality*; Darrow, *Between Light and Shadow*; Pippan, *Förderung der Menschenrechte*.

[89] More on this especially in the chapter on accountability, see *infra* Ch 9 but also in the chapters on decision-making, see especially *infra* Ch 6.B.

German parliament and government decide whether to allocate funds in Mali, German voices would have to speak up, even though only their often rather remote financial or humanitarian interests are at stake. With respect to the recipient authorities that have to agree with the projects, one faces the second disconnect: individual citizens do not have a voice in the international agreements between Mali and Germany that decide about the interventions. Mali citizens who might be affected, for example, because they have to resettle, are not heard. In sum, internationality and the (non-individual/collectivist) structure of public international law have the effect that law- and decision-making and interest representation hardly overlap. Legal protection cannot be demanded by those who would need it. The call for legal regulation, again, is muffled.

Even if there are rules on development cooperation, however, their legal nature might contribute to the neglect of development cooperation in legal academia. Most of the applicable rules, existing in the municipal law of donor states and even more in the internal law of international donor organizations (such as the World Bank) could be characterized as *soft law*. They apply only internally and cannot be called upon in courts. Can we call them law at all? The following chapters will examine the bases and nature of development law.[90] We will see that many aspects of this legal regime consist of only partially formalized law: internal regulations of development administrations and "soft" multilateral agreements will be important sources. Their binding effect may be limited, or may stem from informal enforcement mechanisms. Nevertheless, informality does not necessarily equate with ineffectiveness. To the contrary, national and international law now recognizes the normative power precisely of informal law. To ignore the law of development cooperation simply because of its informality would be shortsighted; in fact, the mixing of formal and informal law can actually be seen as a characteristic feature of this area.[91]

Finally, and perhaps most fundamentally, one can doubt the legitimacy of any legal regulation of development cooperation. This objection might best be labeled as the postcolonial critique of development cooperation, including its law. This critique has two strands: one is postcolonial lawyers who conceive public international law *in general* as a problematic

[90] See *infra* Ch 3.A.–C.

[91] On the legal nature and various modes of application in international institutional law, see A. von Bogdandy, R. Wolfrum, J. von Bernstorff, P. Dann and M. Goldmann (eds.), *The Exercise of Public Authority by International Institutions: Advancing International Institutional Law* (Heidelberg: Springer, 2010).

structure with which Western powers ensure their dominance.[92] The other strand is concerned more specifically with the idea of "development," which is seen as the attempt to mask the old colonial project of subjugation in a new, seemingly humanitarian terminology. Building on both strands, a law of development cooperation can hardly be more than the law of donors that is masking continued inequalities and building a pretense of "partnership" where in fact it is only perpetuating a wrong regime and subjugation. Any law is then only a tool of masquerade. It should not be granted the legitimacy of calling it "law."[93]

In sum, these five considerations might explain to some extent why, rather practically, there has not been much attention from lawyers to the rules on development cooperation. Its political domination, the unusual mode of activity and the dearth of voices in the relevant organs of law-making are part of an explanation. These considerations and objections, more fundamentally, also raise doubts about the legitimacy of such a law. But then again, they also signal where central challenges of the law of development cooperation would lie: in its risk to autonomy, in its soft-law legal nature and in its doubtful legitimacy.

II. Chances: the promise of a legal regulation of development cooperation

Yet thinking about these challenges and the absence of attention also prompts some thoughts about the promises that the inquiry into the law of development cooperation could herald. One can reflect on the functions of law in general that actually urge lawyers to engage especially with a policy field like development cooperation. Three functions are most relevant.

Most fundamentally, law is about justice, the formulation of (counterfactual) *ideals* and hence about providing guidance on reform.[94] Legal rules of development cooperation can lay down goals and principles to ensure that the practice of development cooperation is more closely

[92] For example, Anghie, "Time Present and Time Past"; L. Eslava and S. Pahuja, "Beyond the (Post)Colonial: TWAIL and the Everyday Life of International Law," *Verfassung und Recht in Übersee*, 45 (2012), 195–221.

[93] For more on this position, see *infra* Ch 2.B.IV.

[94] J. Habermas, *Between Facts and Norms: Contributions to a Discourse Theory of Law and Democracy* (Cambridge: MIT Press, 1996) (original: J. Habermas, *Faktizität und Geltung: Beiträge zur Diskurstheorie des Rechts und des demokratischen Rechtsstaats*, 5th edn (Frankfurt: Suhrkamp, 1998), p. 166.

oriented toward them – despite competing priorities and rationalities. Development, collective autonomy and individual freedom are guiding principles of development cooperation which the law can integrate into the daily work of development administrations. Also, the guiding function of law should be mentioned.[95] Like law in general, development cooperation law can help to coordinate actors in the implementation of political priorities. Despite the problems sketched above, the realm of politics (especially of democratic politics) has to use the law to articulate its priorities. Implementation problems certainly call for the improvement of legal technique and institutional frameworks, but hardly for completely abandoning the enterprise of legal regulation.

Secondly, law can have the function of *formalization*. Formalization can help to protect weaker actors by subjecting the naked power politics of donors to rules of equality.[96] True, law can also be abused to legitimize raw power, as one sees in the vote-weighting rules of the World Bank. It can also be simply a smokescreen. Law thus has both negative and positive potential in this regard. Nevertheless, it can still offer genuine protection to smaller and weaker recipient states, especially since they may have no other instruments to protect their interests.

Finally, law and legal scholarship has a *transparency* function which is immensely important in development cooperation. Law's public nature enables participants to understand rules governing procedure, criteria and participation rights that might otherwise have remained largely hidden. Yet, the publicity of rules is only the first step. The task of legal scholarship is to help us to better understand the various rules, enable comparison and, not least, to evaluate and criticize the relevant norms. This function has, up to now, been completely neglected in the development arena. While many complain with good reason about the complexity of the development-aid bureaucracy,[97] it is astounding how little understanding there is among practitioners of development cooperation about the general legal framework in which they operate – to say nothing of their knowledge about other agencies with which they cooperate. Needless to say that transparency is the first step also to accountability.

In sum, there are good reasons to inquire into the law of development cooperation and at least to try to understand what it is. Development

95 Schmidt-Aßmann, *Das allgemeine Verwaltungsrecht*, pp. 18.

96 Koskenniemi, "Constitutionalism," 9.

97 W. Easterly, "Die Entwicklungsideologie west weiter," *Merkur*, 61 (2007), 1084–8 at 1084.

cooperation is without doubt a field that needs critical reflection. Knowledge on what should be the rule can only help. And in the long run: why shouldn't foreign aid also grow out of its politicized niche and become an autonomous legal regime that can be used to effectively check political powers?

PART I

Institutional and intellectual history of development cooperation

1

Formative years

International development policy is a child of the Cold War. As competition between the USA and the Soviet Union intensified, both sides turned their attention to providing not only military but also economic support to economically weaker countries, hoping to pull them into one of the two camps. The Inaugural Address of US President Harry Truman on January 20, 1949, in which he promised to establish programs which would apply scientific knowledge and economic insights to assist less-developed parts of the world, is considered the beginning of development policy.[1] The administrative organizations of development cooperation – that is, the national, supranational and international bodies that organize development policy – were founded in the decade after Truman's speech and reflected a gradual institutionalization and professionalization of development policy. The same is true of theories of development. They also appeared during the 1950s, and gradually developed an understanding of the various perspectives on the goal and the tasks of development cooperation. The genesis of these three components – policy, administration, and theory of development assistance – will be addressed in this first part of the book, providing a context and factual introduction to the field that the law of development cooperation regulates.

There are good reasons to approach the law of development cooperation from a non-legal perspective focusing first on a better understanding of its context and factual subject matter. One such reason is the fact that the subject matter itself is still fairly young, changing and only slowly coming to a solidified understanding of itself. Many aspects of the current system of development assistance (and the law which governs it) are products of its slow and experimental creation. This also goes for the concept

[1] Reprinted in R. A. Goldwin (ed.), *Readings in American Foreign Policy* (New York: Oxford University Press, 1959), p. 542; on the mundane background to the speech see Rist, *History of Development*, pp. 70–1; a fundamentally critical assessment of the rhetoric introduced by the speech is found in G. Esteva, "Development," in W. Sachs (ed.), *The Development Dictionary: A Guide to Knowledge as Power* (London: Zed Books, 1992), pp. 6–25 at p. 6.

of development itself. Another reason for a more contextual approach is the fact that the law of development assistance occupies a field which is strongly influenced by political goals, theoretical frameworks (including the theory of development) and geopolitical circumstances. Indeed, it is one of the peculiarities of development assistance that its goals can be understood both heteronomously and autonomously – aid can be used for external, heteronomous goals (advancing the diplomatic, trade or cultural policies of donor nations) as well as for internal, autonomous goals actually relating to development (principally, to combat poverty). Development theory aims to define what exactly "development" means and how it is to be achieved. The law of development assistance can thus only be understood in a political context which fosters understanding of these autonomous and heteronomous goals. The final factor speaking in favor of a contextual introduction to this area is its very unfamiliarity. Certainly, most people probably have a basic idea of the goals and problems of development assistance. The specific institutions and instruments in use here are nevertheless likely to be unfamiliar to most lawyers.[2] In this first Part, therefore, I will present an introduction to the intellectual and institutional history of development cooperation or foreign aid, laying the groundwork for the later Parts, which will examine the relevant legal structures.

Chapters 1 and 2 will present the history of development assistance in four phases. In each chapter, separate sections will deal with (1) the organizations that administer development aid, (2) development policy, and (3) development theory. Hence, one focus will be on the administrative system of development assistance – that is, the organizations and instruments of development administration. Thereby, the most important objects and subjects of the law of development assistance will be examined. In particular, the similarities and differences between the World Bank, the EU and Germany will be laid out. A second focus in each phase will turn to the geopolitical context of donor and recipient countries, which exerts decisive influence on the contents and structure of development assistance. A particular focus in these sections will be

[2] One factor contributing to this ignorance is the fact that there are overviews of the history of development *theory*, but hardly any studies on the history of development cooperation *itself* – and no comparative studies at all. The work that comes closest to an overall history is Rist, *History of Development*; the most important works on the theoretical history of the area and its political context are U. Menzel, *Das Ende der Dritten Welt und das Scheitern der großen Theorie* (Frankfurt: Suhrkamp, 1992); J. Martinussen, *Society, State and Market: A Guide to Competing Theories of Development* (London: Zed Books, 1997).

on how donors and recipients understand development aid, and who dominates the political agenda. Finally, the most important development theories for each phase will be addressed, focusing on the meaning of autonomous goal setting in the context of development assistance.[3] The sequence of these three aspects (organization, policy, theory) will not always be the same but rather flexible to allow a more coherent narrative.

A Emergence and improvisation (1945–1965)

The history of development administration began with the founding of the World Bank, originally known as the International Bank for Reconstruction and Development (IBRD).[4] The Bank, curiously enough, was founded in 1945, before the modern era of development policy.[5] Only during the 1950s and 1960s – particularly with the 1960 founding of its sister institution, the International Development Association (IDA) – did the IBRD gradually assume its present role as a development bank. As this transformation reflects the geopolitical context after the Second World War and is typical for the foundational phase of development policy, it will briefly be addressed here (I). After this section, the creation of the two additional agencies will be addressed: the development-related organs of the European Economic Community (II) and of the Federal Republic of Germany (III). Finally, the focus will turn to the first theory of the goals and process of development, the modernization theory (IV).

[3] The study of these aspects will not follow the same order in every phase. Further, certain aspects will be treated at greater or lesser length depending on the particular focus.

[4] This acronym for the Bank's English name (International Bank for Reconstruction and Development) is generally used in the literature and will be used here as well. The phrase "World Bank" can be traced to a July 22, 1944 article in the *Economist* on the Bretton Woods Conference which dubbed the IBRD the "World Bank." The Bank has used the phrase officially since 1975. *See* World Bank, *A Guide to the World Bank* (Washington, DC: World Bank Publications, 2003), p. 11.

[5] The development bureaucracies of the former colonial powers (especially France and Great Britain) have roots in their former colonial administrations. A comparative history of development and colonial administrations has yet to be written (and would surely be intriguing) but exceeds the scope of this work. The contrary perspectives on this subject are illustrated by D. H. Lumsdaine, *Moral Vision in International Politics: The Foreign Aid Regime 1949–1989* (Princeton University Press, 1993), pp. 182–220 (affirmative) and Rist, *History of Development*, pp. 47–68 (critical). On the earlier phase of this history see A. Anghie, "Colonialism and the Birth of International Institutions: Sovereignty, Economy, and the Mandate System of the League of Nations," *New York University Journal of International Law and Politics*, 34 (2001), 513–633 at 513.

I. World Bank: Bretton Woods, Wall Street, Washington

1. Foundation and characteristics of the IBRD

Just as generals always fight the last war's battles, the post-war planning of 1944/45 sought to avoid the mistakes of 1919. When the government delegations of the Allied Powers met in 1944 in Bretton Woods, a small town in New Hampshire, to draft a post-war financial system, their primary goal was to develop the institutional architecture for a stable international financial system. The International Monetary Fund (IMF) was created to address this task. John Maynard Keynes and Harry Dexter White, respectively the British and American negotiators, also agreed to create a bank to finance the reconstruction of war-ravaged countries, but conceived of the Bank only as a support to the IMF. This mainly was the task that the IBRD was supposed to fulfill. The idea of using loans from this bank to assist underdeveloped countries was added to the IBRD's agenda unexpectedly, after prompting from Latin American nations.[6]

The experiences of the 1920s had further effects on the structure of the IBRD. The first priority was to create an organization that would not be viewed as hostage to international politics and diplomatic compromises, and thus would be able to win the trust of the financial markets – which, at the time, amounted to winning the trust of Wall Street.[7] Two structural elements were intended to achieve this goal. First, the influence of member states on the Bank's business would not be regulated according to the principle of equality of nations, as was the case with the League of Nations and the United Nations (created at about the same time as the IBRD). Instead, votes in the central decision-making bodies would be weighted according to the financial contributions of the member states.[8] This ensured that the USA, as the wealthiest nation in the world during these years, would play a dominant role.[9] At the same time, it was decided that the financial contributions

[6] D. Kapur, J. P. Lewis and R. Webb (eds.), *The World Bank: Its First Half Century*, vol. II (Washington, DC: Brookings Institution Press, 1997), p. 9; see Art. I Articles of Agreement of IBRD (hereinafter: IBRD Articles).

[7] E. S. Mason and R. Asher, *The World Bank Since Bretton Woods* (Washington, DC: Brookings Institution Press, 1973), pp. 108, 125.

[8] Art. V, Sect. 3 IBRD Articles; G. Wiegand, *Organisatorische Aspekte der internationalen Verwaltung von Entwicklungshilfe: Ein Beitrag zur Organisationsanalyse internationaler Organisationen am Beispiel des UNDP und der Weltbank* (Berlin: Duncker & Humblot, 1978), pp. 216.

[9] The position of the World Bank in the foreign-policy concept of the USA is described in R. Tetzlaff, *Die Weltbank: Machtinstrument der USA oder Hilfe für die Entwicklungsländer* (Munich: Weltforum Verlag, 1980), p. 119.

would be regarded as starting capital, and would therefore not be used for the Bank's ordinary business. Rather, the Bank would finance its operations by loans made in private financial markets. This was the second structural feature designed to guarantee the Bank's independence.[10] This feature was intended to require the IBRD to pay attention to the creditworthiness of projects and loan recipients. In its first years, thus, the struggle to win Wall Street's trust was the main concern of IBRD management.

A third characteristic aspect of the Bank was not established in its founding charter, but rather emerged during the course of the first years. This was the comparatively significant autonomy of the Bank's management as against the Board of Directors, composed of representatives of member countries.[11] This autonomy grew out of a power struggle between the second president of the Bank and the American representative in the Board of Directors.[12] When the first president of the Bank quit after a few months owing to the constant intervention of the American representative, the Truman Administration was hard-pressed to find a successor. Finally, John J. McCloy agreed to fill the role only after receiving assurances from the Board of Directors that the Board would play only a *reactive* role, ratifying or occasionally rejecting Bank projects without attempting to determine the Bank's concrete policies. This understanding secured the principal role of management in directing the Bank's business, a key feature of the Bank to this day.

The dominant role of the Bank's management reflected the aim of its founders to try to make the institution resemble an ordinary commercial bank as far as possible – an approach that also characterized its day-to-day operations.[13] The main business of the IBRD was funding specific projects such as the building of a bridge or coal power plant. The founders wanted to prevent the Bank from losing itself in the funding of vague programs with uncertain goals, and therefore specified in the Bank's charter that it would be limited to financing "specific projects."[14] The charter also prohibited the Bank from interfering in the political affairs of member states or making loan decisions based on political criteria.[15] The duty of political

[10] Mason and Asher, *World Bank Since Bretton Woods*, p. 124.

[11] A systematic presentation of the Bank's organizational structure can be found in Ch 3.A.IV.1.

[12] Ibid., pp. 48–51; Kapur, Lewis and Webb, *The World Bank*, p. 10.

[13] On the relationship of the Bank to the private commerce (on the one hand) and the United Nations (on the other), see Wiegand, *Organisatorische Aspekte*, p. 303.

[14] Art. III Abs. 4 (vii) IBRD Articles, see also Kapur, Lewis and Webb, *The World Bank*, p. 7; Mason and Asher, *World Bank Since Bretton Woods*, p. 230.

[15] Art. IV 10 IBRD Articles.

neutrality was based not only on the conditions of sound banking policy, but also on the hope, not realized in the end, that the Soviet Union could be persuaded to participate in the Bank.[16]

In the 1940s and 1950s, the Bank was an institution with about 400 employees whose backgrounds were largely in economics.[17] Bank staff understood the above-mentioned policies as a suggestion to be very cautious in making loans. They evaluated prospects for success very carefully, specialized in clearly defined projects, and gained a reputation for particularly well-thought-out and successful project financing.[18] Within the first decade of its existence, the Bank won the trust of the private capital markets and earned an AAA rating from ratings agencies.[19] Therefore, during the 1950s, non-industrialized countries increasingly benefited from the Bank's activities, since West European nations had, thanks to Marshall Plan funds which began flowing in 1948, begun to recover economically faster than expected.[20]

Thus, in the 1950s, the IBRD earned a reputation as a reputable bank. However, this development also caused an increasing contradiction between its business model and its client base.[21] According to its business

[16] Despite this clause, the Soviet Union regarded the Bank (not without some justification) as an instrument of the USA and its allies. The Soviet Union did not join the institution, and forced countries within its sphere of influence to steer clear of the Bank. The Soviet Union even forced Poland and Czechoslovakia to cancel their memberships in 1950 and 1954, respectively. Thus, soon after its founding, the IBRD had developed into an institution of western states. See B. Hein, *Die Westdeutschen und die Dritte Welt: Entwicklungspolitik und Entwicklungsdienste zwischen Reform und Revolte 1959–1974*, Quellen und Darstellungen zur Zeitgeschichte (Munich: Oldenbourg Verlag, 2006), vol. LXV, p. 24; Y. Yokota, "Non-Political Character of the World Bank," *Japanese Annual International Law*, 2 (1976), 39–64 at 39; Mason and Asher, *World Bank Since Bretton Woods*, p. 63; on the development policy of the Soviet Union see the essays in A. Hilger (ed.), *Die Sowjetunion und die Dritte Welt: UdSSR, Staatssozialismus und Antikolonialismus im Kalten Krieg 1945–1991*, Schriftenreihe der Vierteljahrshefte für Zeitgeschichte (Munich: Oldenbourg Verlag, 2009), vol. IC.

[17] On the personnel and organizational structure see Wiegand, *Organisatorische Aspekte*, p. 224; Mason and Asher, *World Bank Since Bretton Woods*, p. 66.

[18] Ibid., p. 258.

[19] Kapur, Lewis and Webb, *The World Bank*, pp. 11–12; Mason and Asher, *World Bank Since Bretton Woods*, p. 132.

[20] The first two IBRD loans went to France and Norway. However, the client portfolio changed quickly. For more on this and on the financial dimensions, see R. Mikesell, "The Emergence of the World Bank as a Development Institution," in A. K. Acheson, J. Chant and M. Prachowny (eds.), *Bretton Woods Revisited: Evaluations of the I.M.F. and the International Bank for Reconstruction and Development* (London: Macmillan, 1972), pp. 70–84 at p. 71; Mason and Asher, *World Bank Since Bretton Woods*, pp. 153; 176.

[21] Mikesell, *Emergence of the World Bank*, p. 74; for more on the general discussion see Kapur, Lewis and Webb, *The World Bank*, p. 1121.

model, the Bank was intended to support mainly those creditors who had sufficient expertise to successfully plan and execute projects. However, after the post-war recovery of the financial sector, there were increasing numbers of lenders for these projects and states. Thus, the IBRD was confronted with the problem of how to justify its role, considering especially the transformation brought about by the post-war wave of decolonization.

2. Decolonization and the creation of the IDA

Besides the Cold War, decolonization was the second factor driving the emergence and direction of development policy. At the end of the Second World War, when the Bank was founded, there were approximately sixty states in the world.[22] Great Britain, France and other European powers still possessed extensive colonial territories. The economic and military basis for these "possessions" was, however, permanently shaken by the Second World War. Furthermore, the two post-war superpowers, the USA and USSR (at least officially) demanded self-determination for former colonies. The superpowers declined to support the former colonial powers, a policy that found its final and most dramatic expression in the 1956 Suez crisis. The twenty years since the end of the Second World War – in particular the ten years after the Suez crisis – were marked by a dynamic of increasing emancipation and decolonization. And the trend was evidently successful: by the end of the 1960s, the number of sovereign states had more than doubled, to about 120.[23]

The economic position of the new states, as well as their sheer number and potential collective strength, lent a new dimension to questions of development policy. Although it would take another few years before the countries of the so-called Third World[24] would find a unified voice in world politics and on the distribution of global wealth,[25] the sheer quantity of the new countries shifted the axis of world politics and demanded a new conceptual framework for their political and economic integration. The economic state of the new countries created a particular challenge.

[22] In 1945, the United Nations had 51 founding members.

[23] On the highly diverse processes of decolonization see, e.g. E. Hobsbawm, *Age of Extremes: The Short Twentieth Century, 1914–1991* (London, New York: Viking Penguin, 1994), p. 344; W. Mommsen (ed.), *Das Ende der Kolonialreiche: Dekolonisation und die Politik der Großmächte* (Frankfurt am Main: Fischer Taschenbuch Verlag, 1990). For a critical reading of the decolonization process from a postcolonial perspective see Pahuja, *Decolonising International Law*, p. 54.

[24] On this notion, Intro.A.III.

[25] Discussed further immediately below in section III.

Most of them suffered from massive economic underdevelopment. Even where the colonial powers had left behind some functioning infrastructure, the national economies of these countries were nevertheless still geared toward little more than delivery of raw materials.

In light of this situation, the role of the IBRD in the late 1950s was called into question. President Eisenhower's threat to drastically reduce the USA's support for the IBRD and rely exclusively on bilateral aid during his second term gave a strong impulse to the already-existing idea (supported by developing countries) to address the Third World's new requirements by means of an independent organization specializing in questions of development.[26] The new institution would concentrate entirely on the new clientele of countries without established creditworthiness and offer them a different instrument from what the IBRD offered: the new institution would not offer loans at slightly discounted market rates, but rather concessional loans at steep discounts, or even grants.[27] The new organization was founded in 1960 as the International Development Association (IDA), a sister organization to the IBRD. The IDA's mission to combat poverty was included in its charter. Fifteen years previously, when the IBRD was founded, this goal had been mentioned only in an appendix.[28]

Besides its mandate and financial instruments, the IDA differed from the IBRD in its funding.[29] While the IBRD was able to finance itself by means of its good reputation and its access to loans from the private capital market, this path was essentially unavailable to the IDA. The IDA was founded neither to assist creditworthy parties nor to make genuine loans, but rather to provide grants to the world's poorest nations. Thus, the IDA was dependent on other funding sources – contributions from member states. Every four years, therefore, there was a new round of so-called "replenishments," that is, re-stockings of the IDA's coffers by World Bank donor countries.[30]

[26] For a detailed description of the founding of the IDA, see Kapur, Lewis and Webb, *The World Bank*, pp. 1119–29; Tetzlaff, *Weltbank*, p. 260; Mason and Asher, *World Bank Since Bretton Woods*, p. 381.

[27] IDA loans are essentially interest-free. The only charge is a processing fee of 0.75%. They are repaid over a period of 50 years, and no payments are due during the first 10 years. These conditions are set out in Operational Policy of the World Bank No. 3.10, margin nos. 37–40 (for more on the legal bases of the World Bank see Ch 3.A.IV.2).

[28] Article 1 of the IDA Articles reads: "The purposes of the Association are to promote economic development, increase productivity and thus raise the standard of living in the less-developed areas of the world …"

[29] Wiegand, *Organisatorische Aspekte*, p. 219.

[30] Discussed at length in Kapur, Lewis and Webb, *The World Bank*, pp. 1138–51.

From an organizational perspective, however, the founding of the IDA brought few changes. Certainly it is true that the IDA was, as a matter of international law, an independent legal entity.[31] Nevertheless, the IDA was merged with the IBRD organizationally, and shared personnel, governing bodies and offices with the IBRD.[32] The foundation of the IDA did not even entail a significant change in the number of employees: the total number of employees increased by only nineteen.[33]

For all that the founding of the IDA seemed relatively inconsequential from an external perspective, it marked a significant conceptual transformation.[34] Only at this time did the Bank's second mandate, development, acquire an independent and substantial meaning. Developing countries came to occupy the center of attention. Even though the employees' conception of their own role as bankers rather than development specialists persisted, the first attempts were soon made to strengthen the Bank's knowledge in the area of development, and it began to focus on addressing developmental questions from a planning perspective. New procedures were introduced to study developing countries and to coordinate, in a medium-term framework, the planning of previously independent projects. Hence, the Bank for the Reconstruction of Western Europe had gradually transformed itself into the World Bank as a development bank.

II. The European Economic Community and the formative phase of European development assistance

The creation of European development policy was a classic of French *realpolitik*. Early in the negotiations on the Rome Treaties, the French delegation requested that an "association clause" be integrated into the contract which would require the European Economic Community (EEC) to support the economic and social development of (current or former) colonial possessions of the member states. Germany and the Netherlands opposed

[31] R. T. Libby, "International Development Association: A Legal Fiction Designed to Secure an LCD Constituency," *International Organization*, 29 (1975), 1065–72 at 1065.

[32] Art. II, §1 IDA Articles of Agreement; more details in Ch 3.A.IV.1.

[33] Wiegand, *Organisatorische Aspekte*, p. 235.

[34] The founding of the IDA was only *one* step in the organizational diversification of the original IBRD. The International Finance Corporation was founded in 1956 to specialize in loans to private borrowers. In 1966, the International Center for the Settlement of International Disputes (ICSID) was founded within the same organizational structure. It offers arbitration proceedings between states and private parties. The founding of these organizations permitted the IBRD to diversify functionally. See M. Ragazzi, "World Bank Group," in Wolfrum, *Max Planck Encyclopedia of Public International Law* at margin no. 1.

such a clause on the assumption that it was intended primarily to subsidize French colonial trade, and the topic was abandoned for a time. Shortly before the end of the negotiations, however, the French raised the subject again, and raised the stakes by making their agreement to the entire EEC treaty dependent on the acceptance of the clause. At this time, the German and Dutch delegations had very little bargaining power, and were compelled to agree.[35] France prevailed and was to exert decisive influence on this new policy area.[36] What exactly drove the French administration to deploy this maneuver, and how did it shape the new European policy?

1. Motives, characteristics, and instruments: a development fund for associates

It was the weight of its colonial legacy – rather than the more general concern for a globally oriented, solidarity-based development policy – that led the French delegation to demand a policy of association. At the time of the negotiations, France still possessed approximately twenty dependent territories, which had become an increasing burden to its national economy.[37] Italy, Belgium and the Netherlands also either still had colonies or special relationships with former colonies.[38] The main motives for this approach were thus to maintain these relationships and to spread and

[35] A detailed treatment of this aspect is found in C. Cosgrove Twitchett, *Europe and Africa: From Association to Partnership* (Westmead, England: Saxon House, 1978), pp. 7–9; M. Lister, *The European Community and the Developing World: The Role of the Lomé Convention* (Aldershot: Avebury, 1989), pp. 14–18. A refreshingly honest perspective on the beginnings of European development policy can be found in the contribution of a later General Director, see D. Frisch, "Die entwicklungspolitische Konzeption der Gemeinschaft," in F. Franzmeyer and H. Petersen (eds.), *Neuorientierung in den Beziehungen zwischen der EG und den Entwicklungsländern* (Berlin: Duncker & Humblot, 1984), pp. 13–29 at p. 13.

[36] With respect to the EC, the first period can be described as extending from 1958 to 1972 (that is, until Great Britain joined the community and Community development policy opened up globally). The period from 1945–65, in any case, saw the emergence of the policy in the EEC Treaty, as well as its fundamental transformation by the Yaoundé Convention. This period thus comprises the years in which the EC's specific system of development administration was established.

[37] These areas are largely in Africa: French West Africa (eight territories: Senegal, French Sudan (now Mali), French Guinea (now Guinea), Ivory Coast, Dahomey (now Benin), Mauritania, Niger and Upper Volta (now Burkina Faso)); French Equatorial Africa (four territories: Middle Congo, Ubangui-Sari, Chad and Gabon); French Togoland; additional French territories (St Pierre and Miquelon, the Comoros Archipelago, Madagascar and dependent territories, French Somaliland, New Caledonia, French settlements in Oceania and southern and Antarctic territories).

[38] Italy: Somaliland; Belgium: Belgian Congo, Rwanda, Burundi. The Netherlands still possessed New Guinea, while Indonesia had just recently declared its independence.

socialize the resulting financial burdens. The Association Clause of the Treaty of Rome, the treaty creating the EEC, thus related only to those states which were linked to EEC member states by "special relationships," as provided in Art. 131 I of the Treaty. The provision primarily affected francophone Africa.[39]

The concept of "association" that underlies this relationship had been developed unilaterally by the French. France had developed the concept after the Second World War, when it reorganized its relationships to the colonies and dependencies by creating the French Union in 1946.[40] In contrast to the previous idea of "assimilation," the concept of association emphasized the close connection between France and the colonies, but also expressed the mutual respect for the cultures and histories of the participating countries. The difference between France and the associated countries, thus, was not meant to be erased. Association, however, did not mean equality. It meant, rather, a relationship in which France would be the dominant and controlling center.[41] It was this concept which France brought into the EEC negotiations.[42] The relationships to the associates should be close and custom-tailored, but also clearly dominated by the European countries. The asymmetrical character of the association concept is illustrated by the fact that it was introduced without consultation with the "associated" countries.

The EEC's development policy emerged in the context of this policy of association. Development policy was not a mature field at this time, and there was no general concept underlying it.[43] It was often seen as a mere appendage to trade policy, which was the primary element of the

[39] Except as to the insertion of new Member States such as Great Britain and Denmark, this provision has remained unchanged to this day, see Art. 198 TFEU.

[40] Lister, *EC and the Developing World*, pp. 3–6; extensive discussion in A. Bleckmann, *Das französische Kolonialreich und die Gründung neuer Staaten: Die Rechtsentwicklung in Syrien/Libanon, Indochina und Schwarzafrika* (Cologne: Heymann, 1969), p. 189.

[41] On divisions within the Union with regard to the treatments of colonies and ex-colonies, see E. R. Grilli, *The European Community and the Developing Countries* (Cambridge University Press, 1993), p. 3.

[42] The association of colonies or regions of sovereignty with "special relationships" should not be confused with the option to associate granted to other states, in particular those (such as Greece or Turkey) which saw an opportunity to join the Union. This association was based on Art. 238 of the EEC Treaty (in the version of the Rome Treaties, now Art. 217 TFEU). See also U. Everling, "Die Neuregelung des Assoziationsverhältnisses zwischen der Europäischen Wirtschaftsgemeinschaft und den afrikanischen Staaten und Madagaskar sowie den überseeischen Ländern und Hoheitsgebieten," *Heidelberg Journal of International Law*, 24 (1964), 472–574 at 447.

[43] The European Commission's first conceptual statements on development policy date from the early 1970s. More on this point directly below in Ch 1.B.IV.1.

associations between countries. Trade policies aimed at the mutual opening of markets of EEC countries and associates by means of the abolition of customs tariffs and the reductions of import quotas.[44] France's principal aim was to open new markets in the EEC to associated countries, while simultaneously securing the dominance of its exports in those countries.[45] The aspect of economic aid and development was only added to the "association" regulations as a matter of secondary importance, chiefly due to pressure from Germany.[46]

Despite the fact that European development policy was still in its infancy, we can identify three features that came to define it. First, development was not to be financed from within the EEC budget, but rather from a special fund. To this end, the European Development Fund (EDF) was created. Its funds were to be spent to assist technical and financial development projects in associated countries. Because it was an external fund, it was not set up by the Treaty of Rome, but by a specific implementing agreement between EEC member states. As was characteristic for the time, this agreement was, like the association policy, created unilaterally by the EEC member states, without the participation of the associates. The fund, which operated in a five-year cycle, was stocked by contributions from member states.[47] Development policy thereby became one of the first political domains in which the EEC itself could spend large sums of money – albeit under the control of the member states.

The second feature of European development policy was that the funds from the EDF were to be spent *alongside* the bilateral ODA expenditures of the EEC member states, and thus would not lead to a reduction in the promised spending in respective bilateral relationships.[48] Thus, the funding was organized on the principle of "additionality," although this was never legally formalized. The third feature of European development policy was

[44] An extensive discussion of trade policy between the EEC and developing countries is found in L. Bartels, "The Trade and Development Policy of the European Union," *European Journal of International Law*, 18 (2007), 715–56 at 715; H. P. Ipsen, *Europäisches Gemeinschaftsrecht* (Tübingen: Mohr Siebeck, 1972), p. 968.

[45] On the incompatibility of these agreements with GATT see Bartels, "Trade and Development," 728–9; Grilli, *EC and Developing Countries*, pp. 11–12.

[46] Art. 131 para. 2 EEC Treaty (in the Rome Treaty versions). See ibid., pp. 7–8.

[47] The Germans and the French each assumed one-third of the costs. The First EDF had a volume of US$581 million, the following funds regularly became larger. The third comprised a billion dollars. It was reported that one of the reasons de Gaulle rejected Great Britain's application to join the EEC was to prevent these monies from being shared with other countries – namely, British ex-colonies. On the supplemental character of European aid monies see ibid., p. 94.

[48] Ibid., p. 94.

its continued emphasis on political and economic neutrality.[49] This feature did not particularly distinguish European development policy from that of the World Bank, but did distinguish it from bilateral aid relationships, which were financially more significant. Yet even in comparison to the World Bank, the European Community always saw itself as the more neutral (in particular, less Americanized) donor. This view, however, was more rhetoric than reality. In substance, the policy of early European development was the same as that of the World Bank, in that both entities favored public investment (for example, transport and communication) and allied states.[50]

Although these principles were to define European development policy for the coming decades, the unilateral structure of the EDF was to have a much shorter lifespan. During the process of decolonization, the majority of the associated countries declared their independence within the first few years after the Fund's creation. The Fund's unilateral structure thus became outdated. In recognition of the new status of the associated countries, a new treaty, the so-called Yaoundé Convention, was negotiated after the expiration of the first EDF in 1962. The new agreement entered into force in 1964.[51] In substance, Yaoundé maintained the basic structure of the association policy. A free trade zone was agreed between the EEC and the associated countries. A second five-year extension of the EDF was also approved, and its funds were increased and authorized for a broader spectrum of uses.[52] Training programs were now to run concurrently with infrastructure-related projects. To remedy the association concept's unilateral nature, Yaoundé introduced an institutional structure whose organs (Council, Parliament, Court) were modeled after those of the Community. Donor and recipient countries were equally represented in these organs.[53]

This leads us to consider the organizational structure of European development administration.

2. Administrative structure: the Ferrandi System

The administration of the EDF was from its very beginning in 1958 handled by a dedicated Directorate General (DG) inside the European

[49] Ibid., p. 101; Lister, *EC and the Developing World*, p. 133.

[50] Bartels, "Trade and Development," fn. 73–79; Art. 3, Implementing Convention on the Association of the Overseas Countries and Territories with the Community.

[51] Everling, "Neuregelung des Assoziationsverhältnisses," 484–500, 508; on political problems behind it Grilli, *EC and Developing Countries*, pp. 14–19.

[52] Everling, "Neuregelung des Assoziationsverhältnisses," 535–8.

[53] Cosgrove Twitchett, *Europe and Africa*, p. 109; Everling, "Neuregelung des Assoziationsverhältnisses," 544.

Commission.[54] The DG reflected the extraordinary success France had, in this initial phase, in influencing not only the conceptual but also the administrative form of EEC development policy.[55]

The composition and structure of the EDF drew on the example of the *Fonds d'Investissement pour le Développement Economique et Social* (FIDES), the French development fund established in 1946 for France's overseas possessions.[56] As with the French fund, the EDF would be administered by a specialized bureaucracy. Governments of the associated countries could suggest projects which would then be analyzed and evaluated by the Commission. If the Commission approved, it would forward the project to a committee of the Council, the so-called EDF Committee.[57] The EDF Committee and thus the member states would then be responsible for making the final decision on the disbursement of funds. If the Commission and the Council disagreed, the latter would have the final say.

Developing countries frequently lacked the technical expertise to properly draw up projects. The EDF Committee, for its part, only reviewed completely elaborated proposals, and there were few legal provisions. Thus, it fell largely to the DG for development to determine the contents of the projects. The influence of the French bureaucracy was particularly evident in this process. This influence stemmed in part from the fact that, until 1984, the DG was led solely by French Commissioners.[58] Moreover, the figure with the most *practical* influence over European development

[54] The DG changed its name several times. It was first called the "DG Overseas Development"; in 1967 it was renamed to "DG Aid for Development," then to "Development and Cooperation," and finally renamed DG VIII in 1982. Since 2001, the name has reverted to DG Development, see I. de Chávarri Ureta, "The European Commission's Institutional Framework for Development Policy," in C. Cosgrove-Sacks (ed.), *Europe, Diplomacy and Development: New Issues in EU Relations with Developing Countries* (New York: Palgrave Macmillan, 2001), pp. 52–64 at p. 55.

[55] V. Dimier, "Administrative Reform as Political Control," in D. G. Dimitrakopoulos (ed.), *The Changing European Commission* (Manchester University Press, 2004), pp. 74–85 at p. 78; V. Dimier and M. McGreeve, "Diplomats Without a Flag: The Institutionalization of the Delegations of the Commission in African, Caribbean and Pacific Countries," *Journal of Common Market Studies*, 44 (2006), 483–505 at 492.

[56] Dimier, "Administrative Reform as Political Control," p. 76.

[57] Ipsen, *Europäisches Gemeinschaftsrecht*, §53/13 (p. 970); on the institutional structure of the EEC and hence the role of Council and Commission see P. Dann, "Political Institutions," in A. von Bogdandy and J. Bast (eds.), *Principles of the European Constitutional Law*, 2nd edn (Munich: C.H. Beck, 2010), pp. 234–74.

[58] However, attempts to establish national proportionality have meant that these French Commissioners have always been accompanied by German General Directors.

administration until the early 1970s was also a Frenchman, Jacques Ferrandi. Ferrandi was a former French colonial official in West Africa. From 1953 to 1958, he was Director General of FIDES. In 1958, he became the first Cabinet Chief of the first EEC Commissioner for Development Policy, Robert Lemaignen. In 1963, Ferrandi became Director General in the Development DG and was particularly influential during the ensuing decade.[59]

As with the World Bank, European development policy was characterized by a clear project focus. EDF funds were invested in relatively clear-cut projects primarily in the area of infrastructure, instead of in middle- or long-term projects or strategies. Project selection was done mainly by Ferrandi and his on-site colleagues, on an ad hoc basis. In contrast to the World Bank, whose staff were concerned with the solidity of the loans (to win the trust of financial markets), EEC projects were oriented more toward political prestige and visibility.[60] Visits by European politicians to Africa were often used as occasions to launch high-visibility projects or sign agreements. From the beginning, then, the EEC was more of a "soft" donor. The fund did not make loans, instead providing grants which served political goals.[61] Thus, Ferrandi and his staff had more discretion, which they often used to channel implementation contracts to French firms.[62]

[59] On the figure of Ferrandi and the internal culture within DG VIII see Dimier, "Administrative Reform as Political Control," pp. 75–9; A. Hewitt and K. Whiteman, "The Commission and Development Policy: Bureaucratic Politics in EU Aid from the Lome Leap Forward to the Difficulties of Adapting to the 21st Century," in K. Arts and A. K. Dickson (eds.), *EU Development Cooperation: From Model to Symbol* (Manchester University Press, 2004), pp. 133–48 at pp. 134–7. Ferrandi's influence was a product not just of his position in the administrative hierarchy but also his personal drive to shape policy and, even more, a broad network of personal relationships. His activity in West Africa brought Ferrandi a broad network of contacts in the French colonial administration and diverse African governments. He saw it as one of his main tasks to raise the profile of DG VIII within the Community and also in the eyes of recipient countries, and to support the Directorate's work by private contacts. V. Dimier, "The Invention of a Directorate General for Development (1958–1975)," in A. Smith (ed.), *Politics and the European Commission* (London: Routledge, 2004), pp. 83–95 at p. 83. He was also able to bring some colleagues (largely former French colonial officials) into European development administration. Under the radar of the Commission's leadership and even before the Commission itself had built up an external affairs administration, Ferrandi also established a network of technical inspectors in the capital cities of recipient countries (Dimier and McGreeve, "Diplomats Without a Flag," 483).

[60] Dimier, "Invention of DG Development," pp. 85–9.

[61] Lister, *EC and the Developing World*, p. 135. [62] Ibid., p. 28.

III. Germany: indirect beginnings

1. Motives for development policy? Everything but development

The development policy of the Federal Republic of Germany arose more as an instrument and side-effect of other policies than a decision to engage with poorer countries.[63] In 1956, as the first entry for "development assistance" appeared in the federal budget, there existed no specific conception of German development policy, nor did there appear, at first glance, to be a particular reason to close this gap.[64] Germany did not possess any colonies with whose fate it was particularly closely bound up, nor was there any economic imperative to enter the field of development assistance. The beginnings of German development policy were, rather, driven by considerations deriving from three policy areas: economic policy, foreign policy and, to a limited extent, a genuine impulse to create a German development policy.

External trade was the first driving factor. At the urging of France and Great Britain, who wanted to spur trade with their colonies,[65] and as a welcome replacement for dwindling export markets in Eastern Europe, the German government, in the 1950s, developed a differentiated system of export assistance.[66] Various institutions such as the Ausfuhrkredit-AG (Export-Credit AG) or the Hermes-Kreditversicherungs-AG (Hermes Credit Insurance AG) were commissioned to provide capital for export transactions and to cover the economic and political risks of business

[63] The main sources for the history of German development policy are Hein, *Westdeutschen*; K. Bodemer, "Programmentwicklung in der Entwicklungspolitik der Bundesrepublik Deutschland," in F. Nuscheler (ed.), *Dritte-Welt-Forschung: Entwicklungstheorie und Entwicklungspolitik*. Sonderheft Politische Vierteljahresschrift No. 16 (Opladen: Westdeutscher Verlag, 1985), pp. 278–307 at p. 278 – and understandably in German. For an English-language analysis see H.-I. Schmidt, "Pushed to the Front: The Foreign Assistance Policy of the Federal Republic of Germany 1958–1971," *Contemporary European History*, 12 (2003), 473–507.

[64] Fifty million Deutschmarks were allocated for technical assistance in the Foreign Ministry's budget, see Hein, *Westdeutschen*, pp. 37–9; Bodemer, "Programmentwicklung," pp. 280, 281.

[65] By means of bilateral trade agreements, both nations required Germany to open its market to imports from the two victorious powers' colonies. See Hein, *Westdeutschen*, p. 28.

[66] K. Bodemer, *Entwicklungshilfe – Politik für wen?: Ideologie und Vergabepraxis der deutschen Entwicklungshilfe in der ersten Dekade* (Munich: Weltforum Verlag, 1974), pp. 27–9; Hein, *Westdeutschen*, pp. 27–30; U. Damm, *Die Bundesrepublik Deutschland und die Entwicklungsländer* (Coburg: H. Biehl, 1965), pp. 25–9, pp. 36–8, pp. 46–9; W. W. Kretzschmar, *Auslandshilfe als Mittel der Außenwirtschafts- und Außenpolitik* (Munich: Oldenbourg Verlag, 1964).

with developing countries. The Rourkela project, approved in 1953, is often described as the "first large German business investment project in the Third World."[67] It involved an agreement between the Indian government and the German firms Krupp and DEMAG (which stands for German Machine Factory AG) to build a steelworks in the city of Rourkela in India.[68] When the Indian government was no longer able to meet payment obligations on the project, the German government stepped in with a refinancing loan. The financial dimensions of such export financing grew exponentially in the 1950s: in 1952, there were 1.1 billion Deutschmarks (DM) worth of state-secured loans, while by 1955 the amount had grown to DM 3.5 billion and, by 1957, about DM 10 billion. Accordingly, the first real lobbying group for development aid in Germany was actually formed by export firms.[69] Not least owing to this private-economy dimension, development aid was, until far into the 1960s, considered primarily a field for private firms, in which the state had only a secondary role.[70]

Foreign policy motives played a second important role in the creation of German development policy. Two aspects, in particular, stand out. First, the establishment and rapid growth of German development assistance would have been unthinkable without intense pressure from Western allies.[71] The American government, which had made development policy a systematic instrument of its foreign policy (in particular, containment of the Soviet Union) since Truman's 1949 speech, pressured Germany to step up its foreign-aid activities. Confronted with acute balance-of-payments deficits in the USA and large surpluses in Germany, Presidents Eisenhower and Kennedy demanded increases in German foreign-aid budgets, and even blatantly threatened to make the continued stationing of American troops in Germany dependent on the strengthening of German foreign-aid programs.[72] In addition to feeling pressure

[67] Bodemer, *Entwicklungshilfe*, p. 29.

[68] U. Engelmann, "Das Rourkela-Projekt," in H. Besters (ed.), *Kooperative Entwicklungshilfe: Deutsche und amerikanische Bemühungen beim Aufbau der Entwicklungsländer* (Bielefeld: Bertelsmann Universitätsverlag, 1968), pp. 157–65 at p. 157.

[69] Most important in this respect was the "Working Group for Cooperation with Developing Countries ("Arbeitsgemeinschaft für die Zusammenarbeit mit den Entwicklungsländern" or AGEL), which was founded in 1957 from various industry groups; see Hein, *Westdeutschen*, p. 30; K. Tudyka, *Gesellschaftliche Interessen und Auswärtige Beziehungen* (Katholieke Universiteit Nijmegen, 1978), pp. 94–100.

[70] Bodemer, "Programmentwicklung," p. 281.

[71] The very title of the article expresses the idea in Schmidt, "Pushed to the Front," p. 473; see also Bodemer, *Entwicklungshilfe*, pp. 33–44. Even German participation in the European Development Fund took place, as described, under considerable French pressure.

[72] Hein, *Westdeutschen*, pp. 32–3.

from the USA, West Germany also recognized the usefulness of development assistance as an instrument of its own foreign policy, particularly its claim to be the sole representative of Germany (as opposed to the East German government).[73] This claim to sole representation was the basis of the so-called Hallstein Doctrine, announced in 1955. The doctrine specified that West Germany would regard any diplomatic recognition of the German Democratic Republic government of East Germany as an "unfriendly act," and would reserve the right to react accordingly. Development policy soon proved an appropriate means to flesh out the doctrine, especially when it came to enforcement. Both of these driving factors of German development policy highlight the central role the Cold War played in the establishment and conduct of development policy. It was hardly surprising, then, that the primary recipients of German aid were those newly decolonized states of the Third World which had not yet decided on their political orientation.[74] The countries of the "second," socialist, bloc, by contrast, received no aid, since they were already "lost" for the purposes of German and Western foreign policy.[75]

The questions remains: what role did humanitarianism and solidarity play in the formation of German development policy? It would be unjust to completely neglect this aspect. The Social Democratic parliamentary faction, in particular, a driving factor in German development policy and budgetary appropriations, repeatedly emphasized the role of solidarity.[76] Gratitude for the assistance so recently received by Germany itself also played a role, as did elements of Christian ethics. These aspects were, however, rarely cited as the sole or central motives for development aid, the main focus still resting on the usefulness of development assistance for trade and export policy. In the face of public skepticism, it appeared that humanitarian justifications inspired less confidence than economic ones. Only toward the end of the 1960s would this situation change.

In sum, the motives for the establishment of German development policy were quite varied. Development policy was not made for its own autonomous ends, but served as an instrument for other goals. These

[73] Ibid., pp. 21–2, p. 38, pp. 94–7; Damm, *Bundesrepublik Deutschland und die Entwicklungsländer*, pp. 72–5.

[74] Germany was interested primarily in the young states of Asia and Africa, while Latin America was considered to be within the USA's sphere of influence. From an instrumental perspective, Asian countries tended to receive capital assistance, while African countries were more likely to receive technical assistance. See Bodemer, "Programmentwicklung," p. 283.

[75] Hein, *Westdeutschen*, p. 57 (fn. 106).

[76] Bodemer, *Entwicklungshilfe*, p. 46; Hein, *Westdeutschen*, pp. 37–9.

heteronymous motives were also reflected in the institutions that managed German development policy.

2. First institutional structures and administrative principles

The institutional structure of German development aid was marked from the beginning by differentiation, not to say fragmentation.[77] Development policy was managed primarily by the Bundeswirtschaftsministerium (BMWi/Federal Ministry of Economics) and the Auswärtiges Amt (AA/Foreign Office), but their control was not complete. Rather, in the late 1950s and early 1960s, various administrative units were set up, each of which took on particular aspects of development policy and, in sum, created an entire network of institutions. Even the creation of the Bundesministerium für wirtschaftliche Zusammenarbeit (BMZ/Federal Ministry for Economic Cooperation) in the spring of 1962 led to no short-term changes. Only after the Social Democratic/Liberal coalition took power in 1969, did a second phase ensue that led to a certain amount of consolidation of these administrative structures, and to the BMZ taking on a leading role.[78]

In the first phase, however, the ministries for foreign and economic affairs took a leading role in administering development policy. As early as 1952, the BMWi provided funds to the UN Development Program, and thus became the first German ministry to actually engage in development work. From 1955 on, its budget began to feature independent (if still small) entries for "assistance for the economic support of less-developed countries."[79] As noted above, the Foreign Office received a budget of DM 50 million reserved explicitly for development assistance in 1956 and, two years later, created an independent unit for "Cooperation with Developing

[77] M. Glagow and U. Schimank, "Politisch-administrative Strukturen deutscher Entwicklungspolitik," in Nuscheler (ed.), *Dritte-Welt-Forschung*, p. 313; U. Schimank, "Das außenpolitische Interorganisationsnetz als Hemmnis einer eigenständigen deutschen Entwicklungspolitik," in M. Glagow (ed.), *Deutsche Entwicklungspolitik: Aspekte und Probleme ihrer Entscheidungsstruktur: Beiträge in Zusammenhang mit dem Forschungsprojekt "Handlungsbedingungen und Handlungsspielräume für Entwicklungspolitik"* (Saarbrücken, Fort Lauderdale: Breitenbach, 1983), pp. 51–86 at p. 51; M. Martinek, *Die Verwaltung der deutschen Entwicklungshilfe und ihr Integrationsdefizit: Eine verwaltungswissenschaftliche Struktur- und Funktionsanalyse* (Bad Honnef: Bock und Herchen, 1981).

[78] See Ch 1.B.III; on the present structure see Ch 3.A.II.1. In 1993, the name of the ministry was changed by adding "and Development." However, the regular acronym is still BMZ.

[79] Bodemer, *Entwicklungshilfe*, p. 29; exact figures in K. Billerbeck, *Deutscher Beitrag für Entwicklungsländer* (Hamburg: Verlag Weltarchiv, 1958), p. 45.

Countries."[80] The economics and foreign ministries thus managed the central instruments of development policy: the economics ministry provided financial support, and the foreign ministry gave technical assistance.[81] Quantitatively, the amounts reserved for financial assistance – that is, the provision of public funds to support investment projects – quickly became the leading form of aid.[82] In the first half of the 1960s, DM 10.1 million was provided,[83] not counting extensive contributions to multilateral organizations.[84] The bilateral financial assistance from the economics ministry, was, however, distinguished by its especially harsh conditions in international comparison. While other lenders reduced their interest rates to well under the prevailing market rate, permitted years-long grace periods, and extended the loan terms, the Federal Republic of Germany imposed stricter conditions – on "educational grounds," as it was put.[85] The Foreign Office, on the other hand, was also responsible for technical assistance, which was regarded as particularly important, perhaps more so even than the financial aid.[86] Technical assistance, in this period, comprised everything to do with the transfer of knowledge and skills needed to accomplish tasks for which the developing countries lacked skilled personnel. Between 1956 and 1961, approximately DM 290 million was appropriated for technical assistance.[87] The main focus of German technical assistance was the construction of training centers and model firms in which structures for longer-term knowledge transfer would be established. After a few years, the partner countries would take responsibility for these organizations.[88]

Although the foreign and economics ministries assumed leading roles, other ministries were involved as well. In October of 1956, the

[80] Hein, *Westdeutschen*, pp. 35, 36.

[81] Trade concessions were proclaimed as a third appropriate instrument of development cooperation, but were not put into practice, see ibid., pp. 55, 56.

[82] On the beginnings, see Bodemer, *Entwicklungshilfe*, pp. 31, 32.

[83] Hein, *Westdeutschen*, p. 50.

[84] Germany accordingly paid US$200 million into the first EDF (1958–1963) and US$246.5 million into the second EDF (1963–68) (see Lister, *EC and the Developing World*, p. 27). At the same time, the German Bundesbank (Federal Reserve), in addition to its base capital stock subscription, bought World Bank bonds to the amount of 1.7 billion Deutschmark. See Bodemer, *Entwicklungshilfe*, p. 32; J. White, *German Aid: A Survey of Sources, Policy and Structures of German Aid* (London: Overseas Development Institute, 1965), p. 21.

[85] Hein, *Westdeutschen*, pp. 50–2.

[86] W. Scheel, *Konturen einer neuen Welt* (Düsseldorf: Econ Verlag, 1965), p. 118.

[87] Bodemer, *Entwicklungshilfe*, p. 32.

[88] Hein, *Westdeutschen*, pp. 48–9.

Federal Cabinet set up an inter-ministerial committee "to foster cooperation with developing countries."[89] This committee, to which two sub-committees were added for technical and financial assistance in 1960, was composed of the foreign ministry, as well as the Ministries of Economics, Finance, Labor, and Agriculture.[90] This inter-ministerial committee decided on all West German development projects until the 1970s. The relevant procedure required that each request from a developing country would first be examined by the Foreign Office, then presented to the inter-ministerial committee.[91] If the committee found the request to be appropriate for funding, a detailed request for examination would be sent to the relevant ministry or implementation agency. The result of this examination would then be again presented to the inter-ministerial committee, which would make the final decision on approval of the project. Approval had to be unanimous, which did not exactly increase the frequency of decisions.

The award process of the West German government was guided by three principles: the project principle, the proposal or application principle, and the principle of untied aid.[92] West Germany, like the World Bank and the EEC, followed the *project principle* or project approach, granting assistance only to clearly defined individual projects, avoiding general balance-of-payments or program aid. This principle was intended to secure better control of projects and to increase their visibility.[93] The *proposal or application principle* specified that each project had to be based on a concrete proposal or application stemming from a developing country. This principle was intended to underline the Federal Republic's respect for the sovereignty of recipient countries. Various practical problems, however, led to a softening of this principle during the 1960s.[94] The *untied aid* principle stipulated that the recipient countries should have free choice as to where to place orders with the financial funds provided by the Federal Republic. In other words, the recipient countries should not be required to spend West German aid money in West Germany. This

[89] Ibid., p. 43; on the previous history see J. Dennert, *Entwicklungshilfe – geplant oder verwaltet?* (Bielefeld: Bertelsmann Universitätsverlag, 1968), p. 33.

[90] On the further development of the system of inter-ministerial committees see ibid., p. 37.

[91] Hein, *Westdeutschen*, pp. 44–5; Dennert, *Entwicklungshilfe*, p. 39; Damm, *Bundesrepublik Deutschland und die Entwicklungsländer*, p. 149.

[92] Hein, *Westdeutschen*, pp. 55–60.

[93] Discussed extensively in Bodemer, "Programmentwicklung," p. 299.

[94] On problems with and changes to the proposal principle, see Bodemer, *Entwicklungshilfe*, p. 317.

principle, however, was subject to a few modifications: for one thing, the socialist states were generally excluded as suppliers. German exporters also soon pressed for certain exceptions that would reserve a certain portion of the supply contracts for them.[95] This pressure shows how susceptible development policy was to exporters' interests.

The inter-ministerial committee had already incorporated a large number of departments in the decision-making process on projects. In these years, however, a number of further actors gained influence on development policy.[96] The sheer number of involved parties can be seen as appropriate considering the vast range of policy questions involved. On the other hand, their involvement led to permanent coordination problems and inter-agency conflicts.[97] These circumstances formed the backdrop for the foundation of the Federal Ministry for Economic Cooperation (BMZ) in autumn of 1961.[98] Political motives played an equally important role, though. At the September 15, 1961 elections for the lower house of the German Parliament, the *Bundestag*, the center-right Christian Democratic Union (CDU) lost its absolute majority. Federal Chancellor Konrad Adenauer sought to form a coalition with the liberal Free Democratic Party (FDP), in particular with its young party

[95] Hein, *Westdeutschen*, p. 57; in 1962, however, the Bank for Reconstruction (German acronym KfW) ascertained that 80% of German financial assistance funds flowed back to German firms in any case, ibid., p. 57; see also Bodemer, "Programmentwicklung," p. 276.

[96] At first, the German government assigned two existing privately organized but publicly owned institutions with the implementation of technical and financial assistance. In November of 1957, the Foreign Office concluded a framework agreement with the Deutsche Wirtschaftsförderungs- und Treuhand GmbH (German Economic Support and Trustee GmbH, renamed the Deutsche Förderungsgesellschaft in 1964 and finally incorporated into the GTZ in 1974) and made it the implementation organization for technical assistance. A law was passed in 1960 changing the mission of the KfW, which now became the German "development bank." The German government also created further organizations with specific development tasks, among them the Stiftung für Entwicklungsländer (Foundation for Developing Countries), which was responsible for public education and development training for Germans and citizens from Third World countries. In 1964, the Deutsches Institut für Entwicklungspolitik (German Institute for Development Policy) was founded, dedicated to basic research, political consultation, and the training of young academics. For more on these structures see Hein, *Westdeutschen*, p. 47.

[97] Schimank, "Das außenpolitische Interorganisationsnetz", p. 54.

[98] Dennert, *Entwicklungshilfe*, p. 49; M. Glagow, W. Gotsch and A. Stucke (eds.), *Das Bundesministerium für wirtschaftliche Zusammenarbeit (BMZ): Entstehungszusammenhang, Personalpolitik, Steuerungsfähigkeit* (Pfaffenweiler: Centaurus-Verlagsgesellschaft, 1989), p. 3.

head, Walter Scheel, who had long supported such a coalition. Scheel was an experienced expert in development questions[99] and, during coalition talks, demanded the formation of a new ministry devoted exclusively to the subject. Adenauer approved of the plan, not least because the formation of the BMZ offered him a welcome chance to outflank his rival, the Economy Minister, Ludwig Erhard, who had spoken out strongly against a specialized development ministry, fearing a competitor in the field.

Chancellor Adenauer supported the ministry plan in a note of November 24, 1961, and an executive order from January 29, 1962 led to the formal foundation of the BMZ – and the appointment of Walter Scheel as the first minister heading it. At first, the ministry had very few powers of its own.[100] The BMZ did acquire the authority to lead the interdepartmental steering committee (without, however, power over the sub-committee of department heads within the steering committee), responsibility for two implementing organizations (the German Development Foundation and the German Development Society), and oversight responsibility for the effectiveness of development aid and for any new development plans which might arise in the future. However, changes were made neither to the system of the inter-ministerial committee nor, in particular, to the responsibilities of the Ministry of Economics (for financial assistance) or the Foreign Office (for technical assistance). There was a strategy behind this initial situation: for Scheel, in particular, it had been more important to create the Ministry as quickly as possible, even without all the relevant portfolios, since he assumed that they would all gravitate to the ministry in due course.[101] Since Erhard and his new Foreign Minister Schröder wanted to prevent precisely this, a bureaucratic turf war was in the offing. The conflict proved to be longer term and more problematic than originally surmised. In any event, the newly founded BMZ, with some luck and skilled maneuvering, did indeed eventually provide a basis for the consolidation and gradual centralization of West German development policy, which will be more closely examined when the second phase in the history of international development aid is discussed below.

[99] Scheel was a member of the Parliament of the European Coal and Steel Community from 1955–1958 and, from 1958–61, Member of the Parliament of the EEC and its Development Policy Committee; for more on his biography see W. Gieler, "Walter Scheel 1961–1966," in W. Gieler (ed.), *Deutsche Entwicklungsminister von 1961–2008: Biographien, Konzeptionen und Einfluss auf nationale und internationale Entwicklungspolitik* (Bonn: Scientia Bonnensis, 2008), pp. 12–25 at p. 12; Hein, *Westdeutschen*, p. 45.

[100] Dennert, *Entwicklungshilfe*, pp. 53–6.

[101] Ibid., p. 56.

IV. Development theory as modernization theory and principles of development assistance

The result of the first phase is quite extraordinary: within a few years, a new political field had not only been created, but had also secured an independent institutional existence. Not fifteen years after President Truman first formulated the idea of development policy, various organizations on the national, supranational, and international level had been created to implement the policy.[102] To be sure, the context of the Cold War and decolonization ensured that the circumstances of their creation in each case were widely divergent, and that their administrative form was rather improvised. Nevertheless, these organizations shared a common conceptual basis, substantive orientation and certain principles of development administration. With regard to the conceptual basis, we now turn to the dominant theory of development in the first phase of its existence: the so-called modernization theory.[103]

1. Modernization theory

Development policy in the 1950s and early 1960s was marked by a general technocratic optimism toward the achievability of development goals and by a relative certainty concerning the definition of these goals as well as the steps required to realize them. Modernization theory served as the central conceptual framework. Through its lens, development was seen primarily as the faithful re-creation of the successful economic and social development of modern Western societies, while underdevelopment was regarded as the product of the endogenous defects of traditional societies. Development was seen as a largely economic affair whose success could be measured relatively simply by the rate of economic growth. The path to success was seen primarily as the industrialization of the developing countries, which would increase the effectiveness and efficiency of the productive sectors.

[102] This phase also saw the institutionalization of development administration in other countries (for example, the 1962 establishment of the Agency for International Development (USAID) in the USA and the 1964 creation of the British Ministry of Overseas Development, known since 1997 as the Department for International Development, DFID), as well as the establishment of further multilateral organizations. In the following years, further development banks were created in the mold of the World Bank/IDA (in 1964, the African Development Bank; in 1966 the Asian Development Bank). Within the OECD, the Development Assistance Committee was set up in 1960. The topic is discussed further in Ch 3.C.I.

[103] For an overview see Martinussen, *Society, State and Market*, p. 56; a concise and contextualizing treatment is found in Menzel, *Ende der Dritten Welt*, p. 131.

The central precondition for development, thus understood, was the provision of sufficient capital. Two groups of actors were seen as particularly important protagonists for development processes. First, the upper-income classes of the countries could make the necessary investments if their savings rates were high enough, and if they could be spurred to invest in the relevant areas. However, the more important actor for the first phase was the state.[104] The state should not only take measures to increase the savings rate but also become active in the economy by creating infrastructure, initiating economic activity, or even running businesses itself.[105] It was thought that states, with a "big push," could provide the initial spark for a process of industrialization that would soon develop its own momentum.[106] The ideas of this phase were, therefore, appropriately described as "development Keynesianism."[107]

This concept of development as the step-by-step imitation of the Western path to development was particularly clearly stated in Walt W. Rostow's 1960 book *The Stages of Growth: A Non-Communist Manifesto*, which has had a lasting impact on development economics.[108] Rostow distinguished five idealized stages of development that marked the transition from a traditional to a modern economy. The first phase of a *traditional society* is characterized by the particular importance of agriculture, which contributes little to gross national product.[109] In the second phase, the *preconditions for take-off* are created, in that a willing-to-modernize elite becomes ready to make the necessary investments to drive a radical transformation of the second (industrial) and third (service-related) sectors. The third and central phase, *take-off*, is marked by increased productivity

[104] The nature of the new states and their orientation to the project of development was an important topic of discussion at that time. The discussion came to be known under the rubric of the "developmental state." See also Martinussen, *Society, State and Market*, p. 219.

[105] For a discussion of the role of the state in the development process see D. W. Brinkerhoff, "The State and International Development Management: Shifting Tides, Changing Boundaries, and Future Directions," *Public Administration Review*, 68 (2008), 985–1001 at 985; Leftwich, *States of Development*, p. 152; see also K. König (ed.), *Öffentliche Verwaltung und Entwicklungspolitik* (Baden-Baden: Nomos, 1986).

[106] The idea originated with P. N. Rosenstein-Rodan, "Notes on the Theory of the 'Big Push'," in H. S. Ellis (ed.), *Economic Development for Latin America* (London: Macmillan, 1962), pp. 57–81.

[107] Menzel, *Ende der Dritten Welt*, p. 142.

[108] Martinussen, *Society, State and Market*, p. 61. On the ironic fact that this theory, in the final analysis, reflects a fairly materialistic interpretation of history, see Rist, *History of Development*, pp. 100–1.

[109] W. W. Rostow, *The Stages of Growth: A Non-Communist Manifesto* (Cambridge University Press, 1960), p. 18.

through the application of innovative agricultural techniques and, in particular, by innovations in manufacturing industry. Take-off, however, is impossible to achieve without a massive increase in the savings rate and external capital inflows, since during the critical phase of take-off, net investment rates of between five and seven percent of gross domestic product are necessary. During the fourth phase, called *drive to maturity*, increased productivity is then expanded to further, less-central economic sectors, before, finally, the *age of mass consumption* is achieved, in which the importance of heavy industry declines and consumer-goods production becomes the most important economic driver.

Parallel to an economic theory of development, a more political theory of development also emerged in the 1950s and 1960s. It, too, was generally a modernization theory.[110] Developing countries were again seen as politically and socially underdeveloped, even though it was generally assumed that economic modernization would also lead to the modernization of other sectors. However, it was also assumed that this political-social modernization, as well as a top-down redistribution of growth profits, would take place only in a second step. This delay, considered as a gradual "trickle-down effect" of economic growth, would then lead to urbanization, increased literacy, and finally political participation. Some authors, however, considered this time lag practically as a prerequisite for the successful "big push" and "take-off" phases. Samuel Huntington, in particular, published an influential study arguing that a large degree of political participation could actually endanger the internal stability and growth of societies in transformation.[111]

These theories specified relatively clearly which role development organizations should play. It was generally believed that most countries were in the third phase of the Rostow model, ready for "take-off." Thus, the decisive factor was a massive inflow of capital and technology, to which development organizations would contribute. In the early years, all donors concentrated their attention on support for large infrastructure projects. Energy supply (dams) and transport (roads) played a particularly important role. Such projects, it was assumed, were the primary conditions for industrialization, which would lead to the desired economic

[110] On the close connection between economic and political-social modernization theories see Martinussen, *Society, State and Market*, p. 167; an earlier discussion is found in G. Almond and J. S. Coleman (eds.), *The Politics of the Developing Areas* (Princeton University Press, 1960).

[111] S. Huntington, *Political Order in Changing Societies* (New Haven: Yale University Press, 1968); influential was also M. S. Lipset, "Some Social Requisites of Democracy: Economic Development and Political Legitimacy," *American Political Science Review*, 53 (1969), 69–105.

growth. By contrast, agriculture was considered relatively less important, as were other areas, such as education or health, which were oriented more directly toward basic human needs.

2. Early principles of development cooperation

During this first phase, development assistance shared a common conceptual foundation in modernization theory, which led to a substantive focus on large infrastructure projects. Furthermore, the administrative organization of all three donors was marked by common principles, namely the project principle and the proposal principle. The eventual erosion of these two principles later gave rise to fundamental questions of development cooperation law, which justifies their brief review here. The project principle held that funds would be made available in the main for clearly defined single projects which had a basic productive purpose.[112] These projects were to be distinguished from loans for the support of state budgets or trade balances, implementation of general programs, or import of raw materials. Support for projects appeared, in individual cases, more economically justifiable, easier to monitor in execution, and thus was in the donors' interests. At the same time, the visibility of the projects appealed to both donors and recipients. To be sure, the project principle was never regarded as absolute, but it was always an important aspiration.

At least formally, however, the proposal principle was enforced more strictly. This principle held that it was the exclusive responsibility of recipient countries to formulate and propose projects. This principle sought to respect the recipient countries' decision-making freedom and to emphasize the non-interference of donor countries. This would formalize respect for the sovereignty of the newly formed independent states. In all three institutions, however, the evaluation of the projects and the decision to make loans and implement projects was always the responsibility of the donors. Some countries also lacked the technical resources to develop projects. In light of this fact, the proposal principle had, in point of fact, a somewhat more limited effect. Nevertheless, as a formal matter, it was strictly applied during the first phase.

V. Summary

The first phase marked the gradual emergence of this policy field and its institutional structures. Assistance to poorer countries for its own sake

[112] Particularly explicit in Art. III, Sect 2 (vii) IBRD Articles.

only took shape as a goal gradually, often as an instrument to achieve other goals, particularly those defined by the Cold War or by trade considerations. The process of decolonization, however, made the purpose and the potential applications of development cooperation ever more obvious. Specialized administrative agencies were established quite early, which considerably aided in the process of achieving autonomy and stability in this field of endeavor. By the mid 1960s, specialized administrative agencies had been instituted at all three levels of public authority – national, European, and international – which helped development assistance survive despite changing political circumstances and, in particular, growing doubts about its effectiveness. In the initial phase that has been our focus thus far, however, few doubts had yet been raised about development policy. The field was marked by general technocratic optimism. Development was seen as a clearly defined economic activity that could be achieved by experts according to the standards of modernization theory. Recipient countries did not yet play a significant role as independent actors. They had not yet found a collective voice, and had little effect individually in specific administrative processes, even though the proposal principle demonstrated fundamental respect for their status as states.

B Breakthrough and contestation (1965–1975)

The second phase in this short history of development cooperation is marked by the strength and vigor of the developing countries. It was the decade of young states which took the world stage with increasing confidence and began to test global power relationships. In this phase, which lasted from approximately 1965 to 1975, developing countries began to alter their stance toward their former colonial masters and dominated the international agenda in a manner that hardly seems imaginable today. Often, their assertiveness even overshadowed the Cold War. On the donor side, this is the phase in which development cooperation achieved its political and administrative independence. Development policy achieved a certain amount of autonomy from other policy fields, striving to develop its own independent goals, strategies and methods. This was also a time for reflection on the problematic experiences of the first years, and perhaps also of the realization of just how unbelievably challenging development would be. Toward the end of the 1960s, it became clear that the goals set during the first decade of development would not be achieved, and that the economy-oriented concept of development suggested by modernization theory might need revision. The second phase thus led to political and theoretical paradigm shifts – and they would not be the last.

I. Political and theoretical context: paradigm shift

1. Developing countries in the UN and the NIEO

The decade from 1965 to 1975 was dominated by the effects of decolonization. During the 1955 Bandung Conference of Asian and African countries, the non-aligned nations had announced their intention to pursue their own interests. It can be seen in fact as the starting point of a conscious and self-confident postcolonial perspective on international relations.[113] At first, however, these countries were too disunited to effectively influence the international agenda.[114] Only in the 1960s did the rapidly increasing number of states in the Global South succeed in creating organizational structures that gave them a powerful voice in international politics and permitted their own interests to be heard. The United Nations was a vital instrument in this endeavor.[115]

From the early 1960s, developing countries were in the majority in the United Nations. In December 1962, they used this majority to overcome the resistance of industrialized nations to the formation of the United Nations Conference on Trade and Development, or UNCTAD. They thereby created a forum in which they could, unlike in the World Bank, formulate their own agenda. Already during the very first meeting of the UNCTAD in Geneva in 1964, the developing nations demanded that industrialized countries transfer 0.7 percent of their gross national product to the countries of the Global South in the form of public development assistance ("net-capital inflow"). These first steps, while hardly causing serious concerns in the capitals of industrialized nations, nevertheless marked a clear change. Developing countries had shown that they would use their voting majority to pursue their own interests. At the UNCTAD II Conference in Nairobi in 1968, a general system of customs preferences

[113] R. J. C. Young, *Postcolonialism: A Very Short Introduction* (Oxford University Press, 2003), p. 17; see also Pahuja, *Decolonising International Law*; on postcolonial studies see also, Ch 2.B.IV.1.

[114] W. Link and P. Tücks, *Der Nord-Süd-Konflikt und die Zusammenarbeit der Entwicklungsländer* (Berlin: Colloquium, 1985), p. 26; V. Matthies, *Die Blockfreien: Ursprünge, Entwicklung, Konzeptionen, Analysen* (Opladen: Leske und Budrich, 1985), vol. XXXV; see also literature cited in Menzel, *Ende der Dritten Welt*, p. 147, fn. 17.

[115] J. C. Paul, "The United Nations and the Creation of an International Law of Development," *Harvard International Law Journal*, 36 (1995), 307–28 at 307.

was proposed. In 1970, the UN adopted a highly ambitious program for the second development decade.[116] Finally, UNCTAD III in Santiago de Chile in 1972 started discussions on a general reform of worldwide economic relationships. The increasing discursive power of developing countries, bolstered by their institutionalized power in the UN, was further fueled by the 1973/74 oil crisis and OPEC's highly successful oil embargo. It was widely hoped that other raw material cartels might contribute further to redistribution of wealth from the North to the South.[117] The groundwork was thus laid for the formulation of the Global South's central demands in two 1974 UN Declarations.

In April 1974, a Special General Assembly of the UN convened on the subject of raw materials and development proclaimed a "New International Economic Order" (NIEO[118]).[119] The new order was described in further detail in the "Charter of Economic Rights and Duties of States," adopted during the 29th regular General Assembly on December 12, 1974.[120] This document proposed an agenda of global Keynesianism in which industrialized countries would be bound to active support for the industrialization of developing countries, more equal global trade relations, and the general goal of international social justice and the harmonization of living standards.[121] These declarations did not create any binding legal duties, as they were not even supported by a consensus of the community

[116] UN-GA Res. 2626 (XXV).

[117] On the creation of OPEC see J. P. Terhechte, *OPEC und europäisches Wettbewerbsrecht: Zugleich ein Beitrag zum Phänomen der Fragmentierung des internationalen Wirtschaftsrechts* (Baden-Baden: Nomos, 2008), p. 31; on the aspirations of developing countries see H. Hagemann, *Die Formierung der rohstoffpolitischen Forderungen der Entwicklungsländer auf der Ebene der Vereinten Nationen bis zur Ersten Konferenz für Handel und Entwicklung (UNCTAD 1) 1946*, Schriften des Instituts für Politikwissenschaft der Westfälischen Wilhelms-Universität Münster, (Münster: Institut für Politikwissenschaft der Westfälischen Wilhelms-Universität Münster, 1983), vol. III, p. 201.

[118] The English-language acronym for the New International Economic Order, NIEO, has become standard and will be used here. The acronym typically stands for an amalgam of the two declarations.

[119] UN-GA Res. 3201 (S-VI) and the Action Program in UN-GA Res. 3202 (S-VI).

[120] UN-GA Res. 3281 (XXIX) from December 12, 1974.

[121] A brief overview is found in Menzel, *Ende der Dritten Welt*, pp. 150–3; for a more critical perspective see Rist, *History of Development*, pp. 146–50. Selected contemporaneous commentary includes J. N. Bhagwati, *The New International Economic Order: The North-South Debate* (Cambridge: MIT Press, 1977); J. Galtung, *Poor Countries vs. Rich: Poor People vs. Rich: Whom Will NIEO Benefit?* (University of Oslo, 1977); R. W. Cox, "Ideologies and the New International Economic Order," *International Organization*, 33 (1979), 257–302 at 257; V. Matthies, *Neue Weltwirtschaftsordnung: Hintergründe – Positionen – Argumente, Analysen* (Opladen: Leske und Budrich, 1980), vol. XXVII.

of states. In fact, the Charter was adopted against the explicit opposition of industrialized nations.[122] They did, however, send a signal of confrontation which could not be ignored within the political and economic situation of the time. It called upon industrialized nations to show solidarity with developing countries while at the same time showing respect for their sovereignty in structuring their internal affairs.

Three of the Charter's demands were particularly relevant to development policy: the call for increased ODA payments (Chapter II, Article 22), for the reinforcement of development cooperation through multilateral organizations and the prohibition of tying development assistance to political or military conditions (Chapter II, Art. 17), and, finally, for participation on an equal footing in international decision-making, which referred implicitly to the weighting of votes in the World Bank (Chapter II, Art. 10). Developing countries thus put forward a world-view that aimed primarily at ensuring a generous and uninterrupted flow of resources from North to South, as well as protection for the recipient nation's autonomous authority over these resources. The donor nations' influence was to be clearly limited.

It is somewhat ironic that these UN Declarations, in effect, envisioned a development concept that basically corresponded to modernization theory. The goal of the Declarations was the promotion of economic growth, assistance in industrialization, and the incorporation of developing nations into the system of world trade (under advantageous conditions). The political demands of developing countries were, to a certain extent, less radical than development theory, which by this time had already entered a new and more critical phase.

2. Dependence theory and the basic-needs strategy

While modernization theory had dominated the field in the 1950s and early 1960s, the second half of the 1960s saw the emergence of a fundamental alternative: dependence theory. Dependence theory, developed mainly by North and South American sociologists inspired by neo-Marxist thought, can be described as a nearly point-by-point refutation of modernization theory.[123] Dependence theory posited that the main reasons

[122] One legal analysis is C. Tomuschat, "Die Charta der wirtschaftlichen Rechte und Pflichten der Staaten: Zur Gestaltungskraft von Deklarationen der UN-Generalversammlung," *Heidelberg Journal of International Law*, 36 (1976), 444–90 at 444. In more detail, Ch 4.B.

[123] Important supporters and texts include P. A. Baran and P. M. Sweezy, *Monopoly Capital: An Essay on the American Economy and Social Order* (Harmondsworth: Penguin Press,

for the underdevelopment of the Third World were not to be found in the level of development of particular countries, but rather in their general position in geopolitical and economic structures. Centuries of colonial domination had entrenched power relations resting on a distinction between an economic (and political) center and a periphery, resulting in the degradation of the economies of developing nations into mere sources of raw materials. Within this system, international trade and exchange, instead of benefiting all parties, perpetuated the exclusion and exploitation of developing countries. Thus, it wasn't the developing countries that needed reforming, but rather the structures of international trade. Furthermore – and in clear contrast to modernization theory – the state should not simply accept social inequalities (or even promote them to drive capital accumulation), but should rather actively combat them by redistributive policies such as land reform.

Although the precise consequences of this diagnosis remained unclear or at least highly controversial, there was no question that it was time for a fundamental reform of the basic structures of the international division of labor. The dependence theory, however, offered few recipes for development policy, which was rather oriented toward incremental steps. Not merely because it was seen as a holdover of modernization theory, this incremental strategy was now seen as merely addressing symptoms, while leaving deeper causes unaddressed.

However, it was not only Marxist theoreticians who were skeptical about modernization theory. Based on the meager results delivered by the first development decade (that is, the 1960s) the burgeoning third-world movement in donor states,[124] joined by large sectors of the development "establishment," had begun to express doubts about the previous strategy of growth and industrialization. A particularly visible signal was sent by the so-called Pearson Report, the product of a "Commission for International Development" initiated by the World Bank. The Report, presented in 1969 by former Canadian Foreign Minister Lester Pearson,[125] endorsed several central demands of the UNCTAD.

1968); A. G. Frank, *Capitalism and Underdevelopment in Latin America: Historical Studies of Chile and Brazil* (New York: Monthly Review Press, 1967); F. H. Cardoso and E. Faletto, *Dependency and Development in Latin America* (Berkeley: University of California Press, 1971); see Rist, *History of Development*, p. 109; D. Senghaas, "Elemente einer Theorie des peripheren Kapitalismus," in D. Senghaas (ed.), *Peripherer Kapitalismus: Analysen über Abhängigkeit und Unterentwicklung* (Frankfurt: Suhrkamp, 1974), pp. 7–36; Menzel, *Ende der Dritten Welt*, p. 133.

[124] The example of Germany is described in detail in Hein, *Westdeutschen*, p. 139.

[125] Report of the Commission on International Development 1969 (published as L. Pearson, *Partners in Development: Report of the Commission on International Development* (New

Doubts about previous development policies were particularly evident in the so-called basic-needs approach, which had been developed in the first half of the 1970s by international organizations (in particular, the World Bank), and which was then adopted by many donors.[126] This approach reflected the realization that previous development strategies had done little to improve the living standards of the poorest citizens. Without entirely abandoning the focus on growth, the strategy was to be complemented by policies which would reach the poorest 40 percent in each developing country. These new approaches did not emerge from a unified conceptual system or explanatory model, nor did they give rise to a general overall strategy. The human-needs approaches differed in emphasis.[127] Some, for instance, attempted to ease the access of the poorest citizens to the labor market, while others concentrated on access to public goods. Despite these differences, a common understanding of the three types of basic human needs emerged from these approaches. The first were the needs of daily life, such as nutrition, housing and clothes. A second group related to access to public goods and facilities, such as water, health care and the education system. The third category involved participation in political decision-making processes. Even in its early stages, the human-needs approach endorsed a broad understanding of the relationship between poverty and development, incorporating economic as well as political aspects.[128]

In contrast to the external redistribution from North to South, one of the NIEO's demands, the basic-needs strategy was focused more on an *internal* redistribution within developing countries themselves. The reaction of developing-country governments to the basic-needs approach was, unsurprisingly, quite *guarded*. The approach clearly had nothing to do

York: Praeger, 1969 hereafter referred to as *Pearson Report 1969*); see also D. Nohlen, "Stichwort Pearson-Bericht," in D. Nohlen and S. Arons (eds.), *Lexikon Dritte Welt: Länder, Organisationen, Theorien, Begriffe, Personen* (Reinbek bei Hamburg: Rowohlt, 2002), pp. 667–700 at p. 667.

[126] A fundamental contribution was made by the then-Chief Economist of the World Bank in H. Chenery (ed.), *Redistribution with Growth: Policies to Improve Income Distribution in Developing Countries in the Context of Economic Growth* (Washington, DC: Oxford University Press, 1974) (see Kapur, Lewis and Webb, *The World Bank*, pp. 247); International Labour Organization, *Employment, Growth and Basic Needs: A One-World Problem* (Genf: Council of Foreign Relations, 1976).

[127] The diversity becomes apparent in D. P. Ghai and A. Khan (eds.), *The Basic Needs Approach to Development: Some Issues Regarding Concepts and Methodology* (Genf: Internationale Arbeitsorganisation, 1977); K. Lederer and J. Galtung, *Human Needs: A Contribution to the Current Debate* (Berliner Wissenschaftszentrum: Anton Hain, 1980).

[128] On the context of these approaches see Martinussen, *Society, State and Market*, pp. 298–303; Menzel, *Ende der Dritten Welt*, pp. 166–9.

with the NIEO's growth agenda, and also threatened the interests of ruling elites.[129] In addition to the manifestly confrontational NIEO demands, the human-needs strategy opened up a second field of conflict between developing and industrialized countries. As one of the first grass-roots approaches to development, it did not become the leading developmental theory in the large donor organizations.[130] However, as will shortly be seen, it did have some effect within these organizations. The welter of varying approaches and critical discussions which marked these years was generated in part by internal political developments in industrialized nations. After a phase of economic stagnation during the middle of the 1960s, the economic situation improved toward the end of the decade, laying the groundwork for a liberal reform phase in many Western countries and in the organizations to which they contributed.

II. The World Bank: McNamara and the war on poverty

No other World Bank president shaped the organization as much as Robert McNamara. When he took office in 1968, the former Ford executive was – to put it mildly – seen as a curious choice, given that his many years as Secretary of Defense under Presidents Kennedy and Johnson had made him the face of the Vietnam War. As president of the World Bank, however, he changed its approach both as to substance and administration, showing deep interest in and understanding of the problem of development.[131] In fact, it was McNamara who forged the image of the Bank that it continues to claim as its own to this day: a bank for the poor and the leading development organization in the world.[132]

[129] A contemporaneous discussion is found in M. u. Haq, *The Poverty Curtain: Choices for the Third World* (New York: Columbia University Press, 1976), p. 63. Another critical perspective pointing out not only the interventionist structure of the approach but also its asocial view of the needy individual can be found in Rist, *History of Development*, pp. 162–9.

[130] An indigenous counter-strategy was the self-reliance of developing countries, especially in Tanzania. See ibid., p. 123.

[131] As for McNamara himself, his time at the World Bank appears to have had less of an impact on him. His autobiographical statements revolve almost exclusively around his participation in the Vietnam War. See, in particular, R. S. McNamara, *In Retrospect: The Tragedy and Lessons of Vietnam* (New York: Time Books, 1995) and the film based on the book: *The Fog of War*, 2003.

[132] An interesting commentary on McNamara's role can be found in Tetzlaff, *Weltbank*, p. 67; a current perspective is provided by S. Mallaby, *The World's Banker: A Story of Failed States, Financial Crises, and the Wealth and Poverty of Nations* (New Haven: Yale University Press, 2004), p. 34.

1. Thematic reorientation: the goal of poverty reduction

From the beginning, McNamara put poverty reduction at the center of his efforts.[133] Without abandoning the old paradigm of development, which focused on economic growth, he sought a reorientation of the Bank's priorities, favoring the basic-needs strategy at the Bank. The overriding goal was to reduce poverty. Economic growth was seen as an important factor, but one which did not achieve the hoped-for "trickle-down" effect frequently enough. Poverty reduction, in many instances, required different strategies. Employment, health and demographic (or family) policy – as well as rural development and food security – became the Bank's new themes.[134] Support for agricultural policy, in particular small farmers, became a focus of the Bank. Family planning also increased its profile.

McNamara was not the first who sought to broaden the Bank's vision and areas of activity,[135] but he was especially effective. During his presidency, the Bank not only broadened its perspective and changed its emphasis, but also, to a certain extent, began to see itself in a changed and more complex fashion. The Bank, one might say, became less of a bank and more of a development agency. This change was a necessary consequence of a broader idea of development including (among other things) poverty reduction, and lent the goal of development a certain autonomy from the goal of profitability, which the IBRD had been required to pursue and which, as we have seen, strongly influenced it. The internal relationship between the IBRD and the IDA shifted slightly to the latter leading the Bank to areas which were essentially within the jurisdiction of other UN agencies (such as the World Health Organization, the World Food Organization, and others).[136] The reorientation under McNamara also affected the decision-making structures and procedures of the Bank.

2. Administrative reforms: planning and specialization

McNamara's leadership demonstrated the art of management. Quantitatively as well as administratively, McNamara led the Bank into new territory. During his thirteen-year tenure (1968–81), personnel more than tripled (from 750 to 2,250 employees), and the disbursement volume

[133] Kapur, Lewis and Webb, *The World Bank*, p. 215; on the current importance of this theme in the Bank see R. Kanbur and D. Vines, "The World Bank and Poverty Reduction: Past, Present and Future," in C. Gilbert and D. Vines (eds.), *The World Bank: Structure and Policies* (Cambridge University Press, 2000), pp. 87–107 at p. 87.

[134] Kapur, Lewis and Webb, *The World Bank*, p. 252.

[135] On the beginnings see ibid., pp. 139, 191.

[136] On the rivalry between the IBRD and the IDA see Rist, *History of Development*, p. 169.

more than quadrupled, from US$1 billion per year to US$4.2 billion.[137] Still a small institution at the beginning of the 1960s, the World Bank grew into a large bureaucracy. The massive growth not infrequently conflicted with the Bank's aspirations to quality.[138]

Growth was accompanied by administrative reforms. Four of these reforms are especially important because they signaled new trends in development administration that influenced other donor organizations. First came the introduction of systematic, middle-range program planning for each recipient state.[139] The so-called "country program papers" which McNamara introduced when he took office were meant to sketch the overall planning of the Bank for a period of five years. Without sacrificing the Bank's project focus, these papers permitted McNamara to eliminate arbitrariness from the planning of single projects and to develop a more coherent framework for individual projects. Development cooperation thus moved from being a piecemeal effort to being part of an overall plan. The principle of planning, as well as the integration of projects into an overall plan, remains a fundamental principle of development administration to this day.

McNamara's second reform was a personnel reorganization that better integrated project and regional expertise. McNamara's aim was to unite the two previously separated areas of expertise to enable them better to profit from one another.[140] In 1970, to improve project quality and learn from missteps, McNamara introduced his third key reform, the creation of the operations evaluations unit, now known as the Operations Evaluations Department. After a project was completed, this department was charged with providing as independent an evaluation of the project's success as possible.[141]

Finally, McNamara's fourth innovation was to dramatically expand the Bank's research capabilities. He hired renowned development experts (mostly economists such as Hollis Chenery[142]) and launched a largely successful drive to make the Bank the world's central repository of analytical and empirical development research. Since the mid 1970s, it has been generally agreed that the World Bank is not only the largest

[137] Numbers are also provided in Mason and Asher, *World Bank Since Bretton Woods*, p. 799.

[138] Kapur, Lewis and Webb, *The World Bank*, p. 41.

[139] Ibid., pp. 17, 1185; on the significance of these plans at the time see Wiegand, *Organisatorische Aspekte*, pp. 320–2.

[140] Ibid., p. 226. [141] Kapur, Lewis and Webb, *The World Bank*, pp. 245, 41.

[142] Ibid., pp. 242, 1193.

single development donor, but also has the most expertise in questions of development.[143]

Whether in its emphasis on technical expertise, its advocacy of a broadened idea of development, or the example set by administrative reforms, the influence of McNamara's World Bank on German and European development administration can, as will shortly be seen, hardly be overestimated.

III. Germany: Eppler and the creation of an autonomous development policy

German development administration and policy took a quantum leap forward during the early years of the new left-wing coalition government between the Social Democratic Party and the Free Democrats. Development policy doubtless profited from a favorable political climate. Yet the quantum leap would hardly have been possible without the intellectual gifts and aggressive political support of Development Minister Erhard Eppler, who held that office from 1969 to 1974.[144] Thanks to Eppler, development policy gained a hitherto unknown level of conceptual clarity, autonomy (especially from foreign and economic policy) and independent credibility. Under Eppler, development policy finally attained a level of substantive and administrative consolidation sufficient to justify calling it an independent field of policy.

1. Conceptualizing development policy

The new conceptualization of development policy took place in various stages and aspects. Of crucial importance is Eppler's success in reformulating the purpose and goals of development policy in order to free it from dependence on economic or general foreign policy priorities. Eppler conceived of development policy as a global policy of peace and social justice. In his "General Formula of Development Policy," Eppler early ascertained that the growing gap between developing and

[143] Ibid., p. 1193; on the current concept of the "knowledge bank" see J. Morduch, "The Knowledge Bank," in Easterly, *Reinventing Foreign Aid*, p. 377; L. Squire, "Why the World Bank Should Be Involved in Development Research," in Gilbert and Vines, *The World Bank*, p. 108.

[144] On Eppler as development minister see J. Cernicky, "Erhard Eppler 1968–1974," in Gieler, *Deutsche Entwicklungsminister von 1961–2008*, p. 40. During the 1966 grand coalition government in Germany, the development portfolio was already assigned to the Social Democratic Party (SPD) politician Hans-Jürgen Wischnewski, who exercised relatively little influence. For more on his time in office see ibid., p. 33.

industrialized countries was threatening to increase dramatically.[145] Development policy, therefore, must focus on a "world domestic policy (*Weltinnenpolitik*) … aimed at peace." To achieve this end, development policy would have to pursue the developing nations' goals. At the same time, though, the goals of the developing countries – peace and higher living standards – would also correspond to West Germany's goals in the long term (or, in cases of unrest, the not at all long term).[146] In the struggle for attention or resources of development agencies against other departments of government – which is a fundamental aspect of any development policy at the *national* level – this was a significant step forward.

Soon after, Eppler achieved an equally important step forward in German development policy – the expansion of the idea of development to include questions of redistribution and poverty. In his inaugural speech as Federal Chancellor, Willy Brandt, at Eppler's urging, announced his support for a common development strategy and referred to the recently released and highly progressive Pearson Report.[147] The speech prompted a widening of the thematic spectrum of German development policy making space for a series of new initiatives.

This conceptual transformation was accompanied by material concessions. For the first time, the West German government accepted the goal of dedicating 0.7 percent of its gross national product (GNP) to ODA.[148] Again in the inaugural speech, Brandt also promised to relax conditions for financial aid and dedicate all earnings from such loans to new development projects. He thus transformed one of the previous hallmarks of German development policy: the insistence that aid be subject to strict conditions favorable to West Germany. To an extent, Brandt's speech indicated the "IDA-ization" of German development policy, since the International Development Association as the World Bank's development branch had made it possible to lend to extremely poor (and thus non-creditworthy) countries. And the policy change announced in Brandt's speech was not an empty promise: under Eppler, the budget of the Ministry of Economic Cooperation (BMZ) grew by

[145] An important part of Eppler's political success is seen as stemming from his active critique of the former tradition. He perceived that development policy was especially attractive to young voters and could bind them as new voters to the SPD. See Hein, *Westdeutschen*, pp. 195, 256.

[146] E. Eppler, *Entwicklungspolitik und Eigeninteressen* (Bonn: Deutsche Gesellschaft für Auswärtige Politik, 1971), pp. 187–94; Bodemer, "Programmentwicklung," p. 286.

[147] On this report, see Pearson, *Pearson Report 1969.*

[148] On the discussion of this goal see Bodemer, *Entwicklungshilfe*, pp. 247, 273.

almost 50 percent, and the total development budget doubled in the ten years after he entered office.[149]

The conceptual foundations were finalized in a report entitled the "Development-Policy Principles for the Federal Republic of Germany in the Second Development Decade," which was released in February 1971. It was the first statement of principles of this kind created in the Federal Republic.[150] In this thirty-page document, Eppler set out the central goals, principles and activities of development policy, and sketched its financial framework. The government formulated its goal as "[s]upport for the economic and social progress of developing nations in a system of global partnership." Ten years after the foundation of the BMZ, this document finally provided the first coherent overall concept for development policy in collaboration with foreign and trade policy.[151]

2. Administrative reforms: portfolio acquisition and planning

When it was founded in 1961, the BMZ had no significant portfolios and was more of a coordinating agency than a genuine government organ. During the next ten years, however, the ministry was so successful in acquiring new fields of responsibility that, by Eppler's departure, it had established itself as the main decision-maker in German development policy.[152] A first step was taken in 1964, when the Foreign Office relinquished the authority for planning and implementation of technical assistance to the Development Ministry. At the same time, there was some streamlining of the laborious decision-making process in

[149] Hein, *Westdeutschen*, pp. 198–202; a general assessment of the expansion of the volume of assistance of German development aid is found in R. Stockmann, "Administrative Probleme staatlicher Entwicklungszusammenarbeit," in M. Glagow (ed.), *Deutsche und internationale Entwicklungspolitik: Zur Rolle staatlicher, supranationaler und nicht-regierungsabhängiger Organisationen im Entwicklungsprozeß der Dritten Welt* (Opladen: Westdeutscher Verlag, 1990), pp. 35–75 at pp. 40–4.

[150] BMZ, *Entwicklungspolitische Konzeption der Bundesrepublik Deutschland für die Zweite Entwicklungsdekade*, (Conception) (Bonn, 1971).

[151] The center-right Christian Democratic Union (CDU), rather than sitting idly by as the SPD identified itself with development policy, attacked SPD development policy vehemently. Between 1970 and 1974, the CDU rejected the BMZ's proposed budgets (which had till then been largely approved with all-party support) and sharply attacked individual measures such as preferential tax treatment for private investment in developing countries and the federal government's individual procurement decisions in socialist countries. See Hein, *Westdeutschen*, p. 256.

[152] Stockmann, "Administrative Probleme," pp. 39–40.

the inter-ministerial committee system.[153] However, the Development Ministry still had to share some competencies with other ministries, primarily the Ministry of Economics. Only in 1972 did the Development Ministry finally become responsible for financial assistance, the second main area of German development policy.[154] As had been the case at its foundation, the Development Ministry once again profited from coalition politics. After the 1972 elections, the Free Democratic Party laid a "claim" to two additional Cabinet positions. Since decision-makers wanted to avoid the impression of too much power being given to the FDP, it was decided to transfer some of the portfolio of the Economy Ministry – which was to go to the Free Democrats – to the Development Ministry.[155] The Development Ministry's increasing scope of responsibilities was accompanied by a growth in personnel. The Ministry had 145 employees when it was founded, and 350 by the time Eppler took it over. Under his leadership, the number of employees grew to 500, and remained constant until the 1990s.[156]

Eppler also pursued an ambitious reform of the decision-making process which (as with the World Bank) was intended to improve planning and competence. The system of inter-ministerial decision-making was abolished.[157] The Development Ministry was still obliged to consult a number of other departments before approving a project, but it now had a leading role in the process and could take the most important decisions itself. After much preparation, Eppler also introduced a system of mid-range program planning modeled on the World Bank's.[158] He installed the system of so-called "country assistance programs," which integrated the requirements both of the recipient country and the West German government into a five-year development plan.[159] The decision-making reforms were complemented by a reorganization of the ministry. Regional departments were given leadership of project development, although they were still required to coordinate constantly with relevant technical and supervisory departments.[160] Finally, implementing organizations were consolidated when, in 1974, the Gesellschaft für Technische

[153] Hein, *Westdeutschen*, pp. 112–16. [154] Ibid., pp. 207–11.

[155] Ibid., p. 210. [156] Stockmann, "Administrative Probleme," p. 47.

[157] Hein, *Westdeutschen*, p. 210.

[158] For background see ibid., pp. 149–152, 202; see also Bodemer, *Entwicklungshilfe*, p. 194.

[159] Bodemer, "Programmentwicklung," pp. 287–9 (which, however, points to the rapidly approaching end of this planning form).

[160] Hein, *Westdeutschen*, p. 206.

Zusammenarbeit (GTZ/German Society for Technical Cooperation) was created by the merger of the Bundesstelle für Entwicklungshilfe (BfE/Federal Authority for Development Assistance) and the Deutsche Fördergesellschaft für Entwicklungsländer (German Society to Support Developing Countries).

The Eppler era ended abruptly when Chancellor Brandt resigned, depriving Eppler of his primary supporter in the Cabinet. In July 1974, only weeks after Brandt's successor Helmut Schmidt was sworn in, Eppler submitted his resignation.[161] This ended the most innovative phase German development policy had yet seen. The Eppler era saw the ministry substantially increase its autonomy and independence by refining its conceptual foundations and consolidating its administrative structures and procedures. As in the World Bank, the expansion of what goals development policy should pursue played an important part in the ministry's transformation, moving away from economic growth and donor-state economic interest and toward a policy of poverty reduction, "global domestic policy," and a longer-term conception of donor-state interests.

IV. The European community: Cheysson and the promise of Lomé

On the European level as well, one can discern a second phase both in terms of policy and administrative structures which, even more than in the case of Germany and the World Bank, signaled a rejection of the certainties of the first years. This phase brought about a programmatic and administrative modernization of European development policy, a geographic reorientation, and, finally, liberation from the dominance of French interests. However, the new phase began later at the European level. It began not in the second half of the 1960s, but rather at the beginning of the 1970s; it coincided with the accession of Great Britain into the European Economic Community in 1973, and was marked by the inauguration of Claude Cheysson as Commissioner for Development (also in 1973), and, most importantly, the negotiation and adoption of the Lomé Convention (coming into force in 1975).

1. The new beginning of Lomé

In the second phase the EEC, like Germany, undertook a conceptual reorganization of the goals of an independent development policy,

[161] Ibid., pp. 263–7.

beyond narrower associational and trade interests. A highly influential Commission Paper in 1971 described the necessity of a global perspective.[162] Then, in 1972, development policy, for the first time, was placed on the agenda of a meeting of heads of state and government (later to become the European Council), which led, among other things, to the creation of a separate Council-level committee of development ministers.[163] Although there was already discussion about new directions for development policy at the Commission and Council level, the accession of the UK into the EEC and the expiration of the Yaoundé Convention rendered a revision of policy imperative. It resulted in the conclusion of the Lomé Convention in 1975, which represented a fundamental change in terms of geography, rhetoric, symbolism and substance.[164]

The most obvious change was in the geographic scope and reach of European development policy, bringing about a considerable reorientation and expansion. In contrast to Germany and the World Bank, European development policy had started out with a decidedly regional focus, concentrating on francophone Africa, inviting the criticism that it represented a historically fraught postcolonial arrangement.[165] When the UK entered the EEC, this regional focus became a subject of discussion. The French government was not inclined to permit the UK's accession at the expense of damaging its own relations to its former colonies. It objected in particular to the inclusion of *Asian* members of the Commonwealth, which (particularly in the case of India) would have wildly exceeded the scope of previous programs. However, the French had a simultaneous interest in obtaining British financial contributions to common development projects.[166] To solve the problem, a protocol was added to the accession treaty in which a distinction was drawn between those states that could be associated and those that could not, whereby the "associatable" states would be offered participation in any revised version of the

[162] European Commission, Commission Memorandum on a Community policy for Development Co-operation, from July 27, 1971.

[163] On the background and stages of this reorientation see E. Grabitz, "Die Entwicklungspolitik der Europäischen Gemeinschaften: Ziele und Kompetenzen," *Europarecht*, 12 (1977), 217–39 at 217; Hewitt and Whiteman, "The Commission and Development Policy," pp. 139–41; Frisch, "Die entwicklungspolitische Konzeption," p. 17.

[164] Negotiations on this treaty began on August 1973. It was signed on 28 February 1975 and came into force on 1 April 1976.

[165] As far back as the 1960s there was a certain reorientation occasioned by the expansion of cooperation to states such as Nigeria and the members of the East African Community. See Hewitt and Whiteman, "The Commission and Development Policy," pp. 137, 138.

[166] Lister, *EC and the Developing World*, p. 62.

Yaoundé Convention.[167] This meant that the new treaty (called the Lomé Convention) would include a drastically increased number of signatory states. In addition to the nineteen countries of the Yaoundé Association, twenty-one Commonwealth nations[168] joined the Lomé Convention, as well as six further African countries.[169] The new group of cooperation partners, called the ACP States (African, Caribbean and Pacific) now comprised forty-six countries. The new accord did not represent a true "globalization" of European development aid, since Latin American and many Asian countries were not included, but it did at least end the concentration on former French colonies.

The Lomé Convention was, however, not just a geographic and quantitative transformation. It was also meant to signal a conceptual and rhetorical break with the idea of association. The idea had never lost its connotation of a paternalistic continuation of quasi-colonial power and role relationships. It was replaced by the idea of partnership and cooperation, a step toward cooperation as equals bound by the recognition of the interdependence of all state groups.[170] However, it would be wrong to reduce the changes wrought by Lomé to mere rhetoric, as some commentators did at the time.[171] For one thing, terminology had an important symbolic dimension in this context, particularly for former colonies.[172] For another, the new agreement also marked an important substantive shift on many points. We will briefly examine three of them.[173]

First, EEC–ACP cooperation was now supported by an institutional structure marked by parity between both groups of nations (Art. 69 ff. of the Convention). In a Council of Ministers, a Committee of Ambassadors and a Consultative Assembly, important questions of cooperation would be debated and decided from a position of equality. The second important innovation of Lomé was the introduction of the so-called STABEX

[167] Protocol 22 to the Accession Treaty; see Cosgrove Twitchett, *Europe and Africa*, p. 147; on the states which remained outside of the framework (and who later developed more effectively) see P. Tulloch, *The Seven Outside: Commonwealth's Asia Trade with the Enlarged EEC* (London: Overseas Development Institute, 1973).

[168] In *Africa* they were: Botswana, Gambia, Ghana, Kenya, Lesotho, Malawi, Nigeria, Sierra Leone, Swaziland, Tanzania, Uganda and Zambia. In the *Caribbean*: Bahamas, Barbados, Grenada, Guyana, Jamaica and Trinidad and Tobago. In the *Pacific*: the Fiji Islands, Tonga and West Samoa.

[169] They were Ethiopia, Liberia, Sudan, Guinea, Equatorial Guinea and Guinea-Bissau.

[170] Becker, *Partnerschaft von Lomé*, pp. 51, 52, 153.

[171] For a critical perspective see Lister, *EC and the Developing World*, pp. 59, 103.

[172] Hewitt and Whiteman, "The Commission and Development Policy," p. 140.

[173] An overview of the changes is presented in Grilli, *EC and Developing Countries*, pp. 27–35.

system.[174] STABEX was a stabilizing mechanism designed to compensate for fluctuations in export earnings, a significant problem for the developing economies.[175] A third important innovation was a waiver of reciprocity of trade preferences. In contrast to the Yaoundé Convention, the Community now guaranteed the ACP states free access to Community markets, without demanding free access in return.[176] The elimination of reciprocity had been a key demand of developing nations, in particular the Commonwealth states.[177] Both STABEX and the reciprocity waiver responded to demands that had repeatedly been put forward by UNCTAD.[178] The second pillar of cooperation between the EEC and ACP countries, development cooperation, was also affected by substantive innovations.

2. Development cooperation under Lomé

As with the Yaoundé accord, the Lomé Convention also included provisions governing financial and technical cooperation. Developing countries saw the renewal of the EDF as the most important aspect of the entire accord.[179] It reflected the general paradigm shift in development theory in European countries.[180] Although Lomé did not contain an express commitment to poverty reduction, changes in the approach to development were nonetheless reflected in several other aspects, such as the provision of specific sums for small and micro-enterprises (which included many agricultural operations) and for least-developed countries.[181] Instead of economic growth and infrastructure, these last elements reflected the prevalence of basic-needs theories. At the same time, the grant conditions of the EEC had already been characterized by extremely lenient conditions, which reflected the fact that they served the same clientele as the IDA: 80 percent of the funds were

[174] Art. 16, 17 Lomé Convention.

[175] Bartels, "Trade and Development," 738; J. Ravenhill, *Collective Clientelism: The Lomé Conventions and North-South Relations* (New York: Columbia University Press, 1985), p. 99; Becker, *Partnerschaft von Lomé*, p. 56.

[176] Art. 1 Lomé Convention; see also Bartels, "Trade and Development," 733.

[177] Becker, *Partnerschaft von Lomé*, p. 52.

[178] The significance of the contemporary political-economic context surrounding the negotiations in Lomé – namely, the oil crisis and the general discursive dominance of the developing countries – should also not be underestimated (see, e.g. O. Schmuck and F. Nuscheler (eds.), *Die Süd-Politik der EG* (Bonn: Europa-Union-Verlag, 1993), pp. 38–9).

[179] Lister, *EC and the Developing World*, pp. 131–2.

[180] Grilli, *EC and Developing Countries*, p. 115.

[181] Becker, *Partnerschaft von Lomé*, pp. 81–4; Cosgrove Twitchett, *Europe and Africa*, p. 156.

given as grants, there were relatively broad aid-tying provisions, and social (that is, non-economic) factors were to be taken into account.[182]

The most important component of the Lomé "new beginning" and the goal of teamwork and cooperation, however, was the intensive involvement of the recipient ACP countries in decision-making and mid-range planning, which enabled these countries to plan much more efficiently. The ACP countries, which previously had been authorized only to initiate projects, were now involved in *all phases* of project planning and implementation.[183] In addition, a system of "national authorizing officers" was introduced which made selected recipient-land officials responsible for project supervision.[184] Admittedly, recipient countries did not participate in the final project-funding decisions, which were still taken by the European Commission and the EDF Committee of the EEC's Council of Ministers. However, a system of cooperative planning and implementation had been created that went further in the direction of partnership than any other donor system at that time.[185] In addition, Lomé introduced development program planning for the duration of an EDF fund, which was usually five years (Lomé Convention, Art. 51).[186] ACP countries were also to be involved in this planning, which indeed was usually based on projects they themselves had developed. This system made payments more predictable and, even more importantly, permitted aid recipients to set their own priorities. As was the case in German and World Bank policy, program planning became the norm at the European level as well.

The overall paradigm shift in European development policy was based not least upon a change in leadership of the Commission, which also brought about changes in the internal administrative structure. As discussed above, the European development administration had, until this point, been strongly French-influenced, which essentially meant Gaullist. Under Jacques Ferrandi, former French colonial officials had developed a grant system in which the political relationships of the applicant often

182 Lister, *EC and the Developing World*, p. 149.

183 Discussed in-depth in Becker, *Partnerschaft von Lomé*, p. 86; Cosgrove Twitchett, *Europe and Africa*, p. 157.

184 Lister, *EC and the Developing World*, pp. 139–41.

185 On recipient countries' efforts to obtain greater participation at the UNDP see F. M. Ssekandi and P. L. Johnson, "Law and Development: An Empirical Study of the Evolution of the Legal Framework for Delivery of Multilateral Development Assistance," in S. Schlemmer-Schulte and K.-Y. Tung (eds.), *Liber Amicorum Ibrahim Shihata: International Finance and Development Law* (The Hague: Kluwer Law International, 2001), pp. 753–92 at p. 753.

186 Grilli, *EC and Developing Countries*, p. 11; Becker, *Partnerschaft von Lomé*, p. 86.

appeared more important than whether the project made sense from a developmental perspective. The end of the de Gaulle presidency in 1969 was the beginning of the end of this system. The change was associated primarily with the name of Claude Cheysson, who was appointed Development Commissioner in 1973. Cheysson, a Socialist, was neither close to Ferrandi nor a former colonial official.[187] He brought his own experience and ideas about development policy to the Commission.[188] Within the Directorate General for Development, Cheysson began by dismantling the personalized system Ferrandi had created and instituting more efficiency and transparency in development administration.[189] His program had three main components: greater emphasis on planning, the orientation of the EDF grant procedure toward clearer criteria, and the introduction of the first elements of systematic evaluation into the project cycle.

The actual effectiveness of Cheysson's reforms is difficult to ascertain. In the long term, however, they contributed to internal professionalization, rationalization, and certainly also bureaucratization of European development administration – and as a step toward the approach being used in the World Bank and German development administration.

V. Summary

The second phase in the history of development cooperation saw significant administrative innovations and a strengthened conceptual autonomy of the policy field. It can therefore be seen as a breakthrough in the establishment of the field. However, it also saw development cooperation becoming more controversial politically as well as conceptually, highlighting the potential for conflict in this area. The technocratic optimism

[187] Claude Cheysson was a key figure in French and European foreign policy over a period of several decades. He remained Development Commissioner until 1981, then became Foreign Minister under Mitterrand (1981–84), but then returned to the Commission under Delors (1985–88). Before this he had been cabinet chief under Pierre Mendès-France (1954–55) and General Secretary of the Commission for Technical Cooperation in Africa (1957–1962).

[188] These more resembled the World Bank and the British. His ideas harmonized particularly well with a second influential person in this phase, the high-ranking *British* official in the GD Development, Maurice Foley, who had been sent there from the Overseas Department. For this reason, Cheysson was sometimes described as "Pompidou's gift to the British." See Hewitt and Whiteman, "The Commission and Development Policy," p. 140.

[189] Dimier, "Administrative Reform as Political Control," p. 82.

which had marked the first phase was gone. What follows is a short recap of the hallmarks of the second phase.

Administrative innovations occurred primarily in three areas: first, the introduction of program planning, that is, the idea of multi-year overall plans within which individual projects were integrated; second, the procedural integration of different areas of expertise (in particular, regional and thematic specialization) within the administrations; and third, the introduction of evaluation regimes geared toward a more systematic and independent assessment of projects. Each of these three points was evident (to varying degrees) in each of the three main development organizations studied here. The World Bank modernized itself particularly thoroughly, while the advances in the German foreign-aid administration remained somewhat provisional. Overall, however, the second phase saw increasing professionalization of development administration. The remaining differences in approach between the various donors were clearest with respect to the relation between recipients and donors in development cooperation. The Lomé Convention formally introduced the policy of equal participation by recipient countries in the planning and evaluating of projects – and hence the idea of an equal partnership. However, neither the administrative innovations nor the partnership element in development administration came out of nowhere. Doubts as to the existing system of development cooperation had arisen; the goals of the first development decade had obviously not been reached. The previous approach thus needed re-evaluation. The administrative reforms were, in part, an answer to these questions.

The role of developing countries, however, changed the most. Unified by their recent experience of decolonization and their common poverty, developing countries found a common voice in the 1960s and, especially in the NIEO of 1974, were able to formulate their demands clearly. Their main goal was generous transfers of resources from North to South. They saw industrialized countries as politically and morally (if not legally) obliged to pursue redistribution in the name of international justice. Developing countries demanded solidarity coupled with strict respect for their sovereignty.

However, the confrontation between developed and industrialized countries revolved not just around the demand for funds, but also around the nature of the assistance offered. Reacting to the disappointing effects of previous assistance, donor countries wanted to concentrate more on poverty reduction, in accordance with the basic-needs strategy formulated in the 1970s. Most developing-nation governments rejected the shift, seeing it as an intrusion on their autonomy to use development funds as they saw fit. Although the basic-needs strategy never became the dominant development strategy – perhaps because of resistance to it in recipient countries – it nevertheless still showed a significant change in the understanding of what the purpose of development assistance was. The goal was no longer strictly economic growth, but also social effects, in particular poverty reduction. The change represented a crucial expansion of the idea of development and development cooperation.

2

Years of transformation

A Stagnation and instrumentalization (1975–1990)

The strength of the OPEC countries is shown by the oil crisis, the passage of the NIEO in the UN General Assembly, the Lomé Convention's reputation as being extremely favorable to developing nations: the years 1973–75 were the apex of a development policy – perhaps even international relations in general – dominated by developing countries and their supporters. In hindsight, however, these years also signaled the end of an era. In the third phase of the history of development cooperation, extending from the second half of the 1970s to approximately 1990, the unity of the developing countries – and with it, the basis for their political strength – collapsed. The agenda of development policy came again to be dominated by donor countries.

However, there was to be no return to the status quo of the 1960s. Developing nations had lost not only their unity but also their "innocence." Donor nations began – at first slowly, but increasingly rapidly during the 1990s – to re-evaluate their respect for the sovereignty of developing nations. In a theoretical perspective, there was a renaissance in the orientation toward economic growth instead of poverty reduction and the first signs of concern with the political conditions of development. Development policy again became a tool of specific foreign policy interests, and, occasionally, a mere plaything of economic ideologies. Section I, below, will examine the political and theoretical context of development cooperation. Sections II–IV will then address how the World Bank, the EEC, and Germany reacted to the changing context in their respective development policies and administrations.

I. *Political and theoretical context: revisions*

1. The end of the Third World and the beginning of fragile statehood

The hopes that developing countries had placed in the NIEO did not materialize.[1] The success of OPEC as a raw materials cartel did not carry over to other raw materials. Furthermore, the numerical superiority of developing nations in the UN had not helped to create new binding rules or policies in their favor. The new global economic order remained more a catalog of demands than a concrete obligation. Western countries (and the donor institutions they dominated) responded to further demands with blocking or delaying tactics. Developing nations were indeed able to use their UN majority to keep development issues on the agenda, particularly in the form of the 1986 proclamation of a right to development, which gave the subject a new human rights dimension.[2] At the same time, however, they were confronted both singly and as a group by massive problems which can generally be grouped into two categories: the heterogeneity of the Third World and the emergence of fragile statehood.

a) *Heterogeneity*

Beginning in the mid 1970s, there was an increasing heterogeneity in the camp of developing nations, which finally destroyed their political unity. The "end of the Third World," as Ulrich Menzel has so aptly called it, began at this time.[3] The increasing differentiation initially took a predominantly economic form. On the one side stood a group of countries – mainly from sub-Saharan Africa – where economies stagnated and drastic population increases actually led to an increase in poverty. On the other side there emerged a group of developing nations which generally moved in a progressive direction, albeit in very different ways.[4] Among these were oil-exporting nations, which experienced immense increases in their incomes owing to drastic oil price increases. A group of East Asian countries (especially South Korea, Taiwan, Singapore, Hong Kong, and later Malaysia and Thailand) went through a rapid industrialization. This group of countries, known in the 1980s as the "Asian tigers," demonstrated constant high rates of investment, established themselves

[1] For more on the following discussion see Menzel, *Ende der Dritten Welt*, p. 153.

[2] UNGA Resolution 41/128 from December 14, 1986; see also *infra* Ch 4.D.

[3] Ibid., pp. 28–42; on the notion of Third World, see *supra* Intro.A.III.

[4] D. Messner, "Schwellenländer," in Nohlen and Arons, *Lexikon Dritte Welt*, pp. 708–11.

on the world market, and began to show attributes common to developed Western societies. Finally, there came another group of countries, including Brazil, Mexico and India, which showed high growth rates in certain sectors and income growth among certain population groups. Facets of political differentiation also became clearer. While Africa and the Near East were still generally dominated by autocratic one-party states, the 1980s saw democratization tendencies in South America and the Philippines. The solidarity of the period of decolonization, during which developing countries were united in comparable poverty and shared similar goals, began to fall apart. The once-proud designation "Third World" began to lose its substance.[5]

b) Fragile statehood

At the same time, the domestic political problems of developing countries became more evident. These problems were sometimes severe enough to call their very statehood into question, a phenomenon today commonly known as fragile statehood.[6] Domestic political crises came to be seen as not simply transitory power struggles or ideological contests, but rather as structural weaknesses affecting the very notion of statehood. The term "neopatrimonialism" was coined to refer to this situation. Neopatrimonialism was derived from a contrast with Max Weber's concept of patrimonialism.[7] Weber used the term to describe a form of traditional rule based on a class of administrative and military personnel answerable solely to a ruler. *Neo*patrimonialism referred to a modern type of this form of rule combining patrimonial and rational-bureaucratic elements. While patrimonialism involved rules based solely on personal relationships in which no distinction between private and public existed, neopatrimonialism involves an overlap of traditional and

[5] See Menzel, *Ende der Dritten Welt*, p. 39.

[6] J.-F. Medard, *L'etat sous-develope en afrique: Clientelisme politique du neo-patrimonialisme?* Travaux et Documents, 2nd edn (Bordeaux: Centre d'étude d'Afrique noire, 1983); R. H. Jackson, *Quasi-states: Sovereignty, International Relations and the Third World*, Cambridge Studies in International Relations (Cambridge University Press, 1993), vol. XII; T. Risse and U. Lehmkuhl (eds.), *Regieren ohne Staat? Governance begrenzter Staatlichkeit* (Baden-Baden: Nomos, 2007); S. Weiss and J. Schmierer (eds.), *Prekäre Staatlichkeit und internationale Ordnung* (Wiesbaden: Verlag für Sozialwissenschaften, 2007); R. Rotberg (ed.), *When States Fail: Causes and Consequences* (Princeton University Press, 2004).

[7] I rely here primarily on the presentation in G. Erdmann, "Neopatrimoniale Herrschaft: Der Übergang zur Demokratie ist nicht gelungen," *Entwicklung und Zusammenarbeit*, 42 (2001), 294–7 at 294; there is, however, a large body of work on this subject, see van de Walle, *African Economies and the Politics*, p. 51 (fn. 80).

rational-bureaucratic elements. Here, there is at least a formal differentiation between public and private, even if both spheres are rarely separated in practice. Clientele relationships are of central importance in neopatrimonialism. Clientelism describes the exchange of certain services or resources for political support. Economically, the key feature of neopatrimonialism is the exploitation of public office for the accumulation of private wealth. Political power becomes the basis of economic power.

Neopatrimonial structures are seen by many today as a key factor in the problems of sub-Saharan Africa.[8] Even if neopatrimonialism had roots in colonialism, its effects continue to be particularly evident and particularly harmful, especially for the goals of development cooperation. It leads to massive corruption, the "privatization" of public office, fragile administrative systems, and courts which are only nominally functional. Since the late 1970s, these weaknesses of young states had become increasingly evident. The recognition of these weaknesses meant that, in addition to the large gap in capital between industrialized and developing nations, the political culture of some developing states had also become a structural barrier to capacity increases. The 1980s saw development agencies slowly coming to grips with these problems, which became a central concern of development policy.

c) The debt crisis and the return of the Cold Warriors

The crisis of developing countries in this phase was, however, not solely due to their political culture, but also a result of their economic situation. In the early 1980s, many developing countries plunged into a massive debt crisis.[9] A global increase in interest rates was accompanied by a continuous fall in prices for raw materials. This combination resulted in the insolvency of many states, particularly in Latin America. The affected parties included not only state lenders, but also, and primarily, banks in industrialized nations. On the basis of rising oil prices, these banks had loaned freely to developing countries in the 1970s. Now, they perceived a threat to their very existence, and withdrew from the market for loans to developing countries. These countries, in turn, were then faced with acute liquidity problems and redemption debts.

However, it was not only these internal problems that led to a collapse in the previously strong bargaining position of the developing nations. In 1979, the internal political environment in important donor nations,

[8] Ibid., p. 50; C. Lancaster, *Aid to Africa* (University of Chicago Press, 1999), p. 27.

[9] Todaro and Smith, *Economic Development*, p. 674.

and with it the geopolitical terrain, began to change. The Soviet invasion of Afghanistan served as a reminder that the confrontations of the Cold War were far from over. The revolution in Iran led, after a certain delay, to a second oil crisis. Elections in the USA and Great Britain brought Ronald Reagan and Margaret Thatcher to power, two aggressive politicians who favored a confrontational policy toward the Soviet Union. In addition to global confrontation, they pursued an aggressively liberal economic policy aimed at the privatization of public enterprises and the liberalization of markets.[10] They favored this approach not only for their own countries but also wanted other states to adopt similar strategies. Development policy, too, was seen as a welcome instrument to push these reforms.

2. Dissociation and neoclassicism as new approaches in development theory

In the 1980s, discussion in development circles was marked by two theories which not only offered contrarian perspectives on the issue, but also had very different effects on development cooperation. While neoclassicism became the leading doctrine at the World Bank for several years, the theory of dissociation assigned no particular role to development cooperation and thus had few consequences for it. It will nevertheless be briefly sketched here, since it reflected the state of discussions among dependency theorists.

a) Dissociation

Although there were diverse doubts about various assumptions of dependency theory, many agreed with its basic assumption that the problems of developing countries were not endogenous, but rather were caused by the structure of the international division of labor and the relationship between developing and industrialized nations. The theory of dissociation, mainly formulated by Samir Amin, Dieter Senghaas, and later Ulrich Menzel, suggested an inwardly focused or self-centered (in German: *auto-zentriert*) and occasionally called *dissociative* development path for the countries of the South. These authors suggested a temporary decoupling from the international division of labor.[11] Their theory

[10] Hobsbawm, *Age of Extremes*, pp. 248–9; Menzel, *Ende der Dritten Welt*, p. 171.

[11] D. Senghaas, *Weltwirtschaftsordnung und Entwicklungspolitik: Plädoyer für Dissoziation* (Frankfurt: Suhrkamp, 1977); S. Amin, "Zur Theorie von Akkumulation und Entwicklung," in D. Senghaas (ed.), *Peripherer Kapitalismus: Analysen über Abhängigkeit und Unterentwicklung* (Frankfurt: Suhrkamp, 1974), pp. 71–97 at p. 71; on the context, see Martinussen, *Society, State and Market*, pp. 93.

was based on an analysis of what they considered to be the large disparity in competence between industrialized and developing nations. The gap manifested itself in the different levels of advancement in science, technology and the workforce, as well as the overall level of productivity of the economy and agriculture. The reaction to this disparity, these writers assumed, could take one of two forms: either a submission to better-developed economies within the international division of labor, or an attempt to resist the "peripheralizing pressure" by withdrawing for some time to complete an internal restructuring and thereby achieve a development breakthrough on the state's own terms.[12] Against this backdrop, the authors urged developing nations to undertake a comprehensive, albeit temporary, decoupling from the mechanisms of international trade.

Senghaas's recommendations, in particular, were sharply criticized on the grounds that they called for a radical social transformation that could only have been implemented by a sharply authoritarian regime. The paradigm also offered few suggestions within the existing system of international development, and therefore generated little discussion in these circles. The dissociative idea did, however, emphasize the self-reliance of developing nations, an idea which had many supporters in this period. In addition, it offered alternatives to the discursive power of neoclassicism, which threatened to overwhelm other approaches.[13]

b) Neoclassicism

The starting point for the neoclassical theory was the question of what role the state should take in organizing general welfare. The answer of neoclassical authors such as Deepak Lal,[14] Ian Little[15] or Jürgen Donges[16] was clear: as small a role as possible.[17] Neoclassical writers, who dominated not only development theory but economics in general in these years,

[12] See also U. Menzel and D. Senghaas, "Autozentrierte Entwicklung in historischer Perspektive," in H.-D. Evers and D. Senghaas (eds.), *Auf dem Weg zu einer Neuen Weltwirtschaftsordnung?: Bedingungen und Grenzen für eine eigenständige Entwicklung* (Baden-Baden: Nomos, 1983), pp. 77–96 at p. 79.

[13] A self-critical assessment can be found in Menzel, *Ende der Dritten Welt*, p. 157; on the self-reliance movement see Rist, *History of Development*, p. 123.

[14] D. Lal, *The Poverty of "Development Economics"* (London: Institute of Economic Affairs, 1983).

[15] I. Little, *Economic Development: Theory, Policy and International Relations* (New York: Basic Book, 1982).

[16] J. Donges, *Außenwirtschafts- und Entwicklungspolitik: Die Entwicklungsländer in der Weltwirtschaft* (Berlin: Springer, 1981).

[17] For a contextual assessment see Martinussen, *Society, State and Market*, p. 259; Todaro and Smith, *Economic Development*, p. 126.

radically questioned the role of the state and thus presented a strong contrast to previous theories of development.[18]

Neoclassical economists found all forms of government intervention basically problematic. In their view, only undisturbed market mechanisms could, by permitting prices to reflect the undistorted matching of supply and demand, achieve the best allocation of resources. The state and its bureaucracy were, by contrast, seen as suffering from irremediable deficits. Neoclassicists saw politicians and officials as prone to corruption and the selfish or irrational protection of special interests. Further, state planning was subject to knowledge and competence deficiencies which, the theory posited, did not exist in the free market. State intervention in international economic interaction should, for that matter, also be limited. Here as well, free trade and the international division of labor were the best methods to unleash productive forces. In the final analysis, neoclassical theory held that, in fact, no special measures were needed for developing countries – indeed, such measures could only disturb international markets. The neoclassical strategy was clear. Governments should refrain from exercising any influence on prices. They should not operate their own businesses and should also force the privatization of public enterprises. The retreat of the state also meant the reduction – or better, elimination – of all subsidies. Finally, protectionism should be avoided as far as possible.

Beginning around 1980, neoclassical approaches gained tremendous influence on governments in Washington and London and, through these actors, on the IMF and the World Bank. However, they took on such an ideologically charged form that they soon came to be seen as a "counter-revolution" to existing development theories, and thus triggered opposition beginning in the second half of the 1980s.[19] In the 1990s, a more balanced picture of the relationship between market and state in the development process emerged. We will now examine the practical

[18] It should be kept in mind that, in the early phase of development policy, it was assumed that the state would play a central role (see *supra* Ch 1.A.IV). This could manifest itself in five different tasks and grades of intensity: (1) the establishment of a general institutional structure that establishes market mechanisms by means of freedom of contract and the rule of law, (2) macroeconomic policies such as tax or customs legislation, (3) provision of public goods and services (for example, transport infrastructure), (4) operational control of businesses, up to and including (5) the state's own production of goods and services.

[19] J. Toye, *Dilemmas of Development: Reflections on the Counter-Revolution in Development Theory and Policy* (Oxford: Basil Blackwell, 1987); T. Killick, *A Reaction Too Far: Economic Theory and the Role of the State in Developing Countries* (London: Overseas Development Institute, 1989).

consequences of neoclassicism in the policies of the Bank and other donors in the period of 1975 to 1990.

II. The World Bank: new instruments and the ideology of the Washington Consensus

During the turbulent years of 1973–75, the World Bank acted with cautious pragmatism, trying to avoid staking out definite positions in the increasingly fierce conflicts between North and South.[20] The Bank certainly perceived the effects of geopolitical upheaval, not least because OPEC countries began offering cheaper loans to developing countries, thus competing with it.[21] Substantively, however, the Bank held onto its agenda of economic growth and poverty reduction, with a focus on redistribution, employment, nutrition and, increasingly important, agricultural development. However, the Bank was also confronted with problems for which the neoclassical theories of the time seemed to offer appropriate solutions.

In 1979, Bank President McNamara and his deputy Ernest Stern began, for the first time, to suggest that the unsatisfactory macroeconomic situation of many developing countries (as shown, for example, by their huge current-account deficits) could be best addressed by "structural adjustment programs."[22] These programs were designed along two tracks: on the one hand they contained demands for structural macroeconomic reforms (frequently in legislative form) and on the other hand they provided resources needed to implement these reforms and bridge acute short-term budget deficits. Shortly afterward, a Bank analysis furnished the first signs of fragile statehood – that is, that economic problems, especially in African countries, were caused primarily by internal deficits. The reports pointed in particular to inadequate domestic policies, as well as corruption and inefficiency in public administration.[23]

These conclusions, as well as the idea of structural-adjustment programs and their associated loans,[24] signaled a change in World Bank policy and the advent of two instruments that were to fundamentally

[20] Kapur, Lewis and Webb, *The World Bank*, p. 19.

[21] Ibid., p. 19. [22] Ibid., p. 22.

[23] Ibid., p. 23; I. Shihata (ed.), *The World Bank in a Changing World: Volume I: Selected essays* (Dordrecht: Martinus Nijhoff Publishers, 1991), p. 22; E. J. Berg, *Accelerated Development in Sub-Saharan Africa: An Agenda for Action* (Washington, DC: The World Bank, 1981).

[24] The World Bank does not implement measures itself, it can only finance them. Thus the term structural adjustment *lending* is most appropriate.

change the Bank's work: the so-called "policy lending" and conditionalities. Policy lending in the form of structural-adjustment loans (SALs) was not an entirely new mode in the Bank's operations, but it now became more widely used and noticed since the Bank's previous operations had been focused overwhelmingly on financing long-term and clearly defined projects.[25] SALs were not long-term project financing but rather short-term policy financing – that is, loans for the implementation of macroeconomic reforms, as well as mitigation of their consequences. This policy lending, so called to distinguish it from project or investment lending, was given wide scope for the first time.[26]

SAL or policy lending, however, gave rise to a problem requiring the second new instrument, which continues to be a target for critics of the World Bank. Policy lending, which may require legislative reforms, was (and is) permitted by the Bank's charter only in exceptional circumstances, because it violates the Bank's commitment to a project focus.[27] The loans could therefore be justified only as solutions to *specific* economic problems such as acute balance-of-payments deficits. To ensure such concrete goals were achieved, each SAL was tied to specific conditions, called conditionalities. Such conditionalities were intended to address the root causes of balance-of-payments deficits, and the provision of further loan tranches was made conditional on their implementation. Substantively, these conditions consisted mainly of institutional reforms such as reductions in public employment, restructuring of ministries, the sale of public enterprises and the deregulation of certain markets. The SALs were thus intended not only as incentives to reform but also as the means of mitigating the reforms' direct consequences.[28] However, the tying of SALs to conditionalities was suspected of deeply interfering in the autonomy of recipient countries, particularly as these countries often applied for SALs only when they were under serious economic pressure.[29]

Furthermore, during the 1980s, SALs and conditionalities became identified with a particular ideology and were almost promoted as a panacea, which turned out to be a fateful development both for recipient countries

[25] Ch 1.A.I.; Art. III para. 4 (vii) IBRD Articles; see also Mason and Asher, *World Bank Since Bretton Woods*, p. 260.

[26] Shihata, *The World Bank in a Changing World I*, pp. 25, 58.

[27] More on the legal details *infra* Ch 7.B.I.

[28] More on this point in Kapur, Lewis and Webb, *The World Bank*, pp. 23–4; Shihata, *The World Bank in a Changing World I*, p. 26; later, debt service was also added as a reason (ibid., pp. 27–8).

[29] M. C. Tsai, "Globalization and Conditionality: Two Sides of the Sovereignty Coin," *Law and Policy in International Business*, 31 (2000), 1317–29 at 1317.

and the Bank. SALs were originally intended as specific measures for developing countries with good bureaucracies. With the inauguration of Ronald Reagan, which coincided with that of a new World Bank president, SALs were expanded dramatically. The Bank's new president, Alden W. Clausen, and Anne Krueger, the new chief economist he appointed, brought a team of strict neoclassical economists to the Bank. They eagerly adopted the Bank's analyses pointing to problems with public enterprises in recipient countries and, using SALs, formulated an aggressive agenda of liberalization and privatization.[30] Together with the IMF, which had long advocated similar macroeconomic reforms, the World Bank's new approach came to be known as the so-called *Washington Consensus*, which has dominated the Bank's image since the 1980s.[31] The overall goal of poverty reduction was not abandoned, but it was clearly eclipsed by an increasingly ideological campaign for liberalization and privatization.[32]

Nevertheless, the importance of SALs for the Bank's work should be kept in context. Even though SALs dominated the public perception of the Bank, they still constituted, even in their heyday, only a minority of the Bank's assistance. During the 1980s, SALs comprised approximately 18 percent of the IBRD's loan volume, and 12 percent of the IDA's.[33] SALs were rarely made to Asian countries – the focus was first on African countries, and then, in the late 1980s, also included Latin America. There, the effect of the loans was particularly devastating and they therefore met with a critical public response. Beginning in the mid 1980s, a certain softening of the liberalization agenda took place. In 1986, Barber Conable was appointed new head of the World Bank. From the beginning, he stressed that the goal of poverty reduction was still the Bank's main mission. Environmental protection also became an increasingly important topic in the Bank's political debates. The Washington Consensus had begun to crumble – and with it, the World Bankers' sense of ideological security.

[30] The arrival of these economists was marked by an "abrupt onset of intolerance," (Kapur, Lewis and Webb, *The World Bank*, p. 1194) in the Bank's research department. The department, founded by McNamara as a means of encouraging diverse opinions on Bank policies, was now "brought into line" ideologically.

[31] The phrase "Washington Consensus" is derived in part from J. Williamson, *What Washington Means by Policy Reform in Latin American Adjustment* (Washington, DC: Institute for International Economics, 1990); for more context see Kapur, Lewis and Webb, *The World Bank*, p. 26.

[32] Shihata, *The World Bank in a Changing World I*, p. 33.

[33] Ibid., p. 58 (see also in this book a reference to a report on Adjustment Lending II, Annex 5.2, table 5.3); see also Kapur, Lewis and Webb, *The World Bank*, p. 30.

III. Germany: a return to the priority of short-term interests

A change in German development policy began to show particularly early in this third phase. As the pragmatist Helmut Schmidt took office from the visionary Willy Brandt as Chancellor, a similar transformation took place in the Development Ministry: the realist Egon Bahr replaced Erhard Eppler as Minister in 1974.[34]

Bahr's approach returned development policy to its former status as an instrument of overall foreign policy, thus sacrificing (at least conceptually) its recently won autonomy. Bahr and Schmidt saw development policy not as fundamentally independent, but as part of an "overall policy" (*Gesamtpolitik*) which needed to be coordinated with trade and economic and foreign policy.[35] The overall policy was oriented toward Germany's national interests, which Schmidt and Bahr understood mainly to be Germany's economic interests: encouragement of German exports, securing access to raw materials, and, last but not least, preserving jobs.[36] Short-term interests thus again displaced the longer-term goal of a global policy of peace, which, for its part, had also been driven at least to some extent by the desire to realize certain economic dividends.

Bahr and his successors[37] also tried to adapt development policy to the increasingly obvious differences between developing countries. They aimed to achieve a complementary relationship between public aid and private economic activity in the Third World.[38] While the poorest countries would still receive publicly funded development aid aimed primarily at rural development and the involvement of broad sectors of the population in food production, the so-called emerging countries were to receive forms of development assistance more strongly tied to the private sector, such as support for direct investments or public–private joint ventures.

[34] A portrait of Bahr as development minister can be found in Cernicky, "Erhard Eppler 1968–1974," p. 40.

[35] Number 2 of the so-called "Gymnich Theses" of 1975, see F. Nuscheler, "Partnerschaft oder Ausbeutung?: Die Enwicklungspolitik der sozial-liberalen Koalition," in F. Grube and G. Richter (eds.), *Der SPD-Staat* (Munich: Piper, 1977), pp. 324–46 at p. 334.

[36] Bodemer, "Programmentwicklung," p. 291.

[37] Bahr was in office only until December 1976; his successor was Marie Schlei (until February 1978) and Reiner Offergeld (until 1982), neither of whom established any real profile. See the corresponding entries in W. Gieler (ed.), *Deutsche Entwicklungsminister von 1961–2008: Biographien, Konzeptionen und Einfluss auf nationale und internationale Entwicklungspolitik* (Bonn: Scientia Bonnensis, 2008).

[38] Entwicklungspolitische Grundlinien der Bundesregierung von 1980 [Guidelines on Development Policy of the Federal Government]; see also Bodemer, "Programmentwicklung," p. 294.

The 1982 change of government from a coalition dominated by the center-left Social Democrats (under Chancellor Helmut Schmidt) to the center-right Christian Democrats (under Chancellor Helmut Kohl) actually brought less change than the bold rhetoric of the new Development Minister, Jürgen Warnke, might have suggested. Warnke, a member of the conservative Christian Social Union (CSU) party, was a novice to the Cabinet and did not have any particular reputation in development circles.[39] The new administration's changes to development policy were also limited by existing budget commitments and by the fact that the Foreign Minister, Free Democrat Hans-Dietrich Genscher, remained in office despite the coalition change. Another reason for this continuity was the fact that, during Helmut Schmidt's tenure as Chancellor, development policy had already become a subject of consensus among the various German political parties.[40] The general focus of German policy – rural development, energy-sector support, education and training, and support for trade and industry – remained unchanged.

Thus, the new conservative coalition of the 1980s broadly continued the development policy, albeit with two new accents. First, development policy was to be more clearly oriented toward Germany's own interests, which primarily amounted to the instrumentalization of development policy and its subordination to economic and foreign policy priorities.[41] One can observe a reinforced policy requiring recipients to invest development funds in projects with German companies, more active project development, stricter general loan conditions and a preference for cooperating with more-developed emerging economies.[42]

Furthermore, Germany began using a form of conditionality. The concept was of a "political dialog" with developing countries in which the political situation in the developing countries would be the topic of continuous, albeit informal, discussion between donor and recipient countries.[43] This somewhat diplomatic formulation conveyed the fact that

[39] Gieler, *Deutsche Entwicklungsminister*, p. 89.

[40] Bodemer, "Programmentwicklung," p. 296.

[41] This meant primarily that development policy had to take second place to the required loyalty to NATO and the partnership with the USA, as Helmut Kohl expressed it in his 1982 Government Policy Statement.

[42] Ibid., p. 298. Added to this was an increase in mixed-financing loans (that is, the combination of public funds and commercial export loans); the catchphrase was "job-friendly development policy," Gieler, *Deutsche Entwicklungsminister*, p. 91.

[43] Discussed extensively in D. Radke, *Auflagenpolitik und Politik-Dialog in der entwicklungspolitischen Zusammenarbeit* (Berlin: German Development Institute, 1985); for background since Jimmy Carter's emphasis on human rights in development policy see

donor countries saw it as increasingly necessary not only to provide economic aid, but also to discuss political and human rights problems in the developing countries. During the 1980s, this aspect of development policy was addressed only in a somewhat discreet manner. In the 1990s, however, it became an explicit part of the marked politicization of relationships and the conditionalization of development cooperation.[44]

In this rather pragmatic and instrumental phase of German development policy, few significant changes were made to development administration. Eppler's departure led to a certain relaxation in the methods of planning that he had supported. The country programs were maintained, but they were reduced to a few particularly important nations.[45] In addition, the emphasis on Germany's own national interests led to a noticeable weakening of the proposal principle, which had been intended to protect the sovereign choices of recipient countries.[46] Overall, this era saw a stronger focus on efficiency in development policy and administration. In particular, improved forms of evaluation were introduced with the aim of more carefully observing the efficiency of development policy.[47] The Development Ministry again came under pressure. While its formal powers and competencies had basically stabilized, it registered almost no increase in personnel and was subjected to an informal shift in competencies. Since 1975, there was a noticeable trend toward delegation of tasks to specialized organizations. In particular, the Society for Technical Cooperation (GTZ, now GIZ[48]), which had been founded in 1975 to administer technical assistance, grew both in personnel and in budget. This event led to a reduction in the Development Ministry's substantive authority, which was shifted to the project-related activities of the GTZ, and to reductions in external contacts.[49]

C. Müller, *Die Menschenrechte als außenpolitisches Ziel* (Baden-Baden: Nomos, 1986), p. 36; also briefly discussed in Bodemer, "Programmentwicklung," pp. 292–3; p. 297.

44 Discussed further *infra* Ch 2.B.I.3.

45 Hein, *Westdeutschen*, p. 294.

46 See *supra* Ch 1.A.III.2; J. von Stockhausen, *Theorie und Politik der Entwicklungszusammenarbeit: Eine Einführung in die deutsche bilaterale Entwicklungszusammenarbeit* (Munich: Weltforum Verlag, 1986), pp. 262–70; Gieler, *Deutsche Entwicklungsminister*, p. 88.

47 BMZ, *Grundlinien der Entwicklungspolitik der Bundesregierung*, (Guidelines on German Development Policy) (Bonn, 1986), p. 23; S. Lengl, "Entwicklungspolitik: Administrative Möglichkeiten zur Verbesserung ihrer Wirksamkeit," *Verwaltungsarchiv*, 76 (1985), 427–47 at 427.

48 On the merger of GTZ with other agencies and the subsequent creation of GIZ, see *infra* Ch 3.A.II.

49 Stockmann, "Administrative Probleme," pp. 55–66.

IV. European communities: stagnation within, but dynamism outside the Lomé cooperation

1. Lomé: distortions and practical difficulties

From an external perspective, cooperation with ACP countries as regulated in the Lomé Convention remained the central pillar of European development assistance in the years between 1975 and 1990. During this phase, the Lomé Convention was renewed three times[50] and attracted new members; the group of participating countries increased to fifty-seven ACP countries with Lomé II and to sixty-five with Lomé III. Also from a financial standpoint, the scope of the EDF, out of which ACP development projects were financed, remained significant when measured in nominal and inflation-adjusted terms. After a reduction around the time of Lomé II, it increased again in real terms.[51]

However, the overall atmosphere of cooperation and the relationship between donor and recipient nations changed noticeably. When Lomé I was signed in 1975, it was greeted as a signal of a new era of partnership and a generally valid model for North–South cooperation. But soon it began to lose its progressive image.[52] In particular, the status of the partners changed – the group of ACP countries lost strength. By the end of the 1970s, these countries had lost their influential position of being able to make claims as victims of colonial oppression and were instead forced to explain internal problems such as corruption and, increasingly, human rights violations. Primarily, however, the ACP countries failed to consolidate their unique and therefore privileged group status. While all other developing nations confronted donors on an individual basis, the ACP Group alone had the opportunity to press claims as a group. To make the most of this opportunity, these countries concluded the so-called 1975 Georgetown Agreement. The Agreement aimed to organize internal coordination toward the European Community by creating a Secretariat and by strengthening exchange mechanisms.[53] In practice, however, the Secretariat never really got "off the ground."

[50] Lomé II was signed in 1979 and entered into force in 1981; Lomé III was signed in 1984 and took effect from 1985 onwards; Lomé IV, finally, became effective in 1989 and was replaced in 2000 by the Cotonou Agreement.

[51] Grilli, *EC and Developing Countries*, p. 114; a relative assessment in Lister, *EC and the Developing World*, p. 132 (5% of assistance to ACP).

[52] Hewitt and Whiteman, "The Commission and development policy," p. 140; Grilli, *EC and Developing Countries*, p. 36.

[53] Lister, *EC and the Developing World*, pp. 167; on the special nature of collective of ACP countries Ravenhill, *Collective Clientelism*, pp. 22–34; see also *infra* Ch 3.C.II.

On the donor side, as well, interest in a progressive and autonomous development policy faded. The European Commission, in particular, began to lose zeal and intellectual depth in its approach to development policy. The new Development Commissioner, Edgard Pisani, did try to reinvigorate the Lomé cooperation again in 1982/3, but met with only limited success. At least one reason for this was the lack of interest of the EC member states. They apparently saw ACP–EC cooperation as a less and less appropriate framework for new initiatives. Particularly revealing was the fact that the reaction to the central economic crisis in the Third World in the 1980s, the debt crisis, was handled completely outwith the EC, by the G7 and the Paris Club.[54]

This change in atmosphere and in the political center of gravity manifested itself substantively in the question of the extent to which political and human rights questions could be raised within the Lomé framework and as conditions for aid. The ACP countries had been able to avoid any mentioning of human rights in the Lomé II accord, despite pressure from Great Britain and the Netherlands. In the 1985 Lomé III Convention, however, the topic was broached for the first time, albeit somewhat reluctantly.[55] In return, the ACP nations secured a condemnation of apartheid in South Africa, which the EC had long rejected.[56] The ACP countries were also able to prevent the introduction of a political dialog process into the Convention's text, a provision which the Commission had requested in order to improve control over the choice and implementation of projects.[57] However, the taboo had been broken. Political dialog was introduced increasingly on a bilateral level, and with it came the open discussion of practices which, in the 1970s, would have been regarded as obvious interference in the internal affairs of the developing countries.[58]

Thus, the European Community joined the World Bank and West Germany in making assistance increasingly conditional. The comparison with the World Bank is particularly instructive. Since the beginning of the 1980s, the World Bank, with its SALs, had required broad concessions with respect to the *macroeconomic* sovereignty of recipient countries. The EC, by contrast, paid little attention to this aspect. Only beginning with Lomé IV, in 1989, did the EC also begin using the

[54] Grilli, *EC and Developing Countries*, pp. 39–40.

[55] Discussed in depth in Hoffmeister, *Menschenrechts- und Demokratieklauseln*, pp. 111; Lister, *EC and the Developing World*, p. 157; see also *infra* Ch 4.D.I and Ch 6.B.II.3.

[56] Ibid., p. 158. [57] Ibid., p. 160.

[58] Radke, *Auflagenpolitik*, p. 53; Frisch, "Die entwicklungspolitische Konzeption," p. 25.

instrument of SALs.[59] European and German development policy, however, used this instrument mostly with regard to human rights issues and, later, democratization. These issues were hence instrumental in introducing conditionality, thus raising the question of respect for recipient countries' sovereignty.

On the ground, EC development policies under Lomé had a rather mixed record. There were three main problems. First of all, the intermingling of political and social goals hampered success, at least from the standpoint of development policy. The EC always saw itself as a "soft" donor which paid less heed to the economic or development-related quality of projects than, for instance, the World Bank, instead focusing on political and social questions, as well as the recipient countries' priorities.[60] Second, the reality of program-setting in true partnership was difficult, as donor countries tended to strongly dominate this process.[61] Finally, there were various implementation problems. These were the result of factors including poorly prepared projects, cumbersome approval procedures, and slow disbursements.[62]

2. Development policy beyond Lomé: cooperation with Asia and Latin America

From the beginning, development policy in the European Community had been shaped by a tug of war between so-called regionalists (mainly France) and so-called globalists (Germany and the Netherlands).[63] As the era of development aid began, the regionalists prevailed (especially with the signing of the Yaoundé Convention). However, in a 1972 summit, European heads of state and government signaled that a global approach to development policy was conceivable and desirable. But it was only after the signing of Lomé I that development policy began to include states others than those associated with the ACP Group. Development cooperation began in 1976 with Asian and Latin American (ALA) countries, and in 1978 with North African states.

However, development cooperation with these countries was (and is) marked by a different approach than with ACP countries. Here, there was

[59] H. Lingnau, *Neue Elemente in der Entwicklungszusammenarbeit der Europäischen Gemeinschaft zu Beginn der 90er Jahre: Berichte und Gutachten No. 2* (Berlin: Deutsches Institut für Entwicklungspolitik, 1991), p. 66.

[60] Lister, *EC and the Developing World*, p. 135. [61] Ibid., p. 138.

[62] Becker, *Partnerschaft von Lomé*, pp. 92–3; ECA, Annual Report Concerning the Financial Year 1980 Accompanied by the Replies of the Institutions, OJ C 344/1 of December 31, 1981.

[63] More on the discussion in Grilli, *EC and Developing Countries*, p. 65.

no fine rhetoric about partnership, nor did these states benefit from the practical consequences of this rhetoric. Thus, there was never an overall international-law agreement with groups of these states. Instead, the Community decided itself when and with whom it would cooperate on a bilateral basis. The cooperation with Asian and Latin American states was legally based on the so-called ALA Regulation, promulgated in 1981.[64] An explicit legal basis for such rules on development aid in the European treaties did not exist until the Maastricht Treaty introduced the respective explicit competence.[65] Another difference between the ACP and ALA cooperation was that the participation of recipient countries in programming, project development, and implementation, as agreed with the ACP countries, was never extended to the ALA countries,[66] a distinction that persists to date.[67]

The ALA Regulation permitted development-aid disbursements to eleven Latin American and fifteen Asian nations. The goal in both cases was to improve the living conditions of the poorest residents. Thus, a poverty-oriented focus was adopted. Most of the funds were invested in development of farming and agricultural capacity. The stark disparity between the ACP and ALA countries was also reflected in financial terms: the ALA nations received only a fraction of the sums allotted to ACP countries.[68]

Another aspect and consequence should also be noted. With the introduction of aid to countries outside the ACP Group began the *organizational* fragmentation of development aid within the European Commission. Until this time, the General Directorate for Development had been responsible for all development assistance. The new, non-ACP cooperation programs, though, were to be handled by the General Directorate for External Trade. This division of responsibilities remains a hallmark of European development assistance to this day.[69]

A final characteristic of European development policy and its administration since the 1970s should be noted here. Coordination between donors has become a central theme of development-policy discussions, since the lack of

[64] ALA stands for Asia-Latin America, Council Regulation 442/81 from February 17, 1981; on cooperation with North African states, which will not be further discussed here, see ibid., pp. 193–5.

[65] Pellens, *Entwicklungshilfe Deutschlands*, p. 34; Grabitz, "Entwicklungspolitik," 217.

[66] For a comparison of the legal regimes see *infra* Ch 5.B.II and Ch 6.B.II; a shorter presentation can be found in Dann, *Political Institutions*.

[67] See *infra* Ch 3.A.III.

[68] Grilli, *EC and Developing Countries*, p. 256 (for Latin America), p. 288 (for Asia).

[69] See *infra* Ch 3.A.III.1.

coordination had led to massive extra costs and administrative problems.[70] The European Community, in particular, offered itself as a suitable agent for this coordination, since it comprised the majority of donors. However, the Commission's efforts in this direction, tentatively begun in 1972 and just as tentatively taken up again in 1984(!), have yielded few results.[71] Only in recent years, it seems, have serious coordination efforts begun.[72]

V. Summary

The prevailing winds had changed. Instead of confidently demanding solidarity and money from industrialized countries, developing nations (in the third phase of this short history of development aid) began in the 1970s to face pressure to conform to the demands of donor states. The demands were occasionally formulated in terms of self-interest (as in Germany's case), but also as "objective" requirements of development (as in the case of the World Bank). Whatever the particular justification, donors showed less and less respect for the developing countries' priorities. This priority change was reflected in the instruments of conditionality and political dialog, which were introduced in one form or another by all donor countries during this phase. Donors began to link aid payments to conditions and to address political subjects with recipient nations.

Other than this, there are few common trends or lasting theoretical or administrative innovations. The neoclassical revolution in the World Bank drove an almost crudely economic understanding of development which stressed market liberalization, largely ignoring social questions.[73] This approach was, however, not adopted in this form in other institutions. Although German development officials felt a more self-interested approach to development cooperation was in order, they did not undertake a fundamental reorientation. The EC also adopted the Washington Consensus only after some delay. The third phase of development, rather, sowed the seeds for different approaches, but bore little fruit on its own terms.

[70] Addressed in more detail *infra* Ch 3.A.V and 16.III. Contemporary literature includes J. Betz, *Die Internationalisierung der Entwicklungshilfe* (Berlin: Nomos, 1978); J. Kaplan, *International Aid Coordination*, Studies in Transnational Legal Policy (St. Paul: West Publishing Company, 1978), vol. XVI.

[71] Grilli, *EC and Developing Countries*, pp. 74 (pp.79).

[72] More on this aspect *infra* Ch 3.A.V and 16.III.

[73] Particularly telling are the attempts, during the second half of the 1980s, to imagine "adjustment with a human face," see G. A. Cornia and R. Jolly, *Adjustment with a Human Face: Protecting the Vulnerable and Promoting Growth* (Oxford: Clarendon Press, 1987).

B Expansion and rejection (1990–2000)

Although the 1980s are generally considered a "lost decade" for development work, they can also be seen as a sort of incubation period. Ideas arising in the 1980s began to be conceptualized in the 1990s, and heralded a particularly fruitful phase especially in the theory of development cooperation. This phase saw a wide expansion of the basic understanding of development – but also its first fundamental critique and rejection, formulated by the post-development school.

This blossoming of new thinking about development was connected to the broader political context. The end of the Cold War had significant consequences for development cooperation.[74] The disappearance of the East–West confrontation and the collapse of the Eastern Bloc eliminated the competition for the allegiance of developing nations. As of 1989/1991, Western industrialized nations were suddenly the only donors, and could thus specify their conditions more openly and more politically. This led, most importantly, to a broad expansion of the concept and understanding of development, and of development goals. Sustainability, environmental protection, human rights, democratization and governance reform, which had previously been considered off-limits out of respect for recipient-nation sovereignty, were now openly discussed – and will be recounted below (sections I to III).

However, the "victory" in the Cold War soon also led to a massive questioning of the legitimacy of the development-aid system. It was not only the lack of easily recognizable success that put pressure on development policy.[75] Clear failures, for example, in large dam projects had occurred, which highlighted the dangers of development cooperation for affected citizens.[76] The Cold War as a source of legitimacy for development policy ended. Finally, a large and energized non-governmental organization (NGO) community emerged which was able to formulate

[74] A finely calibrated analysis of the effect of the momentous events of 1990 on North–South relations can be found in A. Hurrell, *On Global Order: Power, Values, and the Constitution of International Society* (Oxford University Press, 2007), p. 210.

[75] Since the late 1960s, which heralded the end of the modernization theory's technocratic optimism, the meagre successes of development cooperation had become apparent, and the search was on for new paths (poverty reduction, structural adjustment). See *supra* Ch 1.B.I.

[76] A particular catalyst was the circumstances surrounding the construction of the Narmada Dam in India, see S. Narula, "The Story of Narmada Bachao Andolan," in D. R. Hurwitz, D. B. Ford and M. L. Satterthwaite (eds.), *Human Rights Advocacy Stories* (New York: Foundation Press, 2009), pp. 351–83 at p. 351.

effective and knowledgeable criticism of development policy. Their effectiveness was demonstrated, for example, to the World Bank. As the Bank proudly planned to celebrate its fiftieth anniversary in 1994, it was instead confronted with vigorous street protests under the slogan "50 years are enough."[77] Criticism was not confined to the World Bank – other institutions also found their credibility sinking to new lows in the 1990s.[78] This crisis initiated a debate on aid effectiveness that will be analyzed in more detail in the next chapter.[79] Already in the 1990s, it had found a conceptual expression in the post-development school. Inspired by the postcolonial studies that had thrived in the 1980s, post-development formulated a stinging critique and rejection (and will be analyzed in section IV below).

One editorial remark might be helpful here: in contrast to the previous sections, the fate of the individual donor organizations will not be discussed in detail here, although important reforms also occurred in this area. Since these reforms involve the present situation, they will be analyzed in Part II of this study.[80]

I. Sustainable development: integration of environmental and social aspects

A first aspect that contributed to the expansion of the idea of development in the early 1990s was the issue of environmental protection and the integration of broader ecological and social needs. These concerns were soon bundled into the key concept of sustainable development.[81] The ideas had,

[77] See R. Tetzlaff, *Weltbank und Währungsfonds: Gestalter der Bretton-Woods-Ära* (Opladen: Leske und Budrich, 1996), p. 191, referencing, among others, the so-called Madrid Declaration of October 1, 1994, which called for the abolition of the World Bank and the IMF. An important polemic for this course of action is S. George and F. Sabelli, *Kredit und Dogma: Ideologie und Macht der Weltbank* (Hamburg: Konkret Literatur, 1995).

[78] Particularly influential was the acid criticism in Hancock, *Lords of Poverty*; a more academic perspective was taken in N. van de Walle, "Aid's Crisis of Legitimacy: Current Proposals and Future Prospects," *African Affairs*, 98 (1999), 337–52 at 337; R. C. Riddell, "The End of Foreign Aid to Africa? Concerns about Donor Policies," *African Affairs*, 98 (1999), 309–35 at 309; C. Burnside and D. Dollar, "Aid, Policies and Growth," *The American Economic Review*, 90 (2000), 847–68 at 847; F. Nuscheler, "Halbierung der absoluten Armut: die entwicklungspolitische Nagelprobe," *Aus Politik und Zeitgeschichte*, B 18–19 (2001), 6–12 at 6. Available at www.bpb.de/system/files/pdf/QZYVRE.pdf (last visited July 2013); a fundamental critique was also articulated in Menzel, *Ende der Dritten Welt*, pp. 202.

[79] See on the aid effectiveness agenda *infra*, Ch 2.C.III.1.

[80] See Ch 3.A and passim.

[81] An introduction can be found in A. Glaser, *Nachhaltige Entwicklung und Demokratie: Ein Verfassungsrechtsvergleich der politischen Systeme Deutschlands und der Schweiz*,

however, been "incubating" for some time in development circles. As early as 1972, the Club of Rome noted the "Limits of Growth" and, more specifically, addressed the interaction between economic growth, population growth and the limits of natural resources.[82] Despite the intensive discussion that the report sparked, however, it had a rather limited effect on the actual practice of development aid or on the behavior of donors and recipients. One reason for this may be the lack of interaction between economists, who dominated development assistance in the 1970s, and ecologists. Furthermore, many of the new states in the Global South wanted most of all to achieve Western standards of living, and viewed environmental concerns as not particularly pressing.

The 1987 Brundtland Report represented a turning point, not least because it meant a decisive conceptual transformation.[83] "Environmental sustainability" was rechristened as "sustainable development," thereby forging a direct link between development and sustainability.[84] The relationship between the different elements (ecological, economic and social) of development became a subject of intense discussion. The Agenda 21 Declaration of the Rio Conference, in which sustainability was introduced into the idea of development, confirmed and sealed this merger.[85] The Declaration proclaimed ecologically sustainable poverty reduction to be a central goal and set out the associated basic strategies, instruments and techniques to achieve the goal in a (non-binding) document which reflected a consensus among participating states. At this time, development organizations, in particular the World Bank, also began addressing environmental issues in their rules.[86] In 2000, sustainable

Recht der nachhaltigen Entwicklung (Tübingen: Mohr Siebeck, 2006), vol. I, pp. 42; A. Grunwald and J. Kopfmüller, *Nachhaltigkeit* (Frankfurt am Main: Campus, 2006); for the development context see N. Michels, *Umweltschutz und Entwicklungspolitik: Mechanismen zur Berücksichtigung von Entwicklungsländern in internationalen Umweltschutzübereinkommen* (Frankfurt: Peter Lang Verlag, 1999).

82 D. H. Meadows and D. L. Meadows, *The Limits to Growth* (New York: Universe Books, 1972).

83 G. H. Brundtland, *Our Common Future* (Oxford University Press, 1987).

84 A critical perspective on the ambiguity of this idea is found in Rist, *History of Development*, pp. 192–6.

85 United Nations Conference on the Environment and Development, Rio de Janeiro, 1992.

86 The World Bank was in the vanguard of creating legal standards for environmental-protection issues. Already in 1989, the Bank required an environmental impact assessment for all of the projects it financed (see Shihata, *The World Bank in a Changing World I*, pp. 135–81). In German and European law, there are still only vague hints in this direction. See also *infra* Ch 6.B.

development (albeit in its narrower environmental sense) was named the 7th Millennium Goal and thus became a part of the central agenda of the world community.[87]

The concept of sustainable development is too broad to permit summary in this short section. The concept addresses primarily the effects of economic and population growth on developing countries (whether in the form of climate change, erosion, depletion of resources or pollution) as well as their inter- and intra-generational dimension.[88] The Brundtland Report thus describes sustainability as "meeting the needs of the present generation without compromising the needs of future generations." Particularly important was developing countries' increasing understanding that Third World nations would be more directly and gravely affected by environmental destruction, not least because their economies are more directly based on natural-resources-intensive activities such as agriculture and fisheries. Another important question was whether the relationship between development, economic growth and environmental protection should be seen as in tension (requiring "trade-offs") or complementary ("win–win"). The 1990s saw an increasing acceptance of the need to balance these demands.[89]

II. Human rights and participation

The second expansion in the notion of development seen in the 1990s relates to the role of the individual in the development process: the individual was increasingly moved to the center of the concept of development. Economic growth was no longer seen as the central goal, but rather as a means to an end. Distribution of wealth and, in particular, the use of profit to advance individual freedom became primary concerns. This change will be presented here in three stages: first, the most influential statements of this broader concept of development – in the works of Amartya Sen and in the definition of development in the UNDP's Development Report of 1990 – will be presented. Next, the implication of these conceptual changes for the role of the individual as participant in

[87] More on the MDGs immediately below in Ch 2.B.I.3.

[88] Comments on this discussion can be found in Martinussen, *Society, State and Market*, p. 143; from an economic perspective Todaro and Smith, *Economic Development*, p. 483.

[89] An expression of this can be found, for instance, in World Bank, *World Development Report 1992: Development and the Environment* (1992). Available at http://documents.worldbank.org/curated/en/home (last visited July 2013).

development cooperation will be addressed. The final section addresses the political implementation and the ambivalence of human rights in the context of development.[90]

1. Development as freedom: Amartya Sen and the UNDP Human Development Report

The work of the Indian economist Amartya Sen is today considered a central point of reference for a broadened understanding of development.[91] Sen conceives development as the process of expanding freedoms and capabilities.[92] For Sen, development is not defined by the goal of increased economic growth, but increased freedoms – the opportunities and skills the individual obtains in order to live according to his or her own priorities.[93] Securing these freedoms is the actual goal of the development process, while economic growth is only the means (although a very helpful means) to securing or expanding freedom.

Sen holds freedoms to have a double function, both evaluative and instrumental. Their *evaluative* function is to serve as yardsticks of development, that is, as ultimate goals.[94] Freedoms, whose definition Sen adopts from the rights mentioned in various human rights treaties, are thus *constitutive* elements of development. Development is measured by their level of realization. To ask whether political rights are necessary or helpful for development efforts, Sen accordingly believes, is asking the wrong question. Political rights are simply a constitutive part of development, which would be deficient insofar as these rights are not developed.

[90] The second expansion of the concept of development also drew upon ideas not drawn from the original discipline of development – economics. These new impulses drew on legal discourse and the perception of individuals in development cooperation. Interestingly, the central concepts were rarely formulated by legal scholars. On the relationship between the discourses of human rights and development see *infra* Ch 4.D.

[91] The central work is Sen, *Development as Freedom*, which grew, interestingly, out of six lectures held in the World Bank. However, it draws on much previous work, including A. Sen, *Commodities and Capabilities* (Amsterdam: Elsevier, 1985); A. Sen, "The Concept of Development," in H. Chenery (ed.), *Handbook of Development Economics* (Amsterdam: North Holland, 1988), pp. 9–25 at p. 9.

[92] On the reception of Sen's work see F. Stewart and S. Deneulin, "Amartya Sen's Contribution to Development Thinking," *Studies in Comparative International Development*, 37 (2002), 61–70 at 62 (and further essays in that work); Todaro and Smith, *Economic Development*, p. 16; B. Chimni, "The Sen Conception of Development and Contemporary International Law Discourse: Some Parallels," *The Law and Development Review*, 1 (2008), 2–22 at 3.

[93] Sen expresses this with the term *capabilities*, Sen, *Development as Freedom*, pp. 10, 75.

[94] Ibid., pp. 4, 36.

Sen argues that freedoms also have an *instrumental* function. He assumes that the "free" person will become an agent of development.[95] Those who are free and use their freedoms contribute to the process of development. As if through Adam Smith's invisible hand, individuals' use of their freedoms and social development are linked and advance in relation to one another. He singles out five types of freedoms that have an instrumental dimension: political freedom, economic facilities, social opportunities, transparency guarantees and protective security. These rights are all interconnected and strengthen each other reciprocally. A good educational and health system, for instance, is no luxury – it strengthens the individual's economic performance and the economy as a whole.[96] In another example, Sen illustrates the relationship between democracy and hunger. He argues that there are no famines in democracies, since such crises can be easily prevented by government efforts, and democratically elected leaders will certainly prevent them.[97]

Sen's work found practical application in the concept of "sustainable human development" (SHD), developed for the UNDP by a research group led by Pakistani economist and development theorist Mahbub ul Haq in 1990.[98] The concept has since become the basis for UNDP development indicators and a generally accepted leading index for the modern understanding of development. Like Sen, the SHD defines development as "expanding human choices," and is thus based on the individual. The generation of economic development and income growth is a central instrument in expanding choices, but remains only a means, and one among many. Ul Haq stresses that social, cultural and political possibilities are central to human flourishing as the goal of development. Securing them is, therefore, a public task and cannot be left solely to the market. Economic and income growth, per se, do not indicate that all parts of society are benefiting.

One central achievement of the UNDP's new paradigm was to specify concretely three essential dimensions of human development, namely the chance to live a long and healthy life, to acquire knowledge, and to

95 Ibid., pp. 10, 37. For a more specific treatment see, e.g. M. Darrow and A. Tomas, "Power, Capture, and Conflict: A Call for Human Rights Accountability in Development Cooperation," *Human Rights Quarterly*, 27 (2005), 471–538 at 471.

96 Sen, *Development as Freedom*, p. 40.

97 For more on this, see his famous earlier work: A. Sen, *Resource, Values and Development* (Cambridge: Harvard University Press, 1984).

98 United Nations Development Programme, *Human Development Report 1990* (New York: Oxford University Press, 1990); see also M. u. Haq, *Reflections on Human Development* (New York: Oxford University Press, 1995).

have access to resources necessary for an appropriate standard of living. These dimensions were then integrated into an indicator model for the yearly UN Human Development Index (HDI). Since the development of the Index, the UNDP has measured developing as well as industrialized countries on three criteria: (1) real average income per capita, (2) average life expectancy, and (3) the illiteracy rate combined with enrollment rates in education institutions of various stages.[99]

The importance of the HDI is that it represents the first alternative and practicable measurement of development; it is the fruit of the paradigm shift in the understanding of development introduced by Sen and others.[100] With it, an idea of development has prevailed that goes beyond economic growth and, with its emphasis on human rights, enters territory familiar to jurists.

2. Participation

One specific aspect of the freedom- and individual-centered reformulation of the idea of development is the participation of citizens and affected parties. This should be addressed separately here, since it is of particular importance for our understanding of development cooperation. During the first decades of development cooperation, there were surprisingly few doubts that the responsible parties for the structuring and organization of development processes were states (both donor and recipient), international organizations and their administrators. Concepts of development that named individuals, groups or civil society as the *main* agents of development were rare.[101]

Nevertheless, since the 1970s, voices have emerged which addressed the participation of affected parties in development projects *in the context* of projects financed at the national or supranational level.[102] As the 1990s saw changes in the understanding of the goals of development, including

[99] More on these indicators and their practical relevance *infra* Ch 3.B.I.

[100] The World Bank also now measures development by a set of indicators called the World Development Indicators. Even the normally critical Rist sees this paradigm change positively, see Rist, *History of Development*, p. 205.

[101] But see, e.g. G. Gran, *Development by People: Citizen Construction of a Just World* (New York: Praeger, 1983); R. Chambers, *Rural Development: Putting the Last First* (London: Longman, 1983). This is not surprising from a political standpoint, however, since the governments of developing nations were very aware of their sovereignty and wanted to control the processes themselves.

[102] See, e.g. P. Streeten and S. J. Burki, *First Things First: Meeting Basic Human Needs in Developing Countries* (New York: Oxford University Press, 1981); on these voices, see Greig, Hulme and Turner, *Challenging Global Inequality*, p. 234.

the gradual focus on individuals, these voices became more important. It is hardly a great step from Sen's conception of the individual as agent of development to the demand for greater individual participation in concrete development projects. As development assistance encountered ever-increased scrutiny from civil society, aid organizations could hardly escape demands for increased civil-society participation. The World Bank's 1995 publication of a *Sourcebook on Participation* is exemplary. The *Poverty Reduction Strategy Paper*, a recipient-driven planning instrument introduced by the World Bank in 1999 and now used by almost all developing countries, sets out the participation of civil-society groups as a precondition.[103]

Nevertheless, the specific form, function and benefit from individuals' participation in planning and implementation of development projects remains controversial and unclear.[104] Critics see them as a Trojan horse, since, in their view, individual participation is only a smokescreen for a continued state monopoly on control over contents and processes.[105] From a technocratic perspective, participation by individuals and civil-society groups can be regarded as helpful even when it doesn't confer any formal voting rights as it creates ownership and responsibility. The concrete importance of participation rights in the disbursement of ODA will be explained more fully in Part III of this investigation.[106]

3. Human rights and development policy: MDGs and conditionality

Human rights and individual freedom were not just theoretical concerns; in the 1990s, they became a concrete component of development policy. Two aspects that put this incorporation into clearer context will be briefly mentioned here. One is the Millennium Development Goals (MDGs), which show the extent to which human rights have penetrated to the core of the development agenda; the other aspect is the political ambivalence

[103] Discussed more extensively *infra* Ch 5.B.II. On the importance of the OECD-DAC in this respect see K. Masujima, "'Good Governance' and the Development Assistance Committee," in M. Boas and D. McNeill (eds.), *Global Institutions and Development: Framing the World?* (Oxon: Routledge, 2003), pp. 151–63 at p. 157.

[104] An overview can be found in L. Groves and R. Hint (eds.), *Inclusive Aid: Changing Power and Relationships in International Development* (London: Earthscan Publications, 2004).

[105] See also B. Cooke and U. Kothari, *Participation: The New Tyranny* (London, New York: Zed Books, 2001).

[106] See *infra* Ch 4.D.III.2 and Ch 5.C and Ch 6.B.

of human rights in development assistance, since they were used not only to protect individual rights but also to foster intervention in and pressure upon recipient states. This ambivalence is chiefly associated with the instrument of conditionality.

The United Nations' MDGs can be seen as a key validation of the human rights orientation of development cooperation. Derived from the UN Millennium Declaration, which was promulgated in 2000 by 147 heads of state (the largest ever assembly of its kind in history), was a consensus document in which the world community agreed on eight goals to be achieved by 2015: (1) halving extreme hunger and poverty, (2) the global introduction of primary education, (3) promoting gender equality, (4) reducing infant mortality by two-thirds, (5) a three-quarters reduction in the maternal mortality ratio, (6) stopping the spread of HIV/AIDS, malaria and other diseases, (7) establishing the principle of ecological sustainability, and (8) introducing a global development partnership.

These eight goals have become the principal yardstick for development cooperation. Certainly, the mere proclamation of impressive goals is hardly a novelty.[107] However, the MDGs mark a new (and controversial) approach to formulating such goals.[108] First, they are not open and vague, but rather precise and quantitative, specifying indicators for measuring achievement. Second, they are time-sensitive – they must be achieved within concrete deadlines. Third, they begin with goals, not with available resources. That is, they require participants to fulfill their duties even if costs increase. Finally, the MDGs were bound to a relatively large institutional structure which was intended to monitor their realization.[109]

What is the concrete relationship of the MDGs to human rights? Clearly, there is a large substantive overlap between the MDGs and central

[107] The UN declared the 1960s, 70s, and 80s each as "development decades" with ambitious goals, but these were never reached. The 1974 NIEO also remained an unfulfilled manifesto. See *supra* Ch 1.B.I.

[108] The MDGs and their structure were prefigured by a 1996 OECD-DAC agenda entitled "Shaping the 21st Century"; see Nuscheler, "Halbierung der absoluten Armut," 6.

[109] Among these was the Millennium Project, a network of politicians, practitioners and researchers under the leadership of Jeffrey Sachs (www.unmillenniumproject.org), whose work has been continued by the UNDP since 2007 (www.undp.org/mdg/), and the Millennium Campaign, which is intended to mobilize civil-society actors and to involve states and international organizations in the realization of the goals, in particular those related to reporting (see www.undp.org/mdg/tracking_countryreports2.shtml) (last visited September 2012); see also P. Alston, "Ships Passing in the Night: The Current State of the Human Rights and Development Debate Seen Through the Lens of the Millennium Development Goals," *Human Rights Quarterly*, 27 (2005), 755–829 at 792.

human rights guarantees. Nevertheless, the first criticism of the MDGs came from the human rights community.[110] Rights advocates complained of the lack of explicit reference to human rights provisions. Others saw the MDGs as too narrow and selective, particularly because they relate "only" to economic and social rights, not political rights. For yet others, the MDGs simply didn't go far enough.[111] And finally, their quantitative, output-oriented approach was criticized.[112]

Some of this criticism does not appear to be wholly justified. Even though human rights are not explicitly mentioned in the MDGs, this doesn't change the fact that the broad *substantive* scope of the goals ensures that their implementation will bring massive improvements in this area. One can criticize the selectivity of the MDGs, yet they arose precisely from the attempt to avoid the over-generality of many former and futile proclamations. Although political rights are not explicitly mentioned in the Goals themselves, they play an important role in the Millennium Declaration on which the MDGs are based. They are thus closely integrated into the context of the MDGs and the strategy for their realization. In the final analysis, it is not particularly productive to set human rights *against* the MDGs rather than viewing them as complementary reinforcements. Considering the role of human rights in development policy from a historical perspective, the MDGs should be recognized as a significant step forward, as they bring basic human rights concerns into the main agenda of development efforts.

In addition to strengthening the human rights orientation of development policy, the MDGs also show how much the balance of power has shifted toward donors in recent years. Human rights as objects of

[110] Discussed in detail ibid., 764.

[111] See, e.g. T. Pogge, *Global Justice and the First Millennium Development Goal.* Available at www.etikk.no/globaljustice/ (last visited September 2012). Others, by contrast, see the danger in the fact that the MDGs are unrealistic and thus risk creating disappointment with respect to development cooperation. See, e.g. M. Clemens, C. Kenny and T. Moss, *The Trouble with the MDG: Confronting Expectations of Aid and Development Progress*, Center for Global Development Working Paper Nr. 40, p. 2. Available at www.cgdev.org/content/publications/detail/2749/ (last visited September 2012).

[112] S. Seppänen, *Possibilities and Challenges of the Human Rights-Based Approach to Development: Erik Castrén Institute research reports No. 17* (Helsinki: The Erik Castrén Institute of International Law, 2005), p. 57; see also Philip Alston's overview of critiques of the MDGs: P. Alston, *A Human Rights Perspective on the Millennium Development Goals*, Paper prepared as a contribution to the work of the work of the Millennium Project Task Force on Poverty and Economic Development, margin nos. 18–23. Available at www.hurilink.org/tools/HRsPerspectives_on_the_MDGs–Alston.pdf (last visited September 2012).

development policy are fraught with political ambivalence, since they implicate the relationship of recipient states to their own citizens, an internal matter and thus a question of autonomy. The human rights discussion may be used not only to improve protection of individuals but also to put pressure on recipient countries. Human rights can thus end up as instruments of political intervention.

Given this historical context, it is understandable that recipient countries long resisted discussion of human rights. Many donors pushed for inclusion of human rights in development cooperation starting in the late 1970s.[113] However, during the 1980s most recipient countries still had enough power to resist this pressure.[114] The end of the Cold War reduced this power considerably. In 1989's Lomé IV Convention, the EC made respect for human rights the basis for its support. In 1991, Germany introduced five political criteria, among them respect for human rights, as conditions for receipt of German development assistance.[115] In the World Bank, as well, human rights became important factors, although the Bank termed them economic rights, in conformity with the Bank's ban on political interference.[116]

In effect, human rights can affect developmental efforts in two ways, namely positively and negatively. Human rights could be the subject of positive support by donors. Thus, the Federal Republic of Germany has made grants for human rights education and legal assistance, to better anchor basic rights in the legal orders of recipient states. But respect for human rights was also used negatively, that is, as a condition for allocation decisions.[117] Human rights became conditions: states which did not respect them could face cuts or the termination of future payments.

Another aspect of human rights in development cooperation that somewhat transcends the double-edged nature of individual protection and interventionist instrumentalization is the question of the extent to

[113] The Presidency of Jimmy Carter is seen as the first time when human rights questions became an important topic in American foreign policy; see *supra* Ch 2.A.III, see also W. Heinz, *Positive Maßnahmen zur Förderung von Demokratie und Menschenrechten als Aufgabe der Entwicklungszusammenarbeit*, Berichte und Gutachten 1994 No. 4 (Berlin, 1994), p. IV.

[114] In Germany, however, political foundations laid preliminary groundwork in this area, albeit as non-state organizations.

[115] Hoffmeister, *Menschenrechts- und Demokratieklauseln*, p. 39; P. P. Waller, "Aid and Conditionality," in O. Stokke (ed.), *Aid and Political Conditionality* (London, Portland: Frank Cass, 1995), vol. XVI, pp. 110–28 at p. 112.

[116] Shihata, *The World Bank in a Changing World I*, p. 97; see *infra* Ch 3.A.IV.3.

[117] A clear description is found in Waller, "Aid and Conditionality," p. 115.

which *donors* themselves are bound by human rights in their activity. This question has often been ignored in the political discussion, but is important to the contours of the law of development cooperation, and will thus be addressed further in Part II.[118]

III. *Stable statehood: democracy and good governance*

As the concept of development, as well as the donor strategies intended to achieve it, began expanding in the early 1990s, a third element of this expansion occurred. The developing countries' form of government and the functioning of recipient states became a focus of development cooperation for the first time. Donor organizations generally had two approaches, which, although springing from different motives and conceptions, were nevertheless typical. As will be seen in Section 1, Germany and the EU, in the exuberant period following the end of the Cold War, tended to emphasize democratization and human rights policies. The World Bank, by contrast, developed the purportedly technocratic instrument of "governance" during the structural-adjustment crisis, as Section 2 explores. Finally, in Section 3, it will be shown that both approaches tended to merge into a general good governance agenda.

1. Human rights and democratization as themes of German and EU development cooperation

In German and EU development policy, the governmental form of recipient states rather unexpectedly became a subject for discussion owing to the sudden collapse of the so-called Second World (i.e. the USSR and communist Eastern Europe) and the end of the Cold War. As has been seen, human rights were already under discussion in the 1980s. The basic structure of state organization, however, was another matter altogether. Even during the period of weakness of developing nations in the 1980s, it was hardly considered an acceptable topic. The end of the Cold War created a different and very specific historical context in three ways.

First, the euphoria caused by the "victory" in the Cold War led industrialized countries to presume the absolute superiority of the Western path. Democracy, human rights and a market economy were now regarded as the obviously superior model, perhaps even the final goal of history.[119]

[118] See Ch 4.D.II.

[119] The classic expression is found in F. Fukuyama, *The End of History and the Last Man* (New York: Free Press, 1992).

Second, this era also saw many developing countries, particularly in Africa, experience an impressive wave of democratization on their own part which seemed to proceed in sync with world-historical developments.[120] In these countries, as well, the "victory" of the Western model seemed to be made manifest. Finally, the end of the Cold War focused attention on the Second World, that is, Eastern Europe. Developing countries in Africa, on the other hand, began to fear being forgotten, which led them to accept even strongly interventionist conditions.[121]

This historical situation allowed Western donors to attach previously unthinkable political conditions to their aid payments. In addition to human rights, donors now openly demanded democratization. In the 1989 Lomé IV Convention, the EC had already prevailed upon the ACP states to endorse a statement that respect and support for human rights is a precondition for development. A 1995 addendum to the agreement established that the recognition and implementation of democratic principles was closely connected to development policy.[122] Already in 1991, Germany had begun linking bilateral assistance to active support for democratic structures and similar measures.[123] The endorsement of democratization as a condition and goal of development assistance was particularly clear in the Charter of the newly founded European Bank for Reconstruction and Development in London. Democracy promotion is a part of its very mandate.[124]

The relatively sudden pressure for democratization is surprising from the perspective of development *theory*. It appears that democratization was seen primarily as a *politically* welcome instrument. There are few scholarly works from this period which analyze the theoretical implications of democratization or which indicate recourse to related ideas by German or European development agencies. It is, of course, possible to describe an outline of the democratization approach, even if it was not explicitly formulated in this way. In the final analysis, it represented a politicized

[120] van de Walle, *African Economies and the Politics*, p. 235.

[121] An example is R. Kappel, "Afrikas Perspektiven in der Entwicklungskooperation mit der Europäischen Gemeinschaft," *Afrika Spectrum*, 25 (1990), 257–82 at 257.

[122] Art. 5 Lomé IV (1989); Art. 5 Lomé IV (1995); this statement of principle was accompanied by a sanctions clause, see Art. 366 II, III Lomé IV (1995); Hoffmeister, *Menschenrechts- und Demokratieklauseln*, pp. 38, 168.

[123] Waller, "Aid and Conditionality," pp. 112, 113; Heinz, *Positive Maßnahmen*, p. 26.

[124] S. Weber, "Origins of the European Bank for Reconstruction and Development," *International Organization*, 48 (1994), 1–38 at 1; I. Shihata, *The European Bank for Reconstruction and Development: A Comparative Analysis of Its Constituent Agreement* (Boston: Martinus Nijhoff Publishers, 1990).

understanding of the development process and its most important actors, as conceived by Amartya Sen and others. Citizens were to play a significant role, requiring the state to respect their rights not only as individuals but also precisely as a democratic collective, thus driving the state to adopt a development-oriented policy. The autonomously and democratically ascertained will of the people, carried out by a responsible government, is considered a critical component, even a precondition, of development. Or, conversely: a developing state requires democracy. Whatever the basis for the approach, however, it can hardly be contested that making aid contingent on democratization was a daring step, both from a political perspective and from the perspective of development theory.[125]

2. Governance as the technocratic strategy of the World Bank

For the World Bank, the role of the state became part of the agenda for other reasons. There, the 1980s had brought two main realizations. First, it became ever clearer how massively a certain group of recipient states (particularly in sub-Saharan Africa) suffered from deficits in their governmental structures, a condition now known as "fragile statehood."[126] At this time a newly formulated and gradually accepted diagnosis, fragile statehood describes a situation in which governments fall short of (Western) expectations of a rational administration that can raise taxes and execute political programs; a court system that can rule impartially, coherently and in a timely manner; and a state that can monopolize force.

Second, it was also recognized that a new balance between the roles of market and state in the development process would have to be found. For one thing, structural-adjustment programs had made it clear that development could not be achieved one-sidedly by bypassing the state – that is, that development could not be achieved solely by "the" market. The strategy of achieving development gains by limiting state involvement and freeing economic initiative had clearly failed. The state had to do more than simply secure the economic rights of investors. However, on

[125] Empirically, the connection between development and democracy remains difficult to prove, see S. Killinger, *The World Bank's Non-Political Mandate* (Cologne: Heymann, 2003), p. 150; on the possibility that there may even be a negative effect see J. Faust and S. Leiderer, "Zur Effektivität und politischen Ökonomie der Entwicklungszusammenarbeit," *Politische Vierteljahresschrift*, 49 (2008), 129–52 at 137–9.

[126] See *supra* Ch 2.A.I.1.

the other hand, the state had also clearly failed at planning the development of the whole economy and running businesses. It became clear that the state must have a role somewhere *between* the minimal state of neoliberals and the planned economy. Its role must include providing public infrastructure (courts, security, transport) as well as distributing wealth.

To address these problems, the World Bank developed the concept of governance as a development strategy and goal of development cooperation.[127] The concept was first formulated in a now-famous 1989 report on the development situation in sub-Saharan Africa.[128] The report argued that "underlying the litany of Africa's development problems was a crisis of governance" and therefore concluded that, in addition to the market, these nations needed to fulfill basic state functions such as efficient public administration, a reliable court system and responsible administration. The report attracted much attention by its use of the word "governance" instead of "government." Governance, defined by the American Webster's dictionary as "the exercise of political power to manage a nation's affairs," had until then been rarely used, whether in the development community or in general speech. The change was driven by the delicate legal question whether the Bank was actually permitted to act in this area, since its founding agreements prohibited interference in recipient countries' political affairs, a restriction that had until then been taken quite seriously.[129]

A 1990 report from the Bank's chief legal counsel, Ibrahim Shihata, became centrally important to the permissibility of the Bank's governance activities, as well as their conceptual structure. Shihata noted that the idea of governance comprised overlapping political and economic aspects, but that the political areas of governance, which were off-limits to the Bank, could nevertheless be separated from the non-political aspects. Shihata marked off five activities that would be prohibited to the Bank[130]

[127] The story of the emergence of the governance policy has been told many times. The most concise presentation is found in Killinger, *The World Bank's Non-Political Mandate*, pp. 10–20.

[128] World Bank, *Sub-Saharan Africa: From Crisis to Sustainable Growth* (Washington, DC: World Bank Publications, 1989). For context see Kapur, Lewis and Webb, *The World Bank*, p. 756.

[129] Art. V, Sect. 10, IBRD Articles; Art. V, Sect. 6, IDA Articles. The provision reads: "The Association and its officers shall not interfere in the political affairs of any member, nor shall they be influenced in their decisions by the political character of the member or members concerned. Only economic considerations shall be relevant to their decisions, and these considerations shall be weighed impartially in order to achieve the purposes stated in this Agreement." Discussed in greater depth *infra* Ch 3.A.IV.3.

[130] Shihata, *The World Bank in a Changing World I*, pp. 81–4. They are: "(i) The Bank should not be influenced by the 'political character' of the member; (ii) The Bank should not

and four areas in which the Bank could legally intervene.[131] On the basis of this memo, the Bank then published two reports outlining its governance agenda. According to the reports, the Bank's activities would be divided into four areas: public sector management, accountability, rule of law, and transparency and the fight against corruption.[132]

Since then, projects and programs to reform governance structures in these areas have become one of the Bank's main activities.[133] At least formally, these projects can be differentiated from the openly political projects of other donors, which, for instance, openly address democratization.[134] Governance consolidation is seen principally as a technical activity which is justified by its positive economic effects. Technocratic consolidation, not political reform, is the Bank's way.[135]

3. (Good) Governance today

At least since the latter half of the 1990s, the World Bank's concept of governance has taken on a life beyond the Bank. An independent, analytical governance discourse outside the development politics emerged, which uses the concept of governance for all questions of control aside from hierarchical statehood.[136] Then, legal scholars took up this analytical

interfere in the domestic or foreign partisan politics of any member; (iii) The Bank, as coordinator of foreign assistance for a given country, should not act on behalf of donor countries influencing the recipient country's political orientation or behavior; (iv) The Bank should not allow political factors or events to influence its decisions unless it is established that they have direct and obvious economic effects relevant to its work; (v) Bank staff should not build their assessment on the possible reaction of any particular Bank member."

131 These are civil service reform, legal reform, accountability of public funds, and budget discipline, see ibid., p. 84.

132 Detailed discussion in Killinger, *The World Bank's Non-Political Mandate*, pp. 20–30. On the importance of institutional economics as a theoretical foundation see C. Theobald, "Die Weltbank: Good Governance und die Neue Institutionenökonomik," *Verwaltungsarchiv*, 89 (1998), 467–87 at 467.

133 Critical was K. Rittich, "The Future of Law and Development: Second-Generation Reforms and the Incorporation of the Social," *Michigan Journal of International Law*, 26 (2004), 199–243 at 243.

134 See Killinger, *The World Bank's Non-Political Mandate*, p. 141.

135 On the technocratic concept of the World Bank regarding the example of rule of law-projects T. Krever, "The Legal Turn in Late Development Theory: The Rule of Law and the World Bank's Development Model," *Harvard International Law Journal*, 52 (2011), 287–319.

136 The ideas of Rosenau are considered the beginning of the debate, J. N. Rosenau and E.-O. Czempiel (eds.), *Governance Without Government: Order and Change in World Politics* (Cambridge University Press, 1992); on the current state of the extensive discussion see, e.g. A. Benz (ed.), *Governance – Regieren in komplexen Regelsystemen: Eine Einführung*

approach.[137] This approach now comes back to discussions of development policy primarily where it relates to the global institutional architecture of development assistance.[138] However, even within the debates about the substance of development policy, the concept of governance has migrated from the halls of the World Bank and become a general model.[139] This is often, but not always, referred to as *good* governance, and always has a normative component, since it serves as a formulation of the goals of development assistance. It combines different aspects of the policies (as presented above) of the World Bank, the EU and Germany.[140]

The core elements of the current concept of good governance include respect for human rights and democratically legitimized exercise of state power complying with the rule of law. The Monterrey Consensus, accepted in 2002 by 147 states and certainly a generally accepted approach, proclaims: "Good governance is essential for sustainable development. Sound economic policies, solid democratic institutions responsive to the needs of the people … are the basis for sustained economic growth, poverty eradication and employment creation."[141] According to a policy paper published in 2009, the German Development Ministry defines good governance as being based on respect for human rights and describes a situation in which "state actors make serious efforts to implement policies that are sustainable, poverty-oriented, and oriented toward meeting the

(Wiesbaden: Verlag für Sozialwissenschaften, 2004); G. F. Schuppert and M. Zürn (eds.), *Governance in einer sich wandelnden Welt* (Wiesbaden: Verlag für Sozialwissenschaften, 2008).

137 H.-H. Trute, W. Denkhaus and D. Kühlers, "Governance in der Verwaltungsrechtswissenschaft," *Die Verwaltung*, 37 (2004), 451–73 at 451; G. F. Schuppert, "Was ist und wozu Governance?" *Die Verwaltung*, 40 (2007), 465–512 at 465 and, for international law, S. Seppänen, *Good Governance in International Law: Erik Castrén Institute research reports No. 13* (Helsinki: The Erik Castrén Institute of International Law, 2003); Kingsbury, Krisch and Stewart, "Emergence of Global Administrative Law"; Bogdandy, Dann and Goldmann, "Developing."

138 For example, J. Faust and D. Messner, "Entwicklungspolitik als Global Governance-Arena," in H. Breitmeier, M. Roth and D. Senghaas (eds.), *Sektorale Weltordnungspolitik: Effektiv, gerecht und demokratisch?* (Baden-Baden: Nomos, 2009), pp. 213–33 at p. 213; more on this debate immediately below in section II.

139 The contributions to H. Weiland, I. Wehr and M. Seifert (eds.), *Good Governance in der Sackgasse?* (Baden-Baden: Nomos, 2009) offer a good overview of the discussion in development-policy circles; on the origins of the concept in the World Bank see Theobald, "Weltbank," 467.

140 The interface between the analytical-institutional and the substantive concept of governance is addressed by C. Möllers, "Die Governance-Konstellation," in G. F. Schuppert and M. Zürn (eds.), *Governance in einer sich wandelnden Welt* (Wiesbaden: Verlag für Sozialwissenschaften, 2008), pp. 238–56 at p. 240.

141 UN-GA, A/Res/56/210 B of 9 July 2002, margin no. 11.

MDGs."[142] A poverty-oriented policy requires that the level of development should be measured by human rights as well as democratic and rule-of-law principles. The World Bank also defines governance in the broadest possible terms as "traditions and institutions by which authority in a state is exercised. This includes the process by which governments are selected, monitored and replaced; the capacity of governments to effectively formulate and implement sound policies, and the respect of citizens and the state for the institutions that govern economic and social interaction among them."[143]

The goal of all these concepts is more stable and responsible statehood, even if reform of the recipient state's political structures is pursued with different levels of intensity, or at least discussed with different levels of directness. All models aim for a rational, transparent, responsible and conscientious polity as a central condition of development. All these concepts also assume that the various aspects they stress mutually influence and reinforce each other.

4. Conclusion: poverty reduction and good governance as development priorities

A final trend in this context should be noted: in recent years, the concentration on poverty reduction as a primary goal of development has become central to the discussion.

This goal is best understood in the context of the definition of poverty. Poverty can be seen as a mirror image of the idea of development as described in the previous sections. There, it was shown that the idea of development underwent fundamental expansion since the early 1990s. It finally broke free of its economic core and took on a more general, holistic character. As it is now understood and supported by basically all development organizations and activists, development involves not only

[142] BMZ, *Förderung von Good Governance in der deutschen Entwicklungspolitik: Konzept Nr. 172*, (Berlin, 2009), p. 6. Available at www.bmz.de/de/publikationen/reihen/strategiepapiere/konzept172.pdf (last visited July 2013).

[143] D. Kaufmann, A. Kraay and M. Mastruzzi, *Governance Matters VIII: Aggregate and Individual Governance Indicators, 1996–2008*, World Bank Policy Research Working Paper No. 4978, p. 5. Available at http://papers.ssrn.com/sol3/papers.cfm?abstract_id=1424591 (last visited July 2013); for a quite critical reading of the World Bank's treatment of the governance idea see Möllers, "Governance-Konstellation," pp. 240–4; an empirical investigation of similar themes is found in G. Harrison, *The World Bank and Africa: The Construction of Governance States* (London: Routledge, 2004). On the question of whether this analysis succeeds as legal interpretation, see the Summary at Ch 7.C.

the liberation of individuals from material want but also the shaping of the individual's social, ecological and political environment. Poverty no longer describes merely material deficits but also the deprivation of social, intellectual and material opportunities. Development thus involves a comprehensive process which is considerably influenced by the political structures of a state, as well as the structure of economic relationships. Good governance becomes particularly important. Goals include the establishment or stabilization of a legal and political system that protects human rights, enforces the rule of law and provides for stable (if not necessarily democratic) national leadership. In the final analysis, this represents a holistic concept of development. At the end of the day, development cooperation is seen to pursue twin goals, namely poverty reduction and the creation of stable and responsive states.

The explicit reference to poverty reduction, however, also serves another purpose: to prevent the abuse of development assistance for illegitimate foreign or economic-policy purposes. This demand has recently become more evident in development law, for instance, in the new British law on development or in the Treaty of Lisbon.[144] Poverty reduction is listed here explicitly as the primary goal of development cooperation – a proviso that simultaneously takes a step toward the autonomization of development aid.

The result is ambivalent: on the one hand, a broader definition of poverty is certainly more appropriate than the narrower definition of earlier models of development. If it is accompanied by an understanding of development as a political process which must also involve the individual not merely as a recipient but also as an active shaper of policy, it comes quite close to Sen's idea of development. On the other hand, the goal is formulated in such a way as to potentially justify far-reaching and intrusive interference to achieve it. The expansion of the concept of development thus justifies an interventionist development policy. This fact, among others, raises the requirements for organization and legitimacy of development assistance, which will be addressed in the last section.

IV. Post-development and the postcolonial critique of development

The 1990s were not only the period in which the concept of development was expanded broadly but also one in which criticism of development

[144] See Art. 1 International Development Act 2002; Art. 209 I para. 1, TFEU; World Bank, Operational Policy 1.00, margin no. 1; see also the section on goals of the Millennium Declaration, UN-GA Res. 55/2 of September 18, 2000, margin nos.11–20.

theory and practice reached a new quality. While substantial criticism of the practice of development cooperation has been a feature almost since its very beginnings,[145] a new school of thought emerged in the early 1990s that questions the very idea of "development." This school is called post-development. It formulates indeed a fundamental rejection of "development" as idea, goal and practice – and provides an important counterpoint to other approaches described so far.

Post-development thinking is closely connected to and based on the thoughts and writings of postcolonial studies. We begin therefore with a brief introduction to postcolonial thinking (Section 1). Against this background, the main ideas of post-development can be presented (Section 2). Finally, we shall ask to what extent the post-development positions have an impact on the current development discourse – and which role the law might play here (Section 3).

1. Postcolonial studies

Postcolonial studies examine the impact of colonialism on the thinking and acting of those living in ex-colonies, as well as on the ex-colonizers. Based on a long tradition of reflection but grown most concretely out of literary and historical studies of the late 1970s and 1980s, they inquire into the consequences of colonial domination in history, psychology and social artifacts.[146] More abstractly, one can say that postcolonial studies are concerned with the "situatedness" or relativity of our thinking and acting, maintaining that any conception of oneself, one's environment or one's opinion is conditioned by where we are, who we are and who we see or hear. Postcolonial thinking hence questions the claims of universal values and concepts. Instead, it observes that much of the narration, description or value construction has been done by the West or Westernized elites. It hence challenges the cultural hegemony of Western and Eurocentric thinking accompanying this and aims to unearth alternative perspectives and voices from the South and from marginalized actors.

[145] See also the famous Pearson Report of 1969, Pearson, *Pearson Report 1969*, especially pp. 124, 168, 208.

[146] E. W. Said, *Orientalism* (New York: Pantheon Books, 1978); H. K. Bhabha, *The Location of Culture* (London, New York: Routledge, 1994); G. C. Spivak and S. Harasym, *The Post-Colonial Critic: Interviews, Strategies, Dialogues* (New York: Routledge, 1990); R. Guha and G. C. Spivak, *Selected Subaltern Studies* (New York: Oxford University Press, 1988); R. Guha, *Subaltern Studies: Writings on South Asian History and Society* (New Delhi, New York: Oxford University Press, 1982); important path-makers were F. Fanon and C. Farrington, *The Wretched of the Earth* (New York: Grove Press, 1963); C. Achebe, *Things Fall Apart* (London: William Heinemann, 1958); S. Ousmane, *Le docker noir*

Postcolonial studies are centrally concerned with language, discourse and representation. They stress the inherently political nature of language and the power that goes along with it.[147] Postcolonial thinkers point out that power and domination are not just functions of the military or the police but can also reside in language and knowledge. Path-breaking in this regard were the literary studies by Edward Said, who analyzed how Western writers had constructed the "Orient" as the "other," formulating assumed characteristics of "the Arabs" while subtly creating perceptions and ingraining prejudices in contrast to the self-perception of Europeans.[148] He examined how such descriptions had more to do with European ideologies, European identities and in fact inherent European problems than with Arab realities, and he analyzed how such writings functioned as important tools to justify colonial domination and subjugation. In consequence, he sharply criticizes Western incompetence or unwillingness (till today) to understand better the realities and complexities of the Middle East (or any postcolonial society). Postcolonial analysis is never far from critical political thinking.

Putting into practice the call to question Western narratives and tell stories from other perspectives, a group of Indian historians in the 1980s created what they called *subaltern studies*.[149] In this second influential strand of postcolonial studies, they shifted the attention from elites and leaders to "subalterns," i.e. to peasants, workers or women, studying economic and political histories rather than literature. Using Gramscian Marxism and French deconstructionism, they studied the participation and role of subaltern groups in the independence struggle and Indian history more generally. They highlighted the special relevance and influence of these groups in the shaping of political processes and economic outcomes – and thus offered a counter-narrative to more bourgeois and elite descriptions.

While postcolonial studies started out in the fields of literature and history, it has been taken up in many other fields, among them law. In

(Paris: Présence africaine, 1956); also W. E. B. Du Bois, *The Souls of Black Folk: Essays and Sketches* (Chicago: A.C. McClurg & Co, 1903). On the intellectual roots of postcolonial studies, see C. McEwan, *Postçolonialism and Development* (London, New York: Routledge, 2009), pp. 38–60.

147 See also J. Berger, "Was behauptet die Modernisierungstheorie wirklich – und was wird ihr bloß unterstellt?" *Leviathan* (1996), 45–62.

148 Said, *Orientalism*; E. W. Said, *The World, the Text, and the Critic* (Cambridge: Harvard University Press, 1983).

149 Spivak and Harasym, *The Post-Colonial Critic*; Guha and Spivak, *Selected Subaltern Studies*; Guha, *Subaltern Studies*.

fact, one might argue that law is an especially fruitful field for the study of postcolonial artifacts, hybridity and deformations.[150] This applies to domestic as well as international law. Domestic law in the colonies and post-colonies is a forceful instrument of constructing social realities. It is used not only to erect structures of government and governmentality but to shape social and economic structures in postcolonial societies.[151] To discern the colonial legacies and postcolonial ruptures can contribute significantly to the understanding of law. And not just domestic, but also international law profits from the critical perspective of postcolonial studies. Public international law especially is shaped by the construction and imposition of supposedly "universal" but actually primarily Western-based values. The postcolonial critique and analysis of international law has become the subject of the Third World Approaches to International Law (TWAIL) since the 1990s.[152]

2. Post-development

Against this background, it is not surprising that postcolonial thinkers would find much to say about the development discourse and the practice of development cooperation. Emerging in the early 1990s, post-development thinking can actually be regarded as an application of postcolonial theory to the field of development, studying language and discourse, practice and politics of development through the lens of the Global South and its subaltern. Though it is probably misleading to understand it as a coherent school of thought, post-development has a number of essential claims and central texts.[153]

[150] U. Baxi, "Postcolonial Legality: A Postscript from India," *Verfassung und Recht in Übersee*, 45 (2012), 178–94; P. Dann and F. Hanschmann, "Post-colonial Theories and the Law," *Verfassung und Recht in Übersee*, 45 (2012), 123–7; with regard to public international law see A. Anghie, *Colonialism, Sovereignty, and the Making of International Law* (Cambridge University Press, 2004); N. Matz, *Wege zur Koordinierung völkerrechtlicher Verträge: Völkervertragsrechtliche und institutionelle Ansätze* (Heidelberg: Springer, 2005); Eslava and Pahuja, "Beyond the (Post)Colonial."

[151] Baxi, "Postcolonial Legality"; H. Kwasi Prempeh and H. Kwasi, "Neither 'Timorous Souls' Nor 'Bold Spirits': Courts and the Politics of Judicial Review in Post-Colonial Africa," *Verfassung und Recht in Übersee*, 45 (2012), 157–77.

[152] Pahuja, *Decolonising International Law*; A. Anghie, "TWAIL: Past and Future," *International Community Law Review*, 10 (2008), 479–82; B. Chimni, "Third World Approaches to International Law: A Manifesto," *European Community Law Review*, 8 (2006), 3–27. On TWAIL as a school of thinkers, see also Eslava and Pahuja, "Beyond the (Post)Colonial." On the European, colonialist and missionary roots of public international law, see M. Koskenniemi, *The Gentle Civilizer of Nations: The Rise and Fall of International Law 1870–1960* (Cambridge University Press, 2006).

[153] For example, Escobar, *Encountering Development*; for an overview see Sachs, *The Development Dictionary*; M. Rahnema and V. Bawtree, *The Post-Development Reader*

Post-development's central claim is that "development" is a Western concept that only serves the aims of the West or Westernized elites but not the well-being of those living in the Global South. It therefore fundamentally rejects the concept of "development" and the idea that certain societies and states should develop and move in a certain direction. While there is certainly no coherent idea of well-being and what the path toward it should be, post-development thinkers demand respect for local, indigenous cultures and prefer grass-roots solutions to wholesale and Western concepts.

On this basis, post-development formulates a rich criticism, which encompasses discourse analysis, economic examinations as well as sociological studies of practices in the development field. It might be broken down to three basic points.

For one, many writers in post-development simply reject the economic and social model underlying almost all theories of development. They perceive them as the projection of an unsustainable and ultimately truly dangerous (Western) model based on a capitalist system geared toward economic growth. Unsustainable in itself, this model is also based on complete ignorance of other concepts of well-being, good life or social and economic structures.

Second, post-development thinkers criticize that inherent to the concept of development is the conception and presentation of another "other," namely the "under-developed." Just as Edward Said had pointed to the binary presentations of the rational, civilized, democratic (etc.) European versus the irrational, barbaric, un-democratic (etc.) Arab, development discourse projects "developing" societies and their subjects as inferior, backward, childish (etc.), which need to develop or be developed. It rejects the often racist foundation of such perception. At the same time it demonstrates the massive influence of such images and perceptions not only on Northern thinking but also on the behavior of development workers.[154] In the practical work of aid agencies the perception of recipients as passive, corrupt, unreliable is a clear expression of the racist and unacceptable prejudices in the development discourse. Aid dependence and the

(London: Zed Books, 1997); A. Ziai, "The Ambivalence of Post-Development: Between Reactionary Populism and Radical Democracy," *Third World Quarterly*, 25 (2004), 1045–61; A. Ziai, *Exploring Post-Development: Theory and Practice, Problems and Perspectives* (London: Routledge, 2007). A historical account of development which is certainly sympathetic to postcolonial perspectives is Rist, *History of Development*.

154 M. E. Baaz, *The Paternalism of Partnership: A Postcolonial Reading of Identity in Development Aid* (New York: Zed Books, 2005).

perception of the recipient as spoiled and inefficient beneficiary are extensions of such thinking.

Finally and most fundamentally, post-development thinking highlights the power of knowledge and criticizes the North's power of definition and representation. It points out that most of the knowledge and data dominant in development agencies is produced in the North, taking into account mostly Northern ideas of social, economic and political structures, actors and relations. A central target here is the World Bank, which describes itself as a "knowledge bank" and hence a big development think tank. While its intention might be to underline its own competence, post-development thinkers perceive it as exclusivist, dominating and largely ignorant of non-Northern approaches. It also questions and rejects the idea that the participation of citizens of recipient countries would change much. Instead, this is criticized as mere façade.[155]

Ultimately, the concept of "development" is conceived of as an instrument of the West to subjugate and dominate the rest of the world. It is understood simply as the continuation of colonialism cloaked in another language but perpetuating the "humanitarian mission" already so central to the colonial endeavor.

3. Criticism, convergence and the (possible) role of law

Post-development itself has been met with criticism. It has been deemed as romanticizing poverty, as too theoretical, impractical and thus neglecting the material needs of the people, or simply as uninformed about the details of the development system.[156] Such criticism, however, seems to be missing the point. The very fact that post-development is formulating a fundamentally contrarian position is very important for the development discourse and for the study of the law of development cooperation – in various respects.

First, there is good reason to argue that despite its very distant and partly hostile stance, the post-development discourse is having a practical effect on the development system. As was described in the previous sections, the 1990s have seen a shift from a dominantly economic to an increasingly cultural and political understanding of the development process. In this context, the role of the individual and of local context has become more important. Community-driven development projects are in fact an important path.

[155] R. Kothari, "On Humane Governance," *Alternatives*, 12 (1987), 277–90.

[156] E. San Juan, *Beyond Postcolonial Theory* (New York: St. Martin's Press, 1999); for a reflection on these criticisms see McEwan, *Postcolonialism*, pp. 112–16.

However, a practical impact is probably not what post-development intends. It rather aims to shake up the system, antagonize and provoke it, without the pragmatic purpose in itself and certainly not to improve the system. But ironically, even if this is not intended, it is nevertheless helpful – intellectually and, in a more indirect way, also practically. People in development cooperation cannot (by profession and inclination) really take such rejection at face value. To be questioned more rigorously, aggressively and from those in the South undercuts certainties and is a tremendous intellectual challenge. But it does have an impact. It changes the balance of power in knowledge, language and ideas, as it questions the overwhelming vocabulary of ideas. And it has an impact especially if combined with other forces. While a first generation of Southern voices (especially in dependence theory) might have had only a very limited impact, the changing context of development cooperation in the "post-Western" twenty-first century certainly provides a different framework.[157]

The debate about the role of law in postcolonial and especially post-development studies has only just begun. On the one hand, some more radical critics see law essentially as an instrument of domination or as an apolitical tool of technical management with little emancipatory potential. On the other hand, law has always been an important instrument to translate political and social criticism into reform. It regulates the mechanisms of power, as it allocates competences (i.e. powers), structures and delineates procedures and sets substantive goals. Law should therefore be understood as a tool to reform the practice of development cooperation. In a sense, the insistence on the political nature of development in post-development is congruent with the approach formulated here, where development is seen primarily as a political process, in which the concrete steps and goals have to be negotiated and agreed upon.[158]

C Development cooperation today

The 1990s mark a threshold in development thinking. They saw new critical as well as practical thinking – and ushered in a new era after 2000. This is characterized by new approaches to development in the era of global governance and a dramatically changing context, symbolized by the rise of emerging economies such as China and India.

[157] On the different path of a new generation of Southern voices, see Eslava and Pahuja, "Beyond the (Post)Colonial"; for an interesting agenda of postcolonial thinking and acting in development, see McEwan, *Postcolonialism*, p. 249.

[158] See *supra*, Intro.A.II.3

This last chapter in our brief history of development cooperation shall now take stock. It will start with a brief retrospective on the first fifty years of development cooperation, as described in the previous sections (I). On this basis, it will highlight some structural problems of development cooperation that have become apparent in this history (II). Against this background, it will look at the current trends and discussions, shaping the system of development cooperation today and providing the current background to the law of development cooperation analyzed in the following parts (III).

I. *In retrospect: the genesis of development cooperation since 1945*

Instead of a full summary, just a short overview of the history of development cooperation since 1945 will be presented here. This will be organized according to the three rubrics which have structured the analysis in this part of the study: donor–recipient relationships, development theory and the goal of development aid, and the system of development administration.

1. Relationship between donors and recipients

The relationship between industrialized and developing countries is central to understanding development assistance. The relationship is marked by dramatic changes in fortune, especially on the recipient side. Their independence won in the process of decolonization and the massive differences in prosperity (magnified by the imperatives of the Cold War) made development aid one of the main tasks of the international community. They soon formed a unified bloc capable of formulating demands on the world stage, facilitated by their common history of colonization, the comparability of their economic situations, and their large number. Drawing on Abbé Sieyès's "Third Estate," they now proudly referred to themselves as the "Third World."[159] The 1960s and 1970s were marked by the rhetorical and political strength of developing countries. For many reasons, they were treated with particular respect by industrialized nations. The concept of development cooperation in the 1975 Lomé Convention embodied the ideal of this phase.[160]

However, the second half of the 1970s saw the strength of developing countries fade and indeed transform into weakness. Two factors drove this change. First, economic differentiation soon developed within the

[159] See *infra* Intro.A.IV [160] See *supra* Ch 1.B.I.1 and Ch 1.B.IV.2.

group, bringing with it divergent interests. Second, the fact of weak state structures in many developing countries soon became evident. The weakness involved capacity deficits as well as the lack of a culture of a reliable bureaucracy and the rule of law.[161]

The end of the Third World as a homogeneous interest group and the recognition of these countries' precarious statehood had profound effects on the development-aid system. The principal effect was a waning respect by donors for recipient countries' sovereignty. In the 1980s, the human rights situation in developing countries became a subject of discussion for the first time, and aid payments were made conditional. The trend became more marked in the 1990s, when donors used ever more intrusive instruments, while developing nations were increasingly perceived as passive and subordinated recipients, incapable of contributing their own ideas, much less taking a leadership role. Concepts such as ownership or partnership, introduced since the late 1990s more by donors than recipients, were meant to counter the perceived passivity. The (re)introduction and protection of the autonomy of recipient countries concerning their own process of development is a central challenge of contemporary development law.

2. Development theory and the goal of development cooperation

With regard to development theory and the understanding of the mission of development aid, a distinction must be drawn between autonomous and heteronomous goals of development aid. *Heteronomous* goals – that is, the instrumentalization of development funds for non-development goals such as to buy support in the Cold War or to finance export subsidies – are a constant feature in the development field, although their importance waxes and wanes. They were particularly apparent in the 1950s/1960s and in the 1980s. The end of the Cold War, however, made them harder to justify.[162] The *autonomous* goals of development assistance – concerning the question of what development actually means and how it may be achieved – are, by contrast, at the heart of development theory. This field has seen enormous changes in the last six decades, which

[161] See *supra* Ch 2.A.I.1.

[162] These motives have, however, hardly disappeared. To be sure, multilateral assistance, which is more strongly oriented toward the autonomous goals of development, has increased. The example of the USA – the largest donor in terms of absolute numbers – shows that support still serves political goals such as the support of politically important partner countries such as Iraq or Egypt.

is hardly surprising considering that these theories address a new, enormously complex, and essentially unprecedented endeavor.

Three distinct stages can be discerned in the genesis of development theory and the articulation of the goals of development.

In the first phase, development was seen primarily in economic terms, and economic growth was considered the basic goal. It is somewhat ironic that both the modernization theory and its ideological opposite, dependence theory, both focus ultimately on economic growth.[163] Only in the second phase of development theory, which begins in the 1970s, do social aspects begin to play a role. Poverty reduction came to be viewed as an additional and direct goal of development.[164] Not until a third phase in the late 1980s did a holistic idea of development emerge – combining ecological and political aspects with economic and social ones. Under this view, development is seen as a comprehensive process improving the chances to realize individual and collective freedom.[165] Interesting from a legal perspective is the fact that human rights (economic and political) have come to be seen as a central concept and driving force of development.[166] Also, the concept of good governance aims at a rule-of-law-based state which is at least transparent and responsive, if not democratic. The genesis of development theory should not, however, be misunderstood as ending in comprehensive consensus, even though an expanded idea of development is now widely accepted. The post-development thinkers have already been mentioned.[167] Donors are still bound by divergent mandates,[168] pursuing a wide range of interests, not to mention the theoretical literature, which is quite polyphonic.

An important driver of the continuous change in development theory could well have been the mixed record of development cooperation. Even as early as the late 1960s, the lack of improvements in recipients' welfare fostered doubts about the understanding of development and the strategies used to further it. Also important were the changing circumstances of aid provisioning and better understanding of development problems, in particular the significant capacity problems of the African states. As the scope of the problem of fragile statehood was gradually recognized, a more interventionist theory and practice of development emerged, which now, in the guise of "governance," dominates the development discourse.

163 See *supra* Ch 1.A.IV and Ch 1.B.I.2.

164 The motto was then "growth and re-distribution," see *supra* Ch 1.B.I.2, Ch 1.B.II.1.

165 Addressed mainly *supra* Ch 2.B.I.–III.

166 See *supra* Ch 2.B.II.

167 See *supra* Ch 2.B.IV.

168 See also *infra* Ch 3.A.IV.3.

Leading participants – first among them the World Bank – also played a central role in the maturation of development theory. The Bank can be understood as a giant think tank which constantly produces new data and theses concerning its own work.[169] Independent think tanks and NGOs have also become increasingly important. Since the 1990s, they have gathered data and fought to open the concept of development to other issues than economy (such as ecology or human rights).[170]

3. The administrative system of development assistance

This short history of development aid has also focused on the emergence of development administrations – that is, the organizations responsible for disbursing ODA and the instruments with which they do so. The point of departure is a fact that seems self-evident today but actually is not: the emergence of administrative structures in industrialized Northern countries that are solely (or principally) concerned with the issue of development. The only other policy field that comes to mind as a newly discovered post-war issue is environmental policy. However, in comparison, development aid was entrusted to dedicated institutions more quickly. Drawing on the examples of the World Bank's IDA, the EU's General Directorate for Development, and the German Development Ministry, it has been shown above how this specialized administrative system was created after Truman's 1949 speech.[171]

These various agencies became autonomous and professionalized in a roughly comparable manner. Milestones in this process included the development of multi-year program planning and the emphasis on poverty eradication, which emerged in all of the organizations studied here. At the same time, the new goals that had been articulated by development theorists were transformed into new instruments. The model of rather narrow project-based assistance based on the proposal principle was complemented in the 1980s with the idea of a broader, programmatic assistance, which was then, again later, coupled with increased use of pol-

[169] On the intellectual role of the World Bank, see Squire, "Why the World Bank," p. 108; N. Stern and F. Ferreira, "The World Bank as 'Intellectual Actor'," in D. Kapur, J. P. Lewis and R. Webb (eds.), *The World Bank: Its First Half Century*, II (Washington, DC: Brookings Institution Press, 1997), pp. 523–610 at p. 523.

[170] Some examples of such organizations are the German Institute for Development Policy (Deutsches Institut für Entwicklungspolitik), the British Overseas Development Institute, or the Center for Global Development in Washington, DC.

[171] Discussed in detail *supra*, Ch 1.A.I. and II. and III.

itical conditionalities. These instruments reflect, among other things, the changed donor–recipient relationship.

Despite such similarities, striking differences remain between these organizations, deriving principally from their nature and mandate. The World Bank's mandate is one of economic assistance, and its approach correspondingly primarily technocratic. The development policy of the European Union was from the very beginning much more politically motivated. In the formative decades, the French took a leading role. France's colonial past ensured that European development policy had a strong regional focus and was closely linked to trade policy, but also that it was inspired by a stronger feeling of partnership and responsibility. German development assistance, by contrast, was not conditioned by a colonial past and oscillated between heteronomous uses and a more autonomous, development-focused mission.

In the final analysis, what is most surprising is how long this administrative system of development organizations escaped analysis of itself. Only in the 2000s, with the debate on aid effectiveness, was the question finally posed whether the manner in which ODA grants were negotiated, agreed, executed and evaluated might have some effect on the success or failure of development cooperation. The governance of donor organizations was addressed only after the governance of recipient countries had been debated. The integration of development cooperation into a system of global governance subject to the rule of law is still in its infancy.

II. Structural problems of development cooperation

The historical perspective clears the path for more structural observations on the development cooperation system and its problems. Such observations can profit from a rich field of new literature and research on development cooperation since the 1990s. One early trigger – next to a general surge in studies on global governance and cooperation – was the World Bank's experiences with structural-adjustment policies. It was asked why these policies of the 1980s – in particular conditionalities – had shown so few positive results. More than before, attention was given to the motives and incentive structures that prevailed during the negotiation and implementation of development projects, and effectiveness became a central concern. Since that time, these questions have been investigated by various research projects with different scientific methods and background assumptions.[172]

[172] To give a broad overview one can distinguish political scientists and economists who use rational-choice approaches, such as game theory (P. Mosley, J. Harrigan and

Even though approaches differ, some of the structural problems of the aid system are clearly recognizable in most of them. These shall be synthesized into three main issues: complexity, power, and knowledge.

1. Complexity

A first problem afflicting development aid is the immense organizational, procedural and terminological complexity. This complexity leads to a fundamental lack of transparency and control. The problem of complexity is caused to a large extent by the inherent distance, in a spatial, cultural as well as social sense, between donors and recipients and the final beneficiaries of aid. Development cooperation organizes, after all, an international transfer of goods and knowledge. However, the problem is more than mere distance; it also derives from the (unnecessarily complex) organization of development-aid programs. The following analysis will distinguish between the complexities in bilateral relationships between donors and recipients (a) and the fragmentation on the donor side (b).

a) Complexity in the bilateral relationships

The planning, award and implementation of development funds is a multi-step, extremely complex process that involves many different actors and agencies.[173] It is never a question of *one* donor and *one* recipient. Rather, relevant actors on the donor side include governments, parliaments and various implementing organizations, which must be distinguished, and the same goes for the recipient side. Furthermore, the national and international administrations responsible for disbursing ODA funds have

J. Toye, *Aid and Power: The World Bank and Policy-Based Lending* (London: Routledge, 1991)) or principal-agent theory (e.g. Killick, *Aid and the Political Economy*; Gibson et al., *Samaritan's Dilemma*; Martens, Mummert and Murrell, *Institutional Economics of Foreign Aid*) and others who provide rather qualitative studies, taking into more account concrete actors and their political, historical and cultural context (see Whitfield, *The Politics of Aid*; Lancaster, *Aid to Africa*; van de Walle, *African Economies and the Politics*; Leftwich, *States of Development*). Within the economic literature, institutional economics has become a central framework (see also Easterly, *Reinventing Foreign Aid*). There is also a burgeoning literature on the implications of new donors on the aid system (see *infra*, Ch 2.C.III.2 and literature cited there). For a good overview see Faust and Leiderer, "Zur Effektivität und politischen Ökonomie," 129 and N. Birdsall, *Seven Deadly Sins: Reflections on Donor Failings*, Center for Global Development Working Paper No. 50. Available at www.cgdev.org/files/2737_file_WP50_rev12_05_2.pdf (last visited July 2013); for an overview on legal approaches see *supra*, Intro.A.1.2.

173 Gibson et al., *Samaritan's Dilemma*, p. 63 create an octagonal(!) diagram containing various cross-linkages to describe the various actors and their interrelationships.

excessively complex organizational structures.[174] The situation is not made easier by the fact that the terminology differs in every organization and every country, and changes frequently.[175] One of the main tasks of harmonizing "soft" laws – and of this book – is to establish a common conceptual and terminological framework.

The complexity of decision-making processes results in distances and a situation in which the recipients and intended beneficiaries may not understand what was decided when and where and by whom. As a result, feedback about particular projects cannot be effectively given, making precisely targeted evaluation more difficult and creating so-called "broken feedback loops."[176] Complex procedures also create misdirected incentives. Donor organizations are often cut off from specific feedback concerning the genuine outcome of projects. Their results are then not measured in terms of their actual effects. Instead, many development organizations measure success by their ability to disburse funds in competition with other agencies, regardless of how the funds are used.[177]

b) Fragmentation among donors

Another aspect of the organizational complexity of development cooperation is fragmentation among donor organizations. Currently, there are about seventy state and international donor organizations and an even larger number of non-state actors. Most of these donors operate simultaneously in the same recipient countries, each of them formulating their own goals and procedural regimes and using their own development instruments.

The consequences are highly problematic.[178] Three problems will be mentioned here. First, the multiplicity of donors increases the transaction

[174] For examples see Lancaster, *Foreign Aid*; equally complex is the structure of UN development aid, or the intricate network of responsibilities and competences that the EU has created (see *infra* Ch 3.A.III).

[175] The best description of the development community's "double-speak" is Easterly, *Cartel of Good Intentions*, pp. 30–5.

[176] See Gibson et al., *Samaritan's Dilemma*, pp. 72, 73; Martens, Mummert and Murrell, *Institutional Economics of Foreign Aid*, pp. 154; 176.

[177] These incentive structures are of particular interest to the institutional-economic analysis of development cooperation (see especially the two essay collections Gibson et al., *Samaritan's Dilemma* and Martens, Mummert and Murrell, *Institutional Economics of Foreign Aid*).

[178] See, in particular, Faust and Messner, "Entwicklungspolitik," p. 213; Lister, *EC and the Developing World*, p. 333; G. Ashoff, *Geberkoordinierung: Eine wesentliche Voraussetzung für eine effizientere und wirksamere Entwicklungszusammenarbeit*, Analysen und Stellungnahmen des deutschen Instituts für Entwicklungspolitik 7/2004. Available at www.die-gdi.de/ (last visited July 2013).

costs of development cooperation. To prepare, execute and assess projects, these organizations use many different procedures, conduct different exploration missions and prepare the necessary analyses and reports. By pursuing these tasks alone, each donor creates an enormous amount of duplicate effort which could have been spared by unified analysis, coordinated projects, and harmonized procedures.

Second, the multiplicity of donors frequently spurs unproductive competition for projects and personnel. This needless competition tends to result in less attractive themes and regions (so-called *aid orphans*) being neglected. Local government employees may be recruited to work for international donors, who pay better salaries. Different donors may also work in the same area, but with divergent and sometimes conflicting conceptual frameworks.

The third and final effect of the fractured donor landscape is that interactions with large numbers of donors may sometimes simply overwhelm the administrative capacity of recipient countries. Complex donor policies on reporting and implementation of projects simply cannot reliably be fulfilled in many developing countries. Some recipient countries have even introduced months-long "quiet periods," during which donors may not pursue missions or other projects in the state while local officials finally find the time to write all the reports demanded by the donor regulations.

It is difficult to think of positive effects of this multiplicity of donors. It could, of course, be the case that the large number of donors fosters productive competition for better concepts, driving weaker donors from the field. Competition could also increase the influence of recipients which can then choose the more effective and perhaps less intrusive donors. The emergence of new donors has given rise to such hopes.[179] However, empirical studies and studies based on institutional-economics approaches do not support these positive assumptions. Because donors, in the final analysis, decide on how funds are spent independently of the concrete consequences of these decisions, there is no market-like constellation which would effectively sanction donors whose projects fail.[180] In addition, donor multiplicity seems actually to create a situation in which recipients play donors off against one another to water down the demands that accompany projects.[181]

[179] See F. Zimmermann and K. Smith, "More Actors, More Money, More Ideas for International Development Cooperation," *Journal of International Development*, 23 (2011), 722–38 and discussion *infra*, Ch 2.C.II.2.

[180] Easterly, *White Man's Burden*, p. 150.

[181] Examples provided in Gibson et al., *Samaritan's Dilemma*, p. 75.

2. Power, identity and autonomy

The second basic problem of development assistance concerns power, identity and autonomy. Development cooperation is not a technical, value-free enterprise. It is a political process involving constant value judgments and decision-making. Regular and unavoidable differences of opinion occur between donor institutions and recipient countries. Donors, of course, pursue their very own interests when giving ODA. These may align with those of the recipient country but often enough do not. Also, within recipient states, development projects require often controversial and hard-to-implement measures such as land reform, resettlements or contentious policy choices (for example on privatization). The interests of the recipient country's government can be at odds with civil society. Decisions made in the development-aid context therefore always involve questions of power and autonomy. This fact, as obvious as it may seem, is addressed surprisingly rarely in the discourse on "aid effectiveness" and "governance," which is conducted in rather technocratic terms.[182]

Decisions on ODA transfers and on the development process take place in a specific context which is shaped profoundly by the power and identity of the actors. The relationship between ODA donors and recipients is anything but neutral. The economic (but often also political or military) weakness of recipients poses a latent danger to their autonomy, growing with increasing dependence on outside support. Here, the sheer degree of imbalance between the parties aggravates the situation. The least-developed nations, most numerously from sub-Saharan Africa, are in a position of fundamental and long-lasting dependence.[183] Several dozen of these states have for decades received ODA assistance that comprises more than 10 percent of their GNP.[184]

[182] This diagnosis is endorsed by the contributions to Bickerton, Cunliffe and Gourevitch, *Politics without Sovereignty*; recent work on the problem of power in development cooperation include Whitfield, *The Politics of Aid*; Hyden, "After the Paris Declaration," 259; Leftwich, *States of Development*; the problem was addressed even earlier in Pearson, *Pearson Report 1969*, pp. 53; 127. Here, in particular, we see confirmation of the preceding observation that the social-scientific discourse on development cooperation is frequently separate and focused on only one approach, while a law of development cooperation may be able to analyze many different principles of development aid simultaneously and point to conflicts and concordances.

[183] On development cooperation in Africa see, e.g. van de Walle, *African Economies and the Politics*; Lancaster, *Aid to Africa*.

[184] On the extent of and problems caused by this dependence see D. Brautigam, *Aid Dependence and Governance*, Expert Group on Development Issues Working Paper 2000/1. Available at www.sti.ch/fileadmin/user_upload/Pdfs/swap/swap404.pdf (last visited July 2013).

At the same time, it is necessary to differentiate carefully between recipient states. India and China receive ODA and are thus recipient states, but their size gives them so much power against donors that there can hardly be any concern about their autonomy.[185] Gambia and Mali, on the other hand, have very little bargaining power.[186] One need not subscribe to the belief that development discourse was invented by the "hegemonic" North to subjugate the South to see the danger to weaker states' autonomy. In some countries, indeed, dependency has gone so far that governments are more beholden to the community of donors than to their own citizens.[187]

Moreover, donor and recipient states frequently share a fraught colonial history. It is therefore crucial to understand development cooperation also in the critical context that postcolonial studies and post-development writers have described.[188] It does not only matter that aid relationships are usually marked by the contrasting ethnic background of the parties, which burdens the relationship with potentially dangerous stereotypes, misunderstandings and conflicts.[189] There also can be and often is a fundamental disconnect and misunderstanding about concepts and instruments of development (such as the law) that is based not only on lack of capacity or lack of "engagement" but on fundamentally different traditions and perceptions of the world. Even more generally, one might say that the whole idea of transferring instruments and concepts to other countries is highly problematic or at least highly contingent.[190] It might be based on misguided intentions of donors as well as misconceptions of recipients.[191] Acceptance of "aid" in the

[185] On the conceptual differentiation between various recipient countries see Gibson et al., *Samaritan's Dilemma*, pp. 65–8; as an empirical matter, the World Bank's so-called *World Development Indicators*, published yearly, are worthy of attention. Differentiation will also be addressed *infra* Ch 3.B.

[186] For numerous case studies on the question of how much autonomy African states have as against the donor community, see Whitfield, *The Politics of Aid*.

[187] T. Moss, G. Pettersson and N. van de Walle, *An Aid-Institution's Paradox? A Review Essay on Aid Dependency and State Building in Sub-Saharan Africa* (Washington, DC: Center for Global Development, 2006), pp. 269–74 with citations to various empirical studies of this problem.

[188] On these schools of thought, see *supra* Ch 2.B.IV.

[189] See S. Carr, E. McAuliffe and M. MacLachlan, *Psychology of Aid* (London: Routledge, 1998); on historical continuities see Rist, *History of Development*, p. 47; Harrison, *World Bank and Africa*, p. 26.

[190] W. Twining, "The Diffusion of Law," *Journal of Comparative Law*, 1 (2006), 237–60; R. Cotterell, "Comparative Law and Legal Culture," in M. Reimann and R. Zimmermann (eds.), *The Oxford Handbook of Comparative Law* (Oxford University Press, 2008), pp. 709–37.

[191] For a fascinating ethnographic analysis of aid see R. Rottenburg, *Weit hergeholte Fakten: Eine Parabel der Entwicklungshilfe* (Stuttgart: Lucius & Lucius, 2002).

context of power and identity between North and South can then rather be based on a feeling of inferiority than on the autonomous voluntary formulation of a need.[192]

Since the 1990s, the problem of power and autonomy in donor–recipient relationships has been exacerbated by one development which reflects the particular contradictions of development cooperation. Donor states, prompted by the expanded understanding of development,[193] have shown an increased "aggressiveness" in formulating and monitoring openly political development goals. As described above, they increased demands that recipient states meet human rights and political standards, or at least formulated "conditionalities" to this effect. ODA was no longer to be paid to corrupt and irresponsible governments.[194] This political aggressiveness often met with unusually lethargic recipient-state governments. Research conducted in the 1990s showed that developing-nation governments frequently accepted conditionalities but then largely ignored them – especially when it came to structural-adjustment measures. These nations lacked the political or administrative commitment, or the autonomy, either to reject the donors' conditions or to actually implement them in the face of domestic political resistance.[195] The self-confidence and positive vision that marked developing countries in the 1970s had been transformed into its opposite. Oddly enough, it was the donors who developed the concept of ownership (or self-responsibility) to address this lethargy.[196] Developing countries should, so some donors thought, take over *ownership* for the development process and independently formulate their own plans and goals, rather than simply adopting them from donors. This would, it was thought, improve the effectiveness of projects. Donors thus "ordered" autonomy, an oxymoron. Here, we see development discourse executing a rather odd about-face, a process that shows the centrality of the question of power in development cooperation.

192 For an analysis of Asian perceptions of Western concepts, see P. Smith, *Somebody Else's Century: East and West in a Post-Western World* (New York: Pantheon Books, 2010).

193 See *supra* Ch 2.B.I–III.

194 See *supra* Ch 2.B.II and III; for a legal analysis of conditionalities see *infra* Ch 6.A.II., in the area of project aid, Ch 6.B.I.2, II.3 and in the area of budget support Ch 7.B.II / III.

195 Mosley, Harrigan and Toye, *Aid and Power*; J. H. Johnson and S. S. Wasty, *Borrower Ownership of Adjustment Programs and the Political Economy of Reform*, World Bank Discussion Papers No. 199. Available at http://gwww.grips.ac.jp/teacher/oono/hp/course/lec03_ownership/paper3_3.pdf (last visited July 2013).

196 An extensive discussion of the origins and the legal classification of this concept is provided *infra* Ch 4.C.I.

3. Knowledge and measurability

The administration of development assistance is also confronted with a third problem. This concerns the possibility of understanding and tracing or measuring development efforts. The problem can be split into three aspects.

First, development management (like risk management in general) faces the problem of inadequate knowledge of the precise problems and development needs faced by developing countries.[197] Administrators in Washington (where the World Bank has its headquarters) or any other aid agency's location have less knowledge per se about the specific preferences and arrangements at the location where their ODA is intended to have its effect, especially in light of the fact that these very preferences and arrangements are disputed and subject to frequent change. The administration's complex procedural policies cut off specific feedback from aid recipients, thus causing a permanent information deficit. Obtaining and analyzing data are therefore a main focus of development management.

Second, the inherent information deficit is aggravated by inadequate capacities in developing nations, one result of which is that accurate and current data are rarely available. Today, inadequate capacity on the recipient side is seen as perhaps the greatest hindrance to development and is addressed by "capacity development," a specific form of technical cooperation.[198] In the meantime, however, these deficits contribute to frequent gaps in knowledge that donors rely on for planning and decision-making.

A third aspect of the knowledge problem concerns the measurability of the results of development. The question of whether a development program has been successful is not as simple as it may seem.[199] In view of widespread doubts concerning the effectiveness of development aid, the question is intensively discussed and there are increasing demands for (supposedly) clearly definable quantitative measurements of aid

[197] This problem is clearly recognized in the principal-agent literature on development aid, see Gibson et al., *Samaritan's Dilemma*, pp. 44–45; 56–7; it is also prominently addressed by those who believe the main problem of development cooperation is its plan-reliant, dirigistic character, see, e.g. W. Easterly, '"Introduction: Can't Take it Anymore?'," in Easterly, *Reinventing Foreign Aid*, p. 5.

[198] Riddell, *Does Foreign Aid*, pp. 163–258; 207–11.

[199] Ibid., pp. 163–258; Burnside and Dollar, "Aid, Policies and Growth," 847; see also D. Dollar and L. Pritchett, *Assessing Aid: What Works, What Doesn't and Why?*, World Bank Policy Research Report (New York: Oxford University Press for the World Bank, 1998); also D. Moyo, *Dead Aid: Why Aid is not Working and How there is Another Way for Africa* (London: Penguin Press, 2009).

effectiveness. The Millennium Development Goals (MDG) or the 2005 Paris Declaration are prominent examples that set forth quantifiable progress indicators.[200] This turn toward quantification, however, is by no means uncontroversial.[201] For one thing, the expansion of the concept of development described in the previous section makes assessment more difficult. Today, the operative concept of development is a holistic one, embracing economic, social and ecological aspects. The broader the concept of development, the more difficult it is to measure. It is also often unclear precisely whose numbers and data should be seen as credible and accurate. The criteria by which the effectiveness of development aid should be measured (and their being set by Western aid agencies) are also controversial. Questions include what time frame the results should be measured in and whether a causal connection exists between the development program and the results it supposedly yielded. In view of these problems, many have concluded that the quantification of development progress is a dead end, since it is virtually impossible to measure the qualitative value of development programs, and attempts to do so usually do not really indicate the program's usefulness.

In the final analysis, complexity, power and knowledge can be seen as three structural issues that generate a host of more specific problems. On the positive side, once these problems are identified, they can be more clearly discussed and addressed, the first step to their solution. Whether there is the political will and cultural aptitude to do so, is, of course, another matter.

III. Current trends: push for effectiveness amid the "rise of the rest"

The crisis of the 1990s and the intensified research on the incentives and structural features driving the aid system have not been without consequences. In fact, the development system has probably never been under more pressure to reform and change than since the 2000s. This pressure informs the two dominant trends that characterize development thinking today: the debate on aid effectiveness (1) and the consequences of the changing tides in the international community, epitomized by the rise of the emerging economies (2).

[200] On these declarations as well as the indicators as instruments of development governance, see *infra* Ch 2.C.III.1.

[201] Critical views include S. Reddy and A. Heuty, "Global Development Goals: The Folly of Technocratic Pretensions," *Development Policy Review*, 26 (2008), 5–28 at 5; Seppänen, *Possibilities and Challenges*, p. 57.

1. Aid effectiveness, indicators and the (good) governance of donors

In the 2000s and arguably for the first time in its sixty-year history, the development system has itself become the object of a critical reform debate.[202] The debate on aid effectiveness, as it is mostly called, turns the table around and inquires as much into the structures of recipients as into the governance structures of donors. Long after good governance has become a central demand leveled against recipients, finally, the good governance of donors has also become a topic.

The motives for this are not entirely voluntary: in the 1990s, the entire development-aid system faced a deep crisis of meaning and legitimacy caused by the end of the Cold War bloc confrontation – a central legitimizing factor – and the broadly shared perception that development assistance had not been as effective and successful as hoped. As a reaction to this crisis, the workings, architecture and structure of the development-aid system became a central focus of discussion. This discussion and the focus of the aid-effectiveness debate is not on the substantive goal of development as such or the deficits of recipient states, but rather the organization of development assistance. Hence for the first time, the governance of donors is more at stake than the governance of recipients.

The following section will first analyze the different stages and subjects of the process (a) and then turn to a central instrument of aid effectiveness and reform in the age of global governance, the so-called indicators (b).

a) *Political process: MDG – Monterrey – Paris – Accra – Busan*

In the late 1990s, a political reform process began that aims to address many of the structural problems described above.[203] The process began with the adoption of the MDG, especially Goal 8, in 2000 and the

[202] This statement needs a bit of explanation. It is not strictly true that nobody has ever addressed the organization of development cooperation. On the contrary: one could even say that the current discussion bears an almost eerie resemblance to previous debates, as it recapitulates subjects and ideas that were being discussed 40 years ago (one needs only read the famous Pearson Report of 1969: Pearson, *Pearson Report 1969*, especially pp. 124, 168, 208). The difference today is in the consequences of the debate. It appears that the reform process which led to the Paris Declaration and beyond has already brought about more changes in development law and practice than all the discussions of the last 40 years. Thus, although the topics and the conclusions may not be new, the way in which they are being dealt with is.

[203] On the creation of the political reform process and, in particular, the influential Agenda of the OECD-DAC "Shaping the 21st Century," see Nuscheler, "Halbierung der absoluten Armut," 6.

Monterrey Consensus of 2002. This was given a stronger organizational structure that led first to the adoption of the 2005 Paris Declaration as well as two further high-level declarations in Accra and Busan. However, criticism of the process and its outcome has also been vocal and shall be described below.

(1) MDG8 and the Monterrey Consensus After the North–South discussion had reached an impasse in the 1980s and 1990s, the first sign that development cooperation (and its management) would again be seen as a collective responsibility of the world community came in the form of the eighth Millennium Development Goal (MDG8). This eighth goal called for a "global partnership for development" and urged donor nations to designate 0.7 percent of their GNP for development aid.[204] This demand had been voiced as early as the 1960s' era, but MDG8 places it in a new context. MDG8 was not meant as a one-sided demand on donors, nor did it envision development solely as a task for developing countries. Rather, it envisions a "partnership" between donor and recipient nations. This goal was rhetorical at first, but was invested with more substance in subsequent declarations, which stressed commitment and constructive cooperation on both sides of the development process.

MDG8 spurred the "International Conference on Financing for Development," which was held in March 2002 in Monterrey, Mexico. At this conference, the heads of state and government in attendance approved the "Monterrey Consensus on Financing for Development."[205] This declaration dealt primarily with the various sources of funding and underlined the insight that development should best be organized and financed by a variety of actors and sources.[206] It was also the first international document that formulated concrete suggestions for

[204] S. Fukuda-Parr, "Millennium Development Goal 8: Indicators for International Human Rights Obligations?" *Human Rights Quarterly*, 28 (2006), 966–97 at 966; another new development is that the indicators specify how the money should be invested, namely for basic social support, for the environment of small island states, and for the transport sector in landlocked states. At the same time, ODA should not take the form of so-called tied aid.

[205] The Consensus was adopted by the UN General Assembly as a Resolution in the same year: A/Res/56/210 B of 9 July 2002. On the role of European countries during the negotiations on the Monterrey Consensus see M. Carbone, *The European Union and International Development: The Politics of Foreign Aid* (London, New York: Routledge, 2007), pp. 71, 92, 113.

[206] Specifically, internal resources of the developing countries (paras. 10–19), foreign direct investment and private sources (paras. 20–25), trade (paras. 26–38), public development aid/ODA (paras. 39–46) and debt reduction (paras. 47–51).

reforming the administrative system of development cooperation. Among other things, the Consensus called for improved harmonization of procedures concerning the programming and evaluation phases to reduce complexity; increased responsibility for developing countries during the formulation of development plans (to address the problem of passivity and reduced autonomy of recipient states); and improved coordination among donors to reduce fragmentation.[207] Finally, the consensus formulated the idea of mutual responsibility for the process of development.

(2) Aid effectiveness in the Paris Declaration (2005) In addition to putting concrete questions of development administration on the agenda, the Monterrey Consensus also sparked a discussion of the basic administrative principles of development cooperation, which culminated in the 2005 Paris Declaration, perhaps the most important document on development reform to date.

The process leading to the Paris Declaration was primarily organized by the Development Assistance Committee of the OECD (OECD-DAC), especially its Secretariat,[208] and coordinated with the World Bank. The process continues to take place on three organizational levels. The so-called "High-Level Forums" meet every two to three years and bring together the ministers of the participating countries and their NGO equivalents. Between these ministerial meetings there is the "Working Party on Aid Effectiveness," which is a regular discussion forum for high-level civil servants and which, according to participants, serves mainly to build trust between the various actors. Finally, on the third level, there are technical working groups, which address individual issues.[209] The diversity of participants in this process is of particular importance. Participants include not only donor nations as OECD members and the primary international organizations (World Bank, IMF, EU) but also many recipient countries and civil-society actors.[210]

The process led in three steps to the Paris Declaration of 2005. A first meeting of the high-level forum in Rome in 2003 addressed procedural

[207] United Nations, *Monterrey Consensus of International Conference on Financing of Development* (2002), margin nos. 43; 69c. Available at www.un.org/esa/ffd/monterrey/MonterreyConsensus.pdf (last visited September 2012).

[208] This Committee is also discussed *infra* Ch 3.C.I.

[209] References to this structure can be found at www.aidharmonization.org, www.acrahlf.net or on the OECD's website (last visited July 2013).

[210] The signatories of the Paris Declaration demonstrate diversity; see Annex B of the Declaration.

harmonization and coordination problems, while a second meeting in Marrakesh in 2004 dealt with inadequate controls and evaluation of results. The subjects of both meetings were united in the Paris Declaration with other topics under the general heading "aid effectiveness."

The Paris Declaration remains the most concrete and comprehensive multilateral document on the question of development management.[211] It is divided into three sections: a Declaration of Resolve, a Commitment, and a list of twelve progress indicators. It envisions a multi-year process in which the parties commit to working more closely together to realize the agreed goals (paras. 8 & 9). As to substance, the document articulated five principles: ownership, alignment, harmonization, managing for results and mutual accountability. They formulate responses to the above-described problems in aid administration. The principles are described in more detail in the following.[212]

The principle of *ownership* stresses that developing countries bear the main responsibility for development policy and that they are responsible for policy planning and coordination. Ownership is a reaction to the relative lethargy of recipient countries and is intended to spur them to greater action. Nevertheless, the fact that this call for more autonomy and sovereignty was formulated mainly by donor nations is rather paradoxical.[213] The second principle, *alignment*, refers to the alignment of donors to the legal and administrative systems of recipient states. Instead of forcing recipient states to conform solely to donor regulations, donors should align their support with recipient nations' procedures for accounting, monitoring, procurement and public finances, among other areas. The goal is to avoid increasing complexity, which additionally taxes the inadequate capacities of recipient states.[214] The third principle calls for the *harmonization* of donor procedures. Donors should harmonize their procedures and make them generally more transparent. This can be achieved by producing common analyses and paying heed to the complementarity of their programs. Both principles, alignment

[211] The Declaration can be found here: www.oecd.org/dataoecd/37/39/35023537.pdf (last visited July 2013).

[212] On the legal classification see *infra* Ch 4.A.III. The particular principles will be analyzed below during the discussion of the principles of development cooperation law with a view to their legal substance and the correspondence to legal principles. At this point, only a short introduction will be provided.

[213] More on the relationship between ownership and sovereignty, see *infra* Ch 4.C.I.

[214] Like the following principles, this one contributes primarily to the principle of coherence and efficiency, see *infra* Ch 4.E.

and harmonization, are meant to reduce procedural complexity. This, in turn, reduces transactions costs and preserves capacity. These principles target mainly donors.

The fourth principle calls for *results-based* management. Recipient countries are to set up monitoring and evaluation systems, while donors should harmonize and simplify their corresponding systems. This is meant to change the incentive structures in development administration, particularly on the donor side. They should no longer reward mere inputs (disbursements of money) but rather outputs and outcomes, that is, the results of investments (projects). More generally, this principle addresses the evaluation problem, yet its focus on quantifiable systems also advances a specific agenda. The fifth principle, *mutual accountability*, stresses the responsibility and accountability on both sides. Stated more concretely, this principle requires developing countries to better integrate their parliaments and civil society into the development process, while donors are supposed to provide timely and comprehensive information.

The manner in which the Paris Declaration is implemented is also noteworthy. As with the MDGs, the Declaration's goals are tied to twelve quantified indicators which are intended to measure progress (para. 8 and Section III of the Declaration). The Declaration also sets deadlines. The end point was the year 2010 (para. 9 and Section III). "Preliminary targets" are to be reached even earlier (para. 9). Participants are also called on to set state-specific goals. Fulfillment of the obligations is to be continually evaluated, both at a state (para. 10) and an international level (para. 11).[215]

(3) Aid effectiveness agenda continued in Accra (2008) and Busan (2011) The Monterrey Process did not end in 2005. In 2008, a High-Level Forum met in Accra (Ghana) to study the progress made.[216] It also adopted the Accra Agenda for Action (AAA).[217] This is mainly a reaffirmation of the targets set in the Paris Declaration and the commitment to

215 Three OECD reviews were to be conducted in 2006, 2008 and 2010. For the final evaluations see http://pd-website.inforce.dk/ (last visited July 2013). On the process in more detail, see *infra* Ch 8.B.V.

216 The OECD-DAC and the World Bank had been tasked with specifying precise indicators and working out concrete criteria. Their reports included: World Bank, *Aid Effectiveness Review 2006*; OECD, *2008 Survey on Monitoring the Paris Declaration: Making Aid More Effective by 2010* (Paris: OECD Publishing, 2008).

217 World Bank, *Accra Agenda for Action: 3rd High Level Forum on Aid Effectiveness, September 2–4, 2008* (2008). Available at http://siteresources.worldbank.org/ACCRAEXT/Resources/4700790-1217425866038/AAA-4-SEPTEMBER-FINAL-16h00.pdf (last visited September 2012).

accelerate and deepen their implementation. No further indicators and time frames were set. In particular, the AAA reaffirmed the need for country ownership (para. 8) and accountability, not least with respect to the taxpayers (paras. 10, 22, 23, 24). Furthermore, the International Aid Transparency Initiative (IATI), a voluntary, multi-stakeholder initiative to help implement the transparency commitments made at the AAA in more consistent and coherent ways, was launched.[218]

A central theme of the Accra meeting was the role of new development actors, such as middle-income countries, global funds, the private sector and civil-society organizations which increasingly change the nature of development cooperation (para. 9). It stressed the necessity of working with all development actors (paras. 19/20). Another central theme was state fragility. In this respect, the AAA acknowledges the need to adapt policies in situations of a recipient state's fragility (para. 21) and committed – on a voluntary basis – to monitor the OECD's Principles for Good International Engagement in Fragile States and Situations.

Three years later, in November 2011, the fourth and final High-Level Forum on aid effectiveness convened in Busan (South Korea). It reviewed the implementation of the Paris Principles and discussed how to maintain the relevance of the aid-effectiveness agenda in the context of the evolving development landscape. Three themes in particular emerge from the Busan meeting and its final declaration the "Busan Partnership for Effective Development Cooperation."[219]

First, the declaration reaffirmed four core principles as "shared principles of cooperation for effective development": ownership (para. 11a), focus on results (11b) as well as transparency and accountability (11d). The remaining ideas of the Paris Declaration (alignment and harmonization) were not addressed. Instead, one new principle of "inclusive development partnerships" (para. 11c) was incorporated.

Second, the declaration addressed the ongoing emergence of new development actors in a "more complex architecture for development cooperation" (para. 5), including South–South and triangular cooperation and the modalities that apply to them (paras. 2, 30). It put forward the idea of a broader partnership and a new principle on inclusive development partnerships (para. 11c) between the different actors. In particular, the need

[218] www.aidtransparency.net/.

[219] Busan Partnership for Effective Development Co-operation, *Outcome Document of the Fourth High-Level Forum on Aid Effectiveness*, Busan, Republic of Korea, 29 November – 1 December 2011. Available at www.effectivecooperation.org/resources.html (last visited July 2013).

to incorporate emerging donors and non-state actors that wish to shape the development agenda that had until recently been dominated by only a handful of Western donors was addressed (para. 7). Following up on this, it was agreed to expand the Working Party on Aid Effectiveness to ensure a broader inclusiveness. At the same time, the "soft" character (that is the voluntary basis of their implementation) was stressed more than in the previous documents.[220] Nevertheless, it was agreed to set up a new monitoring framework and working arrangements by June 2012. The Busan document also aimed to establish a new Global Partnership for Effective Development Cooperation (para. 35b). It seems that this new global partnership will be the new platform to take over the Working Party on Aid Effectiveness responsibility to organize the post-Paris agenda.

The third theme prevalent in Busan again was state fragility and aid. The declaration contained a commitment to promote sustainable development in fragile states and endorsed a "new deal" that aid to fragile states should focus more explicitly on security, justice and "legitimate politics." In this sense, the Busan meeting could have been the first step toward ensuring conflict, security and justice issues – missing from the current MDG agenda – were brought into discussions about what follows the MDGs after 2015. The International Dialog on Peacebuilding and Statebuilding (IDPS) – made up of governments from conflict-affected states (the G7+), donor governments and multilateral agencies – has been working on this new deal since it was established under Accra.[221]

(4) Criticism of the aid-effectiveness agenda Criticism of the described process has been varied. Two main concerns in the beginning of the process were (1) the insufficient participation of civil-society organizations and developing countries in negotiations that were perceived as being dominated by the OECD-DAC,[222] and (2) its overtly technocratic nature concerning a problem that is largely political.[223] Later on, the process was criticized as being too slow,[224] lacking the donors' commitment to achieving the results as well as lack of will *and* ability of many recipients

220 Ibid.

221 www.guardian.co.uk/global-development/poverty-matters/2011/nov/25/busan-explainer-aid-effectiveness (last visited July 2013).

222 See, for example, www.cso-effectiveness.org/-histoire-du-processus,017-.html (last visited July 2013) but which was remedied to some extent later.

223 Brookings, *Opinion: It's Complicated: The Challenge of Implementing the Paris Declaration on Aid Effectiveness*, September 22, 2011. Available at www.brookings.edu/opinions/2011/0922_paris_declaration_chandy.aspx (last visited July 2013).

224 World Bank, *Accra Agenda*.

to implement the agenda[225] – and failing to produce the necessary political pressure for a legally binding framework.[226] As the process moved on, the poor progress in the implementation of the Paris Principles was criticized. Even according to the OECD's own 2011 study on "Aid Effectiveness 2005–10: Progress in Implementing the Paris Declaration" only one out of the thirteen targets has been met, that is the target to raise technical cooperation flows that are implemented through coordinated programs consistent with national development to 50 percent (alignment). Yet, the document stressed that it was important to note that considerable progress had been made toward many of the remaining twelve targets.[227] Finally, the legitimacy of the process and especially of the Working Party as the organizer was questioned. This might have contributed to one of the central failures, namely the difficulty of bringing on board more emerging donors, especially China, which withdrew its support in Busan.[228]

More fundamentally, it should be clear that the process formulates by no means the only conceivable solution to the structural problems of aid. It has, as mentioned, a strongly technocratic impulse, as it envisions governments as the main drivers of development, both on the donor and on the recipient side. Parliaments and civil-society groups are seen only as marginal figures whose main role is to enhance effectiveness. There is little room for political disputes or conflicts of interest. Nor is much thought given to a human-rights-based perspective on the development process. The individual is not even mentioned as actor of the process, and human rights are not accorded any importance.[229] Instead, a vague rhetoric of partnership dominates. Developing nations are called "partner countries" throughout, and partnership is the essential description of the interaction of donors and recipients. Development cooperation is seen first and foremost as a process to be managed as a partnership, subject to quantitatively measurable indicators.

[225] Brookings, *Opinion*.

[226] www.europarl.europa.eu/sides/getDoc.do?pubRef=-//EP//NONSGML+REPORT+A7-2011-0313+0+DOC+PDF+V0//EN, para. E (last visited September 2012).

[227] OECD, *Aid Effectiveness 2011: Progress in Implementing the Paris Declaration* (Paris: OECD Publishing, 2012).

[228] M. Tran, *China Pulls out of Aid Partnership*, The *Guardian*, November 29, 2011 (2011). Available at www.guardian.co.uk/world/2011/nov/29/china-pulls-out-aid-partnership-busan (last visited July 2013).

[229] The extent to which this lack of emphasis ignores a central theme of development should be clear after the preceding section on human rights in development cooperation (Ch 2.B.I.2, see also Ch 4.D).

Against this background, critics doubt whether the aid-effectiveness agenda adequately reflects the nature of development cooperation on at least two grounds. One perspective emphasizes the political nature of the development process and maintains the necessity of creating space and recognition for political processes, particularly on the recipient side, but also between individuals and donors.[230] Another group of critics favors a more market-oriented approach. For them, development aid's basic problems are over-planning and bureaucratization, which, they claim, frustrate smaller, initiative-driven programs. From this perspective, the Paris Declaration is simply further evidence of bureaucratic hubris, not a step toward poverty eradication.[231]

b) *Indicators as new instrument*

As the discussion on aid effectiveness and the ensuing declarations have produced a number of goals, their formulation and fast spread has been accompanied by the rise of a new governance instrument: so-called indicators. Such indicators are used to define, to measure and to evaluate social phenomena (such as human development, ownership or alignment) in concrete numbers and thereby facilitate decision-making. To this end, a social phenomenon is broken down into separate aspects which represent its elements. These elements are then defined in a numerical way, their existence or non-existence measured and the results used to describe the performance of different actors.[232]

Characteristic of indicators is that they represent a social phenomenon not through a textual description or through pictures but through numbers. They do not explain or circumscribe a certain goal in words, which are necessarily open to different understandings and interpretations, but express the state of a phenomenon in the clear, sober and universally understood language of numbers. Being numbers, these indicators can be used especially well in a comparative manner. They are used to indicate

[230] The principal source is Whitfield, *The Politics of Aid* as well as the sources cited in fn. 182.

[231] Easterly, *White Man's Burden*; a short and polemic critique is provided in Easterly, "Entwicklungsideologie," 1084; but the collection edited by him provides a more stimulating perspective, see Easterly, "Introduction."

[232] Kevin Davis, Benedict Kingsbury and Sally Engle Merry define indicators as a "collection of rank-ordered data that purports to represent the past or projected performance of different units. The data are generated through a process that simplifies raw data about a complex social phenomenon. The data in this simplified and processed form, are capable of being used to compare particular units of analysis (such as countries, institutions, or corporations), synchronically or over time, and to evaluate their performance by reference to one or more standards." See Kingsbury, Davis and Merry, "Indicators," 73–4.

the evolution of one aspect over time and can thus serve to evaluate the evolution in the sense of marking progress, standstill or regress. It is also typical that they are produced for policy-makers, to be used in evaluation and decision-making processes.

Since the late 1990s, indicators have become a major instrument of global governance in many fields, such as educational or health policy, human rights regimes or in combating corruption.[233] They have become especially prominent, though, in the field of development policy.[234] UNDP's Human Development Index[235] or the rankings of countries for their classification in the World Bank[236] are especially prominent but mark only a first layer of their use. In the MDG or the Paris Declaration, indicators have come to formulate central targets and standards of the international community. In concrete projects and programs, finally, indicators have become the central tool to organize their evaluation.[237]

The emergence of indicators as an instrument of global governance is certainly connected to the massive increase in the availability and

[233] Generally, see K. E. Davis, A. Fisher, B. Kingsbury and S. Merry, *Governance by Indicators: Global Power Through Classification and Rankings* (Oxford University Press, 2012); on specific uses of indicators see, e.g. A. von Bogdandy and M. Goldmann, "The Exercise of International Public Authority Through National Policy Assessment: The OECD's PISA Policy as a Paradigm for a New International Standard Instrument," *International Organizations Law Review*, 5 (2008), 241–98; G. Backman, "Health Systems and the Right to Health: An Assessment of 194 Countries," *The Lancet*, 372 (2008), 2047–85; A. Rosga and M. L. Satterthwaite, "The Trust in Indicators: Measuring Human Rights," *Berkeley Journal of International Law*, 27 (2009), 253–315.

[234] M. Riegner, *Measuring the Good Governance State: A Legal Reconstruction of the World Bank's "Country Policy and Institutional Assessment,"* IRPA Working Paper 6/2012 (2012) at www.irpa.eu/; C. Arndt and C. Oman, *Uses and Abuses of Governance Indicators* (Paris: Development Centre of the OECD, 2006); S. Morse, *Indices and Indicators in Development: An Unhealthy Obsession with Numbers?* (London: Earthscan, 2004).

[235] United Nations Development Programme, *Human Development Report 2010: The Real Wealth of Nations – Pathways to Human Development.* (New York: Palgrave Macmillan); M. u. Haq, "The Birth of the Human Development Index," in S. Fukuda-Parr and A. K. S. Kumar (eds.), *Readings in Human Development: Concepts, Measures and Policies for a Development Paradigm* (Oxford University Press, 2003), pp. 127–37; E. Stanton, *The Human Development Index: A History*, Political economy research institute working paper series no. 127 (UMass Amherst, 2007). See also above, Ch 2.B.II and below, Ch 3.B.

[236] World Bank, *Doing Business: Making a Difference for Entrepreneurs* (Washington, DC: World Bank Publications, 2011); K. Davis and M. Kruse, "Taking the Measure of Law: The Case of the Doing Business Project," *Law and Social Inquiry*, 31 (2007), 1095–119; H. Spamann, "Large-Sample, Quantitative Research Designs for Comparative Law?" *The American Journal of Comparative Law*, 57 (2009), 797–810.

[237] C. Adam, "Redesigning the Aid Contract: Donor – Use of Performance Indicators in Uganda," *World Development*, 30 (2002), 2045–56.

"process-ability" of data due to progress in computer and data-processing technologies. But indicators are also closely connected to the three long-standing structural problems of development cooperation as outlined above, namely complexity, knowledge and power. On the one hand, they have a number of obvious attractions in this regard. First of all, indicators help to simplify complexity. They easily reduce the necessarily complicated nature of phenomena and present aspects in a (seemingly) unambiguous way. They are also used to harmonize and align multi-donor efforts to common goals, such as the MDGs. Second, indicators are also a way of dealing with information deficits and ambiguity in decision-making, in that they are (seemingly) clear and simple and thus help to increase the efficiency in decision-making or evaluation processes. It is much easier and faster to compare numerical data than worded analysis and description. It seems also more justified and more easily explained to base a decision on clear numbers than on other assessments. For decision-takers in development agencies, for example, it becomes much easier to justify the continued support for a country or project whose evaluative indicators point in the "right" direction. At the same time and third, indicators are attractive because they give the impression of consistency, transparency and impartiality. They appear less ambiguous than language, unequivocal. Numbers also contain a certain "air" of scientific or expert authority. Less obvious and less openly formulated might be another advantage of indicators which is their ability to subtly transport a set of values. While the concrete in this or that indicator might give rise to question, the indicator itself and thereby the standard set by it is often less questioned and easily accepted.

However, as the last point suggests, the use of indicators can at the same time be highly problematic. Three problems shall be highlighted here, others could be added.[238] First, the simplification in the reduction of a complex social phenomenon to simple numbers strips these numbers and underlying data of their context. Any indicator, however, is based on a large number of assumptions, understandings and also omissions. While the compiler of data and even more the developer of an indicator might still know about the problems behind creating and filling the indicator, later users will not know about these and therefore may not know and understand the limitations of the indicated numbers. The indicator then takes on a life of its own.

[238] For a critical assessment of the rise and use of indicators from a more anthropological perspective, see S. E. Merry, "Measuring the World: Indicators, Human Rights, and Global Governance," *Current Anthropology*, 52 (2011), 83–95.

Second, indicators are powerful instruments to define our perception of the world – but who gives actors the power to do so? The production of knowledge has become one of the most important tools of so-called soft power, as well as the ability to influence the direction of what knowledge is produced and used. The traditional and current organization of formal powers, however, hardly grasps this dimension. In this void, many organizations, such as the World Bank as "knowledge bank," but also private actors (rights NGOs as well as businesses) can act with immense discretion and power.

Third, the impression of consistency, impartiality and expertise is deceptive and mostly wrong. Numbers, indicators and statistics are hardly ever impartial or objective. They are invented and developed, which is already a highly discretionary power. But since social phenomena simply do not come in numbers, they also give immense discretion and power to those who compile data and put numbers to evaluate social phenomena. Hence, indicators and their use of seemingly objective numbers is rather a highly political practice.[239]

In sum, indicators have become a central instrument of global governance in general and development governance in particular. They easily captured the imagination of administrations and policy-makers and are now a standard tool that will continue to shape approaches in the field. However, they are not as innocent and easy as they may seem at first sight. They must thus be used and communicated responsibly,[240] and their critical analysis is called for. More so, accountability in their use is called for. Here, law and legal analysis play a crucial role, as law and the rule of law can and should rein in unchecked uses of power. Ideally, law can ensure a framework in which development actors negotiate their preferred measuring techniques on an equal footing and thus contribute to the production of knowledge that is perceived as legitimate by all concerned.[241]

2. Emerging economies and their impact on the development system

The discussion on aid effectiveness has to be seen also in a broader context. One of the central features of this broader and new context is the increasing role and clout of emerging economies. While the development

[239] A. Desrosières, *The Politics of Large Numbers: A History of Statistical Reasoning* (Cambridge: Harvard University Press, 1998).

[240] See e.g. R. Salais, "On the Correct (and Incorrect) Use of Indicators in Public Action," *Comparative Labor Law and Policy Journal*, 27 (2006).

[241] Riegner, *Measuring*, more generally on the role of law in global governance, see Bogdandy, Dann and Goldmann, "Developing".

system was created to support poor countries, the past years have seen an impressive increase in economic output and wealth production in the biggest of these formerly poor countries. China, India and Brazil are often mentioned, but Mexico, Indonesia, Turkey or Nigeria could equally be named. Since around 2000, these countries have produced impressive growth rates.[242] This development, which with some arrogance is sometimes called "the rise of the rest,"[243] has a profound impact on the development system. Three of the most important consequences shall be mentioned.

For one, emerging economies have access to much more funding and many more agents than funding from development agencies. Countries like India, China or Brazil have, by their sheer size, always been and still are important customers of the World Bank and other donors.[244] The dynamic of negotiations with them is profoundly different than with smaller and poorer states. They and others can choose between loans from the public aid agencies or the private sector, i.e. normal business banks. The latter might even be more attractive, since they might come with less stringent conditions attached.[245] They can thus bargain on a wholly different level with the ODA donors. Even though they still receive ODA, they are hardly dependent on it. This has infused an element of competition to the field that was absent until recently.[246]

[242] Data from the IMF World Economic Outlook shows the following average of GDP growth rates for the years 2000–2011: Brazil 3.6%; China 10.2%; India 7.3%; Nigeria 8.5%; Indonesia 5.2%; Mexico 2.2%; Turkey 4.6%. Source: www.imf.org/external/pubs/ft/weo/2012/01/weodata/index.aspx (last visited July 2013).

[243] See F. Zakaria, "The Rise of the Rest," *Daily Beast*, May 3, 2008 (2008). Available at www.thedailybeast.com/newsweek/2008/05/03/the-rise-of-the-rest.html (last visited July 2013); earlier by A. H. Amsden, *The Rise of "the Rest": Challenges to the West from Late-Industrializing Economies* (Oxford University Press, 2003).

[244] OECD statistics database shows that China is the only one of the seven emerging markets where a steady decline of ODA can be observed (from about US$3 billion in the mid 1990s to US$1.7 billion at the turn of the century, to US$648 million in 2010). The numbers for India dropped in the mid 1990s but started increasing again in 2000; numbers for Brazil were fluctuating at a very low level (under US$300 million) until 2007, when they surpassed US$300 million for the first time and reached more than US$600 million in 2010. For the four other countries (Nigeria, Turkey, Mexico and Indonesia) the numbers show no clear trend, but generally went up since 2000. Source: OECD StatExtracts, Geographical Distribution of Financial Flows, Total ODA Net, Online: http://stats.oecd.org/Index.aspx?datasetcode=TABLE1# (last visited September 2012).

[245] On conditionalities in project aid, see *infra* Ch 6.B.I.3 and II.3 – and in budget support *infra* Ch 7.B.II.

[246] N. Birdsall and F. Fukuyama, *The Post-Washington Consensus: Development After the Crisis*, Centre for Global Development Working Paper 244 (2011). Available at www.cgdev.org/content/publications/detail/1424882 (last visited September 2012); Zimmermann and Smith, "More Actors, More Money," 731.

Second, emerging economies have become donors (and lenders) themselves – and change the so-far Western rules of the development system. As so-called "new donors" they provide alternatives for poorer countries to receive loans. They often seek new ways and often give aid with fewer strings attached than loans from traditional Western donors.[247] But they also channel ODA through traditional instruments and institutions and are hence increasingly perceived as "donors" by multilateral development organizations.[248] In this respect, the involvement of China in Africa is already a well-known element of the global economic system. In 2008 China has invested approximately US$1.2 billion in Africa. China's general aid volume was estimated at US$6 billion in 2010.[249] But other emerging economies also have developed aid systems.[250] Their spending might still be relatively small when compared to overall spending by the USA and Western European countries, but in recent years it has been increasing rapidly. From 2005 to 2010, Brazil's assistance spending grew each year by around 20.4 percent, India's by around 10.8 percent, China's by around 23.9 percent, and South Africa's by around 8 percent. Russia's assistance

[247] On the diversity in the group of donors, see Ch 3.A.I.; see also J. Walz and V. Ramachandran, *Brave New World: A Literature Review of Emerging Donors and the Changing Nature of Foreign Assistance*, Center for Global Development, Working Paper 273 (2011). Available at www.cgdev.org/files/1425691_file_Walz_Ramachandran_Brave_New_World_FINAL.pdf (last visited July 2013).

[248] See, for example, the BRICS Report by the Global Health Strategies Initiative from 2012: www.ghsinitiatives.org/downloads/ghsi_brics_report.pdf (last visited July 2013).

[249] For a good introduction to the Chinese aid system but also on the difficulty of how to evaluate Chinese "ODA" see D. Brautigam, "Chinese Development Aid in Africa: What, Where, Why, and How Much?" in Song and Golley, *Rising China*, pp. 215–18; also D. Brautigam, "Aid 'With Chinese Characteristics': Chinese Foreign Aid and Development Finance Meet the OECD-DAC Aid Regime," *Journal of International Development*, 23 (2011), 752–64; C. Lancaster, *The Chinese Aid System*, Centre for Global Development Essay (Washington, DC: Center for Global Development, 2007). Available at www.cgdev.org/files/13953_file_Chinese_aid.pdf (last visited July 2013); see also China's first White Paper on Foreign Aid from April 2011, as translated by China Daily (state-controlled newspaper): "White Paper: China's Foreign Aid," *China Daily*, April 22, 2011.

[250] On India, see I. Taylor, "India's Rise in Africa," *International Affairs*, 88 (2012), 779–98; V. Katti, T. Chahoud and A. Kaushik, *India's Development Cooperation: Opportunities and Challenges for International Development Cooperation*, German Development Institute – Briefing Paper 3/2009 (2009). Available at www.die-gdi.de (last visited July 2013); D. Chananan, "India As an Emerging Donor," *Economic and Political Weekly*, 44 (2009), 11–14. On Brazil, see John Sousa, *Brazil As an Emerging Actor*; B. Ayllon Pino, *Brazilian Cooperation: A Model Under Construction for an Emerging Power (ARI)*. Available at www.realinstitutoelcano.org/wps/wcm/connect/d3dc7f0044b54d2d8c3c8ef55cb546a4/ARI143-2010_Ayllon_Brazilian_Cooperation_emerging_power.pdf?MOD=AJPERES&CACHEID=d3dc7f0044b54d2d8c3c8ef55cb546a4 (last visited July 2013).

increased substantially early in the same period, before stabilizing at around US$450 million per year.[251]

The emergence of new donors has created another element of competition for the established Western donors and that is a competition on the norms ruling the transfer of aid. As will be analyzed in more detail below, the central rules of ODA transfer were traditionally initiated and agreed upon within a relative small club of Western donors, organized in the OECD's Development Assistance Committee (DAC).[252] This rather homogeneous group of countries was able to agree on common approaches more easily, for example, to tie aid to environmental standards or to press for governance programs. The new donors are mostly outside the DAC and thus beyond its rules.[253] A united ideology of donors, as exemplified by the Washington Consensus, is therefore no longer likely to have such a strong impact.

Such competition can be regarded as a good thing. New donors enhance development efforts. They provide new insights and instruments, set other priorities and thus strengthen the system. Poorer countries get an alternative and might rather decide to receive money from less demanding donors, like China. In that sense, not a Beijing Consensus but the Beijing Path is much more likely to emerge, if it hasn't already.[254] Nevertheless, efforts were made to pull new donors into the DAC, which resulted in reforms to make the DAC and its decision-making more open for non-members.[255] So far, there is also only little evidence that the arrival of new donors has undermined governance standards.[256] But changes are not

[251] Global Health Strategies Initiatives, *Shifting Paradigm: How the BRICS Are Reshaping Global Health and Development*, p. 6. Available at www.ghsinitiatives.org/downloads/ghsi_brics_report.pdf (last visited July 2013).

[252] See *infra* Ch 3.C.I.

[253] S. Paulo and H. Reisen, "Eastern Donors and Western Soft Law: Towards a DAC Donor Peer Review of China and India?" *Development Policy Review*, 28 (2010), 535–52.

[254] For a Chinese perspective see J. Xu, *The Anatomy of China's Influence on the International Development Finance System*, RCCPB Working Paper No. 28 (2012). On new terms to which China and India might join aid partnership see *Guardian* article www.guardian.co.uk/global-development/2011/dec/01/china-india-aid-partnership (last visited July 2013).

[255] A formal recognition of the changed environment is apparent in OECD, *Revised Resolution of the Council on a new Governance Structure for the Organisation*, C(2006)78/REV1/FINAL of February 10, 2011. Available at www.oecd.org/legal/41462222.pdf (last visited July 2013).

[256] Paulo and Reisen, "Eastern Donors"; on the role of new donors in the aid system, see the contributions in a 2011 issue of the *Journal of International Development*: S. Kim and S. Lightfoot, "Does 'DAC-Ability' Really Matter? The Emergence of Non-DAC Donors: Introduction to Policy Arena," *Journal of International Development*, 23 (2011), 711–21; Zimmermann and Smith, "More Actors, More Money"; L. Chandy and H. Kharas,

easy and the risk to the DAC's commitment to certain values and competition is real.[257] Some perceive the OECD-DAC, if not the whole ODA transfer, therefore as a dying dinosaur.[258]

There is a third change which is rather conceptual for now but could also have an important impact on the practice of development. This is the shift in focus from poverty to inequality and more precisely from the poverty *of* a country to inequality *within* a country. Until recently, the focus of the development system was to raise countries out of poverty. Especially since the end of the Cold War and with the growing autonomy of the development system, poverty reduction was the central aim.[259] This was mostly understood as lifting societies as such from poverty. At the same time, however, the economic growth in developing countries and emerging economies has highlighted that wealth *within* middle-income or even generally poorer countries is often distributed very unequally.[260] China and India are among the fastest growing economies and at the same time are home to the highest numbers of poor people.[261] This is not just a function of their absolute size but also of domestic policies. If development policy is about poverty reduction, it will increasingly have to press for changes in domestic policies.

Growing wealth and rising standards of living in emerging economies are encouraging signs for those who care about poverty. They might be less so for those in the traditional development system. This raises the question of how much the system of development cooperation contributed here, but more so it has put – as just described – pressures on the system of development cooperation. One path forward is to enhance transparency and accountability in the system. In the rest of this study we will examine to what extent the law of development cooperation can play a role here.

"Why Can't We All Just Get Along? The Practical Limits to International Development Cooperation," *Journal of International Development*, 23 (2011), 739–51).

[257] On the OECD–China relationship (from the perspective of the OECD) see OECD, *OECD–China Co-operation: The First Ten Years* (2005). Available at www.oecd.org/globalrelations/keypartners/37071640.pdf (last visited July 2013); on dangers connected to reforms also Zimmermann and Smith, "More Actors, More Money," 734.

[258] K. Mahbubani, "The OECD: A Classic Sunset Organization," *Global Policy*, 3 (2012), 117–18; Severino and Ray, *The End of ODA*.

[259] See *supra*, Ch 2.B.I.

[260] Brazil (51.9 in 2012, down from 60.7 in 1998) and China (48 in 2009, up from 41,5 in 2005) have a much higher Gini-coefficient compared to India (36.8 in 2004) (see CIA World Fact Book at https://www.cia.gov/library/publications/the-world-factbook/fields/2172.html).

[261] In India 32.6% of the population live with less than US$1.25 a day, in China 13% and in Brazil 6%. Source: World Bank http://povertydata.worldbank.org/poverty/home (last visited July 2013).

PART II

Constitutional foundations of the law of development cooperation

A book on the law of development cooperation must first lay foundations. The Introduction provided a first description and delimitation of this field of law; Part I presented the history of development cooperation by looking at its political, theoretical, and institutional aspects. Now, in Part II, I will analyze the general, one could also say constitutional framework of the development cooperation law. I will proceed in two steps – first addressing the institutional structures and the sources of development cooperation law (Ch 3), and then presenting the principles of this field of law (Ch 4).

3

Institutions and legal framework

A first glance at the institutions and legal frameworks or bases of development cooperation reveals an immense variety. There are almost 70 public donor organizations operating today in about 100 developing states as diverse as India and Zimbabwe, Botswana and China. International organizations such as the UN or the OECD also play an essential role, not as donors but in the preparation or formulation of international standards. Although there are no multilateral agreements or UN conventions on development aid, the disbursement of ODA (official development assistance[1]) is governed not only by the specific regulations contained in bilateral contracts between donors and recipients, but also by the internal law of donors and by general standards, which will be addressed later. How can this institutional and legal diversity be made comprehensible in a more systematic manner?

The present study will attempt the feat through a functional approach. First, donors will be addressed, then recipients, and finally collective actors who help to set standards. With regard to each actor, this study will address organizational laws and then their legal bases, and finally their contribution to the law of ODA allocation. First will be the group of donors (A).[2] They are of primary importance not only from a financial but also from a legal standpoint. Each donor establishes for itself what procedures it will follow to award ODA, what instruments it will use, and what criteria will govern it. After a short overview of the group of donors (A.I), Germany, the European Union and the World Bank will be analyzed in more detail as examples, with particular focus on their organizational structure, their legal framework and their mandate (A.II–IV). Already

[1] On this key term, see *supra* Intro.A.II.2.

[2] In this book, the term donor will generally refer to the legal entity that disburses ODA – for example, the Federal Republic of Germany, the European Community or the World Bank. As a functional matter, the term "development administration" specifically refers to those agencies which organize the award of ODA to third-party organizations which, in turn, may be either donor-country organizations (such as the German Federal Ministry of Development) or, in the case of Europe, the Commission.

this selective portrayal shows a fundamental characteristic of the institutional structures or the global governance structure of development cooperation, namely the particular importance of international organizations such as the EU or the World Bank. This leads to the question of how development cooperation is constituted as a multi-level system, and to the observation that it is, in fact, an unusual *heterarchical* multi-level system (A.V). The results of this analysis will then be summarized by means of a description of the two previously mentioned kinds of development administration (A.VI).

I will then turn to the group of recipient nations and ask to what extent they contribute to the legal framework of ODA and by what criteria they are selected (B). Finally, I will address the question of the extent to which collective actors such as the OECD or the UN set general standards for ODA allocation and for interaction between protagonists (C). By way of summary, I will sketch the characteristics of the institutional structure and legal framework of the development cooperation law (D).

A The donors: organizational structures, legal frameworks, mandates

I. Overview: institutional types and financial dimensions

ODA is disbursed by a large number of public organizations.[3] A characteristic feature of this group is the fact that there are as many international organizations as national ones, yet they all distribute development aid. There is likely no other field in which international organizations have comparable importance. For clarity of presentation, the groups of national and international donors will first be addressed separately.

1. National donors

Looking at the list of *national* ODA donors, it seems evident why development cooperation is largely seen as an element of the North–South conflict. Giving ODA support is traditionally a matter for the prosperous states of the Global North. The largest group of national donors is thus the relevant committee of the OECD, the DAC. Currently, there are twenty-four member states on the DAC.[4] However, this group has been supplemented by new donors over the years, modifying the picture of a pure North–South

[3] A thorough presentation is found in Nuscheler, *Entwicklungspolitik*, pp. 479, 508.

[4] And the EU. For more on the OECD-DAC see *infra* Ch 3.C.I.

transfer. Since the late 1970s, the oil-rich states of the Arabian Peninsula have paid ODA.[5] In addition, since the 1990s, several countries of the former Eastern Bloc have joined the list of donor states.[6] These are the new EU member states Poland, Hungary, Slovakia and the Czech Republic.

Of particular note is the fact that in the last few years, former Third World nations have also become ODA donors. This group includes, in particular, China, India and Turkey, all states that today both give and receive ODA. Discussion here revolves around the question of whether the impulse towards political reform which accompanies ODA payments from OECD countries is undermined and outmoded by these new donors, in particular China.[7] This new diversity among donors, however, should not obscure the question of the financial strength of the new donor nations. The ODA payments from all states that are not members of the OECD-DAC only amount to 5 percent of the DAC members' contributions.[8] Thus, the OECD world still clearly dominates the concessional award of development funds that is at issue in this book.

From a financial standpoint, the USA has always been and still is the largest donor, at least in *absolute* numbers. In 2010, the USA gave US$29.85 billion in ODA.[9] In the same year, Germany, the second-largest donor in absolute terms, gave US$13.27 billion.[10] This was an increase of 9 percent from the previous year, but a decrease of 3 percent compared to 2008, as

[5] These are Saudi Arabia, the United Arab Emirates and Kuwait. See A. Alkazaz, *Arabische Entwicklungshilfe-Institutionen: Organisationsform und Leistungen* (Hamburg: Deutsches Orient-Institut, 1977).

[6] During the Cold War, the Soviet Union also counted as a major development-aid donor, see Hilger, *Die Sowjetunion und die Dritte Welt*; K. von Beyme, *Die Sowjetunion in der Weltpolitik* (Zürich: Piper, 1983), p. 132.

[7] N. Woods, "Whose Aid?: Whose Influence? China, Emerging Donors and the Silent Revolution in Development Assistance," *International Affairs*, 84 (2008), 1205–21 at 1205; R. Manning, "Will 'Emerging Donors' Change the Face of International Co-operation?" *Development Policy Review*, 24 (2006), 371–85 at 371.

[8] And of this percentage, half is contributed by Saudi Arabia. See OECD, *Development Co-operation Report 2009* (Paris: OECD Publishing, 2009). Available at www.keepeek.com/Digital-Asset-Management/oecd/development/development-co-operation-report-2009_dcr-2009-en (last visited September 2012), Table 33. The exact amount of ODA payments from China and India is not known, and would have to be added to this number.

[9] This figure, as well as the following ones, is taken from the OECD, *Development Co-operation Report 2011: 50th Anniversary Edition*, 50th edn (Paris: OECD Publishing, 2011). Available at www.oecd-ilibrary.org/docserver/download/fulltext/4311011e.pdf?expires=1346321629&id=id&accname=guest&checksum=11BDF3A89CF6A88AF45A717199EC07D2 (last visited September 2012), Statistical Annex, p. 228. The figures given for 2010 are preliminary figures, at 2009 prices and exchange rates.

[10] German development aid is financed primarily from the federal budget.

German ODA expenditure had dropped significantly (-13%) in 2009 due to the financial crisis. In the time span between 2000 and 2008 German expenditure had steadily increased.[11] Germany used US$4.3 billion of this amount[12] to support multilateral organizations such as the World Bank or the EU; the German development organizations were themselves responsible for disbursing US$7.9 billion.[13] Overall, the ODA expenditures of the twenty-four OECD-DAC member states have increased significantly in recent years. In 2010, they invested US$127.52 billion, a historical record.[14] In *relative* terms, the rank order of donors looks different. Here, Luxembourg, Norway and Denmark were the leaders in 2010, and the Netherlands and Scandinavian states are traditionally the leaders. They invest over 0.8% of their gross national income in ODA.[15] The figure for Germany is 0.39%, and for the USA, 0.20%. The EU and its member states committed themselves, in the Council of Europe, to increase their ODA funding to 0.56% of their GNP by 2010, increasing to 0.7% by 2015.[16] Another figure may be of interest in this context. States gave almost 70% of their ODA themselves, that is by direct transfer to recipient countries, while 30% of their ODA went to international donor organizations.

2. International donors: development banks and the UN

International donor organizations can be divided into two groups: multilateral development banks[17] and specialized UN organs with a

[11] OECD, *Development Co-operation Report 2011*, Statistical Annex, Table B3, p. 288.

[12] Ibid., Table 15.

[13] A direct comparison of the sums disbursed by Germany to those paid by the EU or World Bank is somewhat misleading, since these latter sums also include money received from Germany and other nations. To convey an impression of the relative amounts, we may compare how much money is under management by these entities. It then becomes clear that the European Union administers about 50% more money than Germany, and the World Bank about 300% more.

[14] ODA transfers from countries which were not members of the OECD-DAC totaled another US$4,7 billion (see ibid., Table B8, p. 237). These figures are for the year 2009. Due to the financial crisis these numbers also show a sharp decline of approximately 27% against the previous year, with Saudi Arabia and the UAE responsible for the largest cuts.

[15] Luxembourg leads this statistic with a ratio of 1.1%, followed by Norway and Denmark with 1.0% and 0.9% respectively. These figures are calculations based on the figures given in OECD, *Development Co-operation Report 2011*, Statistical Annex, Tables B3 and B9, pp. 228, 237.

[16] Council of Europe, Presidency Conclusions, Doc 10255/1/05 Rev 1, margin no. 27 (July 15, 2005); reaffirmed by Council of Europe, Presidency Conclusions, Doc 11018/1/08 Rev 1, margin no. 59 (July 17, 2008).

[17] There are also national development banks, for instance the German *Kreditanstalt für Wiederaufbau* (KfW). More on this bank *infra* Ch 3.A.II.1.

development mandate. One unique international donor is the European Commission, which will be dealt with separately later.[18]

The development banks are a specific type of international organization specializing in the award of loans and grants for development purposes. The first organization of this kind, which has remained a prototype, is the World Bank. Since the 1960s, a series of additional banks has been created which all have a regional focus in their lending, if not always necessarily in their membership.[19] The last to be founded was the London-based European Bank for Reconstruction and Development, established in 1990.[20] In addition to their mandate, development banks are distinguished by their funding and their specific voting system. Regarding their financing, three components have to be differentiated. First, their capital base is furnished by contributions from member states. This basis is, however, not used for ongoing expenses. These are financed by a second source, namely by bonds issued to the capital markets. The banks aim for the best possible rating from the rating agencies and can therefore float attractive bonds in financial markets. The banks can hence finance their loans to middle-income developing countries largely by the income generated from these bonds and fees on loans. These countries are offered loans at conditions only slightly more favorable than the market. Owing to this fact, these loans to middle-income countries are not classified as ODA.[21] For their actual development work – loans at strongly concessional conditions which are classified as ODA – development banks draw on a third source of financing, namely special funds which are replenished at regular intervals by member states.[22] From these funds, they provide discounted loans or direct grants to developing countries; such loans are the only

[18] More on this immediately below in Section III.

[19] There are also, among others, the African, Asian, European, Caribbean, Islamic and Inter-American development banks, see E. Suzuki, "Regional Development Banks," in Wolfrum, *Max Planck Encyclopedia of Public International Law* at margin nos.1; Rigo Sureda, "Law," 13; R. Culpeper, *Titans or Behemoths?* (Boulder: Rienner, 1997); J. Syz, *International Development Banks* (New York: Oceana Publications, 1974); studies of single banks include J. Lehmann, "Die Asiatische Entwicklungsbank im Gefüge der regional governance in Asien," *Verfassung und Recht in Übersee*, 41 (2008), 556–60 at 560, see also literature cited in the following footnotes. On a further group of international financial institutions see M. Ragazzi, "Financial Institutions, International," in Wolfrum, *Max Planck Encyclopedia of Public International Law* at margin no.1.

[20] Weber, "Origins," 1; Shihata, *European Bank*.

[21] For a precise definition of concessionality in the ODA context, see *supra* Intro.A.I.

[22] In the context of the World Bank, this is the IDA. Regional development banks use various organizational models. More precisely defined in Suzuki, "Regional Development Banks," margin nos. 25–33.

workable option for poorer developing countries. For regional development banks, this funding is based on what is called the principle of addition, which also permits states from outside the region to become bank members, thus allowing more resources to be mobilized.[23]

The second special feature of development banks is their voting system. While UN organizations generally give the same weight to votes from all member states,[24] development banks apportion votes according to the amount of capital contributed. States that contribute more capital to the bank are given more votes.[25] In the system of weighted voting, as in its funding, the model for development banks is derived more from corporate law than international law. What differences these modes of organization bring to ODA disbursements will be analyzed in detail when we later look at the World Bank and its International Development Association (IDA).

The second group of international donor organizations operates under the auspices of the United Nations. The UN Development Group, a network of UN organizations which work on development issues was founded in 1997 and counts among its members thirty-two UN special organizations, special funds or programs, most with highly specific missions.[26] The large number and diversity of these organizations is explained in part by the circumstance that developing countries, having obtained a majority in the UN in the 1960s, then used the organization to advance their own interests. The steps they took included founding various new programs, funds and specialist organizations to address development problems.[27] Among these were the UN Conference on Trade and Development (UNCTAD, founded 1964), the UN Development Programme (UNDP/1965), the UN Capital Development Fund (UNCDF/1966), the UN Industrial Development Organization (UNIDO/1966), the International Fund for Agricultural Development (IFAD/1974) and the UN Development Fund for Women (UNIFEM/1976). However, developed countries of the Global North increasingly objected to being used as powerless funders for these organizations and began boycotting them. For this reason, some of the organizations, such as the UNCDF, are largely meaningless today.[28]

[23] Ibid., margin nos. 12–15.

[24] See Art. 18 UN Charter. On voting systems in international organizations in general see H. G. Schermers and N. M. Blokker, *International Institutional Law*, 4th edn (Boston: Nijhoff, 2003), margin nos.791–93; on the aspect of equality see *infra* Ch 4.C.II.

[25] For more details see Rigo Sureda, "Law," 42–4.

[26] See www.undg.org (last visited September 2012).

[27] A detailed discussion of development cooperation in the UN can be found in O. Stokke, *The UN and Development: From Aid to Cooperation* (Indiana University Press, 2009).

[28] P. Dann, "United Nations Development Capital Fund (UNCDF)," in Wolfrum, *Max Planck Encyclopedia of Public International Law* at margin no.1.

The same, however, cannot be said of all UN organizations. One in particular avoided the fate of marginalization to become one of the most important development institutions today: the UNDP was created in 1965 by a UN General Assembly resolution combining a special fund with the "Expanded Programme of Technical Assistance" (EPTA).[29] Today, it is the main organizer of technical assistance, although implementation remains the responsibility of recipient states. The UNDP is administered by an executive council of thirty-six members, as well as an Administrator. Developing countries form a majority in the executive council. However, a custom of reaching decisions by consensus has developed, to avoid out-voting developed nations. Like all UN organizations, the UNDP is financed by member contributions. In 2010, it allocated US$613 million in ODA funds. One particular strength of the UNDP is its global reach. With 132 country and regional offices, it is represented in basically every developing country, often coordinating the efforts of various donors.

Surveying the financial dimensions in which international development administrations operate, one finds significant differences. The development arm of the World Bank, the IDA, emerges as by far the most generous ODA donor. The other development banks are also all better-funded than UN agencies working in this field.[30] Thus, the World Bank, through the IDA, invested US$12.12 billion in 2010, with the IBRD giving a further US$26.5 billion.[31] Most of this money went to African states. The next largest donor among development banks was the Islamic Development Fund, with US$10.3 billion. The UN agency that awarded the most money was (as in most years) UNICEF, but it gave "only" US$1.05 billion; that is, less than a twentieth of the IDA contribution. The UNDP, actually the

[29] UN-GA Res. 2029 (XX), UN-GA Res. 48/162. A thorough discussion of the UNDP is found in S. Klingebiel, *Leistungsfähigkeit und Reform des Entwicklungsprogramms der Vereinten Nationen (UNDP)*, Schriften des Deutschen Instituts für Entwicklungspolitik (DIE) (Köln: Weltforum Verlag, 1999), vol. CXV; M. Hampe and E. Sandschneider, *Das Entwicklungsprogramm der Vereinten Nationen (UNDP): Anspruch-Probleme-Reformen* (Wiesbaden: Deutscher Universitäts-Verlag, 1998); an earlier source is Wiegand, *Organisatorische Aspekte*; D. C. Dicke, *Die administrative Organisation der Entwicklungshilfe durch die Vereinten Nationen* (Frankfurt: Athenäum, 1972); on its legal structure see P. Dann, "Grundfragen eines Entwicklungsverwaltungsrechts," in C. Möllers, A. Vosskuhle and C. Walter (eds.), *Internationales Verwaltungsrecht: Eine Analyse anhand von Referenzgebieten.* (Tübingen: Mohr Siebeck, 2007), vol. XVI, pp. 7–48 at p. 15.

[30] The following information is drawn from 2007 data and from concessional awards – that is, ones that meet only the criteria of ODA. IBRD loans, for example, no longer fit these criteria. See OECD, *OECD Annual Report 2008* (Paris: OECD Publishing, 2008). Available at www.oecd.org/newsroom/40556222.pdf (last visited September 2012), Statistical Annex, Table 17, p. 192.

[31] Based on www.oecd.org/dac/stats/dcrannex (last visited September 2012).

main UN development program, had less than half this amount at its disposal.

In 2010, the EU spent US$12.57 billion on ODA – that is, about as much as the World Bank or Germany.[32] A more exact picture here requires us to acknowledge the two-tiered structure of European development cooperation. ACP states obtain funds through the EDF, which is a separate budget agreed by member-state negotiations.[33] For the years 2008–13, the fund has a total of €22.682 billion, which makes for approximately €3.8 billion per year to be distributed among seventy-eight ACP nations. All other development programs are funded out of the regular EU budget. In all, this provided about €32 billion for the period 2007–13. Of that amount, €21 billion goes to geographic programs in 48 countries and €11 million goes to thematic programs, which are directed at *all* 143 developing countries, including the ACP states.[34]

After this overview, we will now turn to the legal basis and institutional structures of three donors: Germany, the EU and the World Bank. The analysis begins with the example of a national donor as the "normal case," or at least the simplest case.[35]

II. Development administration in Germany

1. Organizational structure

Development policy in Germany is a relatively small policy area, and one that developed relatively late in comparison to foreign or trade policy.[36] Because it came along so late (i.e. in the 1950s), it had to find its own place in the overall administration. This makes it all the more surprising that development policy is organized today by a specially created federal ministry.

[32] Comprehensive statistics in OECD, *Development Co-operation Report 2009*, p. 148.

[33] On the EDF see also K. Schmalenbach, "Art. 177 EGV," in C. Calliess and M. Ruffert (eds.), *EUV/EGV: Das Verfassungsrecht der Europäischen Union mit Europäischer Grundrechtecharta*. Kommentar, 3rd edn (Munich: C.H. Beck, 2007) at margin no.12 and sources cited therein.

[34] See. Art. 1 II DCI Regulation; Art. 3 I 1889/2006; Art. 2 Regulation (EC) 1717/2006.

[35] It is a justified question whether state donors are really the normal case. This is doubtful from a historical perspective, since the World Bank and even the European Commission developed their development-cooperation activities long before most states did so (see *supra* Ch 1.A). On the other hand, from a financial perspective, states are certainly the most important donors. From the legal perspective (which interests us here), state donors, in particular Germany, are the easiest cases.

[36] On the genesis of German development policy and its administration see *supra* Ch 1.A.III, B.III, Ch 2.A.III.

The Federal Ministry for Economic Cooperation and Development (BMZ), founded in 1961, provides the conceptual guidance and overall control of development policy both within and outside the federal government. The ministry formulates the goals, strategies and instruments of German development cooperation, decides on funding, and concludes treaties with partner nations.[37] It acquired these portfolios only gradually, and mostly from the Ministries for Economy, Finance and the Foreign Office. A particular point of controversy concerned which ministry would obtain the authority to disburse funds.[38] Coordination with these ministries in budget matters is still important today.[39]

A further characteristic of the organizational structure of German development administration lies in the separation of institutional political leadership from technical implementation, as well as the organizational fragmentation on the level of implementation. The BMZ is a federal ministry. It collaborates with a number of implementation organizations, in particular the Kreditanstalt für Wiederaufbau Entwicklungsbank (KfW/Bank for Reconstruction) and the Deutsche Gesellschaft für Internationale Zusammenarbeit GmbH (GIZ/German Society for International Cooperation).[40] The KfW Entwicklungsbank is responsible for evaluating and making all grants and loans required for *financial* cooperation, while the GIZ takes care of the corresponding tasks in the area of *technical* cooperation.

The KfW Entwicklungsbank is a public corporation. It was created by a 1948 law, which was updated in 1961 to add capital assistance to developing countries to the bank's areas of activity.[41] Since 1966, the development activity of the KfW has been governed by a general agreement between the

[37] BMZ, *Leitlinien für die bilaterale finanzielle und technische Zusammenarbeit mit Kooperationspartnern der deutschen Entwicklungszusammenarbeit: Konzepte 165*, (Guidelines) (Bonn, 2008). Available at www.bmz.de/de/publikationen/reihen/strategiepapiere/konzept165.pdf (last visited September 2012), no. 15. The legal bases of German development cooperation are addressed immediately below. On the foundation of the Development Ministry see *supra* Ch 1.A.III.

[38] On the evolution of the Development Ministry's portfolio see *supra* Ch 1.A.III.2 and sources cited therein.

[39] U. Kollatz, "Grundlagen der Entwicklungshilfeverwaltung," *Die Öffentliche Verwaltung*, 35 (1982), 561–9 at 564.

[40] On the following discussion see also Pellens, *Entwicklungshilfe Deutschlands*, pp. 43–5; on the organizational structure of German development cooperation see BMZ, *Medienhandbuch Entwicklungspolitik 2008/2009* (Media Handbook 2008/2009) (Bonn, 2008), p. 59. Available at www.entwicklungsdienst.de/fileadmin/Redaktion/Publik_ext/Medienhandbuch2008_2009.pdf (last visited July 2013).

[41] §2 I (h) KfW-Law (Law of November 5, 1948, WiGBl. p. 123).

Federal Republic of Germany and the KfW. The agreement covers questions of financing and budget management, as well as oversight and reporting.[42]

The GIZ is a limited liability company fully owned by the German state.[43] The articles of incorporation, signed on June 23, 1978, declared the goal of the then GTZ ("... supporting the Federal Republic of Germany in realizing its goals in the area of development policy," §2) and set out the internal structures and responsibilities of the organization. There is also a general agreement between the German state and the GIZ, which addresses cooperation between the GIZ and the Development Ministry. This agreement forms the legal basis for commissioning the GIZ with the oversight and implementation of projects. This agreement, however, is not public. The GIZ operates on an independent non-profit basis when implementing BMZ or other German public assignments – it may decide itself how to fulfill the oversight tasks it has been assigned. The GIZ works primarily for Germany, but can also offer its services to other commissioning parties. In terms of employees, the GIZ represents the largest sector of the German development administration. Currently, it employs 17,000 people – around 70 percent as national staff. Additionally, there are 1,110 development workers, 700 integrated and 455 returning experts as well as 700 national skilled workers in partner organizations and 820 "weltwärts" volunteers. In 2010, the GIZ had a business volume of €1.85 billion.[44] By contrast, the Development Ministry has "only" 600 employees and the KfW Development Bank about 400.[45]

One feature of the relationship between the levels of leadership and implementation deserves special mention, since it provides a revealing comparison with the administrative structure of other development agencies. The final decision on loan issuance always rests with the Development Ministry, the BMZ. The ministry does request expert opinions and recommendations from implementation organizations, and these are seldom ignored. However, the formal (funding) decision always remains on the political level.[46]

[42] Vertrag zur Durchführung der bilateralen Kapitalhilfe an Entwicklungsländer (Agreement on the Implementation of Bilateral Capital Assistance to Developing Countries) of May 16/July 4, 1966.

[43] More information can be found in a publication of the Gesellschaft für technische Zusammenarbeit (GTZ, now GIZ), GTZ, *Die Begriffswelt der GTZ: The World of Words at GTZ* (Eschborn: GTZ, 2004), pp. 27–30.

[44] GTZ, *Jahresbericht 2007*, ("Annual Report 2007") (Eschborn: GTZ, 2007), pp. II, 58/9.

[45] BMZ, *Media Handbook 2008/2009*, p. 43; KfW Entwicklungsbank: 400 according to its webpage.

[46] A more concrete description of the process is found *infra* Ch 6.B.III.

Overall, the organizational structure of German development administration is marked by the principal position of the BMZ, the separation of the implementation level from the level of political leadership and policy setting, and a certain fragmentation at the implementation level.[47]

2. Legal framework

The legal foundations of development policy and its administration are comparatively weak in Germany. From a legal perspective, development in Germany has remained a poor cousin, with a home neither in constitutional law nor in normal statutory law. It must content itself with rule by administrative regulation and budget laws. The Social Democratic Party (SPD) did suggest a parliamentary "Law on the Development Policy of the Federal Republic of Germany"[48] in the early 1990s, when it was in opposition. The draft bill did not attract majority support in parliament, however, and when the SPD took power in 1998, the idea of a law for development "suddenly" lost all its supporters.[49] Therefore, development administration remains to this day a kind of fund management with no statutory legal basis.[50]

But does this "lawlessness" of development administration mean that the granting process is not governed by law? This would be the wrong conclusion. German development administration and ODA granting are subject to various legal rules, even if they do not all spring from parliamentary enactments.[51] The first of these is the yearly budgetary law – actually a formal parliamentary enactment given its budget authority – which in its Section 23 specifies the distribution of the budget among recipients and thus sets certain priorities for assistance.[52] The instrument of so-called "appropriations for commitment" was introduced to ameliorate the short-term focus of yearly budget planning, which is hardly conducive to longer time horizons.[53] These appropriations permit multi-year financing commitments.[54]

[47] See D. Brombacher, *Geberstrukturen in der Entwicklungspolitik: Reformansätze für die Steuerung und Koordinierung der deutschen Entwicklungszusammenarbeit* (Berlin: Stiftung Wissenschaft und Politik, 2009), pp. 18, 19.

[48] See *Bundestagsdrucksache* (Parliamentary Report) 12/5960 (of October 22, 1993).

[49] On the discussion of this bill, see Pellens, *Entwicklungshilfe Deutschlands*, p. 49.

[50] Thus argues R. Pitschas, "Recht und Gesetz in der Entwicklungszusammenarbeit," *Verwaltungsarchiv*, 81 (1990), 465–91 at 465.

[51] On the governmental goal of international cooperation see Tietje, *Internationalisiertes Verwaltungshandeln*, pp. 213.

[52] A thorough description of the development-cooperation budget is found in Kollatz, "Grundlagen," 563; Dennert, *Entwicklungshilfe*, pp. 28, 29.

[53] §§11 II, 16, 38 BHO (Federal Budgetary Regulations).

[54] On the legal questions surrounding financing commitments see C. Gröpl, *Haushaltsrecht und Reform: Dogmatik und Möglichkeiten der Fortentwicklung der Haushaltswirtschaft*

The specific administrative procedure for ODA awards is governed by the "Guidelines for Bilateral Financial and Technical Cooperation with Partners in German Development Cooperation," which were issued by the federal government and, in a thoroughly revised version, came into force on March 1, 2007.[55] The Guidelines have the legal status of an administrative regulation that binds the government, implementation organizations and "third parties involved on the German side." Its eighty-nine articles articulate the goals of German development cooperation and specify the procedures and competencies governing the initiation, oversight, implementation and evaluation of projects. This document will be the primary focus of the analysis of the concrete structures of German development cooperation law in Part III of this study.

In addition to these hard-law bases, there are further governmental publications that more precisely define the criteria, goals and instruments of German development administration and policy. They include statements of principles, frequently issued after changes in government, which state the current government's policy orientation.[56] They also include so-called concepts, which set forth the federal government's approach to certain sectors and address certain sectors or subjects more specifically.[57] While some of these concepts are simple position papers reflecting the government's approach to one particular area,[58] others contain important or even dispositive specifications for the shaping of development policy and the procedures of German development administration.[59] As such, they bind implementing organizations. They serve not only to make the policy

durch Flexibilisierung, Dezentralisierung, Budgetierung, Ökonomisierung und Fremdfinanzierung (Tübingen: Mohr Siebeck, 2001), pp. 467–81; on their use in the area of development cooperation see BMZ, *Medienhandbuch Entwicklungspolitik 2004/2005*, (Media Handbook 2004/2005) (Berlin, 2004), p. 42.

55 Also published as BMZ, *Guidelines* (These "concepts" are available on the Ministry's webpage, www.bmz.de/en/index.html (last visited July 2013)). Before this point the 1984 Guidelines, most recently changed in 1999, were in effect.

56 See ibid.; BMZ, *Armut bekämpfen, Gemeinsam handeln. Der Beitrag der Bundesregierung zur weltweiten Halbierung extremer Armut: Aktionsprogramm 2015*, (Defend Poverty) (Bonn, 2003).

57 On the growing importance of "concepts" for the planning direction of administrative action see Schmidt-Aßmann, *Das allgemeine Verwaltungsrecht*, pp. 332–5.

58 See, e.g. BMZ, *Kleine Beiträge – große Sicherheit. Mikroversicherungen im Finanzsystem: Konzept Nr. 176* (Concept No. 176) (Bonn, 2009). Available at www.bmz.de/de/publikationen/reihen/strategiepapiere/Konzept176.pdf (last visited July 2013).

59 See, e.g. BMZ, *Concept No. 172*; BMZ, *Sektorkonzept Soziale Sicherung: Konzept Nr. 180*, (Concept No. 180) (Bonn, 2009). Available at www.bmz.de/de/publikationen/reihen/strategiepapiere/Konzepte180.pdf (last visited July 2013) or BMZ, *Konzept zur Budgetfinanzierung im Rahmen der programmorientierten Gemeinschaftsfinanzierung:*

formation process transparent but also to guarantee rule-based and predictable conduct on the part of the state and those acting on its behalf.

In conclusion, the mere fact that there is no overarching federal parliamentary law on development should not be seen as rendering development administration a "law-free" zone. Admittedly, development is budgeted only by means of overall budgetary laws, not by means of its own specialized framework laid down in parliamentary laws. However, the development administration – that is, the Development Ministry and implementing organizations – receive thorough legal guidance by means of administrative regulations and concepts.

It should nevertheless be noted that the absence of a dedicated legal basis for development cooperation is not the normal case among donor nations. Many other OECD donor states have such laws. The USA passed the "Foreign Assistance Act" in 1961. The law is used intensively by the US Congress to shape development policy.[60] Great Britain and Denmark also have dedicated laws on development aid,[61] while the EU governs development in regulations which have the force of law within the EU framework. Thus, from an international perspective, the lack of a dedicated development cooperation law in Germany is the exception.

3. Mandate

The "mandate" and goals of German development cooperation are set down in the relevant administrative provisions, the guidelines, as well as the (still valid) political plan, the "Action Program 2015," which was adopted in 2001. According to the guidelines, development aid is intended to "combat global poverty, secure peace, realize democracy, make the process of globalization fairer, and protect the environment." The guidelines announce their support for the principles of sustainable development and refer to a series of international declarations (the Millennium Declaration,

Konzept Nr. 146, (Concept No. 146) (Bonn, 2008). Available at www.bmz.de/de/publikationen/reihen/strategiepapiere/Konzepte146.pdf (last visited July 2013).

[60] On American development cooperation see Lancaster, *Foreign Aid*, pp. 62; on the current status of American development cooperation see contributions to L. Brainard (ed.), *Security by Other Means: Foreign Assistance, Global Poverty, and American Leadership* (Washington, DC: Brookings Institution Press, 2007); on the problems caused by Congress's prominent role see C. Flickner, "Removing Impediments to an Effective Partnership with Congress," in Brainard, *Security by Other Means*, pp. 225–54.

[61] Great Britain: International Development Act from February 26, 2002; Denmark: Act on International Development Co-operation, published in Act no. 541 of July 10, 1998. An outstanding comparative analysis not of legal structures but of institutional and intellectual ones is found in Lancaster, *Foreign Aid*; for an overview see also OECD, *Managing Aid: Practices of DAC Member Countries* (Paris: OECD Publishing, 2005).

the Monterrey Consensus and the Paris Declaration) which are meant to give precise contours to the overall concepts. The goal of poverty reduction is particularly highlighted by the Action Program 2015. With reference to the MDG, the plan sets a halving of extreme poverty by 2015 as one of the main goals of German development cooperation, which is to be tackled by the international community as a joint effort.[62] Conceptually, German development cooperation is marked by its global focus, which, in contrast to development aid from the EU or other national donors, is hardly governed by specific regional interests.[63] German development policy is also marked by the policy, followed now for several years, of singling out particular subject areas in order to bundle resources.[64]

In general, the goals and mandate of German development policy are formulated in the broadest possible terms, or, to put it more starkly, marked by an extraordinary lack of clarity. Development cooperation is apparently intended to achieve all things positive. One point which stands out is that all mention of development aid also serving self-interested or financial purposes, which had been included explicitly even into the 1980s, has now been removed. Rather, it is clear that German development cooperation today is intended much more strongly to serve openly political purposes. Democratization and the implementation of human rights are now explicit goals, even as against sovereign recipient countries.[65]

III. Development administration in the European Union

Although the European Union is not the only multilateral organization that awards ODA, it is unique in one respect: almost all of its member states are themselves donors, none is a recipient. The UN, the World Bank and other development banks, by contrast, have a mixed membership, which includes recipient countries. It is also typical for European development policy and administration that it is divided into two parts, namely between regionally focused cooperation with (mostly) former colonies in the context of ACP cooperation, and a globally oriented policy addressing other developing countries. Finally, EU development policy is merely a small policy sector within the EU "portfolio" that does not take center stage. All three aspects (the preponderance of donor states,

[62] BMZ, *Defend Poverty*.
[63] On the corresponding orientation of the EU see Grilli, *EC and Developing Countries*, p. 65.
[64] BMZ, *Guidelines*, no. 2. See also *infra* Ch 5.C.III.
[65] On this change see *supra* Ch 1.B.III and Ch 2.A.III.1.

the distinction between cooperation with the ACP states and others and sectoral competition) also mark the legal structure of European development administration.

1. Organizational structure

The organizational structure of European development administration has been reshaped by the Treaty of Lisbon. This reform concerned on the one hand the creation of the European External Action Service (EEAS), and on the other, the merger of the Commission's DG Development with the implementing agency EuropeAid. This revamp runs the risk of further increasing the already-existing fragmentation. Before the reform, the Commission was responsible for the conception and implementation of European development cooperation. Within the Commission, the prerogative in this area was not in one hand. Responsibilities were split among three commissioners and their respective General Directorates. The "DG Development" was responsible for formulating the general development-policy guidelines for the EU as well as drawing up the more concrete development programs with the seventy-eight ACP countries. It had about 300 employees.[66] In addition, there is the DG for External Relations, which formulated general foreign policy guidelines, handled relations with international organizations, and led the EU's approximately 120 external delegations.[67] The DG also ran concrete development programming with the fifty-five developing countries that do not belong to the ACP Group. The DG for External Relations employed approximately 120 civil servants for development work. Finally, the DG for Humanitarian Assistance (Echo) was responsible for emergency aid in catastrophes.[68]

As in German development administration, European development administration separates the policy-making and political leadership level from the level of technical implementation. The Agency for Cooperation EuropeAid, often called Aidco, was created in 2001 "under" the two General Directorates for Development and External Relations. It is an implementation unit, and is intended to free the General Directorates from the responsibility for concrete implementation and project

[66] OECD, *European Community: Peer Review*, p. 45. Available at www.oecd.org/dac/peerreviewsofdacmembers/38965119.pdf (last visited July 2013); the numbers for the other organs are also for 2006.

[67] This division of responsibilities derives historically from the priority of cooperation with former colonies. See *infra* Ch 1.A.II.1.

[68] This DG will not be addressed here. Further details in Schmalenbach, "Art. 177 EGV," margin no. 9.

supervision.[69] EuropeAid administers programs negotiated on the political level by commissioning and supervising concrete projects. It has approximately 1,000 employees in Brussels. It should be noted, in particular, that the foundation of EuropeAid began an intensive decentralization and regionalization of the organizational structure. Since 2000, almost 1,600 positions have been created in the foreign branches of the EU. These employees are responsible for concrete questions of implementation.[70] Like the GIZ in the German development administration, the number of employees in the EU is matched by at least double that number working in the recipient countries. The complex and conflict-prone division of labor between these three units (DG Development, DG External Relations and EuropeAid) had been governed since 2001 by an *Interservice Agreement.* This Agreement specified the general principles of their joint action (such as cooperation, consultation, basic tasks), as well as specific competences within a particular project cycle.[71]

This structure was changed by the introduction of the Lisbon Treaty and an ensuing reform of 2010. Based on the new Article 27 III TEU, the EEAS was founded.[72] It is "a functionally autonomous body of the Union"[73] which is institutionally separate from both the Commission and the Secretariat of the Council. As an independent institution, it acts under the authority and direction of the High Representative for the Common Foreign and Security Policy (Art. 18, 27 TEU). Certain subject areas and organizational units related to external action are transferred from the Commission to the EEAS, namely the existing delegations abroad, the DG External Affairs and parts of the DG Development.[74] At the same time, the

[69] R. Pitschas, "Art. 177 EGV," in R. Streinz (ed.), *EUV/EGV Kommentar* (Munich: C.H. Beck, 2003) at margin nos. 5; 11.

[70] OECD, *European Community*, pp. 49–50.

[71] Further discussion of these questions *infra* Part III.

[72] Council Decision of July 26, 2010 establishing the organization and functioning of the European External Action Service (2010/427/EU), OJ L 201/39 of 03.08.2010 [hereinafter EEAS Decision]. See S. Vanhoonacker and N. Reslow, "The European External Action Service: Living Forwards by Understanding Backwards," *European Foreign Affairs Review*, 15 (2010), 1–18; G. Quille, "The European External Action Service and the Common Security and Defence Policy (CSDP)," in E. Greco, N. Pirozzi and S. Silvestri (eds.), *EU Crisis Management: Institutions and Capabilities in the Making* (Rome: Istituto affari internazionali, 2010), vol. XIX, pp. 55–78; C. Sichel, "Die Gründung des Europäischen Auswärtigen Dienstes als EU-Organ: Gleichzeitig eine kleine Ordnung der EU-Verwaltungsorganisation," *Europarecht*, 46 (2011), 447–60; G. Sydow, "Der Europäische Auswärtige Dienst," *Juristenzeitung*, 66 (2011), 6–12.

[73] Recital 1, Art. 1 para. 2 EEAS Decision.

[74] See EEAS Decision, Annex, no. 2, as well as Art. 27 para. 3 Lisbon Treaty and Art. 221 para. 1, Treaty on the Functioning of the European Union (TFEU).

EEAS is closely connected to the remaining DGs of the Commission with external relevance (through cooperation procedures and directive competences). The EEAS's staff consists of one-third each of former employees of the Commission, of the Council and delegated national diplomats.

In the area of development cooperation, this means that the EEAS becomes an autonomous actor next to the DG Development.[75] The EEAS will take over the country units for ACP states formerly located with the DG Development and merge them with the country units formerly located with the DG External Action.[76] In addition, the unit for development programming shifts from the DG Development to the EEAS.

Within the Commission, the units remaining with DG Development will be merged with EuropeAid/AidCo, now known together as "Development and Cooperation – EuropeAid."[77] This DG now fulfills certain programming functions in cooperation with the EEAS and is tasked with concrete project implementation.[78] The former EuropeAid employees in the delegations abroad remain with the Commission, but will work under the guidance and supervision of the head of the EU delegation, who is an EEAS official.[79]

This reform can be interpreted in at least two ways. On the one hand, one may be wary of a further fragmentation of Union development administration because it is administered not only by units within the Commission, but also by the EEAS.[80] This creates more departments and increases the need for cooperation and potentially institutional conflicts. On the other hand, the new structure shows a task-specific differentiation and geographical concentration. The separation between ACP and non-ACP countries has been abandoned, and development programming is concentrated at the EEAS, while the Commission is tasked

[75] J. Sattelberger, "Der Europäische Auswärtige Dienst: Chance oder Risiko für die europäische Entwicklungszusammenarbeit?" *Verfassung und Recht in Übersee*, 43 (2010), 381–6 at 381.

[76] EEAS Decision, Annex, no. 2.

[77] According to the DG's Internet site, the combination took place on September 1, 2012, see http://ec.europa.eu/europeaid/who/about/index_en.htm (last visited July 2013). The new organizational structure therefore appears not to be based on a formal legal act, but rather emerges simply from an organizational chart issued on June 1, 2011, see http://ec.europa.eu/europeaid/who/whoswho/index_en.htm (last visited July 2013).

[78] Discussed extensively *infra* Ch 5.C.II and 23.II.

[79] Art. 5 EEAS Decision.

[80] Also critical of this aspect is Sydow, "Europäische Auswärtige Dienst," 10. An overall critical perspective on the EEAS can be found in I. Gräßle, *Die Gründung des Europäischen Auswärtigen Diensts*. Available at www.robert-schuman.eu/doc/questions_europe/qe-194-al.pdf (last visited September 2012).

with project allocation and implementation. This might lead to a certain simplification.

There is another feature that characterizes the European development administration and sets it apart from the German model. The EU development administration is part of a multi-level system. The EU level is continually influenced through the Council, i.e. the member states of the EU. This is effected through a number of committees, of which the Committee on Development (attached to the Council on General Affairs and External Relations) is the most important.[81] The Committees have important competences relating to the formulation and adoption of development programs as well as control over large-scale development projects.[82]

2. Legal framework

In contrast to the situation in Germany, EU development policy is subject to intensive legal regulation.[83] The basis of this legal regulation is a detailed constitutional framework. Article 4 IV of the Treaty on the Functioning of the European Union (TFEU) specifies the competence of the EU to take measures in the field of development cooperation. This is a parallel competence that does not affect the ability of the member states to implement their own development cooperation policies. Nevertheless, under Art. 210 of the TFEU, both parties are obliged to coordinate their policies. The Treaty of Lisbon included a prioritization of the goals of European Union development policy. The main goal of Union policy is now "the reduction and, in the long term, the eradication of poverty" (Art. 208(2)). The new treaty reflects a general trend in development policy since the turn of the millennium, namely an emphasis on poverty reduction. At the same time, however, development policy should still be in line with the principles and goals of the Union's external action (Art. 208 (1)). These include, most prominently, support for democracy, human rights and the rule of law; sustainable development; and the integration of developing countries into the global economy (Art. 21 II(b), (d) and (e)), which the Nice version of the European Community Treaty lists on the same level as the goal of poverty

[81] There was a dedicated council group on development until 2001, see Carbone, *European Union and International Development*, pp. 49, 50.

[82] More details *infra* in Ch 5.C.II.1 and Ch 6.B.II.1.

[83] On these bases see Pitschas, "Art. 177 EGV," margin no. 1 and sources cited therein; on the ultimately minor changes made by the Lisbon Treaty see B. Martenczuk, "Die Kooperation der Europäischen Union mit Entwicklungsländern und Drittstaaten und der Vertrag von Lissabon," in S. Bartelt and P. Dann (eds.), *Entwicklungszusammenarbeit im Recht der Europäischen Union – The Law of EU Development Cooperation: Europarecht-Beiheft Nr. 2* (Baden-Baden: Nomos, 2008), pp. 36–52.

reduction. The Treaty of Lisbon further establishes the Union's law-making competencies (Art. 209(I)) and, in Art. 209(II), its treaty-making authority. The Lisbon Treaty thus furnishes a constitutional framework for Union-level development policy which differentiates it from cooperation with non-developing economies (Arts. 212, 213),[84] the association policy (Arts. 198–204) and, not least, the provisions concerning a common foreign and security policy (Arts. 23–46).[85]

Under this unified constitutional umbrella, the EU development cooperation law is marked by two characteristics: first, the intensive use of regulations (i.e. the legal instrument that is basically the "law" of the EU, see Art. 189 TFEU). The concrete EU decision to grant ODA is thus not just subject to the discretion of the executive or internal guidelines, but is governed by formal laws, namely regulations. Such regulations are adopted by the Council and Parliament in the regular legislative proceedings (Arts. 209 I, 294). The reasons for this formalization can be found in Article 49 of the European Union's "Budget Act," which requires budget items to be based on law (or in EU parlance a "basic" legal act); but this formalization is also a result of the vertical and horizontal separation of powers in the EU, which affords both member states and the European Parliament influence over the actions of the Commission.[86]

The second characteristic is the different legal basis for aid to ACP states as opposed to non-ACP states. Cooperation with ACP states takes place largely[87] on the basis of the Cotonou Agreement, which replaced the Fourth Lomé Convention in 2000,[88] as well as the legal regime of the 10th EDF, which finances aid to the ACP states for the period 2008–13.[89]

[84] ECJ, Case C-155/07, *European Parliament* v. *Council*, [2008] ECR I-08103.

[85] ECJ, Case C-91/05, *Commission* v. *Council* (ECOWAS), [2008] ECR I-3651.

[86] P. Dann, "Programm- und Prozesssteuerung im europäischen Entwicklungsverwaltungsrecht," in S. Bartelt and P. Dann (eds.), *Entwicklungszusammenarbeit im Recht der Europäischen Union – The Law of EU Development Cooperation: Europarecht-Beiheft Nr. 2* (Baden-Baden: Nomos, 2008), pp. 107–38 at pp. 128–30.

[87] Thematic actions can be financed through budgets of other instruments in ACP states as well, see Art. 1 II, DCI Regulation.

[88] Signed on June 23, 2000, OJ L 317/1. Discussed in detail in Martenczuk, "From Lomé to Cotonou"; K. Arts, "ACP-EU Relations in a New Era: The Cotonou Agreement," *Common Market Law Review*, 40 (2003), 95–116.

[89] This legal regime includes the Internal Agreement between the Representatives of the Governments of the Member States on the financing of Community aid (OJ L 247/32 of September 9, 2006); Council Regulation (EC) No. 617/2007 of May 14, 2007 on the implementation of the 10th European Development Fund under the ACP-EC Partnership Agreement(OJ L 152/1 of June 13, 2007) [hereinafter DCI 10th EDF].

Since the EDF is a separate budget negotiated between member states, it is governed by a specific budget law.[90]

EU cooperation outside the group of ACP states is governed on a separate legal basis. The relevant legal framework for this area was fundamentally reformed in 2006 and consolidated. Thirty former legal enactments were consolidated into five.[91] The central act is the regulation called the "Development Cooperation Instrument," or DCI.[92] The DCI regulates the goals and principles governing allocations, as well as their thematic and geographical aspects. Finally, it addresses the procedure for programming and for channeling funds and implementing programs. As will become clear in Part III, its rules are similar to the implementation rules of the EDF, and thus form the basic framework of European development cooperation law. Four further regulations create a means of further differentiating support on geographical and thematic bases.[93] All

[90] Set out in the financing regulation for the 10th EDF, Council Regulation (EC) No. 215/2008 of February 18, 2008 on the Financial Regulation applicable to the 10th European Development Fund (OJ L 78/1 of March 19, 2008) (hereinafter DCI Financing Regulation, 10th EDF). See also Schmalenbach, "Art. 177 EGV," margin no. 12 and sources cited therein. A thorough introduction to the law of the structural fund can be found in B. Schöndorf-Haubold, *Die Strukturfonds der Europäischen Gemeinschaft: Rechtsformen und Verfahren europäischer Verbundverwaltung* (Munich: C.H. Beck, 2005).

[91] On this reform see S. Bartelt, "The Legislative Architecture of EU External Assistance and Development Cooperation," in S. Bartelt and P. Dann (eds.), *Entwicklungszusammenarbeit im Recht der Europäischen Union – The Law of EU Development Cooperation: Europarecht-Beiheft Nr. 2* (Baden-Baden: Nomos, 2008), pp. 9–35 at p. 9.

[92] Regulation (EC) No. 1905/2006 of the European Parliament and of the Council Of December 18, 2006 establishing a financing instrument for development cooperation (OJ L 378/41) [hereinafter DCI Regulation].

[93] As a geographical matter this is governed (in addition to the 48 countries supported by the DCI Regulation) by Regulation (EC) No. 1638/2006 of the European Parliament and of the Council of October 24, 2006 laying down general provisions establishing a European Neighbourhood and Partnership Instrument (OJ L 310/1), which supports the 17 states neighboring the EU. The Council Regulation (EC) No. 1085/2006 of July 17, 2006 establishing an Instrument for Pre-Accession Assistance (IPA), which supports the Balkan countries and Turkey, can be seen as a legal act of development cooperation, insofar as its target is a developing country (e.g. Albania) and its purpose is development. Thus, the monies provided under this agreement can be seen as ODA payments. Thematically, there are three relevant Regulations: Regulation (EC) No. 1889/2006 of the European Parliament and of the Council of December 20, 2006 on establishing a financing instrument for the promotion of democracy and human rights worldwide (OJ L 386/1); Regulation (EC) No. 1717/2006 of the European Parliament and of the Council of November 15, 2006 establishing an Instrument for Stability (ABl. L 327/1) and Council Regulation (Euratom) No. 300/2007 of February 19, 2007 establishing an Instrument for Nuclear Safety Cooperation. 19.2.2007 (OJ L 81/1).

actions based on these legal provisions are financed from the regular EU budget, which means they are governed by EU budgetary regulations.[94] These actions are linked to general cooperation agreements which the EU has concluded with individual countries or small groups of countries on the basis of Art. 181 I 2 of the Lisbon Treaty, in which basic questions of cooperation are addressed.[95]

The legal integration of both regimes (ACP and non-ACP) is driven not only by the overall constitutional commitment to mutual goals and principles, but also by shared "soft law." The European Consensus of December 20, 2005 is particularly important in this respect.[96] The Consensus is a mutual declaration by member states, the Commission, and the European Parliament on European development policy. It formulates the goals, rules and methods of a common European Community development policy. The consensus has no formal binding effect, but has already been cited several times by the European Court of Justice (ECJ) in assessing the scope of development aid.[97] It has also influenced numerous later legal enactments.[98]

3. Mandate

The European laws of European development serve not only economic and social but also political and constitutional aims.[99] The Lisbon Treaty, however, prescribes a clear hierarchy of goals. Poverty reduction is the

[94] Art. 28 DCI Regulation; Council Regulation (EC, Euratom) No. 1605/2002 of June 25, 2002 on the Financial Regulation applicable to the general budget of the European Communities (OJ L 248, 16.9.2002) [hereinafter FR-EU].

[95] A list of these agreements can be found in Schmalenbach, "Art. 181 EGV," at margin no. 5.

[96] European Consensus on Development, OJ C 46/1 of February 24, 2006 [hereinafter European Consensus]; for context see OECD, *European Community*, p. 23; C. Six, *Der Europäische Konsens zur Entwicklungspolitik: Die EU als Geberin in veränderten internationalen Beziehungen*, Österreichische Forschungsstiftung für Internationale Entwicklung, Working Paper No. 10. Available at www.oefse.at/Downloads/publikationen/WP_EuropaeischerKonses_zur_EPolitik_Maerz2006.pdf (last visited July 2013).

[97] ECJ, Case C-91/05 (ECOWAS) and Case C-403/05 (Philippine Border Controls) [2007] ECR I-09045. See T. Wischmeyer, "Europäische Entwicklungszusammenarbeit und evolutionärer Kompetenzbegriff: Urteilsbesprechung von EuGH C-91/05 und C-403/05," *Verfassung und Recht in Übersee*, 41 (2008), 407–12 at 411.

[98] For example in Art. 1 II, III DCI 10th EDF; Art. 2 III DCI Regulation.

[99] These goals are largely uniform for cooperation with ACP states as well as with other states. For one thing, Art. 208 TFEU and Art. 21 of the Lisbon Treaty bind the Union insofar as it (along with Member States) pursues ACP cooperation. In addition, Article 1 of the Cotonou Agreement essentially repeats these two goals.

central goal of EU development cooperation law. Building on the 2000 UN MDG,[100] an international consensus has formed behind poverty reduction as the main goal of development aid as a replacement for the previous mixed approach, which was seen as ineffective. This consensus has been adopted in EU development cooperation law, for example in the Cotonou Agreement,[101] the European Consensus,[102] in secondary law,[103] and now in primary law.[104] The EU remains committed, however, to further economic and social goals, namely the advancement of "the sustainable economic, social and environmental development of developing countries" and the "integration of all countries into the world economy" (Art. 208 I TFEU in connection with Art. 21 II d), e) of the Lisbon Treaty). EU law has thus adopted a broad definition of development that encompasses social issues and sustainability in addition to economic growth.[105]

EU development policy also advances Western-liberal constitutional values. To be sure, this aspiration is no longer explicitly mentioned in the chapter on development aid in the Lisbon Treaty. Nevertheless, the provisions in this chapter refer to the general principles of European foreign policy, which commit the Union to "consolidate and support democracy, the rule of law, human rights and principles of international law" (Art. 21 II b Lisbon Treaty). This rather aggressive formulation of European development aid's political goals may appear unusual, given development aid's role in foreign policy. The World Bank's statutes, by comparison, explicitly forbid it to take account of political aspects, much less to promote political goals.[106] Article 21 of the Lisbon Treaty, which was originally incorporated into the EU law by the Maastricht Treaty on the European Community as Art. 130 u para. 2, marks the decisive change in the paradigm of development and the political context that took place in the early 1990s. Until well into the 1980s, it was taboo to accord development activities a political impetus as partner countries were concerned about their

[100] UN, A/Res/55/2 of September 18, 2000, www.un.org/millenniumgoals/ (last visited July 2013).

[101] Art. 1 para. 2 Cotonou. [102] European Consensus, margin no. 5.

[103] For example Art. 1 I, DCI Regulation.

[104] See also R. Passos and D. Gauci, "European Parliament and Development Cooperation: Shaping Legislation and the New Democratic Scrutiny Dialogue," in S. Bartelt and P. Dann (eds.), *Entwicklungszusammenarbeit im Recht der Europäischen Union – The Law of EU Development Cooperation: Europarecht-Beiheft Nr. 2* (Baden-Baden: Nomos, 2008), pp. 138–61 at pp. 154, 155.

[105] Schmalenbach, "Art. 177 EGV," margin no. 18; Pitschas, "Art. 177 EGV," margin no. 13.

[106] Art. IV Sect. 10 IBRD Articles; see Killinger, *The World Bank's Non-Political Mandate*.

sovereignty. This changed when the Cold War ended.[107] After the Cold War, linking aid to political goals appeared less objectionable.[108] It also became a widespread view that the success of development cooperation was higher when the recipient country was a democracy complying with the rule of law.[109] Nevertheless, the political aspect is still problematic from the perspective of development cooperation law, since these political goals are unilaterally set. In a national context, subsidies are legitimated in part by their orientation toward a "public goal" and agreed upon by the domestic authority whose democratic legitimacy stems from the recipients of the subsidies themselves. In the development context, the goals, be they bilateral, regional, or even cosmopolitan, are dictated by one side.

The above-named goals are, in any event, not exclusive. Art. 208 II of the TFEU requires the Union and member states to "comply with the commitments and take account of the objectives they have approved in the context of the United Nations and other competent international organisations." This provision aims to make the EU's development goals more flexible and internationally dynamic, an important factor considering the static nature of primary law and possible blockades at the level of secondary laws.

In general, the specified goals of European development cooperation law, like the German, appear broad, complex and potentially conflicting. Here we see a general feature of development cooperation law. Unlike policing laws, which prohibit behavior, development law is a kind of social policy, welfare or benefits law which sets positive goals. The goal is not to defend against individual harmful actions but rather to improve conditions by cumulative effects. The concrete behavioral purpose which aims to influence individual actions is meant to give rise to a final goal of overall improvement, which in doubtful cases may end up only being a so-called

[107] On the legal form of a paradigm which tends to preserve sovereignty see Ipsen, *Europäisches Gemeinschaftsrecht*, §53/2, 963; Becker, *Partnerschaft von Lomé*, p. 158; on the step-wise integration of questions of human rights and democracy in the development aid of the then-Community see the thorough discussion in Pippan, *Förderung der Menschenrechte*, p. 32.

[108] However, the limits of the principle of non-intervention are set out in Hoffmeister, *Menschenrechts- und Demokratieklauseln*, p. 183.

[109] On the renaissance and importance of the rule-of-law principle, in particular, see, e.g., O. Meinecke, *Rechtsprojekte in der Entwicklungszusammenarbeit: Theorie und Praxis am Beispiel von GTZ-Projekten zur Konsolidierung des Rechtsstaats in Südafrika und Sambia*, Schriftenreihe der Hochschule Speyer (Berlin: Duncker & Humblot, 2007), vol. CLXXXIIX; Dam, *Law-Growth-Nexus*; Trubek and Santos, *The New Law and Economic*.

"cumulative social effect."[110] The question of goals, however, reveals a further specific problem related to the theme of development. The concept of "development," as such, is open to many interpretations – but it also tends to become intermingled with a series of goals that donor nations pursue under its rubric. Development aid can follow very different goals. Accordingly, the evaluation of the means–ends fit and the monitoring and measuring function of the goals is quite limited.

The goals formulated in development cooperation law share another feature with social policy or benefits law in that many goals typically remain *unstated*.[111] This is especially true of development aid. Political and diplomatic influence and commercial profit, for example, are not mentioned, although they are certainly important objectives. It would be incorrect to assume that only partner countries benefit from development aid. Various donor-nation industries profit from development policy.[112] In the final analysis, these considerations reduce the steering capacity or governance impact of the explicit goals.

IV. The World Bank

When we turn our attention to the World Bank, we encounter a fundamentally different kind of institution. While it is, like the EU, an international donor, it is, in contrast to the EU (and Germany), a specialized agency whose sole purpose is fostering development of its member states. This narrow mandate and specialized instrumentarium has made today's World Bank the world's largest, best-funded, and probably also most intellectually influential development organization.[113] In addition, the World Bank has a near-universal membership, including recipient and donor countries. We will now turn to the distinguishing features of its legal framework and to the law governing the allocation of resources at the Bank.

110 Haverkate, *Rechtsfragen des Leistungsstaats*, p. 25.

111 Ibid., p. 21.

112 It is generally assumed that well over half of all ODA funds flow to donor-state businesses or other organizations tasked with project implementation. On this problem see Nuscheler, *Entwicklungspolitik*, p. 441; the problem of "tied aid" in the European context is addressed in Carbone, *European Union and International Development*, p. 101; see also Grilli, *EC and Developing Countries*, p. 72; see also *infra* Ch 4.D.IV for consideration of whether tied aid infringes autonomy.

113 The Bank's research activities are seldom addressed in depth, but nevertheless play a central role in development-policy discourse. See also Stern and Ferreira, "The World Bank," p. 523; Morduch, "The Knowledge Bank," p. 377.

1. Organizational structure

A legal analysis of the World Bank must begin with an aspect that would likely appear unimportant to an economist or political scientist. The "World Bank" is actually composed of not one but two organizations, which are locked into a symbiosis reminiscent (to Europeans) of organizations such as the European Atomic Energy Community, the European Economic Community and the European Coal and Steel Community. The International Bank for Reconstruction and Development (IBRD) and the International Development Association (IDA), collectively known as the World Bank,[114] are both independent – if similarly structured – organizations. Each was founded by an international treaty (IBRD Articles of Agreement 1944, IDA Articles of Agreement 1960).[115] They possess separate legal personalities which, although not explicitly stated in either treaty, can be deduced from various regulations of the founding treaties.[116] Further, both organizations have different members.[117]

This "duality" is not particularly relevant to the entities' organizational structure. The founding treaties identify the organizational affiliation which attaches to offices and personnel of the two organs. Member-state representatives of the IBRD, as well as its President, also exercise these offices *ex officio* for the IDA.[118] The IDA thus shares the IBRD's institutional structure. Both organizations share a structure whose external contours largely correspond to the traditional model for international

114 The term "World Bank Group" should be broken down. It describes the World Bank (IBRD and IDA) as well as three further sister organizations, the International Finance Cooperation (IFC), the Multilateral Investment Guarantee Agency (MIGA) and the International Centre for Settlement of Investment Disputes (ICSID). Like the IDA, they were created over a longer period of time and each has its own legal personality and functions. On the individual functions of these organizations and their relationships see Ragazzi, "World Bank Group," margin no. 1.

115 The reasons why these organizations were founded separately and 16 years apart are discussed *supra* Ch 1.A.I.2.

116 Especially relevant in this respect are their expressly assumed ability to enter into contracts and to invoke immunities, see Art. VII, Sect. 2 and Sect. 4, 8, 9, IBRD Articles; and parallel to these Art. VIII, IDA Articles. See also A. Broches, *Selected Essays: World Bank, ICSID and Other Subjects of Public and Private International Law* (Dordrecht: Martinus Nijhoff, 1995), p. 19.

117 These are, however, linked to each other. Only IBRD members can become IDA members, but not all IBRD members actually belong to the IDA, see Art. II, Sect. 1, IDA Articles. The IBRD currently has 186 members, of which 169 are also IDA members.

118 Art. VI, Sect. 2 (b), Sect. 4 (b), Sect. 5 (a) IDA Articles; Libby, "International Development Association," 1065.

organizations. The highest decision-making authority rests with a Board of Governors in which every member state is represented and which meets at least once per year.[119] The Board has delegated substantial decision-making authority for conduct of day-to-day business to the Board of Directors, which currently consists of twenty-five Executive Directors. The Executive Directors meet unusually frequently – twice per week – at the Bank's headquarters in Washington, DC, to determine basic Bank policy.[120] Bank employees, equivalent to the Secretariat in other organizations, are led by a President. The President is named for a five-year term by the Board of Directors[121] and is responsible for the "ordinary business of the bank."[122]

As with the EU, the World Bank is thus essentially a multi-level system in which member states can influence development policy. However, EU member states, through the Council, play only a "correcting" role and block financing decisions, for example, only in extremely rare cases. The division of responsibilities at the World Bank is much more complicated. On the one hand, the Executive Directors, as representatives of member states, are "responsible for the conduct of the general operations of the bank," which includes decisions on each loan, credit or grant made by the Bank as well as the approval of the Bank's internal rules. The near-continuous (twice-weekly) meetings of the Directors indicate how broad their responsibilities are. The President leads the bank only "under the direction of the Executive Directors" and can be replaced by them at any time.[123] On the other hand, though, the President determines the Bank's organizational and personnel structures. He also chairs the meetings of the Executive Directors and thus participates in all their discussions, albeit without the right to vote. The powerful role of the President and his management team derives mainly from a very early yet decisive power struggle between the second president of the Bank and the American Executive Director.[124] Although the foundational treaties did not contain specific rules for the distribution of powers, the struggle resulted in the President obtaining

[119] Art. V, Sect. 2, IBRD Articles.

[120] Art. V, Sect. 2 (b), Sect. 4, IBRD Articles; Art. VI Sect. 4, IDA Articles; the authority of the executive directors is spelled out in the by-laws. The role of the executive directors is also addressed in I. Shihata, *The World Bank Legal Papers* (The Hague: Brill Academic Publishers, 2000), p. 639.

[121] Art. V, Sect. 5, IBRD Articles.

[122] Art. V, Sect 5 (b), IBRD; Art. VI, Sect. 5 IDA Articles.

[123] Art. V, Sect. 5 (a), p. 4, IBRD. [124] See *supra* Ch 1.A.I.1.

wide latitude in the Bank's policy formulation, a state of affairs which continues today.[125, 126]

Although the dual legal personality of the World Bank has little organizational significance, the two organizations nevertheless differ in terms of their objectives, their policy instruments and their modes of funding. The IDA was founded in 1960 with the express goal of fostering economic development and raising living standards in particularly poor countries.[127] In pursuing this goal, the organization has been assigned a specific group of client countries and set of instruments. The IDA may direct resources only to the poorest countries (Art. V, Sect. 1 a) and only to projects that "are of high development priority" (Art. V, Sect. 1 b).[128] These countries receive assistance on flexible and concessionary terms that weigh less heavily on recipients' countries budgets than IBRD loans (Art. I).[129] In contrast to the IBRD, the IDA's awards are not based primarily on recipient nations' creditworthiness, but rather on need. This orientation is important to the

[125] The details of the delicate balance between executive directors and the President are addressed in Shihata, *World Bank Legal Papers*, p. 639 (in general), p. 657 (during loan negotiations), p. 676, 677 (chairmanship of the President), p. 695 (budgeting process), p. 705 (organizational power), p. 709 (rule-making).

[126] About 10,000 employees are organized under the President's leadership according to two fundamental criteria, regional and thematic. The six regional concentrations are Sub-Saharan Africa, East Asia and Pacific, Europe and Central Asia, Latin America and the Caribbean, Middle East and North Africa, and South Asia. The thematic concentration groups related thematic responsibilities in different departments. These groupings are also called networks, and are as follows: Environmentally and Socially Sustainable Development, Financial Sector Network, Human Development Network, Poverty Reduction and Economic Management, and Private Sector Development and Infrastructure. Some independent departments are of particular importance. Among these are Operations Policy and Country Services, Operations Evaluations, Development Economics and, last but not least, Legal. The networks are usually run by Vice-Presidents who, along with the President, comprise the Bank's senior management. There is thus no institutional separation between the policy-leadership level and technical implementation organizations, although there is, of course, a hierarchical differentiation of responsibilities. In addition, there has never been a serious attempt at decentralization. By and large, employees work at the Bank's headquarters in Washington, DC. These structures are discussed in more detail in World Bank, *Guide*, pp. 23–8.

[127] Art. I, IDA Articles; see also *supra* Ch 1.A.I.

[128] The Bank classifies member states according to their per-capital incomes as low-, middle- or high-income countries. The IDA lends primarily to low-income countries, while the IBRD lends mostly to middle-income ones. See World Bank, *Guide*, pp. 73–7. The transition from one category into another is called "graduation." Shihata, *World Bank Legal Papers*, p. 493.

[129] The IDA's financing instruments are described in L. F. Guder, "International Development Association," in Wolfrum, *Max Planck Encyclopedia of Public International Law* at margin nos. 10–6.

analysis presented in this book: since only the IDA lends money on a concessional basis, only it (and not the IBRD) qualifies as a provider of ODA according to the OECD definition.[130] Thus, only IDA funding is properly subject to the development cooperation law.

The groups' different goals are also reflected in their different modes of financing. Certainly, both arms of the World Bank operate on the basis of member states' contribution to the capital base of the organization. Nevertheless, this capital is not used in either organization for ongoing expenditures, which are funded from various other sources. The IBRD raises funds primarily by issuing (triple A) bonds on the world's capital markets and from loan proceeds; it can thus properly be called a bank.[131] This option is not available to the IDA, since it issues mainly interest-free loans and earns very little profit. Its operations are funded largely by special contributions from member states. These so-called "replenishments" are negotiated every three years.[132] The funds from replenishments are complemented by loan repayments and by not insignificant cross-financing from the IBRD and the IFC's income.[133] To oversimplify somewhat, one can say that the IBRD is dependent on Wall Street, while the IDA relies on its richer member states.

Another characteristic of the Bank should be remembered: the fact that its membership is almost universal and thus, in contrast to the EU, composed of *both* donor and recipient states. The World Bank is thus in

[130] See OECD, *Development Co-operation Report 2009*, margin no. 192.

[131] Discussed at length in Wiegand, *Organisatorische Aspekte*, pp. 216–19.

[132] In 2008, the 15th Replenishment was agreed. Each replenishment is negotiated between the representatives of the 45 current donor nations, the so-called IDA Deputies (not, however, the Executive Directors, see IDA 14, Replenishment Report, p. i; on IDA Deputies see Shihata, *World Bank Legal Papers*, p. 564. When the replenishment and the associated recommendations have been agreed to, the EDs present the Report with Recommendations to the Board of Governors. If the Board adopts the recommentations, it will then promulgate a Resolution (see IDA 14, Replenishment Report, Annex 3, p. 62). Legally, this is an act of the Board of Governors – which act, in turn, binds the Member States. The donors bind themselves by means of the so-called "Instrument of Commitment," a declaration that contains the specific form and amount of the payment and which is signed by donor state representatives. A model form for this instrument is found in an attachment to the 14th Replenishment Resolution (see IDA 14, Replenishment Report, p. 76, Attachment 1). On the difficult negotiations surrounding the first replenishments see Wiegand, *Organisatorische Aspekte*, pp. 219–21; on the current practice see generally Guder, "International Development Association," margin nos. 18–19 and Rigo Sureda, "Law," 54–6.

[133] In the 15th replenishment, US$41 billion came from donor commitments, while another US$16 billion came from the IBRD and IFC and loan for givenesses (Guder, "International Development Association," margin no. 18.

principle a North *and* South institution.[134] Nevertheless, the fact that a common institution exists does not imply that all members are subject to the same rules. Various special regulations apply. To begin with, the difference between donor and recipient states, which are respectively called Part 1 and Part 2 countries according to the founding treaties, manifests itself in different payment regulations. A country that designates itself as a Part 2 country (i.e. a recipient country) may pay 90 percent of its initial capital contribution in its own currency, while Part 1 countries must pay in gold or a freely convertible currency.[135] Upon accession, each country decides on its own classification.

More importantly, the difference between recipient and donor states is manifested primarily in the weighted voting and representation rules for individual member states. Unlike the UN, these rules are not based on the principle of equality; rather they depend on the amount of a member state's contribution to the Bank's capital base.[136] This has two consequences. First, there is a percentage-based allocation of votes in the various bodies constituted by member states. As the state which has contributed the most capital, the United States has 16.41 percent of the votes; Germany, the third-largest contributor, has 4.49 percent.[137] The weighting system also affects the question of representation through an Executive Director in the Executive Council. Only the five largest contributors have their own Executive Director. The remaining twenty Executive Directors each represent a group of countries. The financial strength of a member state, as well as its willingness to contribute financially, are directly rewarded with an increase of formal powers in the Bank. Thus, although the Bank has almost universal membership, it is dominated by industrialized states.[138]

[134] On the role of the North–South groups see Wiegand, *Organisatorische Aspekte*, pp. 290–303; on the role of the Eastern Bloc states see Mason and Asher, *World Bank Since Bretton Woods*, p. 63.

[135] Art. II, Sect. 2 (d), IDA Articles.

[136] Art. V, Sect. 3, IBRD Articles; Art. VI Sect. 3, IDA Articles; see Ragazzi, "Financial Institutions, International," margin no. 13; with regard to the IDA see Shihata, *World Bank Legal Papers*, pp. 580–90; see also Wiegand, *Organisatorische Aspekte*, pp. 240; 277.

[137] The system is particularly well described in High-Level Commission on Modernization of World Bank Group Governance, *Repowering the World Bank for the 21st Century: Report 10/2009* (Washington, DC, 2009), margin nos. 78–94. Available at http://siteresources.worldbank.org/NEWS/Resources/WBGovernanceCOMMISSIONREPORT.pdf (last visited July 2013) [hereinafter High-Level Commission, *Repowering the World Bank*].

[138] This aspect is often cited as a central critique of the World Bank, see, e.g. N. Woods, "Making the IMF and the World Bank More Accountable," *International Affairs*, 77

The dominance of Western countries in the Bank's governance structure has been criticized for many years. One answer has been to initiate the so-called *Voice and Participation Reform* in 2008. In its second phase, approved by the member states at the spring meeting of 2010, it reorganized the voting weights.[139] The states of Sub-Saharan Africa have now a third Executive Director and the voting bloc of developing countries and emerging economies was lifted by 3.13 percent to 47.19 percent.[140]

The USA is a telling example of one state being more equal than the others. According to an informal agreement with European member states, the American government has the right to nominate Bank Presidents. Up to this point, the USA has nominated exclusively US citizens, in a process that takes place entirely within the American government.[141] This process is a particularly stark example of the oft-criticized influence of the American government on the Bank's operations.[142]

The last component of the Bank's organizational structure that merits our attention is the Inspection Panel. Founded in 1993, it constitutes an unprecedented example of legal control and supervision vested in an entity within an international organization.[143] The Panel has the authority to check whether Bank employees have obeyed internal rules during

(2001), 83–101 at 85–89; see also the recommendations of the High-Level Commission, *Repowering the World Bank*, margin no. 122.

139 Enhancing Voice of and Participation of Developing and Transition Countries, World Bank Group Voice Reform, DC2010-0006 (April 19, 2010), p. 1.

140 World Bank Group Reform: An Update; DC2010-0014 (September 30, 2010), p. 11.

141 In return, Europeans nominate the President of the IMF. This informal practice has been subjected to intensive critique (see World Bank Group Reform: An Update; DC 2010-0014 (September 30, 2010), p. 87). Suggestions for change can be found ibid., margin no. 139.

142 Killinger, *The World Bank's Non-Political Mandate*, pp. 81–3; J. Kranz, *Entre l'influence et l'intervention: Certains aspects juridiques de l'assistance financière multilaterale* (Frankfurt: Peter Lang Verlag, 1994), pp. 248–62; Yokota, "Non-Political Character of the World Bank," 39; see also B. Brown, *The United States and the Politicization of the World Bank* (London: Kegan Paul International, 1992), pp. 170–230.

143 IBRD Resolution, No. 93-10 and IDA Resolution, No. 93-6 of September 22, 1993 (also contained in Operational Policy, Nr. 17.55, Annex A). A considerable body of literature on the Inspection Panel exists, see, e.g. I. Shihata, *The World Bank Inspection Panel* (Oxford University Press, 2000); A. Orakhelashvili, "The World Bank Inspection Panel in Context," *International Organizations Law Review*, 2 (2005), 57–102 at 57; A. Naude Fourie, *The World Bank Inspection Panel and Quasi-Judicial Oversight: In Search of "Judicial Spirit" in Public International Law* (Utrecht: Eleven International Publishing, 2009); E. Baimu and A. Panou, "Responsibility of International Organizations and the World Bank Inspection Panel: Parallel Tracks Unlikely to Converge?" in Cissé, Bradlow and Kingsbury, *International Financial Institutions*, vol. III, pp. 147–72. See also *infra* Ch 9.B.I.1.a.

the planning and implementation of Bank-financed projects. The three-person Panel is independent of the Bank's management, reporting not to the President but only to the Executive Directors. A particularly notable feature of the Panel is that it can receive complaints directly from citizens affected by Bank-financed operations. The Panel thus does not serve state proceedings, but rather ensures the Bank's direct responsibility toward those who are supposed to profit from Bank-financed projects, but are often enough instead harmed by them. The Panel is an innovative approach to ensuring more direct accountability in international organizations. Its effectiveness should not, however, be overestimated. The Inspection Panel is not itself entitled to impose penalties or award compensation. It can only request management to correct mistakes. Its caseload is also limited.[144] Nevertheless, it would be wrong to underestimate the subtle influence of its jurisprudence.[145]

2. Legal framework

What distinguishes the World Bank from other international organizations – and justifies comparison with the EU – is the comparatively intensive and formalized legal regulation of its activities. Two different levels of norms are particularly important here.[146]

The normative framework of the Bank's actions is determined primarily by the founding treaties of 1944 (IBRD) and 1960 (IDA), which represent the Bank's "constitutional" foundations.[147] These so-called Articles of Agreement determine the purpose and mandate of the organizations, their membership and contribution rules, the basic principles governing their activities, and their organizational structure. The Articles also regulate important principles of ODA allocations, for example, the priority given to funding of specific projects, the priority of bank loans as against those from private lenders, or the sovereignty and hence required consent of recipient countries.[148] The right to issue binding, authoritative interpretations of the Articles is reserved for the Bank's Executive Directors.

[144] In its almost 20-year history, it has received 77 cases.

[145] This will become clearer *infra* Ch 6.B.I.

[146] On the Bank's obligation to comply with public international law see D. Bradlow, "International Law and the Operations of the International Financial Institutions," in Bradlow and Hunter, *International Financial Institutions*, pp. 11–23.

[147] Killinger, *The World Bank's Non-Political Mandate*, p. 42. On the importance of the primary law of international organizations for understanding their secondary law, see A. von Bogdandy, P. Dann and M. Goldmann, "Developing the Publicness of Public International Law," *German Law Journal* **9** (2008), 1375–400 at 1391, 1392.

[148] Art. V, Sect. 1 b), c) and e), IDA Articles.

Since 1964, however, the directors have issued such interpretations only after previous consultation with and on the basis of the expert opinion of the Bank's General Counsel. The General Counsel, who heads the Bank's legal department, thus plays a central role in interpreting the Articles.[149]

Of particular importance for ODA allocations (and therefore for our perspective here) is the Bank's secondary law, the formality and precision of which distinguish it from the secondary law of many other international organizations.[150] This secondary law is contained mainly in the so-called Operational Policies (OP) and Bank Procedures (BP).[151] These are legal instruments of general scope that regulate the behavior of the Bank's employees.

More concretely, OPs are described as "short, focused statements that follow from the Bank's Articles of Agreement, the general conditions, and policies approved by the Board. OPs establish the parameters for the conduct of operations," while BPs "explain how Bank staff carries out the policies set out in the OPs. They spell out the procedures and documentation required to ensure Bank-wide consistency and quality."[152] In other words, OPs are rather short provisions that spell out general policies, while BPs provide detailed regulations for concrete procedures and instruments, as well as the substantive standards applicable to loan and other agreements.

OPs and BPs are the product of an internal norm-setting process that reflects a precarious institutional balance.[153] The Articles of Agreement

[149] I. Shihata, "The Creative Role of Lawyers: Example: The Office of the World Bank's General Counsel," *Catholic University Law Review*, 48 (1999), 1041–53 at 1148–50. The interpretive prerogative of the General Counsel became particularly clear in the context of two questions: first, whether the World Bank can support governance projects, and second, the permissibility of structural adjustment measures and budget support (see *supra* Ch 3.A.IV.3 and 26.I). On the Bank's legal department see generally Sarfaty, "Why Culture Matters," 674–7. The Articles are supplemented by By-Laws which contain the specific rules for institutional interaction within the bank and which are adopted by the Board of Governors.

[150] On the broad spectrum of secondary law of international institutions see the contributions to Bogdandy, Wolfrum, Bernstorff, Dann and Goldmann, *Exercise of Public Authority*; Alvarez, *International Organizations*.

[151] On this category of legal instruments see ibid., p. 235; B. Kingsbury, "Operational Policies of International Institutions as Part of the Law-Making Process," in G. Goodwin-Gill and S. Talmon (eds.), *The Reality of International Law* (Oxford University Press, 1999), pp. 323–42 at p. 323.

[152] http://go.worldbank.org/DZDZ9038D0 (last visited June 2013).

[153] See Hunter, "International Law and Public Participation in Policy-Making at the International Financial Institutions," in Bradlow and Hunter, *International Financial Institutions and International Law* (Alphen aan den Rijn: Kluwer Law

do not specify which organ has the power to issue internal secondary norms – in particular, they do not specify whether it is the prerogative of the Board of Directors (and thus the member-state representatives) or the management of the Bank. In the system that has emerged over time and is now consolidated practice, the Board of Directors is responsible for setting out the basic outline of policy, leaving management the prerogative to formulate the concrete rules.[154] In practice, new norms or changes to existing norms are developed by the Bank's Operational Policies and Country Services department and then examined by a committee of the Bank management, the Operational Policies Committee. During this evaluation, the Bank management consults the Board of Directors and obtains its approval of the basic principles of the proposed policy. However, management retains the power to decide on the details of the policy. Further, the general public is increasingly made part of the process. Where policies are under consideration that affect the interests of particular groups, the Bank has published drafts and invited comments from interested parties.[155]

Once adopted, all OPs and BPs become part of the so-called Operational Manual, the compilation of the Bank's internal norms, and are published on the Internet, among other places.[156] Thus, not only the Bank's employees but everybody can see which rules the Bank is obliged to follow and can check compliance.

It is important to note that the Bank's system of legal instruments distinguishes between the Articles of Agreement as "constitutional foundations," binding secondary law as contained in OPs and BPs and other instructions. It hence establishes a clear hierarchy of norms. By differentiating between categories of legal instrument and specifying their respective rank or priority, it lays the foundations for a hierarchy in which the founding treaties have primacy over the OPs and BPs, and these over other, more internal, rules.[157]

International,2010) pp.199–386 at pp. 223–30; on different examples of creating secondary laws in international organizations see Alvarez, *International Organizations*; Bogdandy, Wolfrum, Bernstorff, Dann and Goldmann, *Exercise of Public Authority*; J. D. Aston, *Sekundärgesetzgebung internationaler Organisationen zwischen mitgliedstaatlicher Souveränität und Gemeinschaftsdisziplin* (Berlin: Duncker & Humblot, 2005).

154 See Shihata, *World Bank Inspection Panel*, p. 42.

155 See Kingsbury, "Operational Policies," pp. 324, 325.

156 See http://web.worldbank.org/WBSITE/EXTERNAL/PROJECTS/EXTPOLICIES/EXTOPMANUAL/0,,menuPK:64701637~pagePK:51628525~piPK:64857279~theSitePK:502184,00.html (last visited July 2013).

157 On the features that distinguish various legal instruments and which thus permit judgment of the normativity of norms see M. Goldmann, "Inside Relative Normativity: From

The binding character of the OPs and BPs is underlined by another feature of World Bank law, namely that compliance with the OPs and BPs is monitored by the Inspection Panel to the extent that they relate to the evaluation and implementation of projects or to harm caused by non-observance of the rules. The relevant norm specifies which norms are to be observed in which contexts and where compliance can be monitored.[158] It follows that the regulations concerning the medium-term planning phase are not subject to legal control by the Panel, but only the rules that govern the project cycle in a narrow sense, that is, the elaboration, agreement and implementation of a Bank-financed project.[159] In sum, the concrete procedures of ODA awards and the OPs and BPs which regulate them are subject to largely independent monitoring.

This comparatively formalized legal framework and the system of secondary law in particular has emerged in two main reform periods. The first of these periods was the early 1990s. Massive criticism of the Narmada dam project in India and of the social consequences of the structural-adjustment loans led to a fundamental rethinking of the Bank's governance system, including its internal rule structure. Reports from external experts had identified weaknesses in quality control and accountability on the part of the Bank's employees, and the complexity and vagueness of the Bank's internal rules were seen as major contributors to these weaknesses.[160] In order to address these issues, the Bank decided to establish a more transparent system of legal instruments which would differentiate more clearly between binding and non-binding norms. To that end, it introduced the categories OP and BP in 1992 as binding legal norms, whereas other norms (such as Operational Directives or Good Practices)

Sources to Standard Instruments for the Exercise of International Public Authority," in Bogdandy, Wolfrum, Bernstorff, Dann and Goldmann (eds.), *Exercise of Public Authority*, pp. 661–711 at pp. 684.

158 IBRD Resolution 93–10, margin no. 12. The relevant passage reads: "The affected party must demonstrate that its rights or interests have been or are likely to be directly affected by an action or omission of the Bank as a result of a *failure of the Bank to follow its operational policies and procedures* with respect to the design, appraisal and/or implementation of a project financed by the Bank. … For purposes of this Resolution, 'operational policies and procedures' consist of the Bank's Operational Policies, Bank Procedures and Operational Directives, and similar documents issued before these series were started, and does not include Guidelines and Best Practices and similar documents or statements."

159 These two phases are addressed *infra* Ch 5.C.I. and Ch 6.B.I.

160 For more on the Wappenhans Report in particular, see Darrow, *Between Light and Shadow*, pp. 196–8.

were described as non-binding.[161] Furthermore, there was considerable pressure to establish better oversight as to how the rules are complied with, which led in 1993 to the creation of the Inspection Panel.

The second period of major reforms started around the year 2008. This time, the Bank found itself less confronted with doubts over concrete projects but with the even more fundamental question about its purpose and instruments vis-à-vis private and emerging new donors, as well as its general record of results.[162] And once again, the complexity of a system of norms that has grown incrementally and with little systematic structuring is seen as a major impediment to achieving better results, more accountability and competitiveness in the larger context. The Bank therefore started a major effort to revise and restructure its system of international regulations. Before the reform, the Operational Manual contained some 100 policies, spread out over some 700 pages. A central aim of this second reform was therefore the consolidation and simplification of the system.[163] This affected the Bank's rules on its lending instruments as well as the safeguard policies. With regard to the lending instruments, a central path to achieving a more accessible legal architecture was to organize rules into one major policy for each of the main lending instruments (and hence collate previously scattered norms). These are now OP/BP 10.00 (investment lending), OP/BP 8.60 (development policy lending) and OP/BP 9.00 (program-for-results financing). In particular, the Bank conducted a comprehensive review and consolidation of its regulations on investment lending (10.00).[164] The Bank is also conducting a major overhaul of the normative structure of its safeguard policies.[165] This too aims in particular at providing a more accessible, better structured normative architecture.

[161] On this see L. Boisson de Chazournes, "Policy Guidance and Compliance: The World Operational Standards," in D. Shelton (ed.), *Commitment and Compliance: The Role of Non-Binding Norms in the International Legal System* (Oxford, New York: Oxford University Press, 2000), pp. 281–303 at pp. 283–5.

[162] On the challenging context, see above Ch 2 B.IV and Ch 2. C. III; World Bank, Development Committee, New World, New World Bank Group, Internal Reform Agenda, DC 2010–004 (April 20, 2010).

[163] See World Bank, Committee on Development Effectiveness (CODE), The Bank's Operational Manual: Issues for Reform, Approach Paper, April 2011.

[164] In particular on the Investment Lending reform, see World Bank, Investment Lending Reform Concept note, January 26, 2009 – and World Bank, Investment Lending Reform: Modernizing and Consolidating Operational Policies and Procedures, November 1, 2012. The new OP/BP 10.00 was published on April 8, 2013.

[165] World Bank, The World Bank's Safeguard Policies Proposed Review and Update. Approach Paper, October 10, 2012.

Another aspect of this reform is the Bank's rules on access to documents. These rules are of general importance for making the World Bank's activities both easier to follow and to control. In what was a rather unusual step for an international organization at the time, the World Bank issued a first policy on access to information in the 1980s, which has since been reformed in 1993, 2002 and 2005.[166] The policy introduced a positive list of documents that had to be made publicly available. In 2010, the system was overhauled and access to documents was substantially widened with the "Access to Information Policy" that came into force on July 1, 2010.[167] According to the new policy, all documents are generally available to the public, unless they are subject to an explicit exception. The positive list was therefore replaced by a negative list, establishing the principle of free access to information at the Bank.[168]

In general, it can be said that the World Bank, as an international organization, has a fairly well-consolidated, publicly accessible and systematic internal legal system. The reasons for this "legalization" of the Bank, however, have rarely been discussed. One can assume that the process was probably the result of considerable public pressure since the 1990s, an ongoing struggle between Bank management and member states, who were each seeking autonomy or tighter control over the other, and also the organizational competition between the World Bank and other reform-minded institutions, such as the International Finance Corporation or the Asian Development Bank.

3. Mandate (and the prohibition on political interference)

The question of the Bank's mandate and goals highlights another peculiarity of the Bank's law that differentiates it from German or EU development administrations. On the one hand, the basic mandate of the Bank is relatively broad, requiring it to serve the purpose of member-state development. This basic purpose is shared by other donors as well. On the other hand, the Bank is bound more than others to

[166] This development is described in a table attached as an Annex to World Bank, *Towards Greater Transparency Through Access to Information: The World Bank's Disclosure Policy* (Washington, DC: World Bank Publications, 2009) Annex A.

[167] Ibid.

[168] For an analysis of the new regulations see P. Dann, "Der Zugang zu Dokumenten im Recht der Weltbank: Kosmopolitische Tendenzen im Internationalen Verwaltungsrecht?" *Die Verwaltung*, 44 (2011), 313–25; the origins of the policy are described in Hunter, "International Law and Public Participation," at pp. 221–3. For a critical analysis, see also *infra* Ch 9.B.I.

a solid economic basis for its loans and is also subject to an explicit prohibition on political interference, a unique provision in development law. The ban, in turn, complicates the implementation and fulfillment of the Bank's development goals. These two aspects will be briefly addressed here.

According to Art. I(i) of the IBRD Articles, the IBRD's purpose is "to assist in the reconstruction and development of territories of members by facilitating the investment of capital for productive purposes, including … the encouragement of the development of productive facilities and resources in less developed countries." The IDA's purpose, according to Art. I of its founding treaty, is "to promote economic development, increase productivity and thus raise standards of living in less developed areas of the world." Both organizations are thus obliged to serve the economic development of the Third World. The more explicit focus on promotion of prosperity in the IDA articles is explained by the fact that when the IDA was founded in 1960, decolonization was in progress and it had become clear that a large number of immensely poor new countries would be in need of funds and expertise. The IDA was thus founded with the purpose of extending concessionary loans to these countries.[169] For both organizations, the defining goal of development is defined, as seen above, in a very open fashion and is today consensually conceived of as to encompasses the aim of opening up social, political and cultural opportunities.[170]

However, supporting development in such a broad sense may conflict with the prohibition on political interference in recipient countries, articulated in both founding treaties.[171] During the founding years of the Bank, the prohibition on interference grew naturally from the then-dominant assumptions concerning development, world politics and the Bank's organization. Until well into the 1970s, development was conceived primarily as an economic process oriented towards increasing growth.[172] It was also the case that in the political context of the Cold War, the Bank would have significantly restricted the potential scope and

169 On the background see *supra* Ch 1.A.I.2.

170 For a more thorough discussion of the idea of development, see *supra* Ch 2.B.

171 Art. V, Sect. 10, IBRD Articles; Art. V, Sect. 6, IDA Articles. The provision reads: "The Association and its officers shall not interfere in the political affairs of any member, nor shall they be influenced in their decisions by the political character of the member or members concerned. Only economic considerations shall be relevant to their decisions, and these considerations shall be weighed impartially in order to achieve the purposes stated in this Agreement."

172 See *supra* Ch 1.A.IV.

effectiveness of its activities had it adopted an open political orientation.[173] Furthermore, the early years of the Bank were dominated by the notion of functionalism, as well as a general trust in technocratic-neutral institutions of international cooperation and expertise.[174] The apolitical mandate of the organization which grew from these early assumptions has become deeply rooted in the Bank's self-understanding. The Bank sees itself primarily as a genuine *bank*, which operates according to economic categories and a largely technocratic ethos.[175]

Since the 1980s, and particularly during the 1990s, the Bank's prohibition on political interference has increasingly conflicted with the changing concept of development and the Bank's operational agenda.[176] The Bank at first began making macroeconomic structural-adjustment loans instead of financing specific projects. Even this first step involved conditioning funding on general economic-policy reforms, thus testing the boundaries of the Bank's mandate. Since the early 1990s, under the heading of "governance," the Bank has made institutional reforms the object of its projects, blurring the boundary between its economic mandate and political goals.[177]

Whether these activities can be reconciled with the Bank's apolitical mandate remains controversial.[178] The Bank's long-serving General Counsel, Ibrahim Shihata, who served during this fundamental

[173] It is generally assumed that an important reason for the insertion of the ban on political interference – which did not exist in the original draft of the IBRD articles – was to reassure the Soviet Union. It was thought that the Soviets could thus be convinced to participate in the activities of a clearly Western-dominated bank, see Mason and Asher, *World Bank Since Bretton Woods*, pp. 19, 27; A thorough description of the origins of the clause is found in Killinger, *The World Bank's Non-Political Mandate*, pp. 91–6. On the evolving practice of the Bank regarding the political prohibition and current frontier issues, see H. Cissé, "Should the Political Prohibition in Charters of International Financial Institutions Be Revisited? The Case of the World Bank," in Cissé, Bradlow and Kingsbury, *International Financial Institutions*, pp. 62–81. Cissé concludes that "[t]he interpretation of this clause has served the organization well," p. 90.

[174] D. Mitrany, "The Functional Approach to World Organization," *International Affairs*, 24 (1948), 350–63 at 359; D. Mitrany, *A Working Peace System* (Chicago: Quadrangle Books, 1966).

[175] Sarfaty, "Why Culture Matters," 667–76; Wiegand, *Organisatorische Aspekte*, pp. 303.

[176] On the corresponding development see *supra* Ch 2.A.II, 6.III. Killinger, *The World Bank's Non-Political Mandate* and *infra* Ch 4.C (in particular, Ch 4.C.III.2).

[177] Other practices that are seen as contentious with regard to the political prohibition include criminal justice reforms, engagement in far-reaching reconstruction activities in post-conflict environments, or the decision to engage with extraconstitutional de facto governments.

[178] Extensively discussed in Killinger, *The World Bank's Non-Political Mandate*, pp. 80–9 and sources cited therein.

transformation of Bank policy, saw its activities as consistent with its founding treaties. Since changing the Bank's founding treaties is hardly possible owing to the procedural complexity such an amendment would require, Shihata's 1990 legal opinion on this issue remains the Bank's principal yardstick.[179] In that document, Shihata argued that it is indeed possible to separate permissible economic from impermissible political considerations. The key is whether an aspect has "direct and obvious economic results." Only if this is so can the Bank take it into account in its activities.[180] In the literature, however, there are many critical voices which accuse the Bank of having violated its mandate for many years now and of having hollowed-out the sovereignty of recipient countries.[181] The distinction between political and economic considerations is seen by these critics as unworkable, and its continued observance as more of a strategy of obfuscation than a genuine attempt to circumscribe the Bank's powers. Nevertheless, one can defend the Bank's work, not by Shihata's rather unconvincing distinction but rather by orienting it in the context of an expanded concept of development. Stefanie Killinger has argued convincingly that the ban on political interference can hardly be understood today as binding the Bank to a narrow, purely economic idea of development, which has long been outmoded.[182] To what extent the Bank nonetheless threatens to interfere with recipient-country sovereignty in violation of international law will be addressed later in this book.

V. *Relationships between donors: a heterarchical multi-level system*

Donors do not operate in isolation but interact, particularly when active in the same recipient country. In this section, the question of how – or whether – these relationships are organized will be addressed. The question is not simply of theoretical interest. Rather, the multiplicity of donors has been seen for some time as one of the central problems of development

179 This has been reprinted in (and will be cited as): Shihata, *The World Bank in a Changing World I*, pp. 53 (also reprinted in later collections of his writings, in particular Shihata, *World Bank Legal Papers*, pp. 248–81).

180 Shihata, *The World Bank in a Changing World*, vol. I, p. 94. Shihata prefaces his distinctions with a thorough conceptual analysis (ibid., pp. 67–70, pp. 75–79. He then marks out five activities which are prohibited, contrasting them with four activities which are allowed (ibid., pp. 82–93; see also *supra* Ch 2.B.III).

181 Tsai, "Globalization," 1327; M. Wadrzyk, "Is It Appropriate for the World Bank to Promote Democratic Standards in a Borrowing Country?" *Wisconsin International Law Journal*, 17 (1999), 553–77 at 567.

182 Killinger, *The World Bank's Non-Political Mandate*, pp. 74, 75.

cooperation,[183] since it increases transaction costs, fosters fruitless competition and often overburdens the ministries of recipient countries.[184] The negative consequences of this plurality of donors are mostly practical in nature, as direct or indirect normative conflicts with regard to concrete projects are difficult to imagine.[185] On the other hand, the practical costs of this plurality are sufficiently high to make it worthwhile asking whether there are legal ways to contain them. Are there, in fact, relevant norms that help to coordinate donors?

The first place to look is a series of bilateral cooperation agreements between donors. The World Bank, in particular, has concluded agreements with the UN[186] and the EU.[187] These contain either rather general rules[188] or very specific provisions to regulate the administration of trust funds.[189] They do not contain specific operative rules for cooperation.

Thus, the first answer to the question posed above is no. The relationships between donors in terms of their competences to engage somewhere are, as a legal matter, basically unregulated. This seems obvious with regard to the *horizontal* relationship among national donors, for instance between Germany and the USA. But there are also no rules regulating the vertical relationship between donors. Nor, for that matter, are there general rules governing horizontal divisions of responsibility between international organizations.[190] A ban on interference between organizations

[183] Friedmann, Kalmanoff and Meagher, *International Financial Aid*, p. 135; A. Broches, "International Bank for Reconstruction and Development," in S. Rubin (ed.), *Foreign Development Lending – Legal Aspects*. The papers and proceedings of a conference of legal advisors of national and international development lending and assistance agencies (Leiden: Sijthoff, 1971), pp. 79–93 at pp. 79, 80; Betz, *Internationalisierung*; Kaplan, *International Aid Coordination*.

[184] For a detailed description of the problems, see *supra* Ch 2.C.II.1 and sources cited therein.

[185] On the forms of normative collision and possible solutions see Matz, *Wege zur Koordinierung*, p. 6; International Law Commission, *Fragmentation of International Law: Difficulties Arising from the Diversification and Expansion of International Law*, United Nations Report. Available at http://untreaty.un.org/ilc/sessions/56/56sess.htm (last visited September 2012).

[186] Reprinted in in UN-GA, Res 92 (V), adopted by the Economic and Social Council 1947.

[187] Trust Fund and Co-financing Framework Agreement between the EC and the IBRD, IDA, IFC and MIGA, November 2001.

[188] This is true of the agreement with the UN.

[189] This is true of the agreement with the EU.

[190] On the outlines of a theory of the competences of international organizations see N. Weiß, *Kompetenzlehre Internationaler Organizationen* (Heidelberg: Springer, 2009), pp. 383; see also M. Ruffert and C. Walter, *Institutionalisiertes Völkerrecht: Das Recht der Internationalen Organizationen und seine wichtigsten Anwendungsfelder* (Munich: C.H. Beck, 2009), pp. 76, 77.

in this context has been suggested but has not been realized.[191] Art. 103 of the United Nations Charter could be seen as indirectly committing member states to avoid conflicts, but it regulates only conflicting provisions (a "conflict" of "obligations") and does not guarantee the UN dominance as against other organizations.[192] The legal situation within the UN family could be different. The International Court of Justice has held that a principle of "functional specialization" applies within the UN family.[193] This principle would mean that an organization is only responsible for its own specialized portfolio, and it could be applicable to the World Bank and to UN programs. However, such a principle would make little sense in the context of development aid. There, a large number of UN organizations are active in a variety of closely related and often overlapping areas, making a clear thematic differentiation of competencies near impossible.[194] This fact would also make the practical implementation of a ban on interference impossible.

Nevertheless, it is possible to envisage divisions of responsibility between donors which are part of a *vertically* integrated multi-level system or a federal state. This would apply, for instance, to the EU and its member states or the Federal Republic of Germany and its constituent states.[195] Here, the relationships of the donors would be rather a question of an *internal* division of labor and could conceivably be regulated on a hierarchical basis (i.e. EU would trump member-state action). However, in reality, there are no examples of such a structure – as shown by the example of the EU.

Between the EU and its member states, development cooperation is a parallel competence, where EU activity and member-state activity do not

[191] M. Ruffert, "Zuständigkeitsgrenzen internationaler Organisationen im institutionellen Rahmen der internationalen Gemeinschaft," *Archiv des Völkerrechts*, 38 (2000), 129–68 at 161.

[192] Ibid., 165–7.

[193] International Court of Justice, *Legality of the Threat or Use of Nuclear Weapons* (1996), p. 65. Available at www.icj-cij.org/docket/index.php?p1=3&p2=4&k=e1&p3=4&case=95 (last visited September 2012).

[194] See Killinger, *The World Bank's Non-Political Mandate*, pp. 70–3.

[195] German states (Bundesländer) as well as municipalities may pursue their own development policies. On their respective competences, see J. Wiemann, *Die Neuausrichtung der Entwicklungspolitik der Bundesländer vor dem Hintergrund der veränderten internationalen Rahmenbedingungen: Discussion Paper No. 20.* Available at www.die-gdi.de (last visited July 2013); K. O. Nass, "Recht und Praxis der Entwicklungspolitik der deutschen Länder," *Die Öffentliche Verwaltung*, 49 (1996), 274–82 at 274; M. von Schwanenflügel, *Entwicklungszusammenarbeit als Aufgabe der Gemeinden und Kreise*, Schriften zum Öffentlichen Recht (Berlin: Duncker & Humblot, 1993), vol. DCXXXI.

affect each other. Thus it can be called a heterarchical multi-level system. The EU were allowed autonomous activities in the area of development cooperation only slowly and, at least at first, without an explicit basis in the EC Treaty (excepting the cooperation with ACP states).[196] Only the Maastricht Treaty in 1993 introduced such a basis. Even before, it was assumed that the competencies of the EU and its member states in the field of development cooperation were parallel competencies.[197] Today, Art. 4 IV of the TFEU explicitly formulates a competence of the Union to "conduct a common policy; however, the exercise of that competence shall not result in member states being prevented from exercising theirs."[198] Rather, according to Art. 208 I 2 of the TFEU, the EU development policy should "complement" that of the member states. It can thus be assumed that EU and member-state policies should not fully contradict and undermine each other, but rather coexist. This parallel structure is explained primarily by the fact that in the area of development aid, there is no "implementation federalism," that is, the upper level is not dependent on the lower level for implementation of its laws. Therefore, there is no functional pressure to cooperate. Thus, even within an integrated union such as the EU and its member states, the competences of donors – though not completely legally independent – are nevertheless parallel in status. The multi-level system of development cooperation is thus characterized by heterarchy, not by precedence and hierarchy.

In the final analysis, an unusual situation prevails: the development arena is not only populated by international organizations that, just like their national counterparts, make independent ODA disbursements and are therefore responsible for managing cash flows. They are even legally of the same level. Hence, there is a heterarchy among the national, supranational and international donors.

[196] See *infra* Ch 3.A.III.2. See generally P. Dann, "§34 Europäisches Entwicklungsverwaltungsrecht," in J. P. Terhechte (ed.), *Verwaltungsrecht der Europäischen Union: Zur Ausdifferenzierung und Globalisierung der europäischen Verwaltungsrechtsordnung* (Baden-Baden: Nomos, 2010), pp. 1189–209, Part 1.B.

[197] ECJ, Case 316/91, EU Parliament v Council [1994] ECR I-625, margin no. 26; T. Henze, "Aufgaben- und Ausgabenkompetenzen der Europäischen Gemeinschaft und ihrer Mitgliedstaaten im Bereich der Entwicklungspolitik," *Europarecht*, 30 (1995), 76–86 at 81; B. Martenczuk and A. Zimmermann, "Art. 177 EGV," in J. Schwarze (ed.), *EU-Kommentar*, 2nd edn (Baden-Baden: Nomos, 2009) at margin nos.12, 13 and sources cited therein.

[198] On the category of parallel competences in Union law see A. von Bogdandy and J. Bast, "The Vertical Order of Competences," in A. von Bogdandy and J. Bast (eds.), *Principles of European Constitutional Law* (Oxford: Hart Publishing, 2006), vol. VIII, pp. 335–72 at p. 294.

In view of the practical problems that this situation creates,[199] one might ask whether something like a subsidiarity principle or other rules of precedence might be appropriate. Interestingly enough, the discussions of development policy on this aspect generally tend in the opposite direction. In the current debate (and not just on the side of developing states), the call is for *priority for international donors*, that is, a stronger concentration of competence on the international level leading to the "multilateralization" of development cooperation. Even in the 1970s, it was argued that such multilateralization would limit donor states' frequent and direct instrumentalization of development aid for military, economic or cultural influence on recipient states.[200] Today, there is a similar argument for unifying the competence to make allocations at the level of international donors, on the assumption that this would increase the effectiveness of ODA awards.[201] Donors argued that such pooling would increase the influence of the donors, thereby increasing the potency of the demands associated with the ODA grants.

However, it is exactly this effect that furnishes an argument *against* multilateralization of development aid and against such a "reverse subsidiarity principle." Since such consolidation of power would increase the dominance of donors, it would reduce the negotiating power of recipient nations. Donor dominance is not just a problem because it may facilitate particularly interventionist measures, but also because donors may favor solutions, such as the structural-adjustment loans of the 1980s, that turn out to be simply counterproductive. Authors favoring competition among donors also warn against too much enthusiasm for coordination and multilateralization.[202] For them, pooling or coordination of competences is invariably accompanied by increased planning, which results in an increase in bureaucracy rather than increased problem-solving capacity.

In any event, the discussion remains hypothetical. Although legal efforts to improve donor coordination exist and will be addressed later,[203] there are no hierarchical rules of priority that would regulate the current heterarchy among donors.

[199] See *supra* Ch 2.C.II.

[200] Pearson, *Pearson Report 1969*, pp. 213–15; Betz, *Internationalisierung*, p. 22.

[201] On this discussion see Faust and Messner, "Entwicklungspolitik," p. 228.

[202] D. Whittle and M. Kuraishi, "Competing with Central Planning," in Easterly, *Reinventing Foreign Aid*, p. 461.

[203] Discussed further below in Ch 4.E.III.

VI. Conclusion: two types of development administration

The overview of the institutional structures and legal frameworks generates four basic insights.

First, international donors fulfill basically the same functions as national donors. National as well as international authorities exercise the same authorities by deciding how much and to whom ODA will be given. This is truly unusual. In fact, there might be no other area of global governance where public authorities of different levels execute the same tasks. Thus it is thoroughly appropriate that the present study compares the World Bank, the European Union and Germany – three development administrations on three different levels of public authority.

Second, the analysis has shown that donors generally exercise parallel competencies, making the multi-level system of development aid a *heterarchical multi-level system*. This has various and partly problematic consequences, since it makes coordination among donors as important as it is difficult. These consequences will be addressed later.[204]

The third insight relates to the power to write the laws regulating the ODA transfers. All three donors have adopted extensive rules for ODA allocations. The law of development cooperation is hence clearly dominated by the rules set by donors. The respective rules are of different legal nature. The EU uses its equivalent to a parliamentary law for organizing its ODA activity (regulations). The World Bank issues rules that, at least partly, have external effects (Operational Policies and Bank Procedures). Only Germany has issued exclusively administrative regulations that are merely internally binding. It is striking how little influence recipient states have on the adoption of these regulations. Aside from the EU-ACP context, both the German and the European rules are made in a completely unilateral fashion. It is true that recipient states are represented in the World Bank and are basically involved in the norm-creation process. Nevertheless, their influence is limited by the weighted-voting procedures in the Executive Board, as well as the weak representation of recipient states in the Bank's management. Formally, only the ACP states have considerable influence. The development cooperation between the EU and the ACP Group is governed by the Cotonou Agreement and its appendices.

Finally, comparing donors in terms of mandate, organizational structure and legal frameworks leads to their classification into two general types of development administration. The World Bank represents a

[204] Discussed further in Ch 4.E.III and Ch 5.C.IV.

specialized technocratic organization for development, marked by its focused mandate, centered on development policy, and hence more independent from other policy imperatives. Admittedly, the goal of fostering development is a broad one, and, as we have seen, the borders of the World Bank's mandate are porous. Nevertheless, the Bank is, unlike states or the EU, not required to split its attention among various different tasks, and can focus solely on development. This lends the Bank a technocratic character. This is reinforced by the strong competencies of its management. Of course, member states do play a significant role in the Bank through the Executive Directors. But due to their constant presence in Washington, the Executive Directors share the sectoral focus of the Bank and are therefore somewhat co-opted. The Bank is (more than merely functionally) a *donor* administration. Although its membership is universal, representing both donors and recipients, weighted voting gives donor states the upper hand. In the final analysis, the World Bank can be said to represent a type of technocratic-autonomous development administration.

In the EU, by contrast, development policy is only one part of the wider policy portfolio. The Commission's development administration has to serve a much more thematically diverse foreign policy. This is shaped also by a somewhat "missionary" focus, as the mandate for combating poverty is embedded in the overall goal of exporting constitutional values (such as democracy and human rights). The Commission's orientation is therefore heteronomous – it serves other development goals. Its approach is also more diplomatic than technocratic. The EU, as a whole, is not a technocratic organization, and the rules for development cooperation – in particular with the ACP states – are aligned to diplomatic sensitivities. Another factor explaining development's position within the broader EU foreign policy portfolio is the fact that the issue of development is not necessarily backed by strong leadership within the EU. Development remains the responsibility of several commissioners; it is one aspect among others in the portfolio of a High Representative. Overall, the European Union's development policy is of the diplomatic-heteronomous type, in contrast to the autonomous-technocratic character of the World Bank. Both international development administrations, however, share the fact that they are intensively regulated by law. This distinguishes them, in turn, from German development administration.

German development administration can be seen as a rare refuge for "gubernative" prerogatives. Although subject to legal guidance, the relevant rules are mainly gubernative in character. The general trend in Germany recently for foreign policy to be "legalized" does not really apply to development cooperation.[205] The mandate for development cooperation in Germany is formulated broadly, and is open to goals that relate only indirectly to poverty reduction in recipient states. Typical of the German approach is the organizational separation between political leadership and technical implementation (although both levels cooperate intensively) and the organizational differentiation of the implementation level. In the final analysis, Germany's development administration can be classified as diplomatic-heteronomous, which places it in the same group as its European counterpart.

Obviously, these types have, as of yet, only been sketched very generally. They will be addressed in much more concrete detail in Part III of this book, which will examine the particular structures of ODA award mechanisms. The next step, however, is to examine the counterparties in development cooperation – that is, recipients.

B Recipients: definition, selection, differentiation

Thus far, the parties that cooperate with donors have been described generically and functionally as "recipients." Who are they? How is it determined which countries will receive ODA? The category "developing nations" helps only marginally, as it simply defers the question rather than answering it. Who are these developing countries? Although the category has existed since the end of the Second World War and appears in many multilateral agreements, there is still no general definition of the term.[206] In the following section, various methods for defining this category will be assessed (I). Then, the question of which criteria the donors use – that is, how they select recipients – will be addressed (II). Finally, the recipients themselves will be further differentiated (III).

I. "Developing countries" – methods of definition

The fact that no unified definition of developing nation exists is hardly surprising in light of the fact that there is no unity on the more fundamental question of how development should be measured or, indeed, what should

[205] V. Röben, *Außenverfassungsrecht: Eine Untersuchung zur auswärtigen Gewalt des offenen Staates* (Tübingen: Mohr Siebeck, 2007).

[206] The general context is described in M. Hirsch, "Developing Countries," in Wolfrum, *Max Planck Encyclopedia of Public International Law* at margin nos. 1–8; Bulajic,

count as development.[207] The most frequently used indicator is GNP, which reflects the still-dominant view developed during the first decades of development aid that economic growth is a fundamental component of development. This reflects a further assumption of a correlation between the economic situation of a country and its ability to ensure its citizens' well-being.[208] However, use of GNP as an indicator of development (or at least, as an exclusive measure of development) has been criticized. Briefly summarized, the critique is a methodical one which questions whether GNP really measures the relevant economic activity. GNP does not measure black-market labor, household work or subsistence activity, which play a significant role in developing nations. More fundamentally, critics suggest that economic growth threatens the environment and indigenous (and other) cultures, making it a particularly poor yardstick for general welfare.[209]

For some time now, alternative indices have been developed which use a variety of indicators, especially ones that portray the social dimension of development.[210] The most prominent of these is the Human Development Index (HDI), which the United Nations Development Programme has been measuring since 1993.[211] The HDI measures three essential components of development: (1) health and life expectancy; (2) education, measured by literacy rate and enrolment figures for primary, secondary, and tertiary schools; and (3) the standard of living, measured by GNP.[212] The

Principles of International Development Law, pp. 66–73; on the changing notions Greig, Hulme and Turner, *Challenging Global Inequality*, p. 42.

207 On the breadth of the current concept of development see *supra* Ch 2.B.I–III.

208 This argument is made (among others) by two leading development economists: Collier, *Bottom Billion*, pp. 8–12; W. Easterly, *The Elusive Quest for Growth: Economists' Adventures and Misadventures in the Tropics* (Cambridge, MA: MIT Press, 2002), pp. 1–5.

209 Discussed in depth in Greig, Hulme and Turner, *Challenging Global Inequality*, pp. 32–5 and sources cited therein. A contemporary critique of the current indicators and yardsticks of development can be found in the Report of the Commission on the Measurement of Economic Performance and Social Progress www.stiglitz-sen-fitoussi.fr/documents/rapport_anglais.pdf (last visited September 2012).

210 For an overview consult D. Harris, M. Moore and H. Schmitz, *Country Classifications for a Changing World: Institute for Development Studies Working Paper No. 326* (2009). Available at www2.ids.ac.uk/gdr/cfs/pdfs/Wp326.pdf (last visited September 2012).

211 See *supra* Ch 2.B.II; see also Hirsch, "Developing Countries," margin no. 6; see also the relevant page on the UNDP's website: http://hdr.undp.org/en/statistics/data/ (last visited September 2012).

212 On additional socio-cultural indicators see D. Nohlen, "Stichwort Entwicklungsländer," in Nohlen and Arons, *Lexikon Dritte Welt*, p. 234.

World Bank also publishes each year a comprehensive study on the measurement of poverty and development. It reflects a diverse set of indicators, the so-called World Development Indicators.[213]

In international law, the category "developing country" is important, since it brings with it significant economic and legal advantages that go beyond the mere receipt of aid. Three models for defining developing countries can be distinguished.[214] First, there are organizations that have specified certain *criteria* that define a developing country. Article XVIII of the General Agreement on Tariffs and Trade (GATT), for instance, defines developing countries as countries "the economies of which can only support low standards of living and are in the early stages of development." In Appendix I of the GATT treaty these criteria are fleshed out somewhat.[215] These characteristics are thus made legally binding and explicit, although they remain quite vague. A second example for the definition by criteria, and one that is particularly relevant for ODA, is the category of so-called least-developed countries (LDC), a sub-category of developing nations. Categorization as LDCs has been determined by the Economic and Social Council of the UN every three years since the early 1970s and is oriented toward three significant criteria: income (per-capita GNP, measured in three-year averages, less than US$750); "human resource weakness" (a combination of nutrition, health, education and literacy rate); and a criterion of economic vulnerability.[216] The list of countries satisfying these criteria (currently 50) is then confirmed by the General Assembly.[217]

In addition to the criteria-derived process, there is also the method of self-selection. The UNCTAD supported this method in particular.[218] All members of the Group of 77, for instance, declared themselves

[213] The latest edition can be found at http://data.worldbank.org/indicator (last visited July 2013).

[214] G. Verdirame, "The Definition of Developing Countries under GATT and Other International Law," *German Yearbook of International Law*, 39 (1996), 164–97 at 164; E. U. Petersmann, "Die Dritte Welt und das Wirtschaftsvölkerrecht: 'Entwicklungsland' als privilegierter Rechtsstatus," *Heidelberg Journal of International Law*, 36 (1976), 492–550 at 543.

[215] Verdirame, "The Definition of Developing Countries," 176.

[216] More details on the criteria: www.unohrlls.org/en/ldc/related/59/ (last visited September 2012).

[217] Discussed extensively in Verdirame, "The Definition of Developing Countries," 182–6; U. Simonis, *Review of the List of LDCs* (Berlin: Wissenschaftszentrum Berlin für Sozialforschung, 2003); Nuscheler, *Entwicklungspolitik*, pp. 100–2. The category is also used in development administrative law, see, for instance Art. 85 f. Cotonou; BMZ, *Guidelines*, no. 51.

[218] Verdirame, "The Definition of Developing Countries," 189.

developing countries and, on this basis, sought membership in GATT's "Generalized System of Preferences." However, these unilateral declarations do not bind other states, and developed countries thus frequently ignore them.

Finally, there is the method of creating lists which declare countries to be developed or developing nations. "Negative" lists, which identify countries which must fulfill particular duties, are frequently used in environmental agreements, for instance the Framework Agreement on Climate Change or the Montreal Protocol.[219] Positive lists, by contrast, are often used by bilateral ODA donors.

II. Donors' selection rules

In the area of development cooperation and ODA awards, donors have the right to establish definitions and select recipients.[220] Self-selection by recipient countries is out of the question. Rather, donors use both the criteria as well as the list method. Multilateral donors generally use objectivizing criteria, while bilateral donors generally create autonomous lists. In the context of ODA allocations, it is less important to establish a general definition of the category "developing country" than to select specific ODA recipients. This differentiation is particularly evident with regard to the organizations under review here.

The World Bank uses an economic approach based on gross national income (GNI) per capita per year. GNI includes GNP plus private capital transfers, in particular remittances (transfers from emigrants to their home countries). Bank member states are responsible for providing this information.[221] Based on these data, the Bank distinguishes four categories of country: low-income economies (currently 49)[222] in which average residents earn less than US$935 per year, lower-middle-income countries (54), in which citizens earn between US$936 and US$3,705; upper-middle-income countries (41), in which income ranges upward to US$11,445 and finally 65 high-income countries in which citizens average

[219] United Nations Framework Convention on Climate Change 31 I.L.M. 849 (1992); Montreal Protocol on Substances that Deplete the Ozone Layer, 26 I.L.M. 1541 (1987); more sources in Verdirame, "The Definition of Developing Countries," 192.

[220] The general selection as a country to be supported should be distinguished by the concrete allocation of funds in the respective budgeting processes of donor nations.

[221] The relevant regulations are in Operational Policy Nr. 14.10.

[222] In addition to states, other territories whose state-like character is doubtful or lacking (for instance, areas under the control of the Palestinian Authority) are also evaluated.

over US$11,456 in yearly income. To determine whether a country will receive ODA from the IDA under relaxed conditions, the Bank relies on a country's classification as low-income or lower-middle-income, as well as its loan repayment ability.[223] Depending on the outcome of this analysis, countries may receive loans only from the IDA, only from the IBRD, or from both organizations. This classification is made each year on the first of July and is then published in Annex C to OP 3.10. In the World Bank's terminology, all low- and middle-income countries are developing nations. Thus, the World Bank relies on a largely objective system of classification. There is no (enforceable) right to a particular classification.[224]

EU law follows a different approach.[225] The EU chooses recipients in the ACP area from the parties to the Cotonou Agreement (which established the ACP Group), thus the selection is made on the basis of inviting a country to join this group.[226] Outside of the ACP area, the 2007 DCI Regulation listed, for the first time, the countries eligible to receive assistance. The ordnance uses a two-level system. Art. 1 of the DCI Regulation limits eligibility to those developing countries listed in the OECD-DAC list, which is attached to the regulation as Appendix II.[227] The Commission is then required to narrow the selection further (which it does: Appendix I lists 48 countries and territories, while Appendix II lists 153). By this mechanism, the European Union specifies legally which countries are aid-eligible (all countries on the OECD list), while maintaining control over whom will receive aid. Ultimately, the Commission decides who will receive ODA from the EU, and then communicates this to the Parliament and Council.

[223] The various "products" of the Bank and their conditions are set out in OP / BP 3.10; on the different instruments of the IDA and the IBRD, see *supra* Ch 3.A.IV.1.

[224] One special aspect of a relatively objective system of categorization is that countries can "grow out" of one category, thus going from being recipients to donors. This is called "graduation." On the questions raised by graduation see Shihata, *World Bank Legal Papers*, p. 493.

[225] Martenczuk and Zimmermann, "Art. 177 EGV," margin nos. 15–17.

[226] There are currently 78 countries in this group. On the political dimension of the expansion of the group of ACP countries see *supra* Ch 1.B.II.

[227] The OECD prepares a list of developing countries and ODA recipients every three years. However, this list is oriented exclusively to the World Bank's categories (information at: www.oecd.org/dac/stats/daclist (last visited July 2013)). All low- and middle-income countries in the World Bank's statistics are incorporated in the list of ODA recipients and developing nations. The LDCs are described separately, as is the UN's determination (see *supra*). According to the OECD-DAC, its list serves solely statistical purposes. However, its use as a necessary condition for ODA allocation by the EU gives it a clear normative importance.

In Germany, the decision as to which countries will be invited for development cooperation and thus potentially receive ODA rests solely with the federal government, specifically with the Ministry of Development.[228] The ministry makes a free choice, without relying on abstract categories. Recently, the BMZ has instituted a two-step selection process. It first creates a geographical "country concentration" and thematic focus.[229] Until the end of the 1990s, 120 countries received aid; this number has now been reduced to about 70 and will continue to shrink. There are some criteria spelled out for the decision, but there is no mechanism to determine whether they are being followed. There is generally no possibility for countries to formally protest exclusion.[230] The German ministry also use the concept of "anchor countries."[231] This is not a formal category, but rather a qualitative political choice in which the Ministry of Development focuses on individual developing nations "on the basis of their economic power, their political influence in the region, and their increasing involvement in international processes."[232] There are nine anchor countries: Egypt, Brazil, China, India, Indonesia, Mexico, Nigeria, Pakistan and South Africa.

Compared with the German approach, the World Bank's method, which focuses on the economic situation of a country, is comparatively objective. By contrast, the EU and the Federal Republic of Germany use a procedure in which political discretion plays the key role. Germany, however, does integrate the decision into an overall concept that, while it is non-binding (like the World Bank's), still has been conceptually elaborated and is subject to certain consistency constraints.

III. *Differentiation among recipients*

Another aspect should be addressed, which, although perhaps somewhat obvious, is nevertheless of central importance for development aid and the law governing it: not all recipients are equal. Although they all have the same legal status as subjects of international law,[233] and although they are functionally in the same position insofar as they receive aid, nevertheless,

[228] BMZ, *Guidelines*, no. 15.

[229] Ibid., no. 2; explained in BMZ, *Media Handbook 2008/2009*, pp. 342–4.

[230] Ibid., p. 344.

[231] Discussed in detail in BMZ, *Ankerländer – Partner für globale Entwicklung*, ("Anchor Countries") (Bonn, 2004).

[232] BMZ, *Media Handbook 2008/2009*, p. 448.

[233] On the importance of this formal equality see *infra* Ch 4.C.II.

significant legal and practical differences between them should be kept in mind.

The analysis of the categorization and selection rules for the World Bank has shown that various classes of recipients receive different conditions and instruments. The poorest states, for instance, receive IDA at more favorable conditions than wealthier recipient countries. The EU, by contrast, differentiates between recipient countries by sorting them into the ACP Group and all others, and applying specific formal and procedural legal regimes for each group that frequently differ considerably.[234] Thus, even in legal terms, the field of recipient countries is divided into groups.

Even a legal analysis should, however, take account of the practical differences among recipient countries, to the extent that these affect their legal status. In the institutional economics literature, in particular, there is an important contrast between "strong" and "weak" recipient countries.[235] The literature identifies two aspects that are especially relevant to determining the relative strength of the recipient countries. One is the amount of work a recipient country promises. China, India and Mexico are relatively influential recipient countries, according to this metric, because one can invest a great deal of money and projects in these countries. Donor administrations are always under pressure to (among other things) disburse funds and show how productively they have been used. Large countries and projects are therefore attractive for many donors. The relative strength of recipient countries can also be influenced by whether the country has alternative donors. A recipient country's relative influence and bargaining power is obviously increased when, for instance, it can demonstrate to one donor that it can obtain ODA from another donor at more favorable conditions. This logic was particularly important during the Cold War, during which recipient countries could play the two blocs against one another.[236] This logic remains central even today. Large commercial banks, for instance, often compete with the World Bank to finance large infrastructure projects. China also frequently offers a willing alternative.

A third aspect affecting recipients' practical strength, and therefore the applicable legal regime, is whether it acts alone or as part of a group. Particularly relevant here is the special historical case of the ACP countries, which have always bargained with the EU as a collective.[237] Although

[234] See *infra* Ch 5.C.II.1 and Ch 6.B.II.1.

[235] Gibson et al., *Samaritan's Dilemma*, pp. 65–8.

[236] A well-known example of this phenomenon was Ethiopia, which changed sides twice.

[237] See *supra* Ch 3.A.III.

one should always be careful when attributing causality, it seems reasonable to assume that the particularly favorable conditions under which the ACP states receive ODA may well relate to their negotiating strength as a collective.[238]

The relative strength of a recipient country has many consequences, but is particularly important for the understanding of collective autonomy[239] and in the procedure for planning and allocating ODA.[240] However, our focus will turn next to the third group of institutions, actors who are important to the process of standard setting.

C Standard-promoting collectives: UN, OECD, ACP

Donors and recipients are central actors in development cooperation. But there are other actors which are important since they promote general standards of ODA transfers – beyond the rules of each donor and transaction. In this respect, donors have found an extremely effective forum, the OECD (I), while recipients, though they use various institutions, have so far failed to achieve comparable influence (II).

I. The donor collective: OECD-DAC

Before the multiplicity of donors was seen as a problem – probably even before development aid became generally known as a policy field – aid donors had joined together within the OECD in a group called the Development Assistance Committee, known as the OECD-DAC or simply DAC.[241] Founded on the basis of a ministerial directive, the DAC convenes the most important donor organizations – that is, the thirty-five regular members (34 nations and the EU). The World Bank, the UNDP and the IMF, the three dominant international organizations in this area, are included as permanent observers.

[238] This argument is discussed in depth in Ravenhill, *Collective Clientelism*. On the rules for the ACP countries see *infra* Ch 5.C.II.1 and Ch 6.B.II.1

[239] See *infra* Ch 4.C. [240] See *infra* Ch 5.C, Ch 6.B and Ch 7.B.

[241] On the OECD-DAC see G. Ashoff and German Development Institute, Der *Entwicklungshilfeausschuss der OECD und die deutsche Entwicklungszusammenarbeit: Ein Verhältnis auf dem Prüfstand*, Analysen und Stellungnahmen des deutschen Instituts für Entwicklungspolitik 1/2000. Available at www.die-gdi.de (last visited July 2013); H. Hahn and A. Weber, *Die OECD: Organisation für Wirtschaftliche Zusammenarbeit und Entwicklung* (Baden-Baden: Nomos, 1976), p. 300; S. Rubin, *The Conscience of the Rich Nations: The Development Assistance Committee and the Common Aid Effort* (New York: Harper Row, 1966); and OECD-DAC brochures: OECD, *Inside the DAC* (Paris: OECD Publishing, 2008) and OECD, *The History of the DAC* (Paris: OECD Publishing, 2006).

The DAC is led by a full-time chairperson, which is a distinction shared by only one other Committee of the OECD. The DAC's regular meetings bring together member-state officials and experts fifteen times per year at the DAC's Paris headquarters. Once a year, development ministers join this meeting for a so-called High-Level Forum. The OECD-DAC also has two permanent working groups and six networks devoted to specific subjects.[242] Of particular note is the Working Party on Aid Effectiveness, which has existed since 2003 and which includes representatives of recipient states. The DAC's work is undergirded by a technical and almost obscure-sounding mandate.[243] It is to "consult on methods for making national resources available for assisting countries and areas in the process of economic development and for expanding and improving the flow of long-term funds and other development assistance to them." This technical-sounding mandate, however, does not hinder the DAC's work – in fact, quite the reverse is the case.

The DAC's importance is underlined, ironically, by the fact that it has never issued a formal binding legal instrument in its almost fifty-year history. It operates solely by means of non-binding recommendations and agreements, and through the publication of statistics and standards.[244] It has four main areas of activity. First, it issues development statistics that are the standard worldwide. The Committee's definition of ODA and its yearly statistics are the decisive point of reference for every communication about the amount and form of public disbursement in the area of development cooperation. This gives the DAC a power of definition that can hardly be overstated,[245] since the DAC's work often forms the very basis of understanding and coordination among various actors. Second, the DAC creates so-called "peer reviews" of the development policies and administrations of its member states, a process which every member is required to undergo every four years. These reports are

[242] For detailed discussion of the working groups see Ashoff and German Development Institute, *Der Entwicklungshilfeausschuss der OECD*, p. 1; OECD, *Inside the DAC*, p. 16.

[243] The one-page mandate can be found at: www.oecd.org/dac/thedevelopmentassistancecommitteesmandate.htm (last visited July 2013).

[244] On the importance of the OECD for the global standard-setting process see Bogdandy and Goldmann, "Ausübung internationaler öffentlicher Gewalt," 51; J. Salzman, *Decentralized Administrative Law in the Organisation for Economic Co-operation and Development: International Law and Justice Working Papers No. 17* (New York University, 2005); on the importance of such standards Masujima, "Good Governance," p. 151; Lumsdaine, *Moral Vision*, p. 245.

[245] The controversy this provokes can be seen in such articles as Brzoska, "Extending ODA," 131.

organized according to a uniform process in which the horizontal participation of other members as reporters is of central importance. Third, the Committee develops so-called DAC "best practices" that serve to conceptually coordinate member-state activities. These are "only" non-binding studies. However, only very rarely does the DAC issue recommendations, which, although they do not impose legal duties on states, nevertheless require them to consider the recommended actions.[246] Even the non-mandatory guidelines, however, serve as yardsticks to evaluate donor practices.[247]

Fourth and finally, the DAC serves as a forum, whose importance for communication and collective goal setting by its members can hardly be overestimated. This aspect of the DAC's work has been particularly prominent as forum and driving force behind the "Monterrey Process," a continuing effort to elucidate the basic principles of development cooperation.[248] This process unfolds on three organizational levels of the DAC. At the High-Level Forums, which meet every two to three years, ministers of various states and their counterparts from non-governmental organizations congregate. Between these ministerial forums, the Working Party on Aid Effectiveness meets. This is a continuous discussion forum for high-level officials, which serves, according to participants, to build trust among the various actors. For its part, the Working Party creates "technical working groups" on individual issues. The fact that both donors and recipients meet in these groups adds considerably to their scope and effectiveness. In any case, this dual representation reduces the dominance of the donors. The Secretariat of the DAC coordinates the entire process.[249]

This communication process results in declarations on various aspects of development cooperation, among which the Paris Declaration stands out.[250] Many of these declarations are extremely comprehensive and

[246] Hahn and Weber, *OECD*, p. 99. The last recommendation dates to 2001 and relates to the abolition of tied aid. Earlier recommendations dealt with avoiding corruption (1997), environmental impact assessments during project reviews (1986) and conditions on assistance (1972).

[247] However, a study is currently underway which will illustrate the concrete context empirically.

[248] See *supra* Ch 2.C.III.1.

[249] Its webpage also permits the best understanding of the overall rather intransparent structure of this organ: www.oecd.org/dac/effectiveness and http://www.aidharmonization.org/.

[250] OECD, *Paris Declaration on Aid Effectiveness* (2005). Available at www.oecd.org/development/aideffectiveness/34428351.pdf (last visited July 2013).

detailed. They are not meant to be legally enforceable, but are subject to the explicit approval of participating delegations. The authors of the declaration maintain that their binding nature emerges out of the continuing dialog process, not from abstract legal duties. The Monterrey Process is developing an increasing set of norms in which participants, that is donors and recipients, agree on common principles, goals and standards. The process is, in principle, organized and led by the OECD-DAC.

The DAC thereby emerges as a central instance both for creating norm processes (statistics, guidelines), involving others in their creation (an example being the Monterrey Process) and for starting the evaluation of the norms (for example, by peer reviews). The DAC shows particularly clearly how the multilateral norm-setting process in development aid relies on impulses from donors. Collective standards for donors, as can be seen from the activity of the OECD-DAC, create an increasingly dense network of norms which determines the conduct of donors in awarding ODA.

II. Recipient collectives? UNCTAD, the ACP Group, the UN General Assembly

The OECD-DAC represents a particularly influential donor forum which formulates rules – or consciously refrains from doing so. Although its reports and guidelines are not legally binding, they do indicate precisely how far the donor-side political consensus reaches and thus offer an important basis for effective regulation. What about the recipients? Have they created institutions in which common positions are formulated and brought to bear in donor–recipient relationships? They are obviously at a structural disadvantage, since, as recipients, they are mostly not in a position to dictate the conditions under which ODA transfers are organized. Nevertheless, forums can be helpful in articulating positions, albeit more during the process of preparing rules than actually setting them. Three such institutions will be briefly sketched here: the UNCTAD, the ACP Group (with which the EU traditionally cooperates) and, finally, the UN General Assembly.

The UN Conference on Trade and Development (UNCTAD), founded in 1964, was the central forum for developing nations during the 1960s.[251]

[251] As one example of an extensive literature (and with many sources cited therein) see C. Fortin, "United Nations Conference on Trade and Development (UNCTAD)," in Wolfrum, *Max Planck Encyclopedia of Public International Law* at margin no.1.

Convened "to formulate principles and policies on international trade and related problems of economic development," "to make proposals for putting the said principles and policies into effect" and "to initiate action for the negotiation and adoption of multilateral legal instruments,"[252] and dominated intellectually by Latin American critics of the modernization theory, UNCTAD was the most important forum for the discussion of the weaknesses of alternative perspectives to the international system.[253] With its near-universal membership and a principle of majority rule (observed most consistently at first), the UNCTAD was dominated by developing countries wishing to use the conference principally to prepare multilateral agreements by formulating general principles. The Conference played a crucial role in developing key concepts in international law, such as duality of norms, non-reciprocity and differential treatment.[254] However, they had little wider influence on development law. Their recommendations were not legally binding. Further, development cooperation was only a subordinate theme at the Conference, which was mainly concerned with problems of world trade law. Since the early 1990s, the UNCTAD has increasingly turned away from trying to prepare general treaties and turned toward research and technical assistance. Thus, it has not become an important forum or mouthpiece considering its place in the international-aid system.

Another forum for recipient-side positions could be the ACP Group. It consists of countries from Africa, the Caribbean and the Pacific and has been the main recipient of European development assistance since 1975. After the first Lomé Convention in 1975, these countries, by means of the so-called Georgetown Agreement, created their own international organization, the ACP Group. The group was committed not only to realizing the goals of the Lomé and Cotonou Agreements, but also to formulating general developing-nation goals.[255] The Agreement also creates an institutional structure whose main components resemble that of the EU. The most important organs are an independent Secretariat and an Ambassadorial Committee which formulate positions. In the 1977 Suava Declaration, the ACP Group delivered its first program for action. However, the ACP Group never became an

[252] UN-GA Resolution 1995 (XIX), para. 3.

[253] M. Ruge, *Der Beitrag der UNCTAD zur Herausbildung des Entwicklungsvölkerrechts* (Frankfurt am Main: Haag und Herchen, 1976), pp. 165–99.

[254] P. Berthoud, "UNCTAD and the Emergence of International Development Law," in M. Zammit Cutajar (ed.), *UNCTAD and the North-South-Dialogue* (Oxford: Pergamon Press, 1985), pp. 71–98 at p. 71; Fortin, UNCTAD, margin no. 43.

[255] Extensively Lister, *EC and the Developing World*, p. 167.

important forum outside the context of negotiating particular agreements with the EU. Explanations for this range from the weakness of the Secretariat to conflicting interests among participating countries. In any event, the ACP Group failed to fulfill the potential for discursive power promised by the quantity of allied recipient states and the historical goodwill of the EU countries.

The UN General Assembly is, of course, not primarily an organ of recipient nations. It can, however, be considered a potential third forum, since it has in recent decades adopted a series of resolutions of key significance for development cooperation over the objections of industrialized member states.[256] Among these were the proclamation of the Decade of Development, which, among other things, proclaimed a goal of the transfer of 0.7 percent of the GDP of industrialized countries to developing nations,[257] a New World Economic Order which imposed economic rights and duties on member states,[258] a right to development,[259] and, last but not least, the MDG.[260] In contrast to the UNCTAD and the ACP Group, the General Assembly has also articulated important positions for developing nations with regard to aid, and has thus become the most important forum for the developing world. Nevertheless, the binding nature of General Assembly resolutions remains problematic. While developing countries have always articulated strong objections to the traditional sources of international law (in particular, customary and contract law), they supported General Assembly resolutions as a democratic element in international law-making, and argued they should be considered legally binding. The prevailing opinion in industrial nations, however, overwhelmingly and vehemently denies that UN resolutions have binding character.[261] While it seems fruitless to argue that resolutions are a sort of "instant customary law" or authentic interpretations of the UN Charter (thus giving rise to legal duties), it would also be wrong to dismiss them as completely meaningless. They can be seen

[256] Paul, "United Nations and the Creation," 307.

[257] UN-GA Resolution 1710 (XVI), of December 19, 1961, UN-GA Resolution 2626 (XXV) of October 24, 1970, UN-GA Resolution 35/56 of December 5, 1980 and UN-GA Resolution 45/199 of February 21, 1990.

[258] UN-GA Resolution 3201 and 3202 (XXIX) of May 1, 1974 and UN-GA Resolution 3281 (XXIX) of December 12, 1974; see also *supra* Ch 1.B.I.1.

[259] UN-GA Resolution 41/128 of December 14, 1986.

[260] UN-GA Resolution 55/2 of September 18, 2000.

[261] A good overview of the conflict can be found in M. Kaltenborn, *Entwicklungsvölkerrecht und Neugestaltung der internationalen Ordnung: Rechtstheoretische und rechtspolitische Aspekte des Nord-Süd-Konflikts*, Münsterische Beiträge zur Rechtswissenschaft (Berlin: Duncker & Humblot, 1998), vol. CXIII, p. 87.

as preparations and precursors to slowly developing legal ideas which can consolidate customary laws or even suggest new legal concepts. Thus seen, they fulfill an important function in development cooperation law, as will be seen when their principles are later analyzed.

In the final analysis, then, if there is an important collective forum for developing countries, the UN General Assembly is it. However, it cannot promulgate binding law. Donors have openly rejected this possibility. This is how the donors preserve their dominance over the essential regulations governing development cooperation. It is true that donors do not establish general laws in this area. The OECD-DAC, however, offers them a forum for coordinating common rules, as far as this is desired. These agreements have considerable influence by virtue of the fact that, as donors, these states can unilaterally create ODA procedures and criteria.

D Summary: heterarchy of actors and "donor-bias" of the law

This analysis has so far revealed an unusual institutional arrangement and various legal bases of development cooperation law. While the institutional structure can be characterized by the plurality and heterarchy of the actors, the bases of development cooperation law are characterized by their "donor-bias" and complexity of the legal frameworks.

I. Plurality and heterarchy of actors

The institutional structures in the area of development aid reveal a large number of actors who can be functionally sorted into three groups: donors, recipients and collective actors whose role is primarily to develop general standards.

Within the group of donors, there are national and international donors. National donors are, traditionally, the Western industrialized states of the North, which have created specific administrative structures for this activity. In recent years, they have been joined by some emerging economies, such as China or India. One peculiarity of the institutional structure is the large number of international organizations that independently award ODA. The World Bank and the EU are two of the particularly important institutions, profiled here as examples of a larger group. In the global governance context, these organizations are unusual in that they, just like their national counterparts, decide more or less autonomously concrete cases of ODA transfers. In fact, in financial terms, they are just as important as national donors, if not even more so. Thus, whether one looks at their financial capacities or their competences, they can hardly be considered secondary actors.

A second unusual aspect of the institutional structures is their parallel competences.[262] Even in a quasi-federal organization such as the EU, there is no rule of precedence for member states. Rather, the exercise of one actor's competence has no direct legal consequences for that of any other actor. Instead of hierarchy, then, there is heterarchy. Legally, development cooperation can therefore be characterized as a heterarchical multi-level system.

ODA recipients include a large number of states whose economic performance is particularly weak. A World Bank statistic, compiled yearly, is particularly important in determining a country's relative economic performance.[263] There is no general principle of neediness; every donor decides autonomously which countries it will give ODA to. The group of recipients cannot be described uniformly. In fact, it has become clear that there are important differences between recipients – in particular, between strong and weak recipients. Concepts such as developing country begin to lose their meaning when some countries, such as China, India and Turkey, both receive and give ODA.

The third type of important institution in the development system is that of collectives, which, although they do not award aid, serve to coordinate aid and promote norms.[264] The OECD-DAC plays a central role here, as it unites all important donors and serves as an important coordinator, similar to that of the UN General Assembly. Even though neither the OECD-DAC nor the UN General Assembly can make binding law, they are important as forums for agreeing on common (non-binding) standards and goals. Their importance is based on the diversity of the institutional system of development cooperation. In other words: development aid is a particularly complex arena of global governance which has a correspondingly intense need for coordination and organization. These collective actors attempt to meet the need.

II. Complexity and donor-bias of the laws of development cooperation

In addition to institutional structures, this chapter has addressed the question of the legal sources and legal frameworks of ODA transfers and thus

[262] Ch 3.A.V. [263] Ch 3.B.II. [264] Ch 3.C.

of development cooperation law. Here, three different norm-complexes became apparent that govern this area and should be distinguished: bilateral agreements between donors and recipients, internal rules of donors concerning their own ODA transfers, and, finally, general standards applicable to all actors. The overall view, however, revealed how much development cooperation law is made by donors. Although ODA allocations are governed by individual, bilateral agreements between donors and recipients, these agreements are, at the very minimum, intensively "pre-structured" by the donors' own rules.[265] The development administrations in Germany, the EU and the World Bank all have comprehensive internal rules governing the procedures, criteria and instruments by which ODA will be granted. The actual contracting process thus takes place within the framework of already-existing donor-side law. Generally, recipient countries have very little influence on the creation of these rules. The law of development cooperation can thus be seen as largely "donor-dominated."

The plurality of donors also creates diversity in development cooperation law. This implies diverse substantive and procedural rules, which will be more closely analyzed in Part III of this study. On an abstract level, there is first diversity as to the sources of development cooperation law. Depending on whether the focus is on a state, a supranational organization or an international organization, development law can be national law, supranational law or international law. Even though ODA contracts between donor and recipient are regularly international-law agreements, the procedural and substantive regime preceding and enveloping this agreement is derived from these other sources.

Development cooperation law is also diverse with regard to its rank. In Germany, for instance, development cooperation law is primarily a matter of internal administrative regulations, not of (parliamentary) laws. The World Bank likewise establishes procedures and criteria for its allocations by secondary laws which generally have only an internal binding effect. Development cooperation law is, thus, generally only binding within the respective institution. Since donors see ODA allocations principally through the perspective of their own internal administration, this is only to be expected.

However, this "donor-domination" also has a problematic side. Donors do not just bind themselves by their ODA allocations but also indirectly bind the respective recipient. When a donor imposes environmental or

[265] This will be addressed further in Part III.

social standards, for example, as a condition on its aid allocation, recipients must also meet the standards.

On a third level (that is, besides agreements and donor-nation laws), one can also ask to what extent general norms – binding on all actors – exist for awarding ODA. There are no binding multilateral agreements which set out general rules for ODA and bind all actors. It has recently become clear, however, that the OECD-DAC and the UN General Assembly provide two forums for preparing general norms for development aid. The MDG and the Paris Declaration represent two central documents which, although they do not establish binding law, provide a framework in which donors can promulgate coordinated rules. Since donor law is particularly important, the DAC, by means of its Best Practices and Peer Review, plays an important standard-setting role.

In the next chapter we will clarify whether and to what extent general principles of development cooperation law can be derived from these standards, other sources of development cooperation law or general public international law.

4

Principles of the law of development cooperation

General principles can be central devices to allow us to better understand the manifold rules of a policy field. They can shape the law as normative guideposts and offer insights to its systematic understanding, as well as help us in categorizing and evaluating individual rules. This is also true for development cooperation law. We will now examine its guiding principles and their legal nature. Four concepts are paramount: development, collective autonomy, individual autonomy, and coherence and efficiency.

Development assistance and the law governing it react to the fact of massive material inequalities between states and crushing poverty in developing countries. Development connotes the promise of combating poverty and balancing inequality. A first principle of development cooperation law is thus the principle of development itself. This constitutes the substantive guiding concept and specifies approaches to the problem of poverty (B). If development means the reduction of inequality by international cooperation, it can be seen primarily as a political process, in which the form and substance of this border-crossing cooperation must continuously be negotiated. Securing the autonomy of recipients and donors, as well as finding a compromise between them despite immense inequality, is a second central feature of development cooperation law. Accordingly, the second principle whose legal form we will examine is that of collective autonomy (C). However, development cooperation is not just a process between states – it also affects individual citizens. Their participation, support and protection through human rights guarantees have become important components of the development process and its law. This aspect of development law will therefore be considered under the heading of individual autonomy (D). Finally, development cooperation is shaped by certain normative expectations relating not to participants but to the process itself. The principle of coherence and efficiency is a fourth guiding ideal of the development cooperation law. Its legal form will be considered in Section E.

These four principles have shaped the law of development cooperation and open four perspectives on relevant norms. They help to bring order to the diversity of rules and mechanisms, and pose their own specific questions to the law. They transform established general principles of international law into field-specific sectoral principles of development cooperation law. At the same time, there might also be tensions between them. A final section will look into the individual substance of these principles and highlight areas of tension (F).

At first, though, we will examine the four principles more closely to determine how they relate to the understanding of other principles in the area of law and development.

A Preliminary considerations on principles

In using a principle-based approach, this book enters a broad field. Principles play a central role especially in the context of law and development. The following section will briefly address the attitude toward principles in international development law (I) and then sketch the (slightly different) understanding of principles used by the present work (II). Finally, we will review the relationship of the principles of development cooperation law as set out in this work to those in the Paris Declaration (III).[1]

[1] Since the 1970s, principles have also played an important *political* role for developing nations. They are easier to agree on than concrete obligations and can also be formulated in a way that leaves open more opportunities in the future. The important instruments here were General Assembly Resolutions (especially the NIEO or the right to development, see *supra* Ch 1.B.I.1 and *infra* Ch 4.B.I), on the one hand, and studies on the position of developing countries in international law, on the other. Important documents in the latter category include a UNITAR study from 1984 composed by Georges Abi-Saab (Progressive Development of the Principles and Norms of International Law Relating to the NIEO, UN-Doc A/39/504, Add. 1, Annex III, see W. Benedek, "Progressive Development of the Principles and Norms of International Law Relating to the NIEO: The UNITAR Exercise," *Österreichische Zeitschrift für öffentliches Recht und Völkerrecht*, 36 (1985), 289–328 at 298) and the so-called Seoul Declaration of the International Law Association of 1986 (Declaration on the Progressive Development of Principles of Public International Law Relating to an NIEO, reprinted in T. Oppermann and E.-U. Petersmann, *Reforming the International Economic Order: German Legal Comments*, Tübinger Schriften zum internationalen und europäischen Recht (Berlin: Duncker & Humblot, 1987), vol. I, p. 47). General discussions of the international-law policies of developing countries can be found in Petersmann, "Dritte Welt," 515; A. Cassese, *International Law in a Divided World* (Oxford: Clarendon Press, 1986), pp. 119, 120.

I. *Teleological principles in international development law*

In the school of international development law principles have a mainly teleological function, based on two main considerations.[2] First, international development law is based on the idea of a duality of norms. This idea holds that developing countries should be subject to a specialized legal regime tailored to their specific situation. This duality is derived principally from a (materialistic) reinterpretation of the principle of sovereign equality from Art. 2(I) of the UN Charter, which leads in turn to the reinterpretation of still other norms. The traditional, formal interpretation of the basic UN Charter principle would, it was thought, disadvantage developing nations in practice. A reformulation of the principle tailored to the needs of developing countries was therefore considered essential to an opening-up and transformation of international law in general. This is also true for the second basic idea of this school of thought, which is the "finality" of international law of development. According to its supporters, international law is a so-called "*droit orienté*" or "*droit de finalité*." It is concerned not so much with concrete regulation as with a specific goal, namely overcoming global development disparities.[3] This goal places particular emphasis on prospective, programmatic norms which establish the framework for future development. The legal structure of principles then offers a particularly suitable form.[4]

Principles are thus seen primarily as teleological instruments serving the transformation of general law. They are not primarily intended to serve a systematizing or evaluative function, much less a (stabilizing) ordering function. Instead, they serve the function of programming. As a commentator once put it, they should be the "yeast in the dough of classical international law."[5] However, for the purposes of this book, we will use a different understanding of principles.

[2] On this school, see *supra* Intro.A.I.2. See Kaltenborn, *Entwicklungsvölkerrecht und Neugestaltung*, pp. 25–29, 103–12; Mahiou, "International Law of Development," margin nos. 9, 13.

[3] Flory, *Droit international*, pp. 29; Feuer and Cassan, *Droit international*, p. 24. On this aspect, see Kaltenborn, "Entwicklungs- und Schwellenländer," 207–8.

[4] Among many other sources, see M. Bedjaoui, "General Introduction," in M. Bedjaoui (ed.), *International Law: Achievements and Prospects* (Paris, Dordrecht: Martinus Nijhoff Publishers, 1991), pp. 1–18 at p. 15.

[5] Flory, *Droit international*, p. 31; for a similar approach, drawing on Robert Alexy's work interpreting development-law principles as optimization demands, see Kaltenborn, *Entwicklungsvölkerrecht und Neugestaltung*, p. 122.

II. The distinction between legal and structural principles

The present study reverts to the idea of principles in order to mark basic ideas which transcend particular organizations and levels of authority. The goal is to formulate principles derived from and for the area of development cooperation, so that the systematization and evaluation of development cooperation law is possible. Principles will therefore have primarily a heuristic function.[6] They also help to make the law more intelligible and transparent, especially by highlighting conflicts between simultaneously valid principles and thus areas of tension. But not all principles have the same normative validity. Some of them have been strongly legalized, others less strongly. To denote this difference, we will use the categories of *legal* principles and *structural* principles.[7] What do these categories mean?

A key aspect is the different functions they fulfill: systematization on the one hand, and evaluation on the other. *Structural* principles systematize and order legal materials.[8] They are scholarly abstractions to locate the "defining regularities" in a set of positive legal rules.[9] They can be leading ideas in a particular field, for instance, the principle of cooperation in environmental law, or typical patterns of organizational structures. Structural principles are principally descriptive in character. They primarily serve a doctrinal function and are of interest primarily to legal scholarship.[10] *Legal* principles, on the other hand, have additionally an evaluative function. They help evaluate legal materials on a normative basis. They are fundamental norms of a legal area which can form the basis of a judgment of illegality or, in any event, serve as important resources for argumentation.[11] Even if they are general and vague, they can still provide

[6] On different functions of principles (although in a constitutional context) see F. Reimer, *Verfassungsprinzipien: Ein Normtyp des Grundgesetzes* (Berlin: Duncker & Humblot, 2001), p. 310.

[7] On this distinction see A. von Bogdandy, "Prolegomena zu Prinzipien internationalisierter und internationaler Verwaltung," in H.-H. Trute, T. Groß, C. Möllers and H. C. Röhl (eds.), *Allgemeines Verwaltungsrecht – zur Tragfähigkeit eines Konzepts*. Festschrift für Eberhard Schmidt-Aßmann (Tübingen: Mohr Siebeck, 2008), pp. 683–97 at pp. 692–4; M. Koskenniemi, "General Principles," in M. Koskenniemi (ed.), *Sources of International Law* (Burlinton: Ashgate, 2000), pp. 359–402.

[8] Schmidt-Aßmann, *Das allgemeine Verwaltungsrecht*, margin nos. 3, 5.

[9] Bogdandy, "Prolegomena zu Prinzipien," p. 692.

[10] Koskenniemi, "General Principles," pp. 365; 381.

[11] J. Harenburg, *Die Rechtsdogmatik zwischen Wissenschaft und Praxis: Ein Beitrag zur Theorie der Rechtsdogmatik* (Stuttgart: Steiner Verlag, 1986), p. 6; Bogdandy, "Prolegomena zu Prinzipien," p. 694.

normative guidance and structure for participating actors. According to Stefan Kadelbach and Thomas Kleinlein, they "mark off an area for discretionary action" and provide not so much the legal solution as the contours of one. Nevertheless, they also function as normative yardsticks.[12]

A principle can be both a structural and legal principle. This depends on its own normativity. This observation leads to the second important difference between the two categories. *Structural* principles are the leading ideas of a legal field, but they are not legally binding. They are principally doctrinal-systematizing concepts. *Legal* principles, by contrast, are legal concepts which have stronger normativity; they are legally binding. A conflict between a rule and a legal principle is a powerful argument for the former's illegality.

This chapter will deal with both kinds of principle. The principles of development cooperation law will have a systematizing and heuristic as well as a potentially evaluative function. Every principle must therefore not only be described in substance but also from a normative perspective. This will enable its classification as structural and/or legal. The task will be complex in light of the normative character of development cooperation law as a multi-level legal system and its legal sources. As has been seen above, this area of law is derived from three sources: donor law (which, depending on the donor, can be either national, supranational or international law), international treaty law between donors and recipients, and, finally, overarching principles of international law which set general standards for ODA allocations. This threefold composition affects the analysis of the two kinds of principles.

If the reference is to *legal* principles of development cooperation law, then the third source, i.e. international law, is relevant. Such principles may come from any of the three sources of international law listed in Art. 38 I of the Statute of the International Court of Justice: conventions, customary law and the "general principles of law recognized by civilized nations." It should be noted here that this book will not attempt to formulate any new general principles of law. Thus, there is no need here to broach the ongoing discussion on the development of legal principles.[13]

[12] S. Kadelbach and T. Kleinlein, "Überstaatliches Verfassungsrecht: Zur Konstitutionalisierung im Völkerrecht," *Archiv des Völkerrechts*, 44 (2006), 235–66 at 264; Koskenniemi, "General Principles," p. 380; for a meta-juristic conception of principles as criteria for the evaluation of the legitimacy of the international legal order, see M. Kumm, "The Legitimacy of International Law: A Constitutionalist Framework of Analysis," *European Journal of International Law*, 15 (2004), 907–31 at 907.

[13] See also Kadelbach and Kleinlein, "Überstaatliches Verfassungsrecht," 255–62; N. Petersen, *Demokratie als teleologisches Prinzip: Zur Legitimität von Staatsgewalt im*

Structural principles require another analytical method. Here, it should be noted, we are dealing with principles that are only of *sectoral* importance. They can claim "validity" only for the field of development cooperation and development administrations transferring ODA.[14] This means that they are not to be classified solely as international law, but can rather be assigned to various legal levels (i.e. European or national law). They are generated by a comparative analysis. Since donor law is critical, structural principles must be contained in the law of all such donor-regimes, either in relevant national law, supranational law or international law. Structural principles of development cooperation law tend not only to have an international character but actually to be a kind of *global* law.[15] Development cooperation law is peculiar in that it has not emerged from or built on an existing national law but has rather developed simultaneously at all levels of public authority. Unlike other areas of the law, it hence does not follow national traditions but is inherently international. This leads to an unusual situation with regard to the oft-cited danger that principles of international or global administrative law might be created with Western-hegemonic or parochial methods.[16] On the one hand, the danger of national traditions distorting the view of universal principles is reduced. On the other hand, donor law is still made mostly by Northern countries or organizations in which they are dominant. Thus, it is still emphatically necessary to remain sensitive to the danger of a hegemonically narrowed perspective in this area.

Völkerrecht, Beiträge zum ausländischen öffentlichen Recht und Völkerrecht (Berlin Heidelberg: Springer, 2009), vol. CCIV, p. 68 and sources cited therein; the classic perspective is stated H. Mosler, "General Principles of Law," in R. Bernhardt (ed.), *E-I: East African Community to Italy-United States Air Transport Arbitration (1965)* (Amsterdam: Elsevier, 1995), vol. II, pp. 511–27 at p. 511.

14 On the substance and the limits of development cooperation law see *supra* Intro.A.I.1.

15 On the difficulty of determining the sources in this area see Kingsbury, Krisch and Stewart, "Emergence of Global Administrative Law," 29–31; B. Kingsbury, "The Concept of 'Law' in Global Administrative Law," *European Journal of International Law*, 20 (2009), 23–57 at 23. On the critique, see A. Somek, "The Concept of 'Law' in Global Administrative Law: A Reply to Benedict Kingsbury," *European Journal of International Law*, 20 (2009), 985–95 at 985, for a more broadly conceived approach see A. von Bogdandy, P. Dann and M. Goldmann, "Völkerrecht als öffentliches Recht: Konturen eines rechtlichen Rahmens für Global Governance," *Der Staat*, 49 (2010), 1–128 at 18.

16 C. Harlow, "Global Administrative Law: The Quest for Principles and Values," *European Journal of International Law*, 17 (2006), 187–214 at 207, 208; Kadelbach and Kleinlein, "Überstaatliches Verfassungsrecht," 257, 258.

III. The Paris Declaration and the principles of development cooperation law

A final question one might ask is how the principles of development cooperation law relate to the principles of the 2005 Paris Declaration.[17] As discussed above, the Declaration is a milestone in the history of development aid.[18] It announces five basic considerations or principles for the effectiveness of development aid: ownership, alignment, harmonization, managing for results and mutual accountability. This study, however, does not orient itself more directly towards these principles – for three reasons.

First, the Paris Declaration principles only capture a part of what is of principal importance for development aid and development cooperation law. The Declaration emphasizes the aspect of coherence and efficiency of development aid. Other important topics of the aid system, such as the substantive goal of development or the role of individuals in the aid process are not addressed. Other aspects are addressed only partly so that they seem unsuited as general principles. The principle of ownership, for instance, is only one element of the general concept of collective autonomy which applies both to recipients and donors and is substantively more flexible than the narrow concept of ownership.[19] The Paris Declaration is thus only really important for those dimensions of development cooperation that correspond to a rather functionalist paradigm.

The weak normativity of the Paris Declaration is important. To be sure, the Declaration is a central political document and is of crucial importance for the discourse of development aid. To this extent, its content can be described, to use Armin von Bogdandy's terminology, as fundamental principles which frequently have norm-propositional importance.[20] From a legal perspective, however, the Paris Declaration has little substance. The document was neither discussed nor ratified by any parliament, even though this informality, as is well known, says little about the Declaration's effectiveness in guiding behavior.[21]

[17] At www.oecd.org/dataoecd/37/39/35023537.pdf (last visited July 2013).
[18] See *supra* Ch 2.C.III.1.
[19] Also discussed *infra* Ch 4.C.I.
[20] Bogdandy, "Prolegomena zu Prinzipien," p. 693.
[21] On the Paris Declaration from a legal perspective, P. Dann and L. Vierck, "Paris Declaration on Aid Effectiveness (2005)/Accra Agenda for Action (2008)," in Wolfrum, *Max Planck Encyclopedia of Public International Law*.

Finally, it should be noted that the Declaration, despite its importance, is only intended to have a temporary effect. Like the MDG, the Paris Declaration is subject to a deadline by which its goals are to be reached. In the case of the Paris Declaration, the deadline year was 2010.[22] Although the principles will also be relevant after this point, they are intended to be incorporated into a new Declaration.

Against this background, the Paris Declaration will be used to better grasp certain basic understandings, particularly in the area of collective autonomy of recipients (ownership) or the efficiency and coherence of action (and thus alignment and harmonization). Nevertheless, the Paris Declaration is not a comprehensive statement of aid principles.

B Development

Stark poverty in developing countries and the material asymmetry between countries gave rise to development aid and justifies its continued existence.[23] Development cooperation and the law governing it are practically and normatively oriented towards the solution of this problem. But how is this orientation treated in the law? How does public international law shape this agenda? Our discussion assumes that the relevant norms form the basis of a (structural) principle of development. It gives expression to a more idealistic and liberal paradigm of development aid.[24] According to this principle, states and international organizations are bound to use international cooperation to combat poverty. Both donors and recipients are called to participate in this effort, for example, by making use of ODA transfers. The principle of development expresses thus the central substantive goal of development cooperation, and connects this goal with a duty to cooperate – without, however, this duty being legally binding.

In the following section, we will investigate possible legal bases for such a principle (I). The relevant norms will be examined with regard to their specific substance and how much of a binding character they

[22] See on the follow-up document called Busan Partnership for Effective Development Cooperation, *supra* Ch 2.C.III.1.

[23] On the extent and dimensions of poverty see D. J. Shaw, "Dimensions of Poverty: Status and Solutions Towards the Millennium Development Goals," *Development Policy Review*, 23 (2005), 499–523 at 499; Greig, Hulme and Turner, *Challenging Global Inequality*, p. 10; for an introduction to the ethical discussion on poverty, see B. Bleisch and P. Schaber (eds.), *Weltarmut und Ethik* (Paderborn: Mentis, 2007).

[24] For a theoretical exposition of this, see Lumsdaine, *Moral Vision*.

have (II). Finally, we will turn to the question of who the norms are addressed to (III).

I. Possible legal bases

Various norms can be interpreted to create a "development principle" which requires international cooperation to combat poverty. The first possible legal basis is Art. 2(I) of the UN Charter, which guarantees the sovereign equality of states. This provision has surely traditionally been interpreted to guarantee equality in a merely formal sense. During the 1970s, however, exponents of an international law saw this paragraph as a lever for creating a legal right to substantive compensation. They suggested that Art. 2 be interpreted as a substantive call for equality – in particular a guarantee of equality of economic opportunity among all nations. Art. 2, thus understood, would justify positive discrimination in favor of developing countries.[25] This interpretation, however, did not win much support. A possible "duty to compensate" growing out of Art. 2 was largely rejected, and the formal understanding of equality prevailed.[26]

Nevertheless, the principle of development can be based on other pillars of international treaty law. The first candidates would be Art. 1(III) and 55(a) & (b) and 56 of the UN Charter. These articles require member states to improve living standards and to address international social and economic problems. From a human rights perspective, a meaningful contribution to a principle of development might come from Art. 2(I), 11(I) of the International Covenant on Economic, Social, and Cultural Rights (ICESCR) from 1966. This treaty requires every member state "to take steps, individually and through international assistance and co-operation, especially economic and technical, to the maximum of its available resources, with a view to achieving progressively the full realization of the rights recognized in the present Covenant by all appropriate means, including particularly the adoption of legislative measures."

Besides these international treaties, there are many political declarations (in particular, UN General Assembly Resolutions) which – in their

[25] Bulajic, *Principles of International Development Law*, p. 256; Feuer and Cassan, *Droit international*, pp. 32–4; Flory, *Droit international*, pp. 41–3; see also A. A. Fatouros, "Developing States," in R. Bernhardt (ed.), *A-D: Aalands Islands to Dumbarton Oaks Conference (1944)* (Amsterdam: North Holland Publishing Company, 1992), vol. I, pp. 1017–24 at p. 1021.

[26] A critical linkage of this outcome with the traditions of Western international-law doctrine is found in Kingsbury, "Sovereignty and Inequality," 603.

totality, continuity and degree of acceptance – suggest the existence of a legal consensus and thus a customary-law recognition of the principle of development, even if these would have to be spelled out in more detail to prove customary international law. These documents include Articles 22 and 28 of the Universal Declaration of Human Rights, which guarantee every person the right to a social and international order in which the rights and freedoms contained in the Declaration shall be realized by national measures and international cooperation. The Friendly Relations Declaration stresses the duty of every state to harmonious cooperation in accordance with the UN Charter, including "the promotion of economic growth throughout the world, especially that of the developing countries."[27] Similar sentiments occur in the General Assembly declaration on the creation of a New International Economic Order (NIEO) and other resolutions from the 1970s, although these were passed with only a majority of developing nations.[28] However, development-related instruments from the last ten years – in particular the Millennium Declaration[29] and the Monterrey Consensus – were passed by a consensus of all states.[30] These documents, in particular, stress poverty reduction as a priority of the international community.

This list of potential bases for a principle of development also includes the "right of development" initially discussed in the 1970s[31] and made

[27] UN-GA Res. 2625 (XXV) of October 24, 1970.

[28] UN-Resolution 3201 of May 1, 1974; a detailed discussion of the political background and legal structure of the declarations is found in Bulajic, *Principles of International Development Law*, pp. 126–30; R. Schütz, *Solidarität im Wirtschaftsvölkerrecht: Eine Bestandsaufnahme zentraler entwicklungsspezifischer Solidarrechte und Solidarpflichten im Völkerrecht* (Berlin: Duncker & Humblot, 1994), p. 65; and Kaltenborn, *Entwicklungsvölkerrecht und Neugestaltung*, p. 32 and sources cited therein; on the general politics of international law in the 1970s see, e.g. M. Koskenniemi, "History of International Law: Since World War II," in Wolfrum, *Max Planck Encyclopedia of Public International Law* at margin no. 19; see also *supra* Ch 2.A.1.

[29] UN-GA Res 55/2 of September 8, 2000.

[30] UN-GA Res. A/Res/56/210 B of July 9, 2002; for more background see *supra* Ch 2.C.III.1.

[31] The idea of a right to development (RTD) was first formulated by the Senegalese Kéba M'Baye, who later became a judge on the ICJ (K. M'Baye, "Le droit au developpement comme un droit de l'homme," *Revue des droits de l'homme*, 5 (1972), 505–34 at 505; the right was almost simultaneously also proposed by J. A. Carrillo Salcedo, "El derecho al desarrollo como dereche del person humana," *Revista Española de derecho international*, 25 (1972), 119–25 at 119; the case for an earlier emergence of the right is made in F. Ouguergouz, *The African Charter of Human and People's Rights: A Comprehensive Agenda for Human Dignity and Sustainable Democracy in Africa* (The Hague: Kluwer Law International, 2003), pp. 298, 290). He brought a new idea into the discussion on development in that he viewed the development principle not as a legal-political demand

concrete in the 1986 UN resolution.[32] In this resolution called the "United Nations Declaration on the Right to Development" it is proclaimed as a human right with both individual and collective dimensions, which in turn can justify claims to support in the development process.[33] This right was, however, based solely on nothing other than a UN General Assembly resolution passed over the objections of important donor states.[34] For a long time, it was more a bone of contention than a basis for cooperation. Only in 1998 was there a breakthrough toward a more pragmatic treatment of the issue.[35] We can thus conclude that a "right to development" is not a binding law as such but rather simply an expression of a certain

for solidarity but rather a *human right* that had long been present in international law. Especially since the mid 1970s, when donor countries demonstrated their opposition to legally binding payment obligations, the idea of an RTD offered a new strategy. It portrayed donor activity not as a result of a political struggle, but rather simply as a legal claim arising out of sound legal analysis. On the emergence of the idea see E. Riedel, *Theorie der Menschenrechtsstandards: Funktion, Wirkungsweise und Begründung wirtschaftlicher und sozialer Menschenrechte mit exemplarischer Darstellung der Rechte auf Eigentum und Arbeit in verschiedenen Rechtsordnungen* (Berlin: Duncker & Humblot, 1986), p. 211; S. Bennigsen, *Das "Recht auf Entwicklung" in der internationalen Diskussion* (Frankfurt: Peter Lang Verlag, 1989), p. 19; G. Odendahl, *Das Recht auf Entwicklung: Entstehungsgeschichte, systematische Stellung und Inhalt eines individuellen sowie kollektiven Menschrechts und Grundprinzips der Völkerrechtsordnung* (Aachen: Shaker, 1997), pp. 111–54.

[32] UN-GA Res. 41/128 of December 4, 1986. In 1979, the UN Human Rights Commission presented a 160-page report on the RTD which reflected the entire spectrum of positions. See C. Tomuschat, "Das Recht auf Entwicklung," *German Yearbook of International Law*, 25 (1982), 85–112 at 86–90.

[33] An African perspective is offered by Ouguergouz, *African Charter Of Human and People's Rights*, pp. 297–320 and sources cited therein.

[34] The USA voted against the resolution while Germany, Denmark, Finland, Great Britain, Iceland, Israel, Japan and Sweden abstained from voting. An informative presentation of the USA's attitude toward an RTD in general is found in S. Marks, "The Human Right to Development: Between Rhetoric and Reality," *Harvard Law School Human Rights Journal*, 17 (2004), 137–68 at 141.

[35] The Human Rights Commission recommended by consensus the creation of an open working group as well as the appointment of an independent expert who could create a model for evaluating and operationalizing an RTD (UN Human Rights Commission, Resolution 72/1998, Doc E/CN.4/1998/177 (1998)). This prepared the way for the 2004 creation of a High-Level Task Force which has since applied itself to establishing indicators for implementing and evaluating development partnerships. A surprising convergence of the current discussion of an RTD with international commercial law is noted in C. Tietje, "Internationales Wirtschaftsrecht und Recht auf Entwicklung als Elemente einer konstitutionalisierten globalen Friedensordnung," in K. Dicke, S. Hobe, K.-U. Meyn, A. Peters, E. Riedel, H.-J. Schütz and C. Tietje (eds.), *Weltinnenrecht: Liber amicorum Jost Delbrück* (Berlin: Duncker & Humblot, 2005), pp. 783–813 at p. 803.

point of view.[36] In contrast to the *principle* of development discussed in this book, the right to development is much broader and many-sided, since it calls for development in general as a right meant to be enjoyed by individuals, indigenous peoples and states. The principle of development, by contrast, relates only to institutional cooperation with the goal of reducing poverty by means of ODA transfers.

The legal basis for the principle of development can be drawn from (among other sources) a comparative analysis of the regulations of various donors, in particular the provisions relating to goals and mandates. When the same development-related principles appear in all these legal orders, this could indicate a principle applicable to the entire field. Relevant sources for this inquiry would be the mandate of the World Bank (Art. I of the Articles of the IDA/IBRD), Art. 209 of the TFEU, Art. 21 of the European Union Treaty, Art. 24 of the German Basic Law, and the Guidelines of the German Development Ministry. Finally, the 2005 European Consensus on Development, although it is a non-binding political declaration, is nevertheless another important document for determining EU and member-state policies and priorities.[37]

In the final analysis, there are a number of norms that could form the basis for a principle of development, whether based on treaty, customary law or donor statutes. It remains to be clarified which specific aspects of the principle are supported by which legal basis.

II. Contents

The principle of development basically comprises a general requirement of cooperation and assistance to achieve the goal of poverty reduction. This emerges from Articles 55(a), (b) and Article 56 of the UN Charter, as well as Article 2(1) ICESCR. These oblige the relevant actors to make constructive efforts to forge concrete development goals.[38] The principle

[36] There are, however, dissenting voices such as A. Sengupta, "On the Theory and Practice of the Right to Development," *Human Rights Quarterly*, 24 (2002), 837–89 at 841.

[37] OJ C 46/1 v. Feburary 24, 2006.

[38] The concept of development is addressed in detail *supra* Ch 2.B.I–II I. as well as immediately below in Section 2. On the duty to help in general see M. Sepulveda, "The Obligations of 'International Assistance and Cooperation' Under the International Covenant on Economic, Social and Cultural Rights: A Possible Entry to a Human Rights Based Approach to Millennium Development Goal 8," *The International Journal of Human Rights*, 13 (2009), 86–109 at 89–94; M. E. Salomon, *Global Responsibility for Human Rights: World Poverty and the Development of International Law* (Oxford

of development can thus be seen as particularly close to the principle of solidarity in international law, which likewise is said to give rise to a general duty to help.[39] As will be seen shortly, it is more appropriate in the present context to formulate a specific *development* principle, rather than a general principle of solidarity. The main reason for this is that it allows specification of the concrete goal of development aid – namely, poverty reduction and related goals. Solidarity, by contrast, is not only extremely vague,[40] but is also used in a wide variety of contexts, such as defense situations and natural disasters, as well as long-term support for development processes.[41]

If the principle of development is to be given a specific profile, we will need to determine what aspects of it are suggested by specific provisions.

1. A duty to provide ODA?

The first question is also the most demanding: does the principle of development justify a duty to fund ODA? A duty on the part of industrialized nations to pay 0.7 percent of their GNP as ODA has been a longstanding

University Press, 2008) as well as sources cited in the following footnote; a very early contribution to the discussion is found in B.-O. Bryde, "Von der Notwendigkeit einer neuen Weltwirtschaftsordnung," in B.-O. Bryde and P. Kunig (eds.), *Neuordnung der Weltwirtschaft?* (Baden-Baden: Nomos, 1986), pp. 29–54 at pp. 34–7.

[39] On the principle of solidarity in international law in general see Schütz, *Solidarität im Wirtschaftsvölkerrecht*; R. S. J. Macdonald, "Solidarity in the Practice and Discourse of Public International Law," *Pace International Law Review*, 8 (1996), 259–302 at 259; R. Wolfrum, "Solidarity Amongst States: An Emerging Structural Principle of International Law," in P.-M. Dupuy (ed.), *Völkerrecht als Wertordnung.* Festschrift für Christian Tomuschat (Kehl: Norbert P. Engel, 2006), pp. 1087–101 at p. 1087; M. Kotzur, "Soziales Völkerrecht für eine solidarische Völkergemeinschaft?" *Juristenzeitung*, 63 (2008), 265–72 at 265; on Vattel, a path-maker of this idea, see H. Steiger, "Solidarität und Souveränität oder Vattel reconsidered," in H. Steiger (ed.), *Von der Staatengesellschaft zur Weltrepublik?* (Baden-Baden: Nomos, 2009), pp. 133–41 at p. 133.

[40] On the breadth of the concept in intellectual history see K. Bayertz, "Begriff und Problem der Solidarität," in K. Bayertz (ed.), *Solidarität: Begriff und Problem* (Frankfurt am Main: Suhrkamp, 1998), pp. 11–53 at p. 11; for a particularly stimulating political conception see H. Brunkhorst, *Solidarität: Von der Bürgerfreundschaft zur globalen Rechtsgenossenschaft* (Frankfurt: Suhrkamp, 2002).

[41] On the variety of applications in the legal arena see R. Wolfrum and C. Kojima (eds.), *Solidarity: A Structural Principle of International Law* (Heidelberg: Springer, 2010); which includes my attempt to make the concept bear fruit in the area of development aid, "Solidarity and the Law of Development Cooperation," pp. 55–77 at p. 55.

demand.[42] It has also been intensively discussed,[43] and even assumed by some authors.[44] Nevertheless, doubts are in order.

The aforementioned treaty-based foundations of the development principle do not suggest such a duty. Article 2(I) of the ICESCR, in particular, does not posit a concrete and direct financial duty for donor states.[45] It would, however, remain possible for donor states to voluntarily assume such a duty. One example might be the EU's ODA Level Plan, passed by the Council of Europe in 2005 and reconfirmed in 2008.[46] The plan requires the EU and its member states to raise their ODA contributions to 0.7 percent of their GNP by the year 2015. Nevertheless, the Council's specific conclusions are not legally binding, having more the character of high-level political declarations.[47] Further the Level Plan only suggests abstract amounts, without specifying payment obligations or concrete allocations to specific countries. Thus, the Level Plan creates no binding payment obligations, and in particular no externally binding obligations toward specific recipient states.

[42] The demand is often stated in UN General Assembly Resolutions. The first was Resolution 2626 (XXV) of December 24, 1970 (margin nos. 42, 43), and has recently appeared in the Millennium Goals Declaration (UN-GA Res. 55/2 of September 18, 2000, margin no.15) and the Monterrey Consensus, UN-GA Res. 56/210 of July 9, 2002, margin nos. 41/42. On UN policy in this regard, see Bulajic, *Principles of International Development Law*, pp. 256, 257; Fukuda-Parr, "Millennium Development Goal 8," 966.

[43] Odendahl, *Recht auf Entwicklung*, pp. 268–74; W. Benedek, "Das Recht auf Entwicklung in universeller Sicht und im Rahmen des Afrikanischen Menschenrechtsschutzes," in H.-J. Konrad (ed.), *Grundrechtsschutz und Verwaltungsverfahren, unter besonderer Berücksichtigung des Asylrechts: Internationaler Menschenrechtsschutz*. Referate der 23. Tagung der wissenschaftlichen Mitarbeiter der Fachrichtung "Öffentliches Recht" 22–26 February 1983 in Berlin (Berlin: Duncker & Humblot, 1985), vol. CDLXXXIV, pp. 275–301 at p. 305.

[44] H. Weber, "Der Anspruch auf Entwicklungshilfe und die Veränderungen des internationalen Wirtschaftsrechts," *Verfassung und Recht in Übersee*, 11 (1978), 5–25 at 25; Flory, *Droit international*, pp. 56, 57; Bulajic, *Principles of International Development Law*, p. 256.

[45] On the interpretation of this treaty see M. Sepulveda, *The Nature of the Obligations Under the International Covenant on Economic, Social and Cultural Rights* (Antwerp: Intersentia, 2003), p. 31; more on a thoroughly conceivable indirect duty to provide funds *infra* in Ch 4.D.III.1c.

[46] Council of Europe, Presidency Conclusions, Doc 10255/1/05 Rev 1, margin no. 27 (15.7.2005); Council of Europe, Presidency Conclusions, Doc 11018/1/08 Rev 1, margin no. 59 (17.7.2008); reaffirmed in European Consensus on Development, margin no. 23 (OJ C 46/1 of 24.2.2006).

[47] J.-P. Jacqué, "Art. 4 EUV," in H. von der Groeben and J. Schwarze (eds.), *Vertrag über die Europäische Union und Vertrag über die Gründung der Europäischen Gemeinschaft*. Kommentar, 6th edn, IV (Baden-Baden: Nomos, 2003) at margin nos. 17; 20.

One could, however, also posit a self-imposed obligation emerging from the continued practice of donors in combination with UN Declarations which they often supported. Industrialized states, after all, have made ODA transfers for decades, usually to the same recipient nations. Particularly when recipient states have undertaken complementary activities and plans in reliance on continued ODA payments, one could posit a relationship of trust giving rise to an obligation of continued assistance on donor nations. Donor states, however, have consistently denied that any such concrete, binding obligation exists.[48] In UN votes, donor states have supported the 0.7 percent goal and the increased development efforts required by the MDG, but have always rejected the idea of specific legal obligations. Thus, in the final analysis, there are no grounds for imposing a concrete obligation on donor states to allocate ODA.[49]

Even if the principle of development basically[50] lacks an obligation to make ODA transfers, it still can give rise to specific obligations in the context of ODA transfers. These are based on an if-then logic: *if* ODA allocations are made, *then* the principle of development imposes certain rules on them. To use the language of administrative law, we can distinguish between discretion to decide and discretion to select: although donor

[48] For details see Salomon, *Global Responsibility*, pp. 98–100; the position staked out by the German government's Task Force on Law and Development is particularly clear: http://www2.ohchr.org/english/issues/development/docs/germany.pdf (last visited July 2013).

[49] Skeptical views include Alston, "Ships Passing," 776–8; E. Riedel, "Menschenrechte der Dritten Generation," in E. H. Riedel, C. Koenig and R. A. Lorz (eds.), *Die Universalität der Menschenrechte: Philosophische Grundlagen, Nationale Gewährleistungen, Internationale Garantien* (Berlin: Duncker & Humblot, 2003), pp. 329–61 at p. 352; W. Meng, "Völkerrecht als wirtschaftlicher Ordnungsfaktor und entwicklungspolitisches Steuerungsinstrument," in W. Meng, U. Magnus, S. Schlemmer-Schulte, T. Cottier, P.-T. Stoll and A. Epiney (eds.), *Das internationale Recht im Nord-Süd-Verhältnis* (Heidelberg: C.F. Müller, 2005), vol. XLI, pp. 1–76 at p. 22; C. Tomuschat, "Ensuring the Survival of Mankind on the Eve of a New Century," *Recueil des Cours*, 281 (1999), 9–438 at 265–6; earlier stated H. Neuhold, "Die Pflicht der Staaten zur Zusammenarbeit zwischen Staaten: moralisches Postulat oder völkerrechtliche Norm?" in H. Miehsler and D. Mayer-Maly (eds.), *Ius humanitatis: Festchrift zum 60. Geburtstag von Alfred Verdross* (Berlin: Duncker & Humblot, 1980), pp. 575–606 at p. 600; A. Bleckmann, "Anspruch auf Entwicklungshilfe?" *Verfassung und Recht in Übersee*, 12 (1979), 5–14 at 5; P. Kunig, "Die 'innere' Dimension des Rechts auf Entwicklung: Rechtspolitische Überlegungen zur Inpflichtnahme von Entwicklungsländern," *Verfassung und Recht in Übersee*, 19 (1986), 383–400 at 390.

[50] It should be noted that this assertion relates to the regular allocation of ODA, which is the primary component of development assistance. There are, however, good arguments for a duty to provide assistance in case of catastrophe. See, e.g. Riedel, *Theorie der Menschenrechtsstandards*, pp. 234, 235; Bleckmann, "Anspruch auf Entwicklungshilfe?" 14; see also *infra* Ch 4.D.III.

states have practically unlimited discretion to decide whether to make ODA allocations, they must nevertheless take account of several factors if they choose to do so. We can speak here of "accompanying obligations" that arise from ODA transfers.[51]

2. Poverty reduction and good governance

One primary component of the principle of development concerns the substantive goal of cooperation. This aspect requires the parties not only to pursue the general goal of development, but also the more specific goal of poverty reduction.[52] Development actors (donors as well as recipients) should ensure ODA is not used inappropriately and should concentrate on the goal of (sustainable) poverty reduction. This focus can be derived first and foremost from donor laws specifying the mandate of development aid. Today, all such regulations no longer specify development in general as the goal but explicitly add poverty reduction as well.[53] Poverty reduction is further emphasized by repeated references to the Millennium Declaration and the Millennium Development Goals, which themselves call for poverty reduction (although poverty is defined here rather broadly).[54] This new focus reflects a fundamental change in development law, which in turn grows out of a reaction to the legitimacy crisis that afflicted development work after the Cold War. The legitimacy problems sprang from the suspicion that ODA monies were actually being used to further other goals (fostering donor-state industries or security interests, or pursuing abstract economic theories), leading to the (supposed) failure of development aid. The focus on poverty reduction was meant to address this suspicion. If ODA was to be given at all, then only for the autonomous goal of poverty reduction. Although this focus is quite broad, it can still be used to argue against various inefficient development practices. It is particularly important as an argument against corruption in the context of development assistance, as corruption almost always detracts from legitimate goals of development aid.

It can also be asked whether development includes the goal of establishing good governance in recipient countries, thus making it part of a legally

[51] For a comparable approach see Kaltenborn, *Entwicklungsvölkerrecht und Neugestaltung*, pp. 123, 124.

[52] On the concentration of ODA on poverty reduction see *supra* Ch 2.B.III.

[53] Art. 209 I para. 1, TFEU; BMZ, *Guidelines*, margin no. 1; World Bank, OP 1.00, margin no. 1 (also European Consensus, margin no. 5).

[54] European Consensus, margin no. 6; OP 1.00, margin no. 1; ibid., margin no. 1.

binding principle of development.[55] Elements of the idea of good governance can now be found in many legal and political documents relating to development cooperation, although the phrase "good governance" is not always used explicitly. Both the law of the EU[56] and of Germany[57] contain such references. The European Consensus – the central mission statement of European development cooperation – also names this goal.[58] The World Bank's fundamental secondary-law mission statement discusses a broad concept of poverty that includes the aspect "lack of voice and representation."[59] Even if their provisions do not mention good governance explicitly, their policy documents do so, establishing it as both a goal and a means of development.[60] In general, then, we can say that the goal of good governance, while not legally binding, has nevertheless become a routine entry in the goal-catalog of development. It is therefore clearly a part of the structural principle of development, if not the legal principle.

3. Respect for human rights

Another accompanying obligation which grows out of the development principle – and, in particular, Art. 2(I) of the ICESCR – is respect for human rights during the disbursement and use of ODA funds.[61] Donors must evaluate the human rights consequences of projects they finance and avoid infringements (for instance, mass resettlements). This regulation gives rise, firstly, to a duty to evaluate the human rights consequences of projects before implementation. It also imposes a duty to avoid harmful effects arising from the imposition of conditionalities whose consequences might infringe rights guaranteed in the ICESCR. We can also

[55] On the current meaning of "good governance" in the development cooperation context see *supra* Ch 2.B.III.3; for a good analysis of its legal substance see Seppänen, *Good Governance*, pp. 85–100; a particularly stimulating critical approach is found in Möllers, "Governance-Konstellation," pp. 238, 239, see also C. Möllers, "European Governance: Meaning and Value of a Concept," *Common Market Law Review*, 43 (2006), 314–36 at 314.

[56] For example in Art. 21(II b). Lisbon Treaty; Art. 2(I), DCI Regulation; Arts. 9, 20(I d), Cotonou Agreement.

[57] See BMZ, *Guidelines*, margin no. 1; BMZ, *Concept No. 172.*

[58] European Consensus, margin no. 7.

[59] World Bank, OP 1.00, margin no. 1.

[60] On the openness of the World Bank's concept of development in this regard see Killinger, *The World Bank's Non-Political Mandate*, p. 63.

[61] On the interpretation of Art. 2 of the ECOSOC Treaty, in particular with reference to General Comment No. 3 of the UN Committee on Economic, Social, and Cultural Rights (of December 14, 1990) see Sepulveda, "The Obligations of International Assistance," 90–2.

derive a negative duty to refrain from all activities that undermine the goal of development.[62] Today, procedural aspects that may arise from human rights norms are commonly discussed in the context of an expanded idea of development. However, we will address these issues in other principles of development cooperation law, in particular the principles of collective and individual autonomy.[63]

III. Addressees

Addressees of the principle of development are, first of all, states acting as donors or recipients.[64] They are UN members and thus bound by the UN Charter. Frequently, they have also ratified the ICESCR and have their own development regulations. This means that the development principle also binds recipient countries. They, like donors, must use ODA only for poverty reduction and must respect and foster human rights.

The EU is also an addressee of the development principle based on European treaties, the EU's own secondary law, and Declarations based on these two sources (in particular, the European Consensus), as well as its general requirement to obey international law. Nevertheless, the EU is not a member of the UN member states or an ICESCR signatory.

International organizations are, to greater or lesser degrees, also addressees of the development principle. In the case of the World Bank, the Bank's founding treaties bind it to the basic elements of the development principle, as do secondary legal instruments which – as we have seen – define the goal of poverty reduction. Further, the Bank's status as a "special organization" of the UN is also important. Although scholars dispute whether the Bank is bound by UN General Assembly resolutions,[65] nevertheless, its requirement to follow the UN's basic goals, as defined by Art. 1(III) and Art. 55 of the UN Charter, is clear. Thus, the core substance of the development principle is binding on the Bank, even though the Bank is not bound by the ICESCR.

[62] An early proponent of this idea was Bryde, "Notwendigkeit," p. 43; for more detailed discussion of human rights and their implementation, see *infra* Ch 4.D.

[63] Discussed in detail *infra* Ch 4.C and D.

[64] In the current context of the principles of development cooperation law, we are concerned more with principles, goal statements and key ideas than with concrete, binding rules. Accordingly, the phrase "addressees" will be used instead of "obligees."

[65] This will be discussed in greater detail in the context of a potential binding effect of human rights *infra* Ch 4.D.

IV. Summary

The arrival of developing nations on the international stage appeared to herald a new stage of international law. Until then, the formal principle of sovereign equality had concealed actual inequalities. Many assumed that a new order would now arise in which the material welfare of those in the developing nations would be guaranteed by concrete and binding legal obligations.[66] Political independence, it was thought, was incomplete without an economic basis to permit its realization.

These expectations were not fulfilled. According to the current view among international lawyers, there is *no binding right* to development giving rise to obligations toward developing countries. We will thus here only outline a structural principle of development, without making larger claims. The principle obliges states and international organizations to engage in a political sense in constructive cooperation with the goal of poverty reduction. Rather than imposing material financial obligations, it demands that parties make development cooperation and ODA transfers possible. In particular, it specifies the (accompanying) obligations concerning ODA allocations and the implementation of ODA-funded projects. To use administrative law terminology concerning discretionary action, donors retain generally unlimited discretion *whether* they will make ODA allocations, but once they have decided to give, their discretion during the *selection* process is limited. When it comes to ODA allocations, the development principle imposes certain requirements, such as a focus on poverty reduction or a ban on human rights violations or other damage to developing nations.

The legal status of this principle needs to be assessed with caution. Although there is much support in various provisions for this principle, it is here considered merely as a structural principle. This position is justified because not all actors are bound by the relevant legal instruments

[66] Flory, *Droit international*, p. 51; Bulajic, *Principles of International Development Law*, p. 252; I. Huq, "From Charity to Obligation: A Third World Perspective on Concessional Resource Transfers," *Texas International Law Journal*, 14 (1979), 389–424 at 389; more cautiously, J. Delbrück, "Völkerrecht und Weltfriedenssicherung," in D. Grimm (ed.), *Rechtswissenschaft und Nachbarwissenschaften: Band 2: Geschichte, Logik, Linguistik, Informatik, Friedensforschung, Finanzen, Didaktik*, 2 vols. (Munich: C.H. Beck, 1976), pp. 179–91 at p. 179; Bryde, "Notwendigkeit, "p. 37; and much more cautiously U. Scheuner, "Solidarität unter den Nationen als Grundsatz in der gegenwärtigen internationalen Gemeinschaft," in J. Delbrück, K. Ipsen and D. Rauschning (eds.), *Recht im Dienst des Friedens: Festschrift für Eberhard Menzel zum 65. Geburtstag am 21. Januar 1976* (Berlin: Duncker & Humblot, 1975), pp. 251–77 at p. 251.

(such as the ICESCR), and because some bases of the development principle, such as UN General Assembly resolutions, are not themselves binding law. Nevertheless, important components of the principle can be found in all of the legal regimes which, taken together, constitute development cooperation law as a legal field which encompasses many organizations and levels of government. We can thus plausibly develop a structural principle that is a main component of development cooperation law writ large.

C Collective autonomy and ownership

Development cooperation is not just an economic process but also a political one. The form and substance of cooperation must be continuously negotiated. How donors and recipients can integrate their preferences into this process – that is, how they can legally protect their collective autonomy – is one of the central questions of development cooperation law.[67] This question is particularly pressing in the development context, in which recipients' autonomy is constantly endangered by immense inequality relative to donors and hence the asymmetry in their relationship. This contains the risk that donors simply impose their (political and economic) preference on recipients. The donors, for their part, have a justified interest in controlling the use of their funds, i.e. their taxpayers' money. The respective claims to autonomy are of equal worth. This makes the question of how to preserve autonomy in the face of asymmetry even more pressing. The principle of collective autonomy should provide an answer.[68]

Collective autonomy is the second guiding concept of development cooperation law and is a legal principle. Its normative contours will be outlined in three steps. First, the principle is to be based on the general principle of sovereignty to be found in international law. At the same time, it has seen a certain reformulation in the principle of ownership, particular to the development field. Substantive structure and legal meaning will be discussed below (I). The principle of sovereignty is further concretized by the guarantee of formal equality among sovereign subjects, which should principally benefit weaker states. This guarantee will, however, be critically assessed (II). The final question is how the postulated

[67] On this procedural concept of development, see *supra* Intro.A.II.3.

[68] On the practical problems of preserving autonomy in the face of real-world inequalities see *supra* Ch 2.C.II.1.

equal autonomy can be protected in the case of conflicts and violations. Protection can be found in international treaty law (III.1) and the general principle of non-intervention (III.2). Finally, the results of the discussion will be summarized (IV).

I. *Sovereignty and ownership*

The starting point and legal basis for the principle of collective autonomy is found in the principle of the sovereign equality of states as formulated in Article 2(I) of the UN Charter and as recognized in customary international law.[69] The core principle of sovereignty is found in the Declaration of Principles of 1970: "Each State has the right to freely choose and develop its political, social, economic and cultural system."[70] Sovereignty is thus given a central function in the guarantee of constitutional self-determination: by external means, it protects internal self-determination. Sovereignty secures the right of each state, independent of its size or power, to determine its own internal order. In its inner dimension, sovereignty primarily protects a state's constitutional autonomy and identity.[71]

There can be no doubt of the validity of this principle, nor can it be doubted that it is a legal principle. Also well established is the binding force of this principle of customary international law on supranational organizations such as the World Bank and the EU.[72] Nevertheless, one can imagine additions to the normative basis of this principle. For instance,

[69] Tomuschat, "Ensuring the Survival," 165, 166; B. Fassbender, "Die Souveränität des Staates als Autonomie im Rahmen der völkerrechtlichen Verfassung," in H.-P. Mansel, T. Pfeiffer, H. Kronke, C. Kohler and R. Hausmann (eds.), *Festschrift für Erik Jayme*, 2 vols. (Munich: Sellier, 2004), pp. 1089–101 at p. 1089; on the transformation and change in meaning of the principle see S. Oeter, "Souveränität – ein überholtes Konzept?" in H.-J. Cremer (ed.), *Tradition und Weltoffenheit des Rechts.* Festschrift für Helmut Steinberger (Berlin: Springer, 2002), vol. CLII, pp. 259–90 at pp. 282, 286f.; N. Walker (ed.), *Sovereignty in Transition* (Oxford: Hart Publishing, 2003); for a provocative political-science perspective see S. D. Krasner, *Sovereignty: Organized Hypocrisy* (Princeton University Press, 1999); on the third-world understanding of sovereignty see L. Kühnhardt, *Stufen der Souveränität* (Bonn: Bouvier, 1992).

[70] Declaration of Principles of International Law Concerning Friendly Relations and Co-operation Among States in Accordance with the Charter of the United Nations UN-GA Res. 2625 (XX), of October 24, 1970.

[71] On the core substance, which is binding *ius cogens*, see S. Kadelbach, *Zwingendes Völkerrecht*, Schriften zum Völkerrecht (Berlin: Duncker & Humblot, 1992), vol. CI, pp. 221–3.

[72] R. Hofmann, "Die Rechtskontrolle von Organen der Staatengemeinschaft," in R. Hofmann, A. Reinisch, T. Pfeiffer, S. Oeter and A. Stadler (eds.), *Die Rechtskontrolle von Organen der Staatengemeinschaft: Vielfalt der Gerichte – Einheit des Prozessrechts?*

one could propose basing the principle of collective autonomy on the right to self-determination, as expressed in Art. 1(II) of the UN Charter and Art. 1 of both UN Human Rights Covenants. Especially when one interprets the word "people" to refer not to individual, often ethnically defined groups but rather the population of states, one can derive a second normative basis for the principle of collective autonomy. In the so-called "internal law" to self-determination, the population of a state is seen as the possessor of the right to self-determination.[73] This internal right to self-determination, however, is directed toward a state's leadership. The government may, in turn, face claims for regional autonomy. There is also intensive discussion of the question whether there may be a right to a specific – in particular, democratic – form of government.[74] These internal claims are, however, not relevant to the present discussion. We are concerned with relations between states or between states and international organizations, and the right of a recipient nation to enforce its own preferences as against external donors. In this context, the citizens of a state are represented and mediated through their government. Thus, the right of peoples to self-determination has little import here.[75]

The discussion of sovereignty in the development context also raises the question whether states that do not or cannot fulfill the basic functions of statehood (that is, whose statehood is fragile) lose their sovereignty. This

Referate und Thesen. (Heidelberg: C.F. Müller, 2007), vol. XLII, pp. 1–35 at p. 1; Schermers and Blokker, *International Institutional Law*, margin nos.1572–9; see also A. Bleckmann, "Zur Verbindlichkeit des allgemeinen Völkerrechts für internationale Organisationen," *Heidelberg Journal of International Law*, 37 (1977), 107–21 at 107; on the binding effect of customary international law on the EU see C. Tomuschat, "Art. 281 EGV," in H. von der Groeben and J. Schwarze (eds.), *Vertrag über die Europäische Union und Vertrag über die Gründung der Europäischen Gemeinschaft*. Kommentar, 6th edn, IV (Baden-Baden: Nomos, 2003) at margin no. 43; R. Uerpmann-Wittzack, "Völkerrechtliche Verfassungselemente," in A. von Bogdandy and J. Bast (eds.), *Europäisches Verfassungsrecht*, 2nd edn (Heidelberg: Springer, 2009), pp. 177–226 at pp. 182–5; A. von Bogdandy and M. Smrkolj, "European Community and Union Law and International Law," in Wolfrum, *Max Planck Encyclopedia of Public International Law* at margin nos. 23, 24.

[73] A. Rosas, "Internal Self-Determination," in C. Tomuschat (ed.), *Modern Law of Self-Determination* (Dordrecht: Nijhoff, 1993), pp. 227–8 at p. 227.

[74] J. Klabbers, "The Right to be Taken Seriously: Self-Determination in International Law," *Human Rights Quarterly*, 28 (2006), 186–206 at 186; D. Thürer and T. Burri, "Self-Determination," in Wolfrum, *Max Planck Encyclopedia of Public International Law* at margin nos. 33–9.

[75] However, it would also be possible for non-state actors to invoke this principle to support a right to participate in development-aid processes. This idea is better pursued in a work on the legal position of non-state actors in development cooperation law.

question is addressed more in a practical than legal manner.[76] There are no calls for limitation on legal sovereignty in this context.[77] To do so would be to ignore the formal *legal* character of the attribute of sovereignty.[78]

There is yet another dimension of the autonomy guarantee that bears discussion. It not only gives recipient states the basic right to decide on the use of ODA on their territories, but also permits donor states to administer their own resources. ODA donors also have a right to decide on how their monies are used. The attempt to resolve conflicts between these two claims to autonomy is thus a central question of development cooperation law.

1. Ownership

Sovereignty of states is the central principle of collective autonomy. In recent years, however, it has been reformulated in a rather curious way into the concept of *ownership*, which is now practically ubiquitous in development discourse. Particularly in the Monterrey Consensus and the Paris Declaration, ownership plays an important part in the discussion of division of responsibility in development cooperation.[79] What is ownership, what is its legal status, and how does it relate to sovereignty and collective autonomy?

To understand the concept, it is necessary to know the context in which it emerged. Like governance, it first appeared in the early 1990s in the analyses of the World Bank and IMF,[80] and since 2000, has become extremely common in texts relating to development.[81] Two elements are key. Its emergence is, first of all, associated with the frustration of donors concerning the ineffectiveness of many development projects and

[76] See, e.g. Jackson, *Quasi-states*; D. Williams, "Aid and Sovereignty: Quasi-States and the International Financial Institutions," *Review of International Studies*, 26 (2000), 557–73 at 557.

[77] On the treatment of fragile states in international law see S. Oeter, "Regieren im 21. Jahrhundert: Staatlichkeit und internationales System," in S. Weiss and J. Schmierer (eds.), *Prekäre Staatlichkeit und internationale Ordnung* (Wiesbaden: Verlag für Sozialwissenschaften, 2007), pp. 70–84 at p. 70; M. von Engelhardt, "Reflections on the Role of the State in the Legal Regimes of International Aid," *Zeitschrift für ausländisches öffentliches Recht und Völkerrecht (ZaöRV)*, 71 (2011), 451–74.

[78] There is a more fundamental discussion with regard to illiberal states – to whom, some argue, the egalitarian foundations of international law should not apply. See, e.g. A.-M. Slaughter, "International Law in a World of Liberal States," *European Journal of International Law*, 6 (1995), 503–38 at 534; P. Minnerop, *Paria-Staaten im Völkerrecht?* (Berlin, Heidelberg: Springer, 2004); the clearest statement is Rawls, *Law*, p. 90.

[79] See *supra* Ch 2.C.III.1

[80] Johnson and Wasty, *Borrower Ownership*.

[81] Killick, *Aid and the Political Economy*, p. 86; L. Whitfield and A. Fraser, "Introduction: Aid and Sovereignty," in L. Whitfield (ed.), *The Politics of Aid: African Strategies for*

conditionalities. The failure was explained by a lack of real commitment by recipient nations during implementation of joint projects. At the same time, however, many suspected that there was also a political strategy behind the introduction of the concept, which was devised by donors, in particular the World Bank, the IMF and OECD-DAC. "Ownership" could be seen as a reaction to the strident criticism of World Bank structural-adjustment programs and the (supposed) paternalistic behavior of donors: it is an attempt to share program responsibility.

But what does it mean precisely? Looking at its use in statements of principle in the development area – in particular, the Paris Declaration, which uses it most specifically – ownership calls for a leading role and a leading responsibility for recipient nations in the development process. Recipients should take over an important agenda-setting role during the creation of development strategies, implement the plans in concrete political programs and coordinate donors' funds.[82] They should be independent authors and leading organizers of their development programs and assume responsibility for them. In this context, "recipient" usually means recipient-state governments. These governments are meant to develop programs by means of "broad consultative processes" which foster civil society.[83] Nevertheless, the concept is directed primarily at governing and administrative actors. Non-state entities, as well as legislatures, play a secondary role.

Legally, ownership has remained (up to this point) a non-binding principle. It is thus a structural principle in terms of the definition above.[84] The Paris Declaration and the European Consensus, both of which rely extensively on the idea, are political declarations. The concept has, however, also found use in various legally binding texts.[85] One can expect that the principle will find support in UN resolutions soon, given that

Dealing with Donors (Oxford University Press, 2009), pp. 1–26 at pp. 3–5. A deeper analysis of the emergence of the concept still does not exist.

[82] OECD, Paris Declaration on Aid Effectiveness, margin no. 14. On the conceptions of various donors (before the formulation of the Paris Declaration) O. Johnson, *Country Ownership of Reform Programs and the Implication for Conditionality: G24 Discussion Paper Series No. 35*, pp. 4, 5. Available at www.g24.org/ResearchPaps/ojohnson.pdf (last visited July 2013).

[83] Other legal texts use similar formulations or refer directly to the Paris Declaration, see Arts. 3(VIII), 19, DCI Regulation; Art. 2, 57, Cotonou Agreement; Arts. 1, 4, 6, Regulation (EC) 617/2007 (on the implementation of the Cotonou Agreement); BMZ, *Guidelines*, margin no. 1; European Consensus of December 2005, margin no.14; World Bank, OP 2.11, margin no.8.

[84] *Supra* Ch 4.A.II.

[85] See sources cited in footnote 83.

no group of nations rejects it (although it is noteworthy how it is usually rather included in donor-side regulations).

How does the concept of ownership fit into the overall framework of international law? In particular, how does it relate to the principle of sovereignty as the basis of the principle of collective autonomy? The concept of ownership can be seen, first, as a situation-specific affirmation of sovereignty. It strengthens the right of independence in the formulation of development plans, thus assigning programming competency to recipients. This competence, however, was never really in doubt, given that development programs involve fundamental decisions concerning the structure of a state's internal organization. It cannot be doubted that these decisions are a part of a state's protected area of sovereign self-determination.

Thus, another aspect of ownership – more in the nature of a duty – comes to the fore. Recipients not only have the right, but also now explicitly the *duty* to formulate, coordinate and responsibly implement programs. They must not only write programs but also stand by them. Thus seen, ownership brings an element of reciprocity into development cooperation, more than a mere confirmation of sovereignty. When recipients must present plans as a condition of ODA allocations, the formulation of the plans becomes a precondition for donor participation. This would be problematic from an international-law perspective only if recipient ownership (and the ensuing duties) were introduced unilaterally by donors, to recipients' disadvantage. Whether this problem exists can only be answered by an analysis of the particular structures of development cooperation law and, in particular, programming.[86]

A third aspect of the principle of ownership should be mentioned: as a constraint on donors. Ownership requires donors to implement recipient-developed strategies and projects even when they may not fit with the donors' concepts.[87] It formulates a duty of respect.

In the final analysis, ownership emerges as more complex and ambivalent than we might first have thought. It is a situation-specific affirmation of the autonomy of recipients and, at the same time, an obligation to begin and take responsibility for the process of their own development. This explains, to a certain degree, the seemingly paradoxical fact that donors first created the principle. Ownership represents an intensification of the legal principle of collective autonomy, based primarily on the principle of sovereignty. The concept also constrains donors. They are called upon to

[86] On these duties see *infra* Ch 5.B and C.

[87] See Paris Declaration, margin no.15.

restrain their own parallel planning processes and respect the independently formulated strategies of recipients.

II. *Equal autonomy and its limits*

Collective autonomy is not guaranteed merely on its own. It is also granted to all states in *equal measure*, as the principle of sovereign equality declares.[88] What does this qualification signify?

First, the equality principle guarantees the *formal* equality of all states under law. As seen above, most observers agree that the equality principle is not based on material considerations.[89] Rather, all states are guaranteed legal equality regardless of size or power. In particular, the principle describes an equal right to participate in interstate relations. This includes a right to make treaties, to receive and send diplomats and to take part in the creation of customary law. The principle also constitutes a duty of all nations, from the USA to the Marshal Islands, to obey general rules of international law.[90] In the context of development cooperation law, the principle means that, during bilateral contracting for ODA allocations, both parties are treated formally as equal, even when, in reality, they are immensely unequal. Wealthy donors must, therefore, recognize recipients as equals and negotiate with them as such. The principle could be read to require a kind of legal "equality of arms" between the parties.[91]

Nevertheless, the principle of equality is not unlimited. It is generally taken to be only a rule of *ius cogens* insofar as it applies to the inalienable core of the right of nations to self-determination. Outside this core, it can be modified by mutual consent.[92] This can be both an advantage

[88] (Resolution 2625/XXV); see also U. K. Preuß, "Equality of States – Its Meaning in a Constitutionalized Global Order," *Chicago Journal of International Law*, 9 (2008), 17–49 at 26, 27; J. Kokott, "States, Sovereign Equality," in Wolfrum, *Max Planck Encyclopedia of Public International Law* at margin no. 1; B. Fassbender and A. Bleckmann, "Art. 2 (1) UN-Charta," in B. Simma (ed.), *The Charter of the United Nations: A Commentary*, 2nd edn, II (Oxford University Press, 2002), pp. 68–91 at margin nos.48, 53–58; Tomuschat, "Ensuring the Survival," 161; R. P. Anand, "Sovereign Equality of States in International Law," *Recueil des Cours*, 197 (1986), 9–228; G. Dahm, J. Delbrück and R. Wolfrum, *Völkerrecht*, 2nd edn (Berlin: de Gruyter, 1989), p. 236.

[89] See *supra* Ch 4.B.I.

[90] For an overview of the rights which are specifically protected see Tomuschat, "Ensuring the Survival," 189–95.

[91] The same number of participants in the negotiation and/or jurists, balanced participation in the proceeding, sufficient time for formulation, etc.

[92] Kadelbach, *Zwingendes Völkerrecht*, pp. 224–6.

and a drawback for developing nations.[93] In some legal areas, deviations from the equality principle are consciously used for the benefit of developing nations. This is true particularly in environmental law, where it takes the form of the principle of common, but differential, responsibility,[94] and is also partially true in trade law.[95] In this context, the principle of reciprocity is thought to be relaxed in a *substantive* manner, that is by material concessions. Development aid is also based on a similar kind of relaxing of the principle, since ODA refers only to grants or subsidized loans.[96]

The situation is different when it comes to "procedural reciprocity," that is equal representation in procedures and before agencies. This is particularly applicable to rules of representation in international organizations. In many international organizations, differentiations are based on functional, regional or power-based considerations.[97] One particularly relevant example for development cooperation law is the voting and representation rules in development banks, especially the World Bank. There, voting rights are apportioned basically according to member states' financial contributions, giving donor states clear dominance in the decision-making process.[98] The same goes for the World Bank presidency. Since the 1940s, there has been an informal accord between the USA and European states by which, instead of a principle of rotation or a free choice

[93] C. Warbrick, "The Principle of Sovereign Equality," in V. Lowe and C. Warbrick (eds.), *The United Nations and the Principles of International Law: Essays in Memory of Michael Akehurst* (London, New York: Routledge, 1994), pp. 204–29 at p. 211.

[94] U. Beyerlin, "Bridging the North-South-Divide in International Environmental Law," *Heidelberg Journal of International Law*, 66 (2006), 259–96 at 259; Cullet, *Differential Treatment*; B. Kellersmann, *Die gemeinsame, aber differenzierte Verantwortlichkeit von Industriestaaten und Entwicklungsländern für den Schutz der globalen Umwelt*, Beiträge zum ausländischen öffentlichen Recht und Völkerrecht (Berlin, Heidelberg: Springer, 2000), vol. CXLIII.

[95] Krajewski, *Wirtschaftsvölkerrecht*, p. 264; M. Hilf and S. Oeter, *WTO-Recht: Rechtsordnung des Welthandels* (Baden-Baden: Nomos, 2005), margin no. 31; Thomas and Trachtman, *Developing Countries* and sources cited therein.

[96] The definition of ODA is discussed *supra* Intro.A.I.

[97] Also in the UN (vgl. Art. 23(I), 27(III) UN Charter), and in other organizations. See Schermers and Blokker, *International Institutional Law*, pp. 675, 794; A. D. Efraim, *Sovereign (In)equality in International Organizations* (The Hague: Martinus Nijhoff Publishers, 2000); J. Katz Cogan, "Representation and Power in International Organization: The Operational Constitution and its Critics," *American Journal of International Law*, 103 (2009), 209–63 at 212; see also R. Wolfrum, "Neue Elemente im Willensbildungsprozeß internationaler Wirtschaftsorganisationen," *Vereinte Nationen*, 29 (1981), 50–6 at 50.

[98] See *supra* Ch 3.B.IV.1; see also Rigo Sureda, "Law," 42–4.

of the best candidate, the US administration names the president.[99] Here, then, differentiation works to the disadvantage of developing countries.

Critiques of this policy (mainly but not exclusively from developing countries) fall into two main camps.[100] First, it is argued as a *practical* matter that these representation rules no longer reflect current power relationships in world politics and global commerce and thus need to be changed, not least to preserve the relevance of international institutions such as the World Bank.[101] The second, and more fundamental, point is that developing countries, since the 1970s, have argued for an independent principle which guarantees the effective participation of *all* countries in international decision-making processes. Article 10 of the Charter of Economic Rights and Duties of States prominently states that all states must have the right "to participate fully and effectively in the international decision-making process in the solution of world economic, financial and monetary problems."[102] The principle has since been repeated in many UN Declarations.[103] Nevertheless, Article 10 does not establish a binding legal rule. Thus, the expansion of the principle of formal equality to specifically guarantee procedural equality – especially in international institutions – has not yet occurred.

In the final analysis, then, the equality principle has little real force. It guarantees only a few formal rights to equal participation, and even these can be altered to the disadvantage of weaker nations. Is the equality principle, then, largely obsolete? It would be premature to say so. It is true that its scope is modest, and its mere existence can be seen as a

[99] On the relevant formal and informal rules see Katz Cogan, "Representation and Power," 220, 227.

[100] On the general conflict between developing and industrialized nations on their representation see S. D. Krasner, *Structural Conflict: The Third World Against Global Liberalism* (Berkeley: University of California Press, 1985); for a current analysis see S. Talmon, "Participation of UN Member States in the Work of the Organization: A Multicultural Alternative to Present-Day Regionalism?" in S. Yee and J.-Y. Morin (eds.), *Multiculturalism and International Law: Essays in Honour of Edward McWhinney* (Leiden, Boston: Martinus Nijhoff Publishers, 2009), pp. 239–75 at p. 239; Katz Cogan, "Representation and Power," 241 (who further differentiates critique of the procedure itself, in particular its opacity and informality).

[101] High-Level Commission on Modernization of World Bank Group Governance, *Repowering the World Bank*, margin nos. 84–7; Katz Cogan, "Representation and Power," 240, 241.

[102] UN-GA, Res. 3281 (XXIX) of December 12, 1974; see also Bulajic, *Principles of International Development Law*, pp. 322–30; Kaltenborn, *Entwicklungsvölkerrecht und Neugestaltung der internationalen*, p. 110; Anand, "Sovereign Equality," 138.

[103] For instance, in the Millennium Declaration, UN-GA 55/2 of September 18, 2000, margin no. 5; Monterrey Consensus, UN-GA Res. 56/210 of July 9, 2002, margin no. 62, 63.

smokescreen hiding background ignorance of greater real inequalities.[104] Many authors nonetheless see the insistence on equality, even if counterfactual, as a valuable formal protection for smaller states because it is difficult to evade. Without the principle, the more powerful countries and interests would be able to coordinate and dominate even more directly. The formality of the rules themselves offers weaker states protection, at least in principle.[105] This minimal level of formal protection furnishes a protective barrier (albeit a modest one) against the dominance of stronger states, especially in contract relationships between donors and recipients.

III. Protection of autonomy

Proclaiming collective autonomy is one thing; protecting it against infringement and conflict quite another. Conflicting autonomy claims are inevitable, unless one envisions development cooperation as a primarily technocratic process whose milestones and solutions are agreed in "expertocratic" deliberations. The world-views of donors and recipients are rarely identical, meaning that the use of ODA triggers constant debates and conflict. The mostly[106] superior bargaining position of donors is of particular importance here. We will now assess international-law rules against improper infringements of autonomy. One limit on infringements by donors has already been discussed above in the principle of ownership, which requires respect for the priorities of recipient states. Nevertheless, this is still not a complete answer to how autonomy can be guaranteed in the face of asymmetries.

1. Inadequate protection in international treaty law

We will first examine international treaty law. The rules established therein are of particular importance for development cooperation law, since ODA transfers are agreed on in international agreements. This area of the law seems initially promising as a source of protection against coercion and the redress of inequalities. Nevertheless, two attempts to establish protections for autonomy failed due to opposition from industrialized nations.

[104] Kingsbury, "Sovereignty and Inequality," 600, 601; an equally critical and informative perspective is found in G. Simpson, *Great Powers and Outlaw States: Unequal Sovereigns in the International Legal Order* (Cambridge University Press, 2004).

[105] On the defense of formality see Koskenniemi, "Constitutionalism," 9; Kingsbury, "Sovereignty and Inequality," 603.

[106] Not always do donors have a superior bargaining position. Especially important recipients, such as India, China or Brazil, are (at least) on equal footing with the donors.

At the beginning of the twentieth century, at colonialism's zenith, international law scholars began an intensive discussion of the legal concept of *unequal treaties*.[107] Chinese and Soviet authors, in particular, argued that treaties which qualified as unequal should be held void. This would be the case when the treaty imposed unequal duties, did not entail reciprocity and was imposed in circumstances of extreme restriction on sovereignty or under (political, military or economic) coercion. The historical background of this doctrine was the huge number[108] of treaties of colonial powers with China, in particular, and other Asian nations signed since the mid nineteenth century. In these treaties, the colonial powers granted themselves wide-ranging rights, in particular extraterritorial jurisdiction over their citizens and local operations, unhindered access to ports, the right to their own territorial ownership, and, not least, various trade concessions (in particular, lower tariffs). These contracts, whose substance clearly shows them to be coercive, usually arose under circumstances of massive diplomatic – and even military – coercion. Over time, they came to be seen by Asians as colonial humiliation, and became a rallying-point for national resistance against foreign rule.

The international law of the industrial states, however, never recognized the doctrine of unequal treaties.[109] In any event, the treaties were all dissolved prior to the Second World War. During the Cold War, the doctrine of unequal treaties was a central difference between communist and capitalist international-law thinking. The doctrine disappeared with the end of the Cold War. Most developing countries never really took up the doctrine.

Instead, the developing countries concentrated foremost on the preparation of the 1969 Vienna Convention on the Law of Treaties (VCLT) and the obvious problem of power differentials between Northern and Southern contracting parties.[110] They mainly concentrated, largely unsuccessfully, on increasing protections against all forms of coercion during treaty negotiations. The VCLT contains neither protection against substantively

[107] See A. Peters, "Unequal Treaties," in Wolfrum, *Max Planck Encyclopedia of Public International Law* at margin no. 1.

[108] Anne Peters assumes that 1,000 such treaties exist in the case of China in ibid., margin no. 10.

[109] A fascinating treament of the question why this was so and continues to be so is M. Craven, "What Happened to Unequal Treaties? The Continuities of Informal Empire," *Nordic Journal of International Law*, 74 (2005), 335–82 at 335–82.

[110] On the creation of the VCLT R. D. Kearney and R. E. Dalton, "The Treaty on Treaties," *American Journal of International Law*, 64 (1970), 495–561 at 495.

unequal treaties nor a general protection regime for "weaker" states. The Convention recognizes, in Arts. 46–52, only a very few circumstances that can lead to the invalidity of a treaty. Coercion is addressed in Art. 51, which deals with threats against a country's diplomatic representative, and Art. 52, which invalidates treaties when coercion violates principles of international law as codified in the UN Charter. The reference to UN principles is, however, generally thought to refer only to military coercion (Art. 2(IV) of the UN Charter), not to economic or political pressure.[111] Thus, the law of treaties does not give developing countries the ability to decline pressure to adopt certain projects or programs without losing the entire aid offer.

The genesis of this legal situation is quite revealing: the wording of Art. 52 of the VCLT was extremely controversial.[112] Nineteen governments, largely from the non-aligned movement, insisted that Art. 52 should incorporate a broad notion of coercion which would have included economic and political pressure. This proposal met fierce resistance from industrialized countries. Their primary argument was the stability of treaties, which could be undermined by such a clause. However, other considerations were also in play. Developing countries had let it be known that they would view the withdrawal of development aid or even the threat thereof as coercion that could invalidate treaties. For example, Algeria's representatives argued that colonial oppression would survive in a different form if developing countries could be forced by industrialized states to adopt certain policies. These warring positions threatened to sabotage the entire treaty process. Industrialized countries, which would have been greatly outnumbered in an open vote, made it clear that they would never accept the broad wording of Art. 52. They put enough pressure on developing nations to force a compromise. According to the compromise, a Declaration would be attached to the Convention that would declare all forms of pressure and coercion impermissible. This was done. The industrialized countries had prevailed.

Thus, in international treaty law – and so also in the framework for ODA, which is always treaty-based – there are no specific protections against economic or political pressure during negotiations. Developed nations had prevented the creation of any such rules during the VCLT's new formulation of the law of treaties.

[111] I. M. Sinclair, *The Vienna Convention on the Law of Treaties* (Manchester University Press, 1973), pp. 97, 98; P. Reuter, *Introduction to the Law of Treaties* (London, New York: Kegan Paul International, 1995), pp. 180–2.

[112] Kearney and Dalton, "Treaty on Treaties," 532–5.

2. Weak protection afforded by the principle of non-intervention

A further element of legal protection for collective autonomy is the principle of non-intervention as a principle of non-interference, anchored in the UN Charter (Art. 2(VII)) and the Declaration of Principles of 1970.[113] The principle is intended to delimit the amount of permissible influence one state can exercise on another, thereby protecting the autonomy of each state to create its own internal social, economic or political order.[114] In the development-aid context, the principle could acquire particular resonance by virtue of the thematic broadening of development aid to include demands for human rights protection and good governance.

The recognition of the principle of non-intervention in international law is widely accepted. Certainly, Art. 2(VII) of the UN Charter is applicable only *ratione personae* (to the United Nations) and therefore serves principally to limit UN intervention into member states' affairs. Nevertheless, the applicability of the principle as between states has become customary international law and has been recognized in the Friendly Relations Declaration, among other places. As customary law, it applies to all nations, as well as to international and supranational organizations such as the World Bank and the EU.[115]

Its substantive scope is, however, less clear. What exactly does non-intervention mean in the context of development cooperation? In the following subsections, the meaning of non-intervention will be sketched in three stages. First, the two elements of intervention will be defined: the nature of an intervention (a) which interferes in a state's "internal affairs"

[113] UN-GA Res. 2625 (XXV) of October 24, 1970. Further protection is of course provided by the ban on the use of force, as stated in Art. 2(IV) of the UN Charter. As this subject is not relevant to the subject of this book, it will not be further addressed.

[114] An overview citing many sources is P. Kunig, "Prohibition of Intervention," in Wolfrum, *Max Planck Encyclopedia of Public International Law* at margin no. 1; G. Nolte, *Eingreifen auf Einladung: Zur völkerrechtlichen Zulässigkeit des Einsatzes fremder Truppen im internen Konflikt auf Einladung der Regierung*, Beiträge zum ausländischen öffentlichen Recht und Völkerrecht (Berlin: Springer, 1999), vol. CXXXVI, p. 165; J. A. Frowein, "Die Intervention im heutigen System der Weltverfassung," in H. Jäckel (ed.), *Ist das Prinzip der Nichteinmischung überholt?* (Baden-Baden: Nomos, 1995), pp. 9–26 at p. 9.

[115] On the binding effect on international and supranational organizations see Schermers and Blokker, *International Institutional Law*, margin nos.1572–9; the specific obligation to respect the principle of non-intervention is addressed in H. Fischer, "§59 Gewaltverbot, Selbstverteidigungsrecht und Intervention im gegenwärtigen Völkerrecht," in K. Ipsen, E. Menzel, V. Epping and H.-J. Heintze (eds.), *Völkerrecht*, 5th edn (Munich: C.H. Beck,

(b). The importance of the intervention ban for development aid, in particular, is shown by a nearly identical regulation in the founding treaties of the World Bank (Art. IV, Sect. 10 IBRD), which prohibits the bank from interfering in the political affairs of its members. Finally, in subsection (c), we will analyze how the two regulations interrelate.

a) *Definition of "intervention"*

The prohibition addresses various different kinds of intervention.[116] Development law involves economic intervention, which is particularly difficult to define.[117] A line must be drawn between permissible influence and impermissible intervention. Put otherwise, when does permissible pressure turn into impermissible intervention? The question is particularly hard to answer, since interstate commercial relations generally involve parties intensively and consistently pursuing their own interests. Establishing specific protections for economically weaker countries is difficult. The proper means of doing so was discussed with particular intensity during decolonization, when the influence of developing nations was at its peak. Three approaches can be identified.

Some developing countries favored a broad definition of intervention which largely avoids reliance on the element of coercion.[118] Intervention is here defined as any measure that influences the internal or external affairs of a state, affecting its ability to freely decide on its political, social or economic situation. Even political pressure short of coercion is illegal under this definition. This definition is found in a 1981 UN General Assembly "Declaration on the Inadmissibility of Intervention and Interference in the Internal Affairs of States," which explicitly mentions development aid

2004), pp. 1067–106 at margin no. 52; on the binding effect of international law on the EU see sources cited *supra* on page 228, fn. 5 of Ch 4.C.

116 On the general definition of intervention, especially as set out by the ICJ in the case of *Nicaragua* v. *United States of America* (Judgment of June 27, 1986, ICJ Rep. 1986, esp. Rn. 205) see Kunig, "Prohibition of Intervention," margin nos. 1–6.

117 See W. A. Kewenig, *Die Anwendung wirtschaftlicher Zwangsmaßnahmen im Völkerrecht und im Internationalen Privatrecht: Referate und Thesen der 18. Tagung in Salzburg vom 01. bis 04. April 1981*, Berichte der Deutschen Gesellschaft für Völkerrecht (Heidelberg: C.F. Müller, 1982), vol. XIIX, p. 7; B.-O. Bryde, "Die Intervention mit wirtschaftlichen Mitteln," in I. von Münch (ed.), *Staatsrecht – Völkerrecht – Europarecht*. Festschrift für Hans-Jürgen Schlochauer zum 75. Geburtstag (Berlin: de Gruyter, 1981), pp. 227–45 at p. 227; K. Bockslaff, *Das völkerrechtliche Interventionsverbot als Schranke außenpolitisch motivierter Handelsbeschränkungen* (Berlin: Duncker & Humblot, 1987).

118 H. Neuhold, *Internationale Konflikte – verbotene und erlaubte Mittel ihrer Austragung: Versuche einer transdisziplinären Betrachtung der Grundsätze des Gewalt- und Interventionsverbots sowie der friedlichen Streitbeilegung im Lichte der*

in Section II(k).[119] The mention of development aid, like the discussion of human rights in Section I of this document, was seen as an attempt to declare the suspension of aid because of human rights violations to be illegal.[120] Nevertheless, twenty-two countries voted against the resolution, so it can hardly be seen as consensus-driven customary law. This seems appropriate, since the definition of intervention contained in this document is extremely broad and difficult to define. The principle of non-intervention, rarely used as it is, could be invoked almost constantly under this definition, rendering it (possibly) obsolete.

On the other extreme, some opinions frame the term intervention mostly objectively, according to the alleged intervention's success. Under this definition, interventions are all actions capable of eliminating the freedom of will of the affected state.[121] However, there are doubts about this definition as well. For one thing, it ignores the wording of the Declaration of Principles, which also addresses the intention behind the alleged interference.[122] Further, considering the interdependence and constant interactions in international commerce, defining intervention by any sort of interference in another state's affairs is too broad and requires further qualification.

The third school of thought combines both objective and subjective elements and incorporates an analysis of the relationship between means and ends: an impermissible intervention consists of the use of coercive measures as the manifest intention of changing the subject's will.[123] The intention does not necessarily need to be an intention to harm, as in the criminal use of duress, a frequently cited analogy.[124] The intent to use authoritative measures to exercise coercive influence is sufficient. Thus defined, intervention contains a component of coercion which must nevertheless be coupled to a specific subjective intention. Many authors judge this component by normatively evaluating the goals which the

UN-Prinzipiendeklaration 1970 und der modernen Sozialwissenschaften, Forschungen Aus Staat Und Recht (Wien: Springer, 1977), vol. XXVII, pp. 284–6.

119 UN Resolution 36/103 of December 9, 1981. See also Bockslaff, *Das völkerrechtliche Interventionsverbot*, pp. 68–70, and sources cited therein.

120 Ibid., p. 70; see also C. Tomuschat, "Neuformulierung der Grundregeln des Völkerrechts durch die Vereinten Nationen: Bewegung, Stillstand oder Rückschritt?" *Europa-Archiv*, 38 (1983), 729–38 at 734; on the political context see *supra* Ch 2.A.III.

121 Hoffmeister, *Menschenrechts- und Demokratieklauseln*, p. 187 and sources cited therein.

122 "... in order to obtain the subordination of the exercise of its sovereign rights ..." (Para. 2).

123 One commentator who posits a bundle of criteria, both objective and subjective, is Kewenig, *Anwendung wirtschaftlicher Zwangsmaßnahmen*, p. 16.

124 But see A. Gerlach, *Die Intervention: Versuch einer Definition* (Hamburg: Metzner, 1967), p. 182; D. W. Bowett, "International Law and Economic Coercion," in R. B. Lillich

policy aims to achieve. Intervention exists when those goals violate public policy doctrine, as defined by international law. Public policy is partially defined as "socially appropriate" policy.[125] Brun-Otto Bryde has suggested a less vague alternative that also takes into account the relative position of industrialized and developing countries. His approach permits the use of pressure when it serves not only donor states' interests but also the generally accepted goal of poverty reduction.[126] In light of the increasing tendency to include poverty reduction within the development principle, Bryde's definition appears particularly fitting.

Applying the definition in the development-aid context, an intervention is considered impermissible when economic activity (such as the denial or conditionalization of ODA) is capable of and intended to force the recipient nation into actions that do not (at least in part) serve the goal of poverty reduction.

A special problem of intervention in the development context is the formally voluntary nature of the ODA allocations that are agreed in bilateral treaties.[127] Does this apparent voluntariness always nullify the coercion component of intervention?[128] This would be an over-hasty conclusion, as it fails to acknowledge the practical and legal context in which such treaties are created. From a practical perspective, it is an essential feature of donor–recipient relations that an economic gulf separates them, and that many developing countries – in particular, the smaller ones – are economically dependent on ODA. Their ability to reject or modify contracts is, therefore, quite limited. We can therefore assume a genuine lack of choice. From a legal perspective, it is also worth noting that specific treaties are negotiated in a broader legal context, namely public procurement law and development cooperation law. As we have seen above (in Ch 3.B and D) and will address again in Part III, this law is made essentially by donors. Thus, recipient countries have limited options here, as well. Thus, mere reference to the contractual form of ODA transfer agreements cannot alone negate the application of the intervention ban. Nevertheless, the precise scope of application of the ban remains to be elucidated.

(ed.), *Economic Coercion and the New International Economic Order* (Charlottesville: Michie, 1976), pp. 87–103 at p. 89; p. 93.

125 G. Dahm, *Völkerrecht* (Stuttgart: Kohlhammer, 1958), pp. 206, 207.

126 Bryde, "Intervention," p. 241; an approach stressing the importance of protecting the legal good of sovereignty is Bockslaff, *Das völkerrechtliche Interventionsverbot*, pp. 99.

127 See on such treaties, *infra* Ch 6.B.I.3 / II.3. / II.3.

128 See, e.g. D. C. Dicke, *Die Intervention mit wirtschaftlichen Mitteln im Völkerrecht: Zugleich ein Beitrag zu Fragen der wirtschaftlichen Souveränität* (Baden-Baden: Nomos, 1978), pp. 225–9.

b) *Definition of "internal affairs"*

For the principle of non-intervention to come into play, a second requirement has to be fulfilled, namely that the action invades a protected area: that is, a state's internal affairs. These are defined as all areas not regulated by international law.[129] As soon as a state binds itself in international law in some regard it can no longer proclaim a *domaine réservé* for that subject. In light of the ever-tighter network of international-law regulations, the scope of the principle of non-intervention appears to shrink continuously. By the same token, the continuous expansion of the idea of development and scope of development activities should be considered, as they extend into the area of political reform.[130] Although a legal analysis must always account for the legal position and international-law obligations of individual states, it is nevertheless possible to make several broader points. Which activities might be affected by the principle of non-intervention?

The first issue is the state's internal system of government. A possible right to democracy remains highly controversial, although arguments can be made in its favor.[131] Nevertheless, there is as yet no international-law obligation to respect democratic principles. This implies that the additional elements of a state's government structure and separation of powers would also be included within the *domaine réservé*.[132] In other areas, however, the principle of non-intervention is now more or less obsolete. This is true in particular of human rights. Human rights were the primary "battlefield" on which developing countries sought to limit donor-state influence.[133] However, an attempt to ban human-rights-based conditionalities on aid failed. Human rights guarantees are now so internationalized that assuming them to be part of a state's *domaine réservé* is no longer practicable.[134] The same can be said for anti-corruption measures.[135] The

[129] Fischer, "§59," margin no. 53 and sources cited therein.

[130] See *supra* Ch 2.B.I.

[131] T. Franck, "The Emerging Right to Democratic Governance," *American Journal of International Law*, 86 (1992), 46–91 at 46; Petersen, *Demokratie*.

[132] Citing further sources: G. Nolte, "Article 2 (7): The Charter of the United Nations," in B. Simma (ed.), *The Charter of the United Nations: A Commentary*, 2nd edn, II (Oxford University Press, 2002) at margin nos.62, 63; a contrasting perspective is provided by Christian Tomuschat, who now sees international law as a "comprehensive blueprint for social life" and who posits duties of democracy and good governance, see Tomuschat, "Ensuring the Survival," 63–70; surveying the spectrum of opinion A. von Bogdandy, "Demokratie, Globalisierung, Zukunft des Völkerrechts – eine Bestandsaufnahme," *Heidelberg Journal of International Law*, 63 (2003), 853–77 at 853.

[133] See *supra* Ch 2.B.II / III.

[134] Nolte, "Art. 2 (7) UN Charter," margin nos. 38–44.

[135] On the status of legal measures against corruption see I. N. Androulakis, *Die Globalisierung der Korruptionsbekämpfung* (Baden-Baden: Nomos, 2007).

network of international regulations in the area of the environment and public goods has also become so dense that the environmental demands of donors (for instance, for environmental impact assessments) can hardly be rebuffed by calling them "internal affairs."[136]

In the final analysis, the principle of non-intervention could provide real protection for collective autonomy, which is threatened by the economic power differential between the parties in the development-aid context. The principle is, however, not particularly effective. Proving the use of coercion in the absence of an intent to reduce poverty may well be difficult. Scope for this doctrine has also constantly been shrinking. Nevertheless, the principle of non-intervention should not be dismissed as useless. It allows developing countries at least a legal argument that can enforce limits. In the area of governance reforms, in particular, it can be applicable and useful, at least when proactively used as a barrier of protection.[137] Many developing nations, however, currently seem to adopt more defensive postures. A look at the literature of international law from the 1970s shows just *how* defensive these nations have become. Back then, it was proposed that intervention should actually become the goal of development – intervention, that is, against wealthy states, to combat poverty in developing nations. International development scholars wanted to transform the intervention ban into a pro-intervention principle and use it to oblige donors to grant ODA allocations.[138] Today, this aggressive approach seems farther away than ever.

c) *Comparison: the principle of non-intervention and the prohibition on political interference in the law of the World Bank*

Proof that the idea of non-intervention is a basic component of development cooperation law is furnished by the fact that the World Bank's laws contain a similar idea: the principle of political non-interference, in Art. IV. Sect. 10 of the IBRD Articles and Art. V Sect. 6 of the IDA Articles.[139]

[136] A. Epiney, "Umweltvölkerrechtliche Rahmenbedingungen für Entwicklungsprojekte," in W. Meng, U. Magnus, S. Schlemmer-Schulte, T. Cottier, P.-T. Stoll and A. Epiney (eds.), *Das internationale Recht im Nord-Süd-Verhältnis* (Heidelberg: C.F. Müller, 2005), vol. XLI, pp. 329–72 at pp. 369, 370.

[137] On the universalistic tendency of the governance idea, which seeks to overcome the notion of "internal affairs" see F. Schorkopf, *Grundgesetz und Überstaatlichkeit: Konflikt und Harmonie in den auswärtigen Beziehungen Deutschlands*, Jus Publicum (Tübingen: Mohr Siebeck, 2007), vol. CLXVII, p. 219.

[138] Flory, *Droit international*, p. 46.

[139] See *supra* Ch 3.A.IV.3. The provision reads: "The Association and its officers shall not interfere in the political affairs of any member, not shall they be influenced in their decisions by the political character of the member or members concerned. Only economic

But are the rules identical?[140] The wording of the two provisions is different. While the World Bank prohibits interference in the "political affairs" of member states, Art. 2(VII) of the UN Charter protects the area of "domestic jurisdiction." Political affairs, however, can also relate to foreign relations, and the World Bank is also prohibited from interfering here. Some also argue that the delimitation in the law of the World Bank is not so much between internal and external affairs but between political matters and non-political, economic policy. The legislative history also argues against an identical prohibition: Art. 10 Sect. 10 of the IBRD is more a functional provision than one intended to preserve sovereignty. As convincing as these arguments may be, there is still no way to deny the clear overlaps between the principles of non-interference at the UN and the World Bank. The World Bank's prohibition certainly has a thematic purport, and is therefore more specific. At the same time, however, both principles embody the same basic thought, which is to set limits to the amount of influence one organization or state can bring to bear on another state. Both principles clearly protect a state's internal political constitution. Deciding on its internal order is the protected autonomous right of every state. Both formulations of the non-intervention principle clearly protect this important area and thus reinforce that the core meaning of the principle of collective autonomy is worthy of protection.

IV. Summary

The principle of collective autonomy is a basic element of the law of ODA allocations. As a legal principle, it is founded on the norm of sovereign equality, as guaranteed by international customary law and by Art. 2(I) of the UN Charter. It is both substantiated and protected by further regulations. Its subject matter is also protected by the now ubiquitous principle of ownership in the context of development law. For recipients, ownership entails an ambivalent structure of rights and duties, but at the same time it also includes limitations on the activities of donors. Ownership is, nevertheless, only a structural principle of development cooperation law, not a legal principle. The principle of collective autonomy contains an important qualification, namely the guarantee of *equal* autonomy. This guarantee establishes the fundamental legal right to equal treatment of

considerations shall be relevant to their decisions, and these considerations shall be weighed impartially in order to achieve the purposes stated in this Agreement."

140 See Killinger, *The World Bank's Non-Political Mandate*, p. 103–6.

donors and recipients. Nevertheless, this promise is gravely limited, particularly in the law of international institutions such as the World Bank. The principle of collective autonomy is secured and protected at its core by the principle of non-intervention, even if this principle is small in scope and difficult to define in the context of economic cooperation.

The principle of collective autonomy, as sketched here, is an important normative component of the law of development. It does not compel adherence to any substantive idea, but rather protects the autonomy of each state to pursue its own interests and to structure its internal order and external relations as it chooses. The specific context of development cooperation law, in particular the economic gap between donors and recipients, the limited technical capacities of recipients – but also political disputes – make the principle appear as a sort of counterfactual yardstick for development cooperation law. Although the principle applies to both sides, it has a different meaning for each. For donors, the principle primarily secures their financial sovereignty. For recipients, it applies (more fundamentally) to their ability to freely structure their internal social, economic and political order. The principle thus permits even the smallest developing country to claim sovereignty over what happens inside its borders. It also forms the basis for developing countries' claims to equal participation in the negotiation, planning and permitting of development projects. Finally, it is the basis for recipient countries' supervision of project implementation. Thus, the principle is crucially important in supporting claims for sovereignty and control over development aid being used within a country's own borders. At the same time, claims to autonomy by both sides harbor the potential for conflicts.

The harmonization of these conflicting autonomy claims is the principal object of the specific rules of development cooperation law. Many applications of the principle come to mind. A normative consequence of the principle of collective autonomy in development cooperation law is, for example, the requirement of fair procedures for actors with equal rights. Reconciliation of autonomy claims must take place by means of procedures that afford parties equal chances despite economic and technical inequalities. Another instance of the principle is, for example, the proposal principle, which specifies that every ODA transfer must be started by an autonomous decision of a recipient state. A further consequence of the principle of collective autonomy could (in combination with the development principle) be a prohibition of so-called tied aid, according to which recipients are required to spend ODA monies on goods from the donor country. The development principle and the principle of collective autonomy could form the basis for a legal prohibition on this practice. This would make collective autonomy, in the final analysis, an important precondition for assigning responsibility. Only when parties are free to decide can responsibility be assigned, whether to recipients or donors.

D Individual autonomy and human rights

Today, a law of development cooperation can no longer be conceived of only as a law of states and international organizations. The individual must be a part of the picture. This explains why the principle of individual autonomy and human rights is a foundational idea of development cooperation law. However, individuals' rights were late in taking the stage in development. In its first decades, development cooperation was seen primarily as a question of economic growth driven by states. It was rarely addressed from the perspective of the individual. Also, legally, the individual would play only a minor role in the context of development, which was defined primarily by public international law. The new perspective is connected to the increasing importance of human rights in international relations generally, but also to the profoundly changed concept of development.[141] Now, human rights are a key element of the legal analysis of development processes and strongly influence the contours of development cooperation law.[142] However, in discussions on development cooperation rather disparate aspects of human rights are often addressed in rather poorly differentiated ways. To avoid this error, we will first briefly

[141] On the emergence of human rights in development discourse see *supra* Ch 2.B.II.

[142] Most studies address only one organization. For instance, on the World Bank: Skogly, *Human Rights Obligations*; Darrow, *Between Light and Shadow*; Killinger, *The World Bank's Non-Political Mandate*; S. R. Roos, *Der internationale Menschenrechtsschutz vor entwicklungsbedingten Zwangsumsiedlungen und seine Sicherstellung durch Recht und Praxis der Weltbank*, Schriften zum Völkerrecht (Berlin: Duncker & Humblot, 2008), vol. CLXXIII; on the EU: Bartels, *Human Rights Conditionality*; Pippan, *Förderung der Menschenrechte*; Hoffmeister, *Menschenrechts- und Demokratieklauseln*. There is no monograph on human rights in German development cooperation as yet (but see A. Kämpf and A. Würth, *Mehr Menschenrechte in die Entwicklungspolitik!* Positionspapier Deutsches Institut für Menschenrechte No. 15. Available at www.institut-fuer-menschenrechte.de/uploads/tx_commerce/policy_paper_15_mehr_menschenrechte_in_die_entwicklungspolitik.pdf (last visited July 2013)). The subject is rarely generally addressed (see K. Tomasevski, *Development Aid and Human Rights* (London: Pinter, 1989); R. Tetzlaff (ed.), *Menschenrechte und Entwicklung* (Bonn: Stiftung Entwicklung und Frieden, 1993); P. Uvin, *Human Rights and Development* (Bloomfield: Kumarian, 2004); P. Alston and M. Robinson (eds.), *Human Rights and Development: Towards Mutual Reinforcement* (Oxford University Press, 2005); Seppänen, *Possibilities and Challenges*).

sketch the history of the interaction between human rights and development from which further systematic questions in this Part evolve.

I. The complex relationship between development and human rights

1. History of discourse and contemporary questions

Even into the 1990s (and sometimes to this day), development and human rights were addressed in very different discourses.[143] This separation, which now seems so surprising, was not just a problem of higher respect for sovereignty, but was also probably just as much a product of the diverging interests and cultures of the parties concerned.[144] It is true that at the first World Conference on Human Rights, held in 1968 in Teheran, the connection between human rights and the then-young field of development cooperation was discussed intensively.[145] However, the discussion did not lead to an integration of the two discourses, much less to changes in the law or practice of development cooperation. Human rights experts remained separate from development activists, both personally and conceptually. Donor organizations, at this time, were driven by an economic and technocratic idea of development that favored state-organized top-down approaches. A claim to individual participation and respect for individual rights could hardly be included in such approaches. At the same time, governing elites in recipient countries had little interest in individual rights. They also saw the development process as a state-controlled process that could and should hardly be left to individual initiative or court supervision.

The first signs of a change in this approach can be seen in the late 1970s, with the demand for a right to development.[146] However, this right was characteristically framed as a collective right of states, so that one gains the impression that the promising rhetoric of human rights was merely

143 See Alston, "Ships Passing," 755; however, the MDGs have clearly brought about a fundamental change in this area, see the contributions to the Special Issue of the International Journal of Human Rights, Vol. 13, No. 5 (2009).

144 It is telling that human rights do not feature in the early literature on the international law of development, see, e.g. Feuer and Cassan, *Droit international*; Flory, *Droit international*.

145 P. Alston and M. Robinson, "The Challenges of Ensuring the Mutuality of Human Rights and Development Endeavours," in P. Alston and M. Robinson (eds.), *Human Rights and Development: Towards Mutual Reinforcement* (Oxford University Press, 2005), pp. 1–18 at pp. 1–3.

146 See *supra* Ch 4.B.I.; J. von Bernstorff, "The Changing Fortunes of the Universal Declaration of Human Rights: Genesis and Symbolic Dimensions of the Turn to Rights in International Law," *European Journal of International Law*, 19 (2008), 903–24 at 915.

being paid lip service, and there was no real intention of according individual rights enforceable against donors or recipient-country regimes.

A connection between the two domains first emerged in the 1980s.[147] The demand for greater respect for individual rights in the development context – as well as the interest of human rights activists in development cooperation – was the product of two different approaches, which seem at first glance incompatible.[148] First, neoliberal economic policy focused attention on the importance of individuals' economic rights (protection of property, freedom to contract). The Washington Consensus – in whose name the World Bank, IMF, and Anglo-American donor states focused increased attention on these rights – reflected this approach.[149] At the same time, human rights activists succeeded in incorporating more general human rights themes into development plans. In particular, they focused on the rights of women and children. Human rights activists became convinced that human rights had not only an international dimension, but that their national implementation depended heavily on overall progress toward development.

The fall of the Berlin Wall also brought an even deeper change in perspective among donors. The disappearance of competing political systems permitted donors to make stronger demands for better governance and respect for human rights.[150] At the same time, a human-centered idea of development began winning more adherents within professional discourse.[151] Since the late 1990s, the "rights-based approach to development" has been the battle cry both of human rights and of development experts, reflecting the culmination of their convergence of interests.

Nevertheless, the discourse continues to incorporate various questions and functions of human rights which should be systematically differentiated. What makes human rights so complex and controversial in the development arena is the fact that it involves not just a two-way citizen–state relationship but a triangular relationship: citizen–recipient

[147] Accordingly, studies of this area have emerged only since the early 1980s, see International Commission of Jurists, Development, Human Rights and the rule of law, 1981; G. W. Shepherd and V. P. Nanda, *Human Rights and Third World Development* (Westport: Greenwood Press, 1985); Tomasevski, *Development Aid and Human Rights.*

[148] Trubek, "The 'Rule of Law'," p. 84.

[149] On this development see *supra* Ch 2.A.I.2, II.

[150] This step was particularly explicit in the EU's development cooperation, see W. Benedek, "Die Bedeutung der Menschenrechte in der Entwicklungspolitik der Europäischen Union," *Journal für Entwicklungspolitik*, 10 (1994), 13–31 at 13.

[151] A prominent example is Sen, *Development as Freedom*; on Sen and his role in introducing human rights into development discourse see *supra* Ch 2.B.II.

state / recipient state–donor / donor–citizen.[152] Particularly intense discussion has centered on the relevance of human rights in the relationship between donor and recipient countries – that is, from an objective legal dimension, the fact that donors began in the early 1990s to demand that recipient states respect human rights. Donors have begun increasingly to define development goals in human rights terms – to "use" human rights to pursue development goals. Although this primarily represents the donors' development *policy*, it also has a legal dimension consisting of the question whether donors (in particular, the World Bank) actually have a right or a mandate to demand respect for human rights, and how they can formulate their demands without infringing recipient-state autonomy.[153]

From the perspective of development cooperation law, the relation between donors and citizens of recipient states, another part of the triangular relationship, is of equal interest. The question here is how far donors themselves are bound to respect human rights. Must they take human rights into account when planning, negotiating and implementing ODA transfers? The question has barely been analyzed on its own merits, despite the fact that it is of great practical importance for development cooperation law.

The following section will thus examine this second question. Focusing on Germany, the EU and the World Bank, we will ask to what extent their ODA policies are bound by human rights guarantees (II). We will then examine the substantive obligations which arise from this human rights commitment (III).

2. Human-rights-based approaches

Before we address the concrete question of whether donors are bound to take human rights into account, we will look at two aspects of the discourse of development cooperation and human rights: human-rights-based approaches to development and the many different ways in which human rights are understood in the development context.

Human-rights-based approaches (HRBA) have, in recent years, become as indistinct as they are ubiquitous.[154] At their core, they describe

[152] A fourth relationship exists between the donor state and its citizens, although the principal legal issues here relate to legitimation rather than constitutional questions.

[153] For more on this subject see *supra* Ch 4.C.III.2.b) and the analysis of the mandates in Ch 3.A.

[154] Good overviews include P. Twomey, "Human Rights-Based Approaches to Development," in M. A. Baderin and R. McCorquodale (eds.), *Economic, Social and Cultural Rights in*

a certain basic understanding of the goal, process and actors of development cooperation. Development should no longer be considered just a task for governments, in which recipient-country citizens appear as mere objects whose welfare is being administered. Instead, citizens are seen as possessing rights and the focus should be on their realization. Both the substantive orientation of projects and the process of their negotiation and implementation should be organized with human rights in mind, and citizens should become participants in these processes as well. According to this understanding, the realization of human rights should simply and fundamentally be the goal of development policy. Although this is a normative concept of development cooperation, it is important to realize that the HRBA is not a monopoly of jurists. Quite to the contrary: the HRBA is more often formulated and applied by non-jurists.

Thus, the HRBA consists not only of a fundamental conception of development cooperation, but also as a steering element and "policy instrument." It requires the procedures and policies of donors to be oriented toward protecting human rights. Since the 1990s, various donors have adopted the HRBA as their basic approach to development cooperation and have attempted to give it concrete form. In 2003, for instance, the UN articulated its concept of the HRBA, which governs all UN agencies.[155] German development circles are just beginning to formulate an HRBA policy. There are six core elements to an HRBA: linkage to rights, accountability, empowerment, participation, non-discrimination and attention to vulnerable groups.

A final aspect of the discourse about human rights and development cooperation should be mentioned. It is important to keep in mind that human rights in the development context (and in others as well[156]) can, depending on the observers' perspective, have different functions, different effects and different apparent properties.[157] From a functional-technocratic

Action (Oxford University Press, 2007), pp. 45–70 at p. 45; Seppänen, *Possibilities and Challenges*; Darrow and Tomas, "Power, Capture, and Conflict," 471.

155 United Nations, *The Human Rights Based Approach to Development Co-operation: Towards a Common Understanding Among UN Agencies*. Available at www.undg.org/archive_docs/6959-The_Human_Rights_Based_Approach_to_Development_Cooperation_Towards_a_Common_Understanding_among_UN.pdf (last visited July 2013).

156 M. Koskenniemi, "The Effect of Rights on Political Culture," in P. Alston (ed.), *The EU and Human Rights* (Oxford University Press, 1999), pp. 99–116 at p. 99; K. Günther, "The Legacies of Injustice and Fear: A European Approach to Human Rights and their Effects on Political Culture," in ibid, p. 117.

157 In the development-cooperation context see Darrow and Tomas, "Power, Capture, and Conflict," 511; Seppänen, *Possibilities and Challenges*, p. 7.

perspective, human rights are instruments which foster project efficiency. In a more liberal, activist-oriented perspective, human rights are goals in themselves, expressing a human-centered idea of development. Those who see development as a hegemonic instrument of the Global North, by contrast, see human rights as mere window-dressing, or as a hegemonic strategy to undermine recipient-state sovereignty.[158]

II. *The obligation of donors to respect human rights*

After this long introduction, we can now discuss whether donors are, in fact, bound to consider human rights during the allocation of ODA and implementation of development interventions. The question has to be answered differently for different donors.

1. Germany

Germany's human rights obligations are primarily a question of the scope of its international law obligations, which necessarily implies the much-discussed extraterritorial binding effect of human rights treaties.[159]

The international law[160] obligation of Germany to respect human rights is based first on Germany's ratification of the relevant human rights treaties and conventions. Germany has ratified the most important human

[158] For the so-called post-development approach see M. Rahnema, "Participation," in Sachs, *Development Dictionary*, p. 116; for an approach more attuned to the World Bank's rule-of-law approach see J. M. Ngugi, "The World Bank and the Ideology of Reform and Development in International Economic Development Discourse," *Cardozo Journal of International and Comparative Law*, 14 (2006), 313–45 at 313.

[159] See T. Buergenthal, "The ICJ, Human Rights, and Extraterritorial Jurisdiction," in S. Breitenmoser and L. Wildhaber (eds.), *Human Rights, Democracy and the Rule of Law: Liber Amicorum Luzius Wildhaber* (Zürich, Baden-Baden: Nomos, 2007), pp. 143–50 at p. 143; C. Eick, "Die Reichweite der Bindung menschenrechtlicher Verträge für das auswärtige Handeln von Staaten," in E. Klein (ed.), *Gewaltenteilung und Menschenrechte* (Berlin: Berliner Wissenschafts-Verlag, 2006), pp. 115–28 at p. 115; A. Coomans (ed.), *Extraterritorial Application of Human Rights Treaties* (Antwerp: Intersentia, 2004); on the Bankovic case see G. Ress, "State Responsibility for Extraterritorial Human Rights Violations: The Bankovic Case," *Zeitschrift für europarechtliche Studien*, 6 (2003), 73–89 at 73 and sources cited therein.

[160] It would be possible to develop a *constitutional* obligation, based on Arts. 1(II), (III) of the Geman Basic Law. However, this would apply only to a form of extraterritorial application which is largely absent in development cooperation. See Decisions of the German Constitutional Court, Volume 6, pp. 290 (295); R. Hofmann, *Grundrechte und grenzüberschreitende Sachverhalte*, Beiträge zum ausländischen öffentlichen Recht und Völkerrecht (Heidelberg: Springer, 1994), vol. CXVIII, pp. 10; H. Dreier, "Art. 1 III GG," in H. Dreier and H. Bauer (eds.), *Grundgesetz: Kommentar*, 2nd edn (Tübingen: Mohr Siebeck, 2004–) at margin no. 44.

rights treaties and is thus bound by them.[161] This, however, does not answer the question of whom Germany is bound to – that is, who the actual rights-bearers are. Clearly, in the development-aid context, we are not dealing with the classical situation of a state's obligations to its own citizens, but with the question whether Germany is responsible to those affected by the projects it finances in recipient countries.

There is no general answer to this question; questions of binding effect and rights-bearers can only be answered with reference to the particular jurisdiction provisions of the individual treaties. The relevant provisions of the two 1966 covenants will serve as examples. The ICCPR, in Article 2(1), requires each contracting state to guarantee the rights listed in the treaty "to all individuals within its territory and subject to its jurisdiction." This formulation does not categorically exclude extraterritorial effect, but it does require an element of control over the affected person as a condition for extraterritorial application.[162] The corresponding provision in the ICESCR is more open. Art. 2(1) of this treaty requires each contracting state "to take steps, individually and through international assistance and co-operation … with a view to achieving progressively the full realization of the rights." This provision contains no reference to territoriality or requirement of jurisdiction. There is a dispute as to whether this language is concomitant with extraterritorial obligations for contracting states. It was first thought that the treaty was not intended to give rise to extraterritorial obligations, since the legislative history of the treaty did not lend support to the idea that its drafters intended it to impose specific duties.[163] On the other hand, both the wording of the treaty and recent interpretations of it by the ICESCR Committee support the view that the treaty

[161] These include the International Covenant on Civil and Political Rights (1966 / ICCPR), the International Covenant on Economic, Social and Cultural Rights (1966 / ECOSOC Treaty), Convention on the Elimination of All Forms of Discrimination against Women (1979), Convention against Torture (1984), Convention on the Rights of the Child (1989), and the Convention on the Elimination of all Forms of Racial Discrimination (1965). On the ratification status of these core treaties, see http://www2.ohchr.org/english/law/docs/HRChart.xls (last visited July 2013).

[162] M. Nowak, "Art. 2," in M. Nowak (ed.), *UN Covenant on Civil and Political Rights: CCPR Commentary* (Kehl: N.P. Engel, 2005) at margin nos. 29, 30. Article 1 of the European Convention on Human Rights (ECHR) contains a similar formulation, which formed the bases for the Bankovic decision of the European Court of Human Rights. This judgment called for effective oversight. See Ress, "State Responsibility," 73 and sources cited therein.

[163] P. Alston and G. Quinn, "The Nature and Scope of States Parties' Obligation Under the International Covenant on Economic, Social and Cultural Rights," *Human Rights Quarterly*, 9 (1987), 156–229 at 186–92.

requires certain forms of international cooperation and, in this context, imposes obligations on the parties whenever and to the extent to which they exercise the corresponding influence.[164] Thus, the extent to which the treaty applies to extraterritorial activity must be judged on an individually differentiated, case-by-case basis.

If the basic possibility of an extraterritorial binding effect is assumed, then both treaties require, as a precondition, some sort of control over the affected persons. This, however, is rarely the case in the development law context. Even a technical assistance mission by the GIZ can hardly be said to involve an element of territorial jurisdiction or control over local residents.[165] In fact, donor influence is mediated by cooperation with the recipient government. Acts of German authority in the development-aid context are usually limited solely to signing a project contract and transferring ODA. Does this mean that ODA allocations release Germany from the obligation to guarantee the rights contained in the treaties? This does not necessarily follow, if one looks at the secondary rules of state responsibility in international law. Given that Germany's activities could be seen as assisting the actions of the recipient state rather than as foreign dealings in their own right, this could be construed as a duty to respect the treaties.[166]

Germany could be under obligation if it is at least jointly responsible for the behavior of a recipient state. This case would not require that Germany's *own* jurisdiction apply. Article 16 of the Draft Articles on the Responsibility of States for Internationally Wrongful Acts, promulgated in 2001 by the International Law Commission, recognizes complicity as a form of state responsibility.[167] There are four elements to complicity.[168]

[164] R. Künnemann, "Extraterritorial Application of the International Covenant on Economic, Social and Cultural Rights," in A. Coomans (ed.), *Extraterritorial Application of Human Rights Treaties* (Antwerp: Intersentia, 2004), pp. 201–31 at p. 201; S. Skogly, *Beyond National Borders: States' Human Rights Obligations in International Cooperation* (Antwerp: Intersentia, 2006), pp. 83–9; Sepulveda, *Nature of Obligations*, pp. 272–7; this can also relate to the activities of donors such as the World Bank, see *infra* Ch 4.D.III.1 b).

[165] A perspective that nevertheless stresses the influence of donors is Kämpf and Würth, *Mehr Menschenrechte in die Entwicklungspolitik!*, p. 6.

[166] This approach is rarely used, but has been invoked with a view to the duties imposed by international environmental laws in the development context, see Epiney, "Umweltvölkerrechtliche Rahmenbedingungen," pp. 358–67.

[167] Art. 16 reads: "A State which aids or assists another State in the commission of an internationally wrongful act by the latter is internationally responsible for doing so if (a) that State does so with knowledge of the circumstances of the internationally wrongful act; and (b) the act would be internationally wrongful if committed by that State."

[168] For more on the elements of an offense under Art. 16 see the Reporter's Commentary, J. Crawford, *The International Law Commission's Articles on State Responsibility:*

First, the recipient state must have violated international law. In the present context, this would mean that the recipient state had ratified a relevant human rights treaty, but then violated one of its provisions in the context of an aid project or a specific policy. With respect to the 1966 covenants, it is generally the case that recipients have recognized them and that they apply to relations between the recipient state and its citizens. An aid project which involved mandatory, uncompensated resettlement, for instance, could infringe the right to adequate housing found in Article 11 of the ICESCR.[169]

Complicity also requires that the recipient state is supported in its commission of the act by the donor state, and that (as a third element), the donor state had knowledge of the act. This is also easy to envision. Many aid projects or development policies of recipient states which infringe human rights can only be pursued with donors' financial assistance. As a result, the aid payment is a cause of the human rights infringement. Since projects in project lending and programs in budget support or policy lending[170] are usually very carefully planned, the donors would usually have the knowledge required by Art. 16. Even if it can be assumed that donors, and in particular Germany, do not intend to infringe human rights by means of aid, they will certainly become aware of the danger of human rights violations during negotiations. If they go through with the project without certifying the project's compatibility with human rights guarantees, the necessary subjective element of the complicity test can be assumed to be fulfilled.

The final element to complicity requires that the act would be illegal if committed by the donor state. In this context, this would mean the donor state doing something comparable to its own citizens.[171] Since Germany has ratified the relevant treaties, it is bound by them. Thus, the elements

Introduction, Text and Commentaries (Cambridge University Press, 2002), pp. 148–51; on the doctrine of complicity B. Graefrath, "Complicity in the Law of International Responsibility," *Revue belge de droit international*, 29 (1996), 370–80 at 370; J. B. Quigley, "Complicity in International Law: A New Direction in the Law of State Responsiblity," *British Yearbook of International Law*, 57 (1986), 77–131 at 77; E. Klein, "Beihilfe zum Völkerrechtsdelikt," in I. von Münch (ed.), *Staatsrecht – Völkerrecht – Europarecht*. Festschrift für Hans-Jürgen Schlochauer zum 75. Geburtstag (Berlin: de Gruyter, 1981), pp. 425–38 at p. 425.

169 On ecologically questionable aspects of development projects see Epiney, "Umweltvölkerrechtliche Rahmenbedingungen," pp. 358–67.

170 The difference between project aid and budget support is addressed *infra* in Part III.

171 The examples used in the *travaux préparatoires* related to incidents such as the delivery of money or weapons to regimes that committed clear human rights violations, such as the military junta which governed Chile under Pinochet (see Quigley, "Complicity,"

of complicity according to Art. 16 of the Articles on State Responsibility may therefore be fulfilled. Since the Articles, created by the ILC after forty years of work, are now part of international customary law, they would count, as a matter of German constitutional law, as general rules under Art. 25 of the German Basic Law. This makes them a part of fundamental federal law, with primacy over statutory law.[172] As a result, these international law duties apply to and bind Germany's organs of government.

In the final analysis, Germany's liability for human rights violations which occur with its assistance can be established on the basis of the rules of state responsibility.[173] This analysis circumvents the question of the extraterritorial scope of the covenants. Germany need not exercise its own jurisdiction; its liability can be based on its participation in the human rights violations of the recipient state. Germany essentially participates in the duties of the recipient state. This interpretation appears appropriate in light of the cooperative dimension of development aid. Unlike military interventions, donors are not themselves active in recipient countries, but merely encourage and support recipient regimes. This fact supports a finding of complicity rather than direct responsibility. This approach has another advantage. It helps defuse the question of limitation of sovereignty, always a problem in cases of extraterritoriality. It cannot be assumed that recipient states would always agree with a donor states' active human rights policies. The concept of complicity defines donor obligations as the specific human rights obligations that the recipient state already has towards its citizens.

2. World Bank

The legal situation with respect to the World Bank is clearly different. The Bank is composed of two international organizations that are themselves not signatories to the relevant human rights treaties and covenants.[174] Nor is there any mention of human rights in their founding treaties. Thus, the

92–5). In that discussion, the question was not the responsibility of donor nations toward Chileans but rather the hypothetical pursuit of such activities against its own citizens.

172 *Decisions of the German Federal Constitutional Court* 15, 25 (33); I. Pernice, "Art. 25," in H. Dreier and H. Bauer (eds.), *Grundgesetz: Kommentar*, 2nd edn (Tübingen: Mohr Siebeck, 2004–) at margin no.19; C. Tomuschat, "§172: Die staatsrechtliche Entscheidung für die internationale Offenheit," in J. Isensee and P. Kirchhof (eds.), *Normativität und Schutz der Verfassung – Internationale Beziehungen* (Heidelberg: C.F. Müller, 1992), vol. VII, pp. 483–523 at margin nos.11, 12.

173 Reaching the same results Epiney, "Umweltvölkerrechtliche Rahmenbedingungen."

174 On the question of the status of the IBRD and IDA as international-law subjects (as a precondition to their being bound by international law), see Roos, *Der internationel Menschenrechtsschutz*, p. 352; Skogly, *Human Rights Obligations*, p. 63.

Bank is not bound by treaty law or by its own primary or "constitutional" law to human rights standards. Whether such a commitment arises in other ways is a highly controversial question.[175]

The Bank's legal department has been rather reticent in dealing with this issue up until now,[176] even though the question is hardly new.[177] The question first arose in 1966, when the UN General Assembly passed a resolution calling for the World Bank to cease providing financial assistance to Portugal and South Africa because of those countries' severe human rights violations.[178] The Bank refused, making two arguments. First, owing to the Bank's constitutional prohibition of political activity, it could not allow human rights considerations to influence its lending policy.[179] Second, a resolution of the General Assembly, unlike a Security Council resolution, is not binding on the Bank, according to the wording of the partnership agreement between the Bank and the UN.[180] When it comes to the Bank's human rights obligations,[181] these positions and arguments have remained essentially unchanged to the present day. Nevertheless, the Bank has made certain nuanced changes in its dealings with states which infringe human rights. According to Ibrahim Shihata, the Bank does not lend to states which practice "extensive violation of political rights which takes pervasive proportions."[182]

[175] Hofmann, "Rechtskontrolle von Organen, " pp. 16, 17; J. D. Ciorciari, "The Lawful Scope of Human Rights Criteria in World Bank Credit Decisions: An Interpretive Analysis of the IBRD and IDA Articles of Agreement," *Cornell International Law Journal*, 33 (2000), 331–71 at 331, see also sources cited *supra* in fn. 142. On the binding effect on the UN see M. Darrow and L. Arbour, "The Pillar of Glass: Human Rights in the Development Operations of the United Nations," *American Journal of International Law*, 103 (2009), 446–501 at 446.

[176] Two former General Counsels of the Bank have addressed in detail the different question whether the Bank's mandate permits human-rights related activities despite the general ban on politcal activity. See Shihata, *World Bank Legal Papers*, pp. 33ff.; 815; R. Danino, "The Legal Aspects of the World Bank's Work on Human Rights," in P. Alston and M. Robinson (eds.), *Human Rights and Development: Towards Mutual Reinforcement* (Oxford University Press, 2005), pp. 509–24 at p. 509.

[177] A detailed discussion of the origin of the World Bank's approach to human rights is found in Killinger, *The World Bank's Non-Political Mandate*, pp. 121–7; for a more recent example of the Bank's policy see K. Horta, "Rhetoric and Reality: Human Rights and the World Bank," *Harvard Human Rights Journal*, 15 (2002), 227–42 at 227.

[178] Darrow, *Between Light and Shadow*, pp. 150–2; Killinger, *The World Bank's Non-Political Mandate*, pp. 104–6.

[179] This prohibition is discussed *supra* in Ch 3.A.IV.3 and Ch 4.C.III.

[180] See S. Bleicher, "UN vs. IBRD: A Dilemma of Functionalism," *International Organization*, 24 (1970), 31–47 at 31.

[181] The situation is different with respect to the question whether the Bank may foster such human rights. More immediately below in fn. 176.

[182] Shihata, *World Bank Legal Papers*, p. 235.

This decision, however, is regarded as discretionary, and is based primarily on the economic effects of such human rights violations. No legal obligation is acknowledged. On the contrary, Shihata emphasizes that there is no strict obligation of the Bank to observe human rights under current regulations, and that this could only be achieved by amending the Articles of Agreement.[183]

Three reasonings are commonly put forth to establish the human rights obligations for the Bank: international customary law, the international law obligations of the Bank's member states and, finally, the Bank's status as a specialized agency of the United Nations. These arguments shall now be briefly addressed.

The Bank could, first, be bound by human rights as a matter of international customary law. As an international organization and subject of international law, the Bank is generally bound by the norms of international customary law.[184] It is now widely accepted that core human rights standards form part of customary law. This is especially true if these rules qualify as *ius cogens*.[185] This form of obligation, however, only pertains to the most serious human rights violations. Accordingly, the Bank would not be allowed to support the practice of genocide or systematic racial discrimination.[186] The Bank is, of course, hardly likely to become involved in such actions. Yet it is also frequently argued that at least substantial parts of the Universal Declaration of Human Rights (UDHR) have also become part of international customary law.[187] If this is true, the Bank would be obliged to respect a much wider spectrum of human rights.

Second, it is argued that the Bank is composed largely of member states who themselves have signed and ratified the relevant human rights treaties. It would be paradoxical if these states were able to escape their

[183] Ibid., p. 236.

[184] Schermers and Blokker, *International Institutional Law*, margin no. 1579; on the World Bank specifically see D. Bradlow, "The World Bank, the IMF, and Human Rights," *Transnational Law and Contemporary Problems*, 6 (1996), 47–90 at 63; Skogly, *Human Rights Obligations*, pp. 84–7.

[185] I. Brownlie, *Principles of Public International Law*, 7th edn (Oxford University Press, 2008), pp. 562–4; for a more careful approach based on individual laws and their protection in international humanitarian law and civil human-rights protection regimes, see Kadelbach, *Zwingendes Völkerrecht*, p. 284.

[186] Skogly, *Human Rights Obligations*, p. 89.

[187] Darrow and Arbour, "Pillar of Glass," 470; T. Buergenthal, "The World Bank and Human Rights," in E. Brown Weiss, A. R. Sureda and L. B. de Chazournes (eds.), *The World Bank, International Financial Institutions, and the Development of International Law: A symposium held in honor of Dr. Ibrahim F. I. Shihata*, March 22, 1999 (Washington, DC: American Society of International Law, 1999), pp. 95–104 at p. 96.

obligations by transferring powers to an international organization.[188] The Bank is thus required to respect the duties of its members to observe their human rights obligations and not to undermine their efforts in this respect. The Executive Directors, in particular, are clearly bound by the laws of the states which nominated them.[189] The problem with this argument is that it ignores the World Bank's special status as an independent legal entity. A binding effect mediated through the Bank's member states would violate Articles 34 and 35 of the Vienna Convention on the Law of Treaties and the rule of *pacta tertiis*, whereby a subject of international law cannot be bound except by *its own* written consent.[190,191]

The third argument relies on the status of the World Bank as a specialized agency of the United Nations. Since the implementation of human rights constitutes a core responsibility of the United Nations, its specialized agencies would equally be bound to respect human rights.[192] With respect to the UN's human rights duties, however, this argument is double-edged. First, the World Bank is a rather distant relative within the UN family. The agreements between the World Bank and the UN from 1947 and 1961 explicitly codify the independence the Bank needs in order to be

[188] M. Cogen, "Human Rights, Prohibition of Political Activities and the Lending Policies of World Bank and International Monetary Fund," in S. R. Chowdhury, E. Denters and P. J. I. M. de Waart (eds.), *The Right to Development in International Law* (Dordrecht: Martinus Nijhoff, 1992), pp. 379–96 at pp. 387–8; more cautiously D. Bradlow and C. Grossmann, "Adjusting the Bretton Woods Institutions to Contemporary Realities," in J.-M. Griesgraber and B. Gunter (eds.), *Development: New Paradigms and Principles for the 21st Century: Rethinking Bretton Woods* (London: Pluto Press, 1996), pp. 27–59 at p. 36; a skeptical perspective is found in Killinger, *The World Bank's Non-Political Mandate*, p. 131.

[189] This formulation is also found in the Maastricht Guidelines on the ECOSOC Treaty, see Roos, *Der internationel Menschenrechtsschutz*, p. 368.

[190] C. Schreuer, "Die Bindung internationaler Organisationen an völkerrechtliche Verträge ihrer Mitgliedstaaten: Völkerrecht zwischen normativem Anspruch und politischer Realität," in K. Zemanek and K. Ginther (eds.), *Völkerrecht zwischen normativem Anspruch und politischer Realität: Festschrift für Karl Zemanek zum 65. Geburtstag* (Berlin: Duncker & Humblot, 1994), pp. 223–50 at p. 223; see also M. Singer, "Jurisdictional Immunity of International Organizations: Human Rights and Functional Necessity Concerns," *Virginia Journal of International Law*, 36 (1995), 53–165 at 58.

[191] This, however, does not exclude the contrary argument that member states may not evade their own international-law duties by assigning these tasks to the international organizations of which they are members. See ECHR, *Matthews* vs. *United Kingdom*, 1999-I ECtHR 251; see also Art. 28 of the ILC Draft Articles on the Responsibility of International Organizations, in: UN Doc. A/63/10 (2008).

[192] Skogly, *Human Rights Obligations*, pp. 99–106; Darrow, *Between Light and Shadow*, pp. 124–9.

functional (Art. I(2) of the Treaty).[193] Despite various duties to cooperate (for instance, reciprocal representation, Art. II, or information exchange, Art. V), the autonomy of the Bank's internal decision-making is explicitly recognized (Art. IV(3)). The Bank is only required, by Art. VI, to "take due regard" for decisions of the UN Security Council.[194]

On the other hand, it is true that respect and support for human rights is a core concern of the United Nations, as reflected in Arts. 1(III) and 55 of its Charter. These goals of the UN (improvement of living standards, solution of international economic problems, respect for human rights) bind not only member states, but also specialized UN agencies. The binding effect on the specialized agencies, which include the World Bank, are derived specifically from Arts. 55(c), 57 and 59 of the UN Charter. Article 55(c) requires the United Nations to advance human rights. While Art. 57 only specifies that the UN may create specialized agencies with their own fields of activity, Art. 59 specifies the purpose of these organizations, that is, the implementation of the goals contained in Art. 55. Thus, even in the functionally differentiated organizational structure of the UN, there remains a duty to implement the organization's fundamental goals. These include, it is today assumed, not just support for but also promotion of human rights.[195] The Bank is thus legally bound to respect all human rights such as they are found (at least in part) in the 1948 Universal Declaration.[196]

This fits into the general context. If one accepts the central role that respect for human rights has in the UN legal system, it would be inconsistent to see the Bank's independence as consisting precisely in the nonobservance of this goal. The better argument is that even a comparatively

193 Protocol concerning the entry into force of the Agreement between the United Nations and the International Bank for Reconstruction and Development of November 15, 1947, UNTS 16 (1948), p. 346; Agreement Between the United Nations and the International Development Association (IDA), entered into force March 27, 1961; 394 UNTS 321 (1961), p. 222.

194 On the effect of Security Council resolutions on the Bank's activities see Shihata, *World Bank Legal Papers*, pp. 808–10.

195 ICJ, Effect of Awards of Compensation Made by the United Nations Administrative Tribunal, Advisory Opinion, 1954 ICJ Rep. 47, p. 57; Darrow and Arbour, "Pillar of Glass," 471–2.

196 Darrow, *Between Light and Shadow*, p. 129; Skogly, *Human Rights Obligations*, p. 151; Killinger, *The World Bank's Non-Political Mandate*, pp. 133, 134; P. Klein, "Les institutions financières internationales et les droits de la personne," *Revue belge de droit international*, 32 (1999), 97–114 at 114. On the concrete scope of these duties see *infra* Part III.

independent specialized agency must pursue the fundamental goals of the UN Charter, as specified in the Charter's Article 55. Thus, we see that the World Bank is indeed required to respect human rights, although the exact scope of this duty remains to be determined.[197]

3. The EU

Among all ODA donors, the EU has most expressly underlined the importance of human rights in the development context. Its duty to respect them has many sources.[198]

From an international law perspective, the EU's human rights obligations appear rather limited, as the case of the World Bank has shown. The EU is not a signatory to the various universal human rights covenants. Nor has the EU (yet) formally joined the European Convention on Human Rights, even if the Lisbon Treaty has laid the groundwork for this step.[199] Thus, the EU is only required to observe those human rights that have been recognized in international customary law.[200]

The binding effect of human rights on EU activities in the development context is based on other sources, in particular the human rights recognized by the Union, as well as in the various EU legal instruments that repeatedly emphasize the EU's duty to respect human rights in its foreign and development policy. The extraterritorial binding effect is justified by a two-step argument.

First, according to Arts. 6(I) and (III) of the EU Treaty, the EU is bound to respect basic rights as they are contained in the Charter of Fundamental Rights, the European Convention on Human Rights and the constitutional traditions common to the member states as general principles of

[197] Addressed directly below in Part III. It is, however, hardly possible to argue for assigning to the Bank secondary-law responsibility for human-rights violations of its members, as was postulated previously in the case of Germany. First, one would have to determine the applicability of responsibility rules to IOs. The ILC Articles exclude any direct application (Art. 57). Further, the human-rights violation of the recipient must be portrayed as a violation of a duty owed by the World Bank. This will rarely be possible, since the Bank is only subject to very limited direct obligations.

[198] The literature on the importance of human rights in European development cooperation is extensive, although the question of its *own* duties in this context is rarely addressed explicitly. An article providing a good overview is B. Simma, J. Aschenbrenner and C. Schulte, "Human Rights Considerations in the Development Cooperation Activities of the EC," in P. Alston (ed.), *The EU and Human Rights* (Oxford University Press, 1999), pp. 571–626 at p. 571.

[199] See Art. 6 II, Lisbon Treaty and Art. 218 VI, VIII, TFEU.

[200] Uerpmann-Wittzack, "Völkerrechtliche Verfassungselemente," pp. 182–5 and source above in fn. 72.

the Union's law.[201] Thus, the EU is bound to a comprehensive basic rights regime. This regime is, however, oriented primarily to rights-bearers in the territory of the Union, the primary field of applicability of the treaties. An extraterritorial commitment regarding development aid follows from a series of regulations which lay down support for human rights as one of the core aspects of European development policy. Three norms are of special significance.[202] Article 21 II b TEU declares the promotion of human rights to be a goal of the EU's foreign policy. The same goal is mention in Art. 9(I) of the Cotonou Agreement, which forms the basic legal framework for development aid in the ACP states. Finally, the EU, in Regulation 1889/2006, established its own guideline on development policy which is oriented solely to advancing human rights.[203] The guideline requires the EU to substantively respect human rights as proclaimed in the Universal Declaration and other international and regional human rights instruments.[204]

These norms collectively make the advancement of human rights a core aspect of European development cooperation. But do they also establish an extraterritorial binding effect? One potential objection might be that these regulations nowhere identify individual citizens of recipient states as rights-bearers. On the other hand, these regulations can only make sense if they are interpreted as requiring respect for human rights. It would hardly be consistent for the EU to demand respect for human rights while at the same time pursuing projects which endanger them. In terms of EU law, this behavior would violate the principle of coherence, which forms the basis for EU foreign policy. The EU is thus required to respect the human rights recognized within the Union in its extraterritorial dealings or in its role as financier.[205] The precise content and scope of these obligations will now be addressed.

201 More details in M. Hilf and F. Schorkopf, "Art. 6 EUV," in E. Grabitz and M. Hilf (eds.), *Das Recht der Europäischen Union*, 40th edn, 3 vols. (Munich: C.H. Beck, 2009) at margin nos. 46 and sources cited therein.

202 The EU's "soft law" contains countless additional statements of this idea, see, e.g. European Consensus, 2005, margin nos. 7, 12, 13 as well as sources cited in T. Bruha and M. Rau, "Bedeutung der Grundrechte der EU für Drittstaaten," in S. Heselhaus and C. Nowak (eds.), *Handbuch der Europäischen Grundrechte* (Munich: C.H. Beck, 2006), pp. 105–21, before margin no. 1.

203 Regulation (EC) 1889/2006 of the European Parliament and the Council (OJ 2006 L 386/1). It renews the Regulations (EC) VO 975 and 976/1999 (OJ 1999 L 120/1 and 8).

204 Art. 1 II (a) Regulation (EC) 1889/2006.

205 Stated without extensive discussion in K.-D. Borchardt, *Die rechtlichen Grundlagen der Europäischen Union*, 3rd edn (Heidelberg: C.F. Müller, 2006), margin no. 186;

III. Content of the human rights obligations

Determining that the donors are bound to respect human rights is only the first step. It must now be asked exactly what they have bound themselves to. The problem is complex, since the exact contents are regulated by the particular law that applies and the varied nature of the binding effect on the donor (whether state or international organization).[206] Nevertheless, certain general obligations can be derived in particular from Arts. 2(I), 11, and 23 of the ICESCR and from Arts. 22 and 28 of the Universal Declaration.

To analyze them, we will apply the well-accepted approach among human rights scholars of separating rights into three dimensions. Each right incorporates a duty to respect, a duty to protect, and a duty to fulfill (1).[207] Next, the focus will turn to a more concrete discussion of the frequently asserted right to participation in development processes (2).

1. Duties in the three dimensions of human rights

a) Duty to respect

In their most fundamental meaning, human rights should protect citizens against the arbitrary exercise of state and public authority. This is what the "duty to respect" human rights stands for. Public authorities and other actors bound by human rights treaties must refrain from all activities that violate the protected rights. The invocation of the duty to respect in the development context may appear odd at first. ODA, after all, is basically intended to aid development, thereby fostering and expanding rights. How can ODA transfers endanger human rights? When considered more carefully, it is easy to imagine situations in which ODA allocations could create such dangers. During large infrastructure projects, for instance, such as the construction of a dam, populations might be resettled without compensation, or structural-adjustment programs may trigger budget cuts or other policies with profound social

D. Thym, "Auswärtige Gewalt," in A. von Bogdandy and J. Bast (eds.), *Europäisches Verfassungsrecht*, 2nd edn (Heidelberg: Springer, 2009), pp. 441–88 at p. 464.

206 For an outstanding investigation of the World Bank's duties with respect to the right to education and nutrition see Skogly, *Human Rights Obligations*, pp. 154–62.

207 On this distinction see generally W. Kälin and J. Künzli, *Universeller Menschenrechtsschutz*, 2nd edn (Baden-Baden: Nomos, 2008), p. 110; a fundamental discussion is found in A. Eide, "The Realisation of Social and Economic Rights and the Minimum Threshold Approach," *Human Rights Law Journal*, 10 (1989), 35–51 at 35.

consequences, without the affected parties being afforded a right to participate and be heard.[208] The duty to respect human rights should hinder such projects from being supported by ODA allocations. Donors are therefore required to avoid funding such projects and to respect the rights of affected parties.[209]

All three of the donors under discussion here are bound by human rights in this sense. In Germany's case, this follows from its status as a contracting party to the relevant human rights covenants and treaties and from its potential complicity in violations committed by recipient countries. The EU has also declared itself responsible for respecting human rights in the development context. Most of the individual rights are defined by the Charter of Fundamental Rights and the European Convention on Human Rights, and in any case derive from the rights guaranteed in international law by the Universal Declaration and recognized as customary law. The latter source also defines rights for the World Bank, which is bound to respect them in its role as a subject of international law and its role as a UN specialized agency.[210] Although the binding effect on the World Bank is weaker than on Germany, it nevertheless continues to impose a duty to respect human rights.[211] Further, the precise contents of the duty can only be determined with respect to individual cases and distinct rights. A deeper analysis of each of the individual rights on its own is beyond the scope of this discussion.[212]

[208] An informative discussion is found in I. Hadiprayitno, *Hazard or Right? The Dialectics of Development Practice and the Internationally Declared Right to Development, with Special Reference to Indonesia*, School of Human Rights Research Series (Antwerp: Intersentia, 2009), vol. XXXI, pp. 77–99 (she identifies four main dangers posed by development projects: displacement and landlessness; joblessness and degradation of income; degradation of health, livelihood and morbidity; and food insecurity); on the duties of ECOSOC-contracting states with respect to the implementation of World Bank structural adjustment programs see Sepulveda, *Nature of Obligations*, pp. 218–22.

[209] On the corresponding duties emerging from the ECOSOC Treaty see UN Committe for Economic, Social and Cultural Rights, General Comment, No. 2, margin no. 6 (on technical assistance); General Comment, No. 4, margin no. 19 (on the right to adequate housing); General Comment No. 15, margin no. 33 (right to water); General Comment, No. 19, margin no. 53 (right to social security).

[210] On the internal and external binding effect of this systematization see F. Mégret and F. Hoffmann, "The UN as a Human Rights Violator?" *Human Rights Quarterly*, 25 (2003), 314–42 at 314.

[211] This weaker obligation is sometimes described as an *obligation de vigilance*, see Klein, "Les institutions financières internationales," 113.

[212] For examples drawn from the World Bank and its duties deriving from the right to education and nutrition, see Skogly, *Human Rights Obligations*, pp. 154–62; with respect to its duties in the resettlement context, see Roos, *Der internationel Menschenrechtsschutz*.

b) Duty to protect

A second dimension of human rights protection requires those under obligation to regulate the activities of third parties. The duty is understood as requiring states that are party to human rights treaties to ensure that human rights are not prejudiced by private parties acting in their areas of jurisdiction.[213] In the development context, this dimension is especially relevant as it binds states to their treaty obligations also with regard to their role as members of international organizations. The UN Committee for Economic, Social, and Cultural Rights (CESCR), for example, urged member states, "as a member of international financial institutions, in particular the International Monetary Fund and the World Bank, to do all it can to ensure that the policies and decisions of those organizations are in conformity with the obligations of States parties to the Covenant, in particular the obligations contained in articles 2(1), 11, 15, 22 and 23 concerning international assistance and cooperation."[214] Thus, the behavior of Germany on the Board of the World Bank, but also in EU bodies, is subject to obligations established by human rights treaties.[215] International donors are, of course, not subject to this obligation.

c) Duty to fulfill

The third dimension of human rights can also implicate positive obligations. The so-called "duty to fulfill" requires that public authorities take positive measures to establish the legal, institutional and procedural preconditions so that individuals can actually realize their rights. The principal issue is how the protection of rights is structured. This may involve establishing institutional conditions by enacting laws, or taking positive measures in the form of transfer payments. Nevertheless, state activity in this dimension is often subject to practical limitations (such as lack of financial resources, lack of influence) which human rights treaties take

[213] See generally Kälin and Künzli, *Universeller Menschenrechtsschutz*, pp. 118; for a comparison to the doctrine of the duty to protect in German constitutional law see G. Hermes, *Das Grundrecht auf Schutz von Leben und Gesundheit: Schutzpflicht und Schutzanspruch aus Art. 2 Abs. 2 Satz 1 GG*, Freiburger rechts- und staatswissenschaftliche Abhandlungen (Heidelberg: C.F. Müller, 1987), vol. XLVI.

[214] With respect to Germany see CESCR, Concluding Observations Germany, E/C.12/1/Add. 68, margin no. 31; similar demands emerged with respect to France, Italy and Belgium, see CESCR, Concluding Observations France E/2002/22, margin no. 881; Concluding Observations Italy E/2002/22, margin no. 126; Concluding Observations Belgium E/2001/22, margin no. 493.

[215] Salomon, *Global Responsibility*, pp. 106, 107; Sepulveda, *Nature of Obligations*, pp. 237, 238.

into account. Art. 2(I) of the ICESCR, for instance, provides that a contracting state must employ "the maximum of its available resources" to "progressively" achieve full realization of treaty rights. This is understood to mean that states shall progressively pursue realization of rights to the best of their ability, but that they are always required to guarantee at least a minimum core content.[216]

In the development context, these duties generally apply to recipient states. They are responsible for guaranteeing their citizens' rights. However, donors may also be subject to certain duties to fulfill. The precise scope of these duties is linked to the particular law or right under discussion. Nevertheless, three general approaches merit discussion here: a duty to assess the human rights impact, duties to provide financial assistance and possible duty to reform institutions. It should be kept in mind that even when a certain right is said to exist, this does not necessarily imply a concrete duty to act or even a subjective right which affected parties can claim. It is more a matter of obliging donors to conduct all their activities in a corresponding spirit.

(1) Human rights impact assessment The first question is whether donors have a *duty* to systematically study the potential human rights risks of a project (comparable to an environmental impact study) before agreeing to fund it. This would require donors to ensure that human rights are not jeopardized by the project, both before approval and during implementation. Such a duty – which binds donors directly but recipients only indirectly – might create tension with recipient states, if they are not bound by the same duties themselves. Nevertheless, it is fair to assume that the ICESCR and the Universal Declaration of Human Rights impose corresponding duties on all three donor organizations under study here.[217] A duty to assess the impact on human rights would be an important step towards ensuring respect for human rights by which donors are undoubtedly bound, and could be introduced without major new costs.

216 M. Langford, "The Justiciability of Social Rights," in M. Langford (ed.), *Social Rights Jurisprudence: Emerging Trends in International and Comparative Law* (Cambridge University Press, 2008), pp. 3–45 at p. 21; Sepulveda, *Nature of Obligations*, p. 313.

217 See especially ECOSOC Committee, for instance in Concluding Observations, Germany, E/C.12/1/Add. 68, margin no. 32; on a human rights impact assessment, see Sepulveda, "The Obligations of International Assistance," 92; see also Hofmann, "Rechtskontrolle von Organen," pp. 16, 17 (arguing that this duty can be derived from customary international law); see also J. Cock and E. Webster, "Environmental and Social Impact Assessments," in J.-M. Griesgraber and B. Gunter (eds.), *The World Bank: Lending on a Global Scale* (London: Pluto Press, 1996), pp. 81–100 at p. 81.

In fact, the World Bank has already introduced analogous measures. The Bank has issued many so-called "safeguard policies" which require its employees to consider environmental and social aspects when negotiating projects.[218] EU development cooperation law, by contrast, requires such studies only to a very limited extent, and German law does not impose them at all.[219] Hence, the introduction of human rights impact assessments could be seen as a first test of the seriousness of donors' legal commitment to human rights in development cooperation.[220]

(2) A duty to provide ODA? A much more difficult question is whether donors are obliged to provide material assistance; that is, whether there is a human-rights-based[221] claim to ODA.[222] Here, as well, the legal situation is different for each of the three donors.

With respect to the World Bank, no such duty can be said to exist. The Bank is not a party to the relevant treaties, and the customary international law to which it is subject covers only the core elements of human rights protection but no positive duties.[223]

The situation in the EU is different. The EU is also not a party to the relevant treaties, and is subject only to customary law. However, in both its primary and secondary law, the EU has committed itself expressly and repeatedly to respect and fulfill human rights.[224] This raises the question whether these self-incurred obligations also comprise a duty to provide ODA. In the final analysis, this appears not to be the case. The EU has never embraced a positive duty to provide aid, nor has it granted individual citizens of developing countries a right to ODA. A systematic evaluation of the relevant norms shows that the EU has always insisted on its

[218] The safeguard policies take the form of Bank administrative regulations, as discussed above (see Ch 3.A.IV.2).

[219] Until now the main approach is that of the Bundestag, which submits queries in individual cases as to the potential human-rights risks of projects. This practice, however, does not ensure a systematic evaluation performed in advance of the project.

[220] More details on the structure will be provided in Ch 6.B.

[221] On the (lack of) a claim to ODA arising from the development principle under international law see Ch 4.B.II.1.

[222] T. Pogge, "Recognized and Violated by International Law: The Human Rights of the Global Poor," *Leiden Journal of International Law*, 18 (2005), 717–45 at 717.

[223] A similar conclusion is reached by Skogly, *Human Rights Obligations*, p. 151; Killinger, *The World Bank's Non-Political Mandate*, p. 132; going further, with open advocacy Darrow, *Between Light and Shadow*, pp. 132, 133.

[224] See, e.g. Art. 21(II b), Lisbon Treaty; Art. 9, Cotonou Agreement; Regulation (EC) 1889/2006; Art. 2(I), Regulation (EC) 1905/2006.

sovereign prerogative to decide how and whether aid will be provided.[225] A coherent overview of the legal situation as a whole must conclude that the commitment to human rights in EU development cooperation law is always subject to autonomous financial decision-making. Any duties arising out of human rights law are thus inherently truncated or limited.

The legal situation in Germany is different from both the EU and the World Bank. Germany is a party to the relevant treaties and covenants and thus directly bound by them. As we have seen, Germany, in its development and ODA allocation practices, is hardly in a position to exercise effective control over citizens in recipient states. This deficit is, however, compensated by Germany's responsibility for recipient-state conduct.[226] The question is thus whether Germany, by virtue of the doctrine of state responsibility, may share in the positive duties of protection which recipient states owe to their citizens. This would appear to be the case. Article 16 of the ILC Rules on State Responsibility indicates no differentiation that would exclude the violation of positive duties. On the contrary, Germany shares in the recipient states' duties when it undertakes active cooperation with them. This could well justify a requirement to guarantee protection of recognized rights.

Nevertheless, there are limits to Germany's responsibility. Even from a human rights perspective, the duty to fulfill does not stipulate unlimited obligations but is subject to available resources. The duty also cannot realistically be said to apply to all humans worldwide. Germany's human rights duties also need to be harmonized with its rights under international law. These include sovereignty over its own resources. Provision of aid based on a human rights obligation is therefore contingent on government approval. This does not preclude these rights from turning into a positive duty to provide assistance, e.g. in the extreme case of famine or natural disasters, if the minimum core of rights, such as the right to food, cannot otherwise be protected. But these duties are subject to the availability of funds.

(3) Institutional provisions Finally, human rights treaties may oblige contracting states to undertake further institutional reforms to fulfill treaty rights. States could, for example, be obliged to enhance the effectiveness of rights by establishing channels for complaints in case rights

225 See Arts. 21, 22, Regulation (EC) 1905/2006; Art. 16 Annex IV to the Cotonou Agreement; Art. 7, Regulation (EC) 617/2007 (on the implementation of the Cotonou Agreement).

226 On this transferred responsibility see *infra* Ch 4.D.II.1.

are violated in the context of aid projects. Ombudsmen who could accept complaints from other countries as well would certainly aid in the realization of treaty rights. It should be kept in mind, however, that these are not subjective rights, but rather organizational issues that would be handled, for instance, by German legislation.[227]

This analysis justifies some nuanced, sober conclusions. The World Bank has no duty to provide aid. The EU has committed itself to provide aid, but the regulations can hardly be interpreted to grant rights to any citizens of recipient countries. As to Germany, one could justify a positive obligation on the basis of the ICESCR principles in extreme cases. Any such duty would, however, still be subject to available resources.

2. Participation rights in the development context?

Beyond the question of individual rights and their guarantees stands the larger question whether there is a separate individual right to participate in procedures relevant to the development process, for example the negotiation or structuring of projects. Such a "development-related right to participation" (Roos) would take its place alongside existing rights of participation which have (not without controversy) been derived from individual economic and social rights.[228] Such a right of participation would unquestionably be an important element in making the development process more open. The individual would no longer be treated as an object but as a subject capable of asserting rights and interests. The extent and form of this right could transform a technocratic process in which "stakeholders" are simply consulted on efficiency grounds to a pluralistic-political process in which projects are autonomously (co-)developed, and, when appropriate, rejected.[229]

[227] On the creation of an individual complaint mechanism under the ECOSOC Treaty see Sepulveda, "The Obligations of International Assistance," 98.

[228] See examples presented in A. Eide, C. Krause and A. Rosas, *Economic, Social and Cultural Rights: A Textbook*, 2nd edn (Dordrecht [u.a.]: Nijhoff, 2001), p. 249; p. 318; pp. 380, 381; see also the comments of the ECOSOC Committee in General Comment, No. 11, margin no. 8 (UN Document, E/C.12/1999/4); General Comment, No. 12, margin no. 23 (UN Document E/C.12/1999/5); General Comment, No. 14, margin no. 54 (UN Document E/C.12/2000/4).

[229] See generally F. Bliss, "Von der Mitwirkung zur Selbstbestimmung," *Politik und Zeitgeschichte* (2000), 3–8 at 3; Groves and Hint (eds.), *Inclusive Aid*; Hadiprayitno, *Hazard or Right?*, pp. 105–10; pp. 123–7; The World Bank's attitude to participation is conveyed in Shihata, *The World Bank in a Changing World I*, p. 92 ("participation in concrete project helpful"); see also Shihata, *World Bank Legal Papers*, p. 630 (explaining the term "meaningful consultation").

However, despite the consensus in favor of the practical and conceptual benefits of broad participation in the development process (particularly in the context of HRBA),[230] an arguable basis in international law is much less clear. Most discussion broadly refers to a number of provisions that either directly or indirectly support participation.[231] The UN Declaration on the Right to Development itself, in its Preamble and Art. 2(III), specifies that development should be a comprehensive process "on the basis of ... active, free and meaningful participation in development."[232] The right to shape public affairs[233] is also frequently cited in this context, as well as the rights of particular groups.[234] Finally, proponents of the right of participation refer to guarantees of freedom of opinion, of assembly and of speech.[235]

Although most authors remain somewhat cautious in claiming the existence of a legally binding right in international law that affected parties or NGOs could claim against extraterritorial donors, some authors, in particular Stefanie Ricarda Roos, do posit a right to development-related participation as an independent legal principle of the customary international law of human rights.[236] This right, she claims, gives affected parties a right to be informed and consulted, although it does not yet go so far as to give affected parties a veto right or a right to withhold agreement, in the sense of requiring "free, prior and informed consent."[237]

However, the arguments for this claim seem questionable. The "right to development" formulates an important goal of international law and is clearly on the way to being specified and consolidated. It is, however, not yet binding international law.[238] Freedom of opinion and assembly could certainly be considered core elements of the Universal Declaration of Human Rights, and therefore part of international customary law. However, they hardly guarantee participation in specific processes, in

[230] A perspective skeptical of the mere window dressing of participation is found in Rahnema, "Participation," p. 116; a critique of the possibility of deliberative situations in development cooperation is K. Morrison and M. Singer, "Inequality and Deliberative Development: Revisiting Bolivias Experience with the PRSP," *Development Policy Review*, 25 (2007), 721–40 at 721.

[231] See the descriptions in Darrow and Tomas, "Power, Capture, and Conflict," 506–10; Roos, *Der internationel Menschenrechtsschutz*, pp. 239–56; Hadiprayitno, *Hazard or Right?*, pp. 110–23.

[232] UN-GA, Res. 41/128, December 4, 1986.

[233] Art. 25a ECOSOC, Art. 21, UDHR.

[234] For instance in Article 12 of the Convention on the Rights of the Child, and in Art. 7, 13, 14 II, Convention on the Elimination of all Forms of Discrimination against Women.

[235] Art. 18, 19, 21, ECOSOC; Art. 18–20, UDHR.

[236] Roos, *Der internationel Menschenrechtsschutz*, p. 247.

[237] Ibid., p. 255.

[238] See, with further citations, *supra* Ch 4.B.I.

particular diplomatic ones. In this respect, they set the context for a right of participation rather than forming its concrete basis.

The most important bases for a participation right therefore seem to be Art. 25(a) of the ICCPR and Art. 21 of the Universal Declaration. These provisions guarantee, in practically identical form, the right of a person "to take part in the government of his country, directly or through freely chosen representatives." However, the drafting history of these provisions demonstrates that the question of how states should fulfill this right was intentionally left open.[239] In interpretations of Art. 25(a) of the ICCPR Treaty issued by the UN Committee, it has become clear that the provision is not to be understood as giving directly affected individuals or groups a specific right of participation.[240] An interpretation that did confer a participation right would be very specific and could hardly be considered as a core right protected by customary international law. In any event, Art. 25(a) would have a binding effect only on states, not on the World Bank or the EU.

A particular form of the participation idea can also be found in the idea that indigenous peoples have a right to "free, prior and informed consent," a norm that has become ever more well defined in recent years.[241] It was first mentioned and elaborated in the ILO Conventions,[242] but has been taken up again by a 2007 UN resolution[243] and in various international instruments, not least a World Bank Operational Policy (which speaks of "consultation" though and not of "consent").[244] The right has also recently been recognized by the UN Human Rights Committee.[245] The principle is intended to give indigenous peoples, being a particularly

[239] A. Rosas, "Art. 21," in A. Eide (ed.), *The Universal Declaration of Human Rights: A Commentary* (Oslo: Scandinavian University Press, 1992), pp. 299–317 at pp. 303, 307.

[240] M. Nowak, "Art. 25," in M. Nowak (ed.), *UN Covenant on Civil and Political Rights: CCPR Commentary* (Kehl: N.P. Engel, 2005) at margin no. 15.

[241] K. Göcke, "The Case of Angela Poma Poma v. Peru before the Human Rights Committee: The Concept of Free Prior and Informed Consent and the Application of the International Covenant on Civil and Political Rights to the Protection and Promotion of Indigenous Peoples' Rights," in A. von Bogdandy and R. Wolfrum (eds.), *Max Planck Yearbook of United Nations Law*, 14th edn (Leiden, Biggleswade: Martinus Nijhoff Publishers, 2010), pp. 337–70; R. Wolfrum, "The Protection of Indigenous People in International Law," *Heidelberg Journal of International Law*, 59 (1999), 369–83 at 369.

[242] ILO Conventions No. 107 of June 26, 1957 and No. 169 of June 7, 1989.

[243] UN-GA, Res. 61/295 of September 13, 2007.

[244] World Bank, Operational Policy 4.10 of 2005; on its predecessors see Kingsbury, "Operational Policies"; R. Goodland, "Free, Prior and Informed Consent and the World Bank Group," *Sustainable Development Law and Policy*, 4 (2004), 66–74 at 66.

[245] See Göcke, "Case of Angela Poma Poma v. Peru."

vulnerable group, specific procedural rights in matters – be they legislative or administrative in nature – that relate to their fundamental livelihood. Particularly in the context of development projects, a right not only to participate but also to veto projects would seem appropriate. However, it cannot yet be assumed that this principle is sufficiently established in content and as a prescriptive standard to permit its consideration as a generally accepted principle of customary international law.

Such a right would be unquestionably desirable from a political standpoint. Finally, there are many more or less informal norms that impose a duty on national legislatures to guarantee participation rights in construction law, local government and administrative procedure. However, these principles do not yet provide the foundation for a binding human right as against international donors.

IV. Summary

Human rights are not just rhetorical instruments for donors to control recipient governments, but they also constitute duties. When donors make ODA transfers, they must respect and protect human rights. As the previous analysis has shown, they must secure the protection of human rights both before and during ODA payments and conduct a "human rights impact" assessment. State donors must also pursue these goals as members of international donor organizations. States in particular may be subject to positive duties, although these are likely to take legislative, not financial form. And even when human rights do not entail duties, they guide the planning process for donors and help determine the structure and aim of programs.

The idea of individual autonomy which refers to the protection and promotion of human rights can thus be seen as a further legal principle of development cooperation law. Although its precise content and binding character differ according to the specific right and addressee, they add up to a legal principle of individual autonomy. Recipient-state citizens are thus protagonists of development cooperation and its administrative law. Development cooperation law regulates not only the donor–recipient-state relationship, but is also shaped by the human rights obligations of donor states in particular in the donor–recipient–citizen triangle. Development cooperation is thus not just an international but also a transnational process.

Although human rights confer clear rights on recipient-state citizens as against donors, they are not without their problems. Three are particularly apparent. First, there is tension between the human rights obligations of donors and the sovereignty of recipient states.[246] Human rights restrict the options not only of donors but also of recipient states. The more tightly regulated donors are, the more obliged they are to intervene in the affairs of recipient states. The *safeguard policies* of the World Bank are a good example of this. On the one hand, they represent the Bank's attempt to protect human rights; on the other hand, they impose extensive duties on recipient states. The familiar conflict between sovereignty and human rights appears in a new dimension within the triangular relationship with donors. Duties arising from human rights guarantees also raise the question of enforceability. As convincing as the argument for donors' duties may be, there is a woeful lack of real instruments for their enforcement. This raises the question of whether courts or other adjudicative bodies may be necessary – a question, however, which lies beyond the scope of this book.[247]

Before we can discuss the oversight of human rights and their associated positive duties, we must first address the problem of concretization. Even where human rights are well founded and unquestionably applicable, they remain vague and in need of concretization. This can occur by means of court enforcement or by other legal measures, such as legislation. On the national level, it is generally administrative law which provides for the middle-level enforcement of human rights. In development law as well, specific guarantees are generally addressed in the special part of the law. These guarantees will be addressed in Part III of this book.

E Coherence and efficiency

The fourth principle of development cooperation law does not address the goals or actors of development cooperation but rather its procedural form and its use of resources. The many instantiations of this concept will here be systematized and reduced to the principle of coherence and efficiency. This immediately involves an issue that has been the focus of recent debates on aid effectiveness[248] and which revolves around one

[246] See *supra* Ch 4.C.III.2.

[247] A deeper analysis is not possible in the context of this book. However, the question is addressed in K. Schmalenbach, "Accountability: Who Is Judging the European Development Cooperation?" in S. Bartelt and P. Dann (eds.), *Entwicklungszusammenarbeit im Recht der Europäischen Union: The Law of EU Development Cooperation: Europarecht-Beiheft Nr. 2* (Baden-Baden: Nomos, 2008), pp. 162–90 at p. 162; P. Dann, "Accountability in Development Aid Law: The World Bank, UNDP and Emerging Structures of Transnational Oversight," *Archiv des Völkerrechts*, 44 (2006), 381–404 at 381.

[248] This debate is discussed in detail *supra* Ch 2.C.III.1

important insight: development that is funded by ODA – that is, public funds – must aim at the most efficient possible use of these resources. Efficiency is not just an end in itself; it is also vital to addressing the pressing problem of poverty reduction and is also required simply by virtue of the public nature of the funds.

The current emphasis on this idea is related to the increasing autonomy of development aid since the end of the Cold War. This reduced the use of aid for other, i.e. heteronomous goals (in particular, foreign policy and trade policy) and increased its use for the autonomous goal of poverty reduction. The narrower emphasis on poverty reduction has made it easier to evaluate aid effectiveness. Efficiency, however, also has to do with the discursive hegemony of organizations such as the World Bank or the OECD, which follow a largely functional paradigm of development aid. To put it bluntly, they understand aid at best to be a process in which experts formulate precise goals and then work to achieve them efficiently and according to plan by virtue of comprehensive specialized knowledge.[249] This idea might represent a central insight, but should also be considered in a wider normative context. If efficiency becomes the dominant yardstick for evaluating development aid, as the Paris Declaration itself suggests, this narrow focus may reduce other important values, namely collective and individual autonomy, to mere means to an end. Recipient-state citizens, as well as the states themselves, will become mere extras in the achievement of goals defined elsewhere. As the above discussion of principles shows, this is an unconvincing normative paradigm. The principles, in fact, have significance on their own merits which remains relevant independent of efficiency concerns.[250]

Despite this "appeal" to normative caution, it remains the case that coherence and efficiency represent important conceptual building blocks in development cooperation law. Their legal contours will be explored in the following sections. Three facets of the principle will be analyzed. First, the principle of cost-effectiveness, which is further differentiated in development circles into the idea of result orientation and concentration (I).

[249] A polemical critique intended for a general audience is found in Easterly, "Entwicklungsideologie," 1084.

[250] For a careful integration of the cost-effectiveness principle in national administrative law, mindful of other values, see Schmidt-Aßmann, *Das allgemeine Verwaltungsrecht*, p. 317; see also R. Pitschas, "§42 Maßstäbe des Verwaltungshandelns," in W. Hoffmann-Riem, E. Schmidt-Aßmann and A. Voßkuhle (eds.), *Informationsordnung, Verwaltungsverfahren, Handlungsformen* (Munich: C.H. Beck, 2008), vol. II, pp. 1567–681 at margin no.111.

Then the principle of alignment will be addressed (II), followed by the various embodiments of the ideas of coordination and complementarity in development cooperation law (III). Finally, a summary will portray the status of the underlying norm, which is comprised of the structural principle of efficiency and coherence, but which has not been strengthened into an actual legal principle (IV).

I. Cost-effectiveness, result orientation, concentration

This principle is based on the idea that the allocation and use of ODA should be efficient and cost-effective. The focus here is by no means merely on corruption but more generally on how public funds are to be used. The basic idea is formulated in two ways: first, in general budget law (1) and, with specific reference to development cooperation, in the principles of result orientation and concentration (2).

1. Cost-effectiveness

Development cooperation is, at its core, a financial transfer. Even when the money may be used for various purposes, these uses are all made possible only by the original financial payment. Cost-effectiveness is therefore a basic aspect of development cooperation law. It requires actors to pursue the closest possible relationship between the goal and the means used to achieve it. It can be understood both minimally (a certain result is achieved with the least possible means) or maximally (achieving the best possible result with a defined amount of means). The principle exists in the budgetary laws of all donors and thus also applies to ODA payments. It can be seen, in an inductive and comparative sense, as a typical component of budgetary laws in general.

In Germany, the principle of cost-effectiveness can be found in various forms in various laws.[251] Article 114(II) of the Basic Law gives the *Bundesrechnungshof* (Federal Financial Authority) the responsibility to evaluate the cost-effectiveness and legality of Germany's budget and economic policies. Section 6 of the Budgeting Principles Law (German abbreviation HGrG) and Section 7 of the Federal Budget Ordinance (German abbreviation BHO) contain an identical norm stating that principles of cost-effectiveness and economy must be observed "during the creation and implementation of the budget plan." Sections 14 of the HGrG and

[251] Gröpl, *Haushaltsrecht und Reform*, p. 343; Schmidt-Aßmann, *Das allgemeine Verwaltungsrecht*, pp. 316–20; H. H. von Arnim, *Wirtschaftlichkeit als Rechtsprinzip* (Berlin: Duncker & Humblot, 1988).

23 of the BHO, addressing expenditures outside the area of the federal administration for fulfilling certain purposes (grants), specify that such grants (which include many ODA payments[252]) may only be costed when the federal government has a significant interest at stake that cannot be served (or adequately served) unless the grant is made.

The principle of cost-effectiveness thus consists of both a duty imposed on the *Bundesrechnungshof* to perform an accounting evaluation and a performance yardstick that applies to the executive and the budget lawmaker. Cost-effectiveness has no predefined contents and its intrinsic principle of optimization can only have the desired impact when applied to a concrete goal. In the development context, the relevant goal is poverty reduction. Thus, the funds used to finance ODA must be used as effectively as possible.[253]

In EU law, the principle of cost-effectiveness is found in Art. 317(I) of the Treaty on the Functioning of the European Union (TFEU), which requires the European Commission to implement budget plans "on its own responsibility and within the limits of the appropriations, having regard to the principles of sound financial management." This principle applies to ODA expenditures from the general EU budget. For ODA payments to ACP states from the (currently 10th) Development Fund, Article 11 of Regulation 215/2008 provides that the use of EDF monies "shall be used in accordance with the principles of sound financial management, namely in accordance with the principles of economy, efficiency and effectiveness." Legal definitions of these terms follow: "The principle of economy requires that the resources used for the pursuit of activities shall be made available in due time, in appropriate quantity and quality and at the lowest possible expense." The principle of efficiency "is concerned with the best relationship between resources employed and results achieved." Finally, "[t]he principle of effectiveness is concerned with attaining the specific objectives set and achieving the intended results."

[252] W. Patzig, *Haushaltsrecht des Bundes und der Länder: Band 2: Verwaltungsvorschriften* (Baden-Baden: Nomos, 1982), C/63/7.

[253] In the area of grants in particular, there is a process for evaluating results that has recently been the focus of discussion and reform (H. Dommach, "Das Verfahren der Erfolgskontrolle durch die Bundesverwaltung für zuwendungsfinanzierte Projekte und Institutionen," *Die Öffentliche Verwaltung*, 61 (2008), 282–7 at 282; Gröpl, *Haushaltsrecht und Reform*, p. 560; on financial oversight in general see H. Rischer, *Finanzkontrolle staatlichen Handelns: Wirtschaftlichkeit und Sparsamkeit als Prüfungsmaßstäbe* (Heidelberg: C.F. Müller, 1995); see also contributions in H. Schulze-Fielitz (ed.), *Fortschritte der Finanzkontrolle in Theorie und Praxis: Zum Gedenken an Ernst Heuer. Beiheft Die Verwaltung* (Berlin: Duncker & Humblot, 2000).

These regulations bind the Commission in its use of funds. European law also contains corresponding oversight obligations. Article 287(II) UA(1) of the TFEU sets out sound financial management as the standard that the EU's Court of Auditors must use.[254] Parallel to this, Article 13 of Council Regulation 215/2008 for the EDF specifies concrete requirements for effective financial oversight. Article 124 of the same regulation requires the Court of Auditors to report on the use of funds and (if applicable) issue a yearly report concerning financial management for the previous year. Last but not least, the European Anti-Fraud Office (OLAF) and the Court of Auditors are to be given oversight competencies in specific aid treaties.[255]

World Bank law also contains various regulations which, although they do not specifically establish a principle of cost-effectiveness, effectively pledge the Bank to the equivalent duty of sound financial management of resources. Five provisions will serve as examples. First, the Bank is required to undertake a comprehensive credit evaluation of states which are to receive loans.[256] Second, World Bank monies are to be used only for "specific projects."[257] This rule is intended to enable exact oversight over the use and effectiveness of the funds. There is an explicit exception for "specific circumstances" in the regulation which is now used for budget support, i.e. development policy lending (formerly known as structural-adjustment programs) with the most prominent instrument being budget aid. However, intensive legal discussion preceded the application of this regulation, and it is still regarded as an exceptional clause.[258] A third Bank provision which is applicable to project lending requires Bank employees to ensure that spending is justified not only from a development standpoint but also from an economic perspective.[259] The duty entails an in-depth cost–benefit analysis. A fourth regulation ensures loans are used for the intended purpose by permitting the Bank to disburse monies only when expenses are actually incurred – or as in the case of the recently introduced program-for-results financing, funds can only be disbursed

[254] See W. Schenk, *Strukturen und Rechtsfragen der gemeinschaftlichen Leistungsverwaltung*, Jus Internationale et Europaeum (Tübingen: Mohr Siebeck, 2006), vol. VII, p. 351 and the many further sources cited therein.

[255] Art. 70 IV, 116 III, Regulation (EC) 215/2008.

[256] IBRD, Art. III, Sect. 4(v).

[257] IBRD, Art. III, Sect. 4(vii); IDA, Art. V, Sect. 1(b).

[258] On the beginnings of the use of this clause see *supra* Ch 2.A.II; on its exact interpretation see Shihata, *World Bank Legal Papers*, pp. 157–182; p. 377.

[259] OP 10.00, Rn. 3, OP / BP 10.04.

when the agreed results of a program have been achieved.[260] If the debtor is not a member state but a private entity, the IBRD Articles require that the IBRD can only provide the loan if the entity's home state provides a statutory government guarantee of repayment.[261] This provision does not exist in the IDA articles, as the IDA only lends to governments.[262]

In addition to the above provisions, the Bank's financial regulations are institutionally secured, and the Bank is subject to financial oversight.[263] It is required to subject its budget to an external audit.[264] The Bank also has its own Department of Institutional Integrity, which investigates fraud and corruption, and has also established a whistle-blower hotline.

We have now seen that sound and rational financial management is a basic commitment of every sovereign institution that disburses ODA. The obligation, however, also takes more specific forms in the development context.

2. Result orientation and concentration

In the context of development cooperation, the principle of efficiency has taken two more specific forms, namely the principle of result orientation and the principle of concentration.

According to the Paris Declaration and its successors, development funds are to be administered and used in a result-oriented fashion. This principle aims at defining clear and (when possible) quantitative goals for programming ODA allocations and at erecting precise reporting and evaluation systems with which the use of funds and the realization of goals can be monitored. The Paris Declaration requires recipient countries to create the necessary evaluation systems and indicators, while donor states are obliged to orient their goals and oversight systems to recipient-state development strategies.[265]

European development cooperation law, in particular, has taken up this idea. The 2005 European Consensus, as a general declaration of

260 IBRD, Art. III, Sect. 5; IDA, Art. V, Sect. 1 (h). On Program-for-Results funding, see *infra* Ch 8.

261 IBRD, Art. III, Sect. 4(i). On the legal requirements for Bank financing to NGOs in detail, see I. Shihata, *The World Bank in a Changing World: Volume II: Selected Essays and Lectures* (Dordrecht: Martinus Nijhoff, 1995), p. 268.

262 Shihata, *World Bank Legal Papers*, p. 425; M. Mosler, *Finanzierung durch die Weltbank: Grundlegung und anwendbares Recht der vertraglichen Instrumente* (Berlin: Duncker & Humblot, 1987), pp. 34, 35, on various security arrangements, ibid., pp. 38–41.

263 More discussion on the following points is found in Dann, "Accountability," 389–91.

264 IBRD, Art. V, Sect. 13.

265 Paris Declaration, margin nos. 43–5.

principles, commits the EU and its member states to the principle of result orientation.[266] Development-related regulations issued since 2005, in particular, the so-called Development Cooperation Instrument of 2006 (Regulation 1905/2006, so-called DCI Regulation) also incorporates the idea.[267] Germany adopted result orientation in its 2007 Guidelines for development cooperation and has implemented it in concrete planning rules.[268]

Another principle designed to enhance aid effectiveness is concentration.[269] Concentration calls on donors to concentrate their ODA funds on a few sectors and/or recipient states, to permit a focusing of competences and resources on core problems. Concentrations are to be established in dialog with recipient states and other donors. The Guidelines of the German Development Ministry, as well as the DCI Regulation, now contain thematic concentrations.

II. Alignment with recipients

The Paris Declaration formulates a second approach to increasing the coherence and efficiency of development cooperation, namely the principle of alignment, which requires donors to align programs with the priorities and the institutional, procedural, and regulatory systems of recipient countries. The principle assumes that development cooperation will be more effective if donors respect recipient-country priorities rather than pursuing their own priorities and creating their own rules for public finance management, allocations, etc. The principle evolved not least from the observation that smaller recipient states, in particular, were simply overwhelmed by trying to satisfy the specific demands of over seventy public and many more private donors. It is also closely related to the principle of ownership, indeed it could be said to represent the other side of the coin: wherever recipient countries develop their own poverty reduction strategies, donors should respect these.[270]

The Paris Declaration lists two components of alignment. The first relates to the setting of substantive priorities for development cooperation. It may seem obvious that recipient states should determine what

[266] European Consensus, margin no. 25.

[267] See Art. 3(VIII), 19(IV) Regulation (EC) 1905/2006, OJ L 378, 27.12.2006, pp. 41–71.

[268] BMZ, *Guidelines*, margin nos. 1, 22.

[269] See European Consensus, margin nos. 67–69; Ibid., margin no. 2.

[270] On the principle of ownership see *supra* Ch 4.C.I; on its concrete implementation see *infra*, Ch 5.B and C.

ODA funds are used for and that donors should respect these priorities, but this principle is specifically emphasized here[271] – and for good reason, as we shall later see.[272] Secondly, alignment requires donors, instead of creating their own rules, to channel ODA funds through existing recipient-state structures of public financial administration, auditing or public contracting. Of course, recipient-state systems must be comprehensively evaluated beforehand for reliability.[273] By using recipient-state public finance systems, the recipient states' technical and administrative capacities are strengthened in these areas.[274]

This principle, which was first announced in the Paris Declaration in non-binding form, has since been incorporated into the development cooperation law of many donors.[275] Of particular importance is the orientation toward the substantive priorities of donor states and respect for their planning priorities.

III. Coordination and complementarity

One of the main features of the international aid architecture is not just the plurality of donors but also their non-hierarchical relationship. Plurality and heterarchy have long[276] been recognized as basic problems in development cooperation, since they lead to increased transaction costs, competition between donors and excessive demands on recipient-state administrations.[277] The negative consequences here are mainly practical, since direct or indirect normative conflicts with respect to individual projects are rare and are generally harmless from the perspective of general development goals.[278] Nevertheless, the practical costs are high enough to justify asking for a legal solution to reduce them. If

[271] Paris Declaration, margin no. 16.

[272] On the programming of ODA payments see *infra* Ch 5.B and C.

[273] Paris Declaration, margin nos. 17–21.

[274] Paris Declaration, margin nos. 22–30.

[275] See European Consensus, margin nos. 15, 25, 32, 51, 67; Ibid., margin nos. 2, 8, 38, World Bank, BP 2.10, margin no. 2.

[276] Friedmann, Kalmanoff and Meagher, *International Financial Aid*, p. 135; Broches, "International Bank for Reconstruction and Development," pp. 79, 80; Betz, *Internationalisierung*; Kaplan, *International Aid Coordination*.

[277] For a more detailed discussion of these problems see *supra* Ch 2.C.II.3. See also Faust and Leiderer, "Zur Effektivität und politischen Ökonomie," 145; Ashoff, *Geberkoordinierung*; S. Knack and A. Rahman, "Donor Fragmentation," in Easterly, *Reinventing Foreign Aid*, p. 333.

[278] On the kinds of norm conflicts and possible solutions see International Law Commission, Fragmentation of International Law (Rapporteur Martti Koskenniemi), UN-Doc A/CN.4/L.682 (of April 13, 2006).

there are no clear competence regulations, the question then becomes one of coordination.[279] Three approaches to the problem are of interest: the Paris Declaration, general coordination rules and individual provisions in development cooperation law that contribute to coordination and complementarity.

Coordination is a basic concern of the Paris Declaration. The Declaration imposes a harmonization requirement that requires donors to increase mutual cooperation and complementarity and reduce redundancies.[280] There are three facets to this requirement. First, procedural coordination, which obliges donors to develop common approaches to planning, funding and evaluation of projects. There is also a component which requires donors to create a substantive division of responsibilities and ensure that their programs complement each other. Finally, donors are called upon to create a common approach to assessment of environmental aspects of projects.

Article 210(I) of the TFEU sets forth a general – though regionally based – duty to coordinate.[281] It requires EU and member-state development policies to be complementary.[282] Coordination should happen at three levels. First, it relates to political and strategic decision-making, during which common goals and guidelines are to be established. It should also encompass the operative side of development cooperation – that is, planning and implementation of specific development projects. Finally, the participation of the EU and its member states should be coordinated at international conferences and in international organizations. The duty to coordinate also comprises a duty to cease and desist if the activities of one donor interfere with the activities of another.[283]

[279] See generally Schermers and Blokker, *International Institutional Law*, margin no. 1702; fundamentally C. W. Jenks, "Coordination: A New Problem of International Organization. A Preliminary Survey of the Law and Practice of Interorganizational Relationships," *Recueil des Cours de l"Académie de droit international de la Haye*, 77 (1950), 151–303 at 151.

[280] Paris Declaration, margin nos. 32–36.

[281] A. Schwimmbeck, *Rechtliche Analyse der gegenwärtigen Struktur der regionalen Entwicklungszusammenarbeit in der Europäischen Gemeinschaft* (Frankfurt: Peter Lang Verlag, 2007), p. 159; K. Schmalenbach, "Art. 180 EGV," in C. Calliess and M. Ruffert (eds.), *EUV/EGV: Das Verfassungsrecht der Europäischen Union mit Europäischer Grundrechtecharta*. Kommentar, 3rd edn (Munich: C.H. Beck, 2007) at margin no. 3; on the political background to coordination, which has been demanded for decades but seldom followed, see Carbone, *European Union and International Development*, pp. 51–60; Grilli, *EC and Developing Countries*, pp. 74–84.

[282] Reaffirmed in the European Consensus, margin nos. 30–38.

[283] Schmalenbach, "Art. 180 EGV," margin no. 5.

Finally, there are a large number of more specific coordination rules.[284] They govern three aspects: goals, planning and execution of development cooperation. They can be categorized as conceptual, programming and operative coordination.

Conceptual coordination refers to agreement on common substantive goals to which all or at least many donors agree to be aligned. There are three central documents relating to this form of coordination: first, the Millennium Development Goals, which set out eight specific goals to be reached by 2015; second, the Monterrey Consensus, which also sets goals for global development cooperation; third and finally, the European Consensus on Development Cooperation, which formulates common goals and principles for the EU and its member states.[285] The first two of these documents are UN General Assembly Resolutions, while the European Consensus is a political declaration reflecting the intentions of its signatories. Nevertheless, it has already been used to interpret EU law by the ECJ,[286] and is referred to in many subsequent legislative acts.[287]

Coordination of programming is mainly regulated by two documents. In the European context, a potentially important document is the "Communication from the Commission to the Council and the European Parliament of March 2006: Increasing the impact of EU aid: A common framework for drafting country strategy papers and joint multiannual programming."[288] It addresses the central multi-year planning instrument for development administration and provides a unified format for this activity. If the EU and its member states were to adopt this strategy, it would lead to the comparability and compatibility of costly analyses, thereby saving enormous amounts of work and cost. In 1997, the UN introduced a coordinated planning instrument, the so-called UN Development Assistance Framework. It was meant to draw together the various UN agencies working in development and coordinate them for a three-to-six-year period.[289]

284 Coordination also takes place informally by means of meetings in common forums. See *supra* Ch 3.C.I.

285 On the political context of these documents see *supra* Ch 2.C.III.

286 ECJ, C-91/05 (ECOWAS) and C-403/05 (Philippine Border Controls). See also Wischmeyer, "Europäische Entwicklungszusammenarbeit," 411.

287 For example in Arts. 1(II, III), Regulation (EC) 617/2007; Art. 2(III), Regulation (EC) 1905/2005.

288 KOM (2006) 88, of 2 March 2006; see also European Consensus, 2005, margin no. 31 and the reference thereto in Art. 3 I, DCI 10th EDF.

289 On the UNDAF: Report of the Secretary-General on the Work of the Organization (1999), UN Doc. A/54/1, margin no. 128. On the coordination process within the UN,

Finally, there are various norms that relate to the *coordination of the concrete implementation* of projects and programs. Here as well, there is a new and potentially important EU instrument. The "Code of Conduct on Complementarity and the Division of Labour in Development Policy," issued in May 2007 in the form of a Communication of the Council and the member states there represented,[290] names eleven principles that should guide development cooperation by the EU and its member states in a developing country with a view to improving the division of labor. They include concentration on focal sectors, the acceptance of a lead donorship arrangement for a country or sector, and the aid to so-called *aid orphans*, particularly difficult and therefore often neglected countries.[291] As with the Country Strategy Paper, this Communication is not a binding legal document. It is probably best to have few illusions about how thoroughly these principles will be implemented. They take their place in a long series of pronouncements that have remained largely ignored.[292] Nevertheless, they can also be seen as a new beginning which certainly shows some momentum from the Paris Declaration and the general discussion of aid effectiveness.

Trust funds and co-funding are much better established instruments of operative coordination. Trust funds are special accounts filled by one or more states but which are administered by international development organizations such as the World Bank and used for project financing.[293] Trust funds are generally subject to the law of the administering organizations, although funders have a say in determining the goals for which the funds are used.[294] Trust funds pool resources and subject them to *one* procedural regime and goal instead of many. The World

see *Strengthening of the United Nations: An Agenda for Further Change* Report of the Secretary-General, A/57/387, 9 September 2002, United Nations, New York; see also documents from the UNDG at www.undg.org/content.cfm?id=846 (last visited September 2012); and GA Res. 56/201 (Nov 2000).

290 See Council Document 9558/07 of 15 May 2007.

291 H. Mürle, *Towards a Division of Labor in European Development-Cooperation: Operational Options*, Discussion Paper 6/2007 (Bonn, 2007). Available at www.die-gdi.de (last visited July 2013), which sketches the questions addressed by the Codex.

292 See Schwimmbeck, *Rechtliche Analyse der gegenwärtigen Struktur*, p. 166.

293 See sources cited in I. Bantekas, "Trust Funds," in Wolfrum, *Max Planck Encyclopedia of Public International Law* at margin no. 1; extensively also I. Bantekas, *Trust Funds Under International Law: Trustee Obligations of the United Nations and the Development Banks* (The Hague: Asser Press, 2009).

294 Trust fund activity in the World Bank is regulated by OP / BP 14.40. A framework agreement is reached with a donor on the fundamental questions of trust fund management (for example, the EU-World Bank Framework Agreement of 2001), as well as individual agreements on specific funds. This legal regime appears to have hardly been analyzed up until now.

Bank administers a large number of such funds. A less long-term, more project-specific approach is co-financing. This means the Bank and other donors become collective donors to a common project.[295] Co-financing also requires donors to agree on one procedural regime and project. This reduces complexity for recipients, who need deal with only one counterpart. The instrument of budgetary aid also assists coordination, since it generally involves many different donors acting together.[296]

IV. Summary

This overview has shown that there are many normative bases for deriving a principle of coherence and efficiency in development cooperation law. The principle emphasized the necessity, when planning and implementing ODA, of ensuring cost-effectiveness and rationality, reducing waste and redundancy in their various forms, and measuring aid by verifiable success criteria. In terms of their normative density, however, these ideas take many different forms. Some components of the principle of cost-effectiveness are present in the constitutional and primary law of donors, while others appear only in the Paris Declaration or other merely political documents. Thus, the principle cannot be said to have legal force.

Nevertheless, a structural principle of coherency and efficiency clearly exists. The number and scope of regulations which serve this principle shows it to be a leading concept of development cooperation law. The question of coherence and efficiency can thus serve to systematize the normative material from a doctrinal point of view. The principle, which gives legal form primarily to a functional paradigm of development cooperation, resembles – from a normative point of view – the substantive principle of development, and takes its place alongside the legal principles of collective and individual autonomy. In conclusion, we will now address the content and relationship between these four basic ideas of development cooperation law.

F Summary: substance of and tensions between the principles

Four main principles shape development cooperation law and open up important perspectives on the goal, actors and shape of development cooperation.

295 OP / BP 14.20; Mosler, *Finanzierung durch die Weltbank*, p. 168.

296 Discussed in detail *infra* Ch 7.B.

Substantively, development cooperation law is guided by the development principle. It obliges international organizations and states to cooperate constructively with the goal of reducing poverty. Although it does not establish financial obligations, it does require concrete efforts to make ODA transfers possible. Once it is decided that ODA transfers are to be made, it imposes duties both on donors and recipients. The development principle has many normative bases, but does not have the status of a legal principle. Nevertheless, it formulates the central substantive idea of development cooperation law.

The principles of collective and of individual autonomy, by contrast, mark the status of important actors in development cooperation. Collective autonomy, in particular, sets out a basic concept of development aid: it guarantees the autonomy of every state, whether donor or recipient, big or small, to structure its inner order and external relations without coercion. It is thus a central expression of a realistic legal paradigm of development cooperation. In the context of development cooperation law, collective autonomy is specifically shaped by the principle of ownership, which concretizes the role of recipient states. The principle of collective autonomy fundamentally guarantees that autonomy applies equally to all states, independent of their size or power.

At the same time, however, development cooperation can no longer be thought of only as governed by the law of states and international-law subjects. Rather, individuals and their rights play an important role, too. This role is manifested in the principle of individual autonomy, specifically through human rights. All donors are required to respect human rights. They must ensure protection of human rights before and during ODA expenditures and commission "human rights impact assessments." States, in particular, may be subject to positive duties, although these come more likely in the form of legislative duties than in direct financial obligations. Even where human rights do not impose duties, they create a positive setting for donors' and recipients' planning, serving as substantive guiding principles.

The fourth principle of development cooperation law, coherence and efficiency, is the guiding principle for the procedural organization of development cooperation law and its use of resources. This principle is based on diverse normative foundations that impose a duty to use ODA payments efficiently and monitor their effectiveness, as well as to organize actors to ensure the most coherent and efficient possible use of funds. It is the essential legal expression of a functionalist paradigm of development cooperation. Unlike the principles of collective and individual autonomy, this principle is not a legal principle but a doctrinal-systematizing structural principle.

When positioning these principles normatively within development cooperation law, two things must be kept in mind. *Legal* principles – here collective autonomy and individual autonomy – are based on international law. They take up general principles of international law and then adapt them to the particular area of development cooperation. However, all four principles are also *structural* principles of development cooperation law – doctrinal categories that help systematize legal materials. As such, they serve to systematize norms that may derive from various different legal orders. As structural principles, they even have a multi-level function in that they transcend levels of public authority. The sources for structural principles are thus derived not just from public international law but from all three levels of public authority – national, supranational and international. They provide particular proof of the existence of a global administrative law, which derives its global nature precisely from its transcendence of the international level.[297]

The tension between the principles should also be kept in mind. The individual principles relate to each other in many ways, sometimes complementary, but more often contrary. The collective autonomy of recipient countries can conflict with the autonomy of donors; the duty of solidarity can contradict donor autonomy; human rights can restrict the autonomy of recipient states; efficiency can undermine autonomy. Further conflicts are conceivable. The question of how they are to be resolved is unavoidable. There are no general, binding rules for conflict resolution, nor is a hierarchy among them discernible. Certainly, legal principles have precedence over structural ones, but there is no order of priority between the legal principles of collective and individual autonomy. Creating conflict-resolution rules hardly seems possible, given the many different forms conflicts might take. Instead, it seems that specific solutions will have to be found for individual cases.

A final area of tension should be mentioned; one that affects development cooperation law in particular. This is the tension between the guiding principles of development aid law and its reality in practice. In the face of the enormous inequalities between the parties and the conflicts of interest that in part obviously arise among them, to claim the existence of principles such as autonomy, equality and solidarity seems optimistic – even

[297] Kingsbury, Krisch and Stewart, "Emergence of Global Administrative Law," 29–31; 55.

though this study formulates the claims of these principles rather defensively (in contrast to the international law of development). This discrepancy is irrelevant to the content of the law. It consists, essentially, of the counterfactual postulation of norms. If we wish to understand the law as anything more than an ignorant and cynical pretense, however, we must always keep the tension between law and reality in perspective, and let it inform our understanding of the law.

PART III

Administrative law of development cooperation

While the previous parts conceptualized development cooperation law and sketched its constitutional framework, we have yet to address the rules that govern the concrete process of how ODA is transferred. That will change now. Part III will analyze the laws of ODA transfer. It will examine the procedural rules, legal instruments and substantive standards according to which ODA is awarded – and hence turn to the "administrative law" of ODA transfer. In the course of this analysis, the study will posit two theses: first, it will argue that development cooperation law is not only guided by general principles, but that the law of different donors also shares convergent structures. There is hence a general law of ODA transfer that transcends the boundaries of organizations. Second, Part III will point out that, beyond this convergence, there exist quite diverse forms of development administration and development cooperation law. We especially encounter two general types that have been identified before: one more technocratic-autonomous and one more diplomatic-heteronomous.[1]

Given that the administrative law of development cooperation has hardly been studied yet, we first have to address the question of how to structure our investigation. A first approach could draw upon the perspective offered by the three branches of government. In that line and adopting the perspective of a *legislature*, we could ask how laws and the general ODA budget are set. The focus could then turn to the perspective of *judicial* (or quasi-judicial) institutions, and the question would turn to oversight of development agencies and ODA allocations. The third perspective could take the view of the *executive*. The focus here would be on which rules development organizations and their partners use to plan, negotiate and implement ODA transfers, and which legal doctrines shape the approval process itself. The present study will address the second and third perspective. The perspective of the executive certainly provides most

[1] For more on these types, see *supra* Ch 3.D.

material.[2] Decisions on ODA transfers take place mostly in the executive; it is here that development administration is manifested directly as an exercise of public authority. It also inquires into the rules of accountability and oversight that the judicial perspective lends.[3] Given that ODA are public funds and there is perpetual doubt about the effectiveness of aid, this is an especially important perspective.[4]

Even once we have decided to focus mainly on the rules pertaining to administrative actions regarding ODA payments, we must still organize the material. How is this to be done?

The structure of development cooperation law is easier to grasp when we view the administration in light of its mode of steering behavior. German public law scholarship especially distinguishes between two main modes of steering behavior or governance modes (*Steuerungsmodus*): maintaining public order through public order laws (*Ordnungsverwaltung/Ordnungsrecht*) and providing public benefits law through public benefits laws (*Leistungsverwaltung/Leistungsverwaltungsrecht*).[5] Through that lens, development cooperation law is a form of public benefits law. Development administrations provide benefits, they do not maintain order. The law of development cooperation does not protect against potential dangers, but rather systematically administers expenditures of public funds for the common good. Development administration basically organizes a multi-step and multi-polar process of public contracting. Three phases of this process can be distinguished: first, medium-term planning and programming; second, the agreement on concrete payments in the form of project or budget assistance, and third, the implementation of projects or programs, which may involve procurement processes and include certain forms of oversight (monitoring and evaluation).

This Part will focus on the first two phases, mid-term planning (Ch 5) and agreements on concrete ODA expenditures (Chs 6–8) but it

[2] See *infra*, Chapters 5 to 8.

[3] See *infra*, Chapter 9.

[4] The study of the first perspective must be left to other authors. However fruitful this exploration would be, it exceeds the scope of this book. For a preliminary exploration of the first branch, i.e. the role of the legislature (and in particular the budgeting function), see, e.g. Kollatz, "Grundlagen," 561 and Burall, White and Blick, *Impact of US*.

[5] Schulze-Fielitz, "§12"; M. Nierhaus, "Administrative Law," in M. Reimann and J. Zekoll (eds.), *Introduction to German Law* (Munich: C.H. Beck, 2005), pp. 87–120; G. Jurgens, M. Verhoeven and P. Willemsen, "Administrative Powers in German and in English Law," in L. F. M. Besselink, F. Pennings and S. Prechal (eds.), *The Eclipse of the Legality Principle in the European Union* (Alphen aan den Rijn: Kluwer Law International, 2011), pp. 37–54 at pp. 40–1.

will also examine the rules on accountability and oversight (Ch 9). It will not delve into the implementation, which would involve analysis of procurement law.[6] It will also not analyze in detail the rules on monitoring and evaluation. This would require diving into a gray area between law and administrative management which would certainly be fascinating and break new ground for legal scholarship. However, these questions lie beyond the scope of this book.[7]

[6] On EU procurement law in development cooperation see P. Kalbe, "The Award of Contracts and the Enforcement of Claims in the Context of EC External Aid and Development Cooperation," *Common Market Law Review*, 38 (2001), 1217–67.

[7] There have been several analyses of monitoring and evaluation in development aid, although not from a legal perspective (see K. Hempel, *Erfolgskontrolle in der deutschen Entwicklungszusammenarbeit: Zentrale Herausforderungen unter besonderer Berücksichtigung der Transparenz gegenüber der Öffentlichkeit*, Schriftenreihe des ESB Research Institute (Stuttgart: Ibidem-Verlag, 2006), vol. XL; A. Borrmann and H. Ahrens, *Zur Bewertung der Entwicklungszusammenarbeit* (Berlin: Duncker & Humblot, 2006); A. Coudouel, *Beyond the Numbers: Understanding the Institutions for Monitoring Poverty Reduction Strategies* (Washington, DC: World Bank Publications, 2006)). A legal analysis of evaluations would complement existing analyses of administrative evaluation and be extremely interesting (see articles collected in E. Schmidt-Aßmann and W. Hoffmann-Riem (eds.), *Verwaltungskontrolle*, Schriften zur Reform des Verwaltungsrechts (Baden-Baden: Nomos, 2001), vol. VIII; and, as early as the 1970s, R. Steinberg, "Evaluation als neue Form der Kontrolle final programmierten Verwaltungshandelns," *Der Staat*, 15 (1976), 185–210).

5

Programming the transfer of ODA

Planning is today considered a vital instrument of any modern administration. The euphoria and then deep skepticism about planning which dominated at least German debates in the 1960s and 1970s has given way to a more sober understanding in which prospective planning is regarded as a necessary, but not definitive, element of modern administrative activity.[1] Since the 1960s, development administrations have therefore developed increasingly formalized forms of planning which are usually known as "programming."[2] Programming brings approved – but as yet uncoordinated – projects into an overall framework to increase the effectiveness of aid payments. All three of the development administrations under discussion here have introduced planning regimes.[3] Programming always relates to one recipient country, region or thematic area, and has a medium-term time horizon.[4] It is thus typically a situation-oriented form of planning.

Programming is particularly important in the area of development aid. It is during the programming phase that themes are set out, limits established and, in general, the agenda of cooperation is determined. This phase already raises the first set of problems, relating to who exactly does the planning and therefore sets the agenda. Programming thus serves as the first test of questions of collective autonomy and coordination. In the abstract, it would be possible for both sides to claim influence in the planning process. Since the object is development, recipient states could claim precedence in setting the agenda. However, it is the donors who provide

[1] W. Köck, "§37 Pläne," in W. Hoffmann-Riem, E. Schmidt-Aßmann and A. Voßkuhle (eds.), *Informationsordnung, Verwaltungsverfahren, Handlungsformen* (Munich: C.H. Beck, 2008), vol. II, pp. 1275–339 at margin nos. 2–8 and sources cited therein.

[2] In development-aid texts there is no single term for this activity. In the following discussion the terms "planning" or "programming" will be synonyms for the general task of creating comprehensive plans of several years' duration which involve multiple projects or programs.

[3] See *supra* Ch 1.B.II.2, III.2 and IV.2.

[4] This discussion of planning law focuses on country-based planning, which is the normal case.

the money. This could give them the last word in financial questions. Ideally, the competing claims to influence and autonomy would be fairly balanced. In reality, though, it is mostly donors – as we shall see – who have most competences for planning. It is therefore hardly surprising that programming plays a central role in the discussion about how to foster ownership and autonomy, in particular in the development community's discussion of reforms in these areas.[5]

This chapter will review the current state of planning law in development administration in three steps. We will first address the empirical function and specific challenges posed by development planning (A). We will assume that all development organizations face the same functional tasks, and thus that a *functional* comparison of these agencies (in addition to a comparison based on the principles of development cooperation law from Part II) is particularly appropriate. After this groundwork has been laid, the specific planning laws will then be analyzed. We will begin with a look at the planning instruments of the recipient countries, the so-called Poverty Reduction Strategy Papers (B) and will then move on to the three donor organizations: the World Bank (C.I), the EU (C.II) and Germany (C.III). The coordination strategies used by these donors will also be addressed (C.IV). The third step of the analysis will compare the legal regimes with respect to their functions and the principles (D).

A Functions and problems of programming in development cooperation

Planning, according to Eberhard Schmidt-Aßmann, "consists of the analysis of current situations, the prognosis of future developments, and the tentative draft of a normative order. Its aim is the reconciliation of interests and coordination of activities within a framework of harmonized measures which have been woven into an overall concept. Complexity, connectedness, and structural creativity characterize both the planning process and the plan."[6] Schmidt-Aßmann fittingly describes the task faced by organizations during planning endeavors, and his observations, as will be seen, also apply to development administration.[7]

[5] See *supra* Ch 2.C.III.1, and sources cited therein.

[6] E. Schmidt-Aßmann, "Planung als administrative Handlungsform und Rechtsinstitut," in E. Schmidt-Aßmann (ed.), *Aufgabe und Perspektiven verwaltungsrechtlicher Forschung* (Tübingen: Mohr Siebeck, 2006), pp. 158–76 at p. 159.

[7] Although planning is a central activity particularly in the UN, the process has been subjected to very little study. In particular, there are apparently no studies of questions of

Planning has three principal functions: generation of knowledge, articulation of interests and coordination of activities. The *generation of knowledge* involves a first phase of data collection, the "analysis," which forms the basis for subsequent evaluation of alternatives and formulation of goals.[8] This aspect is particularly important in the development context. Donors planning development projects must necessarily focus on extraterritorial conditions. It is not a matter of District X planning the use of its own land, but (to take one example) the European Commission developing a plan for Kenya. Clearly, the Commission is critically dependent on information from and about Kenya that it will not have internally.[9] Further, the subject matter of development administration is complex and dynamic, such that previous experience with questions of development planning may be of only limited use. In this respect, development cooperation law is related to the law of risk.[10] In both areas, knowledge is typically temporary, subject to change, dynamic and unstable.[11] Planning law must create procedures and instruments which not only provide a base of information for the development administration, but which can also be changed and adapted repeatedly. Achieving this goal is made more difficult by a basic problem in development: the limited capacity of recipient states.[12] They often lack the personnel and specialized resources to master the administrative demands of complex planning.[13] Information that

international and extraterritorial planning from a legal perspective. The following discussion will therefore draw mainly on German planning literature. There are, however, a growing number of authors addressing development planning from a political-science and economic perspective. As far as possible, their findings will be brought into the following discussion.

[8] Köck, "§37," margin no. 26; on the generation of expertise as a way to legitimate decisions, particularly in international organizations, see M. Eifert, "Legitimationsstrukturen internationaler Verwaltung," in H.-H. Trute, T. Groß, C. Möllers and H. C. Röhl (eds.), *Allgemeines Verwaltungsrecht – zur Tragfähigkeit eines Konzepts*. Festschrift für Eberhard Schmidt-Aßmann (Tübingen: Mohr Siebeck, 2008), pp. 307–31 at p. 323.

[9] On these problems, see Gibson et al., *Samaritan's Dilemma*, pp. 41–6; Morrison and Singer, "Inequality and Deliberative Development," 721; see generally M. Behrens, "Global Governance," in A. Benz (ed.), *Governance – Regieren in komplexen Regelsystemen: Eine Einführung* (Wiesbaden: Verlag für Sozialwissenschaften, 2004), pp. 103–24 at p. 107.

[10] This comparison is drawn from K.-H. Ladeur, "Die Internationalisierung des Verwaltungsrechts," in C. Möllers, A. Vosskuhle and C. Walter (eds.), *Internationales Verwaltungsrecht: Eine Analyse anhand von Referenzgebieten* (Tübingen: Mohr Siebeck, 2007), vol. XVI, pp. 375–94 at p. 384.

[11] A. Scherzberg, "Risiko als Rechtsproblem," *Archiv des öffentlichen Rechts*, 84 (1993), 484–513 at 500.

[12] See discussion *supra*, Ch 2.C.II.

[13] Brinkerhoff, "State and International Development Management," 986; V. Fritz and A. Rocha Menocal, "Developmental States in the New Millennium," *European Journal of Development Research*, 25 (2007), 531–52 at 531.

is necessary for sound planning is often unavailable. Knowledge is often limited not only by extraterritoriality but also by inadequate capacity.

Planning also serves the *functions of articulation and reconciliation of divergent interests*. The planning process allows various interests to be heard and considered.[14] It is thus an important channel for expressing the principle of collective autonomy. This is particularly important for development planning, for three main reasons. First, development is a field which is quite loosely defined and open to various approaches.[15] There is no one development ideal which can simply be executed. Even the narrower goal of poverty reduction is vague. For precisely this reason, a procedure that permits the formulation of various interests is centrally important. Second, the articulation function is also important because, in development work, planners and those affected by the plans are separated by a great distance. Donor organizations, as planners, are not in a position of direct responsibility for the affected parties – that is, citizens of developing countries (though human rights obligations can apply).[16] The latter have no other means of voicing their dissatisfaction through, for example, elections or lawsuits. This makes their chance to articulate their interests during planning all the more important.[17]

Third, the articulation function is also connected to a typical problem of development policy, the often weak *motivation of recipients*.[18] Particularly where plans have been made largely without the influence of recipients, the motivation of governments in recipient countries to actively implement the plans and defend them against political opposition is limited.[19] The

[14] On the question of which voices can be given an audience in global administrative questions and how the law should deal with this problem see, e.g. N. Krisch, "The Pluralism of Global Administrative Law," *European Journal of International Law*, 17 (2006), 247–78 at 247.

[15] On the openness of the concept of development see *supra* Ch 2.B.I–III.

[16] See *supra*, Ch 4.D.

[17] The participation of broader society in development planning is a central theme of the development policy discussion. See *supra* Ch 2.B.II. It is discussed particularly often in the context of the newly introduced instrument of national poverty-reduction strategies. See *infra* Ch 5.B; see also Morrison and Singer, "Inequality and Deliberative Development," 721; N. Molenaers and R. Renard, "The World Bank, Participation and PRSP: The Bolivian Case Revisited," *European Journal of Development Research*, 15 (2003), 133–61 at 133.

[18] See *supra*, in particular Ch 2.B.I.

[19] Gibson et al., *Samaritan's Dilemma*, pp. 35; 54; S. Canagarajah and A. van Diesen, "The Poverty Reduction Strategy Approach Six Years On: An Examination of Principles and Practice in Uganda," *Development Policy Review*, 24 (2006), 647–67 at 652. *See also* Killick, *Aid and the Political Economy*, pp. 85–99 (in particular with regard to structural adjustment programs).

concept of *ownership* relates especially to the planning phase.[20] Planning procedures thus serve not only to generate knowledge and to draw up a convincing plan by reconciling interests, but also to improve implementation of the plan by involving the recipient side in the planning.[21]

Thirdly, the planning process, and in particular the plan itself, serves a *coordination function*.[22] The plan presents a "tentative draft of a normative order" (Schmidt-Aßmann) and has the goal of harmonizing individual measures.[23] Depending on how precise and binding the plan is, it can define thematic sectors, structure the interrelation of future actions, and – ideally – bind them all into a meaningful overall context.[24] The planning process and plans themselves not only establish transparency and rationality, but also create a basis for evaluation. Planning also has a rule-of-law component. Development cooperation has a particular need for two kinds of coordination. First, the size and complexity of the field that development cooperation may have in view, as well as the multiplicity of actions even one donor may engage in, must be coordinated within the donor's organization itself. Second, there must also be coordination *among* donors. Plans fulfill the function of signaling externally – that is, to other donors – what one is doing.[25] Plans also help realize the principle of coherence and efficiency.[26]

In addition to these specific functions and problems, the more general difficulties attending planning should be addressed. In general, planning is an easy target for accusations of social-technocratic hubris. The complexity and dynamism of social interactions necessarily make ambitious

[20] See *supra* Ch 4.C.I.

[21] Fritz Scharp maintains that the separation of decision-making and implementation marks (among other things) the differentiation of the roles of participant and affected party, thus revealing the dominance element of the relationship. (F. Scharpf, "Planung als politischer Prozess," in F. Scharpf (ed.), *Planung als politischer Prozess: Aufsätze zur Theorie der planenden Demokratie* (Frankfurt: Suhrkamp, 1973), pp. 33–72 at p. 34)

[22] See generally R. Wahl, *Rechtsfragen der Landesplanung und Landesentwicklung, Band I* (Berlin: Duncker & Humblot, 1978), p. 78; see also W. Thieme, *Verwaltungslehre*, 4th edn (Cologne: Heymann, 1984), margin no. 457.

[23] Schmidt-Aßmann, "Planung als administrative Handlungsform," p. 159.

[24] On the single instrument of programming see Wahl, *Rechtsfragen*, p. 88.

[25] On this problem of coordination see *supra* Ch 2.A.IV. and Ch 2.C.II.1.

[26] On planning in subsidy law, see H. P. Ipsen, "Verwaltung durch Subventionen," in O. Kimminich, P. Pernthaler, H. P. Ipsen and H. F. Zacher (eds.), *Das Staatsoberhaupt in der parlamentarischen Demokratie: Verwaltung durch Subventionen.* Aussprache zu den Berichten in den Verhandlungen der Tagung der Vereinigung der Deutschen Staatsrechtslehrer zu Graz vom 12. bis 15. Oktober 1966 (Berlin: de Gruyter, 1967), vol. XXV, pp. 255–307 at pp. 270, 271.

strategies for the future appear ineffectual.[27] In the development policy discussion, in particular, the most vehement critique of the development aid system is that of donors' over-bureaucratized planning.[28] Instead of global plans, these critics argue, incremental experimentation, competition and market mechanisms offer more effective solutions to development problems. Development planning is thus subject to the double suspicion of both hegemony *and* hubris. This fundamental critique cannot be addressed in the present context. For our purposes, it is more important to understand the present law of development cooperation before making proposals for its improvement (in the area of planning law, among others) or its partial replacement in terms of legal policy.

Before addressing the development planning of recipients (B) and then donors (C), we must note one purpose that the planning phase of development cooperation does *not* serve, namely the allocation of specific budget appropriations. Only the EU decides on budget allocation to individual countries in the programming phase.[29] Under the law of other donors, budget decisions are not made with instruments of medium-term program planning but rather before the planning phase.[30]

B Programming by recipients: the Poverty Reduction Strategy Papers

Programming has been a part of development planning since the 1960s, when the World Bank and other donors began integrating individual projects they were financing into the framework of medium-term program planning.[31] However, one thing has always remained clear: ODA

[27] See contributions to F. Scharpf, *Planung als politischer Prozes*, in particular Scharpf, "Planung," p. 33, as well as F. Scharpf, "Komplexität als Schranke der politischen Planung," pp. 73–113 at p. 73; E.-H. Ritter, "Staatliche Steuerung bei vermindertem Rationalitätsanspruch? Zur Praxis der politische Planung in der Bundesrepublik Deutschland," in T. Ellwein, J. J. Hesse, R. Maynitz and F. Scharpf (eds.), *Jahrbuch zur Staats- und Verwaltungswissenschaft* (Baden-Baden: Nomos, 1987), pp. 321–52 at p. 321.

[28] Easterly, "Introduction," p. 1; Reddy and Heuty, "Global Development Goals," 5.

[29] See *infra* Ch 5.C.II.

[30] An analysis of budgetary laws would be desirable from the perspective of development cooperation law research. Preliminary work in this direction can be found in Kollatz, "Grundlagen"; Dann, *Programm- und Prozesssteuerung*, pp. 118; 125.

[31] See *supra* Ch 1.B.II.2, III and IV; an early assessment of the program as a form of action in development administration can be found in M. Virally, "La Notion de Programme," in M. Virally (ed.), *Le droit international en devenir: Un Instrument de la Coopération Technique Multilatérale* (Paris: Presses universitaires de France, 1990), pp. 427–46 at p. 427.

programming was primarily a task for donors. Recipients were barely involved, and there was no systematic linkage between donor plans and national development plans, which each country developed on its own and for itself. Against this background, the national development plans of recipient countries, the Poverty Reduction Strategy Papers (PRSPs), are a fundamentally new and also somewhat curious instrument of development cooperation law.[32] PRSPs are medium-term development plans drawn up by recipient states at the request of donor nations and according to their specifications. They are intended to increase recipient participation in development planning, placing at least partial responsibility in the hands of those whose fate is being decided. On the other hand, though, such plans are created at the behest of donors. Autonomy and hegemony are found here side by side.

The emergence of this planning instrument is instructive: PRSPs were a result of the harsh critique of the ineffectiveness of development cooperation in the 1990s.[33] It was thought that one significant cause of this ineffectiveness was that recipient countries had too little share in and ownership of development planning, and therefore saw implementation as not really being their responsibility. To strengthen a sense of ownership among recipient states, the World Bank and the IMF, in 1999, made the creation of PRSPs a prerequisite for participation in their debt reduction program, the HIPC.[34] Recipient countries were themselves supposed to initially formulate their preferred medium-term development plans before financial institutions canceled their debts. Soon, however, the World Bank expanded the circle of countries which were obliged to create PRSPs to include all countries which wanted funds from the IDA. The PRSPs were meant to become the foundation for the Bank's own planning. The PRSP was not, however,

[32] For a thorough exploration of the origins of the PRSP, see K. Christiansen and I. Hovland, *The PRSP Initiative: Multilateral Policy Change and the Role of Research* (London: Overseas Development Institute, 2003), pp. 9–30; for general evaluations, see D. Peretz (ed.), *Learning from Experience: Perspectives on Poverty Reduction Strategies from Four Developing Countries* (London: Commonwealth Secretariat, 2009); G. Nankani, J. Page and L. Judge, "Human Rights and Poverty Reduction Strategies: Moving Towards Convergence?" in P. Alston and M. Robinson (eds.), *Human Rights and Development: Towards Mutual Reinforcement* (Oxford University Press, 2005), pp. 475–97 at p. 475; A. Chakravati, *Aid, Institutions and Development: New Approaches to Growth, Governance and Poverty* (Cheltenham: Edward Elgar, 2005), p. 123.

[33] See *supra* Ch 2.C.III.

[34] HIPC stands for Heavily Indebted Poor Country-Initiative. On the role of PRSP for HIPC debt reduction, see L. F. Guder, *The Administration of Debt Relief by the International Financial Institutions: A Legal Reconstruction of the HIPC Initiative* (Berlin: Springer, 2009), pp. 92; 120.

to remain exclusive to the World Bank. The Paris Declaration stressed the importance of PRSPs.[35] Other donor organizations have also made PRSPs the mandatory starting point for their planning.[36]

We will now assess the PRSP from a legal perspective. The first question is the legal nature of the duty to prepare PRSPs (I). The legal regime of the PRSP will then be analyzed from both a procedural and substantive perspective to determine whether recipients' planning can be called genuinely autonomous (II). The results will finally be evaluated in the context of the preceding functional analysis of planning in development cooperation and of the principles of development cooperation law (III).

First, a brief comment about the relationship between PRSPs, the World Bank, and other donors: the concept of the PRSP was invented by the World Bank and the IMF. As will shortly be seen, the World Bank also exercised significant influence over the structure of these documents. We could thus genuinely call the preparation of a PRSP the first phase of World Bank planning. Nevertheless, the PRSP has, in the meantime, expanded to become a general instrument that is intended to guide the efforts of all donors. The Paris Declaration, in particular, stresses this point, as do the various donor regulations which implement the accord. PRSPs will, therefore, be described here in their own terms, rather than being grouped with subsequent elaborations on the planning law of the World Bank.

I. *Legal foundations of the duty to prepare PRSPs*

When the World Bank requests the preparation of a PRSP, the question arises: what is its legal basis for doing so? There is no bilateral international law agreement on the creation of PRSPs. Nor is there a more general multi- or bilateral agreement regulating the details of PRSP preparation. Instead, the World Bank and other donors introduced the PRSP in a unilateral fashion as a prerequisite for application for access to certain financing instruments. The World Bank introduced PRSPs together with the IMF. In September and December of 1999, the Development Committee, a joint organ of the World Bank and the IMF composed of governors of both institutions, endorsed a proposal (created within both institutions) to introduce PRSPs.[37] The legal nature of this "endorsement" is unclear.

[35] Paris Declaration Arts. 14, 16.

[36] On the role of the PRSP in the law of Germany and the EU, see *infra* Ch 5.C.II. and III.

[37] World Bank, *Building Poverty Reduction Strategies in Developing Countries*, DC/99-29 of September 1999 (1999). Available at http://siteresources.worldbank.org/INTPRS1/Resources/383606-1092340662634/build_en.pdf (last visited September 2012); World

The Development Committee does not have its own competence to make legally binding decisions. Rather, it makes proposals to the two institutions which are understood by them as political self-commitments on their part.[38] On this basis, the internally binding law of the World Bank has now been modified to mention PRSPs at various points. One can thus say that the Bank has committed itself to PRSPs.[39] Other donors have copied the technique of incorporating into their internal law a duty to require PRSPs from recipient states.[40] Recipients who seek funds from the World Bank and other donors are thus subjected to norms which were adopted internally and unilaterally by donors.[41]

On the other hand, many recipient states have endorsed the idea of PRSPs. The Paris Declaration in particular places PRSPs in a central role and requires recipients to create and implement them. By accepting the Declaration, recipient states also accept the concept of the PRSP.[42]

In the end, the recipient states' duty to prepare PRSPs is chiefly imposed indirectly. Donors set out the requirement internally and unilaterally. Recipients are then compelled to follow the rules if they seek ODA in the form of financing instruments which require the presentation of a PRSP. Do donors impose further substantive or procedural requirements for PRSPs?

Bank, *Poverty Reduction Strategy Papers – Operational Issues*, September 10, 1999. Available at www.imf.org/external/np/pdr/prsp/poverty1.htm (last visited September 2012). Changes to the original rules were made by a further internal paper, World Bank, *PRSP – Progress in Implementation*, Report September 2004 (2004). Available at http://siteresources.worldbank.org/INTPRS1/Resources/prsp_progress_2004.pdf (last visited September 2012).

[38] For more details see Shihata, *World Bank Legal Papers*, pp. 833–6; Guder, *Administration of Debt Relief*, p. 140.

[39] See World Bank, OP 1.00, margin no. 2; BP 2.11, margin nos. 2, 3, 7; OP 8.60, margin no. 6 (for more on these norm types see *supra* Ch 3.A.IV.2). However, these norms relate primarily to planning. By contrast, there is no *budgetary law* norm of the World Bank that names a PRSP explicitly as a binding prerequisite for the expenditure of IDA funds. The regulations for access to IDA funds (OP 3.10 and the IDA Replenishment Report) do not mention the creation of a PRSP. In budgetary law, it is more accurate to say that the IDA encourages and supports the creation of PRSPs by recipient states (see IDA14-Replenishment Report, Section I D, p. 12/para. 29, Section II E, p. 32/33, para. 96–101).

[40] German law provides for this in its budgeting plan. *See* Bundeshaushalt (German Federal Budget) 2008, Individual Plan 23, Chs. 186 01–23; 166 01–23 (These chapters relate to debt forgiveness within the HIPC area, not to development cooperation in general). European law formulates this in, for example, Art. 25 I b) DCI Regulation.

[41] The exact contents of these donor norms requiring respect for the PRSP will be discussed in the context of limits on donor discretion. *See infra* Ch 5.C.I.2 and II.2.

[42] Paris Declaration, Arts. 14, 16.

II. *Procedural and substantive demands*

PRSPs take the form of national legal acts. They may take the legal form of laws, regulations or programs. However, it would be wrong to conclude from this that recipients enjoy complete autonomy in the creation of PRSPs. The World Bank, in particular, imposes further requirements.

The Bank has formulated a series of specific "expectations" for the creation and content of PRSPs. Nevertheless, the normative quality of these expectations is quite "soft." The requirements are contained in documents which articulate the World Bank's understanding of the procedures and roles of the various participating institutions.[43] These documents are published. However, they have not gone through the regular drafting procedure for internal bank regulations. They are, rather, reports from Bank employees which have been subject to an internal discussion process, but not been endorsed by the President of the Bank or the Executive Board.[44] Legally, these rules are not directly binding. In practice, however, they derive an indirect binding effect from the procedural rules that will be discussed shortly. In addition, some elements of these requirements have been confirmed multilaterally by the Paris Declaration.

With regard to the preparation of PRSPs, the World Bank has specified four aspects that determine the procedure recipient states must follow. The first three relate to the creation of the PRSP. First, it should be drawn up in a broadly based consultative process which can be led either by the government, the national legislature or a ministry. Civil society and especially the poor should be involved in the process.[45] Second, the final promulgation of the PRSP is not left entirely to the recipients. Rather, they must present drafts of their PRSPs to the World Bank and IMF for approval. Both organizations will take a position on the draft by means of a Joint Staff Advisory Note (JSAN) prepared by employees.[46] The draft

[43] The following reports are the most important: World Bank, *Operational Issues*, 1999; World Bank, *PRSP – Progress in Implementation*.

[44] The relevant 1999 Paper describes the process of its creation in concise fashion: "This paper, jointly produced by Bank and Fund staffs, summarizes suggested guidelines for the development of poverty reduction strategies and PRSPs and discusses the role of Bank and Fund staffs." (World Bank, *Operational Issues*, 1999, para. 6).

[45] World Bank, *Operational Issues*, 1999, para. 19; Paris Declaration, para. 14. At the same time, external expertise – that is, help from donors – should be made available, so that the well-known limited administrative capacities of recipient states do not hinder creation of the PRSP. World Bank, *Operational Issues*, 1999, paras. 21, 27/8.

[46] In 2004, the previous name (Joint Staff Assessment) was changed to the present one in order to forestall the impression (which, naturally, remains correct) that the World Bank

of the PRSP must then – on the basis of the JSAN – be endorsed by the Bank's Executive Board. Third, the World Bank requires that the PRSP not be a one-time, static document, but rather a plan that is subject to constant monitoring and further development. It should be updated every three years.[47]

Fourth, the World Bank and the Paris Declaration articulate certain requirements for the content of PRSPs.[48] The plan should, for example, document the participatory, consultative process of its creation.[49] It should analyze the current situation with regard to poverty and economic growth, specify medium- to long-term goals, create structures for monitoring, and estimate to what extent external assistance is needed.[50] Further, the PRSP should be formulated in a result-oriented way and should translate into a program with clear priorities.[51] Finally, the financial dimensions of the development plans should be clarified,[52] with a particular emphasis on improving capacity within the recipient state.[53] All in all, the regulations formulate relatively clear parameters for the creation of PRSPs, and provide specifically for the World Bank's supervision of the strategy papers.

III. Summary

The introduction of PRSPs was a break with previous planning regimes. With respect to the functions of planning in development cooperation sketched at the beginning of the chapter (knowledge generation, articulation, coordination), three aspects of the process should be distinguished. First, by presenting their own situational and poverty analysis, recipients bring their own knowledge to the table, strengthening the knowledge-generating function of planning. Second, recipients are also required, by formulating their version of a development plan, to articulate their own interests and to grant a hearing to civil-society actors. The fact that they

actually approves PRSPs (World Bank, *Progress in Implementation*, 2004, p. 191). The World Bank itself acknowledges the tension with the principle of ownership.

47 World Bank, *Operational Issues*, 1999, para. 22; on monitoring, see in particular Coudouel, *Beyond the Numbers*.

48 In 2002, the World Bank published a so-called "Sourcebook for Poverty Reduction Strategies" in which the question of what should be in a PRSP and how it should be presented is discussed in minute detail (the book consists of two volumes, each over 650 pages!).

49 Ibid. 50 World Bank, *Operational Issues*, 1999, Annex 1.

51 Paris Declaration, para. 14. 52 Paris Declaration, para. 44.

53 Paris Declaration, para. 23.

are responsible for these strategies themselves can give recipient states power to genuinely set the agenda and shape the discourse. Finally, with respect to the coordination function, PRSPs provide a basis and framework for further action and can thus serve as a multi-sector and multi-donor coordination instrument on which the plans of specific donors can build. The process can be described as multi-step planning, in which donor plans have the characteristic of "plan-dependent plans," to use a phrase coined by Rainer Wahl.[54] From this perspective, PRSPs initially appear to be functionally adequate instruments. Upon closer examination, however, some deficiencies emerge – especially with respect to the principles of development cooperation law.

With regard to the principle of collective autonomy, in particular, there is clear tension between recipient states' ownership of a self-directed planning process and control of the procedure by the World Bank. On the positive side, recipient-state governments now have the means to articulate their priorities and integrate them into donors' planning processes. This strengthens collective autonomy, even if the governments' influence is often limited by capacity problems in practice. Many governments cannot meet the technical and administrative demands of creating a PRSP. It is reported that PRSPs are often actually drafted by World Bank consultants.[55] This calls into question whether these strategies can claim to be autonomously formulated. The attempt to generate a broad knowledge base is also called into doubt when it is unclear who the real author of the PRSP is.

Even where recipient-country governments are the actual authors of the report, questions remain as to how autonomous the process is and whether the process may even violate the principle of non-intervention. Both the duty to present a draft of the plan at the beginning of the process and the fact that the PRSP is subject to approval (even though this step is not explicitly so described and may well be loosely applied) pose the risk of impermissible interference in internal affairs. Particularly in countries which are heavily dependent on World Bank loans, the presentation of the plan for approval can hardly be a voluntary process, since the countries have no real choice. The requirement for approval creates the risk that the PRSP will be "tailored" to the World Bank's expectations and that it will thus not represent a genuine autonomous expression of the recipient

54 Wahl, *Rechtsfragen*, pp. 91–5.

55 Easterly, *Cartel of Good Intentions*, pp. 44, 43; on the symbiosis between the World Bank and the administrations of various states – particularly in Africa – see Harrison, *World Bank and Africa* (on participation and PRSPs see in particular p. 103).

country's will.[56] We can thus assume that, under certain circumstances, there is definitely at least a procedural interference in the recipient country's affairs, and the interference may also have a thematic component. Certainly, both recipients and the World Bank are bound by the principle of development and hence committed to pursue development and thus poverty reduction. However, the Bank's expectations, especially in the area of good governance, may affect areas that are protected as internal affairs as provided in Art. 2 of the UN Charter. In the final analysis, it is hard to lay down general rules about the danger of interference; each situation must be analyzed in its own right. It should, however, be clear that the PRSP process can not only strengthen but also endanger collective autonomy.

A differentiated view with respect to the coordination function and the relevant principles of efficiency and coherence is appropriate. Until the advent of the PRSP, each donor developed its own plans and involved the recipient side to varying extents.[57] The PRSPs, however, create a central planning document to which all donors can refer. This should, in principle, ease coordination among donors, serving the principle of coherence. On the other hand, however, the PRSPs are created in addition to donors' pre-existing planning documents. Only when the PRSPs clearly supersede the independent plans of the World Bank, the EU or Germany will coordination be effective.

The dominance of the World Bank in the PRSP process also raises questions about collective autonomy and coherence. This dominance could jeopardize the autonomy of other donors and keep them from according the PRSP anything more than symbolic influence over their own planning. However, the concept of the PRSP was recognized by the general donor community in the 2005 Paris Declaration. Further, the World Bank is itself a forum for donors. As an agent of the donor community, its consent to a PRSP can be understood to imply the consent of its members.

The final question is whether the PRSP requirement enhances the principle of individual autonomy by requiring a broad consultative process.[58] Although this requirement is aimed primarily at increasing civil-society

[56] As a practical matter, this shows a dilemma of development planning: projects often fail because of recipients' limited capacities. Under these circumstances, more autonomy rarely leads to better plans. On the other hand, without the material participation of recipient countries, plans lack the advantage of local knowledge and support for their implementation.

[57] The individual legal regimes are discussed immediately below in Ch 5.C.

[58] World Bank, *Operational Issues*, para. 19; Paris Declaration, paras. 14, 38.

participation, it is nevertheless quite vaguely worded (not least out of respect for collective autonomy). Experience up to now suggests that civil-society involvement is insufficient in many respects. The principal participants are established lobby groups. Smaller interest groups are rarely invited, and representatives of the poor almost never.[59] Furthermore, participation is often understood as consulting these groups in order to win their support, rather than to permit them to make a substantial original contribution.[60] This means that individual autonomy is fostered only to a limited extent, and that the opportunity to increase knowledge and invite alternative points of view is minimal.

In conclusion, PRSPs appear ambivalent as instruments of planning. Whether they are functionally adequate guiding instruments or merely facades depends on the prominence they are given in the donors' laws concerning planning. This question will now be addressed.

C Programming by donors

A recipient country's PRSP can be a starting point for planning, helping the country to realize its claim to shape the planning of development cooperation measures in an equal and self-directed way. For donors, however, planning activity is directed primarily by planning rules which they themselves have created. Recipients may play a major role in this process. How, in general, does the planning law of donors regulate this role? The following parts will present the planning law of the World Bank, the EU and Germany and analyze each, respectively, along three lines. The first subject will be the procedural law of planning. The focus will then turn to the rules which guide the planning. Finally, the legal form and governance modes (*Steuerungsmodus*) of the emerging plan

[59] For an extended discussion, see W. Eberlei, *Stakeholder Participation in Poverty Reduction: Institute for Development and Peace Report 86/2007* (Duisburg, 2007). Available at http://inef.uni-due.de/page/documents/Report86.pdf (last visited July 2013); D. Booth, "Are PRSPs Making a Difference? The African Experience," Introduction and Overview, *Development Policy Review*, 21 (2003), 131–59 at 131; D. Booth, *Missing Links in the Politics of Development: Learning from the PRSP Experiment*, Overseas Development Institute Working Paper No. 256 (London, 2005); G. Dijkstra, "The PRSP Approach and the Illusion of Improved Aid Effectiveness: Lessons from Bolivia, Honduras and Nicaragua," *Development Policy Review*, 23 (2005), 443–64 at 443.

[60] An extensive review of the literature can be found in T. Siebold, *Participation in PRS Processes: A Review of the International Debate*, INEF Report No. 86, p. 15; on the problem of deliberative processes under conditions of inequality, see Morrison and Singer, "Inequality and Deliberative Development," 721.

will be analyzed. A final summary will characterize the respective planning laws of donor organizations and examine their relationship to the principles of development cooperation law. The analysis begins with the World Bank.

I. *The World Bank: Country Assistance Strategy*

The World Bank's medium-term, country-specific planning instrument is the Country Assistance Strategy (CAS). It is valid for four years and is defined by Bank law as "the central tool with which Management and the Board review and guide the Bank Group's support for the country's development programs. Oriented toward results and based on systematic Bank Group collaboration, it is prepared in consultation with country authorities, development partners, and other stakeholders as appropriate."[61] The creation of medium-term country programs was introduced in the 1960s.[62] Since that time, the degree of formality of the Bank's programming has changed. It is now regulated by a Bank Procedure (BP) – that is, a general, internally binding administrative guideline.[63] The current version of BP 2.11 was last revised in 2005 and now specifies, in fifteen sections, the functions of a CAS and the exact procedure for drafting it.[64] Further, there are various informal documents which assist Bank employees in drafting a CAS. These include comprehensive Staff Guidelines for CAS preparation,[65] an internal template to structure the content of the CAS, and some specific provisions for specific situations (such as for countries which have particular natural resources).[66]

BP 2.11 deals principally with the procedure for creating a CAS. What characterizes this procedure? How does it relate to the functions of knowledge generation and interest articulation? Further, how does planning contribute to the implementation of the principles of development cooperation law?

61 World Bank, Bank Procedure (BP) 2.11, margin no. 1.

62 Discussed extensively in Wiegand, *Organisatorische Aspekte*, pp. 317–22 (at that time, planning was more starkly fragmented according to subject matter, being divided into agricultural reports, sector reports, and only then a country program).

63 On the legal form of these guidelines see *supra* Ch 3.A.IV.2.

64 The current BP 2.11 replaces a provisional regulation from 1995.

65 World Bank, *Guidelines to Staff for CAS Products*, March 2006 [hereinafter: CAS-Staff Guidelines].

66 These documents are not generally public, but were made available for research on this book.

1. Procedural rules: "expertocratic" and consultative

A *country team* composed of employees of various Bank departments is responsible for drafting a CAS.[67] The process for preparing a CAS is divided into four phases which constitute the typical pattern of the planning process[68] and which illustrate the importance the Bank places on learning from previous experience and drawing on external expertise. The four-phase structure also underlines how much the planning process is masterminded by the Bank, whereas recipient state governments and beneficiaries only play a subordinate role, even though the advent of PRSPs has increased their participation in recent years.

(1) Conceptualization and Review: In the first phase, the Bank prepares internally to create the CAS. The country team leads conceptual discussions whose content should be shaped by the relevant recipient state's PRSP.[69] These conceptual considerations are complemented by the creation of a "CAS Completion Report" which evaluates the effectiveness of the expiring CAS.[70] The new CAS should incorporate the experiences gained from the old CAS, ideally permitting the creation of the new CAS to be an opportunity for self-reflection and learning. An independent evaluation department within the Bank then reviews and judges the CAS Completion Report.[71] The first phase ends with the first Bank-wide review of the concept draft, which is intended to guide later work on the CAS.[72]

(2) Consultations: The second phase serves the purpose of consultation to acquire external expertise. The country team consults primarily three groups of actors, and the purpose of the consultation changes slightly (but importantly) depending on which group is consulted. To draw on expert knowledge for various aspects of the CAS, the team consults various Bank departments, other donors and external experts.[73] Consultation with civil-society actors in the recipient states serves to increase the team's understanding of conditions in the country and to foster public acceptance of the CAS.[74] The Bank's laws do not mention what exact weight is to be given to

[67] BP 2.11, margin no. 6.

[68] The succession strongly resembles the four phases described in Köck, "§37," margin no. 24.

[69] BP 2.11, margin nos. 2, 10. [70] BP 2.11, margin no. 9.

[71] On the evaluation department see Dann, "Accountability," 392.

[72] BP 2.11, margin no. 10; CAS Staff Guidelines, p. 8.

[73] BP 2.11, margin no. 6. [74] BP 2.11, margin no. 7.

these stakeholders' comments, whether their point of view should be considered, whether their input must be registered in writing in the CAS, or whether their comments are simply to be considered alongside those of all other groups. These civil-society consultations are also subject to initial approval by the recipient state's government, in deference to that state's sovereignty. Finally, the third step in the consultation process involves the government of the recipient state, as well as several of its agencies. There is no functional specification as to what purpose these consultations are to serve – whether, for example, they should involve data collection, feasibility estimates, or overall judgments.[75] The Bank's Executive Director for the relevant country does not appear to be accorded a specific role. He or she is kept informed of the status of the preparations and receives all those documents that are also provided to the state. However, he or she is not consulted separately as an expert.[76] There is no provision for participation by the general public, even in the form of specialists or those affected. Furthermore, the initiative for the consultations always comes from the Bank. Thus, there is no regulation that permits autonomous comments from other actors.

(3) Preliminary Draft and Second Review: Only in the third phase does the country team actually write the CAS. Once the document is drafted, it undergoes a second review by a wide variety of Bank departments, including the legal department.[77] This second review is meant to focus particularly on the selected strategy.[78]

(4) Clearance: The CAS preparation process enters its last phase when the reviewed document is sent for consultation and final clearance by three specialized departments.[79] After having thus been cleared, the CAS is then presented for discussion to the Board of Directors, that is, the representatives of the Bank's member states.[80] Nevertheless, as with decisions about the Bank's internal law, the Board here has no decision-making power.[81] It may discuss the draft, but may not vote on it or even make positive or negative comments about it.[82] This balance of power reflects the strong position of management which the

[75] BP 2.11, margin no. 7. [76] BP 2.11, margin no. 6.
[77] CAS Staff Guidelines, p. 9. [78] BP 2.11, margin no. 10.
[79] To the Finance Department (IBRD or IDA), the Legal Department, and the Regional Department (BP 2.11, margin no. 11).
[80] BP 2.11, margin no. 12.
[81] On the rule-making procedure in the Bank see *supra* Ch 3.A.IV.2.
[82] The CAS Staff Guidelines (p. 12) stress this point expressly.

Bank adopted under its second president.[83] After discussion in the Board of Executive Directors, both the CAS and comments on the Board's discussion of the CAS are made public.[84]

There is another interesting aspect to the decision on the CAS: during the process, there is no single point of time when the document is discussed by all sectors and from all perspectives and a decision taken. Instead, there is a successive evaluation from various sectoral perspectives. Despite its wide-ranging effects, the document is not treated as something that requires broad internal discussion or formal approval from the Bank's political organs.[85]

In general, this comprehensively regulated process has a technocratic character. Procedurally, the leading role is taken by the country team, while the main participants are internal Bank specialists and external experts. The procedure is not open to the public and does not have a political-discursive character. Civil-society actors have no procedural rights but are invited to provide their input. There is no duty to take their views into account. The process can thus hardly be called cooperative. In fact, the Bank controls the entire procedure. Although the process involves consultation with diverse actors, recipient states, for instance, do not play a particularly prominent role. Thus, the process is best described as consultative rather than cooperative.

2. Substantive criteria: (vague) limits of discretion

Development planning is guided not only by procedural law but also by substantive standards. Planning is, to be sure, a type of decision-making that necessarily involves creativity, room for maneuver and a certain amount of discretion. The room for maneuver is, however, limited. The external limits of planning discretion are marked by law, and its analytical implementation is structured. The following section will outline the external limits in the form of strict conditional norms or general objectives (a), and then turn to the question of whether the idea of balancing of interests can be found to represent an inner limit to the discretionary

[83] See *supra* Ch 1.A.I.1.

[84] BP 2.11, margin no. 13; CAS Staff Guidelines, p. 12.

[85] A second phase of the CAS procedure is its review after half of its duration; BP 2.11, margin no. 3. The CAS is meant to be a dynamic document, capable of changing quickly to reflect conditions in the recipient state. For this reason, the Bank creates a CAS Progress Report which describes important developments that have occurred in the meantime and evaluates whether the CAS needs to be corrected. BP 2.11, margin no. 3.

powers of planners in development cooperation law (b).[86] Behind this approach, there are also questions about the substantive orientation that emerges from the norms, the strength of their guiding influence and, not least, whose law does the guiding – that is, who decides on the relevant substantive goals.[87]

a) External limits

There are few norms that set strict and conditional limits on the creation of a CAS. Among these are human rights norms that, as discussed above, bind the World Bank.[88] Another strict limit is imposed by the principle of non-intervention imposed on the Bank by customary law. This principle prevents the Bank from including provisions in the CAS which would force the recipient state to take actions not related to achieving development goals, in particular the goal of poverty reduction.[89] One particular instance of the principle of non-intervention is found in Art. V, §6 of the Articles of the IDA, which forbids the Bank from interfering in the internal affairs of recipient states. In reality, however, these limits have little effect: it is hardly possible that a CAS would be adopted which would, for example, force mass, uncompensated resettlement of indigenous peoples or the adoption of a particular voting law thus violating human rights or constitutional autonomy.

However, the Bank is also subject to limits on its activity by norms formulating binding objectives. These take the form of programming directives which are basically future- and goal-oriented.[90] The norms defining the Bank's mandate are of central importance here. Article I of the IDA Articles of Agreement specifies that the Bank shall "promote economic development, increase productivity and thus raise standards of living

[86] Köck, "§37," margin no. 99; on these normative categories see J. Dreier, *Die normative Steuerung der planerischen Abwägung: Strikte Normen, generelle Planungsleitbegriffe, Planungsleitlinien und Optimierungsgebote* (Berlin: Duncker & Humblot, 1996); for a general discussion of normative control see C. Franzius, "§4 Modalitäten und Wirkungsfaktoren der Steuerung durch Recht," in W. Hoffmann-Riem, E. Schmidt-Aßmann and A. Voßkuhle (eds.), *Methoden, Maßstäbe, Aufgaben, Organisation*, 3 vols. (Munich: C.H. Beck, 2006), vol. I, pp. 177–237 at margin no. 1.

[87] Strict conditionalities and goals set out during the creation of the CAS should be distinguished from criteria for approval of specific projects. These last are oriented toward concrete aspects that are evaluated at a project level and involve criteria such as financial feasibility, environmental impact, and the social consequences of a project. For more discussion see *infra* Ch 6.B.

[88] See *supra* Ch 4.D.II. [89] See *supra* Ch 4.C.III.2.

[90] As regards the concept, see Dreier, *normative Steuerung*, p. 32.

in the less-developed areas of the world." Each CAS must therefore pursue the goal of fostering development. This goal is further specified and updated by secondary law norms such as OP 1.00 and BP 2.11, which specifically deal with CASs. These regulations require the Bank and its planning to be oriented toward the goal of sustainable development and poverty reduction.

Two objectives rely on standards outside of those articulated in Bank law: recipient states' PRSPs and the Millennium Development Goals (MDGs). To what extent is the Bank bound by the PRSP of a recipient state? According to Bank law, the recipient state's PRSP should form the basis for the Bank's CAS, and thus the starting point for the Bank's own planning.[91] The pertinent ruling nevertheless also makes clear that the PRSP is only *one* factor among others that should be taken into account by the Bank (other relevant factors may be the Bank's previous activities, or those of other donors). The CAS can be seen as accessory to the PRSP, but it can also reflect other influences. This is confirmed by the fact that the CAS is expected to record differences of opinion between the Bank and the recipient state,[92] which would only make sense if deviations from the PRSP are permitted.[93] It remains the case, however, that there is a close correspondence between the PRSP and the CAS. The planning process thus has two phases. The plans that recipient states (conditionally) lay down in the first phase then guide the Bank's preparation of a CAS in the second phase.

Another substantive statement of purpose is found in the MDGs. These are not binding international law, it is true.[94] The World Bank has nevertheless committed itself to the goals in official statements, even going so far as to declare them to constitute the core of its work.[95] The Bank has thus committed itself deeply to the goals, and made them instrumental in guiding the preparation of CASs. The unusual aspect of the MDGs is their quantitative structure. The MDGs set a deadline for their achievement: 2015. They

[91] BP 2.11, margin no. 2, p.1: "The CAS starts out from the country's vision of its development goals, which may be set out in a poverty reduction strategy or other country-owned and -led strategy process"; *see also* BP 2.11, margin nos. 3, 7 and OP 8.60, margin no. 6.

[92] BP 2.11, margin no. 3, p. 4.

[93] The Paris Declaration, to which the World Bank subscribes, has not changed this assessment, since the Declaration only requires donors to "respect" the PRSP, not to implement it (Paris Declaration, para. 14).

[94] On the political context of the MDGs see *supra* Ch 2.C.III, on their legal status, see Ch 3.C.II.

[95] *See* World Bank, IDA, 14th Replenishment Report, 2005, p. 1, para. 1; World Bank, IDA, 15th Replenishment Report, 2008, p. 1, para. 2.

also specify numerically measured goals. They do not simply call for poverty reduction, but require the reduction of absolute poverty, as measured by precise indicators, by 50 percent. This quantified structure is intended to improve measurability and ease supervision of poverty reduction efforts. It does not, however, specify how large a role the World Bank should play. MDGs thus guide behavior, but do not determine it.

b) Internal limits: is there a requirement to balance interests in development cooperation law?

In addition to the external limits described above, there could well be internal limits in the form of specifications for analytical structuring. For instance, there may be a requirement that interests of various parties be balanced against each other. This legal principle, which is particularly important in German doctrine, expresses a general rule-of-law principle: when a decision must be made among various options, an appropriate balancing of relevant needs and interests should take place that (ideally) leads to an appropriate compromise solution. In the context of the World Bank, one can ask whether the drafting of a CAS is subject to such a limitation. In general, there is no requirement to balance interests in the Bank's own laws. Nevertheless, there are suggestions which point in this direction. For instance, the Staff Guidelines concerning CASs list the relevant factors which must be considered when preparing the strategy. According to these Guidelines, the following aspects should be considered when choosing which activities the Bank will engage in: the country's needs, policies, institutions, capacities, financial security and level of corruption; other donors' programs; debt sustainability; the Bank's mandate; and its comparative advantages. The decisive factor in the end is achieving the greatest development effect.[96] Nevertheless, this aspect is mentioned only in the Guidelines, which constitute informal advice to Bank employees. It is not a binding legal regulation like a Bank Procedure or other formal law. It would thus be going too far to speak of the Guidelines giving rise to a firm duty to balance interests in development cooperation law.

In the final analysis, substantive specifications such as these have only a weak binding effect on the Bank. Strict limits are, however, imposed by human rights and the principle of non-intervention, although these are not particularly difficult to comply with, since requirements in these areas are broadly formulated. In contrast to procedural law, which regulates the creation of CASs in detail, the regulation of their content is weakly

[96] World Bank, CAS Staff Guidelines, p. 6.

determined. The Bank thus preserves significant autonomy, since neither the Bank's member states (through the Executive Board) nor recipient states (through their development plans) impose significant material restrictions.

3. Legal form and governance mode of the CAS

If programming is to represent a significant step in the process of ODA transfers, the question arises what legal form the resulting program will take. To answer this question, we must address the legal form and governance mode of the CAS. These are of great importance for (among other things) the coordinating function of the plan, as the plan should guide the remaining procedural steps, as well as structuring them and making them more transparent. Nevertheless, the categorization of plans and legal forms is extremely difficult even in domestic law, since plans often do not fit within existing legal forms or instruments. In German law, for example, it is often suggested that plans, in their formal legal sense, be seen as a form *sui generis* or as their own independent form of action.[97] In international law, almost no legal instruments or forms of action are discussed except for treaties, and plans are almost never discussed.[98] Since there are no real precedents or suggestions for determining the legal form of a CAS, the following discussion is only a first attempt and description of this subject. We will take a two-step approach. First, the content and governance mode of the CAS will be evaluated, to arrive at a clearer idea of its rule content. The focus will then turn to the legal form of the CAS, with reference to the criteria of authorship, procedure, publication and addressees.

a) *Governance mode: the CAS as an indicative-influencing plan*

What is the governance mode of a CAS? German administrative law doctrine distinguishes between indicative, influencing and imperative plans.[99] This distinction will be used here, since it might be helpful in categorizing development plans in the context of development cooperation

[97] Schmidt-Aßmann, "Planung als administrative Handlungsform," p. 158; Wahl, *Rechtsfragen*, p. 21.

[98] This will change with the publication of M. Goldmann, *Von der Rechtsquelle zur Handlungsform* (in press). However, his book will not deal with plans. This gap is also found in more recent works which deal with law-making by international organizations, e.g. Alvarez, *International Organizations*; Aston, *Sekundärgesetzgebung*.

[99] Köck, "§37," margin no. 45; W. Hoppe, "§77 Planung," in J. Isensee and P. Kirchhof (eds.), *Aufgaben des Staates*, 3rd edn (Heidelberg: C.F. Müller, 2006), vol. IV, pp. 313–66 at margin no. 17 and sources cited therein.

law. Indicative plans serve to prepare information and do not themselves have any regulatory content. They are regarded as a factual act which is not intended to have legal consequences (*Realakt*). Influencing plans, by contrast, formulate behavioral goals, but use incentives or disincentives to achieve them rather than direct regulatory norms. Finally, imperative plans directly bind their addressees and contain regulations which can be directly implemented.

In this scheme, a CAS can be described as a simultaneously indicative and influencing plan. The regulatory effect of a CAS derives, first, from the analytic contextualization of the country program. Each CAS contains a comprehensive analysis of a country's economic, political and social situation. It has an indicative function in that this analytical report furnishes the foundation for Bank employees' further decision-making. At the same time, the CAS is more than a "mere" collection of information. It also influences and guides action. It sets goals, suggests concrete projects and formulates a strategy. It also determines how much aid will be used either as project or as budget assistance for a particular country.[100] The plan does leave room for later revision, since a project suggested in a CAS must be individually reviewed and may be rejected. However, the plan nevertheless closes off other alternatives. According to BP 2.11, Section 14, the Bank's activities should all relate to the CAS and contribute to the goals articulated in it. This means that projects that are not contemplated by the CAS have little chance of being supported. Since the CAS's contents have this guiding effect, it is appropriate to determine their legal form.

b) Legal form of the CAS

The CAS has its own legal form that is not equivalent to the Bank's internal administrative guidelines, the Bank Procedures and Operational Policies.[101] To begin with, CASs have different authors. The CAS is drawn up in a strongly formalized procedure which is completely in the hands of Bank employees. Although the CAS is presented to the Board of Directors, the Board may discuss it but not pronounce judgment on it. Unlike with OPs or BPs, the Board's approval is not required. Nor is the recipient government involved in the approval process. The CAS is thus a unilateral and internal document that has no contract-like features. The governments of the affected state can, however, influence the publication of the CAS. Since

[100] *See* OP 8.60, margin no. 4.

[101] For a discussion of their legal form see *supra* Ch 3.A.IV.2.

1998 CASs have generally been published.[102] The recipient state is asked for approval for this publication. Any confidential information contained in the CAS will be transferred at the government's request to a confidential "Memorandum of the President." Nevertheless, a state can also completely block publication, although this is only accepted in exceptional cases, since transfer of information to a confidential document is the first choice in resolving such issues. The CAS's addressees are, as with the OPs and BPs, the Bank's employees. They are explicitly required to follow the CAS when developing projects, so the CAS can be said to have an internal binding effect.[103] In the final analysis, a CAS is an instrument that is generated internally by the Bank administration, addressed to Bank employees, is binding upon them and must be published.

4. Summary

To briefly recapitulate the World Bank's planning law, it is of a type that is tailored to the needs of an effective technocracy. It consists mainly of a detailed procedural law that organizes the participation of the broadest range of knowledgeable parties to create the broadest knowledge base possible, while at the same time preserving the Bank's autonomy. The participation of other parties, including recipient governments and civil society, proceeds by consultation – they have no formal right to be heard. The normative framework of the planning by means of substantive specifications is weak. Aside from general definitions of the Bank's mandate or human rights, there are no binding expectations or limits. Although the recipient state's development plan (the PRSP) is an important basis for the Bank's planning, nothing precludes the Bank from diverging from it. Internally, the result of the Bank's planning, the CAS, is accorded significant normative authority. The CAS has an independent legal form and is binding upon all employees. Its regulation is indicative and influencing – it creates both an analytical and a conceptual framework.

How should this planning law be considered in the light of the principles of development cooperation law? The first notable feature is the autonomy the law gives to the Bank. This goes along with a relative[104] lack of influence on Bank planning on the part of recipient governments. Does this clash

[102] World Bank, *Towards Greater Transparency*, margin no. 10; individual CASs can be viewed at www.worldbank.org/cas.

[103] BP 2.11, margin no. 14. It does not, however, have an external binding effect. In particular, it does not constitute an obligation toward recipient states. *See* Shihata, *World Bank Legal Papers*, p. 687.

[104] In this context, it is worth bearing in mind the informal influence of the government and its representatives in the World Bank, and in particular the differences between

with the principle of collective autonomy that applies both to donors and recipients? One contrary argument is that the CAS is not directly binding upon recipient states. Their autonomy is therefore not directly affected; each project or program will be negotiated on its own. Nevertheless, the CAS is binding upon the Bank, which is not permitted to exceed the amounts specified in the plan in future ODA expenditures. There is thus a clear indirect binding effect on recipients. This would conflict with the principle of collective autonomy were it not for the specific sequencing of planning phases. The Bank's law provides for a separation of planning phases, in which recipients first autonomously formulate their PRSPs and then the Bank prepares its CAS on the basis of the PRSP. The requirement that the Bank's actions be in accordance with the PRSP helps secure the collective autonomy of donors. Collective autonomy of recipient states is seriously endangered when this opportunity for influence does not exist.

The relationship between a PRSP and the CAS is also important for a second principle of development cooperation law, coherence and efficiency. This principle aims at coordination among various donors' action plans to prevent misallocation of resources and to harmonize donors' actions with recipients' requirements. If the Bank's planning adheres relatively closely to the PRSP, the principle is satisfied and the Bank's activities are integrated into a "general framework" that can potentially coordinate all donors.

The principles of development and individual autonomy, by contrast, are not particularly relevant to the substantive structuring of Bank planning. The individual plays no role in Bank planning, but his or her rights are also not directly affected by it. Human rights, however, are important from an objective law perspective; plans must respect them. This is also true of the principle of development. The preparation of the CAS should be oriented to the substantive content of this principle. This is a relatively circular assertion, though, since the actual substance of the development principle follows inductively from the donors' mandates.[105]

II. EU: Country Strategy Papers and multi-annual indicative programs

European development programming and ODA transfer take place in two distinct acts that are the product of multi-stage procedures. Nevertheless,

strong and weak recipient states. India certainly exercises immense influence on the very drafting of its CAS, whereas this may well not be the case with Gambia. From a legal perspective, neither has procedural rights.

[105] *See supra* Ch 4.B.II.

they are sometimes published in one single document: the "Country Strategy Paper" and the "multi-annual indicative program." The Country Strategy Paper is an analytical and framework document.[106] It analyzes the current situation of the recipient country, taking into account the status of previous cooperation, and formulates a strategic answer corresponding to the analysis of the situation. It is meant to create a coherent framework for cooperation in the relevant time period. The multi-annual indicative program is based on the strategy paper and complements it by specifying concrete planning (projects, project goals and project costs).[107] Taken together, they form the binding basis for European development administration for regular five-to-seven-year periods. They thus resemble the World Bank's CAS.

What is the legal context for these acts? What is the legal nature of the planning of ODA transfer? Is this process also technocratically dominated and substantively indeterminate? We will now analyze the legal regime of European development planning as we did that of the World Bank, with a view to three aspects: as procedural law, as the law of substantive direction of planning, and with a view to the legal forms of the plans. As we will see, despite functional convergence, EU development planning is clearly different from World Bank planning: it is more cooperative than consultative, and it is guided by more determinate substantive standards.

At the outset, two unusual characteristics of EU planning law should be noted. First is the bipartite structure of Union development cooperation and its law.[108] On the one hand, there is the regionally focused cooperation with ACP states which is based mainly on historical connections to former colonies. On the other hand, the EU also pursues global cooperation with other developing countries. These two spheres of cooperation have different legal bases. For the non-ACP area the DCI Regulation[109] provides the fundamental legal basis for planning law. For cooperation with ACP states, the legal basis is the Cotonou Agreement,[110] its Annex IV, and the associated Council Regulation for the current Tenth European

[106] Art. 4(II) Council Regulation (EC) No. 617/2007 of May 14, 2007 on the implementation of the 10th European Development Fund under the ACP-EC Partnership Agreement [hereinafter CR 10th EDF], Art. 19 II Regulation (EC) No 1905/2006 of the European Parliament and of the Council of December 18, 2006 establishing a financing instrument for development cooperation [hereinafter DCI Regulation]. Both documents are available on the Commission's webpage: http://ec.europa.eu/external_relations/sp/index_en.htm (last visited July 2013).

[107] Art. 4 III CR 10th EDF, Art. 19 IV, 20 I DCI Regulation.

[108] For a thorough discussion see *supra* Ch 2.A.IV.2; Ch 3.A.III.

[109] DCI Regulation.

[110] ACP-EC Partnership Agreement, signed June 23, 2000, OJC L 317/1.

Development Fund (hereinafter CR 10th EDF). It is notable that in the ACP area, two legal bases (the Cotonou Agreement and its Annex) are negotiated *multilaterally*. They are thus not unilateral planning law like World Bank BP 2.11 or the DCI Regulation. The significance of this fact for the planning regime will be addressed later.

Second, the budgetary dimension of the programming phase in the EU's development cooperation law should be noted. Even before the creation of the strategy papers and multi-annual programs, the EU's development planning begins with a provisional allocation of funds to individual countries and to thematic programs. This allocation is made by approval of a multi-year indicative budget by the Commission, a short step whose procedure has not been spelled out in detail.[111] The Commission is not bound to a specific procedure during this step. It need not involve the Council by means of a comitology procedure, nor need partner states be called upon to participate.[112] The decision must nevertheless be justified by "standardized, objective and transparent" criteria which take into account the need and capabilities of the states involved.[113] The orientation to need and capabilities is a conditional element introduced only since the 1980s. While the terms need and capabilities are defined in more detail in secondary law,[114] other criteria for the allocation of funds are not defined, making the process somewhat less transparent. In this respect, the Commission enjoys considerable freedom, a fact which is of great political importance. In contrast to the IDA (the World Bank's development arm), in which the budgeting and allocation of resources is determined in a more cooperative and rather formalized procedural step involving both Bank management and member states, the European Commission itself has the competence to allocate funds to particular states.[115]

1. Procedural rules: executive and (largely) cooperative

What does the thematic programming procedure look like? In terms of the structure of the process, programming in the ACP and non-ACP

[111] Art. 18 II DCI Regulation; Art. 2(IIb), 3(I) CR 10th EDF.

[112] This is very similar to the funds allocation in the area of structural funds. *See* Schenk, *Strukturen und Rechtsfragen*, pp. 288, 289; W. Petzold, "Art. 161 EGV," in H. von der Groeben and J. Schwarze (eds.), *Vertrag über die Europäische Union und Vertrag über die Gründung der Europäischen Gemeinschaft*. Kommentar, 6th edn, vol. IV (Baden-Baden: Nomos, 2003) at margin nos. 11.

[113] Art. 18 II DCI Regulation. [114] Art. 18 II UA 2 DCI Regulation.

[115] On the budgeting process in the World Bank, based in the CPIA, see Riegner, *Measuring*.

areas is generally similar. In both areas, there are four phases: first, strategy papers and multi-annual indicative programs are created by recipient state governments and by the Commission, working with the European External Action Service (EEAS).[116] In the second phase the draft is then examined by a committee of EU member states chaired by the Commission itself. In the third phase, both documents are adopted by a decision of the Commission, and the multi-year indicative program is then confirmed by an agreement with the partner state. Finally, similar to the World Bank, both documents are subjected to a new mandatory review and possible update after at least half of the program time has elapsed.[117]

A main contrast between both areas, however, is the level of participation of the various parties. To approach this issue more closely, we will examine the procedural rights of (1) the governments of the ACP countries, (2) the governments of non-ACP countries, (3) EU member states, and (4) civil society.

(1) Of particular note are the broad procedural rights accorded to ACP state governments during preparation and approval of the documents. Recipient-state governments here actually take over the leading role in drawing up the documents.[118] The strategy paper is prepared jointly by

[116] Cooperation between the Commission and the European External Action Service (EEAS) is regulated by Art. 9 of the Council Decision establishing the organization and functioning of the European External Action Service (2010/427/EU), OJC L 201/30 from August 3, 2010). According to this regulation, decisions on the payment of ODA remain basically the province of the Commission (Art. 9 §1). However, further details are worked out cooperatively between the EEAS and the new GD "Cooperation and Development – EuropeAID." The High Representative is given the responsibility to coordinate all the EU's ODA instruments (Art. 9 §2). For this purpose, the EEAS is tasked with preparing decisions of the Commission on strategic, multi-year measures within a program cycle (Art. 9, §3). Proposals are to be developed jointly by the Commission and the responsible departments within the EEAS and then presented to the Commission for approval in a collegial process (Art. 9, §§3 & 4. Exceptions are certain thematic programs for which the Commission alone is responsible). On the organization see *supra* Ch 3.A.III.1.1. For the previous division of responsibility within the Community see OECD, *European Community*, pp. 44–53.

[117] Art. 5 CR 10th EDF; Art. 19 II U para. 2, IV DCI Regulation. Reviews are undertaken jointly by the Commission and the governments of the partner countries. During these reviews, programs are analyzed according to the current requirements and accomplishments relative to the formulated goals and, when necessary, adjusted. Depending on the results of the evaluation, funds may be increased or decreased.

[118] Art. 4 Cotonou Agreement, Art. 2 III a) CR 10th EDF. This division of responsibility is traditional. Under the previous Lomé Convention recipient countries were also given equal influence over programming (*see* Art. 51 Lomé; Becker, *Partnerschaft von Lomé*, p. 87).

the recipient state, the Commission, and the EEAS,[119] which requires joint analysis of the economic, political and social situation of the recipient country and of previous cooperation programs.[120] Partner states have the first say in transforming these diagnoses into a concrete work program. They are supposed to define the priorities and goals of the indicative programs and to develop them. Only after this is the draft of the indicative program presented to the Commission.[121] The recipient country's government thus formulates the agenda for future cooperation. The indicative program is also the subject of a mutual agreement between the Commission and the recipient state's government.[122] Although the Commission is the first to approve the program, there must be a corresponding decision by the recipient state's government.

(2) The procedural rights of governments of non-ACP states are much more limited. For these countries, strategy papers and indicative programs are produced solely by the Commission and the EEAS.[123] On the other hand, the recipient state's PRSP is of greater importance here. In ACP states, the PRSP is not linked to and does not bind the specific ACP-EU program. For non-ACP states, the DCI Regulation specifies that the development process shall be "partner country led and owned" and that the "Community shall increasingly align its support with partners' national development strategies, reform policies and procedures."[124] Further, "strategy papers shall, in principle, be based on a dialog with the partner country or region which involves … local authorities"[125] and the indicative program "shall be the subject of an agreement with the country or region where possible."[126] These provisions ensure respect for the principles of the Paris Declaration. They are, nevertheless, vaguely formulated. There is no strict requirement that EU planning be in accordance with the recipient state's PRSP.

119 The exact nature of the cooperation between the GD Cooperation and Development – EuropeAID and the EEAS is not specified by the text of Art. 9 of the Establishing Decision for the EEAS. Before the EEAS was founded, the internal Commission cooperation was governed by an Interservice Agreement from June 2001, in Points 2.1.5–2.1.8.

120 Art. 2 I Annex IV Cotonou. The procedure for programming should, according to 2 CR 10th EDF take place "in harmony" with Arts. 1–14 Annex IV.

121 Art. 57 Cotonou Agreement; Art. 4 Annex IV Cotonou.

122 Art. 4 III CR 10th EDF.

123 Art. 18 I DCI Regulation.

124 Art. 3 VIII a) DCI Regulation.

125 Art. 19 III DCI Regulation; consultation with member states, other donors and civil society is also encouraged, in order to increase the complementarity of the programs, Art. 19 VIII, 20 II DCI Regulation.

126 Art. 19 IV UA 1 DCI Regulation.

Thus, the priorities of the recipient states are not strictly binding and are not secured by procedural rights.

(3) Since the EU is a supranational donor and a multi-level system in and of itself, we may ask what procedural rights are accorded to its member states. As mentioned above, strategy papers and indicative programs are presented to member-state governments in a comitology procedure.[127] They can adopt a common position on the documents by a qualified majority (Art. 238 II, III TFEU). If the Commission adopts the paper[128] in contravention of the positions of the member states, they may replace the Commission's adoption order with their own by a qualified majority,[129] although this is extremely rare in practice. In formal terms, the role of EU member states is much stronger than that of the World Bank's member states in this context. The World Bank's Executive Board can discuss the CAS but cannot reject it. Although Bank member states do have a real opportunity to pursue their interests, it must be conceded this comes rather late in the process.[130] It should also be noted that EU member states might be able to take (informal influence) also through the staff that they contribute to the EEAS.

(4) The procedural role of civil society is uncertain and weak. These groups are mentioned specifically,[131] and the Regulation stresses that they should participate in the preparation of the Country Strategy

[127] For non-ACP states, reference is made to Arts. 4 and 7 of the Comitology Decision (Council Decision No. 1999/468) in Art. 21, 35 II DCI Regulation. ACP law contains a parallel regulation (Art. 11 III CR 10th EDF).

[128] Art. 21 DCI, 35 II DCI Regulation combined with 4 II Comitology Decision.

[129] Art. 4 III Comitology Decision.

[130] At this point, the European Parliament is only marginally involved in this process. It is to be kept informed and can issue resolutions on whether the Commission's strategy paper has exceeded the powers granted to it by law (Arts. 7, 8 Comitology Decision). The Commission is, however, not bound by these resolutions. The EP has expanded its information rights by means of a process known as the *democratic scrutiny dialog*. The process was established in Declarations 4 and 5 of an Interinstitutional Agreement on Budgetary Discipline (OJC 2006/C 139 from June 14, 2006, p. 1) and elaborated in greater detail by an exchange of letters between the EP and the Commission during adoption of the DCI Regulation. In practice, the EP takes its right to issue such resolutions quite seriously, and has adopted several critical resolutions (see Passos and Gauci, "EP and Development Cooperation," pp. 146–54). Under the Lisbon Treaty, multi-annual indicative programs (pursuant to Art. 209 TFEU) can be seen as delegated legal acts within the meaning of Art. 290 TFEU. For this to be the case, the delegation regime of the DCI Regulation would have to be changed by the EP and the Council in order to give the EP a right to greater influence (this is, in any case, the argument of ibid., pp. 156–7).

[131] Art. 4 Cotonou Agreement.

> Paper.[132] In ACP law, the meaning of civil society is also spelled out – it includes national legislatures, local agencies, and representative non-state actors. However, these actors are only to be consulted "where appropriate." In this context, as with the World Bank's law, there is no mandatory provision for participation by the general public, for instance, through a general right to comment coupled with a duty to respond to the comments in the final indicative program. The regulations therefore do not provide for serious engagement with a broad spectrum of voices and interests. The programs remain mainly a concern of the executive, and do not enable *societal* ownership of the programs.[133]

In sum, European planning law involves recipients – in particular, the governments of ACP states – more deeply into the planning process than does the law of the World Bank. The EU administration (the Commission and the EEAS) has a leading position in the process. Nevertheless, the governments of the ACP states, in particular, enjoy a basically equal position, and EU member states also have effective procedural rights. The procedures are designed to be cooperative and do not call merely for a voluntary, superficial consultation with partners. On the other hand, the participation rights of non-ACP states and of civil society are weak. How to explain this difference in treatment, especially with respect to non-ACP states? It is certainly relevant that the ACP states, as a group, had the opportunity to negotiate the planning law set out in the Cotonou Agreement with the Union, whereas the non-ACP states did not. The historical background explains why the ACP states were able to operate as a collective. First, almost all countries in the group were former colonies that were regarded by the EEC itself as a group from the beginning.[134] Further, the Lomé Convention, the predecessor to the current regulations, was negotiated during the 1970s, a period during which the Third World enjoyed immense political power.[135]

2. Substantive criteria: many limits on discretion

As we have seen with the law of the World Bank, development planning can be guided not only by procedural rules but also substantive,

[132] Art. 19 III, VIII DCI; Art. 2 III a) CR 10th EDF.

[133] This objection was contained in a Special Report of the EU Court of Auditors, 4/2009, margin nos. 21–27. This is apparently not the case with NGO projects sponsored by the EU, margin no. 37.

[134] See *supra* Ch 1.A.II.

[135] See *supra* Ch 1.B.IV.

programmatic norms. Discretion can be limited by various different kinds of norms. Here as well we will analyze the laws according to the three norm types: strict (conditional) norms, binding goals and, finally, the duty to balance interests.[136] As we will see, the planning law of the EU is subject to much more intensive normative guidance than that of the World Bank. What are the possible explanations for this difference?

In terms of strict norms, there is no difference from the laws of the World Bank. The EU discretion is also limited, primarily by human rights and the principle of non-intervention.[137] Union law does not impose a more specific principle of non-intervention comparable to the World Bank's prohibition on political interference.

However, in stark contrast to the World Bank, EU law does contain many norms which specify binding goals for development planning. There are three categories of binding goals: long-term, quantified and (particularly well developed) medium-term. A separate inquiry concerns the role that PRSPs of the recipient states plays in the development cooperation of the EU.

The basic long-term goals of European development policy, comparable to the mandate provisions of the World Bank, are found mainly in Art. 208(I) TFEU, Art. 21(I) TEU, and Art. 1 of the Cotonou Agreement. They apply to programming in both the ACP and non-ACP areas. These provisions set the goal of poverty reduction, export of constitutional norms, integration into world trade and fostering of sustainable development with respect to the economy, society and the environment.[138] These goals have been further specified by the European Consensus of December 2005.[139] The Consensus adds further contours to these goal formulations principally by emphasizing the commitment of all signatories to the MDG.[140] The Consensus also incorporates a second kind of goal, namely time-limited and quantified goals like those found in the MDGs. European development cooperation law itself, however, does not contain such quantified goals.

EU development cooperation law does, however, thoroughly describe which thematic areas European development aid should address in the

[136] On these types see Köck, "§37," margin no. 99; Dreier, *normative Steuerung*, p. 32.

[137] On the requirement that the EU's development policy protect human rights see *supra* Ch 4.D.II.3, on the principle of non-intervention see *supra* Ch 4.C.III.2. For the context see K. Arts, "The European Union Development Cooperation and Human Rights at a Crossroads," *European Yearbook on Human Rights*, 11 (2011), 283–96.

[138] A more extensive discussion of the EU's mandate is found *supra* in Ch 3.A.III.3.

[139] European Consensus on Development, OJC C Nr. 46/1 from February 24, 2006.

[140] European Consensus, margin nos. 5–8. Nevertheless, there are also "hard" norms in EU law which refer to the binding effect of the MDGs on the EU, among them Art. 5 II a of the DCI Regulation.

medium term. This kind of guidance is completely absent in the World Bank's law. The DCI Regulation and the Cotonou Agreement specify thoroughly and in detail which thematic areas should be addressed in certain regions.[141] These areas are listed by name, and support is often directed toward extremely specific areas. The DCI Regulation, for instance, not only lists education as a central area of cooperation, but also states that the main focus should be on primary education.[142] Further specifications are then made for each region. The document also lists broader themes – such as gender equality or fragile statehood – that should be addressed in all projects. The Consensus also names specific thematic areas that EU development cooperation should address.[143] European development cooperation law also formulates a principle of concentration. This is intended to increase effectiveness by limiting the number of thematic areas in which the EU operates.[144] The density of substantive guidelines for planners is remarkable. It is of particular note that these concrete guidelines are not related to specific programs, but it is the general law of development cooperation of the EU that specifies which thematic areas European ODA disbursements should be directed toward.

With respect to the substantive direction of planning, the question arises what role should be accorded the recipient states' development plans, the PRSPs. In World Bank law, as we have seen, they have become important bases for planning and are binding upon the Bank. They are also playing an increasingly important role in directing the EU's programming. A distinction must again be drawn between ACP and non-ACP-cooperation. In the DCI Regulation, which governs planning for the non-ACP area, Art. 3(II) states that "partner countries or regions are provided with specific, tailor-made cooperation, based on their own needs, strategies, priorities and assets," and Art. 3(VIIIa) states that the Community "shall increasingly align its support with partners' national development strategies, reform policies and procedures." ACP law specifies that programming will be "increasingly aligned with the partner country or region's poverty reduction."[145] While the PRSPs have a guiding function in the non-ACP area (plans shall be "based on" it), the formulation is more open in ACP

[141] E.g. Art. 5–11 DCI Regulation. Arts. 21–33 Cotonou Agreement; *see* Bartelt, *Legislative Architecture*, p. 18.

[142] Art. 5 II b) (iv) DCI Regulation.

[143] In particular, the European Consensus, §§4.3–4.5 (margin nos. 19–22) and §§3.2–3.3 (margin nos. 70–106).

[144] *See* European Consensus, margin no. 67; see also *supra* Ch 4.E.I.2.

[145] Art. 2 IIIa CR 10th EDF.

law. However, even in the non-ACP area, orientation to the PRSPs is still not a mandatory element in the development of EU plans. The binding requirement that planning be in accordance with the PRSP, as is the case in World Bank law, is not provided for here.

A final question is whether EU planning law incorporates some form of the duty to balance interests. As with World Bank law, there is little indication that this is the case. EU law has increased requirements for analytical structuring (particularly with respect to Country Strategy Papers), and specifies what the diagnosis of the current situation, the evaluation of previous cooperation and the sketch of future strategies should look like.[146] Nevertheless, these provisions are intended not so much to provide substantive direction as to ease coordination of analytical activities among the EU and its member states as parallel donors.

In the final analysis, though, EU development planning law displays much more intensive substantive direction than that of the World Bank. Certainly, even in EU law there are no strict norms with conditional effect. Also, the long-term goals laid out within the context of the term "development" go rather far – indeed, farther than those of the World Bank – in that they declare human rights and the rule of law to be goals of European development cooperation. On the other hand, there are an astounding number of medium-term thematic goals. What explains these goals, and what effect do they have?

The first relevant provision is Article 49 of the Council Regulation June 25, 2002 on the Financial Regulation Applicable to the General Budget of the European Communities (hereinafter Budgetary Regulation). It provides that EU budget funds can only be used on the basis of a legal act which justifies their expenditure. Yet Art. 49 only declares the existence of a DCI Regulation as a necessary basic legal act, while not mentioning the density of the contained rules. This follows from the horizontal and vertical distribution of powers within the EU. The density of the regulations is the product of a struggle between European organs concerning leadership in this area.[147] Both the European Parliament (EP) and the Council push for control of development cooperation law. Both of these organs try to determine the Commission's actions by means of thematic

[146] These requirements are derived primarily from the Conclusions of the Council and of the Representatives of the Governments of the Member States Meeting within the Council on Financing for Development and Aid Effectiveness (from April 11, 2006, Council Note No. 8388/06).

[147] On this conflict see Bartelt, *Legislative Architecture*, pp. 12–16; from the EP's perspective Passos and Gauci, "EP and Development Cooperation," p. 138.

requirements. But the question remains whether these requirements actually accomplish much. After all, the requirements remain quite indefinite. In contrast, procedural control instruments, such as the comitology process, are more efficient. Another aspect should be considered: the more the European legislator determines planning, the more limited not only the Commission's planning discretion becomes, but also the autonomy of recipient states. There is, therefore, a certain tension between the goal of recipient-state ownership and the desire to bind the EU to achieving certain goals.

3. Legal form and governance mode

European development planning also faces the question of what legal form and what governance mode the plans have. Last but not least, the transparency, rationality and coordination of the post-planning procedural steps of ODA transfers rely on the answers to these questions.

With respect to the governance mode of the plans, we will return to the three modes described above – indicative, influencing and imperative.[148] Applying this framework reveals clear parallels to the World Bank's regime. In the EU context as well, the plans are both indicative and influencing. The Country Strategy Papers are mainly indicative plans; they are analysis and information documents. They provide an estimate of the political, economic and social situation in a country and an evaluation of the results of previous cooperation. Building on this, they formulate an answering strategy which is intended to ensure coherence with other instruments of European foreign policy and complementarity to the actions of other donors. They impose substantive measurement criteria, but are not regulatory in nature. Indicative programs, by contrast, contain specific rules and are thus influencing in nature. They outline the time period, the projects and sectors and the amounts of money to be invested and also impose performance criteria that are increasingly quantitative in nature.[149] However, they do not impose mandatory conditions, instead formulating options for various kinds of activity. They are thus not imperative, but rather influencing plans.

What is the legal form of these papers and plans? In contrast to the World Bank, the EU's planning actions take a familiar legal form, namely "decisions" of the European Commission.[150] They are binding legal acts

[148] Discussed immediately below in Ch 5.C.I.3 with reference to Köck, "§37," margin no. 45.

[149] Art. 3 III CR 10th EDF; Art. 19 IV DCI Regulation.

[150] Art. 19, 22 DCI Regulation; Art. 4 V CR 10th EDF.

but with a limited obligatory effect in that they are only binding upon EU organs.[151] They have effects both substantively and as organizational law. Substantively, they are relevant to further proceedings in EU development administration, since the next procedural step – the drawing up of an annual work program and the resulting agreement on projects – is intended to be accessory to the relevant strategy paper and the indicative program.[152] Each further measure must therefore fit into the context established by the two planning acts.[153] They also have organizational effects, since, as so-called "orders for service" they form the basis of further action in the implementation units of the Commission and the local EEAS delegations.[154] As with all decisions, these planning acts are not subject to the requirement of publication, unlike the World Bank's CAS documents.[155] In practice, Country Strategy Papers are regularly published, and indicative programs are irregularly published; but only on the Internet, not in the official journal of the EU, nor are they given a document number of the Commission.[156]

As decisions, the plans formally bind firstly only the EU. Nevertheless, the planning documents are effectively not completely unilateral. As noted above, they are negotiated with the recipient states, particularly in the context of EU–ACP cooperation. This raises the question whether they take on a second, distinct legal form. This may especially be the case with indicative programs, since they proceed from first being an internal EU decision to then being the subject matter of agreements between the Commission and recipient countries.[157] The legal nature of this agreement is unclear. It can hardly be called an agreement according to Art. 209(II)

151 On how the decision can be classified as a form of action see J. Bast, *Grundbegriffe der Handlungsformen der EU Entwickelt am Beschluss als praxisgenerierter Handlungsform des Unions- und Gemeinschaftsrecht* (Berlin: Springer, 2006), vol. DLXXXIV (a summary of the individual features is found at pp. 439, 440); but see Schöndorf-Haubold, *Strukturfonds*, pp. 394, 395 (arguing that the programs in the law of the structural fund cannot be said to have any of the legal form of those within the meaning of Art. 249 EC).

152 Art. 22 I DCI Regulation; Art. 7 I CR 10th EDF.

153 Decisions do not themselves have concrete relevance to budgetary law. Only the annual action program has such a binding effect, see *infra* Ch 6.B.II.

154 Point 2.1.11 Interservice Agreement. This document does not distinguish between a strategy paper and an indicative program.

155 Extensive discussion in J. Bast, "Legal Instruments and Judicial Protection," in A. von Bogdandy and J. Bast (eds.), *Principles of the European Constitutional law*, 2nd edn (Munich: C.H. Beck, 2010), pp. 345–97 at pp. 359, 360.

156 The Country Strategy Papers can be found at http://ec.europa.eu/external_relations/sp/index_en.htm.

157 Art. 4 VI CR 10th EDF; Art. 19 IV DCI (here it is qualified only as "where possible").

TFEU and Art. 218 TFEU. It is also not an administrative agreement that the Commission can agree to in the manner described in Art. 220 TFEU since this legal status imposes a strict binding requirement of the recipient state, especially, to spend the entire amount, which is not intended in the case of development cooperation. The mutual "agreements" are therefore best understood as political declarations of intent.[158]

4. Summary

The law of development cooperation of the EU is in many different respects a different type of program planning than that of the World Bank. The process is less oriented toward a technocracy bound only by mandates than to guiding a potentially controversial aspect of foreign policy which is subject to different imperatives and can thus be called heteronomous-diplomatic.[159] The procedures for preparing programs are organized cooperatively, at least as far as the ACP states are concerned. Recipient-state governments are not only consulted, as happens under World Bank law, but also themselves write strategy papers and indicative programs. They have the same rights as the Commission. Non-ACP states are treated differently; their governments are only consulted. At the same time, development planning is not insulated from internal EU politics. In fact the European legislator issues detailed specifications for programming by means of development cooperation law. The legislator thus involves itself further than the World Bank in the thematic orientation of the medium-term ODA allocation and limits the discretion of both the Commission and the recipient states. In both organizations, the plans function in similar ways. There are indicative and influencing plans, which systemize information and concretize options without determining them completely. They are internally binding, but even when they are the subject of agreements with recipients, they are not formally legally binding.

The last question to be addressed here is also how EU planning law relates to the principles of development cooperation law sketched above.[160] As with the law of the World Bank, the principle of collective autonomy merits particular attention. In European development cooperation law, two models of handling the collective autonomy of recipient states must

[158] The fact that only the indicative program (and not the strategy paper) is the subject of the agreement can be explained by the fact that the strategy paper, as a largely diagnostic document, is largely devoid of regulatory content.

[159] On the different types of development administration see *supra* Ch 3.A.VI.

[160] Ch 4.B–E.

be distinguished. In the area of EU–ACP cooperation, there is generally equality between recipient-state governments and the EU during planning. Even though this formal equality cannot conceal real inequality, both sides generally have equal participation rights in the relevant procedures, in which recipient states have priority when it comes to *substantive* priorities, while the EU has sovereignty over the *financial* components of the plans. In development planning relating to non-ACP states, a two-step model is used which resembles World Bank practice. There are two time phases: first, recipients craft their PRSPs autonomously. The EU then builds upon this document in creating its indicative program. In principle, both models can safeguard the collective autonomy of recipients. However, in the second, two-step model, collective autonomy is dependent on a strictly accessory relationship between the PRSP and donor planning. Particularly in the EU context, there are doubts on this point. EU planning is supposed to be based on the PRSP, but this does not establish a strict binding effect. The PRSP is, rather, simply one of several bases for planning. This means weaker protection for the collective autonomy of non-ACP states. EU planning cannot really be considered improper intervention, since it does not result in binding provisions. Yet the process as a whole hardly does justice to the principle of collective autonomy, particularly in the form of the principle of "ownership" as it is used in the development context. European development cooperation law is deficient in this regard.

These considerations give rise to further problems with regard to the principle of coherence. This principle incorporates the idea that different donors should align their programs with recipient states' planning, so that other donors also can align with them. The agreement of exclusively bilateral plans, which is particularly common in the EU–ACP area, is not conducive to this principle and reinforces existing coordination problems. Although EU–ACP law protects the collective autonomy of recipients, it is deficient when it comes to the principle of coherence. By contrast, non-ACP planning, which is based on the PRSP, points in the right direction. However, the weak accessory relationship of donor planning with the PRSP does not adequately realize the principle.

With respect to the principles of development and individual autonomy, the situation is the same as with the World Bank. Both principles serve the substantive structuring of EU planning, but they do not impose strict criteria on planning law.

III. Concepts, papers and (non-existent) German planning law

German development cooperation has used the instrument of medium-term country planning since the 1970s.[161] Nevertheless, the process takes place almost exclusively on a non-legal basis (apart from fiscal and budgetary provisions). The legal regulations of German development cooperation, the Guidelines, only mention the responsibility of the federal government to compile country analyses and to formulate "strategies, goals, and thematic areas with individual partners."[162] They do not specify concrete instruments or relevant procedures. In contrast to the law of the World Bank and the EU, Germany has no real planning law in the policy area of development cooperation. Nevertheless, there is a regular and structured planning practice. The process will be briefly described immediately below. Most of the sources for this description are current publications of the BMZ.

A first stage in planning can be described as the concentration on certain so-called partner countries and thematic areas.[163] This can perhaps be called "planning by selection." At the time of writing (2012), German development aid and planning involves fifty countries as official partner countries, of which nine are designated anchor countries. Anchor countries are selected on the basis of economic power, political influence and participation in international decision-making processes.[164] The designation as partner or anchor country is made by the federal government and, within it, the BMZ, which consults with other government departments.[165] The German federal parliament, the *Bundestag*, has no influence on the process. The designations are updated annually in a multi-agency process. The designations have a binding effect on the work of implementation organizations working on BMZ contracts.[166] The decision as to which countries to assist rests on five political criteria which judge a country's governance capacity. The criteria are (1) poverty-oriented and sustainable

[161] See *supra* Ch 1.B.III.2; Pellens, *Entwicklungshilfe Deutschlands*, p. 93.
[162] BMZ, *Guidelines*, margin no. 15.
[163] Previously discussed *supra* Ch 3.B.II. and Ch 4.E.I.2.
[164] BMZ, *Media Handbook 2008/2009*, p. 344; discussed extensively in BMZ, *Anchor Countries*.
[165] BMZ, *Guidelines*, margin no. 15; Government of the Federal Republic of Germany, *Zwölfter Bericht zur Entwicklungspolitik der Bundesregierung*, ("12th Report"), p. 122. Available at http://dipbt.bundestag.de/dip21/btd/15/058/1505815.pdf (last visited July 2013); see BMZ, *Media Handbook 2004/2005*, p. 278.
[166] BMZ, *Media Handbook 2008/2009*, p. 346.

policies, (2) respecting, protecting and guaranteeing human rights, (3) democracy and the rule of law, (4) performance and transparency of the state, and (5) cooperative behavior in the world community.[167] The criteria are evaluated annually with the help of international indices.[168]

Planning for individual partner countries then takes place by means of various instruments. Country strategies and priority area strategy papers deserve a closer look, as they most closely resemble plans from other donors.[169] Both can be understood as basically political programs. Country strategies are medium-term internal management instruments and are produced for all partner countries.[170] They have an analytical and a planning dimension. They analyze the general conditions of each country, its most pressing problems, its PRSP and the previous experience of Germany and other donors. They also determine the types of support that will be provided, and thus have a significant influence on the subsequent choice of projects.[171] The country strategies are decided on by the BMZ with the assistance of the GIZ and embassy reports from the relevant BMZ regional working groups. The strategies are supposed to be created in a broad and informal dialog process with diverse actors, the so-called country discussions (*Ländergespräche*). The BMZ organizes these discussions and invites other government departments, implementation organizations and civil-society actors. Country strategies form the basis

[167] BMZ, *Concept No. 172*, p. 24; see also Kämpf and Würth, *Mehr Menschenrechte in die Entwicklungspolitik!*, pp. 16–18.

[168] Among these are the "Governance Matters" Index of the World Bank and the Bertelsmann Transformation Index.

[169] In addition, there are regional strategies, sector strategies and multi-sectoral strategies (GTZ, *World of Words at GTZ*, pp. 19–20). The regional strategy can serve as an example of these additional planning instruments, since regional strategies are principally orientation documents. They combine analysis of the political, social, ecological and economic background conditions in a region with a broad designation of priorities for action. The world is divided into five regions: Sub-Saharan Africa, Mediterranean and Near/Middle East, Asia, Latin America, and Europe (Turkey). The regional strategies are published and are intended primarily to provide orientation to private donors or other public donors. There are no general rules for the timeframe of a regional strategy; it may take five to eight years before a strategy is revised. Regional strategies are not concrete working plans and do not have any regulative content. The financial dimension is not made explicit in these reports, which tend to focus more on previous achievements than new planned expenditures. Government of the Federal Republic of Germany, *12th Report*, p. 123; BMZ, *Media Handbook 2004/2005*, p. 283.

[170] Discussed extensively in G. Ashoff, "Die Rolle der Länderkonzepte des BMZ: Schwerpunktsetzung in der deutschen Entwicklungszusammenarbeit," *Entwicklung und Zusammenarbeit*, 39 (1998), 312–16 at 312–16.

[171] Ibid., 314–16.

for discussions about cooperation with other government departments, partner governments and private NGOs. There is no strict timeline for the plan; it is, rather, continuously updated.[172] Substantive criteria for determining targets for support are determined by recipient-state suggestions (especially the PRSP), development policy goals and suggestions from the German government.[173]

Priority area strategy papers "specify the conceptual framework for a particular sectoral support strategy."[174] The PRSP or other partner-country strategies should then be brought into harmony with the BMZ concept. Priority area strategy papers are divided into three parts: first, analysis of the initial situation (core problem, deficits and potential, contributions from other donors), second, a strategic plan for achieving common goals, and third, an implementation plan (taking into account instruments, actors, levels of action, indicators and partners' performance expectations).[175] They are first drafted by the BMZ, then further fleshed out in dialog with the partner country and, finally, subjected to bilateral agreement.[176] Thus, there is a stronger bilateral component to these documents than with the country strategies. Consultations between the German side (BMZ, KfW, the responsible embassy) and the recipient state's government take place every two years. The talks comprise mutual information on the planned projects and the financial volume of future aid according to the planning framework.[177]

Neither country strategies nor priority area strategy papers correspond to an established legal form. Neither their development nor their form is formalized or subject to published regulations. Furthermore, neither of the two documents appears to be subject to a duty to publish. Nevertheless, both plans are seen as internally binding,[178] so it can be assumed that subsequent projects will be in accordance with them. The "agreement" of the priority area strategy papers is not externally binding, and can thus only be regarded as a political (self-)commitment of the German government.

Even if German development planning is not subject to positive procedural laws, it cannot be said to take place in a "legal vacuum." Substantive limitations, at least, exist with respect to human rights and the general

[172] Government of the Federal Republic of Germany, *12th Report*, p. 123; Pellens, *Entwicklungshilfe Deutschlands*, p. 93.
[173] Government of the Federal Republic of Germany, *12th Report*, p. 123.
[174] GTZ, *World of Words at GTZ*, p. 20.
[175] BMZ, *Media Handbook 2004/2005*, p. 284. [176] Ibid., p. 283.
[177] Pellens, *Entwicklungshilfe Deutschlands*, p. 94.
[178] GTZ, *World of Words at GTZ*, pp. 19, 20.

goals of development cooperation, as spelled out in the Guidelines and in the principle of development.[179]

German development administration is a further type of development planning characterized by its considerable flexibility. As the responsible agency, the BMZ has no "duty to plan," nor is it subject to specific procedural or participation rights or forms of planning. Substantive direction is also weak. Development planning is thus clearly a domain of the government. Consequently, other actors, particularly recipient governments, play only a limited role in planning. Their PRSPs should be taken into account, but they have only weak direct participation in the development of plans.

From a normative perspective, in particular with regard to the principles of development cooperation law, this situation is rather unsatisfactory. This is particularly true of the principles of collective autonomy and coherence. The collective autonomy of recipients is not directly limited, it is true, since the plans have a binding effect only on German institutions. Yet the principle of ownership as established in the Paris Declaration and endorsed by the German government requires a substantive involvement of recipients in planning and respect for their PRSPs where available. German development planning does not give recipient states' planning this level of priority. This in turn also hinders implementation of the principle of coherence. This principle requires all donors to align their efforts according to the priorities of donors. Official policy states that German development law should concentrate on sectors and choose them in consultation with the recipient state and with other donors. However, the implementation of this coordination is, in general, not firmly anchored in the basic control instruments of German development policy.[180] The orientation toward guaranteeing human rights is more pronounced in German development cooperation law than the planning law of the World Bank or the EU. The selection of states as cooperation partners depends in particular on the human rights situation in those states. Thus, at least from an objective legal viewpoint, human rights are important.

[179] For more detail on the binding character see *supra* Ch 4.B, Ch 4.D.II.1.

[180] From an empirical perspective as well, German development cooperation still clearly falls short of the goals set by the Paris Declaration, see G. Ashoff, *Die Umsetzung der Paris-Erklärung zur Wirksamkeit der Entwicklungszusammenarbeit: Wo steht Deutschland?* Analysen und Stellungnahmen des deutschen Instituts für Entwicklungspolitik 5/2008, pp. 2, 3. Available at www.die-gdi.de/ (last visited July 2013).

IV. Coordination of planning

Planning and plans serve not only to coordinate the many actions of *one* donor, but to enable coordination *among* donors. They can help address the central problem of development cooperation, namely the complexity of the system created by the sheer number of actors and the heterarchy among them.[181] Coordinating the plurality of donors is not only a basic imperative of development policy but, as seen above, a structural principle of development cooperation law.[182] This raises the question of how much planning law contributes to mutual coordination.

Certain rules require mutual coordination in the *process* of plan development. For example, the World Bank, during creation of the CAS, is required not only to maintain constant contact with other donors to learn their opinion on the Bank's plans, but also to take into account other donors' plans and align them with the Bank's own.[183] The legal situation in the EU is less precise. The EU does, in fact, pledge itself to the principle of coordination (and its binding effect on planning) in both the ACP and non-ACP areas.[184] Nevertheless, it does not specify how and when the coordination with other donors should take place. German development cooperation, as we have just seen, has no explicit procedural law, and thus does not mandate a specific form of exchange with other donors during the planning process. It does, however, pledge itself to the basic idea of development cooperation as a common task, and in particular to the principles of the Paris Declaration.[185] Overall, though, the coordination by procedure is rather weak.

EU law provides for a form of *analytical* coordination. The Council has stipulated principles and a unified scheme for the preparation of Country Strategy Papers.[186] These principles set forth what questions should be answered in which form and with what degree of thoroughness. These principles do not yet amount to plan coordination, but they make mutual alignment easier, since they allow actors to operate from a similar basis of knowledge.

[181] Ch 2.C.II.1 [182] Ch 4.E. [183] BP 2.11, margin nos. 2, 6, 8.

[184] Art. 3 V, 19 I DCI Regulation; Art. 2 III d), Art. 4 I CR 10th EDF.

[185] Government of the Federal Republic of Germany, *12th Report*, margin no. 1; see also margin nos. 15 and 26.

[186] Conclusions of the Council and of the Representatives of the Governments of the Member States Meeting Within the Council on Financing for Development and Aid Effectiveness (from April 11, 2006, Council Note No. 8388/06).

In the final analysis, though, donor coordination is ensured not primarily by procedural law or analytical requirements. Rather, contemporary development cooperation law is based on the principle of coherence and efficiency, but the principle of collective autonomy requires that the leading role be given to recipient states and their development plans. Each recipient state should coordinate donor activities within its borders. To accomplish this, it should put forward its own development plan which can be consulted by all donors who are active in the country. This approach has been adopted in the Paris Declaration in the form of the principle of "alignment" to recipient-country systems, which in turn has been incorporated into relevant planning laws.[187] Donor programming should orient itself toward recipient planning, or, as it is usually put, to act "on the basis of recipient state strategies."

Effective coordination requires more than the existence of a PRSP which is supported by the political will of responsible officials. The key legal question is what binding effect the PRSP has on donors. As already seen, this effect is limited. Only the World Bank's planning law makes the PRSP a binding foundation for planning. In the law of the EU (and even more so in German law) there are merely general acknowledgments that aid should be oriented toward the PRSP. To ensure better coordination, there should be a legally mandatory and regulated procedure in which donors reach agreement with recipient states as to which donor should be responsible for which elements of the PRSP. However, no such framework exists. Although the programming phase would appear ideal for such coordination, the legal instruments for achieving this goal have still not been finalized.

D Comparative summary

Programming organizes an important step in ODA transfers. It sets the agenda for medium-term cooperation and establishes important parameters for the commitment of the respective donor organization. How do the laws of the institutions in this area appear in comparative perspective? In the following sections, each legal regime will be compared with reference to the principles of development cooperation law formulated in Part II and the functions sketched above. At least two things will become clear: the structural convergence in the core areas of each planning-law regime

[187] Paris Declaration, margin no. 16; Art. 2 III d) CR 10th EDF; Art. 2 VI DCI Regulation; BP 2.11 margin no. 2; Ibid., margin no. 1.

and at the same time the occurrence of certain distinctive features in the law of the individual organizations.

Before further discussion of these convergences and typologies, a brief remark on the authorship of law: planning law of ODA transfers is generally donor-made law; they exemplify the "donor-side bias" of development cooperation law which was discussed in more abstract terms above.[188] Donors largely determine the framework in which ODA planning is discussed and decided. The participation with respect to recipients' development plans (PRSP), as called for by the World Bank and the donor community, takes places in a conspicuously indirect manner.[189] Although, in terms of legal policy, the objective of the PRSP was to strengthen the collective autonomy and ownership by recipients, the legal structure of the process instead shows their subordination. They are told when, what and how to plan. In light of this background, the multilaterally agreed law of ACP–EU cooperation is remarkable. Although it is not a guarantee of the actual equality of the parties, it does provide a different basis, namely mutual agreement, on how the planning process should operate.

How do the various planning regimes compare with respect to the function of planning and in light of the principles of development cooperation law?

I. The principle of development and the principle of individual autonomy

The principle of development does not shed much light. Although it forms the basis for all three donors' planning, it has very little guiding force.

More interesting is the comparison among the planning-law regimes with respect to the implementation of human rights. These are not relevant as individual rights, since planning involves either an internal donor-side process or international cooperation between donors and recipient governments, neither of which directly addresses individual rights. Nevertheless, the question arises to what extent human rights, in their legal dimension, influence the plans. As seen above, all three donors are, in principle, bound to respect human rights. Only in German development planning law, however, do human rights considerations become directly relevant, in that German law requires that the human rights situation in the recipient state be evaluated and made a relevant selection

[188] *Supra* Ch 3.D. [189] *Supra* Ch 5.B.

criterion. Neither the law of the World Bank nor that of the EU contains similar requirements.[190]

II. Collective autonomy and three models of recipient–donor cooperation

The principle of collective autonomy is central to planning law. As previously noted, the collective autonomy of recipients finds expression in their ownership of development planning and in the respect shown to them by donors.[191] Recipients should formulate their own development preferences and describe the role they envision for donors in this process. This is one of the central ideas of the Paris Declaration.[192] Collective autonomy is also linked to the function of articulating interests, which was identified above as an important component of development planning.[193]

When we evaluate the specific participation rights of donors and recipient governments from this perspective, three models emerge: a cooperative, a consecutive, and a unilateral model. The law of ACP–EU cooperation can be seen as a cooperative planning model. The EU and ACP recipient governments participate in planning on an equal footing and create a common plan which is then adopted in the form of a bilateral agreement. A consecutive or phased model exists when the recipient creates its PRSP and the donor creates its plan separately, but these are related to each other in a complementary fashion and in such a way that the donor plan is in accordance with the recipient plan. This is true of the law of the World Bank, but also to an extent in European development cooperation with non-ACP countries. Here, donors and recipients plan in separate processes, one after the other. However, insofar as donors are required to make their plans in accordance with the recipients' PRSP, both plans are substantively linked. A unilateral planning process occurs when donors simply create plans on their own (even if they do consult recipient governments and others). This is what happens in the German planning regime.

To evaluate these participation models in light of the principle of collective autonomy, we must distinguish between donors and recipient governments. Donors' right to collective autonomy is hardly ever called into question by any of the three named models. Recipients' collective

[190] Nevertheless, human rights play a central role in the allocation of specific project aid in the law of both the World Bank and the EU, see *infra* Ch 6.B.I.2 and Ch 6.B.II.3.

[191] *Supra* Ch 4.C.I.

[192] Paris Declaration, margin nos. 14–15.

[193] *Supra* Ch 5.A.

autonomy is more clearly preserved in the cooperative model, at least when the mutual negotiations actually occur on an equal footing. If the cooperation is merely a facade behind which powerful donors dictate priorities to recipients, this can lead to a clear violation of autonomy, perhaps amounting even to interference. The consecutive model also basically protects the autonomy and ownership of recipients, although this depends on the exact degree to which recipients' plans are binding upon donors. If there is a strict complementarity, then recipients' independence is guaranteed, and this model could be said to strengthen autonomy and ownership even more than the cooperative model. If PRSPs remain non-binding, however, the autonomous planning of recipients has no effect, and their autonomy is endangered. Unilateral planning by donors largely ignores recipients' collective autonomy. At least since the Paris Declaration, mere consultation with recipient governments can no longer be seen as sufficient. This violates the principle of ownership.[194]

Participation rights for civil-society actors – and hence their chances at articulation – are weak in the law of all three donors. Although there are frequent calls for them to be consulted, the form of the consultation or the weight to be accorded to these actors' views is not further specified. The duty to incorporate civil society into planning is specifically required during compilation of the PRSP, but this duty affects only recipient governments. The legal position of recipient-state legislatures is even weaker. None of the three legal regimes accords them their own role, although this could well be an attempt to respect recipient states' autonomy.

III. *The principle of coherence and efficiency*

The law of the planning phase is particularly relevant to the principle of coherence and efficiency. This is so for at least two reasons: first, effective planning assumes exact knowledge about what is to be planned. An effective plan can only be drawn up on the basis of adequate information on the subject matter of the planning, options and alternatives. In this respect, the function of knowledge generation is linked to the principle of

[194] In addition to the collective autonomy of donor states, questions can be raised about the procedural rights of member states in international organizations. The relative autonomy of the World Bank in relation to its member states is noteworthy. While member states of the EU can block any plan and can derogate relevant Commission Decisions in the comitology proceedings, the Bank's Board of Directors has no power to decide on a CAS. Both organizations, however, guarantee the right of member states to make known their point of view.

coherence and efficiency. The planning phase is also critically important for the coordination of development cooperation activities. A plan is a "tentative draft of normative order" (Schmidt-Aßmann). It is intended to draw various options together into a coherent, well-organized plan which then guides implementation. Here, the principle of coherence and efficiency overlaps with that of collective autonomy. It is, after all, the ideas and plans of the recipients that should guide *all* donors, not just individual ones, in order to achieve not only the collective autonomy of recipients but also coordination of donors.

As for the knowledge-generating aspects of the principle of coherence and efficiency, all three planning regimes approach the task in fundamentally similar ways. Half of the plans consist of situational and need analyses based on the evaluation of past experience. All planning regimes also acknowledge that, in light of constant change and the danger of outdated diagnoses, plans must be subject to regular updates, in fact, constant reflection. European law provides not only for midpoint and final evaluations, but also annual operational and ad hoc reviews. The law of the World Bank provides for regular reviews in the form of "progress reports" and "completion reports."[195] Although this constant self-reflection may seem to address the risks of development cooperation, their intensity raises other questions. The constant reviews require enormous effort and occupy valuable administrative resources, which makes them counterproductive in light of the capacity limitations of development cooperation organizations. These reviews also seem, ironically, to express a certain mistrust in the planning capacity not only of recipient-state governments but also of donors.

The planning regimes of all three donors reflect typical differences as to which actors participate in the planning process. The World Bank seeks the broadest possible base of knowledge, incorporates diverse actors and appears to be the most professional, as it draws on the greatest number of opinions on previous experience and future strategy.[196] The EU's procedural law, by contrast, is less oriented toward plural information sources, focusing more on cooperation between the Commission and the recipient government. A procedure for obtaining outside expertise is not mentioned in the law. The technocratic model of the World Bank here differs considerably from the more diplomatic model used by the EU. Nevertheless, EU planners are also bound to conduct further consultations. For instance,

[195] BP 2.11, margin nos. 3, 9.

[196] Recipient-state governments are consulted on an equal footing with others, in particular technical experts from within the Bank, external specialists, civil-society actors, and other donors.

the law provides for consultation with various departments within the Commission, an evaluation of the plans by an internal inter-service Quality Support Group[197] and exchanges of information with other donors.[198] The German practice in this area appears to follow the example of the EU – however, it is not spelled out in legal rules.

With respect to the function of the plans as a "preliminary draft of normative order" which then guides donor actions and coordinates them in the name of the principle of coherence and efficiency, two aspects should be distinguished. Planning should coordinate later events, but planning *itself* must also be coordinated.

For the first aspect, coordination *by* planning, the legal form of the plans is relevant. There are parallels to this in the law of the EU and the World Bank. In both organizations, development plans are made according to formalized procedures as unilateral, formally standardized legal acts of donor agencies which are internally binding on those agencies and their employees. The subsequent selection of the following project or sectors of commitment is based on the planning decisions, thus contributing significantly to the guidance and control of the ensuing behavior of donor organizations.[199] The question of how the plans provide substantive direction and what their analytical structure is can be answered similarly. All planning regimes envision plans with a double structure: one part diagnosis and one part strategy.

With respect to the second aspect, the coordination of the planning process itself, the substantive requirements should first be discussed. Here, there is a clear difference between the laws of the three organizations. The law of the World Bank is only vaguely defined, mostly by its mission statement and external norms such as the MDGs and PRSPs. EU law, by contrast, specifies in detail what thematic areas should be planned and what the planning should focus on. This shows the priority which the EU legislator (whether the ACP Council or the Council and the European Parliament) places on influencing the thematic focus of development, something the Bank's Board of Directors cannot do. Germany also provides substantive guidance for development planning, in particular by making respect for human rights one of its selection criteria for recipient states.

[197] OECD, *European Community*, p. 49. The Group's responsibilities are set out primarily in internal EU papers. *See* http://ec.europa.eu/europeaid/how/finance/programming_en.htm. (last visited July 2013).

[198] Art. 19 VIII DCI Regulation; Art. 2 III CR 10th EDF.

[199] The plans do not, however, constitute binding legal obligations toward recipient states. The fact that the EU agrees on its indicative programs with recipient states makes more of a political-symbolic difference than a legal one.

The coordinating function of the plans is important in another respect, namely coordination *among* donors. According to the Paris Declaration model, this coordination is ensured primarily by the recipient state's PRSP, which should guide the efforts of all donors.[200] Although there is a convincing argument for transferring the responsibility for coordination to recipient states, since it is their development which is at issue, the PRSPs have only a weak binding force. Procedural law also provides little support for the PRSP. The principle of coherence and efficiency is only partially realized. From a legal perspective, then, guarantees of coordination among donors remain inadequate.

Finally, a comparative analysis of the planning law of the development administrations reveals a structural convergence. To begin with, the organizations have all established legal systems for medium-term planning (although the German version of this is quite rudimentary). Furthermore, they all use comparable instruments, such as sequential participation rights for recipient-side actors, analysis requirements and standardized, internally binding documents. At the same time, a look at the planning law reveals the different types of development administration described above.[201] The planning law of the World Bank confirms its type of technocratic autonomy. The World Bank law secures the Bank's autonomy not only against recipients, whose own planning contributions take place in a separate procedure (the preparation of the PRSP), but also against its own member states, who are prevented by procedural and substantive law from exercising much influence on the drafting of the CAS. Instead, the Bank is required to follow a broad mandate. The development planning law of the EU, by contrast, shows the political heteronomy of development cooperation. EU member states, by means of substantive law-making, can affect planning in general and also intervene in individual planning processes. The relationship to the recipient states, by contrast, is double-faced. With respect to the recipient states of the ACP Group, the picture is one of cooperative planning, while non-ACP states are subject to a largely unilateral process. German planning practice, by contrast, is largely unregulated by formal law. Even so, the German model – at least in the area of planning and despite rhetoric stressing recipients' responsibility – can be seen to regard development administration as a governmental prerogative.

[200] Paris Declaration, margin nos. 14–15. [201] *See supra* Ch 3.D.

6

Transferring ODA through project aid

In the first phase of the ODA process, donors establish a program with a palette of options. In the second phase, to which we will now turn, donors and recipients choose specific development interventions. Only during this phase do the parties determine the contours of their cooperation, agree on financing conditions and determine the specific amount of ODA. On the basis of donors' programs, which have only an internal binding effect, the parties now sign binding project agreements.[1] From unilateral plans emerge mutual agreements.

The parties can generally choose between three financing instruments – and the next three chapters will explore these options. First, the parties can agree on individual projects, and decide by agreement who will administer them, what they will address and what their goals will be. This kind of support is called *project aid*.[2] Alternatively, the parties can agree to directly infuse ODA funds into the recipient state's budget, which it can then use to pursue its own development policies independently. This type of support is called program-based or *budget support*.[3] Since 2012, the World Bank has also offered a third financing instrument which other donors might adopt soon too. It is called *program-for-results* financing and combines features of the previous two. It provides funding for concrete programs that a recipient has developed but links the disbursement of funds to the achievement of concrete results.

1 The description of the contracts differs in the various organizations. The exact definitions will be explained *infra* in B.I.3, II.3 and III.3. For the present, the overall phrase "project contract" will be used.

2 On the nature and general importance of project aid see Riddell, *Does Foreign Aid*, pp. 180–93; the federal government of Germany defines it as "thematically, sectorally, spatially, economically, and temporally limited measures with a clear goal orientation" (BMZ, *Guidelines*, margin no. 7).

3 On budget support see Riddell, *Does Foreign Aid*, pp. 198–202; a much more complex definition of budget support which defines it as program-oriented community funding is contained in BMZ, *Guidelines on German Development Policy*, margin no. 8. More detailed information can be found *infra* Ch 7.A.

The latter two instruments have emerged recently and signal a search for new instruments. In light of the significant capacity limitations of recipients, any financial aid can be seen as a sort of venture capital or risk-prone investment. It is therefore hardly surprising that ODA was originally given only for specific projects. This gave donors better control over the use of their funds and was intended to reduce the risk of projects failing and money "draining away" uselessly. At the same time, however, the focus on financing individual projects required significant effort for relatively limited effects. Thus, starting as early as the 1970s, some donors began bundling individual projects into programs.[4] In the 1980s, the World Bank began to give general budget support in addition to funding individual projects.[5] Other donors soon followed suit, and budget support became more common. Budget support now makes up about 20 percent of the ODA payments of the World Bank and the EU. In the Paris Declaration, Germany committed itself to making more than half of its aid program-based by the year 2010.[6] In the following chapters, we will ask how these instruments are legally structured, what emphasis they place on the aspects of trust and risk control, and how well they serve the principles of development cooperation law.

Answers to these questions are found primarily in the law of donors. This may come as a surprise. When unilateral plans become mutual agreements, one might assume that the relationship between donors and recipients, as well as the applicable law, would change. If the two sides enter negotiations as international law subjects, then the resulting agreement would be subject to general international law principles and the rules of the Vienna Convention on the Law of Treaties (VCLT). Yet this is true only to a limited extent. In addition to the general rules of international law, there are specific donor-imposed rules which set out procedural rules, allocation criteria and general terms and conditions. Without anticipating the results of the discussion below, one characteristic can nevertheless be stated in advance: ODA transfers are not an open and horizontal exchange, but instead are primarily (albeit to varying extents) shaped by donors' law. The extent to which this one-sidedness

[4] For Germany see Bodemer, *Entwicklungshilfe*, p. 299.

[5] *Supra* Ch 2.A.II.

[6] World Bank, *Annual Report 2009* (2009). Available at http://siteresources.worldbank.org/EXTAR2009/Resources/6223977-1252950831873/AR09_Complete.pdf (last visited September 2012), Operational Summary; European Commission, *Better, Faster, More: Implementing EC External Aid 2004–2009* (Luxembourg: Publications Office of the European Union, 2009), p. 15.

also characterizes the transfer process is a further important question which will be addressed here.

In the following three chapters, the legal regimes governing project aid and budget support in the World Bank, the EU and Germany, as well as program-for-results financing in the World Bank will be discussed and compared. The comparative review will be informed by a preliminary empirical analysis of the most important functions and problems which arise during this phase of the aid process (A). Then, the legal regimes of the World Bank, the EU and Germany regarding ODA transfers earmarked for project aid will be analyzed (B) and then compared (C). As with programming, the comparison will highlight typical differences between the legal regimes. The next chapter will then address the more general form of ODA transfers, budget support (Ch 7). A final chapter will examine the latest instrument of program-for-results financing (Ch 8).

A Functions and problems of development finance instruments

In development policy circles, the benefits and drawbacks of various instruments are frequent subjects of discussion. According to its critics, project aid results in overly bureaucratic agreements, patronizes recipient countries and often goes towards unsustainable projects. Particularly in the aid-effectiveness discussion, the recommendation is to focus more on the supposedly more effective tool of budget support or now even program-for-results financing, as reflected and demanded in the Paris Declaration. On the other hand, it is much easier to monitor the effectiveness of individual projects, and they are generally thought to be highly effective. This fact gives rise to the often-noted paradox that the effectiveness of ODA transfers on the micro or project level can easily be proven, while the cumulative effect of these efforts on the macro level remains questionable to this day.[7]

In the following analyses of instruments, the focus will be not on arguing one side or the other of this controversy, but rather on reconstructing their legal structure and judging how well they align with the principles of development cooperation law. The analysis will make clear the inherent problems and deficiencies of each of the instruments, for example, the complexity of evaluating project aid or the human rights blindness of budget support. The analysis can also highlight the tensions between the various principles.

[7] Discussed in depth in Riddell, *Does Foreign Aid*, p. 180.

Before we start the legal analysis of the instruments, however, we shall inquire into the general functions of this second phase of the aid process and the problems attached to it. The second phase serves to identify and evaluate goals and plans, as well as to negotiate and conclude funding agreements between donors and recipients. These agreements require the recipient government either to solicit bids for a specific aid project, conduct the project itself, or follow an agreed policy towards a particular sector. The donor pledges to provide the financial means for this task. Agreements on ODA transfers raise three general problems: gathering information for evaluating the planned project (knowledge generation), articulation and consideration of relevant interests (I) and ensuring that implementation achieves the goal specified in the contract (II).[8]

I. Knowledge generation and articulation of interests

The first two functions in the contracting phase are comparable to similar functions in the planning phase.[9] As in the planning phase, the contracting phase is hampered by a general *information deficit*.[10] In both phases, the problem is that donor organizations have only abstract experience with project design, while local knowledge is rarely available even when the recipient government is consulted.[11] It is also often unclear exactly how particular projects are supposed to work, making it difficult to ascertain whether they have achieved their goals. This makes clear the close relationship, discussed above, between development cooperation law and the law of risk. One of the most important functions of contract negotiations, therefore, is to gain the greatest possible amount of information on the conditions, risks and consequences of the projects.

[8] The problem of coordination will not be addressed here (see *supra* Ch 2.C.II.1 and Ch 4.E.III). To be sure, the problem arises here, as well, of whether to coordinate projects from various donors, and if so, how to do this. However, these questions are generally addressed in the (previous) development planning phase and with its instruments. The law of project assistance affords only sporadic instruments for coordination. The most important is likely the common financing of projects, so-called co-financing. The development cooperation law of all donors specify rules for this (see World Bank, OP/BP 14.40, BMZ, *Guidelines*, margin nos. 67–70, Art. 3 VI, 27 DCI Regulation).

[9] See *supra* Ch 5.A. An overview of the problems in this phase can be found in Pellens, *Entwicklungshilfe Deutschlands*, pp. 97–116; pp. 155–9; from an institutional-economics perspective, Gibson et al., *Samaritan's Dilemma*, pp. 65–74.

[10] *Supra* Ch 5.A; Ibid., p. 41.

[11] Pellens, *Entwicklungshilfe Deutschlands*, p. 97.

The second function of contract negotiations is to organize the *articulation of relevant interests*. In the context of development cooperation, there are two particular problems.[12] The first is how development cooperation law deals with the existing asymmetry between donors and recipients – that is, whether it has instruments at its disposal which can compensate for the economic and political dominance of donor states. Here, the law which drives the process, as well as the roles it assigns to the participants, plays a significant role. There is structural difference between an administrative procedure in which a donor participates not as a party but as an independent referee and a contract negotiation procedure in which the donor is an interested party.[13]

Another question is *whose* interests are heard – in particular, whether potential stakeholders participate in the negotiations. When project agreements are negotiated primarily between donor and recipient *governments*, the two governments are entitled under international law to represent their respective populations. Their participation corresponds to the principle of collective autonomy. In practice, though, this right can be quite problematic, since the special interests of elites or influential lobby groups can influence the positions of recipient country governments more strongly than others.[14] Participation from those affected by the projects can counteract this influence by bringing local and individual interests to the table.[15] There is also the question of if and how the interests of third parties and the general public – in environmental protection, for instance – can be integrated into project agreements. Donors, for their part, can hardly be said to be motivated solely by development-specific motives. Commercial, diplomatic and security considerations, as well as the special interests of particular donor governments, can play a greater or lesser role.[16]

[12] Discussed extensively in ibid., pp. 97–106; Gibson et al., *Samaritan's Dilemma*, p. 73.

[13] On negotiations in German administrative law see H. Bauer, "§36 Verwaltungsverträge," in W. Hoffmann-Riem, E. Schmidt-Aßmann and A. Voßkuhle (eds.), *Informationsordnung, Verwaltungsverfahren, Handlungsformen* (Munich: C.H. Beck, 2008), vol. II, pp. 1155–274 at margin no. 110.

[14] More details in Rauch, *Entwicklungspolitik*, p. 263; D. Brautigam and S. Knack, "Foreign Aid, Institutions, and Governance in Sub-Saharan Africa," *Economic Development and Cultural Change*, 52 (2004), 255–85 at 255.

[15] On participation by affected parties in project design see *supra* Ch 2.B.II and Ch 4.D.III.2.

[16] For an analysis of domestic political influences on development policy and its conceptual framework see Lancaster, *Foreign Aid*, pp. 21, 22; see generally Rauch, *Entwicklungspolitik*, pp. 27–38; Nuscheler, *Entwicklungspolitik*, pp. 432–52.

It should be noted, however, that the interests of affected parties are by their nature constantly in tension with claims to autonomy. This also applies to the relationship between recipients and donors. It also holds true for claims to individual autonomy which can conflict with the state autonomy of recipient governments.

II. *Compliance and conditionality*

A project agreement is an agreement on an activity to be conducted in the future. This phase of the general process serves to prepare instruments for ensuring that the contractually agreed goals are actually met during the subsequent implementation phase. This is a typical problem of public benefits law and subsidy law in particular.[17] A donor pays a beneficiary an amount of money to stimulate certain behavior in the future and thus reach a specific goal. In general, the payment is made at the beginning, and then it is simply expected that the contract will be fulfilled accordingly. The question is how this trust can be safeguarded and the recipient's long-term commitment secured.[18]

Subsidy law provides for a variety of compliance instruments.[19] These can be *ex-ante* instruments, so that requirements for disbursement may be specified by law or in an administrative act that makes payment conditional on meeting such conditions. They can also be construed from the perspective of legal consequences (*ex post*); then subsidy law primarily uses the instrument of a reclaim, punitive instruments (monetary fines, exclusion from future subsidies) or criminal sanctions.

In development cooperation, the problem of compliance is also central, and effectively quite complex. On the one hand, compliance instruments would appear indispensable here, for a number of reasons. Because of

[17] M. Rodi, *Die Subventionsrechtsordnung: Die Subvention als Instrument öffentlicher Zweckverwirklichung nach Völkerrecht, Europarecht und deutschem innerstaatlichen Recht* (Tübingen: Mohr Siebeck, 2000), p. 570; C. Heydemann, *Die Durchsetzbarkeit von Verhaltensbindungen im Recht der begünstigenden Verwaltung*, Münsterische Beiträge zur Rechtswissenschaft (Berlin: Duncker & Humblot, 1995), vol. IXC.

[18] The problem is aggravated when the donor aims to accomplish not just one but several goals, which is the case in development policy (although not only there). In German subsidy law the goals are often not just job creation but also environmental protection; not just support for filmmaking but also protection of public morals. In development law, the additional goals may include country stabilization, protection of human rights or further foreign-policy goals.

[19] A thorough discussion of German and European subsidy law is found in Rodi, *Subventionsrechtsordnung*, pp. 586; 661.

the international dimension and extraterritoriality of transfer payments, these ODA contracts are confronted with the general problem of cross-border contractual monitoring.[20] Furthermore, diplomatic concerns may hinder enforcement of contractual duties even in cases of clear breach.[21] Recipient states' weak motivation leads to frequent non-performance, even though performance should be implicit in the general principle of *pacta sunt servanda*.[22] Thus, effective contract enforcement instruments prove to be indispensable. On the other hand, the agreement and application of such instruments are subject to specific limitations. Every contractual relationship in development cooperation is marked by the existing asymmetry of the contracting parties, such that the inclusion of compliance instruments courts the danger of donor dominance. The donor is not only faced with the political accusation of hegemony but may also encounter limits based on international treaty law or the principle of non-intervention.[23]

Turning to the legal instrumentarium for achieving contractual goals, one particular instrument which has been used frequently in the development context and which is seen as particularly problematic is conditionality. The term emerged first in political science circles.[24] In the legal discussion, it has only been partially analyzed. More general discussion is rare, at least outside the context of development cooperation.[25]

[20] Mechanisms to ensure contract fulfillment are today generally discussed under the rubric of compliance, particularly in international environmental law; see R. Wolfrum, "Means of Ensuring Compliance with and Enforcement of International Environmental Law," *Recueil des Cours*, 272 (1998 (1999)), 9–154; A. Handler Chayes, A. Chayes and R. B. Mitchell, "Active Compliance Management in Environmental Treaties," in W. Lang (ed.), *Sustainable Development and International Law* (London: Graham and Trotman, 1995), vol. VI, pp. 75–96; see also generally A. Chayes and A. Handler Chayes, *The New Sovereignty: Compliance with International Regulatory Regimes* (Harvard University Press, 1995).

[21] For instance, projects may be continued for diplomatic reasons even though the donor knows that funds are being diverted from their proper purposes.

[22] Gibson et al., *Samaritan's Dilemma*, pp. 35–40; p. 67 and sources cited therein; an early analysis can be found in Killick, *Aid and the Political Economy*; see also *supra*, Ch 2.A.II.

[23] Tsai, "Globalization," 1317; A. A. Fatouros, "On the Hegemonic Role of International Functional Organizations," *German Yearbook of International Law*, 23 (1980), 9–36 at 9, see generally also, *supra* Ch 4.C.

[24] O. Stokke (ed.), *Aid and Political Conditionality*, EADI Studies in Development (London, Portland: Frank Cass, 1995), vol. XVI; Nuscheler, *Entwicklungspolitik*, pp. 446–9.

[25] For the beginnings of the discussion see W. Meng, "Conditionality of IMF and World Bank Loans: Tutelage over Sovereign States?" *Verfassung und Recht in Übersee*, 21 (1988), 263–77 at 263; C. Pinelli, "Conditionality," in Wolfrum, *Max Planck Encyclopedia of Public International Law* at margin no. 1; on the EU in particular see Bartels, *Human Rights Conditionality*.

Conditionalities are, however, well known to many donors in development cooperation law and will thus be used somewhat more generally in this book.

The concept and term "conditionality" first emerged in the 1980s in the context of the IMF and World Bank's structural-adjustment programs.[26] The bank began granting ODA not in the form of project aid but rather as budget support – that is, as general budget subsidies. The payments were made conditional on recipient governments implementing certain macroeconomic reforms. These conditions were either imposed as prior actions required before a contract could be agreed or, in the case of ongoing payments, as conditions for the release of further tranches of assistance.[27] Starting in the late 1980s, the EU and Germany linked ODA payments to human rights or democratic norms.[28] This linkage of payment to politically sensitive requirements came to be seen as a characteristic of conditionalities – and a dubious one, since it undermined recipient-state autonomy.[29]

Nevertheless, there is no justification for limiting our consideration of conditionalities only to politically sensitive subjects. The problem of compliance is a general one. Conditions can relate to human rights, economic or environmental goals, as well as to any goals specifically envisioned by the contract itself. Thus, it may be best to define "conditionality" more neutrally, namely as any regulation that a donor attaches unilaterally to an ODA payment or any sanction that it attaches to non-fulfillment. The emphasis is on the *unilateral* nature of the rule. It is characteristic of conditionalities that such rules are non-negotiable between donors and recipients because, for example, they are already established in donor law in the form of general, abstract rules (*ex-ante* conditionality). The legal consequences entailed by such conditionality can include various sanctions such as a suspension of payments, a duty to enter a dialog or even repayment (*ex-post* conditionality). However, this definition does not imply judgment on the legality of a conditionality. Conditionalities can

[26] Killick, *Aid and the Political Economy*; Mosley, Harrigan and Toye, *Aid and Power*; *supra* Ch 2.A.II (as well as immediately below, Ch 6.B.I.2).

[27] On the present legal situation in the World Bank see, World Bank, *Review of World Bank Conditionality 2005* (2005), pp. 3–5. Available at http://siteresources.worldbank.org/PROJECTS/Resources/40940-1114615847489/ConditionalityFinalDCpaperDC9-9-05.pdf (last visited September 2012).

[28] *Supra*, Ch 2.A.II.3; see also e.g. Bartels, *Human Rights Conditionality*; Hoffmeister, *Menschenrechts- und Demokratieklauseln*.

[29] Pinelli, "Conditionality," margin no. 29; Möllers, "Governance-Konstellation," pp. 241, 242.

be justified by Art. 60 of the VCLT or, alternatively, can be considered to satisfy the definition of an illegal intervention.[30] Most important, however, is to understand them as a general means of ensuring compliance both *ex ante* and *ex post*. This will enable us to determine their legal status in the context of development cooperation law. In the following discussion, *ex-ante* instruments of goal attainment will be discussed in the sections dealing with substantive criteria, while the *ex-post* instruments will be dealt with in the sections dealing with contracts.

In the final analysis, there are three main tasks: knowledge generation, reconciliation of interests and achievement of the agreed goals. These three tasks apply to both instruments that are negotiated in this phase – that is, those relating to project aid and those relating to budget support. We will first turn to the legal regime of project aid.

B The legal regime of project aid

The internal legal regimes of donor organizations are of vital importance for the actual disbursement of ODA payments, even though disbursement itself is agreed upon in a bilateral financing agreement with the recipient. The following discussion will therefore analyze the legal regimes regarding the project aid of the three donors that are the objects of this study. Each donor's regime will be analyzed in terms of the questions raised in the preceding section, as well as in light of the general principles of development cooperation law. The discussion begins with the legal regime of the World Bank, since it regulates the instrument of project aid the most intensively and thus affords the most comprehensive insights into possible regulations (I.). The regimes of the EU (II.) and Germany (III.) appear different and more limited in comparison, though not necessarily deficient.

I. The World Bank's legal regime

Project aid or investment project financing, as project aid is called in World Bank law, is the central financing instrument of the World Bank.[31] It consists of interest-free loans (so-called IDA Credits) provided by the

[30] On limits set by international law see Hoffmeister, *Menschenrechts- und Demokratieklauseln*, p. 182.

[31] The name for the instrument of project aid in World Bank regulations has changed over time – from “Project Lending” to “Investment Lending” to nowadays “Investment Project Financing.” Budget support is called “Development Policy Lending” (previously “Structural Adjustment Lending”).

Bank's development arm, the IDA,[32] which are to be repaid after ten years over the course of twenty to forty years with a service charge of 0.75 percent.[33] Through IDA, the Bank has financed an average of approximately 180 plans per year over the last decade, of which about 150 involved project assistance. In 2012 in particular, IDA commitments reached US$14.8 billion, spread over 160 new operations; each project had an average financial volume of about US$92.5 million.[34] A comprehensive legal regime regulates this instrument of ODA transfers. Its core is the Operational Policy and Bank Procedure (OP/BP) 10.00, which sets out basic aims, conditions and procedures. In addition, various rules in the Articles of Agreement and further OP/BPs specify additional substantive and procedural preconditions.[35]

This legal regime for project aid has evolved over time. Originally designed for large infrastructure projects and based in the Articles of Agreement as well as some non-binding internal rules, it had developed incrementally into a complex set of sometimes overlapping rules and procedures, contained in several binding policies (OP/BP) as well as non-binding guidance material. In 2009, the Bank began a comprehensive reform of these rules.[36] The basic idea of the reform was to adapt the relevant law to a different general environment and business model. The old regime in its overly prescriptive, highly complex, detailed and rigid form was considered an impediment to effectiveness as well as accountability. Besides, the Bank's approach had become overly risk-averse while lacking a focus on results and providing mechanisms to monitor their achievement. Prescriptions before approval ("upstream") were intensive, while implementation support after approval ("downstream") was rather vague. Investment Lending

[32] This study, which defines the field of development cooperation law as dealing with the actors, instruments and criteria of ODA transfers (see above, Introduction, A.II), generally looks at IDA, since only IDA funds qualify as ODA. However, the legal regimes of IDA and IBRD (together called the World Bank) regarding project aid are almost identical, so observations here also apply to IBRD and hence to the World Bank in general (on the terminology, see above Ch 1).

[33] The exact conditions are derived from OP 3.10, margin nos. 36–43.

[34] IDA, The World Bank's Fund for the Poorest, October 2012. In comparison, IBRD in 2009 concluded about 110 contracts, of which 90 provided project assistance (World Bank, *Annual Report 2009*).

[35] On the legal instruments of World Bank law generally, see *supra* Ch 3.A.IV.2.

[36] World Bank, *Investment Lending Reform: Concept Note*, Sec M2009-0026 of January 26, 2009. Available at http://siteresources.worldbank.org/PROJECTS/Resources/40940-1240849279648/SecM2009-0026.pdf (last visited September 2012). Investment Lending Reform is part of a larger overhaul of internal World Bank laws. On this larger reform process, see *supra* Ch 3.A.IV.2.

Reform therefore aimed to consolidate and rationalize policies and procedures in order to better secure the achievement of results, openness and accountability by clarifying policy and procedures.[37]

The following discussion will focus on three aspects: the first section will analyze the procedural laws that govern the negotiation and conclusion of project agreements and ask how the problems of knowledge generation and interest articulation are dealt with (1.). The focus will then turn to the substantive side of the regime and hence the criteria for evaluating projects (2.). The contractual form of the project agreements will be studied to determine how they contribute to achievement of results (3.). Finally, a concluding section (4.) will evaluate the regime in light of the general principles of development cooperation law elaborated in Chapter 4.[38]

In general, it will become clear that the World Bank sees the project aid process primarily as an exercise in risk analysis, and that it grants itself intensive monitoring rights. The risk here may be both to the Bank's immediate interests (primarily financial) and more generally, such as the environment or social rights of those affected.[39] Its legal regime allows the World Bank considerable autonomy while involving other participants primarily in a functional manner (as in the programming phase). The aspect of monitoring performance, achieving results and hence the

[37] Investment Lending Reform is complemented by the reform of safeguard policies, started in late 2012 (see World Bank, The World Bank's Safeguard Policies – Proposed Review and Update. Approach Paper, Oct. 2012).

[38] It should be noted that the following doctrinal reconstruction of the relevant law is novel. Only a few aspects have been subject to more intensive analysis (for instance, in the report from Shihata, *World Bank Legal Papers*). An overview of the project negotiations, the so-called project cycle, is found in W. C. Baum and S. M. Tolbert, *Investing in Development: Lessons of World Bank Experiences* (London, New York: Oxford University Press for the World Bank, 1985), pp. 331ff.

[39] This basic understanding has become more relevant in recent times, see the contributions to the 2011 World Development Report, which dealt with post-conflict situations and fragile statehood, and whose conclusions will be incorporated into the procedural rules. See Development Committee, *Operationalizing the 2011 World Development Report: Conflict, Security and Development*, DC 2011-0003 of April 4, 2011, margin no.9. Available at http://siteresources.worldbank.org/DEVCOMMINT/Documentation/22884392/DC2011-0003%28E%29WDR2011.pdf (last visited September 2012): "The Bank is rethinking its definitions of risk tolerance, risk management, and expected results in these contexts, and Senior Management is sending clear signals to staff and codifying the new understanding through revised policies and guidance. As part of on-going reform efforts, the Bank will undertake interim updates to Operational Policies, and will produce Guidance Notes on procurement and financial management, to reflect operational experience and the recommendations of the WDR, provide greater clarity, and facilitate effective implementation support in FCS."

downstream phase has become more prominent in recent reforms but still has weaknesses.

1. Procedural law: risk assessment and implementation support

The procedure for negotiating a contract for project aid is intensively regulated in World Bank law. The basic structure of the procedure is laid out in BP 10.00.[40] This regulation is complemented by others that protect specific legal interests or groups and which establish specific procedural requirements. The general picture emerging is one of a procedural regime that aims to balance the intensive evaluation of a project and its risks before approval and monitoring implementation after approval to ensure that results are achieved (a). Participation by recipient governments (b) and participation of other interested parties (c) are also supposed to help to achieve this goal.

a) Structure of the procedure

The Bank's view of projects as venture capital or risk-prone investments is evident in the way it phrases its general considerations for financing a project. Next to its developmental rationale, risks play a major role.[41] The risks perspective is also apparent in the process of developing a project and concluding a financing agreement. According to BP 10.00, the procedure is divided into four phases leading up to approval (i.e. identification, preparation, appraisal and approval) and two after approval (implementation and completion), the center of which is the appraisal that takes place before any official negotiation begins and contains an intensive economic, ecological, social and technical assessment of the envisioned project.[42] At the same time, the Bank is eager not just to avoid risks but to ensure that the aims envisioned are actually realized. To that end, BP 10.00 stresses the importance of implementation support after approval. The process in general can be summarized as follows.

[40] BP 10.00 – Investment Project Financing (from April 2013).

[41] OP 10.00, paras. 3–9.

[42] The aim of adequate risk assessment is underlined by a differentiation depending on estimated risks. The objective is to install a risk-based management system that will provide the basis for differentiating projects in terms of processing requirements and implementation support (see BP 10.00, para. 2 and 15: "the level and nature of expected results and risks, as well as the specific nature of the project, determine the content, methodology, scope, and depth of the analysis").

The first phase is project identification. After a project has been proposed by the borrower,[43] Bank and borrower cooperate in identifying the "project's overall parameters, objectives, financing requirements."[44] The second phase (preparation) aims to consolidate the concept of the project and identify its central developmental and economic rationale, its expected key results and the scale of the involved environmental risks and financing needs.[45] This includes a first screening of the environmental and social aspects of the planned project. The primary focus is on whether the project presents specific risks to the environment or indigenous peoples, for instance, or whether it would require resettlement.[46] The results of this phase determine the intensity of the assessment which recipients will be required to undertake in the third phase.

Preparation of the project and its comprehensive assessment is primarily the responsibility of the recipient government. It must undertake a comprehensive screening of the risks identified in the first stage, and is under a duty to furnish adequate information.[47] This stage involves verifiable environmental, social and cultural impact assessments, all of which must be performed by the recipient. The relevant Bank guidelines, called "safeguard policies," impose detailed procedural rules on the recipients, which require, among other things, the participation of affected parties and experts.[48] Recipients must also create concepts and plans for dealing with expected problems. However, the Bank is obliged to conduct its own appraisal of the planned project.[49] To that end, it might send a mission to the country and has to draw up a so-called appraisal document.[50] The appraisal document summarizes the evaluation of the feasibility and risk structure (ecological, social and economic) of a project. If the appraisal

[43] BP 10.00, para. 1. [44] BP 10.00., para. 5. [45] BP 10.00, para. 6.

[46] The relevant risks and corresponding investigative duties are named in specific so-called Safeguard Policies, in particular on environmental assessment (OP 4.01, margin no. 4; BP 4.01, margin nos. 2–5), indigenous peoples (OP/BP 4.10, margin nos. 8, 10) and resettlement (OP/BP 4.12).

[47] See BP 4.01, para. 1, 11. On the importance of these assessments see C. Di Leva, "International Environmental Law, the World Bank, and the International Financial Institutions," in Bradlow and Hunter, *International Financial Institutions and International Law*, 2010, p. 350; Cock and Webster, "Environmental and Social Impact Assessments," p. 81.

[48] For example, for the environmental impact assessment, OP 4.01, paras. 4, 15; for resettlements OP 4.12, paras. 6a(i), 7a, 13a; for indigenous peoples OP 4.10, para. 9.

[49] BP 10.00, paras. 15–21, 24. [50] BP 10.00, paras 24 and 25.

comes to a positive result, this is considered within the Bank as a clear signal that the project will be implemented.

Only after these appraisals[51] does the Bank's management decide whether to start the actual contract negotiations for an agreement between the Bank and the recipient government.[52] This first part of the procedure ends with a vote of the Board of Directors (approval).[53] In contrast to the CAS, the Bank's medium-term planning instrument, the approval of a project and the necessary loan or grant must be confirmed by the member states' representatives.[54]

The procedural regime does not end with approval by the Bank and signing of the legal agreements with the borrower. Not least the broader discussion on aid effectiveness has raised awareness for the importance of monitoring and evaluating the implementation of a project. Also, within the Bank it has been recognized that its rules, in particular its safeguard policies, used to focus too heavily on the appraisal phase but neglected the implementation, when actual problems with projects arise and have to be addressed.[55] It was said that the Bank's approach was too "frontloaded" and too little aware of "downstream" problems.

In order to address this imbalance, Bank law now regulates the implementation phase differently.[56] This starts with integrating rules on this phase into BP 10.00, which used to be in the separate BP 13.05 on project supervision. This move consolidates the normative material and makes it more transparent – but only to some extent. Except for a very basic acknowledgment of the relevance of the implementation phase, almost

[51] The effectiveness of these assessments is sometimes doubted. Although the "Task Team" that creates the appraisal has representatives from five Bank directorates (Financial Management, Procurement, Safeguards, Disbursement and Legal), Bank employees report that only Legal and Disbursement are truly "independent" and have an interest in oversight of the project. The others are generally dependent on the Team Leader and less critical in their appraisals.

[52] BP 10.00, paras. 26, 27.

[53] BP 10.00, paras. 28 and 29.

[54] For further procedural rules on how the agreement becomes effective, see BP 10.00, paras. 31–34; OP 10.00, paras. 20 and 21.

[55] For an internal criticism, see Independent Evaluation Group, *Safeguards and Sustainability Policies in a Changing World*, 2010, p. xlviii. On the earlier strategy of clear *ex-ante* prescriptions, see especially World Bank, *Making Sustainable Commitments: An Environment Strategy for the World Bank* (Washington, DC: World Bank Publications, 2001).

[56] Changes are part of the new OP/BP 10.00 and hence "Investment Lending Reform," but are also addressed in the reform of safeguard policies that started in late 2012, see World Bank, *The World Bank's Safeguard Policies – Proposed Review and Update*. Approach Paper, Oct. 2012.

all the other rules in this phase are now relegated to two non-binding Guidance Notes and hence are less directly visible. They are also normatively downgraded, as BP 10.00 hardly mentions the relevant elements and forceful instruments (such as indicators) used here.[57] Within BP 10.00, the rules on the behavior of borrower and Bank now focus more extensively on their roles during implementation in particular. For both actors, their role during implementation and hence their responsibility for monitoring the project implementation, measuring results and proving that objectives have been achieved takes center stage.[58]

Within the Guidance Notes, the first spells out how implementation should be planned, which roles actors should play and how communication through reports, etc. should be conducted.[59] The other Guidance Note prescribes the formulation of a results framework, which should spell out "the underlying logic" of how development objectives are to be achieved.[60] It is supposed to do so by "translating the results chain of an intervention into indicators that measure the degree to which inputs are being transformed into specific activities and outputs, and the degree to which a relevant target population is using those outputs as the anticipated outcomes of the project."[61] Central instruments here are therefore indicators that are supposed to help measure the concrete effects of the project financed.[62]

b) The role of the recipient government

To understand the procedures better, especially with respect to the principle of collective autonomy, it is important to ask specifically about the role that the recipient government is supposed to play. This role, however, is ambivalent. On the one hand, the Bank and the recipient government as borrower are equals under international law and it is stated that the rules concern recipient states' projects, which the Bank merely assists in

[57] BP 10.00, in particular paras. 30, 35–36, 46 (on the contractual instruments of disbursement control and restructuring see below, in 3.b); OP 10.00, para. 18, 19.

[58] OP 10.00, paras. 18, 19; BP 10.00, paras. 35, 36.

[59] World Bank, *Investment Project Financing Implementation Support*, Guidance Note (April 2013).

[60] See World Bank, *Results Framework and M&E*, Guidance Note (April 2013).

[61] Ibid. para 4.

[62] On the important but also ambivalent role of indicators, see Davis, Fisher, Kingsbury and Merry, *Governance by Indicators*; Riegner, *Measuring*; Michael Riegner, "Entwicklungsmessung und Recht," in Dann, Kadelbach and Kaltenborn (eds), *Entwicklung und Recht* (forthcoming fall 2013).

financing.[63] In this vein, recipients, in fact, do have important procedural rights. In particular, a project can only be prepared at the behest of the recipient government, and the Bank can only identify projects at the request of the recipient government.[64] Also, the borrower is responsible for the design and implementation of projects.[65]

On the other hand, the nature and origin of the legal context in itself show that the recipient government is primarily an applicant. It is Bank law, after all, that sets the rules. The Bank determines the relevant procedural rules and manages the procedure. The recipient government must perform the appraisals that the Bank, as funder, demands. The most important function of the recipient appears to be assisting the World Bank in its risk appraisal and hence generating knowledge and information on the project. As shown above, it is primarily the recipients who must perform the appraisals demanded by the Bank, who must furnish information required for risk assessments, and who must also deliver plans for dealing with these risks. Another norm reminds recipients of the duty to support "their" projects, which is in itself a norm that is as curious as it is revealing.[66] Clearly, the borrower's role in securing compliance is seen as crucial though not guaranteed.

A recipient's ability to use its procedural rights and act with collective autonomy, i.e. to be a "weak" or "strong" recipient, depend heavily on non-legal factors.[67] If a state has the administrative and political resources to develop, assess and implement a project, it can do so largely independently. Even though the Bank's law imposes the framework even on "strong" borrowers, Bank law provides flexibility and leeway for such borrowers. But other states do not have such resources. To some extent, the Bank's rules recognize this situation, as the reformed OP 10.00 contains special considerations for "projects in situations of urgent need of

[63] The assisting role of the Bank was more pronounced in the old OP, which stated flatly that "the projects the Bank finances are projects of the borrower" (OP 10.00 (pre-2013), para. 2). The new OP focuses more directly on the Bank itself. The borrower appears more in a complementary role (OP 10.00, para. 18: "the borrower prepares the project for which it seeks investment project financing").

[64] Art. V Sect. 1 d/e, Articles of Agreement, BP 10.00, para. 1.

[65] This is more clearly expressed in World Bank, *Results Framework and M&E*, Guidance Note 2013, para. 11.

[66] See OP 10.00, para 18 ("obligations include the requirement to carry out the project with due diligence ..."), BP 10.00, para. 35 "is responsible for implementing the project."

[67] On the three ideal-typical configurations between "strong" and "weak" donors and recipients, see Gibson et al., Krister, Ostrom and Shivakumar, *Samaritan's Dilemma*, pp. 65–8; see also *supra*, Ch 3.B.I.

assistance or capacity constraints," i.e. fragile states.[68] But many "weaker" countries that do not fall into these special categories may also not have strong enough capacities.[69] Their weakness is compounded by the sheer number and intensity of the Bank's demands. Insofar as the Bank imposes these demands and also offers help in fulfilling them, it places itself legally in the position of taking over the tasks itself.

c) *Participation by affected parties and publicity rules*

One particular feature of the procedural law is the participation of other, private actors. The respective rules on project aid are particularly important since (in contrast to the rules for preparing a CAS) they can be supervised by the Inspection Panel.[70] The Panel can monitor compliance with relevant procedural rules (OP/BP), punish violations, and, by means of its reports, help to elucidate and elaborate the rules.[71] The Bank's procedures involve two groups with distinct participation rights: project-affected people, and indigenous peoples. A third group, namely "stakeholders," used to be expressly mentioned in the OP/BP 10.00,[72] but is no longer mentioned, clearly a loss with regard to preserving individual autonomy in the face of World Bank-financed projects.

The first group with special participatory rights are project-affected people and local NGOs. The Inspection Panel has repeatedly explained the precise meaning of these terms and made them somewhat more specific.[73] For instance, it has determined that those who might only potentially be affected are also included. It has also pronounced on the manner of determining who is affected (the time of the determination, use of census data). These groups have special rights in the context of environmental or social impact assessments. Recipient governments are required to consult these groups as early as possible and to keep them routinely

[68] OP 10.00, paras 10–15; BP 10.00, paras. 47–51. More on these special considerations *infra*, at 2.

[69] On fragile states: B. Kingsbury and K. E. Davis, *Obligation Overload: Adjusting the Obligations of Fragile or Failed States*, Hauser Globalization Colloquium Fall 2010 (2010). Available at www.iilj.org/courses/documents/HC2010Dec01.DavisKingsbury.pdf (last visited September 2012).

[70] In detail: Hunter, "International Law and Public Participation," pp. 199–238.

[71] The jurisdiction of the Inspection Panel is derived from BP 17.55, Annex A, margin no. 12, p. 3.

[72] Stakeholders were supposed to be consulted during project development (BP 10.00 pre-April 2013, paras. 1, 3) and kept informed during official negotiations (BP 10.00 pre-April 2013, paras. 8, 12).

[73] On the relevant 'jurisprudence' see Naude Fourie, *World Bank Inspection Panel*, pp. 238–40.

informed.[74] To ensure "meaningful consultation," the Bank pledges itself and the recipient government to provide timely and sufficient information in a form that these groups will be able to understand.[75] Making environmental reports public is a precondition for the Bank's approval.[76] Similarly, the Bank's law imposes specific information duties on recipients relative to persons who may be resettled,[77] as well as the involvement of the affected persons in the resettlement plans.[78] Here, as well, a "meaningful consultation" is required.[79] The precise meaning of the term "meaningful consultation" has been addressed repeatedly by the Board of Directors and in Inspection Panel reports. A General Counsel of the Bank, Ibrahim Shihata, declared that the term meant that affected parties are provided with sufficient information and have sufficient opportunity to make their views known.[80] The Inspection Panel has stated that affected parties must be able to state their views in a confidential proceeding, not in the presence of government representatives. Consultation must also be understood as not just a one-sided process driven by the Bank or the government, but rather a genuine mutual exchange of opinion.[81]

Consultation with indigenous peoples, the second group, must be even more intensive.[82] The participation and protection rights of indigenous people have been more concretely specified by the concept of "free, prior and informed consultation."[83,84] Recipient governments must create an appropriate framework for consultation with the relevant groups, formulate consultation methods appropriate to the social and cultural practices of the group and provide them with relevant information during the

[74] OP 4.01, margin no. 14. [75] OP 4.01, margin no. 15. [76] OP 4.01, margin no. 17.

[77] OP 4.12, margin nos. 6a(i), 7a, 13a.

[78] OP 4.12, margin nos. 19, 22; or also OP 4.12, Annex A, margin no. 15.

[79] OP 4.12, margin nos. 2a); 14 p. 3.

[80] Shihata, *World Bank Legal Papers*, pp. 630–1.

[81] Naude Fourie, *World Bank Inspection Panel*, pp. 241–4.

[82] On the participation rights of indigenous peoples, see generally Wolfrum, "The Protection of Indigenous People," p. 369.

[83] OP 4.10, margin no. 10; extensive discussion in Roos, *Der internationel Menschenrechtsschutz*, pp. 305ff; Goodland, "Free, Prior and Informed Consent," pp. 66–74; B. Clavero, "The Indigenous Rights to Participation and International Development Policies," *Arizona Journal of Comparative and International Law*, 22 (2005), 41–51; a more general discussion of the position of indigenous peoples in Bank law can be found in Kingsbury, "Operational Policies," pp. 323–42; see also F. MacKay, "Indigenous People and International Financial Institutions," in Bradlow and Hunter, *International Financial Institutions and International Law*, pp. 287–320.

[84] On a similar concept in international environmental law, see K. Peiry Kummer, "Prior Informed Consent," in R. Wolfrum (ed.), *Max Planck Encyclopedia of Public International Law* [online edition] (Oxford University Press, 2008–) at margin no. 1.

process. The Bank may only finance the project when, as a result of this process, the project enjoys "broad support."[85] This last requirement can be seen as giving indigenous groups a practical veto.[86] Thus, the World Bank's procedural law affords indigenous groups the most extensive participation rights, even if it has not decided to go further, for example, by according them an explicit veto right.[87]

"Community-Driven Development" (CDD) initiatives also play a special role, in which the World Bank, with the recipient government's consent, creates local councils on a sub-national level to decide how the Bank's monies should be used. These are generally specially created parallel administrative structures. The local councils are elected, and must be comprised of both women and men.[88]

A further opportunity for "participation" of other actors is provided by the requirement that the documents produced during the process be published. The Project Information document, which concludes the preparation phase of a project, and the integrated safeguard data sheet both have to be disclosed.[89] In this way, NGOs or other groups can at least gradually gather information about projects in the pipeline and, if necessary, organize public pressure.

In sum, one can say that the World Bank law contains participation rights for certain especially affected parties, although the legal implications of these procedural rights remain unclear. For example, neither the Bank nor the recipient-state government must explain why it has not responded to a complaint or offered alternatives to its course of action. The purpose of third-party involvement, as declared in comments to the relevant rule, is revealing: it is primarily intended to ensure the greatest efficiency in planning and projects. Third-party participation thus emerges more as a means to an end than an end in itself. The same is

[85] OP 4.10, margin no. 10.

[86] See also Göcke, "Case of Angela Poma Poma v. Peru," p. 361.

[87] See Roos, *Der internationael Menschenrechtsschutz*, pp. 308–10.

[88] The World Bank, *CDD in the Context of Conlict-Affected Countries: Challenges and Opportunities*, Report No. 36425 GLB (2007). Available at http://siteresources.worldbank.org/EXTSOCIALDEVELOPMENT/Resources/244362-1164107274725/3182370-1164201144397/CDDandConflict-web.pdf (last visited September 2012); See also: F. Rawski, "World Bank Community-Driven Development Programming in Indonesia and East Timor: Implications for the Study of Global Administrative Law," *New York University Journal of International Law and Politics*, 37 (2006), 919–51 at 919.

[89] BP 10.00, para. 8, 23 and OP 10.00, para. 27. See generally World Bank, *Towards Greater Transparency*, pp. 5–6, margin no. 10; documents that relate to specific negotiations are not published (ibid.) as the World Bank policy distinguishes between final documents, which must be published, and process documents, which need not be published.

true of the entire procedural regime. It is intended to intensively structure negotiations, rather than enable consideration of all possible options.

Comparing (for heuristic purposes) the World Bank's procedure with the types of procedure in domestic administrative law reveals its close relation to procedures for knowledge generation as they appear in telecommunication, economic and risk-regulation law.[90] World Bank law closely regulates communication processes for acquiring and evaluating information and the use of medium-term concepts for dealing with unresolved problems (resettlement plans,[91] environmental plans[92]). The recipient side does have significant rights within the process and can, depending on its practical capacities, help determine the content of the plans. However, it remains an applicant, and one which must act subject to external rules.[93]

2. Substantive criteria: safeguard policies and other pre-approval conditions

Beyond the confines of procedural law, one also has to inquire into the substantive legal framework within which project assistance takes place. To what extent and in what form are expenditures conditioned by substantive criteria? Is the autonomy of the contracting parties limited (possibly unilaterally) by these provisions? How do these criteria and instruments serve the above-mentioned functions of generating knowledge and ensuring compliance?

World Bank law regulates substantive requirements extensively and on two normative levels. For one, the Articles of Agreement themselves, the Bank's founding treaty, define the Bank's general mandate and set out concrete preconditions for agreement to ODA payments.[94] Various conditions and requirements are, secondly, put down in the Bank's binding internal regulations, the OPs and BPs. These are primarily contained in OP 10.00 and, to the extent that regulations are intended to protect people and the environment, in the "safeguard policies."[95]

[90] C. C. Röhl, "§30: Ausgewählte Verwaltungsverfahren," in W. Hoffmann-Riem, E. Schmidt-Aßmann and A. Voßkuhle (eds.), *Informationsordnung, Verwaltungsverfahren, Handlungsformen, Grundlagen des Verwaltungsrechts* (Munich: C.H. Beck, 2008), vol. II, pp. 689–750, margin nos. 24–39.

[91] OP 4.12, margin no. 12. [92] OP/BP 4.02.

[93] For an evaluation of the legal situation in light of the general principles, see *infra* 4.

[94] See Art. V, Sect 1 IDA Articles.

[95] On the legal form of the Policies see *supra*, Ch 3.A.IV.2; see generally, e.g. Alvarez, *International Organizations*, pp. 235–40.

The new and much more detailed OP 10.00 of April 2013 considerably restructures the requirements that a project has to fulfill before it can be approved by the Bank.[96] It starts out by defining the general aims that any World Bank-financed project is bound by. The ultimate goal is that of poverty reduction and sustainable development.[97] "Sustainable development" is broken down into "broad-based economic growth," (somewhat circularly) "social and environmental sustainability," and the "effectiveness of public and private sectors." More clearly than before, OP 10.00 stresses that the development objectives and intended results of a project have to be defined, so that the measurement of effects and outcomes of projects becomes easier.

In the second paragraph, OP 10.00 sets down the criteria or conditions that a project has to fulfill. It has to be "productive and necessary to meet the development objectives," its impact has to be acceptable to the recipient country's fiscal sustainability, and it has to provide acceptable oversight arrangements "to ensure that Investment Project Financing proceeds are used only for the purposes for which the financing is granted."[98] The Articles of Agreement furthermore formulate two "negative" criteria, according to which the Bank is not permitted to allow itself to be influenced by political considerations and cannot decree that goods must be obtained from a specific country.[99]

After these conditions for approval, OP 10.00 formulates a longer list of "considerations" that Bank staff and borrowers have to take into account before approval and during implementation, including economic, procurement, social and ecological aspects.[100] These considerations demonstrate the considerable importance that the Bank traditionally attaches to the strict assessment of the projects that it might fund. The oldest and still very prominent consideration concerns the economic justification for a project.[101] The Bank has to analyze the project's economic rationale, the appropriateness of public sector funding and the special value added through Bank support. The economic justification is also demanded by the Articles of Agreement.[102] The Bank also obliges itself and its borrowers to use a specific set of procurement rules.[103]

96 The old OP 10.00 was one page long and had three paragraphs; the new has 27 paragraphs.

97 Art. 1 IDA, Art. V, §1 (a), (b) IDA; OP 10.00, margin no. 1 ("aims to promote poverty reduction and sustainable development …").

98 OP 10.00, para. 2.

99 Art. V Sect. 1 (g) and (f) IDA Articles. On the particularly important prohibition against taking political considerations into account, see *supra* Ch 3.A.IV.3.

100 OP 10.00, paras. 3–15. 101 OP 10.00, para. 5. 102 Art. V Sect. 1 (g) IDA.

103 OP 10.00, para. 7 with reference to OP 11.00.

Since the 1980s, the Bank has also assessed the environmental side of a project.[104] It evaluates every proposed project for environmental risk and classifies the risks into three groups: minimal, medium and high.[105] After this, the recipient is obliged to conduct closer analysis of the environmental risks and prepare plans for addressing them. Policies concerning other specific areas entail other evaluation duties.[106]

In order to safeguard the social acceptability of projects, the Bank has enacted special protective duties when indigenous peoples might be affected or resettlements required.[107] As shown above, these issues trigger special procedural duties (including a hearing) and specific planning requirements. The goal is to prevent resettlements wherever possible. But when they are unavoidable, recipients are required to create adequate resettlement plans and compensation programs.

Next to these general considerations, the new policy also names a number of "special considerations."[108] Here, Bank law carves out two constellations, in which exceptions to the substantive requirements just named will be allowed. These two constellations concern borrowers that are either "in urgent need of assistance because of a natural or man-made disaster or conflict" or that "experience capacity constraints because of fragility or specific vulnerabilities (including small states)." Bank law here picks up on two of the most important discussions in recent years that are closely related to traditional development cooperation but which pose special problems, namely on humanitarian assistance during disaster or conflict and the question of how to deal with fragile states.[109] The

[104] OP/BP 4.01 (Environmental Assessment); extensive discussion of the Bank's environmental policies in Shihata (ed.), *World Bank in a Changing World I*, pp. 183ff.; C. Di Leva, "International Environmental Law and Development," *Georgetown International Environmental Law Review*, 10 (1998), 501–49 at 501; more generally Di Leva, "International Environmental Law, the World Bank," p. 343.

[105] The categories can be found in OP 4.01, margin no. 8.

[106] The Policies protect forests (OP/BP 4.36), dams (OP/BP 4.57), natural resources (OP 4.04) and cultural goods (OP/BP 4.11).

[107] OP/BP 4.10 (indigenous people), OP/BP 4.12 (resettlement); see generally S. R. Roos, "Die Weltbank als Implementierungsgarant menschenrechtsschützender Völkerrechtsnormen," *Heidelberg Journal of International Law*, 63 (2003), 1035–62 at 1040.

[108] OP 10.00, paras. 10–15.

[109] On these discussions, see in particular M. von Engelhardt, *Aiding Fragile States. Development Cooperation between Juridical and Empirical Statehood*, Ph.D. thesis on file with author; K. Boon, "'Open for Business': International Financial Institutions, Post-Conflict Economic Reform, and the Rule of Law," *New York University Journal of International Law and Politics*, 39 (2007), 513–81; World Bank, *2011 World Development Report: Conflict, Security and Development* (Washington DC, 2011).

exceptions allow fiduciary, environmental or social requirements in particular to be dealt with during implementation and not before approval, and hence give everybody more time and more support from the Bank.[110]

The new OP 10.00 and its regime of criteria contain a shift in substance and normative structure. Before the reform of 2013, OP 10.00 on one page prescribed general goals (poverty reduction and sustainability) and named briefly three criteria that any project had to fulfill, namely being economically justifiable, ecologically sound and socially acceptable.[111] OP 10.00 now distinguishes between aims (para. 1), conditions (para. 2) and considerations (paras. 3–15). The normative status of the considerations (including safeguard policies) seems to be reduced in comparison to the conditions in para. 2. OP 10.00 leaves open whether they too must strictly be fulfilled or rather simply taken into account, although from a systematic perspective, considerations, in particular those put down in safeguard policies, are clearly binding. Also, the new OP 10.00 reduces the importance of the Bank's medium-term plan (the Country Assistance Strategy).[112] Though it still is listed as a consideration, it is not per se binding.

In terms of substance, the binding conditions of OP 10.00, para. 2 now put a stronger focus on the fiscal sustainability and financial regularity of project schemes. Overly indebted countries should not be burdened with further obligations. Also, any hint that project funds might be misused has to lead to the abortion of a project plan; it is mandatory that acceptable oversight mechanisms are in place that ensure that proceeds are used economically and efficiently.

At the same time, the new special considerations also introduce a new level of flexibility in dealing with problematic situations. This shift has two sides: on one hand, it contains the risk that standards might be lowered and the important check through environmental and social safeguards fail; on the other hand, the new flexibility might be able to provide more adequate help in difficult constellations.

How can we evaluate these rules in respect to the general functions of generating knowledge and ensuring compliance, as defined in the general introduction above? The various substantive requirements for ODA expenditures can be seen primarily as conditionalities and instruments for ensuring compliance *ex ante*. They try to assure that projects fulfill important criteria before they get started. Their structure and effects

[110] OP 10.00, para. 11 (a). [111] OP 10.00 (pre-2013), para. 3.

[112] Compare OP 10.00 (pre-2013), para. 3 to OP 10.00 (new), para. 1 and BP 10.00, para. 6 a.

are, however, unusual. The Bank's law rarely imposes precise conditionalities or even technical, quantifiable requirements, preferring instead to impose procedural obligations which serve substantive goals. This procedural approach does not make these requirements any less binding. The requirements are imposed primarily in an indirect fashion. The Bank's Articles and the safeguard policies have a directly binding effect only on Bank employees, not on borrowers. Recipients are, however, required to acknowledge these requirements, since the Bank will not issue loans if they do not do so. They acknowledge these duties either by fulfilling them as part of preparation for the agreement or by promising their future fulfillment in the terms of the concluded agreement.[113] In any event, these are unilateral, *ex-ante* conditionalities formulated by the World Bank.

Interesting questions include how to judge the substance of these requirements and, in particular, how they should be evaluated in existing national and international law. Generally, the policies are linked to existing law.[114] Several policies, for instance, specify that when agreeing on environmental duties in project agreements, the Bank will orient itself to the existing domestic regulations of the recipient state.[115] If the Bank lays down specific targets (emissions, for instance[116]), it regards them only as optional standards which should be compared to the national legal situation.[117] Any divergences should be explained. For instance, Bank-financed projects may not contradict standards that the recipient state has pledged to uphold in international law.[118] In many cases, international treaties are specifically mentioned.[119]

Although the safeguards consolidate and implement international standards in the area of environmental law, there are no comparable general clauses in the area of social impact or human rights. As shown above, policies concerning resettlement or indigenous peoples do help protect human rights. Nevertheless, there is no direct reference to relevant

[113] See also Boisson de Chazournes, "Policy Guidance," pp. 289–90.

[114] See also ibid., pp. 297–301.

[115] See, e.g. OP 4.01, margin no. 3 (environmental assessment); on the relevant international environmental-law duties of states see Epiney, "Umweltvölkerrechtliche Rahmenbedingungen," p. 329.

[116] World Bank, *Pollution Prevention and Abatement Handbook: Toward Cleaner Production* (Washington, DC: World Bank Publications, 1998).

[117] See, e.g. OP 4.01 (environmental assessment), margin no. 6.

[118] E.g. OP 4.01, margin no. 3 (environmental assessment); OP 4.36, margin no. 6: "The Bank does not finance projects that contravene applicable international environmental agreements."

[119] E.g. OP 4.11, margin no. 3, fn. 4 (protection of cultural goods).

international law norms for the protection of indigenous peoples.[120] Nor do the policies require a general human rights evaluation.[121]

Overall, the World Bank has an intensive substantive regime that is formulated unilaterally and can also be derogated unilaterally for specific considerations, thus being adaptable to different circumstances and allowing for more rapid response. From an international law perspective, this unilateral shaping of an international treaty is unusual. From the vantage point of domestic law, however, it is quite familiar. There, it is routine that public authorities do not have to accept the complete contractual freedom of their (though mostly private) counterparts, but can also rather pre-configure public contracts.

3. Project agreements and *ex-post* compliance control

The legal regime has a third component besides procedural and substantive law, namely regulations pertaining to the instrument itself. If procedural and substantive law serve primarily to balance interests, gather information and ensure *ex-ante* compliance, the contract itself provides the primary means of ensuring compliance control after signing and during implementation (i.e. *ex-post* approval). The following section will describe the project agreements in more detail, focusing on their structure and legal nature (a) and the instruments for *ex-post* compliance which they contain (b).[122]

a) *Structure and legal nature*

Up to now, we have used the term "project agreements" merely for the purposes of simplification. However, this term stands for many different forms of contract which the World Bank uses to disburse ODA.[123] The main instrument is the loan contract, which the IDA calls a "Financing Agreement" and the IBRD calls a "Loan Agreement." The Bank's contracting partner may be a member state, a state-run enterprise or a private organization which assumes responsibility for implementing the project.[124] This Agreement usually contains the general loan specifications

[120] In particular, the ILO Convention on Indigenous and Tribal Peoples in Independent Countries 1989 (ILO Convention No. 169).

[121] On this discussion, see Roos, "Die Weltbank," 1042–4; Kingsbury, "Operational Policies," pp. 326–7.

[122] On the procedural rules for the implementation phase, see *supra* 1.a (at the end).

[123] Extensively discussed in Mosler, *Finanzierung durch die Weltbank*, pp. 19–41; Rigo Sureda, "Law," 113–20.

[124] Art. III, §4 IBRD Articles; Art. V, §2 (c) IDA Articles.

(amount, interest, repayment conditions) for the project as well as more general aspects (applicability of general conditions, effective date, etc.). Two "schedules" attached to the Agreement contain the details of the project which is being financed.[125]

If the borrower is not implementing the project itself, a "project agreement" will be concluded with the implementing organization. In this agreement, implementation details will be laid out in reference to the loan agreement. If the project is to be carried out by the private sector, the Articles require that yet a third contract be signed, namely a "guarantee agreement."[126] This agreement requires the member state to stand surety for repayment if the private concern is no longer capable of doing so.[127] Thus, a project often results in a large number of different agreements. The recipient state is always involved in these, and often the implementation agency as well.

The second component of every financing agreement is the Bank's so-called General Conditions.[128] These contain the general definitions and conditions (e.g. disbursement conditions, implementation requirements, grounds for termination, arbitration clauses) and other regulations that are highly important to compliance.[129] The general conditions are formulated unilaterally by Bank management, although there are also internal consultations with the Board of Directors. They are, however, non-negotiable for recipients.

The legal nature of the agreements is not explicitly addressed. This fact may, however, be important with regard to realization of the contract goals, where questions of interpretation may well crop up. It is now widely recognized that only international law applies to the Bank's agreements.[130] They are treaties within the meaning of international law, at least

[125] On the structure of this agreement see Mosler, *Finanzierung durch die Weltbank*, pp. 19–23.

[126] Art. III §4 (i) IBRD Articles; Art. V, §2 (d) IDA Articles.

[127] On the structure of this agreement see Mosler, *Finanzierung durch die Weltbank*, pp. 34–6. Nevertheless, contracts between the IBRD or IDA with third parties remain the extreme exception, especially since the 1956 founding of the International Finance Corporation (IFC), which serves as a specialized arm of the bank exclusively handling support for private parties.

[128] IDA, General Conditions for Credits and Grants, July 2005; IBRD, General Conditions for Loans, July 2005; see also J. W. Head, "Evolution of the Governing Law for Loan Agreements of the World Bank and Other Multilateral Development Banks," *American Journal of International Law*, 90 (1996), 214–34 at 218–19.

[129] Discussed in detail immediately below in b).

[130] The first General Counsel of the Bank made this point as early as 1960. See A. Broches, "International Legal Aspects of the Operations of the World Bank," *Recueil des*

when the contracting partner is itself subject to international law, such as a member state. Even when the Bank contracts with private parties, the agreement also partakes of the international character of the relationship between the Bank and the member states.[131] In any event, the recipient state's law is never applicable. The general conditions thus envision that disagreements between the parties should be solved by arbitration.[132]

b) *Contractual instruments for* ex-post *compliance control*

The contract law of the World Bank contains a variety of well-honed instruments to ensure that recipients fulfill their contractual obligations. Since 1984, every financing agreement has been subjected to the so-called Commitment Clause.[133] This clause requires the recipient government to declare that it will be bound by the project's goals. It is in line with the efforts to strengthen or even mandate borrower ownership. The recipient state is responsible for the project's implementation and success. It may be doubted what effect this clause actually has.

The General Conditions also include many contractual oversight mechanisms. The financing agreement itself lays out numerous evaluation criteria and names a Bank supervision team which will monitor and report on implementation.[134] Most importantly, the recipient is required

Cours, 169 (1959), 297–409 at 313; since confirmed by Rigo Sureda, "Law," 113; Head, "Evolution," 214.

131 In exceptional cases, the World Bank has also recognized non-member states as contract partners. For instance, the Bank's activity in East Timor was founded on a contract with UNTAET, the UN's interim administration for the territory. See World Bank, *World Bank Assistance to East Timor: Legal Memorandum of by the Acting Vice-President and General Council*, iii of September 30, 1999 (1999). Available at http://siteresources.worldbank.org/INTTIMORLESTE/Resources/annex+A.pdf (last visited September 2012). Other possible examples are the West Bank/Gaza or Bosnia-Herzegovina, where the justification in each case was that the activity of the World Bank in non-member states was in the interest of all member states. See I. Shihata, H. Abushakra and H.-J. Gruss, "Legal Aspects of the World Bank's Assistance to the West Bank and the Gaza Strip," *Palestine Yearbook of International Law*, 7 (1992/94), 19–43 at 25. In Somalia, the World Bank has not had an active portfolio since 1991, since there has been no effective government to act as a partner, and because the country cannot repay its debts to international financial institutions. Nevertheless, in 1992 the Bank contributed to humanitarian aid through a common Special Emergency Assistance Grant run by UNICEF, WHO and WFP, and finances smaller projects since 2002 with the Post-Conflict Fund.

132 IBRD, General Conditions, §8.04; IDA, General Conditions, §7.03.

133 I. Shihata, "The World Bank and the Environment," in I. Shihata, *The World Bank in a Changing World*, vol. I: Selected essays (Dordrecht: Martinus Nijhoff, 1991), pp. 135–80 at pp. 148–9.

134 See the now extensive description in the Guidance Notes on "Implementation Support" and on "Results Framework and M&E" (both 2013).

to prepare periodic progress reports.[135] The borrower must also prepare many forms of documentation and must grant the Bank the right to visit the project headquarters to inspect those documents at any time.[136]

Finally, the World Bank's law contains various instruments to react to breaches of contract and impose *ex-post* sanctions. The Bank can react to recipients' violations with three levels of intensity: it can suspend the disbursement of ODA, cancel payments, and, as the most drastic measure, demand accelerated repayment of loans. These responses become part of the contracts by means of the General Conditions. The precise implementation of the sanctions is also regulated in the Bank's internal law.[137] Sanctions can be triggered by non-payment by recipients, corruption or mismanagement of Bank funds or breach of contractual conditions. The tools for ensuring *ex-post* goal attainment are comprehensive and minutely adaptable.

4. Summary

Overall, the Bank's legal regime for project lending is intensive and risk-driven. How does it appear with respect to the general principles of development cooperation law as outlined above?[138]

The commitment in the Bank's rules to the principle of development[139] may seem obvious, but is nevertheless worth mentioning. One could, of course, see the entire field of development cooperation law as an implementation of this principle. In project lending, though, the World Bank's law draws specifically on the principle by making the goal of sustainable development the explicit criterion for every project evaluation.[140] The Bank here uses a broad definition of development by referring to the goals of poverty reduction and sustainable development, encompassing broad-based economic growth, social and environmental sustainability and the effectiveness of the public and private sectors.[141]

Also worthy of note is the special status afforded to the principle of cost-effectiveness, which gives legal form to the principle of coherence

[135] At the same time, Bank employees are required to prepare comprehensive reports on the progress and completion of projects, see BP 10.00, para. 46 on Investment Project Completion Report and OP 13.60 (Monitoring and Evaluation).

[136] Art. IV, 4.07–11 General Conditions IDA.

[137] Art. VI General Conditions IDA as well as, in particular, OP 10.00, para. 25 (Recourse and Remedies) and BP 10.00, para. 37 (Disbursements and Suspension of Disbursements) and para. 38/39 (Cancellation).

[138] See Ch 4.

[139] See Ch 4.B.

[140] Art. I, V, §1 (a), (b) IDA Articles; OP 10.00, para. 1.

[141] OP 10.00, para. 1.

and efficiency.[142] The protection of the Bank against economic risk is secured not only by procedural law but also by various substantive criteria regarding ODA allocation. Thus, the conditions for approval mention considerations of economy and efficiency. The procedural law envisions a multi-stage evaluation of project proposals. Participation by the recipient state's government as well as from affected parties is intended (at least in part) to serve the purpose of discovering and evaluating the opportunities and risks of the project in order to influence the planning process accordingly. This risk-averse characteristic of the Bank's law serves primarily to ensure the economic efficiency of projects. Some observers may perceive this emphasis on economic aspects as demonstrating the Bank's technocratic narrow-mindedness. From the perspective of the principle of coherence and efficiency, however, the Bank's policies protect an important norm. Equally important in this respect is that Bank rules also stress the importance of implementation support and control in the name of ensuring compliance and achievement of results. Especially in comparison to the law of other donors (as we will shortly see), this is unusual.

With respect to the principle of collective autonomy, the Bank's law on project lending can be seen as a double-edged sword when it comes to the autonomy of recipients. On the one hand, the recipient must launch the proceeding with a request, bears responsibility for the design of the project, and must, finally, agree to conclude the project agreement. From a procedural law perspective, its position is strong, even if its practical influence depends on its capacities. This is recognized more and more as requirements are now formulated with more flexibility and are receptive to country context, circumstances and capacities. This, however, also gives the Bank more leeway and power to determine the rules. On the other hand, the substantive restrictions and conditionalities, which the World Bank formulates unilaterally, are comprehensive and generally restrict recipient autonomy. The law of the World Bank partially incorporates the domestic law of the recipient state (particularly in the area of environmental law), and thus avoids imposing its own substantive standards on the recipient state. Nevertheless, this is not always the case – in some areas, Bank law contains stricter assessment rules than the domestic law in the recipient state, thus endangering the recipient state's autonomy. This is also true of the considerable oversight rights which each borrower must grant to the Bank. Nevertheless, two aspects deserve mention. For one thing, the Bank is well aware of the sensitivity

[142] *Supra* Ch 4.E.I.

of some of its activities and thus excludes specific substantive areas that are closely connected with the principle of non-intervention, in particular voting and political reform, but also human rights guarantees. The ban on political interference, discussed above, defines exactly these off-limits issues.[143] However, mere reference to the general voluntariness of any contractual agreement – as emphasized by the will theory in domestic contract law – does not keep the Bank from endangering the collective autonomy of borrowers. In reality, only influential borrowers enjoy free will. For smaller recipient states, the threats to autonomy are obvious despite the (principally procedural) protections afforded them in World Bank law. The Bank's duties, in particular to its funders, should also be acknowledged. The Bank imposes many unilateral limits not out of arbitrariness, but (for example, with respect to oversight rights) to ensure that general or specific duties under international law are fulfilled. The autonomy claims of recipient states must be balanced with those of the donor states who finance the World Bank. There is no simple, universal solution to this inherent tension.

A difficult tension also arises with respect to the principle of individual autonomy and thus the safeguarding of human rights, a fourth principle of development cooperation law. World Bank law only partially realizes the principle. Individuals can have participation rights, although modest ones as part of the general public. The rights of indigenous peoples go farther, to the point where they (though not conferring a formal veto) almost constitute a practical right of veto. The Bank also protects the right to be free from uncompensated involuntary resettlement. The respective policies guarantee participation rights to individuals in this context. In general, however, the safeguard policies and general Bank law provide specific protection more for public goods than for individual rights. Social conditions and the environment are granted special protection. The Bank does not bind itself by a general human rights OP. Its approach here thus differs from the environmental area, where the Bank generally works within the recipient state's legal framework and adopts that recipient's (environmental) international law duties as its own criteria. Such an approach, that is, linkage to the domestic human rights obligations of the recipient state, would be conceivable in the area of human rights. According to the legal analysis presented earlier in this book, the World Bank is obliged to do so in order to comply with its human rights obligations.[144] Since the Bank is

[143] Art. V, §6 IDA Articles; Art. IV, §10 IBRD Articles; see *supra* Ch 3.A.IV.3 and Ch 4.C.III.2 c).

[144] On the Bank's human rights duties see *supra* Ch 4.D.II.2.

required to respect and foster human rights, a systematic "human rights impact assessment" should take place to comply with this obligation. This assessment could be sufficiently flexible and be based on the legal situation of the recipient state. By contrast, the articulation of a general human rights policy for the Bank, perhaps based on the contents of the 1966 Covenants, might stand in conflict with the laws of certain recipient states. In this case, the Bank's demand that these rights be respected by recipient countries could conflict with their autonomy. The Bank's restrained policies in this area have the intention of preserving the borrower's collective autonomy. This tension between collective autonomy and human rights could be avoided by linkage to the recipient state's legal system, as described above. In conclusion, the Bank's law contributes to the implementation of the principle of individual autonomy less than it could – and less than it should.

II. The legal regime of the EU

Project assistance is also a central instrument of development cooperation for the EU. About 60 percent of EU disbursements go to projects.[145] There are, however, no exact figures for the number of projects. It can be assumed, though, that the EU finances more projects (and smaller ones) than the World Bank. Another contrast with the World Bank is significant: the EU's project assistance takes the form of direct subsidies, not loans. EU assistance does not have to be repaid.[146] Despite its importance, EU law regulates this second phase of the ODA allocation in a comparatively cursory and neutral fashion. In contrast to the World Bank, where the evaluation and agreement of projects is regulated extensively and is driven by an obvious goal, this phase of the process is subjected to only a few EU provisions. This makes it clear that, for the EU, this phase is not something for development experts and risk examiners, but is rather a

[145] The percentage of project aid is derived from subtracting out the amount of the newer and more-frequently quantified budget support and other instruments from overall budget, see P. Schmidt, *Budgethilfe in der Entwicklungszusammenarbeit der EU*, Studies in Transnational Legal Policy (Bonn, 2005), vol. X, p. 125; European Commission, *Budget Support: A Question of Mutual Trust* (Luxembourg: Publications Office of the European Union, 2008), p. 26. On the various forms of funding besides project aid, see Art. 61 I Cotonou Agreement, Art. 25 DCI Regulation.

[146] See Art. 2 of the Financial Regulation Applicable to the 10th European Development Fund ((EC)215/2008); for a critique of providing subsidies instead of loans, see Moss, Pettersson and van de Walle, *Aid-Institutions Paradox?*, pp. 267, 268 (arguing that subsidies provide a mistaken incentive for recipients to neglect their own taxation systems).

field of foreign affairs and a task for diplomats who are given much discretion. The picture of a diplomatically oriented law of development cooperation, familiar from the first phase, is also evident here. As in World Bank law, though, the donors (here, the EU) essentially control the procedure.

As in the section on planning, the dual nature of EU development cooperation and its law must be taken into account.[147] Cooperation with the ACP Group is based on the Cotonou Agreement and the Council Regulation on Implementation of the 10th EDF, from which the cooperation is currently financed,[148] while work with other states is regulated primarily by Regulation No. 1905/2006 of the European Parliament and of the Council of December 18, 2006, Establishing a Financing Instrument for Development Cooperation (DCI Regulation).[149] Again, we see that the law of ACP cooperation is negotiated multilaterally, while the other law is made unilaterally by the EU. The consequences of this division should be addressed.

In the following sections we will examine, as with the World Bank, the procedural law (1), the substantive criteria (2) and, finally, the form of action of the award process (3), and conclude with an analysis according to the principles of development cooperation law (4).

1. Procedural rules: priority of executive cooperation

a) *Basic structure of the procedure*

The approval of a project is based ultimately on the conclusion of a financing agreement between the Commission and the recipient government.[150] This, however, is only the last of three steps, most of which are laid down in the Union's budgetary law. Three steps must be distinguished: (1) the

[147] Discussed extensively *supra* Ch 3.A.III.2 and Ch 5.C.II.

[148] Of particular relevance for the present discussion are Annex IV to the Cotonou Agreement, the Council Regulation on the Implementation of the 10th European Development Fund (Council Regulation No. 617/2007 from 14 May 2007 (hereinafter Implementation Regulation 10th EDF) and the Financial Regulation for the 10th European Development Fund (Council Regulation No. 215/2008 from 18 February 2008) (hereinafter Financial Regulation 10th EDF).

[149] Regulation (EC) No. 1905/2006 from December 18, 2006, cited under the English abbreviation Development Cooperation Instrument (DCI).

[150] Art. 17 Annex IV Cotonou Agreement, Art. 29 II DCI Regulation. This is a form of decentralized administration in which the recipient government takes over further implementation and the award of specific contracts (see Art. 20 Financial Regulation 10th EDF; Art. 163 EC Financial Regulation). In addition, other non-state actors can become direct contracting partners (see Art. 24 DCI Regulation, Art. 58 Cotonou Agreement (in the revised version: 2005 OJ L 209/39 from August 11, 2005). In this case, the recipient state's government is not involved, and the aid takes the form of direct administration. This form will not be further addressed here.

approval of an Annual Action Program as a Financing Decision within the meaning of the Financial Regulation, (2) the approval of a Financing Proposal as an official commitment of funds, and (3) the conclusion of a Financing Agreement as a legal obligation toward the recipient. In the following, these three steps will be more closely considered.

Each disbursement by the Union must be preceded by a Financing Decision which, although it only has effect within the EU, must nevertheless specify the essential aspects of an activity.[151] With respect to the Union's development expenditures, this Financing Decision takes the form of an Annual Action Program.[152] In this Program, the Commission and the EEAS[153] first determine the goals, action areas and total amount of the financing, then name specific projects and the basic data relevant to them (actors, expected results, evaluation criteria, financing methods).[154] The creation of an Annual Action Program is largely an internal EU affair. Even for the multilaterally negotiated cooperation projects in ACP countries, the relevant provisions are found in the unilaterally decreed Implementing Regulation for the relevant EDF.[155] Action Programs are approved by Commission Decisions after development by the EEAS and consultation with member states in a comitology proceeding, which means approval is also unilateral.[156] In the ACP area, recipient states are consulted, but they are not allowed to have any significant influence. In the non-ACP area, they are not involved at all.[157] Substantively, the Commission is bound by the principle that the Action Programs must be accessory to the Country Strategy Papers.[158] Deviation from the Country Strategy Papers is only permitted in exceptional cases, which are closely regulated.[159] The Commission thus has little chance to shape policy, but

151 This is the legal definition contained in Art. 90 Financial Implementation Regulation (No. 1605/2002); Art. 110 Financial Regulation; Art. 106 Financial Regulation 10th EDF; see also Schenk, *Strukturen und Rechtsfragen*, pp. 152, 153.

152 Art. 7 I Implementation Regulation 10th EDF; Art. 22 I DCI Regulation.

153 The role of the EEAS in this context is not clear. Article 9(IV) of the Council Decision establishing the European External Action Service appears to specify that the Commission will reach a decision, but that this decision will be prepared by the EEAS and the General Directorate for Development.

154 The substantive requirements are listed in Art. 22 II DCI Regulation; Art. 7 II Implementation Regulation 10th EDF; the programs are also listed on the Internet at http://ec.europa.eu/europeaid/work/ap/index_en.htm (last visited July 2013).

155 Art. 7 Implementation Regulation 10th EDF.

156 Art. 22 I, III DCI Regulation; Art. 7 I, III Implementation Regulation 10th EDF.

157 Art. 22 DCI Regulation.

158 Art. 22 I DCI Regulation; Art.7 I Implementation Regulation 10th EDF.

159 Art. 22 I U para. 2 DCI Regulation; Art. 8 Implementation Regulation 10th EDF.

rather can only specify the plan for one year, which was in turn already set out in the multi-annual program.

Of particular importance is the second step, in which a specific Financing Proposal or draft of a Financing Agreement is prepared. These documents set out the exact contours of the project, the financial conditions of the ODA allocation, and the details of the implementation regime. Its approval by the Commission represents a significant commitment of resources for the purposes of budget implementation.[160]

As a matter of budgetary law, the internal EU decision on the Financing Proposal is finally completed by the conclusion of a Financing Agreement with the recipient government.[161] This third step is not further specified in the EU's procedural law.[162] It can be assumed that the Commission simply takes the Financing Proposal, which has already been accepted by the Commission, and converts it into contractual form without making substantive changes. We will now turn to the more important second step and ask whether it serves the purpose of knowledge generation and the inclusion of further participants (recipient governments or third parties).

b) Procedural rights of the recipient government

The decisive step in designing specific projects is the drawing up of a Financing Proposal. When considering the character of this proceeding and the procedural rights of the recipient state's government, the legal regime for ACP and non-ACP states must be distinguished, as was the case in analyzing planning law. In the non-ACP area, the EU dominates the proceeding. It unilaterally determines the relevant procedural law and gives itself the most prominent role within it.[163] True enough, the procedure can only be

[160] Art. 76 Financial Regulation; Art. 70 II Financial Regulation 10th EDF; Art. 28 DCI Regulation in conjunction with Art. 116 Financial Regulation, on the importance of these documents see ECA, *Special Report No 21/2000 On the Management of the Commisson's External Aid Programmes (in Particular on Country Programming, Project Preparation and the Role of Delegations), Together with the Commissions Replies*, OJ C 57/1 of February 22, 2000, margin nos. 36–8. JS:Sonderbericht 1/2011: Dezentralisierung und Qualitätssteigerung; 11/2010: Verwaltung der Budgethilfen in den AKP Staaten durch KOM; 18/2009: Wirksamkeit der EEF Hilfen für regionale Wirtschaftsintegration.

[161] Art. 28 DCI Regulation in conjunction with Art. 166 Financial Regulation (FR); Art. 17 Annex IV Cotonou. On the details of the binding effect of funding agreements see Schenk, *Strukturen und Rechtsfragen*, p. 162.

[162] This is not the case when central, direct funds administration is used; in that case, then there is an approval proceeding (DCI: Arts. 28 I and Art. 114 FR; ACP: Art. 103 and Art. 110 Financial Regulation 10th EDF).

[163] That is, the DCI regulation or other legal act that can form the basis for an ODA allocation. On the potential legal bases, see *supra* Ch 3.A.II.

started by an application from the recipient state. Nevertheless, the process unfolds largely within various EU bodies which evaluate and develop the application.[164] The suspicion that these proposals are in fact usually written by employees of local EU delegations, as was the case in the early years and with World Bank projects, remains strong today.[165] In any case, there is no further recipient-state participation in the form of concrete negotiations, mutual assessment missions or, at the minimum, hearings. There is no specific procedural regime to deal with the problem of lack of information or the practical asymmetry between the contracting parties. The contrast with the World Bank's well-developed procedural law is apparent.

The situation is different with ACP countries. One fundamental difference (with the World Bank as well) is that the process is regulated by a mutually agreed procedural regime set out in the Cotonou Agreement. The regime, which is comprehensive and cooperatively structured, is governed by the basic principles set out in Art. 57 of the Cotonou Agreement.[166] This Article gives ACP countries the responsibility of selecting projects and programs and preparing the necessary paperwork. The countries are to decide the basic structural questions themselves. In practice, the process begins with a recipient's proposal, which is then subjected to a mutual evaluation by both sides.[167] The proposals should contain all relevant information for their evaluation.[168] The evaluation should also be driven by mutually agreed criteria.[169] In sum, the design and selection of projects are the responsibility of the recipient government, while project assessment is the common task of the EU and the recipient government. However, the criteria are not further specified, nor have formal guidelines in this area been published.[170] The Commission prepares a Financing Proposal based on the results of the evaluation. At this step, project design is taken over by the Commission. However, this proposal should also be developed in close consultation with recipients.[171]

164 The rules governing the approval proceeding are applied here; they are found in Art. 162 FR and 114–116 FR; more detailed description in ibid., pp. 156–62.

165 See ECA, *Special Report No 21/2000*, margin no. 31.

166 In addition to the basic principles of Art. 57 Cotonou Agreement there are more details in Arts. 15–17 Annex IV Cotonou Agreement (modified by the Agreement on the Modification of the Cotonou Agreements, OJ L 209 from August 11, 2005, as well as Decision 3/2008 of the ACP-EC Ministers Committee from December 15, 2008, JO L 352/59 from 31 December 2008).

167 Art. 15 I Annex IV. 168 Art. 15 II Annex IV. 169 Art. 15 I Annex IV.

170 Art. 287 of the Lomé IV Convention contains another list of criteria. The substantive criteria will be addressed immediately below in Section 2.

171 Art. 16 I Annex IV. Here as well, the role of the EEAS is not yet clear. The decision establishing the EEAS does not make this explicit, although it may be the case that Art. 9 IV

One peculiarity is contained in Art. 16(V) of the Annex. It permits the recipient state to appeal the denial of a proposal by the Commission to the next highest level (in a Committee composed equally of ACP and EC representatives) or to demand a hearing. The state can present additional information at this stage. ACP countries thus have a right of appeal against denial or modification of their financing proposals. The final step is the Commission's decision on the proposal, which, for projects over a certain size, it makes in cooperation with the member states (in a comitology proceeding).[172] The procedural law in the ACP field is thus much more cooperative, even if the financial decision (because of its financial nature) remains with the EU.[173]

c) Participation of affected parties?

A fair balancing of relevant interests should include not only the EU and the recipient government, but also other stakeholders, in particular affected parties. Where does European development cooperation law stand in this regard? Here, both ACP and non-ACP law are similar, albeit only in the scarcity of rules. The general promise of participatory and inclusive procedures[174] has not resulted in genuine implementation by concrete rules.[175] Third parties can participate at only two points during the process. First, all actors who might have a worthy project have a right to submit proposals for projects.[176] Since this also includes private implementation organizations, they can present their own proposals. This only applies, however, when they themselves want to implement the project. Those who are merely affected do not benefit from this rule.

Second, stakeholders can participate in the non-ACP area when the subject is "environmentally sensitive projects, in particular for major new infrastructure."[177] The nature and consequences of this participation

should be understood as stating that the EEAS will assist in the process, which would seem logical, since it creates on-location delegations.

[172] Member-state influence appears, however, to frequently be minimal, see ibid., margin no. 41.

[173] Art. 57 V Cotonou Agreement.

[174] Art. 2 Cotonou Agreement; Art. 3 VIII DCI Regulation.

[175] For a critique of the practical effectiveness see ECA, *Special Report No 6/2007* on the Effectiveness of Technical Assistance in the Context of Capacity Development Together with the Commission's Replies, OJ C 312/3 of July 21, 2007, margin no. 17.

[176] Art. 24 II DCI Regulation. On this possibility, see Court of Auditors' Special Report No. 4/2009, margin nos. 36–41 (with the somewhat skewed titled "On the Commission's Management of Non-state Actors' (NSAs) Involvement in EC Development Cooperation") (Luxembourg: Publications Office of the European Union, 2009).

[177] Art. 22 IV DCI Regulation.

are, however, not further specified. Nor are there provisions for the systematic participation of third parties by means of mandatory hearings, protection for specific groups, or, at the very least, provisions for submitting comments. The law thus does not match up to the Commission's own principle of inclusivity.[178] If third parties and those potentially affected by projects are not asked for their opinion, they cannot be used as a source of relevant knowledge and local information, and their human rights are not protected. Even when they present their own project proposals, they are required to present all relevant information with the project proposal itself.[179]

In general, the procedural rules only partially fulfill the general function of information acquisition and protection of autonomy. With respect to participation by governments, the procedures have two faces. While non-ACP countries are reduced to the role of applicant, ACP law provides for a genuinely cooperative procedure for developing projects. As in the World Bank's law, recipient governments who submit proposals are responsible for presenting the necessary information and undertake a mutual evaluation of the proposals. In both areas, a project can only be carried out with agreement of the recipient government. Thus, a certain amount of formal autonomy is guaranteed. Participation of affected parties or interested third parties (local NGOs) is not secured in a concrete and legally binding manner in either ACP or non-ACP law.

2. Substantive criteria?

The ODA allocation process can, as we have seen in the case of the World Bank, also be determined and subject to evaluation under substantive law. The relevant regulations present conditionalities and limit the negotiating discretion of the contracting parties, but also serve to secure general goals, such as environmental protection. These rules can be seen as instruments of *ex-ante* goal attainment. In the World Bank's law, in particular its safeguard policies, these instruments are highly regulated.

In this respect as well, the EU's development cooperation law follows a different path than that of the World Bank. Neither in the ACP nor in

[178] In any event, the handbooks created by the Commission for project-cycle implementation recommend the involvement of stakeholders (see European Commission, *Aid Delivery Methods: Volume I: Project Cycle Management Guidelines* (2004), pp. 27; 33. Available at http://ec.europa.eu/europeaid/infopoint/publications/europeaid/documents/49a_adm_pcm_guidelines_2004_en.pdf (last visited July 2013)). However, these are not binding rules. Further, they are extremely vague.

[179] For a somewhat more positive judgment see Pellens, *Entwicklungshilfe Deutschlands*, p. 126.

the non-ACP area are there precise, legally binding criteria for evaluating project proposals. European development cooperation law does not use this instrument.[180] Country Strategy Papers are the strongest influence on thematic project selection.[181] The influence arises from the fact that the creation of Annual Action Programs is subject to the principle that they must be complementary to or in accordance with the Papers, and the individual projects are derived in turn from the Annual Action Program.[182] This is the mechanism by which the thematic orientation of the planning phase is realized within the project phase. This is, however, merely a form of instruction applied at the end of the process. It does not give rise to specific conditional criteria.

Further, there are no genuine, legally binding specifications which direct the selection and evaluation of projects. There is, to be sure, a Commission handbook that lists a series of criteria. Nevertheless, these are broadly formulated and are oriented more toward ensuring that evaluations have taken place rather than imposing substantive binding requirements. Further, they are non-binding.[183] The only exception is the previously mentioned duty, set out in Art. 22(IV) of the DCI Regulation, to undertake a strategic environmental assessment (SEA), in particular for large-scale infrastructure projects. Nevertheless, this duty has not been specified concretely. In particular, there is no reference to the relevant EU Directives which apply within the EU.[184] And in the ACP area, there is not even a duty to perform an SEA. Despite the general proclamations in this area on the ecological and social impact of projects,[185] there is no binding specification of these ideas. Article 15(I) Annex IV does in fact provide that the contracting parties will promulgate appropriate guidelines including criteria. Yet even when they exist, they are not made public and, unlike safeguard policies, cannot be subjected to public oversight.[186]

[180] For a critical perspective on deficient assessment see ECA, *Special Report No 21/2000*, margin nos. 28–30, see also ibid., pp. 124–6.

[181] On these see *supra* Ch 5.C.II.3. A suggestion that this obligation is actually respected in practice is found, for example, in ECA, *Special Report No 6/2007*, margin no. 14.

[182] Art. 22 I DCI Regulation; Art. 7 I Implementation Regulation 10th EDF.

[183] See European Commission, *Aid Delivery Methods 2004*, pp. 30–2; pp. 35–7.

[184] Council Directive of 27 June 1985 on the Assessment of the Effects of Certain Public and Private Projects on the environment, (85/337/EEC), last modified by Directive 2003/35/EC.

[185] Art. 63 Cotonou Agreement; by contrast, Art. 37 of the Lomé IV Convention already imposed such a duty.

[186] A trenchant assessment of the treatment of environmental issues in development cooperation can be found in ECA, *Special Report No 6/2006 Concerning the Environmental*

In stark contrast to the World Bank, the EU has refrained from creating clear, legally binding criteria for ODA allocations in the form of project assistance. In particular, the question of whether projects might endanger human rights, or whether they bring economic benefits, is not raised. Rather, European development cooperation law avoids requiring governments to pledge to respect individual or general interests. The contracting parties are permitted to act on the basis of flexible assessments. This autonomy does, however, have limits. EU law does attach conditions to the receipt of ODA – however, they come into effect later and are much more general in nature. We will now turn to these.

3. Project agreements and *ex-post* compliance: constitutional conditionalities

Although European development cooperation law provides for fewer *ex-ante* substantive compliance criteria, it is much more active in the areas of *ex-post* goal attainment – that is, the conditionalization of cooperation *after* the signing of a Financing Agreement and during project implementation. To analyze the relevant legal instruments, it will be necessary to briefly address the legal nature and structure of Financing Agreements.

The EU concludes such agreements principally with recipient-state governments.[187] Their legal nature is that of an administrative agreement of public international law.[188] They are divided into two components: "special conditions" relevant to the specific project and the "general conditions" of the EU, which are attached as an annex.[189] The special conditions regulate the specific aspects of the project (nature and goal, funding amount from the EU, specific disbursement rules), while the general conditions (similarly to the World Bank) contain general rules for project implementation, payment

Aspects of the Commission's Development Cooperation, Together with the Commission's Replies, OJ C 235/1 of September 29, 2006, margin nos. 39–46.

[187] For ACP states, Art. 17 Annex IV Cotonou; for non ACP states, Art. 29 DCI Regulation, 162 II b) FR EC. See also Pellens, *Entwicklungshilfe Deutschlands*, pp. 160; 168.

[188] Thus argues A. Zimmermann, "Art. 179 EGV," in H. von der Groeben and J. Schwarze (eds.), *Vertrag über die Europäische Union und Vertrag über die Gründung der Europäischen Gemeinschaft*. Kommentar, 6th edn, IV (Baden-Baden: Nomos, 2003) at margin no. 82; Pellens, *Entwicklungshilfe Deutschlands*, p. 160; on the legal nature of financing agreements in EU benefits administration law, see Schenk, *Strukturen und Rechtsfragen*, p. 163.

[189] Form templates for funding agreements, as well as general conditions, can be found on the website of EuropeAid at: http://ec.europa.eu/europeaid/work/procedures/financing/financing_agreement/index_en.htm (last visited July 2013).

modalities, tax rules and arbitration clauses.[190] The main focus of the general conditions, however, is rules concerning the consequences of various violations of the Financing Agreement and cooperation contract – in other words, how fulfillment of the contract's purpose can be secured after it has been agreed. It should be noted that the general conditions, as is the rule for such provisions, are made unilaterally by the EU and are not subject to negotiation by ODA recipients.

The sanctioning clauses relate to two areas: first, ensuring the financial regularity of the implementation, and second, ensuring compliance with general constitutional norms of human rights, democracy and the rule of law.[191] The general conditions first show their teeth when it comes to the EU's financial interests. They require the recipient to undertake to thoroughly investigate irregularities, fraud and corruption.[192] When recipients sign the conditions, they are also giving various EU organs permission to monitor the financial regularity of the implementation. The Commission, the OLAF (the European Anti-Fraud Office) and the Court of Auditors are given the right to inspect the documents and locations of implementation and require recipients to meet the preliminary conditions for these inspections.[193] If inspectors find violations of contractual duties, the Commission can suspend the contractual relationship.[194] If the irregularities are not remedied within four months, either party may cancel the contract.[195] What is particularly remarkable is that European development cooperation law, unlike that of the World Bank, does not provide for repayment of already disbursed ODA as a legal consequence of violations. This ultimate sanction does not exist.

A particular feature of European development cooperation law is the second thematic area of sanctions – that is, the extraordinarily broad constitutional conditionalization of ODA allocation. The general conditions provide that the EU can suspend and later terminate a Financing Agreement if "the Beneficiary breaches an obligation relating to respect for human rights,

[190] General conditions have been separately formulated for the ACP and non-ACP areas, but share the same content. In the following, they will be referred to as GTC 10th EDF (for those that apply to the ACP area and the 10th EDF) and as GTC Budget (for those applicable to the non-ACP area, which are funded from the general EU budget). With respect to the GTC Budget, the comments refer to the GTC for decentralized implementation.

[191] On oversight and accountability, see also *infra* Ch 9.

[192] Art. 18 GTC 10th EDF; Art. 19 GTC Budget.

[193] Art. 19 GTC 10th EDF; Art. 20 GTC Budget.

[194] Art. 22 I GTC 10th EDF; Art. 23 I GTC Budget. It is noteworthy that these clauses are formulated unilaterally, that is they only sanction breaches of contract by recipients, not by the EU.

[195] Art. 23 GTC 10th EDF; 24 GTC Budget.

democratic principles and rule of law and in serious cases of corruption."[196] Thus, the cooperation can be suspended or canceled because of these general concerns, not just for reasons related to the project itself. The regulations make a point of requiring only recipients to observe these constitutional norms. Only a violation by the "Beneficiary" can trigger sanctions.

These regulations are based on specific and well-researched incidents from the legal situation in the early history of development aid.[197] Since the late 1970s, in particular since the dictatorship of Idi Amin in Uganda, the EC has tried to provide for the suspension of ODA disbursements as a sanction for human rights violations.[198] There were, however, international law obstacles to this plan. These did not result from the principle of non-intervention. That principle only comes into play when, owing to the extreme economic dependence of the recipient state, the suspension of ODA disbursements would constitute coercion sufficient to destroy the recipient state's freedom to act, and would also have to relate to the recipient state's internal affairs.[199] This situation occurred but rarely. On the other hand, international treaty law could impose more stringent limits. The suspension or termination of a treaty relationship, which would cover ODA disbursements, can be justified only within the scope of Articles 60–62 of the VCLT. This requires a significant breach of contract. Since human rights guarantees were originally not an important independent component of the majority of ODA allocation and cooperation agreements, it is impossible to justify a politically motivated suspension of performance on these grounds. To overcome this obstacle, the Commission sought to change the contracts. Since 1989, the Commission has been able to insert specific human rights and democracy clauses into the Fourth Lomé Convention and into partnership treaties with non-ACP countries.[200] The "essential elements" clause in use since 1995 now states that respect for human rights and democratic principles are an "essential" element of the contract.[201] The passage of the general conditions excerpted above refers to the corresponding provisions of the Cotonou Agreement

[196] Art. 22 GTC 10th EDF; Art. 23 GTC Budget.

[197] See Bartels, *Human Rights Conditionality;* E. Fierro, *The EU's Approach to Human Rights Conditionality in Practice* (The Hague: Kluwer Law International, 2003); Pippan, *Förderung der Menschenrechte*; Hoffmeister, *Menschenrechts- und Demokratieklauseln.*

[198] See *supra* Ch 1.B; see also Pippan, *Förderung der Menschenrechte*, pp. 32, 33.

[199] *Supra* Ch 4.C.III.2; Pippan, *Förderung der Menschenrechte*, pp. 96–110; Hoffmeister, *Menschenrechts- und Demokratieklauseln*, pp. 183–94.

[200] Art. 5 Lomé IV (in the 1995 revised version).

[201] Art. 9 Cotonou Agreement; a list of cooperation agreements with non-ACP states which include this clause can be found in Bartels, *Human Rights Conditionality*, Annex 1

and the partnership and cooperation treaties with non-ACP countries. Thus, the human rights provisions of those international instruments are incorporated by reference into the aid agreements and can justify the suspension of ODA payments when constitutional norms are violated.

The application of these clauses has also been anchored in procedural provisions. The human rights and democracy clauses have been complemented by a non-fulfillment clause which creates a specific consultation proceeding replacing the general international law procedure of Art. 65ff. of the VCLT.[202] Under this procedure, the "complaining" contract party must first provide relevant information on the situation. After this, consultations must take place. Only if they fail can the complainant take appropriate measures such as suspension or termination of project assistance.

Overall, the development cooperation law of the EU creates a quite specific regime of *ex-post* compliance. The legal consequences of violations are standard – suspension or ending of contract performance – but the events which can trigger a sanction are unusually broadly defined. The EU links its performance under ODA contracts not only to the other side's performance (including limits on corruption) but also to compliance with general principles of constitutional law. This gives the cooperation a strongly political flavor. This hints at a typological distinction between EU and World Bank law, which will be addressed in the conclusion below.

4. Summary

The European legal regime for project lending, looked at as a whole, appears almost as a diametric contrast with the World Bank's law, both from a substantive and procedural standpoint. In the World Bank, projects are seen primarily as venture capital or risk-prone investments which are subject to relatively strict criteria and which are evaluated *before* the agreement is concluded by consulting the broadest possible range of actors, including external experts and affected parties. In EU law, the technical specifics of project allocation are actually "invisible." Rather, the law regulates a diplomatic enterprise whose substance is largely undefined, although it

(p. 241); an extensive history of the emergence of the clause since 1990 can be found in Hoffmeister, *Menschenrechts- und Demokratieklauseln*, p. 88.

202 Art. 96, 97 Cotonou Agreement. On the form and emergence of these clauses see ibid., p. 376; Bartels, *Human Rights Conditionality*, p. 107; on the not-infrequent use of the clause up to now see ibid., Annex II.

is channeled into certain procedural forms. Furthermore, many of the substantive requirements are evaluated *ex post* instead of being integrated *ex ante*.

How does the EU legal regime appear in light of the general principles of development cooperation law?

In European development cooperation law, as elsewhere, the general mandate of development cooperation is realized in specific project allocations, thus underlining the principle of development for this important phase of ODA allocation. For both ACP and non-ACP countries, the orientation toward the goal of poverty reduction is given priority.[203] At the same time, the export of constitutional values such as democracy, human rights and the rule of law are proclaimed to be the goals of each ODA allocation. The principle of development is expressed in a political dimension, other (or perhaps only more explicitly) than in World Bank law.

The principle of cost-effectiveness and thus the principle of coherence and efficiency is also found in the EU's project aid rules, namely in the general conditions. Comparison with the law of the World Bank reveals an interesting difference: the EU's rules have only an *ex-post* effect, being limited to oversight of compliance while the contract is being performed. The World Bank's evaluation of economic efficiency takes place *ex ante*. This reflects a general feature of European development cooperation law.

European development cooperation law acknowledges the principle of individual autonomy in a somewhat ambivalent manner. From a procedural standpoint, there is no protection of the rights of individuals. Neither affected parties nor other third parties are given procedural participation rights. Their opinions, which may convey knowledge of local conditions and reveal potential difficulties, are not solicited. Nor is there a specific right to substantive *ex-ante* evaluation which might serve to incorporate specific human rights guarantees into the project, either directly or by protection of collective goods. On the other hand, the General Conditions, which apply to Financing Agreements and the general cooperation agreements, include a reference to the recipients' duty to respect and protect "human rights," and at the same time enable the EU to sanction violations. These clauses, however, are more geared toward oversight of the general human rights situation in a recipient state, than evaluation toward the human rights risks raised by a specific project. The General Conditions clauses are oriented mainly toward broad-scale and systemic human

[203] Art. 2 I DCI Regulation; Art. 1 Cotonou Agreement.

rights violations.[204] This impression is confirmed by the empirical use of these clauses. The European Parliament routinely inquires into compliance with the clauses, although its inquiries generally focus on political rights rather than economic, social or cultural ones.[205] Compliance with the clauses has up to now focused on the poorest states, with most questions arising in the context of military coups.[206] So the EU human rights clauses do not directly affect the implementation of specific development projects, and the EU pays generally only little attention to the human rights impact of EU-funded development projects. But, unlike the World Bank, the EU cannot convincingly argue that this is due to respect for the recipient countries' collective autonomy, since it generally demands respect for human rights, as the use of human rights clauses and conditionalities in external agreements clearly demonstrates. Yet, as with the World Bank, the EU is also required by its general obligations to ensure respect for human rights in specific situations. To achieve this, the proposal aired for the World Bank should be taken up here as well, namely a systematic human rights impact assessment which would rely on concrete standards, perhaps derived in part from the local legal regime.[207]

European development cooperation law contains only ambivalent protection of the principle of collective autonomy. From a procedural standpoint, ODA allocation is a bilateral process between the Commission and the recipient-state government in which the recipient is accorded the most important formal protection of autonomy (the right to make proposals and conclude contracts). Further specific guarantees, unusual in international law, are given to ACP countries, including a right of objection. As to substance, the executive organs on both sides have very broad discretion. There are no genuine criteria for *ex-ante* project evaluation, nor are there any specific duties to furnish information.

On the other hand, EU law provides for an extremely wide system of conditionality regarding project execution that applies *after* the contract has been signed. Instruments for *ex-post* compliance are oriented not only to the success of the project or the appropriate use of funds, but also

[204] However, they are not required of all states. Cooperation agreements with China and Turkey, for instance, do not contain such clauses. On this phenomenon see Bartels, *Human Rights Conditionality*, pp. 33–5.

[205] Ibid., p. 35.

[206] See in particular E. Riedel and M. Will, "Human Rights Clauses in External Agreements of the EC," in P. Alston (ed.), *The EU and Human Rights* (Oxford University Press, 1999), pp. 723–55 at pp. 739–42.

[207] See *supra* Ch 4.D.II.

(as discussed above) toward general political goals. If there are events in the recipient state which violate the constitutional principles of the EU (human rights, democracy and the rule of law), the EU has created contractual means of imposing sanctions.

In the final analysis, European development law has set out limits on the collective autonomy of recipient states which, although hardly fewer in number, are certainly more diffuse. Nevertheless, the EU does manage to avoid violating the principle of collective autonomy: formally, the principle of non-intervention is respected because the relevant issues are actually discussed in the aid agreements themselves and thus can no longer be designated "internal affairs." While the technocratic mandate of the World Bank and its character as a financial institution result in a project allocation law that is meant to be blind to political considerations, European project law is intentionally open to the political context.

III. The German legal regime

Project aid also plays a central role in German development cooperation.[208] This is attested by the comparatively detailed regulation of project assistance in German development cooperation law, which contrasts with the areas of programming and budget support.[209] In the guidelines for bilateral financial and technical cooperation, which contain the most important regulations, the project aid regulations resemble a mixture of the World Bank and EU models: on the one hand, German law sets out many requirements for the evaluation of the opportunities and risks of projects, which resembles the law of the World Bank. On the other hand, the procedural law is marked by respect for the sovereignty of the recipient state, which suggests parallels to EU law. In the following section, this first impression will be subjected to further analysis. As in the previous sections, German law will first be evaluated from the standpoint of knowledge generation and interest articulation (1). The focus will then turn to the criteria for substantive evaluation,

[208] There are no empirical data on the number of projects supported yearly or on the scope of the project assistance. The German budget plan is more general, and the data of groups that implement the projects (such as the GTZ or KfW) too specialized. According to OECD figures, program-based projects accounted for 34% of German ODA payments in 2007 (OECD, *2008 Survey*, p. 98). It is not clear, however, whether one can extrapolate from this to conclude that almost 70% of the funds were invested in project assistance.

[209] A few general comments on the legal regime can be found in Pellens, *Entwicklungshilfe Deutschlands*, pp. 141–9; Lengl, "Entwicklungspolitik," 432.

particularly in the form of *ex-ante* compliance (2). Finally, the form of action of project agreements will be analyzed (3). The final section will, as before, evaluate the results in light of the general principles of development cooperation law.

1. Procedural law

Allocation of an aid project by Germany begins with the federal government's decision in principle to support appropriate activities in a recipient state.[210] This approval is subject to the condition that suitable projects will be suggested and receive positive evaluations. The procedure consists of three phases: proposal and selection, planning and evaluation and, finally, the conclusion of a treaty under international law to carry out the project. The phases will be briefly sketched here with a focus, as before, on the procedural rights of the recipient regime and affected parties.

The procedure begins with selection from the proposed projects. Recipients must first propose projects.[211] Both the donor and recipient government should then, according to the text of the guidelines, begin a dialog to help flesh out details and then mutually decide whether a more intensive evaluation and planning of the projects is called for.[212] On the German side, the decision will be made by the Federal Ministry for Economic Cooperation and Development (BMZ), which will also solicit a so-called "brief statement" from more specialized development agencies (GIZ or KfW[213]). The statement will evaluate the project idea from the standpoint of development policy and technical criteria. Practitioners report that this step is the central hurdle that a proposal must clear.[214] The second step involves a comprehensive assessment of the project, which involves, among other considerations, the question of possible risk factors.[215] The evaluation is performed unilaterally by German implementation organizations who will request documents from the recipient state and usually send a mission there. The evaluation results in a recommendation to the BMZ.[216] If the BMZ follows the recommendation, the third phase is agreement on relevant measures, which generally means conclusion of a binding treaty under international law between the two

210 BMZ, *Guidelines*, no. 32. 211 Ibid., no. 37. 212 Ibid., no. 21.

213 On these organizations see *supra* Ch 3.A.II.1.

214 Ibid., no. 37; Pellens, *Entwicklungshilfe Deutschlands*, p. 143. According to this study, 30% of proposals fail during this stage, whereas a project that receives a positive appraisal is finally rejected only 1% of the time.

215 BMZ, *Guidelines*, nos. 39–41; nos. 54–7; no. 87. 216 Ibid., Art. 55; 57.

governments and, where relevant, third parties who are responsible for implementation.[217]

What is the relationship between the German government and the recipient state during this procedure – and are affected parties or third parties with interests in the outcome included? The relationship between the governments can be described as cooperative. The German government is required by various provisions to take recipients' priorities into account in their decision-making. Rules governing project selection are characteristic in this regard. At this stage, the recipient government must submit a proposal, which gives them the power of decision over the initiation of a project.[218] Then comes a bilateral decision on the selection from among the proposals. The exclusive prerogative of recipients when proposing projects, which was strictly observed out of deference to recipient-country autonomy in the early years of German development policy, has increasingly yielded to a mutual process of project identification.[219] During selection, the German side is required to support projects in such a way as to "provide the maximum space for the ownership, initiative, and responsibility of the cooperation partner."[220] This regulation is intended to balance the interests of recipients in non-interference with the donor's oversight, but it could also be seen merely as an attempt to obscure the German side's dominant position in the procedure.[221] The recipient government has less influence in the later procedural stages. The substantive evaluation in the second phase is largely the province of the German side. Procedural law affords little opportunity for mutual negotiation of the project contract.

Parties affected by the project do not play an important role in German development cooperation law. They should have a chance to participate[222] and their attitude toward the project should be incorporated into the substantive evaluation of the project proposals.[223] Nevertheless, the rules do not specify who should participate in which phase of planning, nor do they explain what influence the result of the participation should have on

[217] Ibid., nos. 32–6; no. 58. In case of a negative decision, the federal government will communicate the reasons to the partner administration (ibid., no. 41). On the details of the contracting process, see *infra* 3.

[218] Ibid., no. 37.

[219] An early version of this argument is found in Bodemer, *Entwicklungshilfe*, pp. 317–25.

[220] BMZ, *Guidelines*, no. 21 III.

[221] On the difficult balance between recipient ownership and donor's interests in German development cooperation see Meinecke, *Rechtsprojekte*, p. 51.

[222] BMZ, *Guidelines*, no. 22 V.

[223] Ibid., no. 38 II, 4th column.

the decision about the project. The broader public is also not accorded any further role. German law, unlike World Bank law, does not require planning documents to be made public, which would allow the general public to comment on proposals.

Overall, the procedures ensure the formal autonomy of the governments by giving them the right to propose projects and conclude contracts. The recipient government is also called upon for the purpose of providing information. The substantive evaluation of the projects, however, remains the responsibility of the German authorities. Affected parties, third parties and experts are mentioned infrequently in the procedural laws and are not given concrete rights. The collective autonomy of recipients is clearly privileged over the individual autonomy of the affected parties.

2. Substantive criteria

The German procedure is characterized by relatively in-depth evaluation of projects, although the substantive legal guidance of this process is not defined. World Bank law clearly defines development projects as potentially risk-prone investments or as a sort of venture capital investment whose evaluation serves not only to ensure project goals are met, but also that they are economically efficient. It also ensures that the protection of general interests is taken into account during the substantive evaluation of the project according to guidelines such as the safeguard policies. German law follows this example in principle, but does not make the relevant rules and standards transparent. In particular, there are no (published) provisions which specify the procedural rights and material standards relevant to the protection of particular legal interests and groups. Although there are internal guidelines covering these areas, they have not been made public.[224] In contrast to the EU, which contains almost no conditional criteria for the evaluation, instead leaving these matters for later negotiation, German law does at least set out certain broad criteria.[225]

This begins with the selection of proposals and the creation of the "brief statements." In this phase, the law provides that projects should be chosen according to the determinative criteria of effectiveness, sectoral and regional concentration and the potential for wider-ranging effects.[226] In the brief statements, the essential criteria are technical and financial,

[224] See Pellens, *Entwicklungshilfe Deutschlands*, pp. 145–6.

[225] An extensive description of the evaluation can be found in Lengl, "Entwicklungspolitik," 433–45.

[226] BMZ, *Guidelines*, no. 21 I.

as well as the project's impact from the point of view of development policy.[227] In this first phase, it is noteworthy how much weight is assigned to the idea of sustainability. Projects should only be approved when the implementing organization has the relevant qualifications to ensure the project is carried out and when it is clear that the project can be continued within the existing structures of the recipient state.[228] Projects should only be selected if they demonstrate long-term viability. There is also a comprehensive list of specific criteria for the "main evaluation" of the proposal.[229] This phase involves an evaluation of the overall economic situation of the cooperation partner, the need for the project, its technical implementation, and its effects on the economic, socio-cultural, gender-specific and ecological situation in the recipient state.

These rules, however, are vaguely formulated and their priority is not specified. The criteria do not, for example, explain whether ecological concerns should trump economic interests, what socio-cultural aspects of a project should be interpreted positively or negatively, or how macro- or microeconomic interests should be weighed against one another. Nor do they contain conditional criteria or precise indicators. The example of the World Bank shows that technical and ecological evaluation, in particular, can be regulated more precisely, or at least incorporate international law standards. Nor does German law follow a "proceduralization approach" which would counterbalance less precise criteria with the involvement of affected parties or experts. The various criteria do aim to ensure purpose fulfillment *ex ante*, but the projects are generally not subject to an *ex-post* substantive and legal evaluation.

3. Project agreements: multi-stage contractual systems without conditionalities

Ensuring that contractual goals are met can be achieved not only by *ex-ante* assessment but also by contractual clauses that come into play after the contract has been signed. It is thus necessary to consider the form and structure of the project agreements that govern ODA allocation. The German system which forms the contractual basis for ODA allocations can be distinguished from the two previous regimes in two ways. On the one hand, it is very complex: first, because it is in a period of transition at this point, and second, because it distinguishes between technical cooperation and financial cooperation (TC and FC). On the other hand, it also

[227] Ibid., no. 37. [228] Ibid., nos. 23/4. [229] Ibid., no. 38.

appears not to contain any forms of conditionality explicitly spelled out in law. The basic outline of the system will now be examined.[230]

The system in place since April 2009, which has since been supplemented but not replaced, distinguishes between the contractual bases of technical and financial cooperation. TC follows a three-step approach, while FC has two steps. The three-step contracting system in TC is composed of a framework agreement, an international law treaty and an implementation agreement.[231] The multi-year framework agreement between Germany and the recipient state lays down the basic rules and overall structure of cooperation, in particular the form and areas of cooperation, performance and contributions of both sides, and the rights and duties of the technical personnel who will perform the work.[232] These framework agreements are considered treaties that "regulate the political relations of the Federation" within the meaning of Art. 59(2) of the German Constitution, which means that their agreement must be negotiated with the agreement and coordination of the BMZ and the AA (the Foreign Office) according to §72 of the Common Rules of Order for Federal Ministries. After this step is completed, the governments then enter into an international agreement regulating the details of the specific project, either as a treaty or as an exchange of diplomatic notes.[233] The procedural regime described above in Section 1 governs the conclusion of this treaty. The details of implementation of the project are then agreed in the third step, which is an implementation agreement between the implementing organizations. This agreement is usually governed by German private law, not international law.[234]

In the case of financial cooperation, there is only a two-phase process which does not include a framework agreement. Instead, the German federal government declares in an international law agreement that it is prepared to support specific financial aid projects.[235] On this basis, the implementation organizations (usually the KfW) conclude specific agreements which are governed by German private law. These agreements are based on forms that are created in consultation with the federal government. The TC framework agreements and the international agreements on FC are published in the Federal Law Gazette II.[236]

[230] On the structure of project agreements in bilateral cooperation see also L. Gündling, "Foreign Aid Agreements," in R. Bernhardt, *Enclyclopedia of Public International Law* (Amsterdam, 1995), pp. 425–8 at pp. 425–8.

[231] See BMZ, *Guidelines*, nos. 34; 36.

[232] Ibid., no. 34; see also the Law on Development Aid. [233] Ibid., no. 33.

[234] Ibid., no. 33 V 4. [235] Ibid., no. 33. [236] Ibid., no. 35.

In 2009, a model contract for development cooperation was introduced which integrates both systems and is intended to speed up the process. The model contract envisions a two-step contracting system. In the future, the framework contract is to form the basis for the entire state development program and all ODA expenditures, both of TC and FC. This will eliminate the need for individual international law treaties. Under the new regime, measures can be approved by an intergovernmental understanding, which does not amount to a legal agreement. The second step is then the implementation contracts, which, as before, are subject to German private law. The new system is thus built on a framework contract, non-contractual consultations and private-law implementation contracts. The framework contract sets out rules pertaining to sovereignty, such as the tax-free status of delivered goods and services, protection for in-country experts and other state guarantees. Specific projects are mentioned in the intergovernmental consultations, then regulated by the private-law contracts signed by the implementation organizations.

The new system will not apply to all countries. It is primarily intended for recipient states in which the existing international agreements on projects had to be approved by the recipient state's legislature, a process that often involved extensive delay. The new framework contracts are motivated by the questionable intention of bypassing recipient-state legislatures.

What is the position in German development cooperation law with respect to general conditions, oversight rights and sanctions for breach of contract? It is quite surprising that these mechanisms for *ex-post* compliance (that is, conditions that are triggered in the event of non-performance under the contract) are regulated only in a partial and general manner. It appears that neither the former TC framework agreements nor the current general development cooperation framework agreement contains specific sanctioning instruments for contract breaches. Instead, it appears that the sanctioning regime will be included in the individual implementation agreements.[237] General conditions, such as those that govern such matters in the law of the World Bank and the EU, are not applied here, or at least have not been made public.

However, the Guidelines which the federal government applies to project agreements recommend "that specific performance goals or actions by the cooperation partner be recommended or agreed" (Section 25 of

[237] Art. 4 VIII Nr. 8 of the form contract for development cooperation specifies: "In the implementation agreements, binding rules will be agreed especially for ... No. 5 the consequences for breaches of contractual duties."

the Guidelines) "Agreed actions of the cooperation partner or performance goals (results)," the Guidelines continue, "should be in such a form that their fulfilment can be achieved or expected." The subject matter of the goals – in particular, whether they resemble the broad, constitutional goals of the EU or the narrower, project-specific approach of the World Bank – cannot be determined.

4. Summary

In sum, German development cooperation law on project lending offers only very general guidance which, although it does mention certain broad procedural and substantive key factors, affords executive actors broad discretion. The prerogative of executive discretion in development administration, already a feature of German development planning law, is subject only to modest limits. The analysis according to the four general principles of development cooperation law therefore leaves some questions unanswered.

The principle of development is touched on by the selection of projects. German development cooperation law, like its European counterpart, explicitly follows the broad understanding of development: in addition to the priority accorded to the goal of poverty reduction, which must be present in all project proposals, the goals of supporting democracy, human rights and the rule of law are also set out as criteria, albeit in very broad form.

The principle of coherence and efficiency, by contrast, is realized more concretely. Project effectiveness and financial solidity, as well as concentration on specific sectors, are all core ideas of the principle of coherence and efficiency and permeate the German law of development cooperation. Also noteworthy is the repeated emphasis on sustainability in the evaluation and structuring of projects. The principle thus appears to be realized in this context. Nevertheless, it is also clear that there are no specific oversight regulations or sanctions for non-observance, and that the criteria are, overall, relatively vague. This may be a sign of respect for recipients' autonomy.

The collective autonomy of the recipient state and of Germany is clearly the leading principle of the German regime of project lending. Procedural law reflects the formal equality between the German and the recipient government, especially in the requirement that projects be proposed by the recipient government and executed only after the conclusion of a bilateral contract. At the same time, German law imposes fewer (or simply less precise) *ex-ante* demands on the recipients. German agencies are required to undertake a comprehensive evaluation of the projects, but usually without general restrictions on recipients (especially in contrast with, for example, the World Bank). Nor does German law impose explicit *ex-post* conditionalities as does European law. The German government, of course, reserves the right to autonomous decisions on the use of its funds, but this appears to be balanced appropriately with the autonomy of the recipient state's government. The emphasis on collective autonomy which characterizes German law appears, however, to entail a corresponding burden on the principle of individual autonomy.

Although there can be no doubt about the general binding effect of human rights on German development administration, they are but weakly protected in specific project regimes. The first indication of this is the lack of any concrete procedural rules for the participation of affected parties or NGOs. German law affords them no formal participation rights. German law also does not require a focused evaluation of the human rights risks of a project. The duty to introduce a "human rights impact assessment" that would improve respect for (Germany's) human rights duties for each individual project arises from Germany's adherence to the respective treaties. Making the selection of particular countries dependent on the human rights situation there, as provided for under German law,[238] focuses merely on the general situation in a country, not on the potential impacts of particular projects. Despite general rhetoric, there is insufficient protection of human rights. Executive discretion and respect for recipients' collective autonomy must, in legal terms, be bounded by the human rights obligations which Germany has undertaken.

C Comparative summary

The negotiation and agreement of specific ODA transfers in the form of project aid is at the core of development cooperation law. This phase is not about setting preconditions but about making final decisions. Despite broad criticism and proposed alternatives (such as budget support or program-for-results financing), project aid is still quantitatively by far the most important instrument of modern development cooperation. How do the various legal regimes appear in comparative perspective? How do they deal with the functions and problems described at the beginning of this part, and how do they compare in light of the general principles of development cooperation law?

[238] See *supra* Ch 5.C.III.

As with programming, the comparative approach reveals not only a convergence of regulatory structures (which can be explained on functional grounds) but also specific differences explicable in terms of the previously described technocratic-autonomous and diplomatic-heteronomous models.[239] Each regime has developed detailed procedural and substantive provisions to govern this phase. This explains why project assistance is often regarded as a particularly labor-intensive instrument – in each donor's laws, there are many different allocation rules to obey.

This also demonstrates a further oft-remarked characteristic – namely that the law here is also mostly made by donors. Bilateral treaties, of course, are subject to the international law rules of the VCLT. However, all three donors have erected specific frameworks for these treaties by subjecting the contracting process to many procedural and evaluative norms that effectively impose a preliminary normative structure.

The three legal regimes will now be evaluated in light of the four principles of development cooperation law and in light of how well they fulfill the functions set out above.

I. The principle of development

The entire administrative law of development cooperation can be seen as an implementation of the principle of development. Nevertheless, the specific ODA allocation can be seen as a yet more specific instantiation of the principle, in that all three donors focus on the leading idea of development. They also confirm the priority of poverty reduction, which is today considered the primary goal of development cooperation and which has been important in securing the autonomy of development cooperation from other policy areas. The only difference between the various legal orders is how explicitly the goal of constitutional export is formulated in addition to other goals. European development cooperation law is particularly explicit on this point, while the World Bank does not mention it at all.

II. The principle of coherence and efficiency – and the problem of knowledge generation

The principle of coherence and efficiency attains greater importance in this phase, in particular with respect to the requirement of cost-effectiveness. Careful deployment of resources is a particular issue here, where

[239] See *supra* Ch 3.A.VI. and Ch 5.D.

decisions on specific allocations are made. The principle is linked to the empirical problem of knowledge generation, an important problem area in this phase we already touched upon earlier. An effective and sustainable project can be developed only with sufficient information about a plan and its risks, and when alternatives are considered and balanced against each other rationally. It is therefore hardly surprising to find that all three legal orders fundamentally address the problem of knowledge generation. Each provides for an evaluation phase in which proposals are analyzed. It is typical, and revealing, that each procedural regime makes recipients primarily responsible for furnishing information, whether in the context of the proposal or in later stages.

There are, however, clear differences between the legal regimes with respect to the thoroughness of the financial and technical evaluation of the projects. The differences are typical: particularly in World Bank law, projects are seen as a kind of venture capital which must be carefully evaluated and insured before it is made. This purpose is served by diverse procedural and substantive security regulations that take effect before the contract is signed. European development cooperation law, by contrast, provides for hardly any evaluations, limiting itself to oversight rules that take effect after the contract has been signed. Diplomatic harmony appears more important than technocratic risk-minimization. German law resembles World Bank law from a rhetorical standpoint, relying primarily on the idea of sustainability to ensure the efficiency of projects. Nevertheless, the provisions are formulated so vaguely that their steering effect can be questioned. The principle of cost-effectiveness, which is common to the budget law of all three regimes,[240] is spelled out in the most concrete detail in the World Bank's law.

III. *The principle of collective autonomy – and the instrument of conditionalities*

Safeguarding collective autonomy – that is, the right of each state to independently order its own affairs – is one of the most controversial points in development cooperation law, given the real-world power imbalance between donors and recipients. It is particularly relevant during the phase of specific ODA allocations, since this is where it is finally agreed which plans will be approved and how much funding will be provided. The autonomy of donors and recipients may be in tension here, although

[240] See *supra* Ch 4.E.I.1.

the particular situation in each of the legal orders differs in an intriguing fashion.

The formal and procedural equality of the contracting parties is emphasized in generally similar terms in all three legal orders. While recipients are responsible for proposing projects and determining their content, donors retain the right to decide on the approval of ODA resources. The spheres of influence are thus clearly marked. The procedural law governing negotiations is also generally cooperative in form. This is a contrast to the area of planning, in which unilateral elements are present in the law of the World Bank, Germany and the EU's law governing the cooperation with non-ACP states.

Clearer differences can be seen in the stronger substantive demands made with regard to projects, which are mainly framed by donors. This applies especially to the legal tool of conditionalities, a particularly important instrument in development cooperation law. The term "conditionality" refers to provisions which the donor attaches unilaterally – as a condition – to the disbursement of ODA funds, or which provide for sanctions in case of a violation. Conditionalities can be divided into *ex-ante* and *ex-post* forms. These are basically compliance instruments, which also appear in domestic public benefits or subsidy law.[241] The decisive point is that these regulations are formulated by donors, generally unilaterally, and their integration into the contract (and observance) is made a condition of ODA allocation. To the extent that donors generally use conditionalities to implement environmental, labor law or general human rights standards, they can be seen by recipients as constraints on their autonomy, especially since they are generally non-negotiable and often go well beyond the scope of the particular ODA project.

The three legal orders display clear differences in their use of conditionalities. The World Bank has a detailed regime of general rules that requires the technical (for example, environmental) evaluation of projects and must be accepted by all recipients as *ex-ante* conditionalities. European development law, by contrast, contains almost no *ex-ante* conditionalities but links the allocation of ODA to general and constitutional *ex-post* conditionalities relating to respect for democracy, human rights and the rule of law. As far as can be seen, German law contains no general legally defined conditionalities that must be agreed during the project approval process.

[241] For examples in subsidy law see Rodi, *Subventionsrechtsordnung*, p. 586.

Whether these conditionalities infringe recipients' autonomy can be decided only on a case-by-case basis. Certainly, the possibility cannot be excluded. Weaker recipients who depend on ODA may find themselves in a situation in which it is difficult for them to autonomously formulate their priorities. At the same time, the World Bank and the EU have ensured that adherence to their conditionalities is legally enforceable. The World Bank can refer to the principle of non-interference in political affairs, stressing that it does not intend to regulate sensitive matters which would be seen as internal affairs within the meaning of the principle of non-intervention. The EU formulates democracy, human rights and the rule of law as general contract goals and can demand compliance with them as normal contract fulfillment. Nevertheless, the problem of conflicting autonomy claims, which gives rise to these legal provisions, is per se insoluble, and thus persists in this field.

IV. Individual autonomy – and the duty to conduct a human rights impact assessment

Another area of tension in development law surrounds the fourth principle, the guarantee of individual autonomy. As seen above, all three donors are in principle bound by human rights obligations, although the exact degree and nature of the binding effect varies.[242] In contrast to the merely indirect effects decisions during the planning process might have, the concrete allocation of ODA can have a direct human rights impact, since specific projects may very well influence the lives of individuals. The implementation of human rights obligations in the law of all three donors is, however, weak. That this reflects a priority for collective over individual autonomy is only a part of the explanation.

The protection of human rights by securing the participation of individuals in the process of ODA allocation is implemented in the law of only the World Bank and even then, only in special cases such as involuntary resettlement or with regard to the rights of indigenous peoples. Even if a general "development-related right to participation" cannot (yet) be said to exist,[243] various rights do have procedural dimensions that are also binding on donors. Yet the World Bank largely declines to fulfill these duties, and the EU and Germany decline entirely.

[242] For more detail see *supra* Ch 4.D. [243] See *supra* Ch 4.D.III.2.

The substantive evaluation of and respect for the rights of individuals is also neglected in the procedures governing ODA allocation. Until now, none of the donors has fulfilled its obligations by integrating a systematic evaluation of human rights impacts into its ODA procedures. Ironically, it is the World Bank that has come in for renewed criticism for its (supposed) hostility to human rights, despite the fact that its laws best protect the substance of many rights by enacting safeguard policies that usually protect public goods such as the environment, forests and social infrastructure. Neither European nor German development cooperation law contains anything comparable.

Germany and the EU have chosen instead a general approach to protecting human rights. While Germany selects recipient countries based on their human rights situation,[244] the EU requires its ODA recipients to agree contractually to respect "human rights."[245] Neither approach requires the specific analysis of potential human rights impacts caused by individual projects funded by Germany or the EU. Instead, they operate based on the general human rights situation. This approach fails to do justice to their human rights obligations. Further, in the EU's case, the implementation of these provisions is not even monitored coherently.

In sum, the principle of individual autonomy, based on the human rights obligation of donors and also a legal principle of development cooperation law, has been inadequately implemented. This may be because human rights have only recently become an issue in the development arena and are only slowly taking their place in its institutional and legal structures. The weak implementation might also be explained by respect for recipient states' collective autonomy, which prevents donors from making stronger demands on recipients. However, this argument carries little weight with regard to Germany and the EU, since they have for a long time demanded a general respect for human rights. Further, one could always address the human rights duties of the recipient state during the evaluation more flexibly, and demand that they fulfill *their own* duties. This normative request is confirmed by the doctrinal analysis of a donor state's extraterritorial responsibility for certain human rights violations, which was based on the concept of complicity. Since, under international law, complicity requires that the recipient state violate international law, it means that the respective state must have ratified the relevant human rights treaty.[246] Therefore,

[244] See *supra* Ch 5.C.III. [245] See *supra* Ch 6.B.II.3. [246] See *supra* Ch 4.D.II.1.

the human rights obligation as doctrinally constructed on the basis of complicity also requires a "locally tailored" assessment.

What is the situation regarding the legal regime of the second major instrument of ODA, namely budget support? That will be the subject of the next chapter.

7

Transferring ODA through budget support

Budget support is the second main instrument of ODA allocation. It took its present form only recently, but has emerged as an important instrument in the last five to ten years.[1] Budget support follows a fundamentally different path from project aid – indeed, it is almost its opposite, and is intended to remedy its defects. Project aid is the funding of specific activities, while budget support is a subsidy to the general budget of the recipient state meant to support certain sectoral policies.[2] Direct budget subsidies, as budget support is also sometimes called,[3] are bound by two conditionalities: first, states must satisfy institutional and programmatic preconditions to qualify, and second, the phased disbursement of the funds is dependent on the satisfaction of certain performance indicators. The detailed review process attendant on project aid is administratively demanding. Project aid also has only an isolated effect, and usually bypasses recipient-state parliaments. Budget support, by contrast, promises to reduce transaction costs, achieve wider-ranging effects and strengthen political processes in the recipient country. At the same time, however, it shows how comprehensive and deep the cooperation between recipients and donors – as well has how strong donor influence – can be.

How can the budget support process be legally reconstructed? And how can individual regulations be judged against the principles of development cooperation law? A first empirical section will describe the emergence of budget support and clarify the terminology (A). The focus will then turn to the law of budget support (B). It will become clear that there

[1] According to the OECD, Germany has given between 5% and 10% of its ODA in the form of budget support since 2007. In the World Bank, almost 20% of the investments are in the form of budget support. In the 10th European Development Fund, an impressive 25% of funds are reserved for budget support. The signatories to the Paris Declaration, in Indicator 9, pledged themselves to invest 66% of their ODA in program-based activities (in which budget support always plays a significant role) by 2010.

[2] The distinction emerges most clearly in the English-language terminology of the World Bank, which distinguishes between project lending and policy lending.

[3] The terminology will be discussed further immediately below in A.

are comparatively few provisions governing budget support and that all three donors have similar rules. Accordingly, the subsequent examination will be structured somewhat differently from those in the foregoing chapters. The regulations of all three donors will be described and compared at the same time, rather than being compared after being described. The first section will inquire into the permissibility of budget support (B.I). The following analysis of the relevant procedural and substantive law will follow the double conditionality described above in that it will distinguish conditionality at the level of government (B.II) and on the grounds of performance (B.III). Finally, the legal form of budget support agreements will be examined (B.IV). As in the sections on project aid and programming, a concluding section will evaluate the laws against the background of the principles of development cooperation law (C).

A Background and function: from structural adjustment to budget support

Budget support, as such, is not a completely new ODA instrument. Rather, its present incarnation represents the second generation of this tool. General transfers as a method of development aid began in the 1980s with the so-called structural-adjustment measures of the World Bank.[4] The Bank had become convinced that macroeconomic problems frequently destroyed the effects of individual projects and thus of development efforts in general. To influence macroeconomic structures (and economic policy), the Bank began offering countries that were having trouble balancing their budgets rapid disbursements in the form of project-related loans – on condition that recipients, in return, enacted macroeconomic reforms (so-called structural-adjustment measures). These structural-adjustment measures soon became a routine instrument of the Bank, although they were only cautiously adopted by other ODA donors such as the EC and Germany.[5] These measures soon came under heavy fire for imposing a neoliberal agenda of privatization and liberalization that was frequently associated with considerable social disruption. In addition, doubts increased in the 1990s as to whether the measures were actually achieving their stated goals.[6]

[4] See *supra* Ch 2.A.11.

[5] The EC first introduced it in the 4th Lomé Convention, see Simmonds, "Fourth Lomé Convention," 537–40; on the context of this agreement see *supra*, Ch 2.A.IV.1.

[6] Doubts were aired prominently in Mosley, Harrigan and Toye, *Aid and Power*; Killick, *Aid and the Political Economy*; on the Washington Consensus and its decline see S. Maxwell, *The Washington Consensus Is Dead! Overseas Development Institute Working Paper No. 243*. Available at www.odi.org.uk/resources/docs/2476.pdf (last visited July 2013).

At the beginning of this century, the idea of budget support experienced a revival, driven by various factors.[7] First, the introduction of the PRSP created a new basis for budget support.[8] These recipient-formulated programs were intended to emphasize recipient ownership of development planning and to counter the accusation that structural-adjustment measures were intended only to push the donors' agendas. PRSPs appeared to be a credible basis for ODA allocations toward the general budget of a recipient state. At the same time, criticism of the effectiveness of the dominant project-based approach to development cooperation mounted. Within the framework of the discussion on aid effectiveness then taking shape, pressure increased to develop alternative instruments.[9] PRSPs and budget support appeared therefore to be appropriate methods to achieve better effectiveness and stronger coordination of donors' resources. A further – and quite surprising – aspect of budget support's rapid rise in popularity is the sudden increase in funds available to development cooperation since 2005.[10] The reform agenda, coupled with re-emerging attention to the problem of global poverty, led to immense increases in development aid budgets. Budget support is now generally considered to be faster, less bureaucratic and better tailored to recipients' needs. Thus, it promises to be an appropriate tool to implement the fundamental elements of the Paris Declaration and the aid-effectiveness agenda. Whether budget support can fulfill these hopes remains to be seen. The first empirical accounts of its effects are cautiously formulated, in particular because the effects of budget support are difficult to isolate and evaluate.[11]

In addition to these remarks on the background of budget help, some comments about terminology are in order: overall, it is quite disparate. The term describes various instruments that are referred to differently by the various organizations. In the German system, the preferred

[7] For a good introduction from a political-economy perspective, see S. Klingebiel, S. Leiderer and P. Schmidt, *Programme Financing and Public Budgets: New Instruments and Starting-Points of Development Policy*, Discussion Paper No. 3 (Bonn: German Development Institute, 2005).

[8] *Supra* Ch 5.B.

[9] On this general theme see *supra* Ch 2.C.III.1.

[10] See, for example, the numbers in OECD, *Development Co-operation Report 2009*, p. 152, Table 2.

[11] For a precise description see Riddell, *Does Foreign Aid*, pp. 198–202 with particular reference to S. Lister, *Evaluation of General Budget Support: Synthesis Report* (University of Birmingham, 2006); see also P. de Renzio, "Aid, Budgets and Accountability: A Survey Article," *Development Policy Review*, 24 (2006), 627–45 at 627.

description is generally "program-oriented community funding."[12] The definition of the term is "mutual support by multiple donors of the cooperation partner's nationally developed ... reform programs." Budget support describes one of two financing instruments which, from a substantive point of view, may relate to (multi-sector) macro-programs or sector-specific programs[13] and which are characterized, from a technical point of view, by the fact that donor funds flow directly into the recipient's budget, without specifying individual projects.[14] In 2004, the World Bank changed the description of the instrument – and delivered an example of the Bank's rather unwholesome rhetorical slipperiness. To distract from the negative image of structural-adjustment programs, the Bank simply renamed them as "development policy lending."[15] Only EC law explicitly calls it budget support (Art. 25 I (b) DCI), but reference is also made to "direct budgetary assistance" (Art. 61 Cotonou). For the purposes of this discussion it appears sensible to use the simplest term, budget support, which can also serve as a conceptual counterpart to project aid.

Finally, a note on the normative design of budget support. Overall, there are few regulations in this area. European development cooperation law, for instance, mentions budget support only in the two locations cited above.[16] German development cooperation law contains several provisions in the applicable administrative regulation.[17] There is also a concept paper from the BMZ which explains how Germany handles these programs and which paints a comparatively clear and public picture of it.[18] The law of the World Bank is particularly finely structured. There is an OP and a BP (8.60) which set out extensive and binding regulations not only for the substantive core of the activity (OP) but also for the allocation procedure for budget support.

What exactly do these regulations prescribe?

[12] BMZ, *Guidelines*, no. 8.

[13] So-called Sector Wide Approaches (SWAp).

[14] The other instrument for program-based community financing is the so-called basket financing, in which donors fund a precisely specified bundle of measures. A comprehensive description of the various measures can be found in BMZ, *Concept No. 146*, pp. 29–30, Appendix 1.

[15] See World Bank, OP/BP 8.60.

[16] Art. 25 I (b) DCI Regulation; Art. 61 Cotonou Agreement.

[17] BMZ, *Guidelines*, nos. 3; 8; 38; 68.

[18] BMZ, *Concept No. 146*.

B The legal regime of budget support

I. *On the legitimacy of budget support*

The introduction of budget support raises the initial question to what extent development agencies are permitted to subsidize not just individual projects, but rather the general budgets of developing nations.

The law of the World Bank gives a clear answer to this question. Its Articles prescribe that "except in special circumstances, [financing] shall be for specific projects."[19] The term "project" describes a temporally and financially limited activity.[20] General budget subsidies are, therefore, only permissible in exceptional cases. This regulation and its subsequent interpretation have a specific historical background and economic justification.[21] The authors of the Articles wanted to avoid contracts which would repeat the problems of the 1930s, when public funds were spent relatively carelessly – that is, without oversight of the success of the funded endeavors. In the Bank's early practice, the regulation was taken extremely seriously, because the Bank wished to demonstrate its credibility to its main funders, Wall Street.[22] Part of this credibility, it was thought, could be established by funding only limited projects with clearly defined financial and political risks.

Given this legal background, the Bank was required, when it first began regularly funding non-projects, to find a plausible interpretation of the "special circumstances" clause. In various legal opinions, Ibrahim Shihata argued that this regulation should be read in its entire context, and that its most important aspect was its orientation toward the goals of development.[23] Particularly when the economic and productive purpose

[19] Art. V, Sect. 1 (b) IDA Articles: "Financing provided by the Association ... except in special circumstances, shall be for specific projects." Art. III, Sect. 4 (vii) IBRD Articles contains a similar formulation: "Loans made or guaranteed by the Bank shall, except in special circumstances, be for the purpose of specific projects of reconstruction or development."

[20] Kapur, Lewis and Webb, *The World Bank*, p. 8; on the definition of "project" see also Shihata, *World Bank Legal Papers*, pp. 159; 173 (especially pp. 176–8); on the general background and especially interaction with the International Monetary Fund see C. Tan, "Regulation and Resource Dependency: The Legal and Political Aspects of Structural Adjustment Programmes," in Bradlow and Hunter, *International Financial Institutions*, pp. 168–78.

[21] Kapur, Lewis and Webb, *The World Bank*, pp. 7–8.

[22] On the general context see *supra* Ch 1.A.I.1. On the extraordinary political activity of the Bank beyond specific projects see ibid., p. 453.

[23] Shihata, *World Bank Legal Papers*, pp. 159–62; for more discussion of this interpretation see A. Rigo Sureda, "The World Bank and Institutional Innovation," in E. Brown

of a non-project-specific activity can be proven, the Articles of Agreement do not indicate that it is impermissible. Today, there is no doubt that the Bank may also engage in "non-project lending." Nevertheless, every budget support measure still requires proof of "special circumstances."[24] This form of support, therefore, is still seen as an exception. The fact that policy lending makes up a maximum of 20 percent of the Bank's lending is due to this fact. At the same time, the norm clarifies a specific understanding of the Bank's activity and its relationship to recipients. ODA is essentially a risk-prone enterprise that must be subjected to special oversight. Support for general policies instead of specific projects therefore requires a special justification. Given a choice between trusting recipients and exercising its own oversight, the Bank tends to choose the latter.

In the law of other donor organizations, the question of whether budget support is essentially permissible is not addressed. Neither German nor European law contains a norm that restricts ODA to project aid. The special circumstances clause in World Bank law expresses its narrow mandate, while the lack of such a clause in German and European development cooperation law gives those donors more discretion to trust recipients or to designate other factors as more relevant than the strict oversight of the (economic) success of projects.

II. Preconditions for agreement: governmental conditionality

If ODA is understood not as an investment in individual projects but rather as support for a certain sectoral or general policy, then donors' economic, social or development policy criteria for decision-making must logically change as well. The important factor is not the technical structure of a project, but rather the proposed policy – and its author, the recipient state's government. To put it bluntly, the advent of budget support has replaced the technical conditionality of project aid with a kind of "governmental conditionality." Instead of the project being the target of assessment, the focus is shifted to the government, its policy proposals and its budget system.

What is the legal structure of this governmental conditionality? The general preconditions for an agreement are not identical in the various

Weiss, A. Rigo Sureda and L. B. de Chazournes (eds.), *The World Bank, International Financial Institutions, and the Development of International Law: A symposium held in honor of Dr. Ibrahim F. I. Shihata* (Washington, DC: American Society of International Law, 1999), pp. 11–20 at pp. 17–18.

24 See OP 8.60, margin no. 8.

donor organizations, but there are three significant criteria which are common to all three. These preconditions will be addressed first (1). Then, the relevant procedural law will be analyzed (2).

1. Allocation criteria

Budget support will be granted when the recipient state's administration has presented a sectoral or macroeconomic program which is eligible for funding.[25] Only those administrations which demonstrate their commitment and ownership by presenting such a program will receive resources. This gives great importance to the PRSP, which was described above.[26] A fundamentally new aspect of ODA is the consequent direct linkage and complementarity of budget support to the PRSP. As became clear in the previous discussion, project aid also had to be in accordance with broader programs. Those programs themselves, however, were generally created by donor organizations.[27] In the budget support context, donor contributions are thus accessory to the PRSP in a much more direct fashion.

Nevertheless, donors do not "blindly" follow recipients' plans. The PRSP must not only be presented to the donors but also be approved by them. The EC, for instance, requires from ACP and non-ACP states that the proposed policy be "evaluated positively by the most important donors, including international financial institutions when necessary."[28] German law and World Bank law have similar requirements. Thus, although donors do not participate in the formulation, they do have the influence that comes from a right of veto.[29]

Budget support also requires that the public finances of the recipient country must, in the words of the relevant EU norm, be "transparent, reliable and efficient."[30] This provision relates primarily to the fiduciary risks

[25] World Bank, OP 8.60, margin no. 3; Art. 61 II (b) Cotonou Agreement, Art. 25 I (b) DCI Regulation; BMZ, *Guidelines*, no. 8.

[26] Schmidt, *Budgethilfe in der Entwicklungszusammenarbeit*, p. 68; see also BMZ, *Concept No. 146*, p. 30.

[27] *Supra* Ch 5.C.

[28] Art. 25 I (b) DCI Regulation; BMZ, *Guidelines*, no. 38, which specifies that the evaluation can be undertaken mutually or on a division-of-labor basis.

[29] At the same time, budget support must be determined at the phase of medium-term planning. This is specified, for instance, by the law of the World Bank, which sets precise conditions for the exceptional approval of budget support outside of the CAS, see OP 8.60, margin nos. 24–6.

[30] Art. 25 I (b) DCI Regulation, similar formulation in Art. 61 II (b) Cotonou Agreement; Ibid., margin no. 38 (Effectiveness and Transparency); OP 8.60 margin nos. 3; 19. The exact meaning is described in BMZ, *Concept No. 146*, pp. 11–13 and Schmidt, *Budgethilfe in der Entwicklungszusammenarbeit*, p. 88.

which follow from the fact that recipient countries must be trusted to use the funds in ways that serve the overall purpose of the aid. One requirement for this is an effective financial system capable of oversight in the recipient country. This requirement is, however, somewhat problematic in light of the significant capacity problems of recipient states. Almost all developing nations would be unable to meet excessively strict standards. This criterion leads donor states to exercise influence on recipients' financial systems, in particular when "technical" assistance induces donor states to prescribe (or write) the relevant laws or regulations.

Third, budget help is linked to explicit political preconditions, in particular an assessment of the recipient country's good governance (German regulations, in particular, stress this point).[31] According to the definition of the German Ministry of Development, budget support should only be provided to states which "handle political power and public resources in a responsible manner and one which fosters human rights."[32] In the meantime, more detailed definitions of good governance have emerged, and those responsible for assessment (in Germany) must orient themselves to these definitions.[33] The World Bank bases its decision on "an assessment of the country's policy and institutional framework – including the country's economic situation, governance, environmental/natural resource management, and poverty and social aspects."[34]

One particular characteristic of the organization of budget support is that it requires coordination of different donors. The coordination relates primarily to funding, but also to the assessment of the PRSP, carried out by donors either jointly or on a division-of-labor basis. German regulations particularly emphasize that budget support is a form of joint assistance.[35] Thus, the German federal government can, for instance, participate in the funding of World Bank macro-programs.[36] The German government in fact sees this as a special justification of budget support, since it may well increase the impact of German contributions.

To sum up, budget support can be seen as a macroeconomic policy that is (1) formulated and executed independently by recipient states which are

[31] BMZ, *Guidelines*, no. 38; see also OP 8.60, margin no. 3.

[32] BMZ, *Concept No. 146*, p. 15.

[33] Ibid., pp. 31–3, Annex 2; see also especially BMZ, *Concept No. 172*.

[34] OP 8.60, margin no. 3, p. 2. The substantive conditions for awards are even further detailed in World Bank law. The safeguard policies that principally guide the review of project aid (*supra* Ch 6.B.I.2) are not applicable in this context (OP 8.60 margin no. 2, p. 4). Instead, it is specified that the social and environmental impact of the aid be evaluated and compensation plans created when necessary (OP 8.60, margin nos. 10–11).

[35] BMZ, *Guidelines*, margin no. 8.

[36] BMZ, *Concept No. 146*, p. 29, Appendix 1.

(2) economically and politically trustworthy, and which have, in particular, (3) consolidated public finances.

2. The assessment and allocation procedure

How is compliance with the above conditions assessed? In the context of project assistance, it may be remembered, the procedural structures revealed important insights on the attitude of organizations toward recipient countries. The law of the World Bank aimed at a comprehensive risk assessment, while the European and German procedures more resembled diplomatic negotiations. The procedures for assessing budget support differ only minimally from those for project aid. In both European and German development cooperation law, budget support is only one specific form of payment with its own assessment criteria which is evaluated by the same agencies and the same procedures as project aid.[37] This assessment relates to the portion of the PRSP that is to be funded and can – as noted above – be done either jointly or on a division-of-labor basis.

Only the World Bank has enacted targeted procedural guidelines for budget support (BP 8.60, corresponding to OP 8.60). The procedure set out there is a simplified form of the project aid procedure. In this context as well, a World Bank team assists in formulating the program, develops a preliminary document which deals with structures, and then transfers the process to a more general assessment by various Bank departments – all before the beginning of official negotiations with the recipient government.[38] However, there is no extensive appraisal mission – that is, a trip by a Bank team to the recipient land for the purpose of extensive consultations and assessments. What is particularly clear is the increased responsibility placed on the recipient land for the development of the program. In contrast to project aid, which is governed by World Bank law, the recipient country's own constitutional and procedural law determines the structure of the process.[39] Typically for World Bank procedure, as with project aid, the principle of (largely) public documentation prevails.[40] World Bank law does, however, create various options for avoiding publication. Documents can be sequestered based either on the recipient country's

[37] On the relevant procedural rules see *supra* Ch 6.B.II.1., III.1. From a budget-law perspective, budget support in Germany requires individual approval by the Budget Committee of the German Bundestag, according to Kämpf and Würth, *Mehr Menschenrechte in die Entwicklungspolitik!*, p. 19.

[38] BP 8.60, margin nos. 1–6. [39] See OP 8.60, margin no. 6.

[40] OP 8.60 margin no. 29; BP 8.60 margin no. 11.

objection or at the Team Leader's discretion.[41] Although this is quite understandable in view of the political sensitivity of budget support, it does, however, undermine the principles of transparent administration.

Overall, the conditions that donors attach to budget support present a new measure of political conditionality. In contrast to the more focused field of project aid, general budget support is conditional not only on the technical justification for the project but also on the political trustworthiness of the recipient government. The increased trust demanded by transfers of ODA into a country's general budget must be justified *ex ante*. The disbursement stage is attended by yet another form of conditionality, which will now be addressed.

III. Preconditions for disbursement: performance conditionality

The instrument of budget support is marked not only by the careful selection of recipients but also by the continuous oversight of the implementation of the agreed policy. This oversight is a reaction to the fact that the problem of compliance and effectiveness, which is a central challenge of development cooperation law even in relatively simple projects, is even more pronounced in budget support. All three donors thus subject budget support to a contracting technique which ensures oversight of project implementation and reduces the risk which donors encounter in giving general subsidies to the recipient country.[42] The form of conditionality used in this context will be described as performance conditionality. It has three elements.

First, disbursement is linked to contractually agreed performance indicators which demonstrate the contract-compliant implementation and genuine effectiveness of the project. Budget support indicators should be chosen in such a way that they relate to the achievement of measurable results, particularly quantitative ones. There are three different forms of indicators: output, outcome and impact indicators. Output indicators measure the amount of goods or services (such as the number of schools built or teachers trained) created with ODA assistance, while outcome indicators measure the benefit that the goods or services have for the target group. Alternative formulations include results or performance indicators (for example, enrollment rates, percentage of girls among

[41] See BP 8.60, margin nos. 6–8.

[42] Like project aid, budget aid is governed by bilateral contracts. More on this *infra* Section IV.

the enrolled children). Impact indicators describe the intended effects or overall goals of an intervention, which are usually based on several outcomes (literacy rates, unemployment rates, etc.).[43] Performance indicators thus are intended to determine the effectiveness of programs on multiple levels. One important rule is that the performance indicators should, where possible, be derived from the recipient country's PRSP. Recipients thus set the standards by which they wish to be measured.[44]

Another characteristic of the performance conditionality of budget support is relevant, namely the agreement of multiple and *variable* tranches of assistance. For one thing, this means that budget support is not paid "all at once," but rather in stages. This gives donors the possibility of reacting to the fulfillment of indicators. It also means that the amount to be paid can be varied relative to the fulfillment of the indicators. This gives donors an even more finely calibrated tool for improved oversight.[45]

The third characteristic element of budget support is the requirement that donors and recipients remain in continuous dialog during implementation of the supported policies.[46] The focus of these discussions is not only on the implementation of specific programs but also on the general context within which the support takes place, the aim being to both entrench oversight of the indicators and to reduce its intrusiveness. Although donors retain the prerogative to judge fulfillment of the indicators, possible weaknesses or setbacks can be addressed and resolved in this dialog during implementation.[47]

This variant of performance conditionality reflects a generally new approach. Previous regulations envisioned primarily *ex-ante* conditions. This was particularly true of the structural-adjustment measures, the first

[43] For a detailed description, see Schmidt, *Budgethilfe in der Entwicklungszusammenarbeit*, p. 76; for an in-depth discussion of the choice of indicators, see European Commission, *Aid Delivery Methods: Guidelines on the Programming, Design and Implementation of General Budget Support* (2007), pp. 63–6. Available at http://ec.europa.eu/europeaid/what/economic-support/documents/guidelines_budget_support_en.pdf (last visited July 2013).

[44] However, this aspect is not set out in law, but rather in the respective implementation guidelines of each agency, see ibid., p. 64; BMZ, *Concept No. 146*, p. 23.

[45] OP 8.60, margin no. 14; Art. 25 I (b) DCI Regulation (more discussion in European Commission, *Aid Delivery Methods 2007*, p. 17); BMZ, *Guidelines*, margin nos. 8, 25 (more discussion in BMZ, *Concept No. 146*, p. 21 and Appendix 3).

[46] BP 8.60, margin no. 13; ibid., Appendix 3; in the EU, this subject is regulated by the general regulations concerning political dialog with ACP states, Art. 8 Cotonou Agreement.

[47] The actual execution of the performance evaluation, by contrast, is hardly regulated at all, the only provision being OP 8.60, margin no. 16. Some discussion of the subject can also be found in European Commission, *Aid Delivery Methods 2007*, pp. 80–2.

generation of budget support,[48] but was also true of substantive conditions, such as the Bank's safeguard policies. One advantage of the *ex-post* conditionalities linked to phased disbursement is in the improved likelihood of achievement of the agreed purpose during implementation.[49] The phased disbursement also makes it possible to pursue a more programmatic approach. It permits support of more complex programs whose elements take effect gradually and which can be made responsive to one another.[50] On the other hand, this method intensifies donor oversight on recipients. Donors obtain a more precise instrumentarium for evaluation. At the same time, they bind recipients to a more comprehensive system of cooperation, in particular as regards the dialog duty.

IV. Legal form, especially the letter of development policy

The legal form of budget support can be treated relatively briefly here, since it is generally agreed in the same legal form as project aid – that is, in bilateral agreements between donor organizations and recipient-country governments.[51] Nevertheless, two special characteristics should be noted.

The law of the World Bank has a special contractual instrument, the so-called "letter of development policy" (LDP) that accompanies the regular financing agreement on budget support.[52] This document reveals with particular clarity the ambivalence of budget support from the point of view of collective autonomy. The LDP is presented by the recipient country's government and summarizes the entire policy program. In particular, it lists the actions that the recipient state has promised to undertake, which may include the enactment of various legislation. Presentation of this separate document containing binding obligations is a precondition to the approval of budget support by the Bank's Board of Directors, as well as for the later disbursement of funds.[53] The LDP appears to be intended to avoid including language within the actual contract which would impose on the recipient state a duty to pass specific laws. Such language could

[48] See Schmidt, *Budgethilfe in der Entwicklungszusammenarbeit*, p. 74.
[49] If this is not proven to the donor's satisfaction, the donor can react quickly and effectively by not releasing the next tranche. German subsidy law contains a similar provision which is known as the so-called *ex-post* subsidy, see Rodi, *Subventionsrechtsordnung*, p. 576.
[50] On this logic, Martens, Mummert and Murrell, *Institutional Economics of Foreign Aid*, pp. 19, 34.
[51] See *supra* Ch 6.B.I.3 / II.3. / III.3.
[52] OP 8.60 margin no. 30; OP 7.0, margin no. 16; more discussion particularly in Tan, "Regulation," pp. 184–7.
[53] BP 8.60, margin nos. 6; 8; 10.

be interpreted as Bank interference in the recipient country's internal affairs – and thus as a violation of the Bank's mandate.[54]

German development cooperation law provides for a Memorandum of Understanding which accompanies the budget support agreement. The MoU binds the participants to mutually agreed goals. The MoU should require that "good governance, respect for human rights, and the obligation to combat poverty will be understood as the fundamental political basis of trust for budget support cooperation."[55] A material violation of these elements should lead to suspension of assistance.

Both LDPs and MoUs make clear that budget support intrudes into an area that is quite ambivalent from an international law perspective. They promise generous support for recipient nations' policies, but are simultaneously based on a new level of oversight and influence from the donor side, which goes to the very limit of infringing on recipient countries' autonomous decision-making power.

C Summary

Overall, the three legal regimes for budget support show considerable similarities. All three are based on the concept of double conditionality, which makes both conclusion of an agreement and disbursement of individual payments conditional on certain factors. The typological differentiation between the technocratic-autonomous regime of the World Bank and the more diplomatic-heteronomous regime of the EU, which was found with respect to project aid, does not hold here. Rather, the legal regime of budget support is marked by broad convergence among the donors. The Paris Declaration and the discourse on aid effectiveness, which were important factors shaping the legal regime of budget support, have had a clearly harmonizing effect.

How does this regime appear in light of the principles of development cooperation law?

I. Coherence and efficiency

The clear orientation of all legal regimes toward the principle of coherence and efficiency is noteworthy. The law of budget support serves this

[54] The problem was addressed in Shihata, *World Bank Legal Papers*, pp. 384–6 (although these comments were written before the letter of development policy was created). For a comparison with the letter of intent in IMF law see Guder, *Administration of Debt Relief*, pp. 150–4 and sources cited therein.

[55] BMZ, *Concept No. 146*, p. 20.

principle in three respects: result orientation, alignment with recipients and coordination.[56]

More so than with project aid, the law of budget support reacts to the problem of effectiveness and compliance; it attempts to implement the idea of result orientation. The law of budget supports sets up more concrete assessments of quantifiable performance indicators than that of project aid. They are made even more effective by the fact that payments can be made in installments. Further payments can thus be made dependent on the achievement of the desired results. The instrument of budget support also follows the principle of alignment in that recipients alone formulate the content of all programs. In contrast to the preparation process in project aid, which can at the most be called cooperative and which is also sometimes subject to a demanding assessment by donors, budget aid requires recipients to work out their own plans according to their respective domestic procedures. Finally, the rules for budget aid are, in the final analysis, more strongly oriented toward coordination between donors. The very basis of the idea of budget support is not a single project which can be agreed solely between a recipient and an individual donor, but rather support for recipient-state policies in which multiple donors may play a role. The rules also provide that donors will divide the labor of assessing the proposed policy, or even simply adopt the evaluations of other donors.[57]

Although the legal structure is closely bound to the principle of coherence and efficiency (and thus to the Paris Declaration), there are still certain problems. Formulating and evaluating performance indicators has proven extremely difficult in practice. The translation of social goals into quantifiable indicators is a problem, as is the collection of data in the first place. The apparent objectivity of the indicators can obscure the number of underlying problems as well as their complexity.

Coordination is also difficult. This begins with coordination of the donors' various time schedules, in particular with regard to dovetailing evaluation of results and donor budget legislation.[58] Furthermore, coordination is not a purely neutral process, since it involves reconciling the

[56] On the elements of this principle see *supra* Ch 4.E.

[57] Expressly stated in Art. 25 I (b) DCI Regulation; Art. 61 II Cotonou Agreement; BMZ, *Guidelines*, no. 8.

[58] Schmidt, *Budgethilfe in der Entwicklungszusammenarbeit*, p. 69; A. Beasley, D. Colin, J. Malick, A. Melnyk, M. Pitter-Lune and D. Ray, *General Budget Support: Key Findings of Five USAID Studies*, PPC Evaluation Paper No. 7. Available at http://pdf.usaid.gov/pdf_docs/PNADE110.pdf (last visited July 2013).

plans of autonomous donors. In practice, it often appears to entrench the dominance of the World Bank. The Bank offers budget support to which state-level donors contribute.[59] Even more importantly, the Bank decisively influences the formulation of the PRSP.[60] Since this document forms the programmatic framework for budget support, it can fundamentally shape policy. Finally, it is worth noting that the coordination of donor nations strengthens their influence on recipient countries. This concentration may make it more difficult for recipient countries to formulate positions that contradict those of donors. The conflict with the principle of donors' collective autonomy is evident.

II. Collective autonomy

The final judgment on the role of collective autonomy and ownership in the law of budget support must be a complex one. The instrument of budget aid aims at greater ownership. As shown above, the policy disburses ODA for macroeconomic policies which are to be shaped and implemented by recipient nations independently. These policy programs are generally described in national PRSPs. In principle, therefore, recipient countries can be said to make independent offers. Furthermore, performance indicators are also to be derived from the PRSP. This transfers considerable responsibility to recipient states: they define the criteria by which they want to be measured. In contrast to the safeguard policies or other donor-imposed criteria common to project aid, the budget support process strengthens the responsibility and therefore the autonomy of recipient countries.

At the same time, budget support gives donors oversight possibilities that limit recipient autonomy. The first is in the decision whether a recipient state will receive budget support at all. The range of factors that donors can take into account during this process is broader than in project aid. Of course, the decision to furnish project aid already implies a judgment on the recipient state's government. Budget support, however, is explicitly tied to the quality of governance of the recipient state. Political conditionality is, therefore, a critical element of budget support. Only those governments which satisfy donor conceptions of good governance are to receive budget support. Second, the requirement that PRSPs be approved

[59] This reference is, in particular, to the so-called Poverty Reduction Support Credits, to which Germany contributes (see BMZ, *Concept No. 146*, p. 29).

[60] See *supra* Ch 5.B.II.

by donors is in potential conflict with recipients' collective autonomy. Finally, the system of phased and performance-dependent disbursement is a further means of oversight. Overall, budget support is an ambivalent offer of assistance. Only those countries which orient themselves to the basic values of donors and achieve certain kinds of "performance" can then spend the resulting funds largely autonomously. The scope for autonomous decisions is considerably narrowed.

Furthermore, even this remaining margin of discretion is, in political practice, often misleading.[61] The assumption that PRSPs are completely endogenous and independently drafted programs created in a participative process is often questionable. On the one hand, donor influence – and in particular World Bank influence – on the PRSPs is considerable.[62] What is more, the PRSP can also provoke controversy within the recipient state, resulting in limited political will to follow its recommendation.[63] It has also been suggested that program and budget policies are in part merely a facade for donors, and that money is effectively distributed to different places and for different purposes than claimed.[64] To determine whether this is true, one would need effective and reliable evaluation of performance indicators, which could only be undertaken by competent recipient-state administrations. Finally, some commentators claim that the reliance on program-specific conditionalities is beside the point, since donors, in particular the World Bank, have developed a form of "post-conditionality": they have so many current and former employees working in the recipients' ministries and contributing to its policies that the policy development process can no longer be described as autonomous.[65]

Just as with project aid, the level of autonomy in budget support depends on the individual case and the "strength" of the recipient. The

[61] For a review of the critical literature on budget support, see Renzio, "Aid, Budgets and Accountability," 627.

[62] See *supra* Ch 5.B.II.

[63] T. Williamson, "General Budget Support and Public Financial Management Reform," in S. Koeberle, Z. Stavreski and J. Walliser (eds.), *Budget Support As More Effective Aid?* (Washington, DC: World Bank Publications, 2006), pp. 139–53 at p. 147; Renzio, "Aid, Budgets and Accountability," 631.

[64] T. Killick, *The Politics of Ghana's Budgetary System: Overseas Development Institute Policy Brief No. 2*, p. 4. Available at www.odi.org.uk/resources/docs/1963.pdf (last visited July 2013); T. Kelsall, "Shop Windows and Smoke-Filled Rooms: Governance and the Re-politicisation of Tanzania," *Journal of Modern African Studies*, 40 (2002), 597–617 at 605.

[65] Harrison, *World Bank and Africa*, p. 77.

case of Rwanda shows that recipients can indeed operate with considerable freedom. Nevertheless, there remain many areas in which the autonomy of recipients and donors may come into conflict.

III. Individual autonomy?

The principle of individual autonomy is only marginally relevant in the context of budget support. There is little evidence of an individual rights-based approach here, in particular toward donors. Budget support funds domestic programming (namely, the creation of a PRSP) in which donors are only marginally involved. Participation rights, therefore, must relate to this domestic process. To be sure, PRSPs are meant to be drafted in dialog with civil society and to strengthen domestic responsibility. Nevertheless, donors cannot guarantee these effects, nor can one demand that they do so.

However, human rights may be important to the award of budget support from the standpoint of objective law. The selection of countries to which budget support is provided can, for example, be made dependent on the human rights situation there. Moreover, the agreed programs can specify targets with human rights relevance (for example, school enrollment rates) or use them as performance indicators.[66] However, this method, as with human rights-based approaches,[67] is aimed more at directing recipient-state actions than at binding donor nations.

[66] The German Institute for Human Rights (Deutsches Institut für Menschenrechte) has also made similar arguments, see Kämpf and Würth, *Mehr Menschenrechte in die Entwicklungspolitik!*, p. 21.

[67] See *supra* Ch 4.D.I.

8

Transferring ODA through results-based financing

A Background and function: the World Bank's program-for-results financing

In 2012, the World Bank created a third instrument for ODA funding, called the program-for-results financing.[1] The instrument is as much a result of changing demands from the recipients' side as of changing priorities in development policy, expressed especially in the Paris Declaration and its aid effectiveness agenda. As such, it might become a role model for other donor agencies. So far, however, the other donors examined here (EU and Germany) do not have a comparable instrument, so the focus here will be entirely on the World Bank's instrument.

The new instrument will complement the two established mechanisms, analyzed and described above: project aid and budget support. While project aid finances concrete projects with transactions for specific expenditures,[2] and budget support provides funding for policy and institutional reform by paying into a borrower's general budget,[3] the new program-for-results funding sets out on a new path. It provides funding for concrete programs that a recipient has developed but links the disbursement of funds to the achievement of concrete results. Very much in line with the Paris Declaration, it thus aims to strengthen country ownership while shifting the focus from input to results.

The rationale for the introduction of this new instrument becomes clearer against the background of recent trends in the development system and certain Bank objectives.[4] For one, there is a greater demand for

[1] For a detailed description of the new instrument and its creation see World Bank, *A New Instrument to Advance Development Effectiveness, Operations and Country Services*, December 2011, Washington DC [hereinafter World Bank, *New Instrument*]. See also http://web.worldbank.org/WBSITE/EXTERNAL/PROJECTS/EXTRESLENDING/0,contentMDK:22748955~pagePK:7321740~piPK:7514729~theSitePK:7514726,00.html (last visited September 2012).

[2] In detail see *supra*, Ch 6.A and B.I.

[3] In detail see *supra*, Ch 7.A.

[4] On current trends in development systems, see *supra* Ch 2.C.III.

country-driven programs. Larger recipient countries with comparatively stronger capacities increasingly design and implement their own programs, for which they seek supplementary financing and, in particular, technical expertise. The new instrument allows the Bank to co-finance such larger government programs, and provides a good framework for the technical advice and capacity building that the Bank can provide well. In meeting the demands for a different kind of assistance, namely program financing, the Bank seeks to remain a relevant provider of technical and financial assistance in a changing aid landscape.

The new instrument is also, second, a reaction to the demand for less intrusion from the recipient's side. As has been seen, the Bank has comparatively stringent lending conditions, especially those laid down in the safeguarding policies.[5] Given the stronger competition from other funding agents (private banks as well as new donors, such as China), the Bank is clearly under pressure to offer a less demanding and "more flexible" instrument.

But the impetus for program-for-results financing comes as much from donors themselves. As has been described in many places in this study and manifested most prominently in the Paris Declaration, development policy debate in the 2000s has been dominated by a strong demand for a better account and more effective use of the funds invested.[6] A third rationale behind the new instrument is thus the increased demand for aid effectiveness, in particular greater accountability and a focus on results.

Last but not least, the Bank is also interested in increasing the leverage of its technical and financial support. Program-for-results financing is supposed to be a co-financing instrument under which at least 50 percent of the program has to be financed by the recipient. Bank funds can hence trigger other sources, too, and the Bank can more easily team up with partners through pooling resources. Through the co-financing of larger government programs, the Bank's technical assistance, as well as some of its standards in terms of environmental and social impact, fiduciary management and transparency will extend to the country systems involved in the program at large.[7]

I. *The making of the new instrument*

The instrument was developed in the context of a larger reform of the Bank's lending instruments, and is the product of an increasingly public

[5] See *supra*, Ch 6.B.I.2. [6] See *supra*, Ch 2.C.III; Ch 4.E; Ch 7.A.
[7] World Bank, *New Instrument*, paras. 20–21.

and participatory policy-making procedure.[8] The idea and first proposal for the new instrument, voiced in March 2010, stems from the Bank management, and hence not from the member states represented in the Executive Board. It grew out of the discussion on reforming the central instrument of Bank lending, the project or investment lending, in order to offer less stringent or more flexible, rapid and customized assistance to recipient countries. After the green light from the Board's Committee on Development Effectiveness for a draft concept note in October, the revised note from February 2011 served as a basis for broad and public consultations.

Consultations took place in two stages. First, from March to June 2011, consultations within the Bank and around the globe were organized with a broad variety of actors, including governments, other funding agencies, parliamentarians, civil-society organizations and think tanks. The input from these consultations was reflected in a first policy paper, which was then – in the second phase – put on the web and opened for public comment, including on social networks such as Facebook.[9] During the consultations, participants discussed the rationale for a new instrument and its relation with the available instruments of project and budget aid in general, as well as the specific design and process of program-for-results financing, particularly the definition and measurement of results and the design of disbursement-linked indicators. Concerns with the instrument centered on the maintenance of the Bank's environmental, social and fiduciary standards with regard to the supported government programs.[10]

The new financing instrument was formally adopted by the Executive Directors on January 24, 2012, with the corresponding Operational Policy and Bank Procedures OP/BP 9.00 entering into force in February 2012. To mitigate anticipated risks involved in the introduction of a new financing instrument without broad, prior piloting, it was agreed to commit only a maximum of 5 percent of IDA or IBRD funding in the form of program-for-results for the first two years. After that, management will review the implementation of the policy, publish a progress report and engage in discussions with the Executive Directors. The Bank's Independent

[8] On this process see World Bank, *New Instrument*, paras. 2–4; generally on policy-development in the Bank, see *supra* Ch 3.A.II.2.

[9] On the consultations especially, see World Bank, *New Instrument*, Annex A.

[10] World Bank, *New Instrument*, Annex A, paras. 6–12. Comments on the Bank's proposed new instrument were also collected by a number of NGOs on a website "Civil Society Comments and Concerns" (http://p4rcomments.org/).

Evaluation Group is invited to furnish additional, independent input to feed into the ongoing improvements to the instrument.[11]

B The legal regime of program-for-results financing

I. Legal framework

The design and process of program-for-results financing is laid out in the internal law of the Bank. The creation of a formal basis for the new financing instrument is in line with the increasing legalization of the Bank's activities, which is primarily driven by the adoption of binding internal laws, the Operational Policies (OPs) and Bank Procedures (BPs).[12] The legal framework (the Bank calls it the "operational framework"[13]) is briefly described and has four elements.

The instrument is laid out, first of all, in OP/BP 9.00, hence in the form of the two standard instruments that regulate the activities of the Bank and its staff (like project aid is regulated in OP/BP 10.00 and budget support in OP/BP 8.60).[14] While the OP sets out the general idea and basic tenets of the new instrument, including eligibility criteria and the respective responsibilities of the borrower and the Bank, the BP regulates in more detail the process of how program-for-results financing is assessed and agreed upon.

The introduction of the new instrument also has effects on already-existing Bank laws, such as the General Conditions for Loans, Credits and Grants, and a number of other OPs.[15] All of these were changed in the process of introducing the new instrument.

More noteworthy is the third element of the legal framework, the Anti-Corruption Guideline, which the Bank adopted along with the OP/BP for the new instrument.[16] Partly in reaction to concerns voiced during consultations, apparently, the Bank specified rules to react to cases of fraud or corruption in connection with program-for-results financing. The new instrument envisages the use of country systems and reliance on municipal law for the implementation of programs, which are larger government programs that the Bank only contributes to. These are more difficult to

[11] World Bank, *New Instrument*, paras. 111 and 116 and Annex I on the Initial Implementation Review.

[12] See above Ch 3.A.II.2 [13] World Bank, *New Instrument*, paras. 82–87.

[14] On these two instruments, see *supra* Ch 6.B.I, Ch 7.B.I.

[15] Amendments to the General Conditions are reproduced in Annex F of the policy paper World Bank, *New Instrument*, changes to OPs/BPs and Operational Memoranda in Annex H. Most of these changes are self-explanatory or concern language.

[16] "Guidelines on Preventing and Combating Fraud and Corruption in Program-for-Results Financing," February 1, 2012 [hereinafter Guidelines].

monitor than specific projects. The Bank thus cedes considerable control over the use of its resources to the recipient, raising concerns over an increased risk of corruption and fraud.

The legal nature of this "Guideline" is not as apparent as that of the OP/BP. It would be clearer if the rules were themselves put down in an OP; also not helpful is that the Guideline obliges all actors involved to the "highest standards of ethics," instead of law.[17] However, given that the Guidelines were approved in connection with and in the same manner as the OP/BP, that is, by the Board, and that such rules are demanded by the productive-purposes requirement of the Articles of Agreement, and given that they are becoming part of the Loan Agreement itself (just like the General Conditions), it is not to be doubted that they are also legally binding.[18] Since OP and BP 9.00 also refer to the Guidelines,[19] their observation can also be controlled by the Inspection Panel.

A final element has to be mentioned, and that is the compatibility of the new policies with the Articles of Agreement, i.e. the "constitution" of the Bank. It is interesting that the policy paper accompanying the introduction of the new instrument mentions this point only very briefly.[20] Given the intense debate about the legality of structural adjustment, now development policy lending,[21] this compatibility is certainly not a matter of course. According to Art. V, Sect. 1 (b) IDA Articles, financing by IDA shall be for specific projects, except in "special circumstances." It is at least not obvious how the programs that might be funded comply with this requirement, unless the financing instrument relies on "special circumstances," which was not argued. The Bank apparently understood that the approval of the new instrument by the Executive Directors, who are authorized to interpret the Articles, would imply its conformity with the Articles of Agreement.

II. Substantive requirements for funding

Program-for-results financing can be granted as loans, credits or grants. The programs financed can be "national, subnational, multisectoral,

[17] Guidelines, para. 2.

[18] This is in line with the Bank's own understanding that "borrowers will have to comply with new binding Anti-Corruption Guidelines." World Bank, *Program-for-Results Financing: Addressing Fraud and Corruption in the Proposed Program-for-Results Instrument*, November 2011. Available at http://siteresources.worldbank.org/EXTRESLENDING/Resources/7514725-1316733277569/OnepagerfraudandcorruptionOct24.pdf (last visited September 2012).

[19] OP 9.00, para.5 and note 3. BP 9.00, para. 39, 42.

[20] World Bank, *New Instrument*, para. 82. [21] See *supra*, Ch 7.B.I.

sectoral, or sub-sectoral in scope; part of broader, longer-term, or geographically larger programs; and/or carried out by governmental and/or nongovernmental parties."[22]

However, there are a number of requirements that have to be met. Among them, three stand out. First of all, they have to be programs by the recipient itself and use the recipient country's financial, fiduciary and procurement systems, as well as its environmental, social and other laws.[23] Thus, it is not World Bank rules that apply, rather the program relies on and strengthens the country's own legal and institutional structure. Second, program-for-results funding is only co-financing. A minimum of 50 percent of the program has to be financed by the recipient itself, thus making sure that the recipient has a high stake in the program.[24] Both of these requirements aim at fostering ownership and alignment as key principles of the Paris Declaration.

The third and most prominent requirement is also very much in line with the Paris Principles. The disbursement of Bank funds will only take place upon achievement of results that are verified on the basis of so-called disbursement-linked indicators (DLI).[25] Disbursement of Bank funds is triggered not by certain expenditures as it used to be, but by proving the achievement of these results.[26]

The DLI are formulated by the recipient and are assessed by the Bank.[27] Since they play such a central role in verifying the achievement of results and form the basis of disbursements, indicators must be "specific, measurable, and verifiable," while also properly adapted to the circumstances of the program and the implementing government.[28] For each indicator defined for a program, the Bank requires a credible indicator verification protocol, establishing how the indicator will be measured and who is responsible for verifying its achievement.[29]

Apart from these requirements specific to the new instrument, as for all other Bank-financed operations, material conditions for the financing

[22] OP 9.00, para. 2. [23] OP 9.00, para. 2 a) and c).
[24] OP 9.00, para. 3. [25] OP 9.00, para. 2 b), 4.
[26] Disbursement can also be scalable, that is proportional to the progress made in achieving a DLI. In some circumstances, the Bank may allow for necessary advance disbursements for DLI that have not yet been achieved. OP 9.00, BP 9.00 paras. 14–16. See also World Bank, *New Instrument*, paras. 57 and 59.
[27] BP 9.00, para. 22 in connection with paras. 9 and 10.
[28] BP 9.00, paras. 13 and 34 and note 10. World Bank, *New Instrument*, paras. 54, 55.
[29] OP 9.00 para. 11. The Bank only requires that a credible mechanism for monitoring the achievements of results is in place, without prescribing by whom and how verification has to take place. BP 9.00, para. 12 and note 9 and World Bank, *New Instrument*, para. 56.

of government programs include standards of economy and efficiency, and fiduciary, environmental and social standards. The requirements on the environmental and social quality of the co-financed government program have attracted special attention. The traditional project aid by the Bank is linked to rather stringent safeguard policies that the recipient has to respect.[30] Upholding these standards was a contentious issue during the consultations on the new instrument.[31] The final version of OP 9.00 is a sort of compromise.

On the one hand, the safeguard policies do not apply to program-for-results funding.[32] Even though the Bank assesses environmental and social issues before agreeing to fund, it is not bound by the provisions contained in the safeguard policies applicable to project aid. OP 9.00 instead formulates its own standards for assessing environmental and social systems, drawing on the core principles of the safeguards. These standards are, however, much less detailed, and they are assessed only to the extent that they are "applicable or relevant in a particular country, sector, or Program circumstances."[33] On the other hand, the Bank has excluded programs from program-for-results funding that might "have significant adverse impacts that are sensitive, diverse, or unprecedented on the environment and/or affected people."[34] These most sensitive so-called category-A projects thus cannot be financed.[35] Moreover, it may be argued that while the principles adapted from the safeguards for program-for-results financing may go less deep, they have a potentially greater leverage. Program financing is ultimately aimed at strengthening recipients' systems where they fall behind the Bank's standard through targeted activities and implementation support that involve the entire

[30] See *supra*, Ch 6.B.I.2.

[31] See Policy Paper, Annex A: Summary of Consultations, paras. 6, 9. *The Guardian*'s popular Poverty Matters Blog drew attention to the concern among many NGOs that the new instrument would enable countries to circumvent the Bank's strict social and environmental standards, since the existing safeguard policies would be abolished or largely diluted (www.guardian.co.uk/global-development/poverty-matters/2011/oct/21/ngos-criticise-world-bank-lending).

[32] OP 9.00, para. 8; also World Bank, *New Instrument*, para. 45.

[33] OP 9.00, para. 8. The principles established in OP 9.00 are further detailed in the Bank Procedures, see BP 9.00, paras. 28–31.The Bank has argued that "[t]he requirements for the assessment of environmental and social systems are guided in purpose and goals by the environmental and social safeguard policies of Investment Lending projects, adapted to the needs of the Program-for-Results instrument." See World Bank, *New Instrument*, Annex I, Table A1.

[34] OP 9.00, para. 9; BP 9.00, para. 5. Also, World Bank, *New Instrument*, paras. 44–48.

[35] On these categories, see OP 4.01 (environmental assessment), para. 8.

government program. With its ultimate aim of strengthening the capacity of recipient systems, program-for-results financing could be seen as a more sustainable way of ensuring environmental and social standards are upheld.[36]

Less in the public debate but very much at the center of attention for the Bank management was also how the new instrument would deal with questions regarding the fiduciary risks involved. The Bank's OP on Financial Management and its detailed Procurement Guidelines do not apply to program-for-results operations, which instead use the recipient's own standards and procedures. In line with the productive-purposes requirement of its mandate, however, the Bank conducts upfront assessments of a country's financial management and procurement systems, to ensure that they provide for "the appropriate use of Program funds and safeguarding of its assets."[37] As is the case with assessments of the environmental and social systems, where the Bank identifies shortcomings, these can also be addressed during program implementation, through actions aimed at enhancing the recipient's systems.[38]

A central element of ensuring the responsible use of funds is the already-mentioned "Guidelines on Preventing and Combating Fraud and Corruption in Program-for-Results Financing." The Guidelines define the practices that are considered to constitute fraud and corruption, including "collusive," "coercive," or "obstructive" practices in this context.[39] The borrower is not only required to "take all appropriate measures" to prohibit and prevent fraud and corruption, but also to inform the Bank promptly should any substantial allegations arise, to investigate such allegations in cooperating fully with the Bank's staff, and to remedy the situation in a manner satisfactory to the Bank.[40] Further, the Bank maintains the right to conduct investigations of allegations that come to its own attention, also independently of the borrower, and is required only to inform the borrower of the outcome of such investigations.[41] If the Bank (unilaterally) determines that any individual or entity other than a member

[36] OP 9.00 paras. 1 lit. c) and 12; BP 9.00 para 30, which foresees that the Bank will identify the aspects of a country's environmental and social systems that require strengthening, which can then become part of the program's action plan and will be taken on during preparation and implementation of the program.

[37] OP 9.00, para. 7. Also World Bank, *New Instrument*, paras. 38–43.

[38] OP 9.00 para. 1 lit. c) and BP 9.00, para. 27.

[39] Guidelines, para. 4. The five practices listed are referred to collectively in the Guidelines as fraud and corruption (para. 5).

[40] Guidelines, para. 6; BP 9.00, para 40.

[41] Guidelines, para. 7; BP 9.00 paras. 39–40.

country (that is, a national government official or non-autonomous state enterprise) has been responsible for fraud or corruption, it can impose sanctions, including by publicly declaring its ineligibility to benefit from or participate in any Bank-financed project or program.[42] Notably, the Bank's right to investigate and sanction corrupt or fraudulent practices extends to the whole government program, although the Bank finances only parts of it. Together with stringent *ex-ante* assessments also foreseen in OP/BP 9.00,[43] the extensive rights of the Bank to monitor, investigate and sanction in the context of its program-for-results financing aim to uphold the Bank's standards of transparency and accountability.

A final requirement of the program-for-results financing should be mentioned which underlines a central observation of this study:[44] every program has to be in line with the CAS that the Bank has developed on the basis of a Poverty Reduction Strategy Paper (PRSP).[45] With regard to program-for-results financing, the CAS thus maintains its condition-setting or referential nature – it provides the framework to which all instruments and operations must be accessory.

Compared to project lending and budget assistance, the material requirements for program-for-results financing thus appear less predetermined. The Bank seeks to ensure that fiduciary, environmental and social standards are respected also by the recipient's own systems. Rather than formulating detailed and absolute standards, however, the Bank uses an approach based on principles. If a country's systems do not fully meet the Bank's standards, the program is not necessarily excluded from financing. Rather, in line with the new instrument's key objective of capacity building, the achievement of some of the material requirements outlined in OP/BP 9.00 becomes the aim of Bank assistance rather than a precondition.[46] This aspect becomes clearer with regard to the procedure, to which we will turn now.

III. Procedure

Program-for-results financing is driven by the idea of strengthening recipient ownership. One could therefore expect that the procedural rules

[42] Guidelines, para. 7; BP 9.00 para. 41. Sanctions may include temporary suspensions and debarment, that is declaring the ineligibility of an entity to be awarded a World Bank-financed contract.

[43] In particular, BP 9.00 para. 26, referring to the Guidelines in assessing the risk of fraud and corruption in a proposed program.

[44] See *supra*, Ch 5.C.I.3 and II.3 as well as Ch 6.B.II.1

[45] BP 9.00, paras. 4 lit. a) and 20 lit. b).

[46] I am grateful to Marie von Engelhardt for pointing out this element to me.

on how program-for-results financing is agreed upon are less scrupulous than in project financing. While the procedures laid down in BP 9.00 do allow for more flexibility than investment lending in its current form, they are certainly very detailed and thereby comparable to project financing.

The procedure involves four main steps: the proposal of the program by the borrower and preliminary assessment of the Bank, a comprehensive program assessment and appraisal by the Bank, the negotiation of the agreement and approval by the Bank – and finally, implementation support. Just a few remarks on these steps.

First, all instruments of Bank financing rest on a proposal by the recipient. In this sense, program-for-results is not really different. Since the new instrument is one where the Bank only co-finances a government-owned program, which may also be an existing program and one that is financed by other partners besides the Bank,[47] the Bank's role in shaping the objectives and design of a program appears to be limited at first. The provisions of BP 9.00, however, suggest otherwise. The Bank's role in "identifying" and "defining" the program to be financed appears very strong – and one could imagine the Bank taking a fairly proactive role in practice.[48]

At an early stage, the Bank forms a task team responsible for the preliminary assessment of a proposed program in consultation with the borrower. At this stage, assessments concern the program's relation to the CAS, economic aspects, and whether program systems are "broadly adequate" in terms of fiduciary, environmental, social and also governance standards.[49] The assessment of program systems concerns all institutions that are tasked with program implementation, for which the Bank considers the relevant rules and procedures, but also their past implementation performance.[50] New in comparison to project lending is the assessment of program systems at this stage according to general "good governance principles," namely "transparency, integrity, accountability and effectiveness."[51] Apart from the borrower, the Bank must also coordinate with partners and other parties that finance or are involved in the

[47] For this reason BP 9.00 foresees that the "Bank coordinates its preparatory work with development partners and other parties that may co-finance the Program or be otherwise involved in Program-related activities" (para. 6).

[48] BP 9.00, paras. 3 and 4.

[49] BP 9.00 para. 4 lit. e). If a program is seen to have "significant adverse impacts" on the environment or affected people, or if it involves the procurement of goods or services under "high-value contracts," both of which are ineligible for financing and must be excluded from the proposed program at this stage. BP 9.00 para. 5 in accordance with OP 9.00 para. 9.

[50] BP 9.00 para. 4 lit. e) note 4.

[51] BP 9.00 para. 4 lit. e) note 5.

program.[52] The first phase ends with a Concept Review, where it is decided whether the preparation of the operation should continue.[53]

Second, the Bank's assessment and appraisal of the identified program constitutes the central phase of the procedure. The Bank conducts its assessments on the basis of the standards established in OP 9.00 and spelled out in the Bank Procedures.[54] They consist of a technical assessment concerning the strategic relevance and economic soundness of a program, in particular the proposed results framework and DLI, a more comprehensive assessment of fiduciary, environmental and social systems, and an ongoing, integrated risk assessment in parallel. As is the case with regard to projects under the procedures for investment lending, assessments concern the program prepared by the borrower and are the principal responsibility of the Bank; where environmental and social aspects are concerned, it has to consult with "Program stakeholders," which may be any entity involved in the program.[55] The borrower might be under the obligation to include indigenous people, if affected.[56]

Notably, the results of the Bank's fiduciary, environmental and social assessments are seen to "provide a reference," a benchmark for monitoring performance during the program's implementation, but also as a basis to identify activities necessary to strengthen the relevant national capacities and arrangements.[57] The assessments are thus not only *ex-ante* procedural requirements for financing, but translate into an action plan for implementation.

Following the assessments and before a final appraisal, management reviews all relevant aspects of the proposed program's design.[58] The necessary documentation is then prepared for negotiations between the borrower and the Bank, including the design parameters of the program, the main legal terms and conditions, the assessment results and proposed program activities, and particularly the results framework and the DLI verification protocols.[59] The indicators and verification protocols that

52 BP 9.00, para. 6. 53 BP 9.00, paras. 7 and 8.

54 OP 9.00 paras. 6, 7, 8 and 10 and BP 9.00 para. 9, referring to paras. 19–32.

55 OP 9.00 paras. 11 and 12 on the roles and responsibilties of the borrower and the Bank. See also World Bank, *New Instrument*, paras. 90–91 on partners and stakeholders.

56 BP 9.00 para 29 lit. j).

57 BP 9.00 paras. 27 and 30. According to the Policy Paper World Bank, *New Instrument*, as part of implementation support, the Bank provides technical assistance for capacity- and institution-building in a broad range of areas, including fiduciary, environmental and social systems. World Bank, *New Instrument*, para. 100.

58 BP 9.00 para. 10. 59 BP 9.00 para. 12.

constitute the basis for disbursements against results in the program are thus scrupulously assessed and appraised by the Bank.

The negotiations and Board presentation are the third step in the process. Due to the co-financing nature of the instrument, negotiations involve not only the Bank and the borrower, but also any other "program-related parties." Any substantial changes to the design of the program-for-results operation at this stage need to be agreed with management.[60] On the side of the Bank, the process ends with the approval of the program by the Executive Directors.[61]

With the signing of legal agreements between the borrower and the Bank, the borrower accepts the responsibility for implementing the program in accordance with the relevant contractual obligations and for monitoring progress and evaluating results, including through preparing audits and progress reports. In this fourth and final phase, the Bank retains an active role, however, in offering implementation support.[62] The organization closely monitors progress and conducts risks assessments on an ongoing basis, but also offers support to the borrower in the process. Particular attention at this stage goes to the prevention and mitigation of corruption and fraud, in line with the Anti-Corruption Guidelines adopted together with OP/BP 9.00.[63]

In the implementation phase, the Bank also verifies the achievement of the program's results and DLIs. This crucial aspect – disbursements are directly linked to the attainment of results – of the implementation process is not regulated in much detail. Both the Bank and the borrower are responsible for the verification of the DLI. However, there is a notable absence of a procedure for cases where the Bank and the borrower disagree on the achievement of results. BP 9.00 only establishes – placed not very prominently in a footnote – that the Bank retains the right to decide on whether or not the DLI targets have been achieved.[64] While it remains to be seen in practice who determines the design and verification of indicators for results monitoring under the new instrument, the Bank has certainly expressed awareness of the risk that results might end up being imposed by donors with no sense of country ownership, and thus turn into a new form of conditionality.[65]

[60] BP 9.00 para. 17. [61] BP 9.00 para. 18
[62] OP 9.00 para. 13 and BP 9.00 para. 34.
[63] OP 9.00 para. 15 and BP 9.00 paras. 39–42. On the ACG Guidelines, see above Ch 8.B.I
[64] BP 9.00 para. 12, note 9. See also World Bank, *New Instrument*, para. 72.
[65] World Bank, *New Instrument*, paras. 101–102.

In the case of a failure of the borrower to fulfill its contractual obligations vis-à-vis the Bank (not vice versa), the Bank can refer to the same legal remedies as applicable to other financing instruments. The Bank exercises a certain self-restraint in this regard. It commits to exercise remedies only after having paid due regard to the country- and program-specific circumstances, the severity of non-compliance, and the borrower's commitment to tackle the identified problems, generally engaging in consultations with the borrower first.[66]

IV. Control

The lack of control on the part of the Bank over the use of its resources where they contribute to a larger government program implemented using the country's systems and laws, was a major concern in the conception of the program-for-results instrument. Perhaps surprisingly, or as a result of this concern voiced during consultations, the foregoing analysis suggests that program-for-results operations are subject to comprehensive assessments and extensive monitoring by the Bank – from early on and throughout implementation. Moreover, not only has the Bank the right to investigate (through its Integrity Vice Presidency (INT)) allegations of corruption and fraud and impose sanctions accordingly, so too is the World Bank Inspection Panel, the Bank's quasi-judicial mechanism, competent to investigate operations under the new financing instrument.[67] People affected by activities under a Bank-financed program can bring claims to the Inspection Panel if they think that the harm was caused by a failure of the Bank to comply with its Operational Policies and Procedures.[68] However, given that programs are mostly recipient-government designed and run, it might turn out to be difficult in practice to link failures to the Bank.

C Summary

Program-for-results financing clearly is an innovative tool in development finance and development cooperation law. It offers recipients new access

[66] OP 9.00 para. 14 and BP 9.00 para. 43. See also World Bank, *New Instrument*, para. 78.

[67] On the Inspection Panel in general, see *infra* Ch 3.A.IV.1 and *supra* Ch 8.C.I.1.

[68] See World Bank, *New Instrument*, para. 81. In accordance with Resolution IBRD 93–10/IDA 93–6 (the Inspection Panel Resolution); the Review of the Resolution Establishing the Inspection Panel – 1996 Clarification of Certain Aspects of the Resolution; and 1999 Clarification of the Board's Second Review of the Inspection Panel.

to ODA financing and technical support that is based on a different and more flexible set of conditions, stressing the need to show results before receiving funds. It offers donors a tool that has the potential of increasing the effectiveness, results-focus and leverage of their funds, while also improving accountability and transparency.

With the new instrument just entering the first two years of reality testing as this study is written, it is difficult to judge to what extent these promises will be realized in practice. Well aware of some of the risks inherent in the new instrument to support government programs,[69] the World Bank has chosen to so disburse only a small percentage of its funds in the first two years. It has adopted a typically cautious approach, but also one that is very much open to on-the-spot learning and improving, open to public participation.

Based on the previous analysis of its legal design and procedure, how is the instrument to be evaluated with respect to the general normative principles of development cooperation law, as laid out in this study?

I. Efficiency and coherence

The new instrument is surely enforcing the principle of efficiency and coherence.[70] The results orientation through linkage of disbursement to results and through enhanced technical assistance and capacity development can be expected to increase efficiency. The Bank has surely created an instrument that puts into practice important ideas here. But there are also concerns inherent in the indicator-based approach to measuring results. As discussed above, results are not always easy to measure, in particular if the objective is not to build a dam but to improve the health-care system, for instance. There is also the issue of independent evaluation of results.

Coherence will be strengthened through the alignment to and use of country systems, a central element of the new instrument. There is an increased emphasis on coordination with partners, who will regularly be co-financing partners. Consultation with such partners is explicitly required in the process, not only other development organizations but also private entities, enterprises and NGOs. It is not clear, however, how the Bank will coordinate and collaborate with partners in practice. This

[69] On the challenges and risks from the perspective of the Bank, see World Bank, *New Instrument*, paras. 92–107.

[70] On the content of this principle, see *supra* Ch 4.E.

will require a lot of coordination that international organizations have seldom been very good at.

The danger also remains that it will be hard to actually control the use of the Bank's resources if they are thrown into a large pot with financing coming from other sources, and in addition are spent through country systems. The Bank's own relatively high standards regarding anti-corruption, environment and social protection will certainly be compromised here.

Despite these doubts on specific aspects, the general evaluation regarding the principle of efficiency and coherence is positive.

II. Collective autonomy

The new instrument has at least the potential to also enhance the principle of collective autonomy and ownership.[71] The programs supported have to be designed by the recipient government. This is, in theory, nothing new, since every project financed by project aid, for example, is supposed to be proposed by the recipient. In practice, however, poorer countries with fewer capacities often rely heavily on input from the donors. This could be the case here, too. However, ownership of the government program will be strong, in particular where a program already exists and the Bank comes in later with additional financing and technical assistance. Also, the option of capacity building during the program has a good potential to strengthen ownership and hence collective autonomy.

The Bank itself has voiced concerns that indicators might end up being imposed on recipients. This would turn them into a new form of conditionality. It is notable here that the Bank ultimately decides on its own whether results are achieved and disbursements can continue.

Recipient autonomy is also restricted where Bank standards become applicable to the whole government program not just the parts financed by the Bank.

In the end, the extent of ownership will (as always) likely depend on the kind of recipient. The new instrument is open and very much adaptable to all, from larger to smaller and weaker (expressly including post-conflict and fragile states, too). Depending on how strong and able the Bank's counterpart is (and how proactively the Bank tries to shape programs), autonomy and ownership will be more or less preserved.

[71] On this principle, see *supra* Ch 4.C.

III. *Individual autonomy and human rights*

The new instrument is clearly deficient, however, from the perspective of human rights and individual autonomy. The relevant rules hardly mention the role of "stakeholders"; this vague catch-all phrase is typical for the Bank law. Environmental and social safeguards (for example, to protect indigenous peoples or those involuntarily resettled) are not applicable and the few hints at these standards are much less detailed and demanding.

However, the argument can also be flipped around. If the promise of leveraging Bank standards to the entire program turns out to be true, then a much broader impact could be expected and, for example, domestic rules on the protection of indigenous rights could benefit. On the positive side with respect to individual autonomy is also the increased transparency that comes with the Bank's involvement. Bank rules on transparency, which are comparatively strict,[72] could here also have a leveraging effect. It could benefit individuals, providing a basis to hold their governments to account.

A final thought: the new instrument contains a very important capacity-building component. It is based on the idea that the Bank concentrates on offering its assistance in achieving certain standards rather than making them an *ex-ante* assessment. This might, however, also blur the line between what standards must be met to be eligible and what standards can be achieved throughout the program.

All in all, the new program-for-results instrument is an innovative tool that reacts to changing demands and circumstances. Many aspects are difficult to evaluate today, as there has been little practical experience of it at the time of writing (September 2012).

[72] See *infra* Ch 9.A.II.

9

Accountability in ODA transfers

Once the transfer of ODA is agreed upon, projects or programs have been implemented and the funds are spent, the question of accountability can arise. How to make sure that projects are effective, that funds are not misused, that goals are achieved – and that in the case of misbehavior consequences follow? These questions have been at the heart of the policy discussions on development cooperation in the past years. They are also at the heart of a law of development cooperation for it is only the law that can provide reliable mechanisms and standards.[1]

This chapter will recast the broader policy discussion in legal terms. As in the chapters before, it will proceed in three steps. First, the concept and functions of accountability will be clarified (A). This seems especially necessary since the concept is hardly established in legal doctrine. In the second and main step, the concrete accountability mechanisms will be analyzed (B). This section will analyze the World Bank, the EU and Germany, but also look at the accountability of recipients of ODA as well as mechanisms of peer control among the donors. Finally, a comparative summary will review the findings against the principles of development cooperation law but also point out some structural problems of accountability in development cooperation law (C).

A Concept and functions of accountability in development cooperation

I. Concept of accountability

The concept of accountability is hard to grasp, for at least two reasons. First, accountability is a fairly elusive term for it is not anchored in any conventional legal concept. Even in the English-speaking world, accountability (in contrast, for example, to responsibility) is not a fixed concept,

[1] On the discussions on aid effectiveness and accountability, see *supra* Ch 2.C.III.1.

neither of domestic administrative law, nor of public international law, although international lawyers in particular have started to adapt and clarify the notion.[2] Perhaps not surprisingly, political scientists seem therefore more comfortable with the term.[3]

Even so, one can employ the term and use it rather more restrictively in the sense of a rule-of-law-based understanding of administrative control and oversight. Then, however, one faces a second difficulty, as one has to acknowledge that our understanding of the concept of domestic administrative control is itself profoundly changing. The traditional concept of administrative control, based primarily on judicial review, covers only a very limited aspect of what administrations do.[4] Instead, more cooperative and dynamic forms than *ex-post* control and more actors than courts have come to be analyzed.[5] But then again, this broadened horizon also facilitates the transfer of domestic administrative law concepts to the global sphere,[6] since it eases the fixation on courts as the dominant means of accountability. In a way, the vagueness and blur might even be the actual allure of the term "accountability." Precisely its imprecision makes it

[2] For an analysis of the domestic usage, see R. Mulgan, "'Accountability': An Ever-Expanding Concept?" *Public Administration Review*, 78 (2000), 555–73; for attempts to clarify the notion in the vocabulary of public international law, see International Law Association Committee, *Accountability of International Organisations: Berlin Conference (2004)*. Available at www.ila-hq.org/en/committees/index.cfm/cid/9 (last visited April 2013); Pauwelyn, *Informal International Lawmaking*; J. G. S. Koppell, *World Rule: Accountability, Legitimacy, and the Design of Global Governance* (University of Chicago Press, 2010); Dann and Engelhardt, "Legal Approaches"; E. de Wet, "Holding International Institutions Accountable: The Complementary Role of Non-Judicial Oversight Mechanisms and Judicial Review," in A. von Bogdandy, R. Wolfrum, J. von Bernstorff, P. Dann and M. Goldmann (eds.), *The Exercise of Public Authority by International Institutions: Advancing International Institutional Law* (Heidelberg: Springer, 2010), pp. 855–82; Harlow, "Global Administrative Law."

[3] See Grant and Keohane, "Accountability and Abuses," 29 and references therein.

[4] Seminal: Schmidt-Aßmann, *Das allgemeine Verwaltungsrecht*, p. 229; W. Kahl, "§47: Begriff, Funktionen und Konzepte von Kontrolle," in W. Hoffmann-Riem, E. Schmidt-Aßmann and A. Vosskuhle (eds.), *Personal, Finanzen, Kontrolle, Sanktionen, Staatliche Einstandspflichten* (Munich: Beck, 2009), pp. 427–541; S. G. Breyer, R. Stewart, C. Sunstein and A. Vermeule, *Administrative Law and Regulatory Policy: Problems, Text and Cases*, 6th edn (New York: Aspen Publishers, 2006), pp. 160, 161.

[5] See the contributions in Schmidt-Aßmann and Hoffmann-Riem, *Verwaltungskontrolle*; also D. Oliver and G. Drewry, *Public Service Reforms: Issues of Accountability and Public Law* (London, New York: Pinter, 1996), p. 4.

[6] On such transfers, see R. Stewart, "U.S. Administrative Law: A Model for Global Administrative Law?" *Law and Contemporary Problems*, 68 (2005), 63–104 at 63, 76; D. Sarooshi, "Essentially Contested Nature of the Concept of Sovereignty: Implications for the Exercise by International Organizations of Powers of Government," *Michigan Journal of International Law*, 25 (2004), 1107–39 at 1121.

attractive as a "buckle-notion" between domestic and international law, and between law and other disciplines.

Nevertheless, the concept of accountability has to be clarified in order to facilitate legal analysis. A rather restrictive approach appears the most promising. On a basic level, accountability means "to have to answer for one's action or inaction, and depending on the answer, to be exposed to potential sanctions."[7] Starting from that point, accountability here shall contain three elements.

First, accountability involves a certain *distance* between the power wielder and those who hold him accountable (the accountability holder, as Grant and Keohane put it[8]), including a certain degree of independence of the accountability holder. Self-control thus does not qualify. Second, accountability is based on the possibility of a *sanction*. This does not have to be a formal fine or penalty; public outcry can be quite an effective sanction, too. But accountability has an amendatory character, based on the effect of sanctions. And, thirdly, accountability in principle presupposes the existence of certain fixed and legitimate *standards* of review. There are certainly exceptions to this third element; the vote in an election, for example, could be regarded as an accountability mechanism but it is not based on a general standard and therefore does not fall within our definition.

The concept of accountability should be distinguished from two related concepts. First of all, it differs from the legal concept of *responsibility*, especially from state responsibility in public international law. Responsibility connotes a strictly legal set of secondary rules that apply when the breach of a legal obligation is at stake.[9] It is therefore narrower than accountability since the standards of an accountability review may also be non-legal standards of fiscal correctness or even political appropriateness. Second, accountability should be distinguished from the concept of *participation*. Accountability does not include just any influence on a decision-making process but rather involves a certain element

[7] R. J. Oakerson, "Governance Structures for Enhancing Accountability and Responsiveness," in J. L. Perry (ed.), *Handbook of Public Administration* (San Francisco: Jossey-Bass, 1989), pp. 110–25 at p. 114.

[8] Grant and Keohane, "Accountability and Abuses," 36.

[9] H. C. Black, *Black's Law Dictionary: Definitions of the Terms and Phrases of American and English Jurisprudence Ancient and Modern*, 5th edn (St. Paul: West Publishing Company, 1979), defines "responsibility" as "the state of being answerable for an obligation," the "obligation to answer for an act done, and to repair or otherwise make restitution for an injury one may have caused"; J. Crawford, "State Responsibility," in Wolfrum, *Max Planck Encyclopedia of Public International Law*.

of transgression and retrospective review. The distinction between participation and accountability is especially important since many writers conflate them, on the grounds that both are supposed to contribute to the legitimacy of public authority.[10] However, even though both accountability and participation can contribute to legitimacy, they generate *different types* of legitimacy. While participation generally contributes to *democratic* legitimacy, accountability generates *legal* legitimacy, such as the rule of law does; it is not a concept of democratic legitimacy. It is in that sense not an input-oriented form of legitimacy, but rather a form that is based on the fairness of rules and compliance with them.

In sum, this study uses a narrow concept of accountability that focuses on the retrospective review of a power wielder's behavior by an independent accountability holder based on previously fixed and legitimate standards of review and including the possibility of sanctions.

II. Elements of accountability in development cooperation: accountability of whom, to whom, and according to which standards?

In order to better understand the concrete meaning of accountability in our context of development cooperation (and to structure the latter analysis), three elements of accountability should be distinguished: first, the object of accountability (accountability of whom?); second, the standards and mechanisms of accountability (against which standards and in which procedures is accountability "measured"?) and finally, the subjects of accountability (accountable to whom?). All three will briefly be explained.

The first element is the question of *whose accountability* is at stake. Who is to be held accountable? In the context of the law of development cooperation, the central focus has to be on the donor organizations – given the uneven allocation of power in the donor–recipient relationship and their primary responsibility for the transfer of ODA.[11] Yet, the limited success of aid efforts has also led to questions concerning the ways in which recipients use the aid and to international efforts to increase transparency and accountability in recipient-country regimes.[12] It is

[10] Pauwelyn, "Informal International Lawmaking," Section III.1c; see also Naude Fourie, *World Bank Inspection Panel*, p. 3.

[11] See *infra* Ch 9.B.I.-III.

[12] See the United Nations, *Monterrey Consensus*, margin nos. 13, 15; OECD, *Paris Declaration on Aid Effectiveness*, margin nos. 43–6 and the accompanying report, esp. pp. 49–53, paras. 19, 20, 48; OECD, *Donor Approaches to Governance Assessments: A*

therefore expedient to examine the legal regime of accountability pertaining to the recipients. Since recipient governments are entrusted with public money, they too should be held accountable as to how they use this money. However, since this study cannot cover the domestic laws of all recipient countries, it will focus on those rules that are internationally agreed and thus common to all.[13]

The second element relates to the *standards of accountability* and the mechanisms by which they are checked. Four different types of standard can be distinguished.[14] A first standard of review may be *legal* rules to be checked in judicial or quasi-judicial procedures. In the context of development cooperation law, this is difficult. Given the fact that development cooperation is a transnational system, we will have to analyze carefully whether there are any courts available or other, perhaps quasi-judicial bodies. A second type of standards concerns rules of *fiscal* propriety. These are of special importance here, since development cooperation is ultimately based on financial transactions. It has to be investigated whether there are Courts of Auditors or other auditing institutions involved. The third type of standard could be termed standards of *substantive or impact* scrutiny, concerning the assessment of the results and effectiveness of interventions. This mechanism refers mostly to evaluations, which are a long-established and an especially rich mechanism in the area of development cooperation.[15] Finally, as a fourth standard of review there may also be the constitutional rules that contain standards for *political* scrutiny. The question here would be to what extent other branches of the organization control the staff that are handling the concrete transfer of ODA. It should be pointed

Sourcebook: A Sourcebook (2009). Available at www.oecd.org/development/governanceanddevelopment/42472200.pdf (last visited July 2013); G. Cremer, *Korruption begrenzen: Praxisfeld Entwicklungspolitik*, 2nd edn (Freiburg im Breisgau: Lambertus, 2008); A. Alesino and B. Weder, "Do Corrupt Governments Receive Less Foreign Aid?" *The American Economic Review*, 92 (2002), 1126–37.

13 See *infra* Ch 9.B.IV.

14 Dann, "Accountability," 385; Grant and Keohane, "Accountability and Abuses," 29; for an analysis of mechanisms also E. Mitzmann, "The Proliferation of Independent Accountability Mechanisms in the Field of Development Finance," *Rivista trimestrale di diritto pubblico*, 62 (2012), 93–134.

15 See *supra*, Ch 1.B.II.2 / V. On evaluations in development cooperation generally OECD, *Evaluation in Development Agencies* (Paris: OECD Publishing, 2010); Hempel, *Erfolgskontrolle in der deutschen Entwicklungszusammenarbeit*; E. Duflo and M. Kremer, "Use of Randomization in the Evaluation of Development Effectiveness," in Easterly, *Reinventing Foreign Aid*, p. 93; L. Pritchett, "It Pays to Be Ignorant: A Simple Political Economy of Rigorous Program Evaluation," in ibid, p. 121.

out that within these four types of review, legal standards go along with standards of practicality (*Zweckmäßigkeit*). This is not unusual for the control and oversight of executive agencies, given that they often have fairly wide discretion.

One element of accountability has to be mentioned separately, as it perhaps forms their very basis: transparency. All of the mechanisms listed above actually presuppose that the relevant information on the standards applicable and the behavior in question is available. This seems obvious, yet access to relevant documents and information in organizations is not obvious at all.[16]

Finally, there is a third element of accountability to be concretized in the context of development cooperation, and that is the question of the *subjects of accountability*. If the objects of accountability are donors and recipient governments, who are they accountable to? This question touches on a particularly complex element, since development cooperation, as has been observed before,[17] involves a great number of actors. Here, we have to distinguish (at least) four relevant holders of accountability. There are, first, other organs or branches within the donor organization, which enact checks and balances. This would be, for example, the Board of Executive Directors holding the World Bank's management accountable or the German parliament holding the Federal Ministry for Development accountable. Second, there is the relation between the donor organization and the recipient state. Here, we are seeing a relationship of mutual accountability as donor and recipient have entered into bilateral contractual relations. Third, and perhaps most importantly, there is the question to what extent those who are affected by the projects and policies, i.e. citizens in the recipient countries, can activate accountability mechanisms. And finally, one can inquire whether the general public and peers can hold the donors (and each other) accountable – and how.

[16] R. Vaughn, "Transparency in the Administration of Laws: The Relationship Between Differing Justifications for Transparency and Differing Views of Administrative Law," *American University International Law Review*, 26 (2011), 969–82; J. Bröhmer, *Transparenz als Verfassungsprinzip: Grundgesetz und Europäische Union* (Tübingen: Mohr Siebeck, 2004); A. Roßnagel, "Möglichkeiten für Transparenz und Öffentlichkeit im Verwaltungshandeln – unter besonderer Berücksichtigung des Internet als Instrument der Staatskommunikation," in W. Hoffmann-Riem and E. Schmidt-Aßmann (eds.), *Verwaltungsrecht in der Informationsgesellschaft* (Baden-Baden: Nomos, 2000), vol. VII, pp. 257–332 at pp. 264–70.

[17] See *supra* Ch 3.D.

III. *Functions of accountability*

Having clarified the conceptual features of accountability, we should also explain the functions of accountability. Three functions stand in the foreground.[18]

A first function is ensuring compliance. Accountability mechanisms are supposed to make sure that the relevant actors adhere to the applicable rules and that misbehavior is sanctioned. In the area of development cooperation this means that projects should be implemented as planned and, more fundamentally, ODA funds invested as agreed upon. In this sense, accountability is a central mechanism to ensure that corruption and misuse do not occur (or occur less).

A second function is providing information and contributing to organizational learning. By giving accountability holders the opportunity to complain and competent organs the power to check what happened in projects or programs, accountability mechanisms help to find out what worked and what results they had. Accountability helps to create more transparency and provide feedback. It is not surprising that aid organizations headline evaluation mechanisms often as "lessons learned," indicating this function. Altogether it is necessary to understand accountability as part of a cyclical process and element of learning. Information gained through reviews feeds into new programs and projects and hence (ideally) helps improve them.

A third function is generating legitimacy. Even though accountability, in our understanding, does not contribute to democratic or input legitimacy, it does create responsiveness and legal legitimacy. It involves the affected, who are able to name and sanction those who misbehave. This can foster trust in the procedures or organizations. It also helps to clarify responsibilities. Accountability mechanisms often include the chance to answer the question of who did what (wrongly). In a sense, accountability is also supposed to enhance the effectiveness of regimes and thus to contribute to their output. If, for example, auditing and other rules are supposed to protect the financial interests of those involved (donors as well as recipients), their accurate application helps to provide the intended outcomes.

[18] On more functions see E. Mitzmann, *The Proliferation of Independent Accountability Mechanisms in the Field of Development Finance*, The Jean Monnet Center for International and Regional Economic Law & Justice Working Paper 14/10, pp. 15–17. Available at http://centers.law.nyu.edu/jeanmonnet/papers/10/101401.pdf (last visited July 2013); also Kahl, "§47," margin no. 8.

B Accountability of donors and recipients

I. World Bank

1. Standards and mechanisms: how the bank can be held accountable

a) Legal accountability: the Inspection Panel and its context

Considering that this is a book on the *law* of development cooperation and that one of its main arguments is the legalization of development cooperation, legal accountability is of special importance. Yet, legal accountability is also a rather delicate issue in the given political and economic context. The option for recipient governments to sue donors exists mostly in theory. Although every legal agreement between recipient government and the Bank contains clauses on arbitration,[19] these clauses have never (sic!) been invoked. The World Bank, moreover, has mostly succeeded in shielding itself against legal action in domestic courts by reference to its privileges and immunities.[20] Even though the World Bank does not enjoy full functional immunity from law suits in member states' courts, an "indirect immunity" clause essentially precludes access to national courts for two categories of claimants most relevant here: firstly, member states themselves or litigants deriving claims from them, and secondly, third parties which have not entered into a contractual relationship with the Bank beforehand.[21] In these cases, domestic courts generally grant the Bank immunity from suit.

[19] See, for example, the General Conditions of the International Bank for Reconstruction and Development, March 12, 2012, Art. VIII, Sect. 8.04. The General Conditions set forth the terms and conditions generally applicable to the legal agreements between the Bank and the recipient, see Head, "Evolution," 218–22; see also *supra*, Ch 3.A.IV.2.

[20] See Art. VII Articles of Agreement IBRD /Art. VIII IDA Articles of Agreement: See also A. Reinisch and J. Wurm, "International Financial Institutions before National Courts," in Bradlow and Hunter, *International Financial Institutions*, pp. 123, 124 (who point out, though, that there is a rich case law brought by *private* creditors and contractors of the Bank, not their public partners).

[21] Cf. Art. VII Sect. 3 IBRD Articles of Agreement/VIII Sect. 3 IDA Articles of Agreement. This provision is usually interpreted (beyond its wording) to contain a limited "functional waiver" of the Bank's immunity that only applies to contractual debtors, creditors and bondholders, which are allowed to sue the Bank in domestic courts as this is functionally necessary to ensure the Bank's creditworthiness. This waiver generally does not apply to employees and third parties. For respective case law see ibid., p. 111, also with reference to possible exceptions. See also Shihata, *World Bank Inspection Panel*, pp. 122, 123.

However, in an unprecedented step, in 1993 the World Bank established an institution of legal review, the Inspection Panel.[22] The Panel has the task of scrutinizing whether the Bank adheres to its operational policies and procedures in the design, preparation and implementation of projects. The Panel consists of three external experts who are appointed by the Board for non-renewable periods of five years. The Panel is separated from the Bank's management in that it does not report to the Bank's President but to the Executive Board and its staff is separated from the Bank's staff. More importantly, the Panel is open not only to the complaints of states but also to the complaints of affected third parties and individuals. Any group of two or more individuals who claim to have been harmed by a World Bank project can request the Panel to investigate whether the Bank has complied with its own Bank Procedures and Operational Policies in its operations.[23] This makes the Panel a unique institution.

The Panel is generally termed a "quasi-judicial" accountability mechanism for it bears traits of both judicial and administrative internal review.[24] The Panel process follows a formalized two-step procedure, including an eligibility stage and an investigation stage. It results in a Panel report, which is routinely endorsed by the Executive Directors. However, the Panel's findings themselves are not binding on management, and it cannot enforce its recommendations or order payment of damages. The scope of scrutiny is limited to Bank-internal rules and does not explicitly encompass, namely, international human rights law. In addition, given

[22] IBRD Resolution, No. 93–10 and IDA Resolution, No. 93–6 of September 22, 1993 (also Operational Policy 17.55). There is plenty of literature on the Panel, see Shihata, *World Bank Inspection Panel*; Naude Fourie, *World Bank Inspection Panel*; Orakhelashvili, "World Bank Inspection Panel," 57ff.; for an internal perspective, see World Bank, *Accountability at the World Bank: The Inspection Panel 10 Years On* (2003). Available at http://siteresources.worldbank.org/EXTINSPECTIONPANEL/Resources/TenYear8_07.pdf (last visited September 2012), *Accountability at the World Bank: The Inspection Panel at 15 Years* (2009). Available at http://siteresources.worldbank.org/EXTINSPECTIONPANEL/Resources/380793-1254158345788/InspectionPanel2009.pdf (last visited September 2012). On these, see also E. van Waeyenberge, "Accountability at the World Bank," *Development and Change*, 43 (2012), 615–21.

[23] IBRD Resolution, No. 93–10 and IDA Resolution, No. 93–6 of September 22, 1993, para. 12.

[24] It would be fascinating to compare its role and genesis to other organs that have started as internal review mechanisms and later evolved into full-fledged courts, such as the French Conseil d'État or the Dutch Raad van State. See on them T. Koopmans, *Courts and Political Institutions: A Comparative View* (Cambridge University Press, 2003), pp. 69, 70.

the strong role of the Executive Directors in the Panel process, its institutional independence is weak on paper. However, in practice its independence and influence has increased considerably.[25] By 2012, the Panel had reviewed a total of seventy-seven requests, often finding instances of at least partial non-compliance, and has had an appreciable impact on the legalization of and compliance with the Bank's internal rules.[26]

b) Financial accountability: audits, anti-corruption, whistle-blowing

Development aid is about money. Public money is used to finance projects intended to support economic growth and development in developing countries. Despite good intentions, the susceptibility of donors to corruption, fraud and simple waste is immense.[27] The system of financial control is therefore especially important. It involves a range of mechanisms and employs a number of actors: audits are performed by external experts, internal investigators are charged with the investigation of fraud and corruption, and whistle-blowers are asked to report misconduct.

Auditing as an instrument of fiscal accountability is well known in domestic systems and also in the law of IOs.[28] The audit of the financial statement of the World Bank is prescribed by Art. V, Sect. 13 of the Articles of Agreement IBRD. It is performed by an external private company, which is chosen by the Audit Committee of the Board of Executive Directors.[29] Audits are performed according to the auditing standards generally accepted in the United States and International Standards of Accounting. These involve compliance with the respective laws of sound management. The sanctions at hand, however, are mild: the audit reports are published and reaction is thus left to a vigilant public.[30]

[25] Naude Fourie, *World Bank Inspection Panel*, pp. 185–96; pp. 213–54.

[26] See the case list on www.worldbank.org/inspectionpanel and the discussion of landmark cases at ibid., pp. 197, 198.

[27] See generally Riddell, *Does Foreign Aid*, pp. 179, 180. Specifically on corruption, see ibid., pp. 185, 226 and L. J. Dumas, J. R. Wedel and G. Callman, *Confronting Corruption, Building Accountability: Lessons from the World of International Development Advising* (New York: Palgrave Macmillan, 2010); Cremer, *Korruption begrenzen*; J. Svensson, "Foreign Aid and Rent-Seeking," *Journal of International Economics*, 51 (2000), 437–61.

[28] H. G. Schermers and N. Blokker, *International Institutional Law: Unity Within Diversity*, 5th edn (Leiden, Boston: Martinus Nijhoff Publishers, 2011), margin nos. 1123–1125.

[29] See World Bank, *Annual Report 2010: Internal Audit Vice Presidency*. Available at http://siteresources.worldbank.org/EXTANNREP/Resources/IAD-FY10-Annualreport.pdf (last visited September 2012).

[30] Even this can be ineffective. For years, the Court of Auditors in the EU did not approve the financial statement of the EU, but with no effect.

Audits serve the financial credibility of these institutions, which are, last but not least, dependent on the trust of donating member states or financial markets. If audits are hence indispensable, they are also toothless. To battle the persistent problem of *fraud and corruption*, donor institutions have established new institutional and legal means for more proactive efforts.[31] In 2001, the World Bank created the Department of Institutional Integrity (INT), basically a prosecutor's office within the Bank.[32] This unit has the mandate to investigate allegations of fraud and corruption in World Bank projects and of misconduct of staff within the World Bank.[33] It has unrestricted access to Bank records, documents and properties, is institutionally separated from regular staff and reports directly to the President. Its mandate as well as definitions of fraud and corruption are laid out in its Terms of Reference (ToR)[34] and in Sections 1 a (3) and 3 of the Sanctions Committee Procedures, which were approved by senior management and endorsed by the Board of Executive Directors in July 2004. If allegations prove substantiated, sanctions can involve the termination of contract with the Bank and a debarment from rehiring, or disciplinary actions.[35] The INT has today a staff of fifty-five professionals. According to its Annual Report, it investigated 125 cases in 2003 and 151 in 2004.[36]

The World Bank also adopted the concept of *whistle-blowing*, which has been known in private business and national labor law for quite some time.[37] It is in itself not an accountability mechanism, but contributes to the accountability of institutions.[38] The Bank appeals to individuals

[31] On such efforts in international organizations generally, C. de Cooker, "Ethics and Accountability in International Civil Service," in C. de Cooker (ed.), *Accountability, Investigation and Due Process in International Organizations* (Leiden, Boston: Martinus Nijhoff, 2005), pp. 1–51 at pp. 42–9.

[32] See www.worldbank.org/integrity.

[33] It also investigates external cases.

[34] See http://siteresources.worldbank.org/INTDOII/Resources/Integritytermsofreference.doc (last visited September 2012).

[35] On the rights of the staff in such investigations, see H. Dean, "Due Process: The Rights of World Bank Staff in Misconduct Investigations," in de Cooker, *Accountability, Investigation and Due Process*, p. 97.

[36] See World Bank, *Annual Report on Investigations and Sanctions of Staff Misconduct and Fraud and Corruption in Bank-Financed Projects* (2004). Available at http://siteresources.worldbank.org/INTDOII/Resources/INTFY04AnnualReport2005.pdf (last visited September 2012).

[37] See de Cooker, "Ethics and Accountability," pp. 39–42; C. F. Alford, *Whistleblowers: Broken Lives and Organizational Power* (Ithaca: Cornell University Press, 2001).

[38] Whistle-blowing has been described as appealing to the "active responsibility" of individuals, see M. Bovens, *The Quest for Responsibility: Accountability and Citizenship in Complex Organisations* (Cambridge University Press, 1998), pp. 190.

within and outside the institution to report any suspicious behavior and to that end provide open and potentially anonymous channels and protection. It provides a secret channel (telephone hotline, email submission formula and postal address) and advises on how to report.[39] Its Staff Rule 8.01 prohibits any retaliation against informants.

c) Substantive accountability: evaluations and impact assessments

The instrument of evaluations has become a central tool to check on the substantive outcomes of projects and programs and recount their impact. Over many years, the Bank has created an internal but fairly independent evaluation system. The Independent Evaluation Group (IEG), established under President McNamara in the early 1970s, is headed by a Director General, who is appointed by the Board of Executive Directors.[40] It is organizationally independent from the Bank's other departments and reports directly to the Board.[41] The IEG rates the efficacy and efficiency of World Bank's operational programs. It has developed a set of tools to review projects and country programs, to perform sector or thematic reviews or undertake impact evaluations. These reviews rate performance according to a set of four criteria: outcome, sustainability, institutional impact, Bank and Borrower performance. The concrete standards applied are derived from the objectives which the Bank and projects set for themselves.[42]

Sanctions in the evaluation system have different, although rather mild forms. For one, the units report their findings to the Senior Management of World Bank as well as to the representation of member states. At the same time, most of these reports are made public.[43] The most important point, however, is that management has to respond to the report. The form and content of such a response, however, seem hardly regulated.

d) Political accountability

Finally, the World Bank is also subject to those retrospective supervisory mechanisms of accountability by which the member states typically

[39] See FAQ section on webpage (www.worldbank.org/integrity).

[40] Until 2002, the office was called the Operations Evaluations Department (OED), on its history see P. Grasso et al. (eds.), *The World Bank's Operations Evaluations Department: The First 30 Years* (World Bank Publications, 2003). Evaluations are also performed by Bank's project teams themselves. Since these evaluations lack the element of distance, we will not analyze them. But see World Bank's Operational Policy (OP) 13.55.

[41] See generally www.worldbank.org/ieg/about.html.

[42] See also OP 13.60 on Monitoring and Evaluation, June 2007 (which superseded the old Operational Directive (OD) 10.70 on Project Monitoring and Evaluation).

[43] See *World Bank Policy on Access to Information*, effective July 1, 2010, paras. 48–50.

hedge and influence the actions of international organizations.[44] For example, member states hold sway over the appointment and dismissal of the head of the organization. It is the Board of Executive Directors, the representation of member states in the Bank, which appoints the Bank's president.[45] Through their representations, member states can also control policies and concrete decisions of the Bank. As analyzed above, the Board of Executive Directors meets twice per week and is responsible for deciding about the general policies guiding the Bank's operations as well as for the approval of all loans and of the annual administrative budget.[46]

However, the existence of these instruments does not necessarily mean that they are used or used equally by all member states. In fact, the lack of effective member-state oversight or the circumvention of formalized mechanisms has been stated as a main problem and reason for the perception of a lack of accountability.[47] The sheer amount of activity and information generated by the vast and largely autonomous Bank bureaucracy with its 10,000 staff often exceeds the member-state representatives' capacity to process information and single out the problematic cases where political scrutiny would have to be exercised.[48] Moreover, high-income states and especially the USA and European states exert a much stronger influence and hold organizations almost unilaterally accountable, for example, by determining who is president of the World Bank. While

[44] On the notion of supervisory accountability, see Grant and Keohane, "Accountability and Abuses," 36. On the delicate relationship between member states and international organizations generally N. Blokker, "International Organizations and their Members: International Organizations Belong to All Members and to None," Variations on a Theme, *International Organizations Law Review*, 1 (2004), 139–61 at 140–52.

[45] Art. V Sect. 5 Articles of Agreement IBRD. This is, of course, only the formal side. Informally and based on a compromise between the USA and Western European countries, the Bank president is always chosen by the US administration, whereas the Europeans determine who heads the IMF, see Woods, "Making the IMF," 85–6; Mallaby, *World's Banker*, p. 174. On the reform of the Bank's governance structure, including the weighted voting scheme, see also World Bank, *Synthesis Paper: New World, New World Bank Group*, DC 2010–0002/1 of April, 25, 2010. Available at http://siteresources.worldbank.org/DEVCOMMINT/Documentation/22555916/DC2010-0002-1_E_SynthesisPaperRevised.pdf (last visited September 2012). Recommending a more rules-based and transparent leadership selection process: High-Level Commission on Modernization of World Bank Group Governance, *Repowering the World Bank*, p. 42.

[46] See Art. V Sect. 4a Articles of Agreement IBRD and *supra*, Ch 3.A.IV.1.

[47] See Woods, "Making the IMF," 84–90; Chimni, "International Institutions," 20, 21; N. Woods, *The Globalizers: The IMF, the World Bank, and Their Borrowers* (Ithaca: Cornell University Press, 2006), pp. 190, 191.

[48] See generally on the de facto independence of international bureaucracies from member state control von Bernstorff, "Procedures of Decision-Making," 1939, 1942, 1943.

mechanisms of political accountability are hence certainly existent, they can effectively be used only by a small group of members.

2. Transparency: the 2010 Access to Information Policy – and the mobilization of citizens

To a growing degree, donor institutions are also held accountable by the general public. Such control, however, is possible only if information on the actors is actually accessible. The World Bank has a long history here. In what was a rather unusual step for international organizations back then, the World Bank issued a first policy on access to information in the 1980s and has since reformed it in 1993, 2002 and 2005.[49] It established the system of a positive list of documents that had to be made publicly available. In 2010, this system was reformed comprehensively and access substantially widened.[50] According to the new 2010 policy, *all* documents are now generally available to the public, *unless* they are subject to an explicit exception. The positive-list approach was therefore replaced by a negative list, establishing the principle of free access to information at the Bank.[51]

But the new policy goes even further than that. It also introduced an enforcement mechanism: applicants can appeal to an independent panel of external experts if their request for disclosure of particular documents has been denied by the Bank and by an internal review process. The new policy enables civil-society organizations to proactively uncover information needed for increased public scrutiny of the Bank.

In theory, the new policy provides a promising basis for the engagement of the general public with the Bank. It could almost be seen as an attempt to mobilize citizens as agents for the Bank, contributing to the improvement of operations by learning from their complaints and inquiries. In this perspective, it contains a fascinating appeal to a cosmopolitan model of a global discourse as well as local engagement. At the same time, this appeal has a somewhat cunning side, since it could also be seen as circumventing the member states. As the Bank has a huge amount of data on every member state, the Access to Information Policy could be seen as mobilizing citizens to put pressure on their governments.

Whether the Policy will make a difference in reality, however, will depend on the handling of the list of exceptions by the Bank and the

[49] For an overview see World Bank, *Towards Greater Transparency.*

[50] World Bank, *The World Bank Policy on Access to Information* (Washington, DC: World Bank Publications, 2010).

[51] In detail Dann, "Zugang zu Dokumenten im Recht der Weltbank," 313; on the evolution of the policy, Hunter, "International Law and Public Participation," pp. 221–3.

Appeals Panel in practice. It also depends on a vigilant public that sustains a certain level of continuous engagement with the Bank.[52]

3. Relational summary: who is the Bank effectively accountable to?

The legal regime governing the World Bank provides a multitude of accountability mechanisms. If we recapitulate and summarize them from the perspective of the accountability holders, hence by asking to whom the Bank is effectively accountable, the picture becomes simpler.

The Bank is most prominently accountable to its (rich) member states. The mechanisms of political and financial accountability especially empower the member states to interfere and react to or sanction wrongful behavior. However, legally as well as politically, it is only the rich member states that can effectively wield these instruments. Given the weighted system of voting rights they dominate decision-making in the Executive Board. They are also responsible for financing IDA and hence are in a very strong position to shape Bank policies in the way they want. This situation of rich states driving the Bank agenda is increasingly unsatisfactory. The financial crisis in the North and emerging economies in the South have changed the global context profoundly.[53] In the Bank, reform and rethinking processes are cautiously under way.[54]

The Bank is effectively accountable to the recipient states to a much lesser extent. Though they are also member states and can hence use internal mechanisms, as recipients of loans and hence contracting partner of the Bank, they are in a more dependent position. In consequence, they hardly use tools of legal accountability, for example. At the same time, one has to distinguish carefully here between the recipients. Some bigger economies (such as China, India or Mexico) have considerable clout within the Bank since they are important customers. Others become important as role models. The greater number of poorer, and especially the least-developed countries, however, are hardly in a position to hold the Bank accountable.

[52] For a critical assessment of the 2005 policy, see N. Bernasconi-Osterwalder and D. B. Hunter, "Democratizing Multilateral Development Banks," in C. Bruch (ed.), *The New "Public": The Globalization of Public Participation* (Washington, DC: Environmental Law Institute, 2002), pp. 151–64 at pp. 152–6.

[53] On how these developments affect the development system, see *supra* Ch 2.C.III.2.

[54] High-Level Commission on Modernization of World Bank Group Governance, *Repowering the World Bank*, http://siteresources.worldbank.org/DEVCOMMINT/Documentation/22335196/DC2009-0011%28E%29Voice.pdf (last accessed September 2012).

There is a considerable void concerning the accountability of the Bank towards the affected citizens in recipient states. The potentially most effective path for them is the Inspection Panel, since it gives direct access and voice to them. It is of central importance for accountability (and hence legitimacy) of the Bank. However, it has the mentioned flaws, especially the fact that the management is not bound by its reports and cannot be forced to live up to its obligations. The impact of the new Access to Information Policy is not yet clear. This too could be an important tool in the hands of affected citizens and activists. But its interpretation in practice is not yet clear.

These results point to structural problems in the accountability mechanisms. Member states who could have the most resources to hold the Bank accountable are also stakeholders in its governance. Their "appetite" for sharp control is therefore impaired. Those having the most vital and immediate interest in control, the affected citizens, on the other hand, have much fewer possibilities. This only underlines the necessity for the general public to be able to monitor the Bank. The surprisingly progressive transparency regime of the Bank, although it still has to pass the reality check, could be an important tool here. Not least the publicity of project documents and evaluation results can help here. However, a more nuanced appraisal of the Bank's accountability will emerge once we have studied the other institutions.

II. European Union

Accountability in EU development cooperation concerns two actors: the European Commission and the European External Actions Service (EEAS). In programming, the EEAS has mainly a preparatory role, while eventual decision-making essentially rests with the Commission. In contrast, implementation is largely handled by the EEAS country delegations. Accountability patterns will have to follow the split responsibilities, not really enhancing transparency.[55]

1. Standards and mechanisms: how the EU can be held accountable

a) Legal accountability: the difficult path to the ECJ and Ombudsman

In contrast to the World Bank, the EU has, of course, a court, and is generally subject to more and stricter judicial review than any other

[55] On this split responsibility, see *infra* Ch 3.A.III.1.

international organization.[56] The question of standards and mechanisms is therefore easily answered – at least in principle. More concretely, however, the question is to what extent the EU's ODA transfer and development cooperation is indeed scrutinized by the ECJ. This shall be analyzed first (1). Then the quasi-judicial mechanisms of legal accountability through the EU Ombudsman will be examined (2).

(1) Proceedings before the ECJ Different parties can have different legal paths to a proceeding before the ECJ. One has to distinguish between the claims of other organs, recipient governments and affected citizens.[57]

(i) Most cases concerning development policies before the ECJ are brought by the organs and concern the proper use of competences. Such disputes have arisen in two varieties. In one variety it is questioned whether the Commission is overstepping its competences in making certain financing decisions. Most famous here is the Philippines case, in which the European Parliament doubted whether approving an EU project that was financing security measures in the Philippines could be considered as a *development* project.[58] The court analyzed in detail the aims and objectives of EU development cooperation and found that the Commission had indeed acted ultra-vires. The other variety concerns the choice of a legal basis when dealing with development issues. A recent case scrutinized the relation between (former) Community competences on development and (former) Union competences in the Common Foreign and Security Policies (CFSP) under the Art. 40 TEU.[59] The court here curtailed the Council's preference to base programs on bases in the CFSP instead of on development. In both varieties, however, the court is faced with certain limits of its own competence. Since actions by the Commission or the Council in this policy area often involve a high degree of political and economic assessment, the Court normally refrains from a too-detailed review.[60]

56 Klabbers, *An Introduction*, p. 220; Bast, "Legal Instruments," p. 345.

57 Disputes concerning dissatisfied tenderers and contractors of the EU will not be considered here, since they concern the implementation of contracts. See extensively Kalbe, "Award of Contracts," 1217.

58 ECJ, C-403/05 (Parliament v. Commission), 23 October 2007, ECR 2007, I-9045, paras. 39, 40.

59 ECJ, C-91/05 (ECOWAS), ECR 2008, I-3651, para. 60.

60 ECJ, C-402/05 P, (*Kadi*), ECR 2008, I-6351, para. 360; ECJ, C-347/03, (*Regione autonoma Friuli-Venezia Giulia*), ECR 2005, I-1875, para. 131; CFI, T-572/93 (*Odigitria*), ECR 1995, II-2025, para. 38.

EU organs have another potential avenue to hold the Commission legally accountable and that is the action for the failure to act (Art. 265 TFEU) despite a poor human rights record of a recipient country.[61] Such an action could be lodged if the Commission does not initiate pre-suspension consultation with a beneficiary country,[62] if it has abstained from proposing a Council decision on suspension[63] or if it has abstained from suspending the financing agreement with the beneficiary country on the basis of the latter's "General Condition" provision. However, EU organs, especially the European Parliament, have never chosen such action. Given that any decision to act upon human rights violations involves very complex assessment, the EP's reluctance seems reasonable.

(ii) Governments of a recipient country could also bring legal action against the EU. There are many conceivable constellations in which they could regard the EU's actions as violating the terms of respective programs or Financing Agreements. But how and where could they sue the EU? Two paths seem possible: arbitration and again the EJC. Arbitration is the most common path of dispute resolution between subjects of international law and, indeed, Art. 98 of the Cotonou Agreement allows for such action.[64] In reality, however, as with the World Bank, such clauses have never been used – most likely for political reasons. Equally difficult is the second path, namely actions of annulment according to Art. 263 IV TFEU before the ECJ. Even though the wording of this provision might include third states as "legal persons" to have standing, a more convincing systematic and teleological reading of it has to exclude them. It is hardly conceivable that the *acta iure imperii* of two international legal persons should be settled in the court of one of them (unless it is explicitly regulated this way).[65]

(iii) The EU's legal accountability towards affected citizens of the recipient states can rest on two pillars. At least briefly to be mentioned is,

[61] On the human rights obligations of the EU, see *supra* Ch 4.D.II.3.

[62] Cf. Art. 96 Cotonou Agreement and Art. 37 of the DCI Regulation (Regulation (EC) No. 1905/2006 of the European Parliament and of the Council of 18 December 2006 establishing a financing instrument for development cooperation (OJ L 378/41) [hereinafter DCI Regulation].

[63] Cf. Art. 300 TEC and Art. 37 DCI Regulation.

[64] By contrast, most bilateral partnership agreements with non-ACP countries are reluctant with regard to arbitration and simply contain a clause to the effect that every party may take "appropriate measures" in line with general international law if a political solution fails. Cf. Art. 19 Cooperation Agreement between European Community and the Kingdom of Cambodia, OJ 1999 No. L 269/18. See also Schmalenbach, "Accountability," p. 176.

[65] See ibid., pp. 176–7.

first, the possibility of judicial proceedings *before national courts* in the respective country.[66] This route, however, is quickly blocked by the jurisdictional immunity of international organizations, which is widely recognized by customary international law and explicitly stipulated in many partnership agreements.[67] More important is the second possible pillar, namely *proceedings before the ECJ*. Is there a way that an affected person, for example in Mozambique, who suffers human rights violations from projects financed and supervised by the EU, can sue the EU?

Two judicial actions seem possible. The first is the action of annulment, pursuant to Art. 263 IV TFEU. Yet the chances for an affected person to fulfill the requirements are less than slim. No affected person will ever itself be addressed by an EU act (first option in Art. 263 IV TFEU). But even if the citizen is not itself addressed by the act yet the act is of "direct concern" to him or her (second option), then he or she would still only have standing if the act "does not entail implementing measures."[68] Since development projects, as decided by the EU, always need further "implementing measures," i.e. decisions on who will conduct the project or program, this requirement will hardly ever be fulfilled.

The other and slightly more realistic judicial action would be an action for damages (Art. 268 TFEU). To trigger non-contractual liability pursuant to Art. 340 para 2 TFEU, the Commission must have acted in a way that constitutes a "sufficiently flagrant violation of a superior rule of law" which confers rights on individuals.[69] This could be the case if binding human rights were violated (see Art. 6 TEU). However, proof of a direct causal link between the unlawful conduct and the alleged damage is difficult to establish. One way to overcome the difficulties could be to hold the Commission accountable for its duties to supervise and monitor its agreements, based on Art. 41 Charter of Fundamental Rights.[70] However, here again, the hurdles for the plaintiff are high.

In sum, legal accountability of the EU for its development interventions is not very strong. While the internal distribution of powers can be and is clearly checked by the Court, other parties, such as the recipient government or affected individuals, hardly have the chance to succeed.

[66] For the respective problematic concerning the World Bank, see *supra* Ch 9.B.I.1a.

[67] See generally A. Reinisch, *International Organizations Before National Courts* (Cambridge University Press, 2000). Specifically for the EU, see P. Craig and G. de Búrca, *EU Law: Text, Cases, and Materials*, 5th edn (Oxford University Press, 2011), p. 307.

[68] On the requirements for standing in Art. 263 IV, see ibid., pp. 491, 492.

[69] ECJ, Case 5/71 (Schöppenstedt v. Council), *ECR* 1971, p. 975, para. 11.

[70] On this argument see Schmalenbach, "Accountability," pp. 182–3.

(2) The European Ombudsman This shifts the focus to another institution that can provide a forum for individual complaints: the European Ombudsman (Art. 228 TFEU). The European Ombudsman is elected by the EP and is an independent organ of the Union. It can receive complaints not only from EU citizens but from any natural or legal person residing in the EU. It has also been established that a complainant does not have to be directly or personally affected by the contested measure. Therefore, European NGOs or committed individuals of any nationality can put forward an *action popularis* on behalf of project-affected individuals. The approval of the affected person is not necessary.

The mandate of the Ombudsman covers investigations into the "maladministration in the activities of EU institutions." Hence, issues of ill-conceived development projects can be investigated and evaluated against the existing legal standards and those agreed upon in the project agreement. In practice, there have been many complaints concerning the area of development cooperation. However, most of them have been driven by (economic) self-interest.[71] Clearly, the potential of such proceedings has not been fully developed yet. One reason might be the rather toothless tools that the Ombudsman can use. It concludes its investigations with decisions and reports to the concerned institution, the EP and the public. The Union organs are obliged to cooperate with it and respond to its statement. However, its reports are not legally binding.

Certainly, the Ombudsman stands in the shadow of the European courts. But can it not bear comparison with the World Bank Inspection Panel, as Kirsten Schmalenbach has pointed out?[72] There are certain differences which weaken the position of the EU Ombudsman in comparison to the Inspection Panel. Since World Bank regulations are generally more explicit and concrete than those of EU development cooperation law, the Panel can make more concrete statements and judgments. Also, the Panel's reports have to be approved by the Board of Executive Directors, while the reports of the Ombudsman are simply presented to the organs. Hence, the institutional attention to the Panel's findings might be higher than to the reports of the Ombudsman. Finally, the fact that the World

[71] The vast majority of these complaints were related to the termination of contracts, unsuccessful tenders, outstanding payments and the rejection of proposed projects. However, some cases also concerned damage caused to complainants affected by an EU-financed road project in Nairobi and complaints against continued cooperation with Vietnam despite a poor human rights record. Cf. ibid., p. 184.

[72] Ibid., pp. 183–5.

Bank is a specialized, single-issue organization grants its Panel more publicity. In the EU, the Ombudsman has many more issue areas to report on and is also in "competition" with other actors. Nonetheless, both organs are indeed comparable and perform a very similar function. Civil society should make much more use of the pulpit that an Ombudsman can provide.

b) Financial accountability: Court of Auditors, OLAF and whistle-blowing

Financial accountability of EU development cooperation rests on two shoulders: the European Court of Auditors and the OLAF anti-corruption agency. In addition, a framework for the encouragement and protection of whistle-blowers complements these two.

Auditing by the European Court of Auditors (ECA) is a central accountability mechanism. Based on Art. 287 TFEU, the ECA's task is to examine all revenue and expenditure accounts of the EU with regard to legality, regularity and sound financial management.[73] Its standard of review goes beyond the legal rules. It is therefore especially positioned to control what is now called aid effectiveness, namely the impact and effects of ODA funds spent. The relevant EU financial regulations extend the ECA's mandate to external action, including development cooperation.[74] The ECA's role in the area of EU development cooperation covers ODA expenditures from the general budget, but also the financial activities funded out of the EDF.[75] The investment facility under the EDF is subject to a special audit report based on a tripartite agreement between the Commission, the ECA

[73] H. Hofmann, G. C. Rowe and A. Türk, *Administrative Law and Policy of the European Union* (Oxford University Press, 2011), pp. 729–40; B. Laffan, "Financial Control: The Court of Auditors and OLAF," in J. Peterson and M. Shackleton (eds.), *The Institutions of the European Union*, 2nd edn (Oxford University Press, 2006), pp. 210–28; M. Freytag, *Der Europäische Rechnungshof: Institution, Funktion und politische Wirkung* (Baden-Baden: Nomos, 2005); J. Inghelram, "The European Court of Auditors: Current Legal Issues," *Common Market Law Review*, 37 (2000), 129–46 at 129.

[74] See Regulation 1605/2022 on the Financial Regulation applicable to the general budget of the European Communities. Art. 162 para. 1 makes the provisions concerning audit by the ECA applicable to external action; Art. 170 provides that financing agreements must provide for powers of audit by the ECA.

[75] Art. 11 para. 7 of the Internal Agreement between Representatives of the Governments of the Member States, meeting within the Council, on the financing of Community aid under the multiannual financial framework for the period 2008–2013 in accordance with the ACP-EC Partnership Agreement, OJ 2006 No. L 247/32. On these two budgets and their background in the early ACP cooperation and the later added cooperation with other countries, see *supra* Ch 3.A.III.

and the European Investment Bank (EIB).[76] The ECA acts by investigating and publishing reports. It presents annual reports but can also investigate special issues and then publish the results. The annual reports are adopted in confidential contradictory procedure and then published in the EU Official Journal.[77] In the area of development cooperation, the ECA reports are among the most qualified and biting assessments of the ongoing waste and inefficiencies.[78]

As mentioned before, auditing is important but can be toothless. Specific structures against corruption are necessary. Even before the World Bank, the European Union in 1999 established a special office that is tasked with combating corruption, called OLAF.[79] Art. 325 TFEU lays down that the Union and its member states are obliged to counter fraud and any other illegal activities affecting the financial interests of the Union.[80] Of course, the scope of OLAF's mandate and work is much broader, given the immense sums that are, for example, spent on the European agricultural policies. Still, investigations into irregularities and fraud in the Union's external action are part of OLAF's mandate and play a considerable role in its work.[81]

[76] Tripartite agreement between the European Commission, the ECA, and the EIB concerning cooperation for the purposes of the Court of Auditors' audit rights with respect to the EIB of 27 October 2003.

[77] Art. 143 para. 2–6 of the General Financial Regulations No. 1605/2002, OJ 2002 No. L 246/1 (made applicable to the EEAD by Regulation No. 1081/2010, OJ No L 311/9); third parties are not party to this contradictory procedure even if they are critically mentioned in the Annual Report, see CFI, T-277/97 (*Ismeri Europe* v. *Court of Auditors*), *ECR* 1999, II-1825.

[78] See, for example, ECA, Annual Report Concerning the Financial Year 2010, OJ C 326 of November 10, 2011; ECA, Annual Report Concerning the Financial Year 2009, OJ C 303 of November 9, 2010; ECA, Annual Report on the Activities Funded by the Eighth, Ninth and Tenth European Development Funds (EDFs), OJ C 326/02 of November 10, 2011; ECA, *Special Report No 4/2009: The Commission's Management of Non-State Actors' Involvement in EC Development Cooperation* (Luxembourg: Publications Office of the European Union, 2009); ECA, *Special Report No 10/2008 EC Development Assistance to Health Services in Sub-Saharan Africa: (pursuant to article 248(4), second subparagraph, EC)* (Luxembourg: Publications Office of the European Union, 2009); ECA, *Special Report No 6/2006.*

[79] This acronym is based on the French name of the European Anti-Fraud Office: Office Européen de Lutte Anti-Fraud / OLAF; for its legal base see Commission's Decision of April 28, 1999 to establish OLAF (OJ 1999, L136).

[80] J. Inghelram, *Legal and Institutional Aspects of the European Anti-Fraud Office (OLAF): an Analysis with a Look Forward to a European Public Prosecutor's Office* (Groningen: Europa Law Pub., 2011).

[81] OLAF's competences are contained in the specific sectoral legislative acts, including the ones applicable to development cooperation, see namely Art. 30 DCI Regulation No 1905/2006. In 2009, OLAF investigated irregularities in external aid (which goes beyond

One specific mechanism that is also promoted by OLAF is that of whistle-blowing.[82] The EU mechanisms in place also apply to development cooperation, and the EU actively encourages partner countries to institute complementary mechanisms on their side.[83]

c) Substantive accountability: evaluations

Evaluation of EU development cooperation has evolved considerably over the years. Since 1997 it has been carried out by the "Joint Evaluation Unit," which performs a common function for DG External Affairs, DG Development and EuropeAid. It enjoys a measure of independence in that it reports directly to the Commissioners, bypassing the respective hierarchies. The DG External Affairs having been merged into the EEAS, the work program of the Evaluation Unit is decided by the Commissioner for Development in agreement with the High Representative for Foreign Affairs and the Commissioner for Enlargement and European Neighbourhood Policy.[84] The budget of the Evaluation Unit is determined by the EU Parliament and the EU Commission. Independence is ensured by direct reporting to the political level and by the standing of the head of Evaluation. He or she is posited at the highest level of seniority before political function.

The Evaluation Unit is in charge of the evaluation of the Commission's cooperation and development programs in third countries, excluding the enlargement candidate countries and humanitarian aid. It covers all geographical regions and the corresponding EC external cooperation programs. There are evaluations of country programs, sectors and different instruments. Concrete evaluations are carried out by external consultants under the quality control of the Evaluation Unit.

development cooperation) in 86 cases with a total volume of 153.31 million euro, cf. European Commission, *Protection of the European Union's Financial Interests-Fight Against Fraud-Annual Report 2009*, Report from the Commission to the Council and the European Parliament, COM (2010) 382 final of July 14, 2010, p. 16. Available at http://ec.europa.eu/anti_fraud/documents/reports-commission/2009_en.pdf (last visited July 2013).

82 See European Commission, *Protection of the Financial Interests of the Communities – Fight Against Fraud – Annual Report 2006*, Report from the Commission to the European Parliament and the Council, COM (2007) 390 of July 6, 2007, pp. 19–21. Available at http://ec.europa.eu/anti_fraud/documents/reports-commission/2006_essn.pdf (last visited July 2013)

83 ECA, *Supporting Anti-Corruption Reform in Partner Countries: Concepts, Tools and Areas for Action* (Luxembourg: Publications Office of the European Union, 2011), pp. 42; 65.

84 See OECD, *Evaluation in Development Agencies*, p. 73; see also the webpage of the unit at http://ec.europa.eu/europeaid/how/evaluation/index_en.htm, in particular http://ec.europa.eu/europeaid/how/evaluation/work_program/documents/note_ap_2011_en.pdf (last visited July 2013).

The EU's law of development cooperation contains explicit legal bases for evaluations. For ACP countries, the Cotonou Agreement explicitly lays down objectives and modalities of evaluation.[85] It provides for joint evaluations of the EU and its partner countries, but does not explicitly require stakeholder involvement as a matter of the Agreement itself. Outside the ACP context, the DCI Regulation and respective thematic instruments explicitly require the Commission to evaluate its programs and send reports to the European Parliament. The DCI also requires the commission to "associate all relevant stakeholders, including non-State actors and local authorities."[86]

The details of the evaluations, namely the substantive standards, are not legally regulated and are left to the discretion of the Evaluation Unit. In practice, the standards used are essentially the self-set targets of the respective programs or projects.[87] There remains considerable difference in evaluation between project aid and budget support. However, the overall evaluation methodology is influenced considerably by more general OECD-DAC standards.[88]

The EU evaluation regime does not provide for any specific sanctions for negative evaluation results. The legal bases stipulate that evaluation results shall inform future planning, and since 1997 evaluation reports are routinely published on the Commission website. Otherwise, specific reactions to negative evaluations are left to the established channels of administrative and parliamentary oversight. In that sense, evaluation provides the informational basis and necessary evidence for accountability and complements other mechanisms, but is not in itself a sufficient instrument for substantive accountability.

d) *Political accountability*

The political accountability of the EU development administration, as primarily located in the European Commission, is the task of the European Parliament (EP) as well as the Council, in which the member states are

[85] Articles 31 and 32 of Annex IV of the Cotonou Agreement.

[86] See e.g. Article 33 DCI Regulation (EC, No 1905/2006).

[87] See European Commission, *Evaluation Methods for the European Union's External Assistance* (Luxembourg: Publications Office of the European Union, 2006). Available at http://ec.europa.eu/europeaid/evaluation/methodology/examples/guide4_en.pdf (last visited July 2013).

[88] See OECD, *Quality Standards for Development Evaluation*, DAC Guidelines and Reference Series (Paris: OECD Publishing, 2010). Available at http://www.oecd.org/development/evaluationofdevelopmentprogrammes/dcdndep/44798177.pdf (last visited July 2013); OECD, *Evaluation in Development Agencies*.

represented. The EP has a Committee on Development which is the parliament's most important actor in this respect.[89] It shares its task (or competes) with the Committee on External Relations. Besides the parliament, the Council also has working groups dealing with development, namely the ACP Working Group and the Development Cooperation Working Group.

The EP and Council share a central mechanism of scrutiny: their budgetary power, based on Art. 314 TFEU. With their power of the purse they can react to previous results of policies, hence reward successful projects or shut down others. In support of this function, they receive the European Court of Auditor's Annual and Special Reports on the implementation of the development policy together with the Statement of Assurance within the context of the discharge procedure (Art. 319 TFEU) and thus have detailed information on the proper management of most aspects of the EDC.[90]

Besides, the EP has the task of general political control (Art. 14 para. 1 TEU). In this respect, it is dependent on detailed information at an early stage, provided either by the Commission[91] or gathered through other sources (e.g. the European Ombudsman). It can also unearth the relevant information through its right to question the Commission.

2. Transparency: only for EU citizens?

Transparency of EU development operations rests, first of all, on the general access to information regime. Article 15 para. 3 TFEU lays down a right of access to Union documents for every resident or citizen of the EU in line with secondary legislation. The latter is based on legislation enacted in 2001.[92] On this basis, applicants have a right of access to documents of the Commission, Council and Parliament, unless it falls under a

[89] On the central role of committees in the EP in general, Dann, *Political Institutions*.

[90] It has been criticized that the EDF's investment facility that is managed by the EIB is not covered by the discharge procedure even though the operations under this instrument are conducted by the EIB on behalf of the Community that keeps bearing the risk (see the ECA, *Opinion No 9/2007 on the Proposal for a Council Regulation on a Financial Regulation Applicable to the 10th European Development Fund*, OJ 2008 C 23/3 of January 28, 2008, margin no. 6).

[91] E.g. through its Annual Report for the implementation of the European Community Policy (cf. the European Consensus of Development, OJ 2006 No. C 46/01, para. 125).

[92] Regulation (EC) No 1049/2001 of the European Parliament and the Council of 30 May 2001 regarding public access to European Parliament, Council and Commission documents. On the regulation see M. Broberg, "Access to Documents: a General Principle of Community Law?" *European Law Review*, 27 (2002), 194–205.

negative list of exceptions. Refusal of access is subject to complaint to the European Ombudsman or appeal to the Court (formerly Court of First Instance).

The present regime displays two weaknesses which are particularly relevant in development cooperation: firstly, non-residents of the EU do not have a right of access but are subject merely to a discretionary decision by the respective institution. Secondly, the old legislative regime does not extend to all EU institutions, and specifically not to the EEAS. Repeated proposals for reform have not resulted in amendments so far, even though Article 15 para. 3 TFEU now provides a basis for extending access rights to all EU institutions, bodies and agencies.[93]

In addition to the general legal regime, transparency in EU development cooperation is governed by self-commitments. The Commission signed up to the International Aid Transparency Initiative in September 2008 as part of the Accra Agenda for Action and Aid Effectiveness.[94] In line with the standards of this initiative, it discloses all available information on volume, allocation and results of its aid expenditure on its website.

3. Relational summary: who is the EU development administration effectively accountable to?

As before, we shall summarize the accountability structures by asking to whom the EU development administration is accountable. Here, a similar picture emerges as in the World Bank, with rather effective accountability towards Europeans but fewer possibilities for recipients and recipient citizens.

European development administration is effectively accountable to the other organs of the EU. The Council and European Parliament can and do deploy legal accountability mechanisms, namely lawsuits before the ECJ, in order to check the use of competences. They also have means of political accountability. With the Court of Auditors as well as OLAF, two more organs of the EU check on the financial propriety of development operations, even though with fewer sanctioning powers. Internal checks and balances are therefore available and used.

[93] On recent developments see D. Adamski, "Approximating a Workable Compromise on Access to Official Documents: The 2011 Developments in the European Courts," *Common Market Law Review*, 49 (2001), 521–58.

[94] Cf. Accra Agenda for Action, para. 24 a) and the Commission's website at http://ec.europa.eu/europeaid/how/accountability/iati_en.htm (last visited July 2013). More on this, see *infra* V.3.

The European general public also has various means to hold the EU administration accountable. It can activate the Ombudsman, and use its report to publicize or scandalize wrong-doing. It can also rely on the often very well-informed and detailed reports of the Court of Auditors. And finally it can use its strong right to access EU documents.

The EU is much less accountable, however, to recipient states and their citizens who might be affected by EU financed projects. Since they cannot use political and financial accountability mechanisms, which are reserved for internal EU actors, they are left with legal and substantive accountability. Yet recipient governments have no regular standing at the ECJ and do not use arbitration. Affected citizens in the recipient countries equally cannot access the European courts. They could, however, file complaints with the Ombudsman. This is, however, not a very resourceful and effective organ but it could provide more help than it is currently asked to give. What is very problematic indeed is the fact that access to documents is especially hampered for non-EU citizens. Clearly, the EU law of development cooperation provides even less protection for non-EU parties than the law of the World Bank.

III. Germany

Accountability of German development administration is the accountability of a regular national executive and its (private) cooperation partners (here especially the KfW and GIZ). One is therefore confronted with the regular instruments of executive oversight. At the same time, one can inquire into more specialized mechanisms that apply in the area of development cooperation (such as evaluations).

1. Standards and mechanisms: how Germany can be held accountable

a) Legal accountability: courts, Integrity Advisor, Ombudsman

Courts are the first forum of legal accountability to think of. The rule of law including the access to justice is a central principle of German constitutional law (Articles 19 para. 4 and 20 para. 3 German Constitution). But in the area of development cooperation access to justice and legal accountability is harder to obtain. The situation resembles that in the EU. Similarly, we have to distinguish between different actors.

There are, first, organs of the other branches of government (especially the parliament). Judicial control of their respective competences is possible (cf. Art. 93 para. 1, no.1 German Constitution) and hence the accountability of the German development administration assured in principle. Yet, there is no relevant case law regarding the use of competences by the government in the area of development cooperation. Only the vertical distribution of competences, especially the question of whether municipalities could establish their own development programs, was briefly contested.[95]

Recipient governments as well as affected citizens, on the other hand, face major legal hurdles to gaining judicial protection. There is no information on arbitral proceedings between Germany and recipient states. Even if there were arbitral clauses in the cooperation agreements of which we are not aware, such clauses are not really used in practice. With respect to normal court action, there are further hurdles. If a recipient state wanted to sue Germany for not providing as much ODA as agreed upon in an agreement (and assuming that no primary arbitration is agreed upon), the foreign government would be faced in Germany (and any other donor country) with the principle of state immunity.[96] This would prevent German courts from accepting such actions.

Affected citizens of recipient countries, finally, would be faced with a restrictive understanding of their standing in German procedural law. This is not a problem of nationality. The problem rather lies in the narrow German concept of standing. This requires the claimant to show the violation of a norm that intended to give the affected a subjective right.[97] Development agreements as agreed upon by the German state do not contain such norms.[98] They do not address the affected citizen but grant rights only to the contracting parties, i.e. the government. Affected citizens therefore cannot claim to be entitled by them.

Project-affected individuals might possibly rely on human rights treaties to gain standing in German courts. As has been argued above, Germany is bound extraterritorially, namely by the International Covenant on Economic, Social and Cultural Rights.[99] Ratified treaty law is applicable in German courts, and human rights provisions certainly grant rights to individuals. However, there is no case law in these matters, and litigants would face additional hurdles regarding proof, causation and attribution

[95] Schwanenflügel, *Entwicklungszusammenarbeit als Aufgabe der Gemeinden*, p. 81.

[96] M. N. Shaw, *International Law*, 5th edn (Cambridge University Press, 2003), pp. 621, 622.

[97] M. P. Singh, *German Administrative Law in Common Law Perspective*, 2nd edn (Berlin, New York: Springer, 2001), pp. 214, 215.

[98] On the legal nature of such agreements, see *supra* Ch 6.B.III.3.

[99] See *supra* Ch 4.D.II.1.

of violations. The case law from German courts that does exist rather concerns criminal prosecutions of German officials for corruption,[100] labor disputes[101] or tax matters.[102]

Another question is, again, whether there are further, quasi-judicial institutions that help to provide (quasi-)legal accountability. There is no general Ombudsman for development cooperation or the like. Instead, one has to look into the different organizations that effectively decide about the transfer of ODA, mainly the GIZ (responsible chiefly for expertise in technical assistance) and the KfW (responsible for expertise in the financial assistance).[103] Both organizations have certain structures, yet none of them are very satisfactory.

In the German development bank (KfW), compliance with and the respect for relevant rules have become a noted topic, but mostly concern financial integrity (and are thus dealt with below at b). The GIZ has an Integrity Advisor[104] as well as an external Ombudsman – and it is not quite clear from the publicly available sources why there is such duplication. Both of them can be approached by anybody, namely project partners, clients or the public at large as well as staff of the organization. Both are supposed to oversee that standards of integrity, as laid down in a Code of Conduct, are upheld.[105] The main focus of this Code is the rules on financial behavior, i.e. the prohibition of corrupt practice (active or passive bribery, accepting gifts/advantages), and the obligation to remain neutral and avoid conflicts of interest. Both of them seem to be tasked with mediating in conflicts. The only difference appears to be their status within the organization: while the Integrity Advisor is a GIZ employee, the Ombudsman is an external lawyer. However, even the Integrity Advisor is guaranteed certain independence, as he or she reports directly to the Management Board, and is obliged to be impartial, autonomous and bound to confidentiality.

However, it is important to note that it would be false to conceive these bodies as providing judicial or even quasi-judicial accountability. They do not judge by legal rules; they have only limited autonomy; and they

[100] Bundesgerichtshof, judgment of 19.12.1997, Az. 2 StR 521/97 (holding that GIZ employees are criminally liable just as other public officials).

[101] Bundesarbeitsgericht, judgment of 12.12.1990, Az. 4 AZR 238/90 (on working hours for experts employed abroad).

[102] Finanzgericht Rheinland-Pfalz, Urteil v. 30.04.2007, Az. 5 K 2884/03 (on taxation of experts employed abroad).

[103] For an introduction to them, see *supra* Ch 3.A.II.1. and 23.III.

[104] See www.giz.de/en/aboutgiz/integrity_advisor.html (last visited July 2013).

[105] See www.giz.de/en/downloads/giz-en-code-of-conduct.pdf (last visited July 2013).

cannot prescribe any sanctions. Instead, they should be seen as mediators and sensitizers. They can moderate conflicts, help to create mutual understanding and inform organizations about feedback. But they hardly hold the organizations accountable for their behavior.

In sum, it is difficult to hold the German development administration legally accountable. While other branches of government have the respective rights, recipient states and affected citizens in the recipient countries face high hurdles and there is no respective practice. There is a trend, though, to establish less-formalized structures, but their effect is still to be proven.

b) Financial accountability: audits and anti-corruption measures

Given the poor record with regard to *legal* accountability, the issue of financial accountability gains importance in the German context. Here again, we differentiate between *general auditing* and more specific structures dealing with *corruption*.

Regarding *general auditing* requirements, the German Court of Auditors is especially important. It annually checks the expenditure of the German government, including that of the BMZ (Art. 114 para. 2 German Constitution). The Court is an independent institution and reports directly to parliament. Discharge by parliament of the financial operations of the branches of government depends on the Court's report.[106] In its annual reports, the Court of Auditors also reports regularly on the expenditures of the German Ministry for Development. The reports generally comment on the evolution and structure of development expenditure and the effectiveness of the implementing structures. In recent years, the Court specifically criticized the use of personnel from GIZ for ministerial tasks and commented skeptically on the merger of GIZ with other implementing organizations. It did not, however, analyze individual projects or programs in recipient countries.[107] Its role seems to be more to control

[106] §§42–47 Gesetz über die Grundsätze des Haushaltsrechts des Bundes und der Länder (Haushaltsgrundsätzegesetz – HGrG / Law on Budget Principles for the Federal and State Government); §§88–104 Bundeshaushaltsordnung (BHO / Federal Budget Order); §§1Gesetz über den Bundesrechnungshof (Law on the Federal Court of Auditors).

[107] See e.g. Bundesrechnungshof, *Bemerkungen 2011 zur Haushalts- und Wirtschaftsführung des Bundes* (2011), p. 36. Available at http://bundesrechnungshof.de/veroeffentlichungen/bemerkungen-jahresberichte/Bemerkungen-2011.pdf (last visited July 2013); pp. 279–85 (Ch. 75); Bundesrechnungshof, *Bemerkungen 2010 zur Haushalts- und Wirtschaftsführung des Bundes* (2010), p. 36. Available at http://bundesrechnungshof.de/veroeffentlichungen/bemerkungen-jahresberichte/bemerkungen-2010.pdf (last visited July 2013); pp. 166–8 (Ch. 33).

organizational structures and general procedures rather than the actual use of funds by implementing agencies, even though the Court's powers extend to the latter.

The BMZ itself takes on an increasingly important role in the auditing of public expenditures here.[108] It has established a separate auditing division within its structure. Given that most development projects are not implemented by the BMZ itself but by specialist organizations, the division is mainly concerned with examining the way they and other grant recipients have used those funds. The division has three responsibilities, which we shall briefly review: external auditing, auditing of equity holdings and auditing of contract awards.[109]

The first and main task is the external auditing of grant recipients (*Außenrevision*). Two (or in larger projects more) auditors conduct such review, normally within nine months after the final use of funds. Secondly, the BMZ has to report to the Court of Auditors with regard to its shareholdings in other publicly owned institutions (such as the GIZ), so-called *Beteiligungsprüfung*.[110] It is obliged to audit the federal government's holdings and report to the Federal Court of Audit on the annual accounts and all relevant occurrences in the past financial year. The head of the division, as the person responsible for auditing equity holdings, must send a report to the Federal Court of Audit within three months of the annual accounts being adopted. Finally, the Ministry has a special procurement control unit (*Vergabeprüfungsstelle*) that checks whether the respective rules on public procurement have been complied with. It also has the power to oblige units to suspend wrongful transactions.

Development agencies such as the GIZ, which is a privately organized company (even though owned by the German state), have to comply with the general auditing rules applicable to any company.[111] The KfW is subject to the general rules of auditing that apply to any bank according to German law.[112] In terms of internal structures, the KfW also has an audit committee, which (according to its web page) "deals with monitoring the accounting process, the effectiveness of the internal controlling system,

[108] See www.bmz.de/en/what_we_do/approaches/evaluation/revision.html#t1 (last visited July 2013).

[109] On the evaluation of partner organizations by the BMZ see BMZ, *Guidelines*, Point 44.

[110] §53–55 HGrG; §65–69, 112 para. 2 BHO.

[111] See §§316 *et seq*. Handelsgesetzbuch (Commercial Code).

[112] Here audit is based on §§340a *et seq. Handelsgesetzbuch* (Commercial Code) in connection with §9 KfW-Gesetz (Act on the Kreditanstalt für Wiederaufbau), available at www.kfw.de (last visited July 2013).

the internal audit system and the risk management system, auditing the annual and group financial statements, the required independence of the auditor and determines the main points of the audit."[113] Given the prominence of its members (mainly ministers from the federal and regional level) it seems unclear how effectively this committee works.

Besides securing the general financial regularity of their operations, GIZ and KfW also provide certain internal structures to combat *corruption*. As mentioned above, GIZ has appointed an external lawyer as Ombudsman, responsible for dealing with questions of corruption. The Ombudsman can be contacted by anybody. GIZ also adopted a Code of Conduct that deals specifically with the issue of corruption. The KfW has also addressed the issue of corruption more forcefully since the 1990s. Like GIZ, it adopted a Code of Conduct and states that "these rules ensure transparency and encourage employees to deal with possible conflicts of interest openly. The conduct of KfW's employees may not at any time jeopardize the interests of KfW, nor may it lead to any dependencies or obligations. The bank's employees are familiarized with and regularly informed about these rules. The task force working on corruption prevention comprises employees from all of KfW's departments and continues to meet in order to exchange experiences gathered in the individual departments and add to organisational regulations and procedures already in place."[114] KfW also aims to combat money-laundering. It has, to this end, joined a number of international initiatives and regularly trains its employees on the relevant rules and risks.

c) Substantive accountability: evaluations

Evaluations have become a major topic also in the German development system.[115] The Evaluation and Audit Division of the ministry (BMZ-E) has become the central actor here. It has the overall responsibility for the evaluation system of German development cooperation and is tasked with providing guidance and quality assurance of evaluation systems of implementing agencies. A new evaluation policy and guidance for German development cooperation evaluation system was adopted in 2006.[116] Besides, BMZ-E is charged to conduct evaluations of German

[113] At www.kfw.de (last accessed July 2013).

[114] At www.kfw.de (last accessed July 2013).

[115] See OECD, *Evaluation in Development Agencies*, p. 81.

[116] BMZ, *Evaluierungskriterien für die deutsche bilaterale Entwicklungszusammenarbeit: Eine Orientierung für Evaluierungen des BMZ und der Durchführungsorganizationen* (2006). Available at www.bmz.de/de/zentrales_downloadarchiv/erfolg_und_kontrolle/evaluierungskriterien.pdf (last visited July 2013).

development cooperation as a whole. BMZ-funded interventions of all implementing agencies and NGOs, as well as contributions to multilateral organizations are covered on a selective basis. About one-third of its evaluations are conducted jointly with other donors and partner countries.

BMZ-E operates independently from BMZ policy divisions. As a separate unit within the Central Management and NGOs Directorate, its head reports to the deputy minister through the Director General. All evaluations are conducted by external consultants, usually contracted following an EU tender process, who have the final say on the content of the reports. The evaluation reports are available to the public (but only upon request) and executive summaries are published on BMZ's website. Quality is aimed for through a stepwise process, including a mandatory inception report and involvement of stakeholders and, increasingly, external experts through establishment of a reference group for each evaluation. The Evaluation Unit undertakes a quality control of evaluation reports using a related checklist based on OECD standards. It covers six main criteria: relevance, effectiveness, efficiency, overarching development impact, sustainability and coherence.[117]

Participatory evaluation processes that involve all stakeholders, including those at the local level (without compromising the independence of evaluations) are supposed to enhance the use of evaluation results and recommendations. In addition to fostering such participation, BMZ-E also actively engages in disseminating findings and tracks the implementation of recommendations. A formal procedure for follow-up has been in operation since 2001.

KfW and GIZ as implementing agencies have their own evaluation units. KfW has an evaluation department that concentrates on *ex-post* and thematic investigations. It is an independent entity reporting to the Board. Manuals and guidelines help ensure the quality of evaluations. For decentralized evaluations self-reviews are done for certain topics. The evaluations can be conducted by KfW staff or others, as long as they have not been involved in the project at hand.

GIZ also has an internal, but organizationally separate evaluations unit. It develops the GIZ-evaluation system (concepts, procedures, methods and instruments), advises the operative departments on decentralized evaluation, analyzes evaluation findings for learning and accountancy purposes, and communicates evaluation methods and results to the external and internal public. It is separate from the operative departments and

[117] Ibid.

reports directly to the Office of the Managing Directors. Independence is furthermore promoted by contracting independent consulting firms and independent institutes to conduct evaluations. The head of the unit participates in meetings of senior management but not in the highest management team.[118]

d) *Political accountability*

The core actor with regard to the political accountability of the German development administration is the German parliament, the Bundestag. The parliament can hold the government, including the Minister for Economic Cooperation and Development, i.e. the head of the BMZ, responsible for its activities.[119] Within the Bundestag, the Committee for Economic Cooperation and Development is the lead actor and conducts hearings on relevant topics and informs the parliament at large. The Bundestag's competence has two components: for one, it has to approve the annual budget, including those funds reserved for ODA. Here, the Bundestag can and does concretely influence which issues and which countries or regions receive German aid. Beyond its budgetary power, the Bundestag can hold the government accountable by investigation and questioning. Here, the mentioned Committee and its members is a central forum. In addition, the parliament's Budgetary Committee is involved in the financial aspects of development cooperation. In terms of accountability, the parliamentary committees generally require the administration to report on deviations from the planned expenditures as laid down in the budgetary legislation. Due to the wide formulation of the budgetary appropriations, and the merely indicative and confidential nature of more concrete annexes, such deviations are, however, hardly a suitable basis for parliamentary sanction of development administration.

Recounting formal powers can be deceptive, though. In the political reality, development cooperation has seldom been an issue of contention between the political parties in parliament. Only during a short period in the late 1960s and early 1970s was the especially progressive minister attacked more forcefully by its political opponents.[120] Ever since, there has again been a fairly broad consensus on development issues. Hence, while budgetary power is an ongoing and relevant instrument of political and parliamentary oversight, questioning and public debate hardly is.

118 See www.giz.de/en/aboutgiz/monitoring_and_evaluation.html (last visited July 2013).

119 Kollatz, "Grundlagen," 563; 566.

120 *Supra* Ch 1.B.III.

2. Transparency

Transparency of German development cooperation rests, firstly, on the general legal regime for freedom of information in German law. Article 5 para. 1 of the German Constitution guarantees everyone the right to inform themselves without hindrance from generally accessible sources. The 2005 Freedom of Information Act concretizes this right.[121] It firstly makes documents and other pieces of information in the possession of the federal government and agencies such a "generally accessible" source, and secondly grants everyone access to them. Exceptions apply to certain forms of privileged information listed in the Act. According to case law, access to information also encompasses the entire operations of all federal ministries.[122] This includes the Ministry for Economic Cooperation and Development. Indeed, the Ministry has published its archiving system online to facilitate requests for information.[123] The Act is equally applicable to legal persons of private or public law to the extent they exercise public functions, which would encompass GIZ and KfW.[124]

Beyond strictly legal rules, BMZ and the implementing agencies have, secondly, committed themselves to additional non-binding transparency standards. In the context of the Paris Declaration and Accra Agenda for Action, as of 2009, the BMZ has committed itself to the International Aid Transparency Initiative (IATI)[125] and to make information about all allocations and disbursements available to partners and the general public.[126] However, at the time of writing, the BMZ website lacked an easily accessible and comprehensive database of all aid flows to individual countries and individual measures. More information, namely on individual projects, is, however, available on the websites of the GIZ and KfW. GIZ has also subjected itself to an internal transparency policy.[127] In addition,

[121] Gesetz zur Regelung des Zugangs zu Informationen des Bundes, BGBl. I S. 2722. On this, see D. Kugelmann, "Das Informationsfreiheitsgesetz des Bundes," *Neue Juristische Wochenschrift*, 58 (2005), 3609–13 at 3609.

[122] Bundesverwaltungsgericht, judgment of November 3, 2011, Az. 7 C 4.11.

[123] www.bmz.de/de/service/IFG/index.html (last visited July 2013).

[124] §1 para. 1. [125] www.aidtransparency.net/. See *supra*, Ch 2.C.III.1.

[126] BMZ, *Operationsplan zur Umsetzung der Pariser Erklärung 2005 und des Accra Aktionsplans 2008 zur Steigerung der Wirksamkeit von Entwicklungszusammenarbeit* (2009). Available at www.bmz.de/de/zentrales_downloadarchiv/grundsaetze_und_ziele/OP_Paris_Accra_03_2009.pdf (last visited July 2013). See also www.bmz.de/de/was_wir_machen/themen/goodgovernance/korruption/deutscherbeitrag/index.html (last visited July 2013).

[127] GIZ, Policy Transparenz und Informationsaustausch, available at www.giz.de/de/downloads/giz2011-de-policy-transparenz_1.pdf (last visited September 2012).

GIZ and KfW have committed themselves to the "Public Corporate Governance Codex" adopted by the federal government on July 1, 2009. This non-binding codex formulates standards of corporate governance designed to make the management and supervision of publicly owned companies more transparent and easier to understand.[128]

3. Relational summary: who is German development administration effectively accountable to?

The accountability of German development administration is a patchwork that is growing thicker but still has big holes. German development administration is, like the development administrations in the EU, mostly accountable to other branches of government. Parliament or states can check its competences in court; parliament can use means of political accountability (through parliamentary inquiries or budget control). But there is, in effect, no pertinent case law and hardly any parliamentary inquiries. At least in public, there is relatively little debate.[129] Instead, development cooperation in Germany is mostly supported by a broad political consensus. The certainly ongoing political control of ODA in parliament is therefore a rather silent affair. The Court of Auditors, on the other hand, certainly watches over expenditures but has so far rarely engaged in detailed controls of projects and programs.

And again, recipient governments and affected citizens cannot effectively intervene and hold the German administration accountable. There are no (at least no public information on) arbitral proceedings and standing in court is hampered. Less than the World Bank (Inspection Panel) or the EU (Ombudsman), the German institutions hardly provide quasi-legal venues of accountability. Even though the GIZ has an Ombudsman and an Integrity Advisor, who can be called upon by anybody, there is no information on their "cases," reports or effects. Participation in evaluation would be the only possible way for affected citizens to voice their opinions.

[128] The Codex is available in English at www.bundesfinanzministerium.de/nn_39010/DE/Wirtschaft__und__Verwaltung/Bundesliegenschaften__und__Bundesbeteiligungen/Public__corporate__governance__Kodex/AnlagePCGKengl,templateId=raw,property=publicationFile.pdf (last visited September 2012). See also www.kfw.de/kfw/de/KfW-Konzern/Unternehmen/Verantwortung_und_Corporate_Governance/Corporate_Governance55703/index.jsp (last visited September 2012).

[129] Current discussions on the activities of the Minister are rather based on his overly partisan distribution of jobs at the ministry, see M. Schäfers, "Das System Niebel," *Frankfurter Allgemeine Zeitung* (January 1st, 2012). Available at www.faz.net/aktuell/wirtschaft/entwicklungshilfeministerium-das-system-niebel-11609182.html (last visited July 2013).

More effective than in other cases are the legal regimes on transparency and access to documents. Here, it is the role of the general public to make use of them.

All in all, the accountability of German development administration leaves familiar elements to be wished for. The voices of affected people especially have no venue here, which is a problem of individual justice as much as a missed opportunity for institutional learning on the side of German actors. It should be noted that Canada adopted a special Official Development Assistance (ODA) Accountability Act in 2008.[130] However, this Act mainly serves the purpose of ensuring that all ODA expenditures focus on poverty reduction and respect human rights (Art. 4), on which the relevant authorities have to report regularly (Art. 5). Beyond this, it does not provide for more specialized accountability mechanisms or grant access to non-Canadian citizens. It is not clear that this Act effectively increases the accountability of actors but it does signal a clear acceptance of the importance of the issue. A German debate on stronger legal grounds for accountability would be useful.

IV. Recipients

Donors are not the only objects of accountability in the law of development cooperation. On the contrary, in the popular mindset it is primarily the recipients who have to be held responsible for their (mis-)use of development funds. With regard to recipients, different accountability mechanisms of different levels have to be distinguished. There are, first, the domestic mechanisms of accountability in the aid-receiving countries. These may include various forms of political, legal or financial control, used by national parliaments, courts and publics. These mechanisms are beyond the reach of this study, however, given their domestic nature and multitude.[131]

130 For information see www.acdi-cida.gc.ca/acdi-cida/acdi-cida.nsf/eng/FRA-121185349-JB8 (last visited July 2013).

131 On a new approach to strengthen domestic systems of accountability and its application in Kenya, see J. M. M. Akech, "Development Partners and Governance of Public Procurement in Kenya: Enhancing Democracy in the Administration of Aid," *New York University Journal of International Law and Politics*, 37 (2006), 829–68. See generally L. Pritchett and M. Woolcock, "Solutions When the Solution Is the Problem: Arraying the Disarray in Development," in Easterly, *Reinventing Foreign Aid*; R. Reinikka, "Donors and Service Delivery," in ibid., pp. 179–99. For an examination of recipient strategies for managing aid in the 1990s, see J. Carlsson, G. Somolekae and N. van de Walle, *Foreign Aid in Africa: Learning From Country Experiences* (Uppsala: Nordiska afrikainstitutet,

Yet fully within our scope are those mechanisms with which donors supervise the use of "their" money. Donors have installed mechanisms of fiscal accountability to control the implementation of projects (1a). Secondly, we examine the fascinating system by which the World Bank can hold individual contractors accountable (1b). And, thirdly and equally fascinating, is a new mechanism involving the peer review of recipients by other recipients (2).

1. Accountability towards donors

a) *Supervision and sanctions against recipient governments*

The system by which donors hold the governmental recipients of ODA accountable has two elements: one is a set of contractual tools of supervision, the other their sanction mechanisms.

The World Bank obliges itself to supervise the implementation of Bank-financed projects and has, to that end, developed an extensive system regarding its own monitoring, evaluation reviews and reporting.[132] Its internal law also states, however, that the recipient's project team is primarily responsible for overviewing a project's implementation and outcome. It spells out precisely which procedures the recipients have to obey in monitoring and evaluating the project's process and outcome, and what to report to the Bank.[133] The General Conditions, which set forth the terms and conditions generally applicable to the legal agreements between the Bank and the recipient, and which are regularly incorporated into its legal agreements with borrowers, specify these obligations. These General Conditions also add the duty of recipient governments to periodically audit their financial statements.[134]

These duties of the recipient to monitor, evaluate, report and audit are backed in the internal regulations of the World Bank by the possibility of legal sanctions. These include the possible suspension or even termination

1997). On the interaction between African political and administrative systems with the aid system in specific country contexts, see Whitfield, *The Politics of Aid*; A. Rocha Menocal, *Learning From Experience: A Review of Recipient Government Efforts to Manage Donor Relations and Improve the Quality of Aid*, Overseas Development Institue Working Paper No. 268. Available at www.odi.org.uk/resources/docs/2027.pdf (last visited July 2013).

[132] World Bank Operational Policy 13.05, Operational Policy 13.55.

[133] World Bank Operational Policy 13.55, para. 1 and 3.

[134] General Conditions IBRD (fn. 19), Art. V, Sect. 5.08 and 5.09; General Conditions IDA, Art. IV, Sect. 4.08 and 4.09 (different as there is no equivalent to Art. V, Sect. 5.09 b (iii) IBRD which states that it must make the audited Financial Statements, or cause the audited Financial Statements to be made, publicly available in a timely fashion and in a manner acceptable to the Bank.

of the financing of projects. Here again it is the General Conditions that regulate in detail under which circumstances the Bank can suspend or cancel its financial support for a project.[135] The Bank can go further still. It can declare the acceleration of its payment of dues or even demand a refund of already paid sums.[136] These sanctions can be triggered in cases of corrupt, fraudulent or collusive behavior on the side of the recipient. However, such sanctions can also be based on performance failure on the part of the recipient. And, obviously, they are imposed unilaterally by the Bank.

The EU also supervises the implementation of its projects by recipients. This ongoing task is mainly carried out by the country delegations now integrated into the EEAS.[137] The Commission's general conditions for Financing Agreements also require beneficiaries to check regularly that operations financed with EU funds are properly implemented and to take appropriate measures to prevent irregularities, fraud and corruption.[138]

In all likelihood, German project agreements have similar clauses, but they are not known to us. Given that GIZ, for example, implements many of the projects itself, accountability is more a question of the internal oversight and evaluation within the GIZ.

b) Sanctioning contractors

In recent years, the World Bank has also developed an elaborate sanctioning system that is geared not towards the recipient government but targets individual contractors, consultants, bidders or other individuals. The system has evolved since the late 1990s and is now formally based on the Sanctions Committee Procedures (SCP), as approved by the Board of Executive Directors in 2004.[139]

The process starts with the above-mentioned Department of Institutional Integrity (INT)[140] investigating any allegation of fraud and

[135] General Conditions IBRD, Art. VII; General Conditions IDA, Art. VI, see also Shihata, *World Bank Legal Papers*, p. 619.

[136] General Conditions IBRD, Art. VII, Sect. 7.06 and 7.07, General Conditions IDA, Art. VI, Sect. 6.06.-6.07.

[137] See Article 36, Annex IV Cotonou Agreement. See also Article 30 DCI Regulation on the requirement that agreements concluded with beneficiaries provide for investigation rights of OLAF and the ECA.

[138] See e.g. Article 19, Financing Agreement – Annex I – General Conditions, available at http://ec.europa.eu/europeaid/work/procedures/financing/financing_agreement/documents/2011_cf_cg_bud_essn.pdf (last visited July 2013).

[139] See also the so-called Thornburg Report at http://siteresources.worldbank.org/PROCUREMENT/Resources/thornburghreport.pdf; also de Cooker, "Ethics and Accountability," pp. 48–9.

[140] See *supra* Ch 9.B.I.1b.

corruption in a Bank-financed project (Sect. 3 SCP). If it finds sufficient evidence, the INT notifies the so-called Sanctions Committee, which is composed of five members of the World Bank staff.[141] The Sanctions Committee then assesses the charges in a strictly formalized, quasi-judicial procedure. In that procedure, it has to inform the respondent, who has the right to submit their own written arguments (Sect. 5 SCP). The Committee then conducts a hearing (Sect. 9, 10) in which the respondent as well as the INT is represented. If the Committee finds the evidence sufficient, it can impose sanctions on the respondent. These sanctions can range from reprimanding the respondent in a formal letter of censure to declaring the respondent ineligible to be awarded future bank contracts, to "any other sanctions that the Committee deems appropriate under the circumstances" (Sect. 13c).

The EU also provides explicit legal bases to exclude contractors from further procurement processes.[142] These provisions of its general budgetary law also apply to development cooperation. It requires the exclusion of contractors who were declared in serious breach of a past contract. Such a declaration is made by the Commission in a formalized procedure and can be based specifically on instances of irregularities and corruption.

In Germany, the BMZ's procurement control unit (*Vergabeprüfstelle*) also investigates individual allegations of misconduct. In terms of sanctions, the unit itself can only require the annulment of individual contract awards, but serious irregularities are subject to the ordinary criminal proceedings under German anti-corruption law. In addition, German procurement law contains numerous sectoral legal bases for the exclusion of contractors from future public procurement procedures in certain cases of prior irregularities.[143]

c) *Brief summary*

In sum, donors have (to varying degrees) installed a system to control the fiscal accountability of recipients that provides potentially effective instruments. The practical application and hence its "bite" is unclear, but given the power dynamic between "rich lender" and "poor recipient," one could imagine a strict application. Whether donors actually do so is

[141] Two Managing Directors, the General Counsel as well as two senior members of the Bank staff, all appointed by the President, Sect. 1 a SCP.

[142] See Financial Regulation No. 1605/2002, Articles 93, 96, 114.

[143] See e.g. §6 para. 5, §6 EG para. 4 of the Vertrags- und Verdingungsordnung für Leistungen, Teil A (VOL/A), 20 November 2009.

probably again a political question. Often enough, enforcement of the law might take a back seat.

In relation to the other areas of accountability of recipients, however, financial accountability is strongest in a formal sense. Political accountability of recipients towards donors is hardly put in formal terms. And with regard to mechanisms of substantive accountability, recipient governments are no less responsible to evaluate than the donors themselves.

2. Accountability among peers: NEPAD's African Peer Review Mechanism

Holding the recipients of development aid accountable is not a task of the donors alone. In an unprecedented move in 2001, a number of African countries created a mechanism to hold each other accountable. The "African Peer Review Mechanism" (APRM) is embedded in the New Partnership for Africa's Development (NEPAD), which was founded by five countries (Algeria, Egypt, Nigeria, Senegal, South Africa) and today comprises thirty-three members. NEPAD has the objective to establish conditions for sustainable development by promoting policy reforms and mobilizing resources.[144] The APRM is a central building block of this endeavor.[145] It is formally regulated in the Base Document, approved by the Heads of States and Government Implementation Committee of NEPAD and endorsed by the African Union Summit in 2002.[146]

The APRM is open to all member states of the African Union which adopt the Declaration on Democracy, Political, Economic and Corporate Governance.[147] By adoption, the country commits itself to a set of reviews, starting with a base review within eighteen months of signing up to the APRM, with periodic reviews every two to four years and special reviews

[144] A. Bing-Pappoe, *Reviewing Africa's Peer Review Mechanism: A Seven Country Study* (Ottawa: Partnership Africa Canada, 2010). Available at www.pacweb.org/Documents/APRM/APRM_Seven_countries_March2010-E.pdf (last visited July 2013); for an early appraisal see C. Jakobeit, "Fünf Jahre NEPAD," *Aus Politik und Zeitgeschichte*, 32–33 (2006), 21–5 at 21; A. Marong, "New Partnership for Africa's Development (NEPAD)," in Wolfrum, *Max Planck Encyclopedia of Public International Law*; Z. Ndayi, "Contextualising NEPAD: Regionalism, Plurilateralism and Multilateralism," *South African Journal of International Affairs*, 16 (2009), 371–87. The central document, the Strategic Framework Document, was formally adopted in 2001.

[145] See A. M. B. Mangu, "What Future for Human and Peoples' Rights Under the African Union, New Partnership for Africa's Development, African Peer-Review Mechanism and the African Court?" *South African Yearbook of International Law*, 29 (2004), 136–63 at 147–51.

[146] At www.uneca.org/aprm/ (last visited July 2013). [147] Ibid.

if so desired (according to Base Document, para. 14). Reviews are undertaken by a Country Review Team which is appointed by the standing Panel of Eminent Persons, composed of five to seven experts overseeing the APRM process (para. 6–8).

The reviews are geared toward two sets of standards. One is the Program of Action, which every participating country has to develop and which sets out its development agenda (para. 17). The other standard used to review the country's performance is the Declaration on Democracy, Political, Economic and Corporate Governance, which endorses a clear set of objectives, standards, criteria and indicators (para. 15). The Country Review Reports are adopted by the Heads of States and Governments (Implementation Committee), including recommendations on the follow-up and are published. A monitoring of the follow-up process is envisioned.

This, however, was only the theory. The first decade showed a mixed outcome. So far (2012), fourteen countries have taken part in the mechanism or are close to finishing the review; four more are currently beginning. Twelve countries have not yet taken part in the mechanism, a clear contravention of the agreement, which obliges every new entry to start a base review within eighteen months of accession.[148] Altogether, a number of problems have evolved with regard to the mechanism. A first problem lies in the duration of the reviews. They take up to four years; in particular, the time-lags between presentation, discussion and publication of the reports hamper public interest. Another problem concerns the publication of the reports. So far, self-assessments are not published at all and regular reports have also been presented incompletely.[149] It has also been noted that the APRM institutional structure is rather weak and perhaps overwhelmed by its task.[150] Finally, some commentators have been critical

[148] For a map detailing the participation across the continent see www.uneca.org/aprm/ (last visited July 2013); for critical analysis of the experiences so far D. M. Hamam and B. I. Ouédraogo, *Africa: Improving Africa's Governance, Before It's Too Late.* Available at http://allafrica.com/stories/201202271025.html (last visited July 2013); Bing-Pappoe, *Reviewing Africa's Peer Review Mechanism*, p. 19.

[149] See the official webpage at http://aprm-au.org/category/document-categories/country-annual-progress-reports); helpful also is the Africa Governance Institute: www.iag-agi.org/bdf/en/thesaurus_thema/motcle-thema-2998.html (last visited July 2013).

[150] H. Maihack and M. Öhm, *Dynamik im African Peer Review Mechanism (APRM): Kritischer Mosambikbericht bringt dem Gesamtprozess neue Glaubwürdigkeit*, Friedrich-Ebert-Stiftung Perspektive. Available at http://library.fes.de/pdf-files/iez/07269.pdf (last visited July 2013); Bing-Pappoe, *Reviewing Africa's Peer Review Mechanism*, p. 20.

with the content and spirit of the reports, characterizing them as too timid, uncritical and thus useless.[151]

In any event, it is difficult to attribute concrete positive developments to the mechanism. Nonetheless, the APRM might be regarded as a valuable mechanism for socializing countries into a culture of constructive review and comparison.

V. *Peer accountability among donors*

Donors are subject to a number of instruments that aim at legal, financial, political and substantive accountability. Accountability holders are here normally, as seen above, other branches of government, such as the legislature, courts of auditors or, in case of the World Bank, the wealthy member states. The level of scrutiny seems rather low, however.

Donors are, however, also increasingly subject to review among their peers. Such scrutiny can also fail for reasons of diplomatic diffidence or a collective disregard for such mechanisms (as the NEPAD example seems to indicate). In case of aid donors, it seems to be driven by the aid-effectiveness agenda as the latest meta-topic – and by a dedicated and driven international expert organization, the OECD.

1. Peer reviews by the OECD-DAC

Since its creation in 1961, the OECD has been using peer reviews in various policy fields, including development cooperation.[152] The organization claims credit for having pioneered the use of peer reviews among member states of international organizations, and for being the organization that has developed the method most extensively. Review processes differ for each policy field, but the stated objectives are the same: to make national policies more effective through learning from the experience of other countries, to identify best practices, and to trigger policy changes where needed through "peer pressure."[153]

[151] P. Fabricius, "Africa's Cracked Mirror: the African Peer Review Mechanism Is Valuable, but Its Strides Are Few and Small," *Daily News South Africa* (2010).

[152] See Dann, "Accountability," 393; and on the peer review as a mechanism to raise compliance with soft law, Paulo and Reisen, "Eastern Donors."

[153] The different procedures for different policy fields share certain structural elements, namely "a basis for proceeding; an agreed set of principles, standards and criteria against which the country's performance will be reviewed; designated actors to carry out the review; and a set of procedures leading to the final result." See online, www.oecd.org/site/0,3407,en_21571361_37949547_1_1_1_1_1,00.html (last visited July 2013) and the study by F. Pagani, *Peer Review: An OECD Tool for Co-operation and Change* (Paris:

Every member state of the OECD-DAC is obliged to participate in the peer review, both as reviewer and as subject of review.[154] The key principal of the OECD's peer-review method is "cooperation" – all member states are involved in the review, which is conducted on an equal basis, through a consultative process, and which serves as a mutual learning exercise. Since the establishment of the Network on Development Evaluation, multilateral aid agencies like the World Bank have observer status and have come to be reviewed, too.

At the outset of the process, each year the OECD-DAC Secretariat chooses five members to be reviewed and ten members to conduct the reviews; each donor is thus assessed every four to five years.[155] From then on, the process is conducted under the auspices of the DAC's Peer Review and Evaluation Division, by a review team that regularly consists of one or two representatives from each examining country, two or three Secretariat staff and one expert on humanitarian assistance.[156] The role of the Development Co-operation Directorate is generally one of analytical support and developing and updating the conceptual framework for the review, contained in the DAC *Peer Review Content Guide* that is approved by the DAC for a two-year period.[157] It consists of six sections: strategic orientations, policy coherence, aid flows and allocations, management and organization, aid effectiveness, and humanitarian assistance.[158] Subject to review are thus the structures, policies and implementation of national

OECD Publishing, 2003). On the potential exercises of public authority implied in evaluations, see Bogdandy and Goldmann, "The Exercise."

154 OECD, *Information Note on the DAC Peer Review Process: DCD(2009)6/REV1 of September, 6, 2012* (2012). Available at www.oecd.org/dac/peerreviewsofdacmembers/46127335.pdf (last visited July 2013) [hereinafter OECD, Information Note], para. 4: "Membership of the Development Assistance Committee obliges members to undergo, and to serve as 'examiners' in Peer Reviews."

155 The Secretariat seeks to choose members for review that have an aid program of comparable size and complexity so as to maximize the comparability and thus learning opportunity. On the process in detail, see ibid.

156 Ibid., margin no. 8. Donors which are not members of the DAC may participate in the process as external observers, if the reviewed member and its examiners agree, and on the basis of a "Code of Conduct" that lays out the procedure for observers.

157 OECD, *DAC Peer Review Content Guide: DCD/DAC(2010)33/FINAL of September, 27, 2010* (2010). Available at www.oecd.org/dac/peerreviewsofdacmembers/43569829.pdf (last visited July 2013), applicable for all reviews completed in the 2011–12 biennium [hereafter OECD, *Content Guide*].

158 For each section, the *Content Guide* provides standard questions and allows for reporting to the DAC on lessons learned. It is structured to provide for a headquarters and a field perspective on each issue, and includes questions addressed to partners. ibid., margin no. 4.

aid programs. They are assessed against a compilation of internationally agreed benchmarks and nationally selected reference points, as well as DAC guidelines and criteria agreed by the Committee, set out at the beginning of each section as key references for accountability purposes.[159] Key references include, for example, the Millennium Development Goals and the Paris Declaration regarding strategic orientations; the UN target of 0.7 percent of ODA/GNI regarding ODA volume; and the Principles and Good Practice of Humanitarian Donorship for humanitarian assistance.

The peer-review process itself is structured into five phases: (1) preparation and planning, (2) fact-finding, analysis and report writing, (3) the Peer Review Meeting, (4) approval and publication, and (5) follow-up. Before the review team begins with the examination, the reviewed member submits a country memorandum that is based on the *Peer Review Content Guide*. By preparing its own memorandum, the reviewed member not only provides information to the reviewers, but also has the opportunity to express itself on outstanding reforms and challenges. The memorandum is published and serves as a basis for consultations between the review team and the member concerned, which also take into account other background material such as key written documents, evaluations and audits and information provided by research institutions or the media.[160]

The review team compiles information and analyzes the reviewed national aid program on the basis of the *Content Guide*. Central to the fact-finding stage are comprehensive consultations with the reviewed member, facilitated through missions to the capitals and field missions to examine how the national aid program is being implemented. Next, the Secretariat drafts the Peer Review Report, which is discussed with the review team. Before the Report is published, the reviewed member has the opportunity to comment on the second part of the report containing factual information on the national aid program, but not on the first part, which contains the main findings and recommendations.[161] In the third phase, the Report is discussed at a Peer Review Meeting with all DAC members, providing the reviewed member with the opportunity to respond to the Report. The Report is revised accordingly during an editorial session that again includes the review team and the reviewed member, and the final Report is published after a three-day period in which the DAC delegates are asked

[159] Ibid., margin no. 3. The *Content Guide* thus serves as a common analytical framework and reference for reviews rather than a standard-setting document.

[160] Ibid., margin no. 13. [161] Ibid., margin no. 18.

for final approval. Finally, during the follow-up phase, the DAC Chair or a senior representative of the Secretariat may visit the reviewed member eighteen to twenty-four months after the Peer Review Meeting, to discuss implementation of the Report's recommendations and to report thereon. Such mid-term reviews have become standard process, but members may decide to opt out "if circumstances dictate."[162] No sanctions are provided for the case of non-implementation of the recommendations, since the primary purpose of the peer-review process is to facilitate mutual learning on a voluntary basis.

In sum, OECD-DAC reviews are based on the principle of cooperation and consultation. While there might be findings that the reviewed party does not agree with, it can respond to and identify them. The applicable standards are compiled by and partly set by the OECD; in other parts they are taken from international (or EU) commitments and benchmarks. All of them are soft law and the OECD decides which commitments/benchmarks will be used as key references. Human rights are not part of these key references.

2. The Paris Declaration and its follow-up process: mega-evaluation

The OECD-DAC conducts, as just seen, the most comprehensive regular peer reviews of donor systems.[163] In the past years, however, it has helped establish and drive an even more fundamental process of peer review and reform, namely the donor reviews initiated and framed by the Paris Declaration of 2005.[164] Linked to this declaration is an intensive process of progress examination and review, which by itself constitutes an accountability mechanism on donor aid effectiveness. "Paris" thus stands not just for a static document, but for a dynamic process that started in 2004, in which the parties agreed to work towards the agreed goals and hold each other accountable for their commitments.

For this purpose, the Paris Declaration included twelve quantifiable progress indicators and targets and fifty-six explicit actions and established precise deadlines. Indicators seek to help evaluate the implementation of the five key Paris Principles (e.g. by asking to what extent mutual accountability mechanisms and result-oriented frameworks are in use) or aid flows more generally (e.g. by measuring the percentage of untied

[162] OECD, *Information Note*, margin no. 25.

[163] See Harrison, *World Bank and Africa*; Gardner, *Legal Imperialism*; Dijkstra, "PRSP Approach."

[164] On the Paris Declaration, see *supra* Ch 2.C.III.1.

and predictable aid).[165] Progress was to be evaluated continually, both at the national and international level. The key tool for reviewing progress were Monitoring Surveys, prepared under the auspices of the OECD Working Party on Aid Effectiveness in 2006, 2008 and 2011,[166] in developing countries that agreed to participate in the process.[167] The surveys process involved a national coordinator nominated by his/her government to manage the process at the national level, and if desired, a donor focal point appointed by the national coordinator to assist him/her in managing the survey. National coordinators were further encouraged to involve civil-society organizations and parliamentarians in discussions on the survey.[168] All surveys were published, including individual country chapters and all data sets.[169] The survey process follows the stated objective of "providing a means of making sure that donors and partner countries act upon the commitments they have made" and is thus a more genuine accountability mechanism than the OECD Peer Review process, which is rather a collaborative exercise aimed at fostering mutual learning and identifying best practices. However, the Paris Declaration does not provide for legal or stricture sanctions in the case of non-compliance other than public criticism.[170]

[165] The list of Indicators of Progress, together with targets for 2010, is contained in part III of the 2005 Paris Declaration and has thus been agreed by its signatories, donor and recipient countries alike.

[166] The Working Party is a multi-stakeholder group consisting of developing and developed countries, South–South cooperation providers and civil-society organizations. See online, www.oecd.org/document/4/0,3746,en_2649_3236398_43414212_1_1_1_1,00.html (last visited July 2013).

[167] The 2006 Survey established the baseline for measuring future progress; 34 developing countries and 55 donors participated. In the 2008 Survey, an additional 21 developing countries participated; the Survey provided evidence for the stocktaking in Accra. In the last survey, 78 countries and territories participated. The synthesis report OECD, Aid Effectiveness 2005–10: Progress in implementing the Paris Declaration, 2011 and detailed country reviews are available online, www.oecd.org/document/1/0,3746,en_2649_3236398_48725569_1_1_1_1,00.html (last visited July 2013). In the 2011 round of monitoring, progress against the Principles for Good International Engagement in Fragile States and Situations was reviewed in a separate but parallel process.

[168] On the process in detail, see OECD, *Survey Guidance: 2011 Survey on Monitoring the Paris Declaration* (2011), p. 2. Available at www.oecd.org/site/dacsmpd11/46138662.pdf (last visited July 2013).

[169] The results of the 2011 Survey on Monitoring include disaggregated data for each participating developing country and indicator, and for each donor and indicator. Statistical appendices A-D, OECD, *Aid Effectiveness 2005–10: Progress in Implementing the Paris Declaration* (2011). Available at www.oecd.org/dac/aideffectiveness/48742718.pdf (last visited July 2013).

[170] OECD, *2011 Survey on Monitoring the Paris Declaration: Key Facts* (2011). Available at www.oecd.org/development/aideffectiveness/44807435.pdf (last visited September 2012).

In addition to the Monitoring Surveys aimed at tracking progress made against an agreed set of indicators, members of the OECD-DAC Network on Development Evaluation agreed that an independent group should evaluate the impact of the implementation of the Paris Declaration, i.e. the degree of implementation and its results in developing countries.[171] This evaluation was a more in-depth process, conducted in fewer countries in 2007 and 2010 and aimed at examining and explaining the overall implementation performance in individual countries as seen from the donors' perspective.[172]

The High-Level Forums in Accra in 2008 and in Busan in 2011 constituted key milestones for taking stock of progress. In Accra, participants agreed to accelerate and deepen the implementation of the Paris Principles; implementation of the corresponding recommendations was also reviewed in the Monitoring Surveys.[173] In Busan, delegates met for a last time to assess whether the targets agreed in 2005 had been met, but also to discuss the continued relevance of the aid effectiveness agenda beyond 2012. Accordingly, its outcome document, the Busan Partnership for Effective Development Co-operation, not only reaffirms the Paris Principles but also contains new commitments for improving aid effectiveness.[174] Importantly, it calls for the set-up of new monitoring frameworks at the level of individual developing countries and agreement on a new set of indicators and targets.[175] The Paris commitments to improving aid effectiveness, subsequently deepened in Accra and carried further in Busan, therefore remain an important benchmark for assessing ODA delivery.

[171] D. Booth and A. Evans, *Evaluation Network Follow-up to the Paris Declaration on Aid Effectiveness: An Options Paper*, Submitted for discussion at the fourth meeting of the DAC Evaluation Network, 30–31 March 2006. Available at www.oecd.org/development/evaluationofdevelopmentprogrammes/dcdndep/36303226.pdf (last visited July 2013). On the Evaluation in detail, see OECD, *The Evaluation of the Paris Declaration: Phase 2*, Final Report of May 2011 (2011). Available at http://pd-website.inforce.dk/content/content-en.html (last visited July 2013). On the results of country evaluations, donor and agency studies conducted as part of the Paris Evaluation, see ibid.

[172] On the difference between the Monitoring Surveys and the independent evaluation process, see OECD, *Paris Declaration Monitoring and Evaluation: Complementarities and Differences*, Explanatory Note (2011). Available at www.oecd.org/development/evaluationofdevelopmentprogrammes/dcdndep/44729491.pdf (last visited July 2013).

[173] OECD, Aid Effectiveness 2005–10, p. 15.

[174] Busan Partnership for Effective Development Co-operation, *Outcome Document*. As a new principle, the Busan Partnership contains a commitment to fostering "Inclusive Development Partnerships," para. 11 lit. c.

[175] Ibid., margin no. 35. The new indicators are to be formulated until June 2012. Moreover, for certain commitments, the document formulates timeframes in paras. 23–25.

All in all, the Paris Declaration and its ensuing reform process have certainly set a new record in public analysis and criticism of governance structures in donor as well as recipient countries. It has created an unprecedented level of scrutiny and comparison between these systems. However, its overall result seems ambiguous. First, one can question the general direction and substance of the process. It has been criticized for being overly technocratic and giving little or no regard to individual actor participation and human rights standards.[176] Second, one can question its effect more directly. The record of implementation seems sketchy and one might wonder whether the resources were well spent.

3. IATI – transparency initiative

A third donor peer-review mechanism should be mentioned that might have a longer-lasting effect into the future and also encourage public participation in the aid system. As a result of the High-Level Forum in Accra, the International Aid Transparency Initiative (IATI) was launched in 2008.[177] IATI is a voluntary, multi-stakeholder initiative (not an institution),[178] involving donors as well as recipient countries and civil-society organizations.[179] It is based on the commitments made in the Accra Agenda for Action to "publicly disclose regular, detailed and timely information on volume, allocation, and when available, results of development," support information systems for managing aid, and "provide full and timely information on annual commitments and actual disbursements."[180] Accordingly, it is focused on donor transparency, not transparency in recipient countries. Central to the initiative is its international standard, developed and used as a guideline for the publication of aid spending.[181]

176 On the critique see *supra*, Ch 2.C.III.1.; on its evaluation against the principles of development cooperation law, *infra* Ch 8.C.I.

177 International Aid Transparency Initiative, Accra Statement (September 4, 2008) and online, www.aidtransparency.net/.

178 The initiative is administered by a "virtual secretariat," consisting of DFID, UNDP, and the NGO "aidinfo." The secretariat acts under the auspices of the IATI Steering Committee, which meets 2–3 times per year and comprises donor and recipient governments, civil-society organizations and independent experts. The Steering Committee is assisted by a Technical Advisory Group. On the governance of the IATI, see online, www.aidtransparency.net/.

179 Current membership consists of 19 donors that have signed up to IATI and 19 developing countries that have endorsed it. See online, www.aidtransparency.net/about/whos-involved (last visited September 2012).

180 Accra Agenda for Action, paras. 24 lit. a), 23 lit c) and 26 lit. b).

181 The IATI Standard was adopted by all donors signatory to the IATI and the IATI Steering Committee, which also represented the developing countries that had endorsed

This is not aimed at creating a new mechanism for data appraisal and connection, in order not to duplicate the work already being done elsewhere, in particular at the OECD-DAC, but rather to provide detailed definitions and common formats for the publication of aid information. It thus aims to address the challenge identified in developing countries of access to information about aid flows and hence to conduct accurate budgeting, accounting and auditing.

C Comparative summary

The issue of accountability lies at the heart of development cooperation and its law. Accountability is central to making sure that control and learning can take place – and it is organized best in a rule-bound system. The law is hence an essential instrument to ensure accountability – and accountability is essential to ensure effective development cooperation. The previous sections have shown, however, how difficult it is to hold those accountable who exercise public authority in the trans- and international process of development cooperation.[182] Though there is no dearth of accountability mechanisms, they vary greatly as to *who* is held accountable and *by whom*. Recipient states and especially their citizens mostly lack a strong voice in the system. Also, independent and sanction-backed review is rather rare. It is thus questionable whether a satisfactory degree of legitimacy is generated, though this is a central function of accountability structures (besides ensuring compliance and learning).[183]

Yet, changes are taking place and structures are evolving. This concluding section will appraise the findings of this chapter with respect to the general principles of development cooperation law that have been proposed in Part II as overarching normative yardsticks of the law of development cooperation (I).[184] It will conclude with thoughts on structural deficits of accountability in development aid, as the limitations are all too visible (II).

I. Appraisal with respect to principles

The foregoing analysis used a narrow concept of accountability in order to make sure that it remains a reasonably precise and hence clearly applicable

the initiative but had no separate voting right. For more information on the standard, see the IATI Standard website, http://iatistandard.org/.

182 On the broader debate on accountability of international organizations, see literature in *supra* fn. 2.

183 On the general functions of accountability, see *supra* Ch 9.A.III.

184 See *supra*, Ch 4.

concept. It understood accountability as the retrospective review of a power wielder's behavior by an independent accountability holder based on previously fixed and legitimate standards of review and including the possibility of sanctions.[185]

Among the four principles that have been formulated in Part II, the focus here will be on individual autonomy, collective autonomy and efficiency. These are most directly supported (or undercut) by existing accountability structures, whereas the principle of development has a less direct connection. Of course, it also profits from stricter control, since all mechanisms that serve compliance and learning within the system also serve the broader substantive goal of development. But the impact here is indirect.

1. Principle of individual autonomy

The first principle which comes to mind as benefiting from stricter accountability and as a yardstick to evaluate the law is the principle of individual autonomy. Individuals can be active participants in the development process as well as passively affected.[186] Their freedoms are at stake in both roles – and (in a purely traditional domestic setting) it would be the prime task of courts to uphold their rights. Legal accountability is a central precondition for individual autonomy. Another path to the protection of individual autonomy could be the individuals' active participation in evaluations, i.e. in substantive accountability. Finally, transparency serves individual accountability. Only where information is available can individuals engage and make their case as autonomous actors.

With regard to legal accountability, individuals should be able to trigger judicial review of donors and recipient governments. But a number of problems are encountered. The World Bank is not subject to any control by a formal court accessible by individuals. European and German exercise of public authority is generally subject to judicial control when it comes to extraterritorial constellations.[187] But the rules on legal standing for affected individuals turned out to be impassable hurdles in both polities.

Interest therefore turns to *quasi*-judicial mechanisms.[188] In this regard, the World Bank provides a more accountable structure than the other two

[185] See *supra*, Ch 9.A.I.

[186] On this concept of development cooperation as a political and transnational process (and not as one only between governments and governmental organizations), see *supra* Ch 2.B.II and Ch 4.D.

[187] See *supra*, Ch 4.D.II.

[188] On this notion Naude Fourie, *World Bank Inspection Panel*.

organizations. The Inspection Panel is not to be mistaken for a court but it does provide a venue in which individual instances of wrongful behavior can be independently assessed against a clear set of rules and a response to the wrongful act can be proposed. Even though it is beset with many problems,[189] the Inspection Panel is an important provider of (quasi-)legal accountability. The Ombudsman of the EU has much less clear standards, no procedural set-up and even less chance of sanctioning the administration, except for reports to the European Parliament and an obligation of the institution concerned to respond. German development administration lacks even this. The BMZ, as the central development agency, and KfW have no structures accessible by individuals. The Integrity Advisor and the Ombudsman of the GIZ seem to be accessible also by private individuals, but their procedures, their standards of review and especially their competence to sanction wrong-doing are not known. Overall, legal or quasi-legal accountability to ensure the principle of individual autonomy is very weak.

Individual participation in evaluations would give individuals a controlling voice through concrete feedback. While there are likely to be procedures that involve affected individuals, these procedures are (as far as we could see) not set forth in general rules that could be considered legal. If they exist and if they are really intended to have a stronger effect, they would profit from formalization.

The situation with regard to transparency is slightly better. All three organizations have extensive regulations governing access to documents and information. The laws in the EU and Germany, however, make a clear distinction between citizens and non-citizens. While the former have fairly strong rights, non-citizens have not. Clearly, these laws are not adequate for development cooperation as a transnational system and process. The World Bank as a specialized international organization has developed a regime that is better in the sense that it is accessible for all.

All in all, accountability structures further the principle of individual autonomy only to a very limited extent. It is virtually impossible for individuals to trigger and use them – and those in the recipient countries especially are almost entirely excluded.

2. Principle of collective autonomy

The principle of collective autonomy, i.e. the idea that a society should freely determine which path it chooses, provides another yardstick

[189] See *supra*, Ch 9.B.I.1a.

to evaluate the law.[190] It focuses on different actors than the principle of individual autonomy, as it does not refer to individuals but societies represented through their state governments. And since development cooperation is largely driven by governments and governmental organizations, it provides a central perspective. Accountability here would mean that governments can control whether the rules that they agreed upon are complied with – and can sanction non-compliance. Mechanisms of legal, financial and especially political accountability are the most relevant elements here. The existing instruments in and between the organizations are diverse and (not surprisingly) more numerous than for individuals. But here again, donor and recipient states have very different chances of preserving their autonomy.

A central instrument with regard to mutual legal accountability could be arbitration proceedings, which are provided for in transfer agreements of all donors. However, these are not used.[191] Legal accountability of donors towards recipients in their own courts (in the EU or Germany) or in domestic courts of the recipients (all donors) is prevented by rules of standing, immunity clauses or inadmissibility. Equally, recipient governments hardly face legal accountability in courts. In effect, mutual legal accountability between donors and recipients is therefore almost non-existent. However, development administrations face the risk of being held legally accountable by their domestic or internal counterparts. The European Commission indeed faces legal action by the Council or the European Parliament, and the German government could be sued by the German parliament or states (this has never happened, though). In this regard, the EU development administration especially is held legally accountable.

Important though much less effective are mechanisms of financial accountability (i.e. audits, anti-corruption rules, etc.). These are well established in all organizations examined here. The EU and the World Bank have stricter policies and stronger institutional structures to prosecute and sanction misbehavior, especially with regard to corruption.

Especially important for the protection of collective autonomy are mechanisms of political accountability. Since development cooperation is a policy field with large discretion for governments, it is understandable that accountability works along political rather than legal or substantive lines. Structures of political accountability are different, though, in the

[190] On the principle of collective autonomy and sovereignty, see *supra* Ch 4.C.

[191] See *supra*, Ch 9.B.I.

respective organizations due to their differing nature. In Germany as a nation-state, political control is mainly exercised by the national parliament (Bundestag). It has, as we saw, important budgetary and inquisitional powers. The fact, however, that Germany has a parliamentary system (i.e. the majority running the government) and a fairly broad consensus in matters of development means that control is gentle. In the EU as a quasi-federation, control is exercised by the European Parliament as well as the member states assembled in the Council. Due to the political dynamics in the EU institutional system, control through both is strong.[192] The World Bank as an international organization has no parliament. Instead, member states can hold the Bank accountable. Here, however, we saw that only the rich member states, which have more voting rights, appointment powers and budgetary influence, are actually influential. Comparing all three, political control is probably the strongest in the EU and least biting in Germany.

In sum and again not surprisingly, the collective autonomy of (rich) donor and member states is well protected, especially through mechanisms of political accountability. Recipient states, on the other side, have far fewer instruments to use. There are very few legal accountability mechanisms, while financial accountability is as much targeted at them as at donors.

3. Principle of efficiency

The principle of efficiency is the third yardstick to evaluate and compare accountability structures. It holds that cost-effectiveness, result orientation and coordination are important elements laid down and demanded by law.[193] Accountability structures can help to promote these values – but they do so to different degrees in structures of financial, substantive, legal and political accountability. Mechanisms of *financial* accountability squarely serve the goal of cost-effectiveness. Audits, anti-corruption policies and institutions as well as whistle-blower programs aim at checking the use of funds and holding those accountable who waste funds. Similarly, the structures of *substantive* accountability, mainly evaluations, aim at an improved result orientation of operations. They are intended to

[192] On the institutional structures of the EU and mechanisms of control P. Dann, "The Political Institutions," in A. von Bogdandy and J. Bast (eds.), *Principles of European Constitutional Law* (Oxford: Hart Publishing, 2006), vol. VIII, pp. 229–80 at pp. 246, 256.

[193] On the content and legal contours of the principle, see *supra* Ch 4.E.

ensure that development interventions actually achieve their goals. *Legal* and *political* accountability can contribute to efficiency, too, and are complementary as they are linked to other standards. To some extent, however, they also serve more as back-up mechanisms, coming into play when others have failed and failures cross certain thresholds.

There are clear differences in the way the three donors organize financial and substantive accountability. With regard to *financial* accountability we found that all institutions are subject to external auditors, be they Courts of Auditors (as in the EU or Germany) or private auditing firms (as with respect to the Bank). We can assume that their standards and methods are similar and in this regard result in a similar level of scrutiny. We also observed that all of them have by now adopted explicit anti-corruption policies and set up institutional structures to address this issue.[194] However, differences pertain especially to the organization of control. Both the Bank and the EU have established specialized internal anti-corruption units (INT and OLAF) with far-reaching powers of investigation and partly sanctioning,[195] while in Germany no specific unit exists. GIZ and KfW have no proactive, investigative units here but they can, of course, use the general prosecutors. Despite organizational differences, one can therefore state a general similarity of mechanisms and standards with respect to financial accountability.

More differences appeared with regard to *substantive* accountability through evaluations. This area has seen much reform in the last years under the influence of the aid-effectiveness debate. Even though evaluations are scarcely a new topic, the level and thoroughness of their organization have improved. In terms of substantive standards, there is clearly a trend towards harmonization under the guidance of the OECD.[196] Comparing the organizational structures, the World Bank has created the most extensive and influential unit (the IEG). The EU and Germany have also created units that are outside the regular hierarchies but have fewer resources at their disposal.[197] In terms of independence of evaluation units, the number of evaluations and the public availability of reports, the World Bank has the most advanced system.

Central to advancing the principle of efficiency are also the various mechanisms of peer review among donors, and to a lesser extent among recipients.[198] The reviews among OECD-DAC members and

[194] See *supra* at Ch 9.B.I.1b / II.1b / III.1b. [195] Ibid. [196] See Ch 9.B.V.
[197] See *supra* Ch 9.B.I.1c / II.1c / III.1c. [198] See *supra* Ch 9.B.V.

those connected to the Paris Declaration have clearly contributed to strengthened systems of evaluation.

In sum, the principle of efficiency has certainly become more formalized, more important and better fulfilled over the years.

II. Structural problems of accountability in development cooperation

The foregoing description revealed a perhaps surprising number and variety of accountability mechanisms. At the same time, structural problems surfaced time and again. This final section summarizes and highlights them. It will start by looking at the three defining elements of accountability: the relation between power wielders and accountability holders, applicable standards and possible sanctions.

1. Power wielders and accountability holders, standards and sanctions

Accountability is based on a *power wielder* being answerable to an *accountability holder*. Distance between these two is necessary to ensure the independence of the accountability holder.[199] The critical question here is who is held accountable and who should be an accountability holder.

It is primarily the donor institutions that are to be held accountable, i.e. those who have the power to decide to whom to grant ODA and under which conditions. Yet, the recipient governments should also be answerable to power wielders. They are entrusted with public money and should be accountable as to how they use this money. The analysis therefore inquired into the accountability of both donors and recipients.

The more important question is to whom are donors and recipients accountable. Who are the accountability holders?[200] The analysis showed that accountability holders are often internal control units or detached external experts. Internal control was found in the evaluation and investigation units charged with substantive and financial scrutiny.[201] External experts were found to be relevant actors in the Inspection Panel as a legal accountability mechanism, in audit mechanisms as fiscal accountability, but also in peer reviews. One can ask whether they have the necessary distance from the actual power wielders.

[199] On the concept of accountability see *supra*, Ch 9.A.I.

[200] Krisch, "Pluralism."

[201] See *supra* Ch 9.B.

The more serious problem, however, is not the lack of distance of internal control units but the inadequate voice of three other constituencies: the people affected by projects in developing countries, the recipient governments and taxpayers in donor countries. The affected people in developing countries have only very few direct mechanisms against the donors, namely the Inspection Panel and, to some extent, the European Ombudsman. All other mechanisms are indirect or beyond their influence. In German development law, an effective mechanism for individual complaints is missing. And the European Ombudsman is hardly an effective agent of control. This state of affairs is clearly deficient in comparison to international agencies, where such procedures have become frequent.[202] In order to protect the rights of affected people, Germany and the EU are obliged to provide better mechanisms.[203] The position of the recipient governments is hardly better in practice. Even though they are represented in the World Bank Executive Board, their position there is weak.[204] They are not able to hold the EU or Germany accountable. Finally, taxpayers are equally barred from direct influence.

The general public, on the other hand, has become a relevant accountability holder, be it as a global civil society or as national publics in developing or developed countries. Many of the rules that establish accountability mechanisms are geared towards public scrutiny (publication of reports, of evaluation or audit results, of peer reviews). Transparency rules have evolved and become more stringent but they too often exclude affected citizens.[205]

Standards are a second element of accountability – and indicate a second structural problem. Standards define where conduct turns into "misconduct." But the question arises whether there are standards and who is there to set them. The study has shown that standards vary according to the area concerned. Most clearly stated are standards of legal accountability, as used, for example, by the Inspection Panel. Standards of financial accountability, to take another example, are contained in several sources and include auditing rules. These standards are mostly set in legal rules. The standards for substantive and political accountability are often less precise.

Most of the standards are set by power wielders themselves and not by independent, external legislators and are thus often internalized. Exceptions to this rule are the standards for external expert mechanisms,

[202] Mitzmann, "Proliferation of Independent Accountability."

[203] See also *supra* Ch 4.D.II – on their human rights obligations.

[204] See *supra* Ch 3.A.IV.1.

[205] See *supra* Ch 9.B.I.1/2/3 and Ch 9.B.II.2/III.2.

such as auditing or peer reviews. Here, the applied standards are general laws or global best practices. The standards pertaining to the transnational accountability of recipients are set by donors or peers.

Finally, accountability mechanisms can be evaluated also with regard to their *potential sanctions*. Again, one has to distinguish between sanctions against donors and against recipients. The sanctions against donors point to another general weakness of the legal regimes which is that accountability mechanisms in development cooperation law are mostly devoid of hard and curtailing sanctions. Most mechanisms only result in publicized reports, such as audit reports, Inspection Panel investigation reports, evaluation reports or peer reviews. These appeal to the public for some kind of reputational sanctioning, but are not followed by any legally enforceable reactions. In contrast to these mild sanctions against donors, sanctions against recipients are of a different kind. As we have seen, donors can react to the recipient's misconduct with the end of funding or even the demand to pay back the received funds.[206] These are certainly effective instruments. Hence, again, we see a striking imbalance between the accountability of global donor organizations and recipients.

2. On sources and gaps

This leads finally to two more general observations, on the sources containing accountability mechanisms and the question of whether these mechanisms provide a satisfactory level of accountability.

From a legal perspective, it is striking that accountability mechanisms in development institutions are undergoing an increasing formalization and legalization.[207] The majority of the rules and institutions described here have developed only since the 1990s. These new rules establish new accountability holders (like the Inspection Panel or internal oversight units) and formalize the procedures of mechanisms of accountability. However, if these rules and mechanisms fall into the scope of *legal* analysis, as proposed here, one has to adopt a broad notion of law. The institutional or procedural structures observed were only to a limited extent prescribed by primary (treaty) or parliamentary laws. More are organized by "secondary" law (like Operational Policies), or in even "softer" internal rules (like guidelines for evaluation, policy papers, etc.).[208] In this respect,

[206] See *supra* Ch 9.B.IV.

[207] This is the underlying thesis of this study, see *supra* Intro.A.II.

[208] On the legal character of such rules, see *supra* Ch 3.A.II.2 / IV.2; also Kingsbury, "Operational Policies."

our analysis of the law of development cooperation confirms a broader trend towards new sources in international law.[209]

This leads to the second issue of whether the described mechanisms provide a satisfactory level of accountability. This question is difficult to answer since it is unclear what the appropriate level of accountability should be. This study proposed to use general principles as standards. Compliance with them has been mixed (to put it mildly), as the previous section showed. For now, we can only point out some obvious aspects and deficits. We might begin by stating that the accountability mechanisms of donor institutions show a somewhat surprising similarity. Except for the Inspection Panel, most instruments are to be found in World Bank, the EU and Germany. All currently stress especially financial, substantive and also peer accountability, while mechanisms of legal accountability are weak. On second glance, however, one also has to point out that the World Bank's mechanisms are often more advanced in the sense that they are often more transparent and supported by more resources.[210]

Problematic are the obvious gaps and imbalances in the system, especially the lacking voice of affected people and the muzzled voice of recipient governments. It is in this regard that the imbalance of economic power is indeed continued in legal structures. The central problem of accountability in the global development system does not lie in the absence of mechanisms. On the contrary, at least with respect to the World Bank, one can argue that it is very accountable – but only to a few member states, especially the USA. The problem is rather that aid organizations are not adequately accountable to those who are the intended beneficiaries of aid and are too accountable to actors who pursue their own national interests.[211] A global civil society might have increasing information about the work of the donor organizations and perhaps reputational leverage. But it

[209] See G. Hafner, "Diversity or Cacophony? New Sources of Norms in International Law," *Michigan Journal of International Law*, 25 (2004), 845–1375; also N. Krisch and B. Kingsbury, "Global Governance and Global Administrative Law in the International Legal Order," *European Journal of International Law*, 17 (2006), 1–13 at 12.

[210] The reasons for this seem to be (at least) twofold. For one, the World Bank has been the object of much more attention and public scrutiny than other donors and appears to have reacted at least to some extent to the public pressure (cf. Mallaby, *World's Banker*, pp. 44–8, 58–64). And, secondly, the Bank has not only more financial resources to deploy, for example, a bigger evaluation unit, but it also has a self-understanding and "corporate culture" which is geared more towards private-sector banks than international bureaucracies. This might also contribute to its openness to more efficient structures (Wiegand, *Organisatorische Aspekte*, pp. 359, 360).

[211] Similarly, Grant and Keohane, "Accountability and Abuses," 37, 39.

too lacks mechanisms that are not dependent on the benevolence of the donors.

The problem of imbalance of influence and interests runs through all levels of development cooperation law, national, supranational and global alike. It is rooted in the transnational nature of development cooperation law, in which the most affected party, the people in developing countries, is structurally excluded from holding the donors directly accountable. Global development-aid law, as we have seen, provides a number of alternative devices. But these seem often to miss the political dynamics at work.

Conclusions and future prospects

Development cooperation is an unusual subject for legal analysis. Its very nature – in particular, its internationality, its political instrumentality, and its dealing with informal asymmetries in the North–South relationship – would appear to make it difficult to be controlled by law. It is therefore hardly surprising that legal scholars so far have not addressed development cooperation very extensively. This book suggests a new perspective: it conceives of development cooperation as an activity centered around the transfer of development funds and organized by agencies on a national, supranational, and international level. Their activity is, to a significant and growing extent, regulated by law. It can, accordingly, be understood and investigated as a multi-level field of law.

This book has analyzed this law in three steps. The first part tried to illuminate the political and theoretical background by reconstructing the institutional and intellectual genesis of development cooperation. Building on this historical foundation, the second part considered the institutions, legal bases and principles of development cooperation law and sketched the general, quasi-constitutional structures of this legal field. The third part, finally, systematized the legal rules which regulate the ODA allocation process and examined the specific administrative law structure of the relevant laws. The approach and the issues are set in context of a number of current relevant academic discussions. The analysis first incorporated the discussion of an international administrative law and the legal structures of global governance. It is guided by the *hope* for a rationalization and legal control of international (but also domestic) institutions, the *concern* over the legitimacy of law as a means of integrating these bureaucracies and the *interest* in marking these questions out as important areas of research.[1]

[1] Bogdandy, "General Principles"; Kingsbury, Krisch and Stewart, "Emergence of Global Administrative Law"; Dann and Engelhardt, *Legal Approaches*.

This conclusion will recount the most important results of the discussion (A). It will become clear that this book only begins the discussion on development cooperation law. It offers a framework and suggestions, but can hardly be considered the last word. A final section therefore sketches some promising subjects for future research (B).

A Central features and problems of development cooperation law

The most important conceptual aim of this study was to make the broad and diverse field of development cooperation accessible to legal analysis. This was done by focusing on a relatively abstract element which is regulated legally. The law of development aid, as it has been described here, is focused on the activity of allocating ODA. This abstraction permits a focus on development cooperation independent of organization or level of public authority, thus enabling comparison of diverse legal entities. This conceptual definition of development cooperation law delimits it from other materials and regulations that foster development by means such as trade or property law.[2] It also complements well the procedural approach to the concept of development proposed in this study.[3]

This basic approach afforded a view of a specific institutional and normative structure whose essential features will be summarized here.

I. Institutional structure and legal bases: heterarchical multi-level systems

Many institutions are active in development cooperation. Current estimates hold that about seventy state and inter-state organizations are involved in granting ODA. Proliferation and fragmentation, which characterizes the entire field of international organizations, is a particular problem in the development context.[4] Not only the number, but also the competences of the various organizations are unusual. In the area of ODA allocation, organizations – and especially supranational and international ones – pursue fundamentally administrative activities in that

[2] On the definition of ODA and the distinctions between ODA and other legal institutions see *supra* Intro.A.I.

[3] See Introduction A.II.2.

[4] *Supra* Ch 3.A.I; see generally N. M. Blokker and H. G. Schermers (eds.), *Proliferation of International Organizations: Legal Issues* (The Hague: Kluwer Law International, 2001); International Law Commission, Fragmentation of International Law (Rapporteur Martti Koskenniemi), UN-Dok A/CN.4/L.682 (from April 13, 2006).

they decide on individual loans and grants. The World Bank and the EU, to remain with the organizations that have been the subject of this book, do not act primarily to coordinate standards or collect and process information (the normal function of international organizations), but rather perform fundamentally executive tasks, and do so with a remarkable degree of autonomy. It may be surprising to note, but financing development is more internationalized than many other fields.

Furthermore, the institutional structure of development cooperation is marked by a basic heterarchy between the different levels of public authority.[5] That is, the competences of national and international organizations are not integrated into a hierarchical relationship of supervision and subordination, but rather exist parallel to one another. Thus, a decision by the EU to provide aid to Namibia has no effect on Germany's competences or scope of action. Hence, development cooperation law is a heterarchical multi-level system whose study can provide relevant insights concerning the general problem of fragmentation and coordination.

However, the fact that the relevant law has the character of a multi-level system makes it particularly complex. The laws governing a particular award of ODA stem from diverse legal orders, among which the most important are the donor laws governing legal actions, which specify the procedures, instruments and criteria pursuant to which ODA is authorized.[6] The legal form of these provisions is variable. In the EU's development cooperation law, they take the form of regulations and agreements with recipient states. In the case of the World Bank, some of the rules are found in the Articles of Agreement, but many are increasingly set out in astoundingly detailed and formalized internal administrative regulations (the Operational Policies and Bank Procedures). German development cooperation law is the least legally formalized and the least transparent, as it is governed only by an administrative regulation. Comparison with the laws and regulations governing development cooperation in the USA, Great Britain and Denmark shows that the situation in Germany is not routine among aid-granting nations, but rather unusual – and not particularly rule-of-law compliant.[7] In addition to the laws of donors, there is the less prominent category of bilateral rules to coordinate laws between donors and recipients and among donors themselves. These include

[5] *Supra* Ch 3.A.V.

[6] On the legal bases see *supra* Part II, Ch 3.A.II.2, III.2 and IV.2.

[7] On the legal situation in Britain see, e.g. P. McAuslan, "The International Development Act, 2002: Benign Imperialism or a Missed Opportunity?" *Modern Law Review*, 66 (2003), 563–603.

a growing number of international declarations on the purposes and principles of development cooperation (such as the MDGs or the Paris Declaration).[8]

The normative structure of development cooperation law is also unusual for another reason: although this field involves an immense diversity of institutions whose laws are not at all hierarchically organized, a doctrinal analysis reveals convergent structures among these multiple heterarchical systems. A central result of the comparative approach used in this book is that when one surveys the different organizations and levels of sovereignty, a general law of ODA allocation procedures emerges. What are its contours?

II. *Typical doctrinal features: complementarity and conditionality*

Development cooperation law regulates the systematically planned allocation of public resources for general welfare, even when the recipient is extraterritorial. The task of development administration is a multi-step decision-making process. After the amount of available resources has been determined, a medium-term program is planned,[9] then the actual allocation of funds is decided, which is done primarily through three instruments: project aid, budget support or program-for-results financing.[10] This is followed by the implementation phase, which is not a focus of this book. In planning and allocation, some doctrinal building blocks are of particular importance.

Complementarity is the first important legal doctrine in development cooperation law. It links various phases of the process and plays a significant role.[11] Development cooperation organizes the step-by-step transformation of goals into concrete actions. The various phases of this process of "concretization" (budget allocation, recipient planning, donor planning, award and implementation) are the responsibility of different actors during each phase. Therefore, the granting of autonomous decision-making power in *one* phase to *one* actor is combined with the obligation (and thus the complementarity) of *following* decisions and actors to respect the previous decision. For example, recipient autonomy can only be assured when donors' planning is determined by the previous

[8] For more on these declarations see *supra* Ch 2.B.II.2.
[9] More on this subject *supra* Part III, Ch 5.
[10] More on these instruments, *supra* Part III, Chs 6–8.
[11] See *supra* Part III, Ch 5.C.I.2/3, II.2/3, Ch 6.B and Ch 7.B.II.

plans drawn up by recipients. Planning complementarity is, therefore, an important instrument for linking the phases of development cooperation law and preserving autonomy.

Further characteristic doctrines of development cooperation law can be explained by the fact that this field must deal, among other things, with financial and technical risks. Donors' aid may be misused, which violates their own duty of economic efficiency. Also, development interventions (such as dams, structural-adjustment projects / budget support, etc.) can present serious risks for the economic, environmental and social system of the recipient country or region. Development cooperation law can therefore profit when analyzed from the perspective of risk-management law, which comprises various procedural law elements such as analysis duties, reporting duties and periodic review.[12]

A particular instrument of this "risk oversight" – and a typical doctrine of development cooperation law – is *conditionality*, which is basically similar to typical compliance methods used in welfare administration law in general. A conditionality can be understood as a rule which makes the disbursement of ODA dependent on a certain condition or which attaches sanctions to non-compliance.[13] One can distinguish between *ex-ante* and *ex-post* conditionalities. Although this doctrine appears in the development cooperation law of all organizations, its precise structure indicates typical differences between the various regimes. World Bank law, for instance, makes particularly intensive use of *ex-ante* conditionalities typically linked to environmental or social rights norms, while the EU uses *ex-post* conditionalities concerned with constitutional norms such as human rights generally and democracy.[14]

The use of indicators and other forms of quantification in development cooperation law has to date hardly been addressed, but will surely meet with increased interest in the future. Since 2000, under the rubric of results orientation, quantitatively measurable and time-limited goals have become a standard instrument of development cooperation law.[15] Since that time, they have developed into an important instrument of oversight.[16]

[12] This is particularly clear in the law of the World Bank, *supra* Ch 6.B.I.
[13] Discussed in more detail *supra* Part III, Ch 6.A.II.
[14] See *supra* Part III, Ch 6.B.I.2/3 and 23.II.2/3.
[15] See *supra* Part I, Ch 2.B.II.
[16] See Kingsbury, Davis and Merry, "Indicators"– and discussion *supra* Ch 2.C.III.1.

III. Legitimation problems of development cooperation and principles of development cooperation law

In addition to the rather technical side of regulating the ODA procedure, development cooperation law must also confront the fundamental conflicts inherent in the enterprise of development cooperation. Christoph Möllers, for instance, describes the activities of the World Bank as governance and as a constellation in which external control, informality and asymmetrical responsibility are combined to grant actors like the World Bank obscure yet immense power over recipient states, which in turn generates a fundamental legitimacy problem.[17] Another approach argues that ODA allocations are actually an exercise of international public authority, since ODA donors possess the final legal power to unilaterally determine recipient states' actions, thus limiting their autonomy.[18] Others counter these arguments by pointing to the freely agreed nature of contracts for ODA transfers. But this argument is weakened by the insight of this study that the contracting process takes place in a procedural and substantive framework which is strongly determined by donors.[19] Taking into account the economic pressure of the situation and the communicative power of donors to shape development discourse, a strong argument can be made that donors unilaterally condition the behavior of recipients in a manner that qualifies as an exercise of public authority. A serious legitimacy problem for development cooperation emerges under both perspectives.

Do these arguments undermine the analysis of development cooperation law as legitimate law? Do they expose it as a mere facade for a politically dominated process? This interpretation does not do justice to development cooperation law – not because there is no dependence or dominance, which indeed is the case, but rather precisely because the exercise of international public authority should itself be subject to legal regulation. It would, therefore, be shortsighted to focus on donor power without also taking into account that development cooperation is marked by many value conflicts, not just those between donors and recipients. There are also conflicts among different donors, between recipient governments and their citizens and between donors and affected citizens. Various questions hint at these conflicts: can donor power be considered legitimate when it is used to protect human rights in recipient nations?

[17] Möllers, "Governance-Konstellation," pp. 240–4; p. 254.

[18] On the idea of international public authority see Bogdandy, Dann and Goldmann, *Developing*, pp. 8–10

[19] Discussed in detail *supra* Part III, Ch 5.C.

What about the interests of citizens whose taxes are used for ODA? Do they have less of a right to determine what happens with their funds than recipient states? And must we perhaps accept compromises on the goal of poverty reduction to ensure corruption-free use of ODA?

One of the central tasks of development cooperation law is to organize a response to these questions and visualize various areas of tensions or even internal contradictions which characterize development cooperation and the law governing it.[20] Law and legal analysis can help classify arguments, examine the normative justifications for various approaches and rationalize the discourse. To this end, this book has identified four principles of development cooperation law: *development*, which requires cooperation for the purpose of poverty reduction;[21] *collective autonomy*, which is the right of each donor and recipient to independently decide on its domestic order and the use of its resources (and which, in the development context, also takes the form of the principle of ownership);[22] human rights as the third principle of *individual autonomy*;[23] and finally the principle of *coherence and efficiency*, which is manifested in the principles of economic efficiency and coordination which apply to the allocation process.[24] These principles transcend levels of public authority (national, supranational, international and organizational barriers, and can thus be used to analyze all institutions and situations in the area of development cooperation law. Nevertheless, they do not all display the same level of normativity.[25] While collective and individual autonomy can be described as *legal* principles, the principles of development and coherence and efficiency are merely *structural* principles. In cases of conflict, legal principles trump structural principles. However, there is no order of priority between the two legal principles (collective and individual autonomy), in particular because collective autonomy is not equivalent to democratic self-rule. Indeed, it is precisely the question of how to deal with authoritarian regimes or even dictatorships in developing countries which is one of the central problems of development cooperation law.

Analysis of development cooperation law from these perspectives illuminates how the different organizations (and their administrative guidelines) approach the normative challenges of development cooperation and what they focus on. In fact, the comparison itself yielded surprising results. The law of the World Bank was, in the final analysis, more open to

[20] See *supra* Part II, Ch 4.A.II and Ch 4.F. [21] Part II, Ch 4.B.
[22] Part II, Ch 4.C. [23] Part II, Ch 4.D.
[24] Part II, Ch 4.E. [25] More details *supra* Part II, Ch 4.A.II.

human rights protection and thus the principle of individual autonomy.[26] Even if this focus can be seen as "only" serving the technocratic purpose of contributing to project success, it nevertheless still has a mitigating effect, at least in principle. In the development cooperation law of the EU, by contrast, human rights are addressed generally as the context of development cooperation, but there is no later oversight of whether they are respected in specific projects. This is also true of German development cooperation law.[27]

On the other hand, European development cooperation law displays particular respect for the collective autonomy of recipient states.[28] Particularly in the ACP context, the EU has established a level playing field which protects recipient ownership both in planning and in negotiating specific measures. The World Bank's development cooperation law focuses more on its own autonomy and takes fewer precautions to secure that of recipients. German law can here be said to occupy a middle position.[29]

It is perhaps less surprising that the World Bank implements the principle of coherence and efficiency better than the other legal regimes under study here. The Bank's particular concern for financial security leads to a better *ex-ante* evaluation of economic efficiency. Although German law contains similar ideas, it sets out only vague benchmarks for the evaluation, while European law ignores this point entirely.[30] The element of coordination, which is an essential part of the principle of coherence and efficiency, is particularly well respected by the World Bank, since the Bank's planning is more strongly oriented towards recipient needs than that of other donors. This policy eases coordination. The partnership-oriented – yet exclusively bilateral – planning under the law governing EU-ACP cooperation is less open, as is the German planning regime.[31]

If one combines the individual elements, we can distinguish two basic forms of development cooperation law, namely an autonomous-technocratic form (in the World Bank) and a more heteronomous-diplomatic one (as in the EU and Germany).[32] The first form is more strongly oriented

[26] *Supra* Part III, Ch 6.B.I.1c) and 2.

[27] *Supra* Part III, Ch 6.B.II.1c) and 2., see also Ch 6.B.III.1 and 2. A comparative analysis of all three organizations is found in Ch 6.C.

[28] *Supra* Part III, Ch 5.C.II.1, Ch 6.B.II.1b.

[29] *Supra* Part III, Ch 5.C.I.1, Ch 6.B.I.1.b) and Ch 6.B.III.1.

[30] Part III, Ch 6.B.I.1.a) and 2 (World Bank) vs. Ch 6.B.II.2 (EU) and Ch 6.B.III.2 (Germany).

[31] Part III, Ch 5.C.I.3.a) (World Bank) vs. Ch 5.C.II.2 (EU) and Ch 5.C.III (Germany).

[32] Part II, Ch 3.A.VI. and Part III, Ch 5.D.

toward the autonomous goals of development cooperation (development and poverty reduction) and uses various elements, some technocratic, to achieve these goals. Under this approach, development cooperation is less an open, politically contested process than a relatively clearly defined technical problem which can be addressed with expertise. In the heteronomous-diplomatic type, by contrast, the goals are less explicitly oriented to poverty reduction and development, since development cooperation can, of course, pursue other goals. Particular weight is assigned to the political process of negotiation between governments.

B Development cooperation law: agenda for future study

This book has argued that the rules which govern development cooperation can be understood, doctrinally and systematically, as one field of law. It is the law governing a policy area which not only has its own institutional structures but also its specific doctrinal forms. This book, however, marks only the beginning of the exploration of this area of law. The discussion in this book has revealed a broad spectrum of issues, indeed an entire research agenda.[33]

Four main groups of issue and research areas can be identified: first, research could address the law of *further phases* of the ODA transfer process. The present work has concentrated on the constitutional elements (organizations, mandates, legal sources and principles), as well as the administrative law core of ODA law (i.e. planning and concrete agreement on development interventions). It also studied the accountability structures. A further research area could address how ODA funds are allocated *before* planning. This would require an analysis of donors' budgetary laws, and in particular the role of donor-state legislatures. Budget allocation rules of the international actors would also be fascinating from a legal perspective – the World Bank, in particular, has developed a budgetary law oriented toward indicators and quantifiable criteria which could be profitably compared to conventional budgetary law. Also, the phases after agreement should be studied, especially the procurement law of development financing and the evaluation and monitoring phase.

A further promising area might be the investigation of the development cooperation law of *other actors*. The law of other donors might well display different doctrinal structures than the ones assessed in this

[33] A research agenda focusing more on instruments than institutions is set forth in Davis, *Financing Development*.

book. A horizontal comparison of various state actors would deepen the understanding of this area of law, in view of the fact that other important donor states (especially the USA, Great Britain and Canada) have comprehensive laws governing development cooperation which await doctrinal analysis and contextualization.[34] A comprehensive understanding of development cooperation law would also require careful examination of the *law of recipients*. Here, the question would be how these states deal with ODA funding from the perspective of organizational and procedural law. A comparative approach to the various recipient states would be particularly intriguing.[35] One last further approach would be to include private development actors. Examining the role of churches, the Gates Foundation, and mixed private–public partnerships would add greatly to the understanding of the legal structures of development cooperation.

A further area of study would be the *special parts* or neighboring areas of development cooperation law: that is, regulations which have been developed for specific subject areas or instruments. They should be assessed not only in their own right, but also in relation to the general structures of development cooperation law, as laid out here. Funding for humanitarian aid or disaster relief are considered as ODA, but are subject to their own rules and procurement principles.[36] Another area which has generated regulatory interest in recent years is fragile states. This area, as well, has so far received only minimal legal analysis.[37] One area which is not thematically delimited but which has emerged as an important instrument is the law of trust funds, which has yet to be examined in depth.[38] There are, in addition, other thematic areas and instruments which could further deepen our understanding of this legal domain.

Fourthly and finally, we should consider the possibility of more interdisciplinary research and contextualization of development cooperation law. Clearly, an intensified *historical* consideration – in particular, possible continuities between forms of former colonial and present-day

[34] On British law see, e.g. McAuslan, "The International Development Act, 2002."

[35] A promising contribution can be found in Akech, "Development Partners."

[36] H.-J. Heintze and A. Zwitter, *International Law and Humanitarian Assistance: A Crosscut Through Legal Issues Pertaining to Humanitarianism* (Berlin, Heidelberg: Springer, 2011); Engelhardt, "Reflections."

[37] K. E. Boon, "'Open for Business': International Financial Institutions, Post-Conflict Economic Reform, and the Rule of Law," *New York University Journal of International Law and Politics*, 39 (2007), 513–81; M. von Engelhardt, *Aiding Fragile States*, Ph.D. thesis (forthcoming 2013).

[38] Work has begun in this area, but has yet to exhaust its possibilities, see Bantekas, *Trust Funds*.

development administration – would be fruitful areas for future research.[39] While this book has drawn primarily on a familiar legal perspective, one could also subject the laws discussed here to *other* theoretical approaches. A postcolonial perspective could be particularly fruitful, as well as an approach oriented toward economic analysis of law, in particular institutional economics.[40]

In summary, the research agenda for development cooperation law is broad. A (legal) *policy* agenda can also easily be envisioned. A particular focus could be on more transparent rules and improved compliance oversight through quasi-judicial bodies or ombudsmen, similar to the approach taken by the World Bank through its Inspection Panel. A legal research agenda could go hand-in-hand with improved rule-of-law and good governance of donors. However, there has been little activity in this area so far. The potential of law in the context of development cooperation has yet to be fully realized.

[39] H. Sieberg, *Colonial Development: Die Grundlegung moderner Entwicklungspolitik durch Grossbritannien, 1919–1949* (Stuttgart: Steiner, 1985).

[40] A postcolonial critique is presented in Anghie, "Time Present and Time Past"; on the analysis of welfare law from an economic perspective see, e.g. U. Sacksofsky, "§40 Anreize," in W. Hoffmann-Riem, E. Schmidt-Aßmann and A. Voßkuhle (eds.), *Informationsordnung, Verwaltungsverfahren, Handlungsformen* (Munich: C.H. Beck, 2008), vol. II, pp. 1459–517 at margin no. 29.

REFERENCES

Abi-Saab, Georges, "The Third World and the Future of the International Legal Order," *Revue égyptienne de droit international*, 29 (1973), 27–66.

Achebe, Chinua, *Things Fall Apart* (London: William Heinemann, 1958).

Acheson, A. L. Keith, Chant, John and Prachowny, Martin (eds.), *Bretton Woods Revisited: Evaluations of the IMF and the International Bank for Reconstruction and Development* (London: Macmillan, 1972).

Adam, Christopher, "Redesigning the Aid Contract: Donor–use of Performance Indicators in Uganda," *World Development*, 30 (2002), 2045–56.

Adamski, Dariusz, "Approximating a Workable Compromise on Access to Official Documents: The 2011 Developments in the European Courts," *Common Market Law Review*, 49 (2001), 521–58.

Akech, J. M. Migai, "Development Partners and Governance of Public Procurement in Kenya: Enhancing Democracy in the Administration of Aid," *New York University Journal of International Law and Politics*, 37 (2006), 829–68.

Alesino, Alberto and Weder, Beatrice, "Do Corrupt Governments Receive Less Foreign Aid?" *The American Economic Review*, 92 (2002), 1126–37.

Alford, C. Fred, *Whistleblowers: Broken Lives and Organizational Power* (Ithaca: Cornell University Press, 2001).

Alkazaz, Aziz, *Arabische Entwicklungshilfe-Institutionen: Organisationsform und Leistungen* (Hamburg: Deutsches Orient-Institut, 1977).

Almond, Gabriel and Coleman, James S. (eds.), *The Politics of the Developing Areas* (Princeton University Press, 1960).

Alston, Philip, (ed.), *The EU and Human Rights* (Oxford University Press, 1999).

A Human Rights Perspective on the Millennium Development Goals, Paper prepared as a contribution to the work of the work of the Millennium Project Task Force on Poverty and Economic Development. Available at www.hurilink.org/tools/HRsPerspectives_on_the_MDGs–Alston.pdf (last visited September 2012).

"Ships Passing in the Night: The Current State of the Human Rights and Development Debate Seen Through the Lens of the Millennium Development Goals," *Human Rights Quarterly*, 27 (2005), 755–829.

Alston, Philip and Quinn, Gerard, "The Nature and Scope of States Parties' Obligation Under the International Covenant on Economic, Social and Cultural Rights," *Human Rights Quarterly*, 9 (1987), 156–229.

Alston, Philip and Robinson, Mary (eds.), *Human Rights and Development: Towards Mutual Reinforcement* (Oxford University Press, 2005).

"The Challenges of Ensuring the Mutuality of Human Rights and Development Endeavours," in P. Alston and M. Robinson (eds.), *Human Rights and Development: Towards Mutual Reinforcement* (Oxford University Press, 2005), pp. 1–18.

Alvarez, Jose E., *International Organizations as Law-Makers* (Oxford University Press, 2005).

Amin, Samir, "Zur Theorie von Akkumulation und Entwicklung," in D. Senghaas (ed.), *Peripherer Kapitalismus: Analysen über Abhängigkeit und Unterentwicklung* (Frankfurt: Suhrkamp, 1974), pp. 71–97.

Amsden, Alice H., *The Rise of "the Rest": Challenges to the West from Late-Industrializing Economies* (Oxford University Press, 2003).

Anand, Ram Prakash, "Sovereign Equality of States in International Law," *Recueil des Cours*, 197 (1986), 9–228.

Androulakis, Ioannis N., *Die Globalisierung der Korruptionsbekämpfung* (Baden-Baden: Nomos, 2007).

Anghie, Antony, "Colonialism and the Birth of International Institutions: Sovereignty, Economy, and the Mandate System of the League of Nations," *New York University Journal of International Law and Politics*, 34 (2001), 513–633.

Colonialism, Sovereignty, and the Making of International Law (Cambridge University Press, 2004).

"Time Present and Time Past," *New York University Journal of International Law and Politics*, 32 (2000), 243–90.

"TWAIL: Past and Future," *International Community Law Review*, 10 (2008), 479–82.

Arndt, Christiane and Oman, Charles, *Uses and Abuses of Governance Indicators* (Paris: Development Centre of the Organisation for Economic Co-operation and Development, 2006).

Arnim, Hans Herbert von, *Wirtschaftlichkeit als Rechtsprinzip* (Berlin: Duncker & Humblot, 1988).

Arts, Karin, "ACP-EU Relations in a New Era: The Cotonou Agreement," *Common Market Law Review*, 40 (2003), 95–116.

"The European Union Development Cooperation and Human Rights at a Crossroads," *European Yearbook on Human Rights*, 11 (2011), 283–96.

Arts, Karin and Dickson, Anna K. (eds.), *EU Development Cooperation: from Model to Symbol* (Manchester University Press, 2004).

Ashoff, Guido, *Der Entwicklungshilfeausschuss der OECD und die deutsche Entwicklungszusammenarbeit: Ein Verhältnis auf dem Prüfstand*, Analysen und Stellungnahmen des deutschen Instituts für Entwicklungspolitik 1/2000. Available at www.die-gdi.de/CMS-Homepage/openwebcms3.nsf/%28ynDK_contentByKey%29/ENTR-7BSKLC?Open (last visited July 2013).

Geberkoordinierung: Eine wesentliche Voraussetzung für eine effizientere und wirksamere Entwicklungszusammenarbeit, Analysen und Stellungnahmen des deutschen Instituts für Entwicklungspolitik 7/2004. Available at www.die-gdi.de/CMS-Homepage/openwebcms3.nsf/%28ynDK_contentByKey%29/ENTR-7BRHES (last visited July 2013).

"Die Rolle der Länderkonzepte des BMZ: Schwerpunktsetzung in der deutschen Entwicklungszusammenarbeit," *Entwicklung und Zusammenarbeit*, 39 (1998), 312–16.

Die Umsetzung der Paris-Erklärung zur Wirksamkeit der Entwicklungszusammenarbeit: Wo steht Deutschland?, Analysen und Stellungnahmen des deutschen Instituts für Entwicklungspolitik 5/2008. Available at www.die-gdi.de/CMS-Homepage/openwebcms3.nsf/%28ynDK_contentByKey%29/ANES-7HXFTL?Open (last visited July 2013).

Aston, Jurij Daniel, *Sekundärgesetzgebung internationaler Organisationen zwischen mitgliedstaatlicher Souveränität und Gemeinschaftsdisziplin* (Berlin: Duncker & Humblot, 2005).

Ayllon Pino, Bruno, *Brazilian Cooperation: a Model Under Construction for an Emerging Power (ARI)*. Available at www.realinstitutoelcano.org/wps/wcm/connect/d3dc7f0044b54d2d8c3c8ef55cb546a4/ARI143-2010_Ayllon_Brazilian_Cooperation_emerging_power.pdf?MOD=AJPERES&CACHEID=d3dc7f0044b54d2d8c3c8ef55cb546a4 (last visited September 2012).

Baaz, Maria Eriksson, *The Paternalism of Partnership: A Postcolonial Reading of Identity in Development Aid* (New York: Zed Books, 2005).

Backman, Gunilla, "Health Systems and the Right to Health: An Assessment of 194 Countries," *The Lancet*, 372 (2008), 2047–85.

Baderin, Mashood A. and McCorquodale, Robert (eds.), *Economic, Social and Cultural Rights in Action* (Oxford University Press, 2007).

Baimu, Evarist and Panou, Aristeidis, "Responsibility of International Organizations and the World Bank Inspection Panel: Parallel Tracks Unlikely to Converge?" in H. Cissé, D. Bradlow and B. Kingsbury (eds.), *International Financial Institutions and Global Legal Governance*, The World Bank Legal Review (Washington, DC: World Bank Publications, 2012), vol. III, pp. 147–72.

Bantekas, Illias, "Trust Funds," in R. Wolfrum (ed.), *Max Planck Encyclopedia of Public International Law* [online edition] (Oxford University Press, 2008–). Available at www.mpepil.com (last visited April 2013).

Trust Funds Under International Law: Trustee Obligations of the United Nations and the Development Banks (The Hague: Asser Press, 2009).

Baran, Paul A. and Sweezy, Paul M., *Monopoly Capital: An Essay on the American Economy and Social Order* (Harmondsworth: Penguin Press, 1968).

Baron Maydell, Bernd von and Eichenhofer, Eberhard (eds.), *Abhandlungen zum Sozialrecht* (Heidelberg: C.F. Müller, 1993).

Barry, Christian and Pogge, Thomas (eds.), *Global Institutions and Responsibilities: Achieving Global Justice* (Malden: Blackwell, 2005).

Bartels, Lorand, *Human Rights Conditionality in the EU's International Agreements* (Oxford University Press, 2005).

"The Trade and Development Policy of the European Union," *European Journal of International Law*, 18 (2007), 715–56.

Bartelt, Sandra, "The Legislative Architecture of EU External Assistance and Development Cooperation," in S. Bartelt and P. Dann (eds.), *Entwicklungszusammenarbeit im Recht der Europäischen Union – The Law of EU Development Cooperation: Europarecht-Beiheft Nr. 2* (Baden-Baden: Nomos, 2008), pp. 9–35.

Bartelt, Sandra and Dann, Philipp (eds.), *Entwicklungszusammenarbeit im Recht der Europäischen Union – The Law of EU Development Cooperation: Europarecht-Beiheft Nr. 2* (Baden-Baden: Nomos, 2008).

Bast, Jürgen, *Grundbegriffe der Handlungsformen der EU: Entwickelt am Beschluss als praxisgenerierter Handlungsform des Unions- und Gemeinschaftsrechts*, Beiträge zum ausländischen öffentlichen Recht und Völkerrecht (Berlin: Springer, 2006), vol. DLXXXIV.

"Legal Instruments and Judicial Protection," in A. von Bogdandy and J. Bast (eds.), *Principles of the European Constitutional law*, 2nd edn (Munich: C.H. Beck, 2010), pp. 345–97.

Bauer, Hartmut, "§36 Verwaltungsverträge," in W. Hoffmann-Riem, E. Schmidt-Aßmann and A. Voßkuhle (eds.), *Informationsordnung, Verwaltungsverfahren, Handlungsformen*, Grundlagen des Verwaltungsrechts (Munich: C.H. Beck, 2008), vol. II, pp. 1155–274.

Baum, Warren C. and Tolbert, Stokes M., *Investing in Development: Lessons of World Bank Experiences* (London, New York: Oxford University Press for the World Bank, 1985).

Baxi, Upendra, "Postcolonial Legality: A Postscript from India," *Verfassung und Recht in Übersee*, 45 (2012), 178–94.

Bayertz, Kurt, "Begriff und Problem der Solidarität," in K. Bayertz (ed.), *Solidarität: Begriff und Problem* (Frankfurt am Main: Suhrkamp, 1998), pp. 11–53.

(ed.), *Solidarität: Begriff und Problem* (Frankfurt am Main: Suhrkamp, 1998).

Beasley, Anne, Colin, David, Malick, Jeff, Melnyk, Andrew, Pitter-Lune, Maxine and Ray, Diane, *General Budget Support: Key Findings of Five USAID Studies*, PPC Evaluation Paper No. 7. Available at http://pdf.usaid.gov/pdf_docs/PNADE110.pdf (last visited July 2013).

Becker, Jürgen, *Die Partnerschaft von Lomé: Eine neue zwischenstaatliche Kooperationsform des Entwicklungsvölkerrechts* (Baden-Baden: Nomos, 1979).

Bedjaoui, Mohammed, "General Introduction," in M. Bedjaoui (ed.), *International Law: Achievements and Prospects* (Paris, Dordrecht: Martinus Nijhoff Publishers, 1991), pp. 1–18.

(ed.), *International Law: Achievements and Prospects* (Paris, Dordrecht: Martinus Nijhoff Publishers, 1991).

Behrens, Maria, "Global Governance," in A. Benz (ed.), *Governance – Regieren in komplexen Regelsystemen: Eine Einführung* (Wiesbaden: Verlag für Sozialwissenschaften, 2004), pp. 103–24.

Beitz, Charles, *Political Theory and International Relations* (Princeton University Press, 1979).

Benda-Beckmann, Franz von, "'Recht und Entwicklung' im Wandel," *Verfassung und Recht in Übersee*, 41 (2008), 295–308.

Benda-Beckmann, Franz von, Benda-Beckmann, Keebet von and Wiber, Melanie, *Changing Properties of Property* (New York: Berghahn Books, 2006).

Benedek, Wolfgang, "Die Bedeutung der Menschenrechte in der Entwicklungspolitik der Europäischen Union," *Journal für Entwicklungspolitik*, 10 (1994), 13–31.

"Progressive Development of the Principles and Norms of International Law Relating to the NIEO: The UNITAR Exercise," *Österreichische Zeitschrift für öffentliches Recht und Völkerrecht*, 36 (1985), 289–328.

"Das Recht auf Entwicklung in universeller Sicht und im Rahmen des Afrikanischen Menschenrechtsschutzes," in H.-J. Konrad (ed.), *Grundrechtsschutz und Verwaltungsverfahren, unter besonderer Berücksichtigung des Asylrechts: Internationaler Menschenrechtsschutz*. Referate der 23. Tagung der wissenschaftlichen Mitarbeiter der Fachrichtung "Öffentliches Recht" 22–26 February 1983 in Berlin (Berlin: Duncker & Humblot, 1985), vol. CDLXXXIV, pp. 275–301.

Bennigsen, Sabine, *Das "Recht auf Entwicklung" in der internationalen Diskussion* (Frankfurt: Peter Lang Verlag, 1989).

Benz, Arthur (ed.), *Governance – Regieren in komplexen Regelsystemen: Eine Einführung* (Wiesbaden: Verlag für Sozialwissenschaften, 2004).

Berg, Elliot J., *Accelerated Development in Sub-Saharan Africa: An Agenda for Action* (Washington, DC: The World Bank, 1981).

Berger, Johannes, "Was behauptet die Modernisierungstheorie wirklich – und was wird ihr bloß unterstellt?" *Leviathan* (1996), 45–62.

Berger, Peter L., "Speaking to the Third World," in P. L. Berger and M. Novak (eds.), *Speaking to the Third World: Essays on Development and Democracy: Studies in Religion, Philosophy, & Public Policy* (Washington, DC: Aei Press, 1985), pp. 4–20.

Berger, Peter L. and Luckmann, Thomas, *The Social Construction of Reality* (New York: Anchor Books, 1966).

Berger, Peter L. and Novak, M. (eds.), *Speaking to the Third World: Essays on Development and Democracy: Studies in religion, philosophy, & public policy* (Washington, DC: Aei Press, 1985).

Bernasconi-Osterwalder, Nathalie and Hunter, David B., "Democratizing Multilateral Development Banks," in C. Bruch (ed.), *The New "Public": The Globalization of Public Participation* (Washington, DC: Environmental Law Institute, 2002), pp. 151–64.

Bernhardt, Rudolf (ed.), *A-D: Aalands Islands to Dumbarton Oaks Conference (1944), Encyclopedia of Public International Law* (Amsterdam: North Holland, 1992), vol. I.

(ed.), *E-I: East African Community to Italy-United States air transport arbitration (1965), Encyclopedia of Public International Law* (Amsterdam: Elsevier, 1995), vol. II.

Bernstorff, Jochen von, "Procedures of Decision-Making and the Role of Law in International Organizations," *German Law Journal*, 9 (2008), 1939–64.

"The Changing Fortunes of the Universal Declaration of Human Rights: Genesis and Symbolic Dimensions of the Turn to Rights in International Law," *European Journal of International Law*, 19 (2008), 903–24.

Berthoud, Paul, "UNCTAD and the Emergence of International Development Law," in M. Zammit Cutajar (ed.), *UNCTAD and the North-South-Dialogue* (Oxford: Pergamon Press, 1985), pp. 71–98.

Besselink, Leonard F. M., Pennings, F. and Prechal, Sacha (eds.), *The Eclipse of the Legality Principle in the European Union* (Alphen aan den Rijn: Kluwer Law International, 2011).

Besters, Hans (ed.), *Kooperative Entwicklungshilfe: Deutsche und amerikanische Bemühungen beim Aufbau der Entwicklungsländer* (Bielefeld: Bertelsmann Universitätsverlag, 1968).

Betz, Joachim, *Die Internationalisierung der Entwicklungshilfe* (Berlin: Nomos, 1978).

Beyerlin, Ulrich, "Bridging the North-South-Divide in International Environmental Law," *Heidelberg Journal of International Law*, 66 (2006), 259–96.

Beyme, Klaus von, *Die Sowjetunion in der Weltpolitik* (Zürich: Piper, 1983).

Bhabha, Homi K., *The Location of Culture* (London, New York: Routledge, 1994).

Bhagwati, Jagdish N., *The New International Economic Order: The North-South Debate* (Cambridge: MIT Press, 1977).

Bickerton, Christopher J., Cunliffe, Philip and Gourevitch, Alexander (eds.), *Politics Without Sovereignty: A Critique of Contemporary International Relations* (University College London Press, 2007).

Billerbeck, Klaus, *Deutscher Beitrag für Entwicklungsländer* (Hamburg: Verlag Weltarchiv, 1958).

Bing-Pappoe, Adotey, *Reviewing Africa's Peer Review Mechanism: A Seven Country Study* (Ottawa: Partnership Africa Canada, 2010). Available at www.pacweb.org/Documents/APRM/APRM_Seven_countries_March2010-E.pdf (last visited July 2013).

Birdsall Nancy, *Seven Deadly Sins: Reflections on Donor Failings*, Center for Global Development Working Paper No. 50. Available at www.cgdev.org/files/2737_file_WP50_rev12_05_2.pdf (last visited September 2012).

Birdsall, Nancy and Fukuyama, Francis *The Post-Washington Consensus: Development After the Crisis*, Centre for Global Development Working Paper 244 (2011). Available at www.cgdev.org/content/publications/detail/1424882 (last visited July 2013).

Black, Henry Campbell, *Black's Law Dictionary: Definitions of the Terms and Phrases of American and English Jurisprudence Ancient and Modern*, 5th edn (St. Paul: West Publishing Company, 1979).

Bleckmann, Albert, *Das französische Kolonialreich und die Gründung neuer Staaten: Die Rechtsentwicklung in Syrien/Libanon, Indochina und Schwarzafrika* (Cologne: Heymann, 1969).

"Zur Verbindlichkeit des allgemeinen Völkerrechts für internationale Organisationen," *Heidelberg Journal of International Law*, 37 (1977), 107–21.

"Anspruch auf Entwicklungshilfe?" *Verfassung und Recht in Übersee*, 12 (1979), 5–14.

Bleicher, Samuel, "UN vs. IBRD: A Dilemma of Functionalism," *International Organization*, 24 (1970), 31–47.

Bleisch, Barbara and Schaber, Peter (eds.), *Weltarmut und Ethik* (Paderborn: Mentis, 2007).

Bliss, Frank, "Von der Mitwirkung zur Selbstbestimmung," *Politik und Zeitgeschichte* (2000), 3–8.

Blokker, Niels, "International Organizations and their Members: International Organizations Belong to All Members and to None," Variations on a Theme, *International Organizations Law Review*, 1 (2004), 139–61.

Blokker, Niels M. and Schermers, Henry G. (eds.), *Proliferation of International Organizations: Legal Issues* (The Hague: Kluwer Law International, 2001).

Boas, Morten and McNeill, Desmond (eds.), *Global Institutions and Development: Framing the World?* (Oxford: Routledge, 2003).

Bockslaff, Klaus, *Das völkerrechtliche Interventionsverbot als Schranke außenpolitisch motivierter Handelsbeschränkungen* (Berlin: Duncker & Humblot, 1987).

Bodemer, Klaus, *Entwicklungshilfe – Politik für wen?: Ideologie und Vergabepraxis der deutschen Entwicklungshilfe in der ersten Dekade* (Munich: Weltforum Verlag, 1974).

"Programmentwicklung in der Entwicklungspolitik der Bundesrepublik Deutschland," in F. Nuscheler (ed.), *Dritte-Welt-Forschung: Entwicklungstheorie und Entwicklungspolitik*. Sonderheft Politische Vierteljahresschrift No. 16 (Opladen: Westdeutscher Verlag, 1985), pp. 278–307.

Bogdandy, Armin von, "Demokratie, Globalisierung, Zukunft des Völkerrechts – eine Bestandsaufnahme," *Heidelberg Journal of International Law*, 63 (2003), 853–77.

"General Principles of International Public Authority: Sketching a Research Field," *German Law Journal*, 9 (2008), 1909–38.

"Prolegomena zu Prinzipien internationalisierter und internationaler Verwaltung," in H.-H. Trute, T. Groß, C. Möllers and H. C. Röhl (eds.), *Allgemeines Verwaltungsrecht – zur Tragfähigkeit eines Konzepts*. Festschrift für Eberhard Schmidt-Aßmann (Tübingen: Mohr Siebeck, 2008), pp. 683–97.

Bogdandy, Armin von and Bast, Jürgen (eds.), *Principles of European Constitutional Law*, Modern Studies of European Law (Oxford: Hart Publishing, 2006), vol. VIII.

"The Vertical Order of Competences," in A. von Bogdandy and J. Bast (eds.), *Principles of European Constitutional Law*, Modern Studies of European Law (Oxford: Hart Publishing, 2006), vol. VIII, pp. 335–72.

Europäisches Verfassungsrecht, 2nd edn (Heidelberg: Springer, 2009).

Principles of the European Constitutional Law, 2nd edn (Munich: C.H. Beck, 2010).

Bogdandy, Armin von, Cassese, Sabino and Huber, Peter Michael (eds.), *Verwaltungsrecht in Europa: Wissenschaft*, Ius Publicum Europaeum (Heidelberg: C.F. Müller, 2011), vol. IV.

Bogdandy, Armin von, Dann, Philipp and Goldmann, Matthias, "Developing the Publicness of Public International Law: Towards a Legal Framework for Global Governance Activities," *German Law Journal*, 9 (2008), 1375–400.

"Developing the Publicness of Public International Law," in A. von Bogdandy, R. Wolfrum, J. von Bernstorff, P. Dann and M. Goldmann (eds.), *The Exercise of Public Authority by International Institutions: Advancing International Institutional Law* (Heidelberg: Springer, 2010), pp. 3–32.

"Völkerrecht als öffentliches Recht: Konturen eines rechtlichen Rahmens für Global Governance," *Der Staat*, 49 (2010), 1–28.

Bogdandy, Armin von and Goldmann, Matthias, "The Exercise of International Public Authority Through National Policy Assessment: The OECD's PISA Policy as a Paradigm for a New International Standard Instrument," *International Organizations Law Review*, 5 (2008), 241–98.

"Die Ausübung internationaler öffentlicher Gewalt durch Politikbewertung: Die PISA-Studie als Muster einer neuen völkerrechtlichen Handlungsform," *Heidelberg Journal of International Law*, 69 (2009), 51–102.

Bogdandy, Armin von and Smrkolj, Maja, "European Community and Union Law and International Law," in R. Wolfrum (ed.), *Max Planck Encyclopedia of Public International Law* [online edition] (Oxford University Press, 2008–). Available at www.mpepil.com (last visited April 2013).

Bogdandy, Armin von and Wolfrum, Rüdiger (eds.), *Max Planck Yearbook of United Nations Law*, 14th edn (Leiden, Biggleswade: Martinus Nijhoff Publishers, 2010).

Bogdandy, Armin von, Wolfrum, Rüdiger, Bernstorff, Jochen von, Dann, Philipp and Goldmann, Matthias (eds.), *The Exercise of Public Authority by International Institutions: Advancing International Institutional Law* (Heidelberg: Springer, 2010).

Boisson de Chazournes, Laurence, "Policy Guidance and Compliance: The World Operational Standards," in D. Shelton (ed.), *Commitment and Compliance: The Role of Non-Binding Norms in the International Legal System* (Oxford University Press, 2000), pp. 281–303.

Boon, Kristen E., "'Open for Business': International Financial Institutions, Post-Conflict Economic Reform, and the Rule of Law," *New York University Journal of International Law and Politics*, 39 (2007), 513–81.

Booth, David, "Are PRSPs Making a Difference? The African Experience," Introduction and Overview, *Development Policy Review*, 21 (2003), 131–59.

Missing Links in the Politics of Development: Learning from the PRSP Experiment, Overseas Development Institute Working Paper No. 256 (London, 2005).

Booth, David and Evans, Alison, *Evaluation Network Follow-up to the Paris Declaration on Aid Effectiveness: An Options Paper*, Submitted for discussion at the fourth meeting of the DAC Evaluation Network, 30–March 31, 2006. Available at www.oecd.org/development/evaluationofdevelopmentprogrammes/dcdndep/36303226.pdf (last visited July 2013).

Borchardt, Klaus-Dieter, *Die rechtlichen Grundlagen der Europäischen Union*, 3rd edn (Heidelberg: C.F. Müller, 2006).

Borrmann, Axel and Ahrens, Heinz, *Zur Bewertung der Entwicklungszusammenarbeit* (Berlin: Duncker & Humblot, 2006).

Bothe, Michael, "Environment, Development, Resources," *Recueil des Cours*, 318 (2005), 323–516.

Bovens, Mark, *The Quest for Responsibility: Accountability and Citizenship in Complex Organisations* (Cambridge University Press, 1998).

Bowett, Derek W., "International Law and Economic Coercion," in R. B. Lillich (ed.), *Economic Coercion and the New International Economic Order* (Charlottesville: Michie, 1976), pp. 87–103.

Bradlow, Daniel, "International Law and the Operations of the International Financial Institutions," in D. Bradlow and D. B. Hunter (eds.), *International Financial Institutions and International Law* (Alphen aan den Rijn: Kluwer Law International, 2010), pp. 11–23.

"The World Bank, the IMF, and Human Rights," *Transnational Law and Contemporary Problems*, 6 (1996), 47–90.

Bradlow, Daniel and Grossmann, Claudio, "Adjusting the Bretton Woods Institutions to Contemporary Realities," in J.-M. Griesgraber and B. Gunter (eds.), *Development: New Paradigms and Principles for the 21st Century: Rethinking Bretton Woods* (London: Pluto Press, 1996), pp. 27–59.

Bradlow, Daniel and Hunter, David B. (eds.), *International Financial Institutions and International Law* (Alphen aan den Rijn: Kluwer Law International, 2010).

Brainard, Lael (ed.), *Security by Other Means: Foreign Assistance, Global Poverty, and American Leadership* (Washington, DC: Brookings Institution Press, 2007).

Brautigam, Deborah, *Aid Dependence and Governance*, Expert Group on Development Issues Working Paper 2000/1. Available at www.sti.ch/fileadmin/user_upload/Pdfs/swap/swap404.pdf (last visited July 2013).

"Aid 'With Chinese Characteristics': Chinese Foreign Aid and Development Finance Meet the OECD-DAC Aid Regime," *Journal of International Development*, 23 (2011), 752–64.

"Chinese Development Aid in Africa: What, Where, Why, and How Much?" in L. Song and J. Golley (eds.), *Rising China: Global Challenges and Opportunities* (Acton: ANU E Press, 2011), pp. 203–22.

Brautigam, Deborah and Knack, Stephen, "Foreign Aid, Institutions, and Governance in Sub-Saharan Africa," *Economic Development and Cultural Change*, 52 (2004), 255–85.

Breitenmoser, Stephan and Wildhaber, Luzius (eds.), *Human Rights, Democracy and the Rule of Law: Liber amicorum Luzius Wildhaber* (Zürich, Baden-Baden: Nomos, 2007).

Breitmeier, Helmut, Roth, Michele and Senghaas, Dieter (eds.), *Sektorale Weltordnungspolitik: Effektiv, gerecht und demokratisch?* (Baden-Baden: Nomos, 2009).

Breyer, Stephen G., Stewart, Richard, Sunstein, Cass and Vermeule, Adrian, *Administrative Law and Regulatory Policy: Problems, Text and Cases*, 6th edn (New York: Aspen Publishers, 2006).

Brinkerhoff, Derick W., "The State and International Development Management: Shifting Tides, Changing Boundaries, and Future Directions," *Public Administration Review*, 68 (2008), 985–1001.

Broberg, Morten, "Access to Documents: a General Principle of Community Law?" *European Law Review*, 27 (2002), 194–205.

Broches, Aron, "International Bank for Reconstruction and Development," in S. Rubin (ed.), *Foreign Development Lending – Legal Aspects*. The papers and proceedings of a conference of legal advisors of national and international development lending and assistance agencies (Leiden: Sijthoff, 1971), pp. 79–93.

"International Legal Aspects of the Operations of the World Bank," *Recueil des Cours*, 169 (1959), 297–409.

Selected Essays: World Bank, ICSID and Other Subjects of Public and Private International Law (Dordrecht: Martinus Nijhoff, 1995).

Bröhmer, Jürgen, *Transparenz als Verfassungsprinzip: Grundgesetz und Europäische Union* (Tübingen: Mohr Siebeck, 2004).

Brombacher, Daniel, *Geberstrukturen in der Entwicklungspolitik: Reformansätze für die Steuerung und Koordinierung der deutschen Entwicklungszusammenarbeit* (Berlin: Stiftung Wissenschaft und Politik, 2009).

Brookings, *Opinion: It's Complicated: The Challenge of Implementing the Paris Declaration on Aid Effectiveness*, September 22, 2011. Available at www.brookings.edu/opinions/2011/0922_paris_declaration_chandy.aspx (last visited July 2013).

Brown, Bartram, *The United States and the Politicization of the World Bank* (London: Kegan Paul International, 1992).

Brown Weiss, Edith, Rigo Sureda, Andres and Boisson de Chazournes, Laurence (eds.), *The World Bank, International Financial Institutions, and the Development of International Law: A symposium held in honor of Dr. Ibrahim F. I. Shihata*, March 22, 1999 (Washington, DC: American Society of International Law, 1999).

Brownlie, Ian, *Principles of Public International Law*, 7th edn (Oxford University Press, 2008).

Bruch, Carl (ed.), *The New "Public": The Globalization of Public Participation* (Washington, DC: Environmental Law Institute, 2002).

Bruha, Thomas and Rau, Markus, "Bedeutung der Grundrechte der EU für Drittstaaten," in S. Heselhaus and C. Nowak (eds.), *Handbuch der Europäischen Grundrechte* (Munich: C.H. Beck, 2006), pp. 105–21.

Brundtland, Gro Harlem, *Our Common Future* (Oxford University Press, 1987).

Brunkhorst, Hauke, *Solidarität: Von der Bürgerfreundschaft zur globalen Rechtsgenossenschaft* (Frankfurt: Suhrkamp, 2002).

Bryde, Brun-Otto, "Die Intervention mit wirtschaftlichen Mitteln," in I. von Münch (ed.), *Staatsrecht – Völkerrecht – Europarecht*. Festschrift für Hans-Jürgen Schlochauer zum 75. Geburtstag (Berlin: de Gruyter, 1981), pp. 227–45.

"Von der Notwendigkeit einer neuen Weltwirtschaftsordnung," in B.-O. Bryde and P. Kunig (eds.), *Neuordnung der Weltwirtschaft?* (Baden-Baden: Nomos, 1986), pp. 29–54.

Bryde, Brun-Otto and Kübler, Friedrich (eds.), *Die Rolle des Rechts im Entwicklungsprozess* (Frankfurt am Main: Metzner, 1986).

Bryde, Brun-Otto and Kunig, Philip (eds.), *Neuordnung der Weltwirtschaft?* (Baden-Baden: Nomos, 1986).

Brzoska, Michael, "Extending ODA or Creating a New Reporting Instrument for Security-related Expenditures for Development?" *Development Policy Review*, 26 (2008), 131–50.

Buergenthal, Thomas, "The ICJ, Human Rights, and Extraterritorial Jurisdiction," in S. Breitenmoser and L. Wildhaber (eds.), *Human Rights, Democracy and the Rule of Law: Liber Amicorum Luzius Wildhaber* (Zürich, Baden-Baden: Nomos, 2007), pp. 143–50.

"The World Bank and Human Rights," in E. Brown Weiss, A. R. Sureda and L. B. de Chazournes (eds.), *The World Bank, International Financial Institutions, and the Development of International Law: A symposium held in honor of Dr. Ibrahim F. I. Shihata*. Sponsored by the Georgetown University Law Center and the World Bank in association with the American Society of International Law, March 22, 1999 (Washington, DC: American Society of International Law, 1999), pp. 95–104.

Bulajic, Milan, *Principles of International Development Law*, 2nd edn (Dordrecht: Martinus Nijhoff, 1993).

Bundesministerium für wirtschaftliche Zusammenarbeit und Entwicklung (BMZ), *Ankerländer – Partner für globale Entwicklung* (Anchor countries) (Bonn, 2004).

Armut bekämpfen, Gemeinsam handeln. Der Beitrag der Bundesregierung zur weltweiten Halbierung extremer Armut: Aktionsprogramm 2015 (Defend Poverty) (Bonn, 2003).

Entwicklungspolitische Konzeption der Bundesrepublik Deutschland für die Zweite Entwicklungsdekade (Conception) (Bonn, 1971).

Evaluierungskriterien für die deutsche bilaterale Entwicklungszusammenarbeit: Eine Orientierung für Evaluierungen des BMZ und der Durchführungsorganisationen (2006). Available at www.bmz.de/de/zentrales_downloadarchiv/erfolg_und_kontrolle/evaluierungskriterien.pdf (last visited July 2013).

Förderung von Good Governance in der deutschen Entwicklungspolitik: Konzept Nr. 172 (Concept No. 172) (Berlin, 2009). Available at www.bmz.de/de/publikationen/reihen/strategiepapiere/konzept172.pdf (last visited July 2013).

Grundlinien der Entwicklungspolitik der Bundesregierung (Guidelines on German Development Policy) (Bonn, 1986).

Kleine Beiträge – große Sicherheit. Mikroversicherungen im Finanzsystem: Konzept Nr. 176 (Concept No. 176) (Bonn, 2009). Available at www.bmz.de/de/publikationen/reihen/strategiepapiere/Konzept176.pdf (last visited July 2013).

Konzept zur Budgetfinanzierung im Rahmen der programmorientierten Gemeinschaftsfinanzierung: Konzept Nr. 146 (Concept No. 146) (Bonn, 2008). Available at www.bmz.de/de/publikationen/reihen/strategiepapiere/Konzepte146.pdf (last visited September 2012).

Leitlinien für die bilaterale finanzielle und technische Zusammenarbeit mit Kooperationspartnern der deutschen Entwicklungszusammenarbeit: Konzepte 165 (Guidelines) (Bonn, 2008). Available at www.bmz.de/de/publikationen/reihen/strategiepapiere/konzept165.pdf (last visited July 2013).

Medienhandbuch Entwicklungspolitik 2004/2005 (Media Handbook 2004/2005) (Berlin, 2004).

Medienhandbuch Entwicklungspolitik 2008/2009 (Media Handbook 2008/2009) (Bonn, 2008). Available at www.entwicklungsdienst.de/file-admin/Redaktion/Publik_ext/Medienhandbuch2008_2009.pdf (last visited July 2013).

Operationsplan zur Umsetzung der Pariser Erklärung 2005 und des Accra Aktionsplans 2008 zur Steigerung der Wirksamkeit von Entwicklungszusammenarbeit (2009). Available at http://www.bmz.de/de/zentrales_downloadarchiv/grundsaetze_und_ziele/OP_Paris_Accra_03_2009.pdf (last visited July 2013).

Sektorkonzept Soziale Sicherung: Konzept Nr. 180 (Concept No. 180) (Bonn, 2009). Available at www.bmz.de/de/publikationen/reihen/strategiepapiere/Konzepte180.pdf (last visited September 2012).

Bundesrechnungshof, *Bemerkungen 2010 zur Haushalts- und Wirtschaftsführung des Bundes* (2010). Available at http://bundesrechnungshof.de/veroeffentlichungen/bemerkungen-jahresberichte/bemerkungen-2010.pdf (last visited July 2013).

Bemerkungen 2011 zur Haushalts- und Wirtschaftsführung des Bundes (2011). Available at http://bundesrechnungshof.de/veroeffentlichungen/bemerkungen-jahresberichte/Bemerkungen-2011.pdf (last visited July 2013).

Burall, Simon, White, Jonathan M. and Blick, Andrew, *The Impact of U.S. and U.K. Legislatures on Aid Delivery*, Economic Policy Paper Series 09. Available at www.odi.org.uk/resources/docs/4652.pdf (last visited July 2013).

Burnside, Craig and Dollar, David, "Aid, Policies and Growth," *The American Economic Review*, 90 (2000), 847–68.

Busan Partnership for Effective Development Co-operation, *Outcome Document of the Fourth High-Level Forum on Aid Effectiveness*, Busan, Republic of Korea, 29 November – December 1, 2011. Available at www.aideffectiveco-operationresources.html (last visited July 2013).

Calliess, Christian and Ruffert, Matthias (eds.), *EUV/EGV: Das Verfassungsrecht der Europäischen Union mit Europäischer Grundrechtecharta*, Kommentar, 3rd edn (Munich: C.H. Beck, 2007).

Canagarajah, Sudharshan and van Diesen, Arthur, "The Poverty Reduction Strategy Approach Six Years On: An Examination of Principles and Practice in Uganda," *Development Policy Review*, 24 (2006), 647–67.

Carbone, Maurizio, *The European Union and International Development: The Politics of Foreign Aid* (London, New York: Routledge, 2007).

Cardoso, Fernando Henrique and Faletto, Enzo, *Dependency and Development in Latin America* (Berkeley: University of California Press, 1971).

Carlsson, Jerker, Somolekae, Gloria and van de Walle, Nicolas, *Foreign Aid in Africa: Learning from Country Experiences* (Uppsala: Nordiska afrikainstitutet, 1997).

Carothers, Thomas (ed.), *Promoting the Rule of Law Abroad: In Search of Knowledge* (Washington, DC: Carnegie Endowment for International Peace, 2006).

Carr, Stuart, McAuliffe, Eilish and MacLachlan, Malcolm, *Psychology of Aid* (London: Routledge, 1998).

Carrillo Salcedo, Juan A., "El derecho al desarrollo como dereche del person humana," *Revista Española de derecho international*, 25 (1972), 119–25.

Cassese, Antonio, *International Law in a Divided World* (Oxford: Clarendon Press, 1986).

Cernicky, Jan, "Erhard Eppler 1968–1974," in W. Gieler (ed.), *Deutsche Entwicklungsminister von 1961–2008: Biographien, Konzeptionen und Einfluss auf nationale und internationale Entwicklungspolitik* (Bonn: Scientia Bonnensis, 2008), pp. 40–56.

Chahoud, Tatjana, *Southern Non-DAC Actors in Development Cooperation*, German Development Insitute – Briefing Paper 13/2008 (2008). Available at www.die-gdi.de/CMS-Homepage/openwebcms3.nsf/%28ynDK_contentByKey%29/ANES-7LTH4R/$FILE/BP%2013.2008.pdf (last visited July 2013).

Chakravati, Ashok, *Aid, Institutions and Development: New Approaches to Growth, Governance and Poverty* (Cheltenham: Edward Elgar, 2005).

Chambers, Robert, *Rural Development: Putting the Last First* (London: Longman, 1983).

Chananan, Dweep, "India as an Emerging Donor," *Economic and Political Weekly*, 44 (2009), 11–14.

Chandy, Laurence and Kharas, Homi, "Why Can"t We All Just Get Along? The Practical Limits to International Development Cooperation," *Journal of International Development*, 23 (2011), 739–51.

Chávarri Ureta, Iciar de, "The European Commission's Institutional Framework for Development Policy," in C. Cosgrove-Sacks (ed.), *Europe, Diplomacy and Development: New Issues in EU Relations with Developing Countries* (New York: Palgrave Macmillan, 2001), pp. 52–64.

Chayes, Abram and Chayes, Antonia Handler, *The New Sovereignty: Compliance with International Regulatory Regimes* (Harvard University Press, 1995).

Chayes, Antonia Handler, Chayes Abram and Mitchell, Ronald B., "Active Compliance Management in Environmental Treaties," in W. Lang (ed.), *Sustainable Development and International Law*, International Environmental Law and Policy Series (London: Graham and Trotman, 1995), vol. VI, pp. 75–96.

Chenery, Hollis (ed.), *Redistribution with Growth: Policies to Improve Income Distribution in Developing Countries in the Context of Economic Growth* (Washington, DC: Oxford University Press, 1974).

Handbook of Development Economics (Amsterdam: North Holland Publishing Company, 1988).

Chimni, Bhupinder, "International Institutions: An Imperial Global State in the Making," *European Journal of International Law*, 15 (2004), 1–37.

"The Sen Conception of Development and Contemporary International Law Discourse: Some Parallels," *The Law and Development Review*, 1 (2008), 2–22.

"Third World Approaches to International Law: A Manifesto," *European Community Law Review*, 8 (2006), 3–27.

Chowdhury, Subrata Roy, Denters, Erik and Waart, Paul J. I. M. de (eds.), *The Right to Development in International Law* (Dordrecht: Martinus Nijhoff Publishers, 1992).

Christiansen, Karin and Hovland, Ingie, *The PRSP Initiative: Multilateral Policy Change and the Role of Research* (London: Overseas Development Institute, 2003).

Christodoulidis, Emilios and Tierney, Stephen (eds.), *Public Law and Politics: The Scope and Limits of Constitutionalism* (Aldershot: Ashgate, 2008).

Ciorciari, John D., "The Lawful Scope of Human Rights Criteria in World Bank Credit Decisions: An Interpretive Analysis of the IBRD and IDA Articles of Agreement," *Cornell International Law Journal*, 33 (2000), 331–71.

Cissé, Hassane, "Should the Political Prohibition in Charters of International Financial Institutions Be Revisited? The Case of the World Bank," in H. Cissé, D. Bradlow and B. Kingsbury (eds.), *International Financial Institutions and Global Legal Governance*, The World Bank Legal Review (Washington, DC: World Bank Publications, 2012), vol. III, pp. 59–92.

Cissé, Hassane, Bradlow, Daniel and Kingsbury, Benedict (eds.), *International Financial Institutions and Global Legal Governance*, The World Bank Legal Review (Washington, DC: World Bank Publications, 2012), vol. III.

Clavero, Bartolome, "The Indigenous Rights to Participation and International Development Policies," *Arizona Journal of Comparative and International Law*, 22 (2005), 41–51.

Clemens, Michael, Kenny, Charles and Moss, Todd, *The Trouble with the MDG: Confronting Expectations of Aid and Development Progress*, Center for Global Development Working Paper Nr. 40. Available at www.cgdev.org/content/publications/detail/2749/ (last visited July 2013).

Cock, Jacklyn and Webster, E. C., "Environmental and Social Impact Assessments," in J.-M. Griesgraber and B. Gunter (eds.), *The World Bank: Lending on a Global Scale* (London: Pluto Press, 1996), pp. 81–100.

Cogen, Marc, "Human Rights, Prohibition of Political Activities and the Lending Policies of World Bank and International Monetary Fund," in S. R. Chowdhury, E. Denters and P. J. I. M. de Waart (eds.), *The Right to Development in International Law* (Dordrecht: Martinus Nijhoff Publishers, 1992), pp. 379–96.

Collier, Paul, *The Bottom Billion: Why the Poorest Countries Are Failing and What Can Be Done About It* (Oxford University Press, 2007).

Cooke, Bill and Kothari, Uma, *Participation: The New Tyranny* (London, New York: Zed Books, 2001).

Cooker, Chris de, "Ethics and Accountability in International Civil Service," in C. de Cooker (ed.), *Accountability, Investigation and Due Process in International Organizations* (Leiden, Boston: Martinus Nijhoff, 2005), pp. 1–51.

(ed.), *Accountability, Investigation and Due Process in International Organizations* (Leiden, Boston: Martinus Nijhoff, 2005).

Coomans, Alphonsus (ed.), *Extraterritorial Application of Human Rights Treaties* (Antwerp: Intersentia, 2004).

Cornia, Giovanni A. and Jolly, Richard, *Adjustment with a Human Face: Protecting the Vulnerable and Promoting Growth* (Oxford: Clarendon Press, 1987).

Cosgrove Twitchett, Carol, *Europe and Africa: From Association to Partnership* (Westmead, England: Saxon House, 1978).

Cosgrove-Sacks, Carol (ed.), *Europe, Diplomacy and Development: New Issues in EU Relations with Developing Countries* (New York: Palgrave Macmillan, 2001).

Cotterell, Roger, "Comparative Law and Legal Culture," in M. Reimann and R. Zimmermann (eds.), *The Oxford Handbook of Comparative Law* (Oxford University Press, 2008), pp. 709–37.

Coudouel, Aline, *Beyond the Numbers: Understanding the Institutions for Monitoring Poverty Reduction Strategies* (Washington, DC: World Bank Publications, 2006).

Cox, Robert W., "Ideologies and the New International Economic Order," *International Organization*, 33 (1979), 257–302.

Craig, Paul and Búrca, Gráinne de, *EU Law: Text, Cases, and Materials*, 5th edn (Oxford University Press, 2011).

Craven, Matthew, "What Happened to Unequal Treaties? The Continuities of Informal Empire," *Nordic Journal of International Law*, 74 (2005), 335–82.

Crawford, James, *The International Law Commission's Articles on State Responsibility: Introduction, Text and Commentaries* (Cambridge University Press, 2002).

"State Responsibility," in R. Wolfrum (ed.), *Max Planck Encyclopedia of Public International Law* [online edition] (Oxford University Press, 2008–). Available at www.mpepil.com (last visited April 2013).

Cremer, Georg, *Korruption begrenzen: Praxisfeld Entwicklungspolitik*, 2nd edn (Freiburg im Breisgau: Lambertus, 2008).

Cremer, Hans-Joachim (ed.), *Tradition und Weltoffenheit des Rechts*, Festschrift für Helmut Steinberger, Beiträge zum ausländischen öffentlichen Recht und Völkerrecht (Berlin: Springer, 2002), vol. CLII.

Cullet, Philippe, *Differential Treatment in International Environmental Law* (Aldershot: Ashgate, 2003).

Culpeper, Roy, *Titans or Behemoths?* (Boulder, CO: Rienner, 1997).

Dahm, Georg, *Völkerrecht* (Stuttgart: Kohlhammer, 1958).

Dahm, Georg, Delbrück, Jost and Wolfrum, Rüdiger, *Völkerrecht*, 2nd edn (Berlin: de Gruyter, 1989).

Dam, Kenneth, *The Law-Growth-Nexus: The Rule of Law and Economic Development* (Washington, DC: Brookings Institution Press, 2006).

Damm, Ulrich, *Die Bundesrepublik Deutschland und die Entwicklungsländer* (Coburg: H. Biehl, 1965).

Danino, Roberto, "The Legal Aspects of the World Bank's Work on Human Rights," in P. Alston and M. Robinson (eds.), *Human Rights and Development: Towards Mutual Reinforcement* (Oxford University Press, 2005), pp. 509–24.

Dann, Philipp, "Accountability in Development Aid Law: The World Bank, UNDP and Emerging Structures of Transnational Oversight," *Archiv des Völkerrechts*, 44 (2006), 381–404.

Entwicklungsverwaltungsrecht (Tübingen: Mohr Siebeck, 2011).

"§34 Europäisches Entwicklungsverwaltungsrecht," in J. P. Terhechte (ed.), *Verwaltungsrecht der Europäischen Union: Zur Ausdifferenzierung und Globalisierung der europäischen Verwaltungsrechtsordnung* (Baden-Baden: Nomos, 2010), pp. 1189–209.

"Grundfragen eines Entwicklungsverwaltungsrechts," in C. Möllers, A. Vosskuhle and C. Walter (eds.), *Internationales Verwaltungsrecht: Eine Analyse anhand von Referenzgebieten*, Jus Internationale et Europaeum (Tübingen: Mohr Siebeck, 2007), vol. XVI, pp. 7–48.

"Political Institutions," in A. von Bogdandy and J. Bast (eds.), *Principles of European Constitutional Law*, Modern Studies of European Law (Oxford: Hart Publishing, 2006), vol. VIII, pp. 229–80.

"Political Institutions," in A. von Bogdandy and J. Bast (eds.), *Principles of the European Constitutional Law*, 2nd edn (Munich: C.H. Beck, 2010), pp. 234–74.

"Programm- und Prozesssteuerung im europäischen Entwicklungsverwaltungsrecht," in S. Bartelt and P. Dann (eds.), *Entwicklungszusammenarbeit im Recht der Europäischen Union – The Law of EU Development Cooperation: Europarecht-Beiheft Nr. 2* (Baden-Baden: Nomos, 2008), pp. 107–38.

"Solidarity and the Law of Development Cooperation," in R. Wolfrum and C. Kojima (eds.), *Solidarity: A Structural Principle of International Law* (Heidelberg: Springer, 2010), pp. 55–77.

"United Nations Development Capital Fund (UNCDF)," in R. Wolfrum (ed.), *Max Planck Encyclopedia of Public International Law* [online edition] (Oxford University Press, 2008–). Available at www.mpepil.com (last visited April 2013).

"Der Zugang zu Dokumenten im Recht der Weltbank: Kosmopolitische Tendenzen im Internationalen Verwaltungsrecht?" *Die Verwaltung*, 44 (2011), 313–25.

Dann, Philipp and Engelhardt, Marie von, "Legal Approaches to Global Governance and Accountability: Informal Lawmaking, International Public Authority, and Global Administrative Law Compared," in J. Pauwelyn, R. Wessel and J. Wouters (eds.), *Informal International Lawmaking* (Oxford University Press, 2012) pp. 106–121.

Dann, Philipp and Hanschmann, Felix, "Post-colonial Theories and the Law," *Verfassung und Recht in Übersee*, 45 (2012), 123–7.

Dann, Philipp, Kadelbach, Stefan and Kaltenborn, Markus (eds.), *Entwicklung und Recht* (forthcoming fall 2013).

Dann, Philipp and Vierck, Leonie, "Paris Declaration on Aid Effectiveness (2005)/Accra Agenda for Action (2008)," in R. Wolfrum (ed.), *Max Planck Encyclopedia of Public International Law* [online edition] (Oxford University Press, 2008–). Available at www.mpepil.com (last visited April 2013).

Darrow, Mac, *Between Light and Shadow: The World Bank, the International Monetary Fund and International Human Rights Law* (Oxford: Hart Publishing, 2003).

Darrow, Mac and Arbour, Louise, "The Pillar of Glass: Human Rights in the Development Operations of the United Nations," *American Journal of International Law*, 103 (2009), 446–501.

Darrow, Mac and Tomas, Amparo, "Power, Capture, and Conflict: A Call for Human Rights Accountability in Development Cooperation," *Human Rights Quarterly*, 27 (2005), 471–538.

Davis, Kevin E., *"Financing Development" as a Field of Practice, Study and Innovation*, New York University Institute for International Law and Justice Working Paper 2008/10 (New York, 2008). Available at http://papers.ssrn.com/sol3/papers.cfm?abstract_id=1341291## (last visited July 2013).

Davis, Kevin E., Fisher, Angelina, Kingsbury, Benedict and Merry, Sally Engle, *Governance by Indicators: Global Power Through Classification and Rankings* (Oxford University Press, 2012).

Davis, Kevin E. and Gelpern, Anna, "Peer-to-Peer Financing for Development: Regulating the Intermediaries," *New York University Journal of International Law and Politics*, 42 (2010), 1209–68.

Davis, Kevin E. and Kruse, Michael, "Taking the Measure of Law: The Case of the Doing Business Project," *Law and Social Inquiry*, 31 (2007), 1095–119.

Dean, Howard, "Due Process: The Rights of World Bank Staff in Misconduct Investigations," in C. de Cooker (ed.), *Accountability, Investigation and Due Process in International Organizations* (Leiden, Boston: Martinus Nijhoff, 2005), pp. 97–110.

Delbrück, Jost, "Völkerrecht und Weltfriedenssicherung," in D. Grimm (ed.), *Rechtswissenschaft und Nachbarwissenschaften: Band 2: Geschichte, Logik, Linguistik, Informatik, Friedensforschung, Finanzen, Didaktik*, 2 vols. (Munich: C.H. Beck, 1976), pp. 179–91.

Delbrück, Jost, Ipsen, Knut and Rauschning, Dietrich (eds.), *Recht im Dienst des Friedens: Festschrift für Eberhard Menzel zum 65. Geburtstag am 21. Januar 1976* (Berlin: Duncker & Humblot, 1975).

Dennert, Jürgen, *Entwicklungshilfe – geplant oder verwaltet?* (Bielefeld: Bertelsmann Universitätsverlag, 1968).

Desrosières, Alain, *The Politics of Large Numbers: A History of Statistical Reasoning* (Cambridge: Harvard University Press, 1998).

Deutsche Gesellschaft für Technische Zusammenarbeit (GTZ), *Die Begriffswelt der GTZ: The World of Words at GTZ* (Eschborn: Deutsche Gesellschaft für Technische Zusammenarbeit, 2004).

Jahresbericht 2007 (Annual Report 2007) (Eschborn: Deutsche Gesellschaft für Technische Zusammenarbeit, 2007).

Development Committee, *Operationalizing the 2011 World Development Report: Conflict, Security and Development*, DC 2011-0003 of April 4, 2011. Available at http://siteresources.worldbank.org/DEVCOMMINT/Documentation/22884392/DC2011-0003%28E%29WDR2011.pdf (last visited September 2012).

Dezalay, Yves and Garth, Bryant (eds.), *Lawyers and the Rule of Law in an Era of Globalization*, Law, Development and Globalization (Oxon, New York: Routledge, 2011).

Di Leva, Charles, "International Environmental Law and Development," *Georgetown International Environmental Law Review*, 10 (1998), 501–49.

"International Environmental Law, the World Bank, and International Financial Institutions," in D. Bradlow and D. B. Hunter (eds.), *International Financial Institutions and International Law* (Alphen aan den Rijn: Kluwer Law International, 2010), pp. 343–86.

Dicke, Detlev Christian, *Die administrative Organisation der Entwicklungshilfe durch die Vereinten Nationen* (Frankfurt: Athenäum, 1972).

Die Intervention mit wirtschaftlichen Mitteln im Völkerrecht: Zugleich ein Beitrag zu Fragen der wirtschaftlichen Souveränität (Baden-Baden: Nomos, 1978).

Dicke, Klaus, Hobe, Stephan, Meyn, Karl-Ulrich, Peters, Anne, Riedel, Eibe, Schütz, Hans-Joachim and Tietje, Christian (eds.), *Weltinnenrecht: Liber amicorum Jost Delbrück* (Berlin: Duncker & Humblot, 2005).

Dijkstra, Geske, "The PRSP Approach and the Illusion of Improved Aid Effectiveness: Lessons from Bolivia, Honduras and Nicaragua," *Development Policy Review*, 23 (2005), 443–64.

Dimier, Véronique, "Administrative Reform as Political Control," in D. G. Dimitrakopoulos (ed.), *The Changing European Commission* (Manchester University Press, 2004), pp. 74–85.

"The Invention of a Directorate General for Development (1958–1975)," in A. Smith (ed.), *Politics and the European Commission* (London: Routledge, 2004), pp. 83–95.

Dimier, Véronique and McGreeve, Mike, "Diplomats Without a Flag: The Institutionalization of the Delegations of the Commission in African, Caribbean and Pacific Countries," *Journal of Common Market Studies*, 44 (2006), 483–505.

Dimitrakopoulos, Dionyssis G. (ed.), *The Changing European Commission* (Manchester University Press, 2004).

Dollar, David and Pritchett, Lant, *Assessing Aid: What Works, What Doesn't and Why?*, World Bank Policy Research Report (New York: Oxford University Press for the World Bank, 1998).

Dommach, Hermann, "Das Verfahren der Erfolgskontrolle durch die Bundesverwaltung für zuwendungsfinanzierte Projekte und Institutionen," *Die Öffentliche Verwaltung*, 61 (2008), 282–7.

Donges, Juergen, *Außenwirtschafts- und Entwicklungspolitik: Die Entwicklungsländer in der Weltwirtschaft* (Berlin: Springer, 1981).

Dreier, Horst, "Art. 1 III GG," in H. Dreier (ed.), *Grundgesetz: Kommentar*, 2nd edn (Tübingen: Mohr Siebeck, 2004–).

Dreier, Horst (ed.), *Grundgesetz: Kommentar*, 2nd edn (Tübingen: Mohr Siebeck, 2004–).

Dreier, Johannes, *Die normative Steuerung der planerischen Abwägung: Strikte Normen, generelle Planungsleitbegriffe, Planungsleitlinien und Optimierungsgebote* (Berlin: Duncker & Humblot, 1996).

Du Bois, William Edward Burghardt, *The Souls of Black Folk: Essays and Sketches* (Chicago: A.C. McClurg & Co, 1903).

Duflo, Esther and Banerjee, Abhijit, *Poor Economics: A Radical Rethinking of the Way to Fight Global Poverty* (New York: PublicAffairs, 2011).

Duflo, Esther and Kremer, Michael, "Use of Randomization in the Evaluation of Development Effectiveness," in W. Easterly (ed.), *Reinventing Foreign Aid* (Cambridge: MIT Press, 2008), pp. 93–120.

Dumas, Lloyd J., Wedel, Janine R. and Callman, Greg, *Confronting Corruption, Building Accountability: Lessons from the World of International Development Advising* (New York: Palgrave Macmillan, 2010).

Dupuy, Pierre-Marie (ed.), *Völkerrecht als Wertordnung*, Festschrift für Christian Tomuschat (Kehl: Norbert P. Engel, 2006).

Easterly, William, *The Cartel of Good Intentions: Center for Global Development Working Paper No. 4*. Available at www.cgdev.org/content/publications/detail/2786/ (last visited July 2013).

The Elusive Quest for Growth: Economists' Adventures and Misadventures in the Tropics (Cambridge, MA: MIT Press, 2002).

"Die Entwicklungsideologie west weiter," *Merkur*, 61 (2007), 1084–8.

"Introduction: Can't Take it Anymore?" in W. Easterly (ed.), *Reinventing Foreign Aid* (Cambridge: MIT Press, 2008), pp. 1–43.

The White Man's Burden: Why the West's Efforts to Aid the Rest Have Done So Much Ill and So Little Good (New York: Penguin Press, 2006).

(ed.), *Reinventing Foreign Aid* (Cambridge: MIT Press, 2008).

Eberlei, Walter, *Stakeholder Participation in Poverty Reduction: Institute for Development and Peace Report 86/2007* (Duisburg, 2007). Available at http://inef.uni-due.de/page/documents/Report86.pdf (last visited July 2013).

Efraim, Athena Debbie, *Sovereign (In)equality in International Organizations* (The Hague: Martinus Nijhoff Publishers, 2000).

Eick, Christoph, "Die Reichweite der Bindung menschenrechtlicher Verträge für das auswärtige Handeln von Staaten," in E. Klein (ed.), *Gewaltenteilung und Menschenrechte* (Berlin: Berliner Wissenschafts-Verlag, 2006), pp. 115–28.

Eide, Asbjørn, "The Realisation of Social and Economic Rights and the Minimum Threshold Approach," *Human Rights Law Journal*, 10 (1989), 35–51.

(ed.), *The Universal Declaration of Human Rights: A Commentary* (Oslo: Scandinavian University Press, 1992).

Eide, Asbjørn, Krause, Catarina and Rosas, Allan, *Economic, Social and Cultural Rights: A Textbook*, 2nd edn (Dordrecht [u.a.]: Nijhoff, 2001).

Eifert, Martin, "Legitimationsstrukturen internationaler Verwaltung," in H.-H. Trute, T. Groß, C. Möllers and H. C. Röhl (eds.), *Allgemeines Verwaltungsrecht – zur Tragfähigkeit eines Konzepts*. Festschrift für Eberhard Schmidt-Aßmann (Tübingen: Mohr Siebeck, 2008), pp. 307–31.

"Das Verwaltungsrecht zwischen 'klassischer' Dogmatik und steuerungswissenschaftlichem Anspruch," in C. Hillgruber, U. Volkmann, G. Nolte and R. Porscher (eds.), *Die Leistungsfähigkeit der Wissenschaft des Öffentlichen Rechts: Berichte und Diskussionen auf der Tagung der Vereinigung der Deutschen Staatsrechtslehrer in Freiburg im. Breisgau vom 3. bis 6. Oktober 2007*, Veröffentlichungen der Vereinigung der Deutschen Staatsrechtslehrer (Berlin: de Gruyter, 2008), vol. LXVII, pp. 286–333.

Ellis, Howard S. (ed.), *Economic Development for Latin America* (London: Macmillan, 1962).

Ellwein, Thomas, Hesse, Joachim Jens, Maynitz, Renate and Scharpf, Fritz (eds.), *Jahrbuch zur Staats- und Verwaltungswissenschaft* (Baden-Baden: Nomos, 1987).

Engelhardt, Marie von, "Reflections on the Role of the State in the Legal Regimes of International Aid," *Zeitschrift für ausländisches öffentliches Recht und Völkerrecht (ZaöRV)*, 71 (2011), 451–74.

Aiding Fragile States. Development Cooperation between Juridical and Empirical Statehood, Ph.D. thesis (forthcoming 2013).

Engelmann, Ulrich, "Das Rourkela-Projekt," in H. Besters (ed.), *Kooperative Entwicklungshilfe: Deutsche und amerikanische Bemühungen beim Aufbau der Entwicklungsländer* (Bielefeld: Bertelsmann Universitätsverlag, 1968), pp. 157–65.

Epiney, Astrid, "Umweltvölkerrechtliche Rahmenbedingungen für Entwicklungsprojekte," in W. Meng, U. Magnus, S. Schlemmer-Schulte, T. Cottier, P.-T. Stoll and A. Epiney (eds.), *Das internationale Recht im Nord-Süd-Verhältnis*, Berichte der Deutschen Gesellschaft für Völkerrecht (Heidelberg: C.F. Müller, 2005), vol. XLI, pp. 329–72.

Eppler, Erhard, *Entwicklungspolitik und Eigeninteressen* (Bonn: Deutsche Gesellschaft für Auswärtige Politik, 1971).

Erdmann, Gero, "Neopatrimoniale Herrschaft: Der Übergang zur Demokratie ist nicht gelungen," *Entwicklung und Zusammenarbeit*, 42 (2001), 294–7.

Escobar, Arturo, *Encountering Development: The Making and Unmaking of the Third World* (Princeton University Press, 1995).

Eslava, Luis and Pahuja, Sundhya, "Beyond the (Post)Colonial: TWAIL and the Everyday Life of International Law," *Verfassung und Recht in Übersee*, 45 (2012), 195–221.

Esteva, Gustavo, "Development," in W. Sachs (ed.), *The Development Dictionary: A Guide to Knowledge as Power* (London: Zed Books, 1992), pp. 6–25.

European Commission, *Better, Faster, More: Implementing EC External Aid 2004–2009* (Luxembourg: Publications Office of the European Union, 2009).

Budget Support: A Question of Mutual Trust (Luxembourg: Publications Office of the European Union, 2008).

Evaluation Methods for the European Union's External Assistance (Luxembourg: Publications Office of the European Union, 2006).

European Court of Auditors (ECA), *Special Report No 4/2009: The Commission's Management of Non-State Actors' Involvement in EC Development Cooperation* (Luxembourg: Publications Office of the European Union, 2009).

Special Report No 10/2008 EC Development Assistance to Health Services in Sub-Saharan Africa: (pursuant to Article 248(4), second subparagraph, EC) (Luxembourg: Publications Office of the European Union, 2009).

Supporting Anti-Corruption Reform in Partner Countries: Concepts, Tools and Areas for Action (Luxembourg: Publications Office of the European Union, 2011).

Everling, Ulrich, "Die Neuregelung des Assoziationsverhältnisses zwischen der Europäischen Wirtschaftsgemeinschaft und den afrikanischen Staaten und Madagaskar sowie den überseeischen Ländern und Hoheitsgebieten," *Heidelberg Journal of International Law*, 24 (1964), 472–574.

Evers, Hans-Dieter and Senghaas, Dieter (eds.), *Auf dem Weg zu einer Neuen Weltwirtschaftsordnung?: Bedingungen und Grenzen für eine eigenständige Entwicklung* (Baden-Baden: Nomos, 1983).

Fabricius, Peter, "Africa's Cracked Mirror: the African Peer Review Mechanism Is Valuable, but Its Strides Are Few and Small," *Daily News South Africa* (2010).

Fanon, Frantz and Farrington, Constance, *The Wretched of the Earth* (New York: Grove Press, 1963).

Fassbender, Bardo, "Die Souveränität des Staates als Autonomie im Rahmen der völkerrechtlichen Verfassung," in H.-P. Mansel, T. Pfeiffer, H. Kronke, C.

Kohler and R. Hausmann (eds.), *Festschrift für Erik Jayme*, 2 vols. (Munich: Sellier, 2004), pp. 1089–101.

Fassbender, Bardo and Bleckmann, Albert, "Art. 2 (1) UN-Charta," in B. Simma (ed.), *The Charter of the United Nations: A Commentary*, 2nd edn, vol. II (Oxford University Press, 2002), pp. 68–91.

Fatouros, Arghyrios A., "Developing States," in R. Bernhardt (ed.), *A-D: Aalands Islands to Dumbarton Oaks Conference (1944)*, Encyclopedia of Public International Law (Amsterdam: North Holland Publishing Company, 1992), vol. I, pp. 1017–24.

"On the Hegemonic Role of International Functional Organizations," *German Yearbook of International Law*, 23 (1980), 9–36.

Faundez, Julio and Tan, Celine (eds.), *International Economic Law, Globalization and Developing Countries* (Cheltenham: Edward Elgar, 2010).

Faust, Jörg and Leiderer, Stefan, "Zur Effektivität und politischen Ökonomie der Entwicklungszusammenarbeit," *Politische Vierteljahresschrift*, 49 (2008), 129–52.

Faust, Jörg and Messner, Dirk, "Entwicklungspolitik als Global Governance-Arena," in H. Breitmeier, M. Roth and D. Senghaas (eds.), *Sektorale Weltordnungspolitik: Effektiv, gerecht und demokratisch?* (Baden-Baden: Nomos, 2009), pp. 213–33.

Feuer, Guy and Cassan, Hérve, *Droit international du développement*, 2nd edn (Paris: Dalloz, 1991).

Fierro, Elena, *The EU's Approach to Human Rights Conditionality in Practice* (The Hague: Kluwer Law International, 2003).

Fischer, Horst, "§59 Gewaltverbot, Selbstverteidigungsrecht und Intervention im gegenwärtigen Völkerrecht," in K. Ipsen, E. Menzel, V. Epping and H.-J. Heintze (eds.), *Völkerrecht*, 5th edn (Munich: C.H. Beck, 2004), pp. 1067–106.

Fischer-Lescano, Andreas and Teubner, Gunther, "Regime-Collisions: The Vain Search for Legal Unity in the Fragmentation of Global Law," *Michigan Journal of International Law*, 25 (2004), 999–1046.

Flickner, Charles, "Removing Impediments to an Effective Partnership with Congress," in L. Brainard (ed.), *Security by Other Means: Foreign Assistance, Global Poverty, and American Leadership* (Washington, DC: Brookings Institution Press, 2007), pp. 225–54.

Flory, Maurice, *Droit international du développement* (Paris: Presses universitaires de France, 1977).

Fortin, Carlos, "United Nations Conference on Trade and Development (UNCTAD)," in R. Wolfrum (ed.), *Max Planck Encyclopedia of Public International Law* [online edition] (Oxford University Press, 2008–). Available at www.mpepil.com (last visited September 2012).

Franck, Thomas, "The Emerging Right to Democratic Governance," *American Journal of International Law*, 86 (1992), 46–91.

Fairness in International Law and Institutions (Oxford University Press, 1995).

Frank, Andre Gunder, *Capitalism and Underdevelopment in Latin America: Historical Studies of Chile and Brazil* (New York: Monthly Review Press, 1967).

Franzius, Claudio, "§4 Modalitäten und Wirkungsfaktoren der Steuerung durch Recht," in W. Hoffmann-Riem, E. Schmidt-Aßmann and A. Voßkuhle (eds.), *Methoden, Maßstäbe, Aufgaben, Organisation*, Grundlagen des Verwaltungsrechts, 3 vols. (Munich: C.H. Beck, 2006), vol. I, pp. 177–237.

Franzmeyer, Fritz and Petersen, Hans (eds.), *Neuorientierung in den Beziehungen zwischen der EG und den Entwicklungsländern* (Berlin: Duncker & Humblot, 1984).

Freytag, Michael, *Der Europäische Rechnungshof: Institution, Funktion und politische Wirkung* (Baden-Baden: Nomos, 2005).

Friedmann, Wolfgang, "The Changing Dimensions of International Law," *Columbia Law Review*, 62 (1962), 1147–65.

Friedmann, Wolfgang, Kalmanoff, George and Meagher, Robert F., *International Financial Aid* (New York: Columbia University Press, 1966).

Friedrich, Carl J., *Constitutional Government and Democracy* (Boston: Ginn, 1950).

Frisch, Dieter, "Die entwicklungspolitische Konzeption der Gemeinschaft," in F. Franzmeyer and H. Petersen (eds.), *Neuorientierung in den Beziehungen zwischen der EG und den Entwicklungsländern* (Berlin: Duncker & Humblot, 1984), pp. 13–29.

Fritz, Verena and Rocha Menocal, Alina, "Developmental States in the New Millennium," *European Journal of Development Research*, 25 (2007), 531–52.

Frowein, Jochen A., "Die Intervention im heutigen System der Weltverfassung," in H. Jäckel (ed.), *Ist das Prinzip der Nichteinmischung überholt?* (Baden-Baden: Nomos, 1995), pp. 9–26.

Fukuda-Parr, Sakiko, "Millennium Development Goal 8: Indicators for International Human Rights Obligations?" *Human Rights Quarterly*, 28 (2006), 966–97.

Fukuda-Parr, Sakiko and Kumar, A. K. Shiva (eds.), *Readings in Human Development: Concepts, Measures and Policies for a Development Paradigm* (Oxford University Press, 2003).

Fukuyama, Francis, *The End of History and the Last Man* (New York: Free Press, 1992).

Galanter, Marc, "The Modernization of Law," in M. E. Weiner (ed.), *Modernization: The Dynamics of Growth* (New York: Basic Books, 1966), pp. 153–65.

Galtung, Johan, *Poor Countries vs. Rich: Poor People vs. Rich: Whom Will NIEO Benefit?* (University of Oslo, 1977).

Gardner, James, *Legal Imperialism: American Lawyers and Foreign Aid in Latin America* (Madison: University of Wisconsin Press, 1980).

George, Susan and Sabelli, Fabrizio, *Kredit und Dogma: Ideologie und Macht der Weltbank* (Hamburg: Konkret Literatur, 1995).

Gerlach, Axel, *Die Intervention: Versuch einer Definition* (Hamburg: Metzner, 1967).

Ghai, Dharam P. and Khan, A. R. (eds.), *The Basic Needs Approach to Development: Some Issues Regarding Concepts and Methodology* (Genf: Internationale Arbeitsorganisation, 1977).

Gibson, Clark C., Krister, Andersson, Ostrom, Elinor and Shivakumar, Sujai, *The Samaritan's Dilemma: The Political Economy of Development Aid* (Oxford University Press, 2005).

Gieler, Wolfgang (ed.), *Deutsche Entwicklungsminister von 1961–2008: Biographien, Konzeptionen und Einfluss auf nationale und internationale Entwicklungspolitik* (Bonn: Scientia Bonnensis, 2008).

"Walter Scheel 1961–1966," in W. Gieler (ed.), *Deutsche Entwicklungsminister von 1961–2008: Biographien, Konzeptionen und Einfluss auf nationale und internationale Entwicklungspolitik* (Bonn: Scientia Bonnensis, 2008), pp. 12–25.

Gilbert, Christopher and Vines, David (eds.), *The World Bank: Structure and Policies* (Cambridge University Press, 2000).

Gillespie, John and Nicholson, Penelope, *Law and Development and the Global Discourses of Legal Transfers* (Cambridge University Press, 2012).

Glagow, Manfred (ed.), *Deutsche Entwicklungspolitik: Aspekte und Probleme ihrer Entscheidungsstruktur: Beiträge in Zusammenhang mit dem Forschungsprojekt "Handlungsbedingungen und Handlungsspielräume für Entwicklungspolitik"* (Saarbrücken, Fort Lauderdale: Breitenbach, 1983).

(ed.), *Deutsche und internationale Entwicklungspolitik: Zur Rolle staatlicher, supranationaler und nicht-regierungsabhängiger Organisationen im Entwicklungsprozeß der Dritten Welt* (Opladen: Westdeutscher Verlag, 1990).

Glagow, Manfred, Gotsch, Wilfried and Stucke, Andreas (eds.), *Das Bundesministerium für wirtschaftliche Zusammenarbeit (BMZ): Entstehungszusammenhang, Personalpolitik, Steuerungsfähigkeit* (Pfaffenweiler: Centaurus-Verlagsgesellschaft, 1989).

Glagow, Manfred and Schimank, Uwe, "Politisch-administrative Strukturen deutscher Entwicklungspolitik," in F. Nuscheler (ed.), *Dritte-Welt-Forschung: Entwicklungstheorie und Entwicklungspolitik*. Sonderheft Politische Vierteljahresschrift No. 16 (Opladen: Westdeutscher Verlag, 1985), pp. 308–32.

Glaser, Andreas, *Nachhaltige Entwicklung und Demokratie: Ein Verfassungsrechtsvergleich der politischen Systeme Deutschlands und der Schweiz*, Recht der nachhaltigen Entwicklung (Tübingen: Mohr Siebeck, 2006), vol. I.

Global Health Strategies Initiatives, *Shifting Paradigm: How the BRICS Are Reshaping Global Health and Development*. Available at www.ghsinitiatives.org/downloads/ghsi_brics_report.pdf (last visited July 2013).

Göcke, Katharina, "The Case of Angela Poma Poma v. Peru before the Human Rights Committee: The Concept of Free Prior and Informed Consent and the Application of the International Covenant on Civil and Political Rights to the Protection and Promotion of Indigenous Peoples Rights," in A. von Bogdandy and R. Wolfrum (eds.), *Max Planck Yearbook of United Nations Law*, 14th edn (Leiden, Biggleswade: Martinus Nijhoff Publishers, 2010), pp. 337–70.

Goldmann, Matthias, "Inside Relative Normativity: From Sources to Standard Instruments for the Exercise of International Public Authority," in A. von Bogdandy, R. Wolfrum, J. von Bernstorff, P. Dann and M. Goldmann (eds.), *The Exercise of Public Authority by International Institutions: Advancing International Institutional Law* (Heidelberg: Springer, 2010), pp. 661–711.

Von der Rechtsquelle zur Handlungsform (in press).

Goldwin, Robert A. (ed.), *Readings in American Foreign Policy* (New York: Oxford University Press, 1959).

Goodland, Robert, "Free, Prior and Informed Consent and the World Bank Group," *Sustainable Development Law and Policy*, 4 (2004), 66–74.

Goodwin-Gill, Guy and Talmon, Stefan (eds.), *The Reality of International Law* (Oxford University Press, 1999).

Grabitz, Eberhard, "Die Entwicklungspolitik der Europäischen Gemeinschaften: Ziele und Kompetenzen," *Europarecht*, 12 (1977), 217–39.

Grabitz, Eberhard and Hilf, Meinhard (eds.), *Das Recht der Europäischen Union*, 40th edn, 3 vols. (Munich: C.H. Beck, 2009).

Graefrath, Bernhard, "Complicity in the Law of International Responsibility," *Revue belge de droit international*, 29 (1996), 370–80.

Gran, Guy, *Development by People: Citizen Construction of a Just World* (New York: Praeger, 1983).

Grant, Ruth Weissbourd and Keohane, Robert O., "Accountability and Abuses of Power in World Politics," *American Political Science Review*, 99 (2005), 29–43.

Gräßle, Ingrid, *Die Gründung des Europäischen Auswärtigen Diensts*. Available at www.robert-schuman.eu/doc/questions_europe/qe-194-al.pdf (last visited September 2012).

Grasso, Patrick G., Wasty, Sulaiman S., and Weaving, Rachel V. (eds.), *The World Bank's Operations Evaluations Department: The First 30 Years* (World Bank Publications, 2003).

Greco, Ettore, Pirozzi, Nicoletta and Silvestri, Stefano (eds.), *EU Crisis Management: Institutions and Capabilities in the Making*, IAI Quaderni English Series (Rome: IIstituto affari internazionali, 2010), vol. XIX.

Greig, Alastair, Hulme, David and Turner, Mark, *Challenging Global Inequality: Development Theory and Practice in the 21st Century* (Basingstoke: Palgrave Macmillan, 2007).

Griesgraber, Jo-Marie and Gunter, Bernhard (eds.), *Development – New Paradigms and Principles for the 21st Century: Rethinking Bretton Woods* (London: Pluto Press, 1996).

(eds.), *The World Bank: Lending on a Global Scale* (London: Pluto Press, 1996).

Grilli, Enzo R., *The European Community and the Developing Countries* (Cambridge University Press, 1993).

Grimm, Dieter (ed.), *Rechtswissenschaft und Nachbarwissenschaften: Band 2: Geschichte, Logik, Linguistik, Informatik, Friedensforschung, Finanzen, Didaktik*, 2 vols. (Munich: C.H. Beck, 1976).

Groeben, Hans von der and Schwarze, Jürgen (eds.), *Vertrag über die Europäische Union und Vertrag über die Gründung der Europäischen Gemeinschaft*, Kommentar, 6th edn, vol. IV (Baden-Baden: Nomos, 2003).

Gröpl, Christoph, *Haushaltsrecht und Reform: Dogmatik und Möglichkeiten der Fortentwicklung der Haushaltswirtschaft durch Flexibilisierung, Dezentralisierung, Budgetierung, Ökonomisierung und Fremdfinanzierung* (Tübingen: Mohr Siebeck, 2001).

Groves, Leslie and Hint, Rachel (eds.), *Inclusive Aid: Changing Power and Relationships in International Development* (London: Earthscan Publications, 2004).

Grube, Frank and Richter, Gerhard (eds.), *Der SPD-Staat* (Munich: Piper, 1977).

Grunwald, Arnim and Kopfmüller, Jürgen, *Nachhaltigkeit* (Frankfurt am Main: Campus, 2006).

Guder, Leonie F., *The Administration of Debt Relief by the International Financial Institutions: A Legal Reconstruction of the HIPC Initiative* (Berlin: Springer, 2009).

"International Development Association," in R. Wolfrum (ed.), *Max Planck Encyclopedia of Public International Law* [online edition] (Oxford University Press, 2008–). Available at www.mpepil.com (last visited April 2013).

Guha, Ranajit, *Subaltern Studies: Writings on South Asian History and Society* (New Delhi, New York: Oxford University Press, 1982).

Guha, Ranajit and Spivak, Gayatri Chakravorty, *Selected Subaltern Studies* (New York: Oxford University Press, 1988).

Gündling, Lothar, "Foreign Aid Agreements," in R. Bernhardt, *Enclyclopedia of Public International Law* (Amsterdam, 1995), pp. 425–8.

Günther, Klaus, "The Legacies of Injustice and Fear: A European Approach to Human Rights and their Effects on Political Culture," in P. Alston (ed.), *The EU and Human Rights* (Oxford University Press, 1999), pp. 117–44.

Habermas, Jürgen, *Between Facts and Norms: Contributions to a Discourse Theory of Law and Democracy* (Cambridge: MIT Press, 1996).

Faktizität und Geltung: Beiträge zur Diskurstheorie des Rechts und des demokratischen Rechtsstaats, 5th edn (Frankfurt: Suhrkamp, 1998).

Hadiprayitno, Irene, *Hazard or Right?: The Dialectics of Development Practice and the Internationally Declared Right to Development, with Special Reference to Indonesia*, School of Human Rights Research Series (Antwerp: Intersentia, 2009), vol. XXXI.

Hafner, Gerhard, "Diversity or Cacophony? New Sources of Norms in International Law," *Michigan Journal of International Law*, 25 (2004), 845–1375.

Hagemann, Hermann, *Die Formierung der rohstoffpolitischen Forderungen der Entwicklungsländer auf der Ebene der Vereinten Nationen bis zur Ersten Konferenz für Handel und Entwicklung (UNCTAD 1) 1946*, Schriften des Instituts für Politikwissenschaft der Westfälischen Wilhelms-Universität Münster, (Münster: Institut für Politikwissenschaft der Westfälischen Wilhelms-Universität Münster, 1983), vol. III.

Hahn, Hugo and Weber, Albrecht, *Die OECD: Organisation für Wirtschaftliche Zusammenarbeit und Entwicklung* (Baden-Baden: Nomos, 1976).

Hamam, David Mehdi and Ouédraogo, Ben Idrissa, *Africa: Improving Africa's Governance, Before It's Too Late*. Available at http://allafrica.com/stories/201202271025.html (last visited July 2013).

Hampe, Michael and Sandschneider, Eberhard, *Das Entwicklungsprogramm der Vereinten Nationen (UNDP): Anspruch-Probleme-Reformen* (Wiesbaden: Deutscher Universitäts-Verlag, 1998).

Hancock, Graham, *Lords of Poverty: The Power, Prestige, and Corruption of the International Aid Business* (London: Macmillan, 1989).

Haq, Mahbub ul, "The Birth of the Human Development Index," in S. Fukuda-Parr and A. K. S. Kumar (eds.), *Readings in Human Development: Concepts, Measures and Policies for a Development Paradigm* (Oxford University Press, 2003), pp. 127–37.

The Poverty Curtain: Choices for the Third World (New York: Columbia University Press, 1976).

Reflections on Human Development (New York: Oxford University Press, 1995).

Harenburg, Jan, *Die Rechtsdogmatik zwischen Wissenschaft und Praxis: Ein Beitrag zur Theorie der Rechtsdogmatik* (Stuttgart: Steiner Verlag, 1986).

Harlow, Carol, "Global Administrative Law: The Quest for Principles and Values," *European Journal of International Law*, 17 (2006), 187–214.

Harris, Dan, Moore, Mick and Schmitz, Hubert, *Country Classifications for a Changing World: Institute for Development Studies Working Paper No. 326* (2009). Available at www2.ids.ac.uk/gdr/cfs/pdfs/Wp326.pdf (last visited July 2013).

Harrison, Graham, *The World Bank and Africa: The Construction of Governance States* (London: Routledge, 2004).

Haslam, Paul, Schafer, Jessica and Beaudet, Pierre (eds.), *Introduction to International Development: Approaches, Actors, and Issues* (Oxford University Press, 2009).

Haverkate, Görg, *Rechtsfragen des Leistungsstaats: Verhältnismässigkeitsgebot und Freiheitsschutz im leistenden Staatshandeln* (Tübingen: Mohr Siebeck, 1983).

Head, John W., "Evolution of the Governing Law for Loan Agreements of the World Bank and Other Multilateral Development Banks," *American Journal of International Law*, 90 (1996), 214–34.

Hein, Bastian, *Die Westdeutschen und die Dritte Welt: Entwicklungspolitik und Entwicklungsdienste zwischen Reform und Revolte 1959–1974*, Quellen und Darstellungen zur Zeitgeschichte (Munich: Oldenbourg Verlag, 2006), vol. LXV.

Heintze, Hans-Joachim and Zwitter, Andrej, *International Law and Humanitarian Assistance: A Crosscut Through Legal Issues Pertaining to Humanitarianism* (Berlin, Heidelberg: Springer, 2011).

Heinz, Wolfgang, *Positive Maßnahmen zur Förderung von Demokratie und Menschenrechten als Aufgabe der Entwicklungszusammenarbeit*, Berichte und Gutachten 1994 No. 4 (Berlin, 1994).

Hempel, Kevin, *Erfolgskontrolle in der deutschen Entwicklungszusammenarbeit: Zentrale Herausforderungen unter besonderer Berücksichtigung der Transparenz gegenüber der Öffentlichkeit*, Schriftenreihe des ESB Research Institute (Stuttgart: Ibidem-Verlag, 2006), vol. XL.

Henze, Thomas, "Aufgaben- und Ausgabenkompetenzen der Europäischen Gemeinschaft und ihrer Mitgliedstaaten im Bereich der Entwicklungspolitik," *Europarecht*, 30 (1995), 76–86.

Hermes, Georg, *Das Grundrecht auf Schutz von Leben und Gesundheit: Schutzpflicht und Schutzanspruch aus Art. 2 Abs. 2 Satz 1 GG*, Freiburger rechts- und staatswissenschaftliche Abhandlungen (Heidelberg: C.F. Müller, 1987), vol. XLVI.

Heselhaus, Sebastian and Nowak, Carsten (eds.), *Handbuch der Europäischen Grundrechte* (Munich: C.H. Beck, 2006).

Hestermeyer, Holger, *Human Rights and the WTO: The Case of Patents and Access to Medicines* (Oxford University Press, 2007).

Hewitt, Adrian and Whiteman, Kaye, "The Commission and Development Policy: Bureaucratic Politics in EU Aid from the Lomé Leap Forward to the Difficulties of Adapting to the 21st Century," in K. Arts and A. K. Dickson (eds.), *EU Development Cooperation: From Model to Symbol* (Manchester University Press, 2004), pp. 133–48.

Heydemann, Christoph, *Die Durchsetzbarkeit von Verhaltensbindungen im Recht der begünstigenden Verwaltung*, Münsterische Beiträge zur Rechtswissenschaft (Berlin: Duncker & Humblot, 1995), vol. IXC.

High-Level Commission on Modernization of World Bank Group Governance, *Repowering the World Bank for the 21st Century: Report 10/2009* (Washington,

DC, 2009), margin nos. 78–94. Available at http://siteresources.worldbank.org/NEWS/Resources/WBGovernanceCOMMISSIONREPORT.pdf (last visited September 2012).

Hilf, Meinhard and Oeter, Stefan, *WTO-Recht: Rechtsordnung des Welthandels* (Baden-Baden: Nomos, 2005).

Hilf, Meinhard and Schorkopf, Frank, "Art. 6 EUV," in E. Grabitz and M. Hilf (eds.), *Das Recht der Europäischen Union*, 40th edn, 3 vols. (Munich: C.H. Beck, 2009).

Hilger, Andreas (ed.), *Die Sowjetunion und die Dritte Welt: UdSSR, Staatssozialismus und Antikolonialismus im Kalten Krieg 1945–1991*, Schriftenreihe der Vierteljahrshefte für Zeitgeschichte (Munich: Oldenbourg Verlag, 2009), vol. IC.

Hillgruber, Christian, Volkmann, Uwe, Nolte, Georg and Porscher, Rolf (eds.), *Die Leistungsfähigkeit der Wissenschaft des Öffentlichen Rechts: Berichte und Diskussionen auf der Tagung der Vereinigung der Deutschen Staatsrechtslehrer in Freiburg im. Breisgau vom 3. bis 6. Oktober 2007*, Veröffentlichungen der Vereinigung der Deutschen Staatsrechtslehrer (Berlin: de Gruyter, 2008), vol. LXVII.

Hirsch, Moshe, "Developing Countries," in R. Wolfrum (ed.), *Max Planck Encyclopedia of Public International Law* [online edition] (Oxford University Press, 2008–). Available at www.mpepil.com (last visited April 2013).

Hobart, Mark (ed.), *An Anthropological Critique of Development: The Growth of Ignorance* (London: Routledge, 1993).

Hobsbawm, Eric, *Age of Extremes: The Short Twentieth Century, 1914–1991* (London, New York: Viking Penguin, 1994).

Hoffmann-Riem, Wolfgang and Schmidt-Aßmann, Eberhard (eds.), *Verwaltungsrecht in der Informationsgesellschaft*, Schriften zur Reform des Verwaltungsrechts (Baden-Baden: Nomos, 2000), vol. VII.

Hoffmann-Riem, Wolfgang, Schmidt-Aßmann, Eberhard and Voßkuhle, Andreas (eds.), *Informationsordnung, Verwaltungsverfahren, Handlungsformen*, Grundlagen des Verwaltungsrechts (Munich: C.H. Beck, 2008), vol. II.

(eds.), *Methoden, Maßstäbe, Aufgaben, Organisation*, Grundlagen des Verwaltungsrechts, 3 vols. (Munich: C.H. Beck, 2006), vol. I.

(eds.), *Personal, Finanzen, Kontrolle, Sanktionen, Staatliche Einstandspflichten* (Munich: C.H. Beck, 2009).

Hoffmeister, Frank, *Menschenrechts- und Demokratieklauseln in den vertraglichen Außenbeziehungen der Europäischen Gemeinschaft*, Beiträge zum ausländischen öffentlichen Recht und Völkerrecht (Berlin/ New York: Springer, 1998), vol. CXXXII.

Hofmann, Herwig, Rowe, Gerard C. and Türk, Alexander, *Administrative Law and Policy of the European Union* (Oxford University Press, 2011).

Hofmann, Rainer, *Grundrechte und grenzüberschreitende Sachverhalte*, Beiträge zum ausländischen öffentlichen Recht und Völkerrecht (Heidelberg: Springer, 1994), vol. CXVIII.

"Die Rechtskontrolle von Organen der Staatengemeinschaft," in R. Hofmann, A. Reinisch, T. Pfeiffer, S. Oeter and A. Stadler (eds.), *Die Rechtskontrolle von Organen der Staatengemeinschaft: Vielfalt der Gerichte – Einheit des Prozessrechts? Referate und Thesen.*, Berichte der Deutschen Gesellschaft für Völkerrecht (Heidelberg: C.F. Müller, 2007), vol. XLII, pp. 1–35.

Hofmann, Rainer, Reinisch, August, Pfeiffer, Thomas, Oeter, Stefan and Stadler, Astrid (eds.), *Die Rechtskontrolle von Organen der Staatengemeinschaft: Vielfalt der Gerichte – Einheit des Prozessrechts? Referate und Thesen.*, Berichte der Deutschen Gesellschaft für Völkerrecht (Heidelberg: C.F. Müller, 2007), vol. XLII.

Hoppe, Werner, "§77 Planung," in J. Isensee and P. Kirchhof (eds.), *Aufgaben des Staates*, Handbuch des Staatsrechts der Bundesrepublik Deutschland, 3rd edn (Heidelberg: C.F. Müller, 2006), vol. IV, pp. 313–66.

Horta, Korinna, "Rhetoric and Reality: Human Rights and the World Bank," *Harvard Human Rights Journal*, 15 (2002), 227–42.

Hossain, Kamal, *Legal Aspects of the New International Economic Order* (London, New York: Frances Pinter, 1980).

Hunter, David B., "International Law and Public Participation in Policy-Making at the International Financial Institutions," in D. Bradlow and D. B. Hunter (eds.), *International Financial Institutions and International Law* (Alphen aan den Rijn: Kluwer Law International, 2010), pp. 199–386.

Huntington, Samuel, *Political Order in Changing Societies* (New Haven: Yale University Press, 1968).

Huq, Inamul, "From Charity to Obligation: A Third World Perspective on Concessional Resource Transfers," *Texas International Law Journal*, 14 (1979), 389–424.

Hurrell, Andrew, *On Global Order: Power, Values, and the Constitution of International Society* (Oxford University Press, 2007).

Hurwitz, Deena R., Ford, Douglas B. and Satterthwaite, Margaret L. (eds.), *Human Rights Advocacy Stories* (New York: Foundation Press, 2009).

Hyden, Goran, "After the Paris Declaration: Taking on the Issue of Power," *Development Policy Review*, 26 (2008), 259–74.

Inghelram, Jan, "The European Court of Auditors: Current Legal Issues," *Common Market Law Review*, 37 (2000), 129–46.

Legal and Institutional Aspects of the European Anti-Fraud Office (OLAF): an Analysis with a Look Forward to a European Public Prosecutor's Office (Groningen: Europa Law Pub., 2011).

International Labour Organization, *Employment, Growth and Basic Needs: A One-World Problem* (Genf: Council of Foreign Relations, 1976).

International Law Commission, *Fragmentation of International Law: Difficulties Arising from the Diversification and Expansion of International Law*, United Nations Report. Available at http://untreaty.un.org/ilc/sessions/56/56sess.htm (last visited September 2012).

Ipsen, Hans Peter, "Verwaltung durch Subventionen," in O. Kimminich, P. Pernthaler, H. P. Ipsen and H. F. Zacher (eds.), *Das Staatsoberhaupt in der parlamentarischen Demokratie: Verwaltung durch Subventionen*. Aussprache zu den Berichten in den Verhandlungen der Tagung der Vereinigung der Deutschen Staatsrechtslehrer zu Graz vom 12. bis 15. Oktober 1966, Veröffentlichungen der Vereinigung der Deutschen Staatsrechtslehrer (Berlin: de Gruyter, 1967), vol. XXV, pp. 255–307.

Europäisches Gemeinschaftsrecht (Tübingen: Mohr Siebeck, 1972).

Ipsen, Knut, Menzel, Eberhard, Epping, Volker and Heintze, Hans-Joachim (eds.), *Völkerrecht*, 5th edn (Munich: C.H. Beck, 2004).

Isensee, Josef and Kirchhof, Paul (eds.), *Aufgaben des Staates*, Handbuch des Staatsrechts der Bundesrepublik Deutschland, 3rd edn (Heidelberg: C.F. Müller, 2006), vol. IV.

(eds.), *Normativität und Schutz der Verfassung – Internationale Beziehungen*, Handbuch des Staatsrechts der Bundesrepublik Deutschland (Heidelberg: C.F. Müller, 1992), vol. VII.

Jäckel, Hartmut (ed.), *Ist das Prinzip der Nichteinmischung überholt?* (Baden-Baden: Nomos, 1995).

Jackson, Robert H., *Quasi-states: Sovereignty, International Relations and the Third World*, Cambridge Studies in International Relations (Cambridge University Press, 1993), vol. XII.

Jacqué, Jean-Paul, "Art. 4 EUV," in H. von der Groeben and J. Schwarze (eds.), *Vertrag über die Europäische Union und Vertrag über die Gründung der Europäischen Gemeinschaft*. Kommentar, 6th edn, IV (Baden-Baden: Nomos, 2003).

Jakobeit, Cord, "Fünf Jahre NEPAD," *Aus Politik und Zeitgeschichte*, 32–33 (2006), 21–5.

Jenks, Clarence Wilfried, "Coordination: A New Problem of International Organization. A Preliminary Survey of the Law and Practice of Interorganizational Relationships," *Recueil des Cours de l'Académie de droit international de la Haye*, 77 (1950), 151–303.

John Sousa, Sarah-Lea de, *Brazil As an Emerging Actor in International Development Cooperation: a Good Partner for European Donors?*, German Development Institute – Briefing Paper 5/2010 (2010). Available at www.die-gdi.de/CMS-homepage/openwebcms3.nsf/%28ynDK_contentByKey%29/ANES-83EH29/$FILE/BP%205.2010.pdf (last visited July 2013).

Johnson, John H. and Wasty, Sulaiman S., *Borrower Ownership of Adjustment Programs and the Political Economy of Reform:* World Bank Discussion Papers No. 199. Available at http://gwww.grips.ac.jp/teacher/oono/hp/course/lec03_ownership/paper3_3.pdf (last visited July 2013).

Johnson, Omotunde, *Country Ownership of Reform Programs and the Implication for Conditionality: G24 Discussion Paper Series No. 35*. Available at www.g24.org/ResearchPaps/ojohnson.pdf (last visited July 2013).

Jurgens, Gerdy, Verhoeven, Maartje and Willemsen, Pauline, "Administrative Powers in German and in English Law," in L. F. M. Besselink, F. Pennings and S. Prechal (eds.), *The Eclipse of the Legality Principle in the European Union* (Alphen aan den Rijn: Kluwer Law International, 2011), pp. 37–54.

Kadelbach, Stefan, *Zwingendes Völkerrecht*, (Berlin: Duncker & Humblot, 1992), vol. CI.

Kadelbach, Stefan and Kleinlein, Thomas, "Überstaatliches Verfassungsrecht: Zur Konstitutionalisierung im Völkerrecht," *Archiv des Völkerrechts*, 44 (2006), 235–66.

Kahl, Wolfgang, "§47: Begriff, Funktionen und Konzepte von Kontrolle," in W. Hoffmann-Riem, E. Schmidt-Aßmann and A. Vosskuhle (eds.), *Personal, Finanzen, Kontrolle, Sanktionen, Staatliche Einstandspflichten* (Munich: Beck, 2009), pp. 427–541.

Kalbe, Peter, "The Award of Contracts and the Enforcement of Claims in the Context of EC External Aid and Development Cooperation," *Common Market Law Review*, 38 (2001), 1217–67.

Kälin, Walter and Künzli, Jörg, *Universeller Menschenrechtsschutz*, 2nd edn (Baden-Baden: Nomos, 2008).

Kaltenborn, Markus, "Entwicklungs- und Schwellenländer in der Völkerrechtsgemeinschaft: Zum Stand und zu den Perspektiven des Entwicklungsvölkerrechts," *Archiv des Völkerrechts*, 46 (2008), 205–32.

Entwicklungsvölkerrecht und Neugestaltung der internationalen Ordnung: Rechtstheoretische und rechtspolitische Aspekte des Nord-Süd-Konflikts, Münsterische Beiträge zur Rechtswissenschaft (Berlin: Duncker & Humblot, 1998), vol. CXIII.

Kämpf, Andrea and Würth, Anna, *Mehr Menschenrechte in die Entwicklungspolitik!: Positionspapier Deutsches Institut für Menschenrechte No. 15*. Available at www.institut-fuer-menschenrechte.de/uploads/tx_commerce/policy_paper_15_mehr_menschenrechte_in_die_entwicklungspolitik.pdf (last visited July 2013).

Kanbur, Ravi and Vines, David, "The World Bank and Poverty Reduction: Past, Present and Future," in C. Gilbert and D. Vines (eds.), *The World Bank: Structure and Policies* (Cambridge University Press, 2000), pp. 87–107.

Kaplan, Jacob, *International Aid Coordination*, Studies in transnational legal policy (St. Paul: West Publishing Company, 1978), vol. XVI.

Kappel, Robert, "Afrikas Perspektiven in der Entwicklungskooperation mit der Europäischen Gemeinschaft," *Afrika Spectrum*, 25 (1990), 257–82.

Kapur, Devesh, Lewis, John P. and Webb, Richard (eds.), *The World Bank: Its First Half Century*, vol. II (Washington, DC: Brookings Institution Press, 1997).

Katti, Vijaya, Chahoud, Tatjana and Kaushik, Atul, *India's Development Cooperation: Opportunities and Challenges for International Development Cooperation*, German Development Institute – Briefing Paper 3/2009

(2009). Available at www.die-gdi.de/CMS-Homepage/openwebcms3.nsf/%28ynDK_contentByKey%29/ANES-7QAGRV/$FILE/BP%203.2009.pdf (last visited July 2013).

Katz Cogan, Jacob, "Representation and Power in International Organization: The Operational Constitution and its Critics," *American Journal of International Law*, 103 (2009), 209–63.

Kaufmann, Daniel, Kraay, Aart and Mastruzzi, Massimo, *Governance Matters VIII: Aggregate and Individual Governance Indicators, 1996–2008*, World Bank Policy Research Working Paper No. 4978. Available at http://papers.ssrn.com/sol3/papers.cfm?abstract_id=1424591## (last visited July 2013).

Kearney, Richard D. and Dalton, Robert E., "The Treaty on Treaties," *American Journal of International Law*, 64 (1970), 495–561.

Kellersmann, Bettina, *Die gemeinsame, aber differenzierte Verantwortlichkeit von Industriestaaten und Entwicklungsländern für den Schutz der globalen Umwelt*, Beiträge zum ausländischen öffentlichen Recht und Völkerrecht (Berlin, Heidelberg: Springer, 2000), vol. CXLIII.

Kelsall, Tim, "Shop Windows and Smoke-Filled Rooms: Governance and the Re-politicisation of Tanzania," *Journal of Modern African Studies*, 40 (2002), 597–617.

Kennedy, David, "The 'Rule of Law,' Political Choices and Development Common Sense," in D. Trubek and A. Santos (eds.), *The New Law and Economic Development: A Critical Appraisal* (Cambridge University Press, 2006), pp. 95–173.

Kewenig, Wilhelm A., *Die Anwendung wirtschaftlicher Zwangsmaßnahmen im Völkerrecht und im Internationalen Privatrecht: Referate und Thesen der 18. Tagung in Salzburg vom 01. bis 04. April 1981*, Berichte der Deutschen Gesellschaft für Völkerrecht (Heidelberg: C.F. Müller, 1982), vol. XIIX.

Killick, Tony, *Aid and the Political Economy of Policy Change* (London: Routledge, 1998).

The Politics of Ghana's Budgetary System: Overseas Development Institute Policy Brief No. 2. Available at www.odi.org.uk/resources/docs/1963.pdf (last visited July 2013).

A Reaction Too Far: Economic Theory and the Role of the State in Developing Countries (London: Overseas Development Institute, 1989).

Killinger, Stefanie, *The World Bank's Non-Political Mandate* (Cologne: Heymann, 2003).

Kimminich, Otto, Pernthaler, Peter, Ipsen, Hans Peter and Zacher, Hans F. (eds.), *Das Staatsoberhaupt in der parlamentarischen Demokratie: Verwaltung durch Subventionen*, Aussprache zu den Berichten in den Verhandlungen der Tagung der Vereinigung der Deutschen Staatsrechtslehrer zu Graz vom 12. bis 15. Oktober 1966, Veröffentlichungen der Vereinigung der Deutschen Staatsrechtslehrer (Berlin: de Gruyter, 1967), vol. XXV.

Kim, Soyeun and Lightfoot, Simon, "Does 'DAC-Ability' Really Matter? The Emergence of Non-DAC Donors: Introduction to Policy Arena," *Journal of International Development*, 23 (2011), 711–21.

Kingsbury, Benedict, "The Concept of 'Law' in Global Administrative Law," *European Journal of International Law*, 20 (2009), 23–57.

"Operational policies of international institutions as part of the law-making process," in G. Goodwin-Gill and S. Talmon (eds.), *The Reality of International Law* (Oxford University Press, 1999), pp. 323–42.

"Sovereignty and Inequality," *European Journal of International Law*, 9 (1998), 599–625.

Kingsbury, Benedict and Davis, Kevin E., *Obligation Overload: Adjusting the Obligations of Fragile or Failed States*, Hauser Globalization Colloquium Fall 2010 (2010). Available at www.iilj.org/courses/documents/HC2010Dec01.DavisKingsbury.pdf (last visited July 2013).

Kingsbury, Benedict, Davis, Kevin and Merry, Sally Engle, "Indicators as a Technology of Global Governance," *Law and Society Review*, 46 (2012), 71–104.

Kingsbury, Benedict, Krisch, Niko and Stewart, Richard, "The Emergence of Global Administrative Law," *Law and Contemporary Problems*, 68 (2005), 15–62.

Klabbers, Jan, "The Right to be Taken Seriously: Self-Determination in International Law," *Human Rights Quarterly*, 28 (2006), 186–206.

An Introduction to International Institutional Law, 2nd edn (Cambridge University Press, 2009).

Klein, Eckart, "Beihilfe zum Völkerrechtsdelikt," in I. von Münch (ed.), *Staatsrecht – Völkerrecht – Europarecht*. Festschrift für Hans-Jürgen Schlochauer zum 75. Geburtstag (Berlin: de Gruyter, 1981), pp. 425–38.

(ed.), *Gewaltenteilung und Menschenrechte* (Berliner Wissenschafts-Verlag, 2006).

Klein, Pierre, "Les institutions financières internationales et les droits de la personne," *Revue belge de droit international*, 32 (1999), 97–114.

Klingebiel, Stephan, *Leistungsfähigkeit und Reform des Entwicklungsprogramms der Vereinten Nationen (UNDP)*, Schriften des deutschen Instituts für Entwicklungspolitik (DIE) (Köln: Weltforum Verlag, 1999), vol. CXV.

Klingebiel, Stephan, Leiderer, Stefan and Schmidt, Petra, *Programme Financing and Public Budgets: New Instruments and Starting-Points of Development Policy*, Discussion Paper No. 3 (Bonn: German Development Institute, 2005).

Knack, Stephen and Rahman, Aminur, "Donor Fragmentation," in W. Easterly (ed.), *Reinventing Foreign Aid* (Cambridge: MIT Press, 2008), pp. 333–48.

Köck, Wolfgang, "§37 Pläne," in W. Hoffmann-Riem, E. Schmidt-Aßmann and A. Voßkuhle (eds.), *Informationsordnung, Verwaltungsverfahren, Handlungsformen*, Grundlagen des Verwaltungsrechts (Munich: C.H. Beck, 2008), vol. II, pp. 1275–339.

Koeberle, Stefan, Stavreski, Zoran and Walliser, Jan (eds.), *Budget Support As More Effective Aid?* (Washington, DC: World Bank Publications, 2006).

Kokott, Juliane, "States, Sovereign Equality," in R. Wolfrum (ed.), *Max Planck Encyclopedia of Public International Law* [online edition] (Oxford University Press, 2008–). Available at www.mpepil.com (last visited April 2013).

Kollatz, Udo, "Grundlagen der Entwicklungshilfeverwaltung," *Die Öffentliche Verwaltung*, 35 (1982), 561–9.

König, Klaus (ed.), *Öffentliche Verwaltung und Entwicklungspolitik* (Baden-Baden: Nomos, 1986).

Konrad, Hans-Joachim (ed.), *Grundrechtsschutz und Verwaltungsverfahren, unter besonderer Berücksichtigung des Asylrechts: Internationaler Menschenrechtsschutz*, Referate der 23. Tagung der wissenschaftlichen Mitarbeiter der Fachrichtung "Öffentliches Recht" 22 – 26 February 1983 in Berlin. (Berlin: Duncker & Humblot, 1985), vol. CDLXXXIV.

Kooiman, Jan, "Findings, Speculations and Recommendations," in J. Kooiman (ed.), *Modern Governance: New Government-Society Interactions* (Thousand Oaks, CA: Sage Publications, 1993), pp. 249–62.

(ed.), *Modern Governance: New Government-Society Interactions* (Thousand Oaks, CA: Sage Publications, 1993).

Koopmans, Thijmen, *Courts and Political Institutions: A Comparative View* (Cambridge University Press, 2003).

Koppell, Jonathan G. S., *World Rule: Accountability, Legitimacy, and the Design of Global Governance* (University of Chicago Press, 2010).

Koskenniemi, Martti, "Constitutionalism as Mindset: Reflections on Kantian Themes About International Law and Globalization," *Theoretical Inquiries in Law*, 8 (2007), 9–36.

"The Effect of Rights on Political Culture," in P. Alston (ed.), *The EU and Human Rights* (Oxford University Press, 1999), pp. 99–116.

"General Principles," in M. Koskenniemi (ed.), *Sources of International Law* (Burlinton: Ashgate, 2000), pp. 359–402.

The Gentle Civilizer of Nations: The Rise and Fall of International Law 1870–1960 (Cambridge University Press, 2006).

"History of International Law: Since World War II," in R. Wolfrum (ed.), *Max Planck Encyclopedia of Public International Law* [online edition] (Oxford University Press, 2008–). Available at www.mpepil.com (last visited April 2013).

"Human Rights Mainstreaming as a Strategy for Institutional Power," *Humanity*, 1 (2010), 47–58.

(ed.), *Sources of International Law* (Burlinton: Ashgate, 2000).

Kothari, Rajni, "On Humane Governance," *Alternatives*, 12 (1987), 277–90.

Kotzur, Markus, "Soziales Völkerrecht für eine solidarische Völkergemeinschaft?" *Juristenzeitung*, 63 (2008), 265–72.

Krajewski, Markus, *Wirtschaftsvölkerrecht* (Heidelberg: C.F. Müller, 2009).

Kranz, Jerzy, *Entre l'influence et l'intervention: Certains aspects juridiques de l'assistance financière multilaterale* (Frankfurt: Peter Lang Verlag, 1994).

Krasner, Stephen D., *Structural Conflict: The Third World Against Global Liberalism* (Berkeley: University of California Press, 1985).

Sovereignty: Organized Hypocrisy (Princeton University Press, 1999).

Kretzschmar, Winfried Walter, *Auslandshilfe als Mittel der Außenwirtschafts- und Außenpolitik* (Munich: Oldenbourg Verlag, 1964).

Krever, Tor, "The Legal Turn in Late Development Theory: The Rule of Law and the World Bank's Development Model," *Harvard International Law Journal*, 52 (2011), 287–319.

Krisch, Niko, "The Pluralism of Global Administrative Law," *European Journal of International Law*, 17 (2006), 247–78.

Krisch, Niko and Kingsbury, Benedict, "Global Governance and Global Administrative Law in the International Legal Order," *European Journal of International Law*, 17 (2006), 1–13.

Kugelmann, Dieter, "Das Informationsfreiheitsgesetz des Bundes," *Neue Juristische Wochenschrift*, 58 (2005), 3609–13.

Kühnhardt, Ludger, *Stufen der Souveränität* (Bonn: Bouvier, 1992).

Kumm, Matthias, "The Legitimacy of International Law: A Constitutionalist Framework of Analysis," *European Journal of International Law*, 15 (2004), 907–31.

Kunig, Philip, "Die 'innere' Dimension des Rechts auf Entwicklung: Rechtspolitische Überlegungen zur Inpflichtnahme von Entwicklungsländern," *Verfassung und Recht in Übersee*, 19 (1986), 383–400.

"Prohibition of Intervention," in R. Wolfrum (ed.), *Max Planck Encyclopedia of Public International Law* [online edition] (Oxford University Press, 2008–). Available at www.mpepil.com (last visited April 2013).

Künnemann, Rolf, "Extraterritorial Application of the International Covenant on Economic, Social and Cultural Rights," in A. Coomans (ed.), *Extraterritorial Application of Human Rights Treaties* (Antwerp: Intersentia, 2004), pp. 201–31.

Kwasi Prempeh, Henry "Neither 'timorous souls' nor 'bold spirits': Courts and the politics of judicial review in post-colonial Africa," *Verfassung und Recht in Übersee*, 45 (2012), 157–77.

Ladeur, Karl-Heinz, "Die Internationalisierung des Verwaltungsrechts," in C. Möllers, A. Vosskuhle and C. Walter (eds.), *Internationales Verwaltungsrecht: Eine Analyse anhand von Referenzgebieten*, Jus Internationale et Europaeum (Tübingen: Mohr Siebeck, 2007), vol. XVI, pp. 375–94.

Laffan, Brigid, "Financial Control: The Court of Auditors and OLAF," in J. Peterson and M. Shackleton (eds.), *The Institutions of the European Union*, 2nd edn (Oxford University Press, 2006), pp. 210–28.

Lal, Deepak, *The Poverty of "Development Economics"* (London: Institute of Economic Affairs, 1983).

Lancaster, Carol, *Aid to Africa* (University of Chicago Press, 1999).

The Chinese Aid System, Centre for Global Development Essay (Washington, DC: Center for Global Development, 2007). Available at www.cgdev.org/files/13953_file_Chinese_aid.pdf (last visited July 2013).

Foreign Aid: Diplomacy, Development, Domestic Politics (University of Chicago Press, 2007).

Lang, Winfried (ed.), *Sustainable Development and International Law*, International Environmental Law and Policy Series (London: Graham and Trotman, 1995), vol. VI.

Langford, Malcolm (ed.), "The Justiciability of Social Rights," in M. Langford (ed.), *Social Rights Jurisprudence: Emerging Trends in International and Comparative Law* (Cambridge University Press, 2008), pp. 3–45.

Social Rights Jurisprudence: Emerging Trends in International and Comparative Law (Cambridge University Press, 2008).

Lederer, Katrin and Galtung, Johan, *Human Needs: A Contribution to the Current Debate* (Berliner Wissenschaftszentrum: Anton Hain, 1980).

Leftwich, Adrian, *States of Development: On the Primacy of Politics in Development* (Cambridge: Polity Press, 2000).

Lehmann, Julia, "Die Asiatische Entwicklungsbank im Gefüge der regional governance in Asien," *Verfassung und Recht in Übersee*, 41 (2008), 556–60.

Lengl, Siegfried, "Entwicklungspolitik: Administrative Möglichkeiten zur Verbesserung ihrer Wirksamkeit," *Verwaltungsarchiv*, 76 (1985), 427–47.

Libby, Ronald T., "International Development Association: A Legal Fiction Designed to Secure an LCD Constituency," *International Organization*, 29 (1975), 1065–72.

Ligustro, Aldo and Sacerdoti, Giorgio (eds.), *Problemi e tendenze del diritto internazionale dell'economia: Liber amicorum in onore die Paolo Picone* (Naples: Editoriale Scientifica, 2011).

Lillich, Richard B. (ed.), *Economic Coercion and the New International Economic Order* (Charlottesville, VA: Michie, 1976).

Lingnau, Hildegard, *Neue Elemente in der Entwicklungszusammenarbeit der Europäischen Gemeinschaft zu Beginn der 90er Jahre: Berichte und Gutachten No. 2* (Berlin: Deutsches Institut für Entwicklungspolitik, 1991).

Link, Werner and Tücks, Paul, *Der Nord-Süd-Konflikt und die Zusammenarbeit der Entwicklungsländer* (Berlin: Colloquium, 1985).

Lipset, Martin Seymour, "Some Social Requisites of Democracy: Economic Development and Political Legitimacy," *American Political Science Review*, 53 (1969), 69–105.

Lister, Marjorie, *The European Community and the Developing World: The Role of the Lomé Convention* (Aldershot: Avebury, 1989).

Lister, Stephen, *Evaluation of General Budget Support: Synthesis Report* (University of Birmingham, 2006).

Little, Ian, *Economic Development: Theory, Policy and International Relations* (New York: Basic Book, 1982).

Loewenstein, Karl, *Political Power and the Government Process* (University of Chicago Press, 1957).

Loughlin, Martin, *Foundations of Public Law* (New York: Oxford University Press, 2010).

"Reflections on 'the Idea of Public Law'," in E. Christodoulidis and S. Tierney (eds.), *Public Law and Politics: The Scope and Limits of Constitutionalism* (Aldershot: Ashgate, 2008), pp. 47–68.

Lowe, Vaughan and Warbrick, Colin (eds.), *The United Nations and the Principles of International Law: Essays in Memory of Michael Akehurst* (London: Routledge, 1994).

Lumsdaine, David H., *Moral Vision in International Politics: The Foreign Aid Regime 1949–1989* (Princeton University Press, 1993).

Macdonald, Ronald St. John, "Solidarity in the Practice and Discourse of Public International Law," *Pace International Law Review*, 8 (1996), 259–302.

MacKay, Fergus, "Indigenous People and International Financial Institutions," in D. Bradlow and D. B. Hunter (eds.), *International Financial Institutions and International Law* (Alphen aan den Rijn: Kluwer Law International, 2010), pp. 287–320.

Mahbubani, Kishore, "The OECD: A Classic Sunset Organization," *Global Policy*, 3 (2012), 117–18.

Mahiou, Ahmed, "International Law of Development," in R. Wolfrum (ed.), *Max Planck Encyclopedia of Public International Law [online edition]* (Oxford University Press, 2008–). Available at www.mpepil.com (last visited April 2013).

Maihack, Henrik and Öhm, Manfred, *Dynamik im African Peer Review Mechanism (APRM): Kritischer Mosambikbericht bringt dem Gesamtprozess neue Glaubwürdigkeit*, Friedrich-Ebert-Stiftung Perspektive. Available at http://library.fes.de/pdf-files/iez/07269.pdf (last visited July 2013).

Mallaby, Sebastian, *The World's Banker: A Story of Failed States, Financial Crises, and the Wealth and Poverty of Nations* (New Haven: Yale University Press, 2004).

Mangu, André Mbata B., "What Future for Human and Peoples' Rights Under the African Union, New Partnership for Africa's Development, African Peer-Review Mechanism and the African Court?" *South African Yearbook of International Law*, 29 (2004), 136–63.

Manning, Robert, "Will 'Emerging Donors' Change the Face of International Co-operation?" *Development Policy Review*, 24 (2006), 371–85.

Mansel, Heinz-Peter, Pfeiffer, Thomas, Kronke, Herbert, Kohler, Christian and Hausmann, Rainer (eds.), *Festschrift für Erik Jayme*, 2 vols. (Munich: Sellier, 2004).

Marks, Stephen, "The Human Right to Development: Between Rhetoric and Reality," *Harvard Law School Human Rights Journal*, 17 (2004), 137–68.

Marong, Alhagi, "New Partnership for Africa's Development (NEPAD)," in R. Wolfrum (ed.), *Max Planck Encyclopedia of Public International Law* [online edition] (Oxford University Press, 2008–). Available at www.mpepil.com (last visited April 2013).

Martenczuk, Bernd, "Die Kooperation der Europäischen Union mit Entwicklungsländern und Drittstaaten und der Vertrag von Lissabon," in S. Bartelt and P. Dann (eds.), *Entwicklungszusammenarbeit im Recht der Europäischen Union – The Law of EU Development Cooperation: Europarecht-Beiheft Nr. 2* (Baden-Baden: Nomos, 2008), pp. 36–52.

"From Lomé to Cotonou: The ACP-EC Partnership Agreement in a Legal Perspective," *European Foreign Affairs Review*, 5 (2000), 461–87.

Martenczuk, Bernd and Zimmermann, Andreas, "Art. 177 EGV," in J. Schwarze (ed.), *EU-Kommentar*, 2nd edn (Baden-Baden: Nomos, 2009).

Martens, Bertin, Mummert, Uwe and Murrell, Peter (eds.), *The Institutional Economics of Foreign Aid* (Cambridge University Press, 2002).

Martinek, Michael, *Die Verwaltung der deutschen Entwicklungshilfe und ihr Integrationsdefizit: Eine verwaltungswissenschaftliche Struktur- und Funktionsanalyse* (Bad Honnef: Bock und Herchen, 1981).

Martinussen, John, *Society, State and Market: A Guide to Competing Theories of Development* (London: Zed Books, 1997).

Mason, Edward S. and Asher, Robert, *The World Bank Since Bretton Woods* (Washington, DC: Brookings Institution Press, 1973).

Masujima, Ken, "'Good Governance' and the Development Assistance Committee," in M. Boas and D. McNeill (eds.), *Global Institutions and Development: Framing the World?* (Oxon: Routledge, 2003), pp. 151–63.

Matthies, Volker, *Neue Weltwirtschaftsordnung: Hintergründe – Positionen – Argumente, Analysen* (Opladen: Leske und Budrich, 1980), vol. XXVII.

Die Blockfreien: Ursprünge, Entwicklung, Konzeptionen, Analysen (Opladen: Leske und Budrich, 1985), vol. XXXV.

Matz, Nele, *Wege zur Koordinierung völkerrechtlicher Verträge: Völkervertragsrechtliche und institutionelle Ansätze* (Heidelberg: Springer, 2005).

Maxwell Simon, *The Washington Consensus Is Dead! Overseas Development Institute Working Paper No. 243*. Available at www.odi.org.uk/resources/docs/2476.pdf (last visited July 2013).

M'Baye, Keba, "Le droit au developpement comme un droit de l'homme," *Revue des droits de l'homme*, 5 (1972), 505–34.

McAuslan, Patrick, "The International Development Act, 2002: Benign Imperialism or a Missed Opportunity?" *Modern Law Review*, 66 (2003), 563–603.

McEwan, Cheryl, *Postcolonialism and Development* (London, New York: Routledge, 2009).

McNamara, Robert S., *In Retrospect: The Tragedy and Lessons of Vietnam* (New York: Time Books, 1995).
Meadows, Donella H. and Meadows, Dennis L., *The Limits to Growth* (New York: Universe Books, 1972).
Medard, Jean-Francois, *L'etat sous-develope en afrique: Clientelisme politique du neo-patrimonialisme?*, Travaux et Documents, 2nd edn (Bordeaux: Centre d'étude d'Afrique noire, 1983).
Mégret, Frédéric and Hoffmann, Florian, "The UN as a Human Rights Violator?" *Human Rights Quarterly*, 25 (2003), 314–42.
Meinecke, Oliver, *Rechtsprojekte in der Entwicklungszusammenarbeit: Theorie und Praxis am Beispiel von GTZ-Projekten zur Konsolidierung des Rechtsstaats in Südafrika und Sambia*, Schriftenreihe der Hochschule Speyer (Berlin: Duncker & Humblot, 2007), vol. CLXXXIIX.
Meng, Werner, "Conditionality of IMF and World Bank Loans: Tutelage over Sovereign States?" *Verfassung und Recht in Übersee*, 21 (1988), 263–77.
"Völkerrecht als wirtschaftlicher Ordnungsfaktor und entwicklungspolitisches Steuerungsinstrument," in W. Meng, U. Magnus, S. Schlemmer-Schulte, T. Cottier, P.-T. Stoll and A. Epiney (eds.), *Das internationale Recht im Nord-Süd-Verhältnis*, Berichte der Deutschen Gesellschaft für Völkerrecht (Heidelberg: C.F. Müller, 2005), vol. XLI, pp. 1–76.
Meng, Werner, Magnus, Ulrich, Schlemmer-Schulte, Sabina, Cottier, Thomas, Stoll, Peter-Tobias and Epiney, Astrid (eds.), *Das internationale Recht im Nord-Süd-Verhältnis*, Berichte der Deutschen Gesellschaft für Völkerrecht (Heidelberg: C.F. Müller, 2005), vol. XLI.
Menzel, Ulrich, *Das Ende der Dritten Welt und das Scheitern der großen Theorie* (Frankfurt: Suhrkamp, 1992).
Menzel, Ulrich and Senghaas, Dieter, "Autozentrierte Entwicklung in historischer Perspektive," in H.-D. Evers and D. Senghaas (eds.), *Auf dem Weg zu einer Neuen Weltwirtschaftsordnung?: Bedingungen und Grenzen für eine eigenständige Entwicklung* (Baden-Baden: Nomos, 1983), pp. 77–96.
Merry, Sally Engle, "Measuring the World: Indicators, Human Rights, and Global Governance," *Current Anthropology*, 52 (2011), 83–95.
Messner, Dirk, "Schwellenländer," in D. Nohlen and S. Arons (eds.), *Lexikon Dritte Welt: Länder, Organisationen, Theorien, Begriffe, Personen* (Reinbek bei Hamburg: Rowohlt, 2002), pp. 708–11.
Michels, Natalie, *Umweltschutz und Entwicklungspolitik: Mechanismen zur Berücksichtigung von Entwicklungsländern in internationalen Umweltschutzübereinkommen* (Frankfurt: Peter Lang Verlag, 1999).
Miehsler, Herbert and Mayer-Maly, Dorothea (eds.), *Ius humanitatis: Festchrift zum 60. Geburtstag von Alfred Verdross* (Berlin: Duncker & Humblot, 1980).
Mikesell, Raymond, "The Emergence of the World Bank as a Development Institution," in A. K. Acheson, J. Chant and M. Prachowny (eds.), *Bretton*

Woods Revisited: Evaluations of the I.M.F. and the International Bank for Reconstruction and Development (London: Macmillan, 1972), pp. 70–84.

Minnerop, Petra, *Paria-Staaten im Völkerrecht?* (Berlin, Heidelberg: Springer, 2004).

Mitrany, David, "The Functional Approach to World Organization," *International Affairs*, 24 (1948), 350–63.

A Working Peace System (Chicago: Quadrangle Books, 1966).

Mitzmann, Elena, *The Proliferation of Independent Accountability Mechanisms in the Field of Development Finance*,: The Jean Monnet Center for International and Regional Economic Law & Justice Working Paper 14/10. Available at http://centers.law.nyu.edu/jeanmonnet/papers/10/101401.pdf (last visited July 2013).

"The Proliferation of Independent Accountability Mechanisms in the Field of Development Finance," *Rivista trimestrale di diritto pubblico*, 62 (2012), 93–134.

Molenaers, Nadia and Renard, Robrecht, "The World Bank, Participation and PRSP: The Bolivian Case Revisited," *European Journal of Development Research*, 15 (2003), 133–61.

Möllers, Christoph, *Gewaltengliederung: Legitimation und Dogmatik im nationalen und internationalen Rechtsvergleich* (Tübingen: Mohr Siebeck, 2005).

"Die Governance-Konstellation," in G. F. Schuppert and M. Zürn (eds.), *Governance in einer sich wandelnden Welt* (Wiesbaden: Verlag für Sozialwissenschaften, 2008), pp. 238–56.

"European Governance: Meaning and Value of a Concept," *Common Market Law Review*, 43 (2006), 314–36.

"§3 Methoden," in W. Hoffmann-Riem, E. Schmidt-Aßmann and A. Voßkuhle (eds.), *Methoden, Maßstäbe, Aufgaben, Organisation*, Grundlagen des Verwaltungsrechts, 3 vols. (Munich: C.H. Beck, 2006), vol. I, pp. 121–76.

Mommsen, Wolfgang (ed.), *Das Ende der Kolonialreiche: Dekolonisation und die Politik der Großmächte* (Frankfurt am Main: Fischer Taschenbuch Verlag, 1990).

Morduch, Jonathan, "The Knowledge Bank," in W. Easterly (ed.), *Reinventing Foreign Aid* (Cambridge: MIT Press, 2008), pp. 377–97. Available at https://www.nyu.edu/projects/morduch/documents/chapters/2008-Morduch-the-Knowledge-Bank-Easterly-%20Reinventing-Foreign-Aid.pdf (last visited July 2013).

Morgenthau, Hans, "A Political Theory of Foreign Aid," *The American Political Science Review*, 56 (1962), 301–9.

Morrison, Kevin and Singer, Matthew, "Inequality and Deliberative Development: Revisiting Bolivias Experience with the PRSP," *Development Policy Review*, 25 (2007), 721–40.

Morse, Stephen, *Indices and Indicators in Development: An Unhealthy Obsession with Numbers?* (London: Earthscan, 2004).

Mosler, Hermann, "General Principles of Law," in R. Bernhardt (ed.), *E-I: East African Community to Italy-United States Air Transport Arbitration (1965)*, Encyclopedia of Public International Law (Amsterdam: Elsevier, 1995), vol. II, pp. 511–27.

Mosler, Matthias, *Finanzierung durch die Weltbank: Grundlegung und anwendbares Recht der vertraglichen Instrumente* (Berlin: Duncker & Humblot, 1987).

Mosley, Paul, Harrigan, Jane and Toye, John, *Aid and Power: The World Bank and Policy-Based Lending* (London: Routledge, 1991).

Moss, Todd, Pettersson, Gunila and van de Walle, Nicolas, *An Aid-Institution's Paradox?: A Review Essay on Aid Dependency and State Building in Sub-Saharan Africa* (Washington, DC: Center for Global Development, 2006).

Moyo, Dambisa, *Dead Aid: Why Aid Is not Working and How There Is Another Way for Africa* (London: Penguin Press, 2009).

Mulgan, Richard, "'Accountability': An Ever-Expanding Concept?" *Public Administration Review*, 78 (2000), 555–73.

Müller, Christoph, *Die Menschenrechte als außenpolitisches Ziel* (Baden-Baden: Nomos, 1986).

Münch, Ingo von (ed.), *Staatsrecht – Völkerrecht – Europarecht*, Festschrift für Hans-Jürgen Schlochauer zum 75. Geburtstag (Berlin: de Gruyter, 1981).

Murkens, Jo Eric Khushal, "The Future of Staatsrecht: Dominance, Demise or Demystification?" *Modern Law Review*, 70 (2007), 731–58.

Mürle, Holger, *Towards a Division of Labor in European Development-Cooperation: Operational Options*, Discussion Paper 6/2007 (Bonn, 2007). Available at www.die-gdi.de/CMS-Homepage/openwebcms3.nsf/%28ynDK_content-ByKey%29/ADMR-7BRJA4/$FILE/6-2007.pdf (last visited July 2013).

Nankani, Gobind, Page, John and Judge, Lindsay, "Human Rights and Poverty Reduction Strategies: Moving Towards Convergence?" in P. Alston and M. Robinson (eds.), *Human Rights and Development: Towards Mutual Reinforcement* (Oxford University Press, 2005), pp. 475–97.

Narula, Smita, "The Story of Narmada Bachao Andolan," in D. R. Hurwitz, D. B. Ford and M. L. Satterthwaite (eds.), *Human Rights Advocacy Stories* (New York: Foundation Press, 2009), pp. 351–83.

Nass, Klaus Otto, "Recht und Praxis der Entwicklungspolitik der deutschen Länder," *Die Öffentliche Verwaltung*, 49 (1996), 274–82.

Naude Fourie, Andrea, *The World Bank Inspection Panel and Quasi-Judicial Oversight: In Search of "Judicial Spirit" in Public International Law* (Utrecht: Eleven International Publishing, 2009).

Ndayi, Zoleka, "Contextualising NEPAD: Regionalism, Plurilateralism and Multilateralism," *South African Journal of International Affairs*, 16 (2009), 371–87.

Neuhold, Hanspeter, *Internationale Konflikte – verbotene und erlaubte Mittel ihrer Austragung: Versuche einer transdisziplinären Betrachtung der Grundsätze des Gewalt- und Interventionsverbots sowie der friedlichen Streitbeilegung im Lichte der UN-Prinzipiendeklaration 1970 und der modernen Sozialwissenschaften*, Forschungen Aus Staat und Recht (Wien: Springer, 1977), vol. XXVII.

"Die Pflicht der Staaten zur Zusammenarbeit zwischen Staaten: moralisches Postulat oder völkerrechtliche Norm?" in H. Miehsler and D. Mayer-Maly (eds.), *Ius humanitatis: Festchrift zum 60. Geburtstag von Alfred Verdross* (Berlin: Duncker & Humblot, 1980), pp. 575–606.

Ngugi, Joel M., "The World Bank and the Ideology of Reform and Development in International Economic Development Discourse," *Cardozo Journal of International and Comparative Law*, 14 (2006), 313–45.

Nierhaus, Michael, "Administrative Law," in M. Reimann and J. Zekoll (eds.), *Introduction to German Law* (Munich: C.H. Beck, 2005), pp. 87–120.

Nohlen, Dieter, "Stichwort Entwicklungsländer," in D. Nohlen and S. Arons (eds.), *Lexikon Dritte Welt: Länder, Organisationen, Theorien, Begriffe, Personen* (Reinbek bei Hamburg: Rowohlt, 2002), pp. 233–5.

"Stichwort Pearson-Bericht," in D. Nohlen and S. Arons (eds.), *Lexikon Dritte Welt: Länder, Organisationen, Theorien, Begriffe, Personen* (Reinbek bei Hamburg: Rowohlt, 2002), pp. 667–700.

Nohlen, Dieter and Arons, Steven (eds.), *Lexikon Dritte Welt: Länder, Organisationen, Theorien, Begriffe, Personen* (Reinbek bei Hamburg: Rowohlt, 2002).

Nolte, Georg, "Article 2 (7): The Charter of the United Nations," in B. Simma (ed.), *The Charter of the United Nations: A Commentary*, 2nd edn, vol. II (Oxford University Press, 2002).

Eingreifen auf Einladung: Zur völkerrechtlichen Zulässigkeit des Einsatzes fremder Truppen im internen Konflikt auf Einladung der Regierung, Beiträge zum ausländischen öffentlichen Recht und Völkerrecht (Berlin: Springer, 1999), vol. CXXXVI.

Nowak, Manfred, "Art. 2," in M. Nowak (ed.), *UN Covenant on Civil and Political Rights: CCPR Commentary* (Kehl: N.P. Engel, 2005).

"Art. 25," in M. Nowak (ed.), *UN Covenant on Civil and Political Rights: CCPR Commentary* (Kehl: N.P. Engel, 2005).

(ed.), *UN Covenant on Civil and Political Rights: CCPR Commentary* (Kehl: N.P. Engel, 2005).

Nuscheler, Franz, (ed.), *Dritte-Welt-Forschung: Entwicklungstheorie und Entwicklungspolitik*, Sonderheft Politische Vierteljahresschrift No. 16 (Opladen: Westdeutscher Verlag, 1985).

Entwicklungspolitik: Lern- und Arbeitsbuch, 5th edn (Bonn: Dietz, 2004).

"Halbierung der absoluten Armut: die entwicklungspolitische Nagelprobe," *Aus Politik und Zeitgeschichte*, B 18–19 (2001), 6–12. Available at www.bpb.de/system/files/pdf/QZYVRE.pdf (last visited September 2012).

"Partnerschaft oder Ausbeutung? Die Enwicklungspolitik der sozial-liberalen Koalition," in F. Grube and G. Richter (eds.), *Der SPD-Staat* (Munich: Piper, 1977), pp. 324–46.

Oakerson, Ronald J., "Governance Structures for Enhancing Accountability and Responsiveness," in J. L. Perry (ed.), *Handbook of Public Administration* (San Francisco: Jossey-Bass, 1989), pp. 110–25.

Odendahl, Guido, *Das Recht auf Entwicklung: Entstehungsgeschichte, systematische Stellung und Inhalt eines individuellen sowie kollektiven Menschrechts und Grundprinzips der Völkerrechtsordnung* (Aachen: Shaker, 1997).

Oeter, Stefan, "Regieren im 21. Jahrhundert: Staatlichkeit und internationales System," in S. Weiss and J. Schmierer (eds.), *Prekäre Staatlichkeit und internationale Ordnung* (Wiesbaden: Verlag für Sozialwissenschaften, 2007), pp. 70–84.

"Souveränität - ein überholtes Konzept?" in H.-J. Cremer (ed.), *Tradition und Weltoffenheit des Rechts*. Festschrift für Helmut Steinberger, Beiträge zum ausländischen öffentlichen Recht und Völkerrecht (Berlin: Springer, 2002), vol. CLII, pp. 259–90.

Oliver, Dawn and Drewry, Gavin, *Public Service Reforms: Issues of Accountability and Public Law* (London, New York: Pinter, 1996).

Oppermann, Thomas and Petersmann, Ernst-Ulrich, *Reforming the International Economic Order: German Legal Comments*, Tübinger Schriften zum internationalen und europäischen Recht (Berlin: Duncker & Humblot, 1987), vol. I.

Orakhelashvili, Alexander, "The World Bank Inspection Panel in Context," *International Organizations Law Review*, 2 (2005), 57–102.

Organisation for Economic Co-operation and Development (OECD), *2008 Survey on Monitoring the Paris Declaration: Making Aid More Effective by 2010* (Paris: OECD Publishing, 2008).

Aid Effectiveness 2011: Progress in Implementing the Paris Declaration (Paris: OECD Publishing, 2012).

Development Co-operation Report 2009 (Paris: OECD Publishing, 2009). Available at www.keepeek.com/Digital-Asset-Management/oecd/development/development-co-operation-report-2009_dcr-2009-en (last visited September 2012).

Development Co-operation Report 2011; 50th Anniversary Edition: 50th edn (Paris: OECD Publishing, 2011).

European Community: Peer Review. Available at www.oecd.org/dac/peerreviewsofdacmembers/38965119.pdf (last visited July 2013).

Evaluation in Development Agencies (Paris: OECD Publishing, 2010).

The History of the DAC (Paris: OECD Publishing, 2006).

Inside the DAC (Paris: OECD Publishing, 2008).

Managing Aid: Practices of DAC Member Countries (Paris: OECD Publishing, 2005).

OECD Annual Report 2008 (Paris: OECD Publishing, 2008)

Quality Standards for Development Evaluation, DAC Guidelines and Reference Series (Paris: OECD Publishing, 2010). Available at www.oecd.org/development/evaluationofdevelopmentprogrammes/dcdndep/44798177.pdf (last visited September 2012).

Orwell, George, *1984* (London: Secker and Warburg, 1949).

Ouguergouz, Fatsah, *The African Charter of Human and People's Rights: A Comprehensive Agenda for Human Dignity and Sustainable Democracy in Africa* (The Hague: Kluwer Law International, 2003).

Ousmane, Sembène, *Le docker noir* (Paris: Présence africaine, 1956).

Pagani, Fabrizio, *Peer Review: An OECD Tool for Co-operation and Change* (Paris: OECD Publishing, 2003).

Pahuja, Sundhya, *Decolonising International Law: Development, Economic Growth, and the Politics of Universality* (Cambridge, New York: Cambridge University Press, 2011).

Passos, Ricardo and Gauci, Daniela, "European Parliament and Development Cooperation: Shaping Legislation and the New Democratic Scrutiny Dialogue," in S. Bartelt and P. Dann (eds.), *Entwicklungszusammenarbeit im Recht der Europäischen Union – The Law of EU Development Cooperation: Europarecht-Beiheft Nr. 2* (Baden-Baden: Nomos, 2008), pp. 138–61.

Patzig, Werner, *Haushaltsrecht des Bundes und der Länder: Band 2: Verwaltungsvorschriften* (Baden-Baden: Nomos, 1982).

Paul, James C., "The United Nations and the Creation of an International Law of Development," *Harvard International Law Journal*, 36 (1995), 307–28.

Paulo, Sebastian and Reisen, Helmut, "Eastern Donors and Western Soft Law: Towards a DAC Donor Peer Review of China and India?" *Development Policy Review*, 28 (2010), 535–52.

Paulus, Christoph G., "What Constitutes a Debt in the Sovereign Debt Restructuring Context?" in A. Ligustro and G. Sacerdoti (eds.), *Problemi e tendenze del diritto internazionale dell"economia: Liber amicorum in onore die Paolo Picone* (Naples: Editoriale Scientifica, 2011), pp. 231–48.

Pauwelyn, Joost, "Informal International Lawmaking: Framing the Concept and Research Questions," in J. Pauwelyn, R. Wessel and J. Wouters (eds.), *Informal International Lawmaking* (Oxford University Press, 2012).

Pauwelyn, Joost, Wessel, Ramses and Wouters, Jan (eds.), *Informal International Lawmaking* (Oxford University Press, 2012).

Pearson, Lester, *Partners in Development: Report of the Commission on International Development* (New York: Praeger, 1969).

Peiry Kummer, Katharina, "Prior Informed Consent," in R. Wolfrum (ed.), *Max Planck Encyclopedia of Public International Law* [online edition] (Oxford University Press, 2008–). Available at www.mpepil.com (last visited April 2013).

Pellens, Martin, *Entwicklungshilfe Deutschlands und der Europäischen Union: Rechtsgrundlagen und Verfahren bei der finanziellen und technischen Zusammenarbeit*, Berliner Europa-Studien (Berlin: Verlag Dr. Köster, 1996), vol. IV.

Pellet, Alain, *Le droit international du développement*, 2nd edn (Paris: Presses universitaires de France, 1987).

Peretz, David (ed.), *Learning from Experience: Perspectives on Poverty Reduction Strategies from Four Developing Countries* (London: Commonwealth Secretariat, 2009).

Pernice, Ingolf, "Art. 25," in H. Dreier (ed.), *Grundgesetz: Kommentar*, 2nd edn (Tübingen: Mohr Siebeck, 2004–).

Perry, James L. (ed.), *Handbook of Public Administration* (San Francisco: Jossey-Bass, 1989).

Peters, Anne, "Unequal Treaties," in R. Wolfrum (ed.), *Max Planck Encyclopedia of Public International Law* [online edition] (Oxford University Press, 2008–). Available at www.mpepil.com (last visited April 2013).

Petersen, Niels, *Demokratie als teleologisches Prinzip: Zur Legitimität von Staatsgewalt im Völkerrecht*, Beiträge zum ausländischen öffentlichen Recht und Völkerrecht (Berlin Heidelberg: Springer, 2009), vol. CCIV.

Petersmann, Ernst-Ulrich, "Die Dritte Welt und das Wirtschaftsvölkerrecht: 'Entwicklungsland' als privilegierter Rechtsstatus," *Heidelberg Journal of International Law*, 36 (1976), 492–550.

Peterson, John and Shackleton, Michael (eds.), *The Institutions of the European Union*, 2nd edn (Oxford University Press, 2006).

Petzold, Wolfgang, "Art. 161 EGV," in H. von der Groeben and J. Schwarze (eds.), *Vertrag über die Europäische Union und Vertrag über die Gründung der Europäischen Gemeinschaft*. Kommentar, 6th edn, vol. IV (Baden-Baden: Nomos, 2003).

Pinelli, Cesare, "Conditionality," in R. Wolfrum (ed.), *Max Planck Encyclopedia of Public International Law* [online edition] (Oxford University Press, 2008–). Available at www.mpepil.com (last visited April 2013).

Pippan, Christian, *Die Förderung der Menschenrechte und der Demokratie als Aufgabe der Entwicklungszusammenarbeit der Europäischen Gemeinschaft*, Europäische Hochschulschriften (Frankfurt: Peter Lang Verlag, 2002), vol. MMMCDLX.

Pitschas, Rainer, "§42 Maßstäbe des Verwaltungshandelns," in W. Hoffmann-Riem, E. Schmidt-Aßmann and A. Voßkuhle (eds.), *Informationsordnung, Verwaltungsverfahren, Handlungsformen*, Grundlagen des Verwaltungsrechts (Munich: C.H. Beck, 2008), vol. II, pp. 1567–681.

"Art. 177 EGV," in R. Streinz (ed.), *EUV/EGV Kommentar* (Munich: C.H. Beck, 2003).

"Recht und Gesetz in der Entwicklungszusammenarbeit," *Verwaltungsarchiv*, 81 (1990), 465–91.

Pogge Thomas, *Global Justice and the First Millennium Development Goal*. Available at www.etikk.no/globaljustice/ (last visited September 2012).

"Recognized and Violated by International Law: The Human Rights of the Global Poor," *Leiden Journal of International Law*, 18 (2005), 717–45.

Preuß, Ulrich K., "Equality of States – Its Meaning in a Constitutionalized Global Order," *Chicago Journal of International Law*, 9 (2008), 17–49.

Pritchett, Lant, "It Pays to Be Ignorant: A Simple Political Economy of Rigorous Program Evaluation," in W. Easterly (ed.), *Reinventing Foreign Aid* (Cambridge: MIT Press, 2008), pp. 121–40.

Pritchett, Lant and Woolcock, Michael, "Solutions When the Solution Is the Problem: Arraying the Disarray in Development," in W. Easterly (ed.), *Reinventing Foreign Aid* (Cambridge: MIT Press, 2008), pp. 147–78.

Quigley, John B., "Complicity in International Law: A New Direction in the Law of State Responsiblity," *British Yearbook of International Law*, 57 (1986), 77–131.

Quille, Gerrard, "The European External Action Service and the Common Security and Defence Policy (CSDP)," in E. Greco, N. Pirozzi and S. Silvestri (eds.), *EU Crisis Management: Institutions and Capabilities in the Making*, IAI Quaderni English Series (Rome: Istituto affari internazionali, 2010), vol. XIX, pp. 55–78.

Radke, Detlef, *Auflagenpolitik und Politik-Dialog in der entwicklungspolitischen Zusammenarbeit* (Berlin: German Development Institute, 1985).

Ragazzi, Maurizio, "Financial Institutions, International," in R. Wolfrum (ed.), *Max Planck Encyclopedia of Public International Law [online edition]* (Oxford University Press, 2008–). Available at www.mpepil.com (last visited April 2013).

"World Bank Group," in R. Wolfrum (ed.), *Max Planck Encyclopedia of Public International Law [online edition]* (Oxford University Press, 2008–). Available at www.mpepil.com (last visited April 2013).

Rahnema, Majid, "Participation," in W. Sachs (ed.), *The Development Dictionary: A Guide to Knowledge as Power* (London: Zed Books, 1992), pp. 116–31.

Rahnema, Majid and Bawtree, Victoria, *The Post-Development Reader* (London: Zed Books, 1997).

Rauch, Theo, *Entwicklungspolitik* (Braunschweig: Westermann, 2009).

Ravenhill, John, *Collective Clientelism: The Lomé Conventions and North-South Relations* (New York: Columbia University Press, 1985).

Rawlings, Richard (ed.), *Law, Society, and Economy: Centenary Essays for the London School of Economics and Political Science, 1895–1995* (Oxford University Press, 1997).

Rawls, John, *A Theory of Justice* (Harvard University Press, 1971).

The Law of Peoples (Cambridge: Harvard University Press, 1999).

Justice as Fairness: A Restatement, edited by Erin Kelly (Harvard University Press, 2001).

Rawski, Frederick, "World Bank Community-Driven Development Programming in Indonesia and East Timor: Implications for the Study of Global Administrative Law," *New York University Journal of International Law and Politics*, 37 (2006), 919–51.

Reddy, Sanjay and Heuty, Antoine, "Global Development Goals: The Folly of Technocratic Pretensions," *Development Policy Review*, 26 (2008), 5–28.

Reimann, Mathias and Zekoll, Joachim (eds.), *Introduction to German Law* (Munich: C.H. Beck, 2005).

Reimann, Mathias and Zimmermann, Reinhard (eds.), *The Oxford Handbook of Comparative Law* (Oxford University Press, 2008).

Reimer, Franz, *Verfassungsprinzipien: Ein Normtyp des Grundgesetzes* (Berlin: Duncker & Humblot, 2001).

Reinikka, Ritva, "Donors and Service Delivery," in W. Easterly (ed.), *Reinventing Foreign Aid* (Cambridge: MIT Press, 2008), pp. 179–99.

Reinisch, August, *International Organizations Before National Courts* (Cambridge University Press, 2000).

"Securing the Accountability of International Organizations," *Global Governance*, 7 (2001), 131–49.

Reinisch, August and Wurm, Jakob, "International Financial Institutions before National Courts," in D. Bradlow and D. B. Hunter (eds.), *International Financial Institutions and International Law* (Alphen aan den Rijn: Kluwer Law International, 2010), pp. 103–35.

Renzio, Paolo de, "Aid, Budgets and Accountability: A Survey Article," *Development Policy Review*, 24 (2006), 627–45.

Ress, Georg, "State Responsibility for Extraterritorial Human Rights Violations: The Bankovic Case," *Zeitschrift für europarechtliche Studien*, 6 (2003), 73–89.

Reuter, Paul, *Introduction to the Law of Treaties* (London, New York: Kegan Paul International, 1995).

Riddell, Roger C., *Does Foreign Aid Really Work?* (Oxford University Press, 2007).

"The End of Foreign Aid to Africa?: Concerns about Donor Policies," *African Affairs*, 98 (1999), 309–35.

Riedel, Eibe, "Menschenrechte der Dritten Generation," in E. H. Riedel, C. Koenig and R. A. Lorz (eds.), *Die Universalität der Menschenrechte: Philosophische Grundlagen, Nationale Gewährleistungen, Internationale Garantien* (Berlin: Duncker & Humblot, 2003), pp. 329–61.

Theorie der Menschenrechtsstandards: Funktion, Wirkungsweise und Begründung wirtschaftlicher und sozialer Menschenrechte mit exemplarischer Darstellung der Rechte auf Eigentum und Arbeit in verschiedenen Rechtsordnungen (Berlin: Duncker & Humblot, 1986).

Riedel, Eibe H., Koenig, Christian and Lorz, Ralph Alexander (eds.), *Die Universalität der Menschenrechte: Philosophische Grundlagen, Nationale Gewährleistungen, Internationale Garantien* (Berlin: Duncker & Humblot, 2003).

Riedel, Eibe and Will, Martin, "Human Rights Clauses in External Agreements of the EC," in P. Alston (ed.), *The EU and Human Rights* (Oxford University Press, 1999), pp. 723–55.

Riegner, Michael, "Entwicklungsmessung und Recht," in Dann, Kadelbach and Kaltenborn (eds), *Entwicklung und Recht* (forthcoming fall 2013).

Measuring the Good Governance State: A Legal Reconstruction of the World Bank's "Country Policy and Institutional Assessment," IRPA Working Paper 2012 (in press) at www.irpa.eu.

Riegner, Michael and Wischmeyer, Thomas, "'Rechtliche Zusammenarbeit' mit Transformations- und Entwicklungsländern als Gegenstand öffentlich-rechtlicher Forschung," *Der Staat*, 50 (2011), 436–68.

Rigo Sureda, Andres, "The Law Applicable to the Activities of International Development Banks," *Recueil des Cours*, 308 (2004), 13–249.

"The World Bank and Institutional Innovation," in E. Brown Weiss, A. Rigo Sureda and L. B. de Chazournes (eds.), *The World Bank, International Financial Institutions, and the Development of International Law: A symposium held in honor of Dr. Ibrahim F. I. Shihata* (Washington, DC: American Society of International Law, 1999), pp. 11–20.

Rischer, Herbert, *Finanzkontrolle staatlichen Handelns: Wirtschaftlichkeit und Sparsamkeit als Prüfungsmaßstäbe* (Heidelberg: C.F. Müller, 1995).

Risse, Thomas and Lehmkuhl, Ursula (eds.), *Regieren ohne Staat? Governance begrenzter Staatlichkeit* (Baden-Baden: Nomos, 2007).

Rist, Gilbert, *The History of Development: From Western Origins to Global Faith*, 3rd edn (London: Zed Books, 2008).

Ritter,Ernst-Hasso,"StaatlicheSteuerungbeivermindertemRationalitätsanspruch? Zur Praxis der politische Planung in der Bundesrepublik Deutschland," in T. Ellwein, J. J. Hesse, R. Maynitz and F. Scharpf (eds.), *Jahrbuch zur Staats- und Verwaltungswissenschaft* (Baden-Baden: Nomos, 1987), pp. 321–52.

Rittich, Kerry, "The Future of Law and Development: Second-Generation Reforms and the Incorporation of the Social," *Michigan Journal of International Law*, 26 (2004), 199–243.

Röben, Volker, *Außenverfassungsrecht: Eine Untersuchung zur auswärtigen Gewalt des offenen Staates* (Tübingen: Mohr Siebeck, 2007).

Rocha Menocal, Alina, *Learning From Experience: A Review of Recipient Government Efforts to Manage Donor Relations and Improve the Quality of Aid*, Overseas Development Institue Working Paper No. 268. Available at www.odi.org.uk/resources/docs/2027.pdf (last visited July 2013).

Rodi, Michael, *Die Subventionsrechtsordnung: Die Subvention als Instrument öffentlicher Zweckverwirklichung nach Völkerrecht, Europarecht und deutschem innerstaatlichen Recht* (Tübingen: Mohr Siebeck, 2000).

Röhl, Carl Christian, "§30: Ausgewählte Verwaltungsverfahren," in W. Hoffmann-Riem, E. Schmidt-Aßmann and A. Voßkuhle (eds.), *Informationsordnung, Verwaltungsverfahren, Handlungsformen*, Grundlagen des Verwaltungsrechts (Munich: C.H. Beck, 2008), vol. II, pp. 689–750.

Roos, Stefanie Ricarda, *Der internationale Menschenrechtsschutz vor entwicklungsbedingten Zwangsumsiedlungen und seine Sicherstellung durch Recht und Praxis der Weltbank*, Schriften zum Völkerrecht (Berlin: Duncker & Humblot, 2008), vol. CLXXIII.

"Die Weltbank als Implementierungsgarant menschenrechtsschützender Völkerrechtsnormen," *Heidelberg Journal of International Law*, 63 (2003), 1035–62.

Rosas, Allan, "Internal Self-Determination," in C. Tomuschat (ed.), *Modern Law of Self-Determination* (Dordrecht: Nijhoff, 1993), pp. 227–8.

"Art. 21," in A. Eide (ed.), *The Universal Declaration of Human Rights: A Commentary* (Oslo: Scandinavian University Press, 1992), pp. 299–317.

Rosenau, James N., "Governance, Order, and Change in World Politics," in J. N. Rosenau and E.-O. Czempiel (eds.), *Governance Without Government: Order and Change in World Politics* (Cambridge University Press, 1992), pp. 1–29.

Rosenau, James N. and Czempiel, Ernst-Otto (eds.), *Governance Without Government: Order and Change in World Politics* (Cambridge University Press, 1992).

Rosenstein-Rodan, Paul Narcyz, "Notes on the Theory of the 'Big Push,' in H. S. Ellis (ed.), *Economic Development for Latin America* (London: Macmillan, 1962), pp. 57–81.

Rosga, AnnJanette and Satterthwaite, Margaret L., "The Trust in Indicators: Measuring Human Rights," *Berkeley Journal of International Law*, 27 (2009), 253–315.

Roßnagel, Alexander, "Möglichkeiten für Transparenz und Öffentlichkeit im Verwaltungshandeln – unter besonderer Berücksichtigung des Internet als Instrument der Staatskommunikation," in W. Hoffmann-Riem and E. Schmidt-Aßmann (eds.), *Verwaltungsrecht in der Informationsgesellschaft*, Schriften zur Reform des Verwaltungsrechts (Baden-Baden: Nomos, 2000), vol. VII, pp. 257–332.

Rostow, Walt W., *The Stages of Growth: A Non-Communist Manifesto* (Cambridge University Press, 1960).

Rotberg, Robert (ed.), *When States Fail: Causes and Consequences* (Princeton University Press, 2004).

Rottenburg, Richard, *Weit hergeholte Fakten: Eine Parabel der Entwicklungshilfe* (Stuttgart: Lucius & Lucius, 2002).

Rubin, Seymour, *The Conscience of the Rich Nations: The Development Assistance Committee and the Common Aid Effort* (New York: Harper Row, 1966).

(ed.), *Foreign Development Lending – Legal Aspects: The Papers and Proceedings of a Conference of Legal Advisors of National and International Development Lending and Assistance Agencies* (Leiden: Sijthoff, 1971).

Ruffert, Matthias, "Perspektiven des Internationalen Verwaltungsrechts," in C. Möllers, A. Vosskuhle and C. Walter (eds.), *Internationales Verwaltungsrecht: Eine Analyse anhand von Referenzgebieten.*, Jus Internationale et Europaeum (Tübingen: Mohr Siebeck, 2007), vol. XVI, pp. 395–419.

"Zuständigkeitsgrenzen internationaler Organisationen im institutionellen Rahmen der internationalen Gemeinschaft," *Archiv des Völkerrechts*, 38 (2000), 129–68.

Ruffert, Matthias and Walter, Christian, *Institutionalisiertes Völkerrecht: Das Recht der Internationalen Organisationen und seine wichtigsten Anwendungsfelder* (Munich: C.H. Beck, 2009).

Ruge, Martin, *Der Beitrag der UNCTAD zur Herausbildung des Entwicklungsvölkerrechts* (Frankfurt am Main: Haag und Herchen, 1976).

Sachs, Wolfgang (ed.), *The Development Dictionary: A Guide to Knowledge as Power* (London: Zed Books, 1992).

Sacksofsky, Ute, "§40 Anreize," in W. Hoffmann-Riem, E. Schmidt-Aßmann and A. Voßkuhle (eds.), *Informationsordnung, Verwaltungsverfahren, Handlungsformen*, Grundlagen des Verwaltungsrechts (Munich: C.H. Beck, 2008), vol. II, pp. 1459–517.

Said, Edward W., *Orientalism* (New York: Pantheon Books, 1978).

The World, the Text, and the Critic (Cambridge: Harvard University Press, 1983).

Salais, Robert, "On the Correct (and Incorrect) Use of Indicators in Public Action," *Comparative Labor Law and Policy Journal*, 27 (2006), pp. 237–256.

Salomon, Margot E., *Global Responsibility for Human Rights: World Poverty and the Development of International Law* (Oxford University Press, 2008).

Salzman, James, *Decentralized Administrative Law in the Organisation for Economic Co-operation and Development: International Law and Justice Working Papers No. 17* (New York University, 2005).

San Juan, E., *Beyond Postcolonial Theory* (New York: St. Martin's Press, 1999).

Sands, Philippe and Klein, Pierre, *Bowett's Law of International Institutions*, 6th edn (London: Sweet & Maxwell, 2009).

Sarfaty, Galit A., "Why Culture Matters in International Institutions: The Marginality of Human Rights at the World Bank," *American Journal of International Law*, 103 (2009), 647–83.

Sarooshi, Dan, "Essentially Contested Nature of the Concept of Sovereignty: Implications for the Exercise by International Organizations of Powers of Government," *Michigan Journal of International Law*, 25 (2004), 1107–39.

Sattelberger, Julia, "Der Europäische Auswärtige Dienst: Chance oder Risiko für die europäische Entwicklungszusammenarbeit?" *Verfassung und Recht in Übersee*, 43 (2010), 381–6.

Schäfers, Manfred, "Das System Niebel," *Frankfurter Allgemeine Zeitung* (January 1, 2012). Available at www.faz.net/aktuell/wirtschaft/entwicklungshilfeministerium-das-system-niebel-11609182.html (last visited July 2013).

Scharpf, Fritz, "Komplexität als Schranke der politischen Planung," in F. Scharpf (ed.), *Planung als politischer Prozess: Aufsätze zur Theorie der planenden Demokratie* (Frankfurt: Suhrkamp, 1973), pp. 73–113.

(ed.), *Planung als politischer Prozess: Aufsätze zur Theorie der planenden Demokratie* (Frankfurt: Suhrkamp, 1973).

"Planung als politischer Prozess," in F. Scharpf (ed.), *Planung als politischer Prozess: Aufsätze zur Theorie der planenden Demokratie* (Frankfurt: Suhrkamp, 1973), pp. 33–72.

Scheel, Walter, *Konturen einer neuen Welt* (Düsseldorf: Econ Verlag, 1965).

Schenk, Wolfgang, *Strukturen und Rechtsfragen der gemeinschaftlichen Leistungsverwaltung*, Jus Internationale et Europaeum (Tübingen: Mohr Siebeck, 2006), vol. VII.

Schermers, Henry G. and Blokker, Niels, *International Institutional Law: Unity Within Diversity*, 5th edn (Leiden, Boston: Martinus Nijhoff Publishers, 2011).

International Institutional Law, 4th edn (Boston: Nijhoff, 2003).

Scherzberg, Arno, "Risiko als Rechtsproblem," *Archiv des öffentlichen Rechts*, 84 (1993), 484–513.

Scheuner, Ulrich, "Solidarität unter den Nationen als Grundsatz in der gegenwärtigen internationalen Gemeinschaft," in J. Delbrück, K. Ipsen and D. Rauschning (eds.), *Recht im Dienst des Friedens: Festschrift für Eberhard Menzel zum 65. Geburtstag am 21. Januar 1976* (Berlin: Duncker & Humblot, 1975), pp. 251–77.

Schimank, Uwe, "Das außenpolitische Interorganisationsnetz als Hemmnis einer eigenständigen deutschen Entwicklungspolitik," in M. Glagow (ed.), *Deutsche Entwicklungspolitik: Aspekte und Probleme ihrer Entscheidungsstruktur: Beiträge in Zusammenhang mit dem Forschungsprojekt "Handlungsbedingungen und Handlungsspielräume für Entwicklungspolitik"* (Saarbrücken, Fort Lauderdale: Breitenbach, 1983), pp. 51–86.

Schlemmer-Schulte, Sabine and Tung, Koh-Yung (eds.), *Liber Amicorum Ibrahim Shihata: International Finance and Development Law* (The Hague: Kluwer Law International, 2001).

Schmalenbach, Kirsten, "Accountability: Who Is Judging the European Development Cooperation?" in S. Bartelt and P. Dann (eds.), *Entwicklungszusammenarbeit im Recht der Europäischen Union: The Law of EU Development Cooperation: Europarecht-Beiheft Nr. 2* (Baden-Baden: Nomos, 2008), pp. 162–90.

"Art. 177 EGV," in C. Calliess and M. Ruffert (eds.), *EUV/EGV: Das Verfassungsrecht der Europäischen Union mit Europäischer Grundrechtecharta*. Kommentar, 3rd edn (Munich: C.H. Beck, 2007).

"Art. 180 EGV," in C. Calliess and M. Ruffert (eds.), *EUV/EGV: Das Verfassungsrecht der Europäischen Union mit Europäischer Grundrechtecharta*. Kommentar, 3rd edn (Munich: C.H. Beck, 2007).

"Art. 181 EGV," in C. Calliess and M. Ruffert (eds.), *EUV/EGV: Das Verfassungsrecht der Europäischen Union mit Europäischer Grundrechtecharta*. Kommentar, 3rd edn (Munich: C.H. Beck, 2007).

Schmidt, Heide-Irene, "Pushed to the Front: The Foreign Assistance Policy of the Federal Republic of Germany 1958–1971," *Contemporary European History*, 12 (2003), 473–507.

Schmidt, Petra, *Budgethilfe in der Entwicklungszusammenarbeit der EU*, Studies in transnational legal policy (Bonn, 2005), vol. X.

Schmidt-Aßmann, Eberhard, *Das allgemeine Verwaltungsrecht als Ordnungsidee: Grundlagen und Aufgaben der verwaltungsrechtlichen Systembildung*, 2nd edn (Berlin: Springer, 2004).

(ed.), *Aufgabe und Perspektiven verwaltungsrechtlicher Forschung* (Tübingen: Mohr Siebeck, 2006).

"Die Herausforderung der Verwaltungsrechtswissenschaft durch die Internationalisierung der Verwaltungsbeziehungen," *Der Staat*, 45 (2006), 315–38.

"Planung als administrative Handlungsform und Rechtsinstitut," in E. Schmidt-Aßmann (ed.), *Aufgabe und Perspektiven verwaltungsrechtlicher Forschung* (Tübingen: Mohr Siebeck, 2006), pp. 158–76.

Schmidt-Aßmann, Eberhard and Hoffmann-Riem, Wolfgang (eds.), *Verwaltungskontrolle*, Schriften zur Reform des Verwaltungsrechts (Baden-Baden: Nomos, 2001), vol. VIII.

Schmuck, Otto and Nuscheler, Franz (eds.), *Die Süd-Politik der EG* (Bonn: Europa-Union-Verlag, 1993).

Schönberger, Christoph, "§71 Verwaltungsrechtsvergleichung: Eigenheiten, Methoden und Geschichte," in A. von Bogdandy, S. Cassese and P. M. Huber (eds.), *Verwaltungsrecht in Europa: Wissenschaft*, Ius Publicum Europaeum (Heidelberg: C.F. Müller, 2011), vol. IV, pp. 493–540.

Schöndorf-Haubold, Bettina, *Die Strukturfonds der Europäischen Gemeinschaft: Rechtsformen und Verfahren europäischer Verbundverwaltung* (Munich: C.H. Beck, 2005).

Schorkopf, Frank, *Grundgesetz und Überstaatlichkeit: Konflikt und Harmonie in den auswärtigen Beziehungen Deutschlands*, Jus Publicum (Tübingen: Mohr Siebeck, 2007), vol. CLXVII.

Schreuer, Christoph, "Die Bindung internationaler Organisationen an völkerrechtliche Verträge ihrer Mitgliedstaaten: Völkerrecht zwischen normativem Anspruch und politischer Realität," in K. Zemanek and K. Ginther (eds.), *Völkerrecht zwischen normativem Anspruch und politischer Realität: Festschrift für Karl Zemanek zum 65. Geburtstag* (Berlin: Duncker & Humblot, 1994), pp. 223–50.

Schulze-Fielitz, Helmut (ed.), *Fortschritte der Finanzkontrolle in Theorie und Praxis: Zum Gedenken an Ernst Heuer. Beiheft Die Verwaltung* (Berlin: Duncker & Humblot, 2000).

"§12 Grundmodi der Aufgabenwahrnehmung," in W. Hoffmann-Riem, E. Schmidt-Aßmann and A. Voßkuhle (eds.), *Methoden, Maßstäbe, Aufgaben, Organisation*, Grundlagen des Verwaltungsrechts, 3 vols. (Munich: C.H. Beck, 2006), vol. I, pp. 761–838.

Schuppert, Gunnar Folke, "Was ist und wozu Governance?" *Die Verwaltung*, 40 (2007), 465–512.

Schuppert, Gunnar Folke and Zürn, Michael (eds.), *Governance in einer sich wandelnden Welt* (Wiesbaden: Verlag für Sozialwissenschaften, 2008).

Schütz, Raimund, *Solidarität im Wirtschaftsvölkerrecht: Eine Bestandsaufnahme zentraler entwicklungsspezifischer Solidarrechte und Solidarpflichten im Völkerrecht* (Berlin: Duncker & Humblot, 1994).

Schwanenflügel, Martin von, *Entwicklungszusammenarbeit als Aufgabe der Gemeinden und Kreise*, Schriften zum Öffentlichen Recht (Berlin: Duncker & Humblot, 1993), vol. DCXXXI.

Schwarze, Jürgen (ed.), *EU-Kommentar*, 2nd edn (Baden-Baden: Nomos, 2009).

Schwimmbeck, Andrea, *Rechtliche Analyse der gegenwärtigen Struktur der regionalen Entwicklungszusammenarbeit in der Europäischen Gemeinschaft* (Frankfurt: Peter Lang Verlag, 2007).

Seidman, Ann (ed.), *Making Development Work: Legislative Reform for Institutional Transformation and Good Governance* (The Hague: Kluwer Law International, 1999).

Sen, Amartya, *Resource, Values and Development* (Cambridge: Harvard University Press, 1984).

Commodities and Capabilities (Amsterdam: Elsevier, 1985).

"The Concept of Development," in H. Chenery (ed.), *Handbook of Development Economics* (Amsterdam: North Holland, 1988), pp. 9–25.

Development as Freedom (New York: Knopf, 1999).

Senghaas, Dieter, "Elemente einer Theorie des peripheren Kapitalismus," in D. Senghaas (ed.), *Peripherer Kapitalismus: Analysen über Abhängigkeit und Unterentwicklung* (Frankfurt: Suhrkamp, 1974), pp. 7–36.

Peripherer Kapitalismus: Analysen über Abhängigkeit und Unterentwicklung (Frankfurt: Suhrkamp, 1974).

Weltwirtschaftsordnung und Entwicklungspolitik: Plädoyer für Dissoziation (Frankfurt: Suhrkamp, 1977).

Sengupta, Arjun, "On the Theory and Practice of the Right to Development," *Human Rights Quarterly*, 24 (2002), 837–89.

Seppänen, Samuli, *Good Governance in International Law: Erik Castrén Institute research reports No. 13* (Helsinki: The Erik Castrén Institute of International Law, 2003).

Possibilities and Challenges of the Human Rights-Based Approach to Development: Erik Castrén Institute research reports No. 17 (Helsinki: The Erik Castrén Institute of International Law, 2005).

Sepulveda, Magdalena, *The Nature of the Obligations under the International Covenant on Economic, Social and Cultural Rights* (Antwerp: Intersentia, 2003).

"The Obligations of 'International Assistance and Cooperation' Under the International Covenant on Economic, Social and Cultural Rights: A Possible Entry to a Human Rights Based Approach to Millennium Development Goal 8," *The International Journal of Human Rights*, 13 (2009), 86–109.

Severino, Jean-Michel and Ray, Olivier, *The End of ODA: Death and Rebirth of a Global Public Policy*, Working Paper Number 167 (2009). Available at www.cgdev.org/files/1421419_file_End_of_ODA_FINAL.pdf (last visited July 2013).

Shadlen, Kenneth C., Guennif, Samira, Guzmán, Alenka and Lalitha, N. (eds.), *Intellectual Property, Pharmaceuticals, and Public Health: Access to Drugs in Developing Countries* (Cheltenham: Edward Elgar, 2011).

Shaw, D. John, "Dimensions of Poverty: Status and Solutions Towards the Millennium Development Goals," *Development Policy Review*, 23 (2005), 499–523.

Shaw, Malcolm N., *International Law*, 5th edn (Cambridge University Press, 2003).

Shelton, Dinah (ed.), *Committment and Compliance: The Role of Non-Binding Norms in the International Legal System* (Oxford University Press, 2000).

Shepherd, George W. and Nanda, Ved P., *Human Rights and Third World Development* (Westport: Greenwood Press, 1985).

Shihata, Ibrahim, "The Creative Role of Lawyers: Example: The Office of the World Bank's General Counsel," *Catholic University Law Review*, 48 (1999), 1041–53.

The European Bank for Reconstruction and Development: A Comparative Analysis of Its Constituent Agreement (Boston: Martinus Nijhoff, 1990).

"The World Bank and the Environment," in I. Shihata (ed.), *The World Bank in a Changing World*, Volume I: Selected essays (Dordrecht: Martinus Nijhoff, 1991), pp. 135–80.

(ed.), *The World Bank in a Changing World: Volume I: Selected Essays* (Dordrecht: Martinus Nijhoff, 1991).

(ed.), *The World Bank in a Changing World: Volume II: Selected Essays and Lectures* (Dordrecht: Martinus Nijhoff, 1995).

The World Bank Inspection Panel (Oxford University Press, 2000).

The World Bank Legal Papers (The Hague: Brill Academic Publishers, 2000).

Shihata, Ibrahim, Abushakra, Hadi and Gruss, Hans-Jürgen, "Legal Aspects of the World Bank's Assistance to the West Bank and the Gaza Strip," *Palestine Yearbook of International Law*, 7 (1992/94), 19–43.

Sichel, Christian, "Die Gründung des Europäischen Auswärtigen Dienstes als EU-Organ: Gleichzeitig eine kleine Ordnung der EU-Verwaltungsorganisation," *Europarecht*, 46 (2011), 447–60.

Sieberg, Herward, *Colonial Development: Die Grundlegung moderner Entwicklungspolitik durch Grossbritannien, 1919–1949* (Stuttgart: Steiner, 1985).

Siebold, Thomas, *Participation in PRS Processes: A Review of the International Debate*, INEF Report No. 86.

Simma, Bruno (ed.), *The Charter of the United Nations: A Commentary*, 2nd edn, 2 vols. (Oxford University Press, 2002).

Simma, Bruno, Aschenbrenner, Jo and Schulte, Constanze, "Human Rights Considerations in the Development Cooperation Activities of the EC," in

P. Alston (ed.), *The EU and Human Rights* (Oxford University Press, 1999), pp. 571–626.

Simmonds, K. R., "The Fourth Lomé Convention," *Common Market Law Review*, 28 (1991), 521–47.

Simonis, Udo, *Review of the List of LDCs* (Berlin: Wissenschaftszentrum Berlin für Sozialforschung, 2003).

Simpson, Gerry, *Great Powers and Outlaw States: Unequal Sovereigns in the International Legal Order* (Cambridge University Press, 2004).

Sinclair, Ian Moe, *The Vienna Convention on the Law of Treaties* (Manchester University Press, 1973).

Singer, Michael, "Jurisdictional Immunity of International Organizations: Human Rights and Functional Necessity Concerns," *Virginia Journal of International Law*, 36 (1995), 53–165.

Singh, Mahendra P., *German Administrative Law in Common Law Perspective*, 2nd edn (Berlin, New York: Springer, 2001).

Six, Clemens, *Der Europäische Konsens zur Entwicklungspolitik: Die EU als Geberin in veränderten internationalen Beziehungen*, Österreichische Forschungsstiftung für Internationale Entwicklung, Working Paper No. 10. Available at www.oefse.at/Downloads/publikationen/WP_EuropaeischerKonses_zur_EPolitik_Maerz2006.pdf (last visited July 2013).

Skogly, Sigrun, *The Human Rights Obligations of the World Bank and the International Monetary Fund* (London: Cavendish, 2001).

Beyond National Borders: States' Human Rights Obligations in International Cooperation (Antwerp: Intersentia, 2006).

Slaughter, Ann-Marie, "International Law in a World of Liberal States," *European Journal of International Law*, 6 (1995), 503–38.

Slinn, Peter and Snyder, Francis (eds.), *International Development Law* (Abingdon: Professional Books, 1987).

Smith, Andy (ed.), *Politics and the European Commission* (London: Routledge, 2004).

Smith, Patrick, *Somebody Else's Century: East and West in a Post-Western World* (New York: Pantheon Books, 2010).

Somek, Alexander, "The Concept of 'Law' in Global Administrative Law: A Reply to Benedict Kingsbury," *European Journal of International Law*, 20 (2009), 985–95.

"The Indelible Science of Law," *International Journal of Constitutional Law*, 7 (2009), 424–41.

Song, Ligang and Golley, Jane (eds.), *Rising China: Global Challenges and Opportunities* (Acton: ANU E Press, 2011).

Spamann, Holger, "Large-Sample, Quantitative Research Designs for Comparative Law?" *The American Journal of Comparative Law*, 57 (2009), 797–810.

Spivak, Gayatri Chakravorty and Harasym, Sarah, *The Post-Colonial Critic: Interviews, Strategies, Dialogues* (New York: Routledge, 1990).

Squire, Lyn, "Why the World Bank Should Be Involved in Development Research," in C. Gilbert and D. Vines (eds.), *The World Bank: Structure and Policies* (Cambridge University Press, 2000), pp. 108–30.

Ssekandi, Francis M. and Johnson, Peri Lynne, "Law and Development: An Empirical Study of the Evolution of the Legal Framework for Delivery of Multilateral Development Assistance," in S. Schlemmer-Schulte and K.-Y. Tung (eds.), *Liber Amicorum Ibrahim Shihata: International Finance and Development Law* (The Hague: Kluwer Law International, 2001), pp. 753–92.

Stanton, Elizabeth, *The Human Development Index: A History*: Political economy research institute working paper series no. 127 (University of Massachusetts Amherst, 2007).

Steiger, Heinhard, "Solidarität und Souveränität oder Vattel reconsidered," in H. Steiger (ed.), *Von der Staatengesellschaft zur Weltrepublik?* (Baden-Baden: Nomos, 2009), pp. 133–41.

(ed.), *Von der Staatengesellschaft zur Weltrepublik?* (Baden-Baden: Nomos, 2009).

Steinberg, Rudolf, "Evaluation als neue Form der Kontrolle final programmierten Verwaltungshandelns," *Der Staat*, 15 (1976), 185–210.

Stern, Nicholas and Ferreira, Francisco, "The World Bank as 'Intellectual Actor'," in D. Kapur, J. P. Lewis and R. Webb (eds.), *The World Bank: Its First Half Century*, II (Washington, DC: Brookings Institution Press, 1997), pp. 523–610.

Stewart, Frances and Deneulin, Severine, "Amartya Sen's Contribution to Development Thinking," *Studies in Comparative International Development*, 37 (2002), 61–70.

Stewart, Richard, "US Administrative Law: A Model for Global Administrative Law?" *Law and Contemporary Problems*, 68 (2005), 63–104.

Stockhausen, Joachim von, *Theorie und Politik der Entwicklungszusammenarbeit: Eine Einführung in die deutsche bilaterale Entwicklungszusammenarbeit* (Munich: Weltforum Verlag, 1986).

Stockmann, Reinhard, "Administrative Probleme staatlicher Entwicklungszusammenarbeit," in M. Glagow (ed.), *Deutsche und internationale Entwicklungspolitik: Zur Rolle staatlicher, supranationaler und nicht-regierungsabhängiger Organisationen im Entwicklungsprozeß der Dritten Welt* (Opladen: Westdeutscher Verlag, 1990), pp. 35–75.

Stokke, Olav (ed.), *Aid and Political Conditionality*, EADI Studies in Development (London, Portland: Frank Cass, 1995), vol. XVI.

The UN and Development: From Aid to Cooperation (Indiana University Press, 2009).

Streeten, Paul and Burki, Shahid Javed, *First Things First: Meeting Basic Human Needs in Developing Countries* (New York: Oxford University Press, 1981).

Streinz, Rudolf (ed.), *EUV/EGV Kommentar* (Munich: C.H. Beck, 2003).

Suzuki, Eisuke, "Regional Development Banks," in R. Wolfrum (ed.), *Max Planck Encyclopedia of Public International Law [online edition]* (Oxford University Press, 2008–). Available at www.mpepil.com (last visited April 2013).

Svensson, Jakob, "Foreign Aid and Rent-Seeking," *Journal of International Economics*, 51 (2000), 437–61.

Sydow, Gernot, "Der Europäische Auswärtige Dienst," *Juristenzeitung*, 66 (2011), 6–12.

Syz, John, *International Development Banks* (New York: Oceana Publications, 1974).

Talmon, Stefan, "Participation of UN Member States in the Work of the Organization: A Multicultural Alternative to Present-Day Regionalism?" in S. Yee and J.-Y. Morin (eds.), *Multiculturalism And International Law: Essays in Honour of Edward McWhinney* (Leiden, Boston: Martinus Nijhoff Publishers, 2009), pp. 239–75.

Tan, Celine, "Regulation and Resource Dependency: The Legal and Political Aspects of Structural Adjustment Programmes," in D. Bradlow and D. B. Hunter (eds.), *International Financial Institutions and International Law* (Alphen aan den Rijn: Kluwer Law International, 2010), pp. 167–97.

Taylor, Ian, "India's Rise in Africa," *International Affairs*, 88 (2012), 779–98.

Terhechte, Jörg Philipp, *OPEC und europäisches Wettbewerbsrecht: Zugleich ein Beitrag zum Phänomen der Fragmentierung des internationalen Wirtschaftsrechts* (Baden-Baden: Nomos, 2008).

(ed.), *Verwaltungsrecht der Europäischen Union: Zur Ausdifferenzierung und Globalisierung der europäischen Verwaltungsrechtsordnung* (Baden-Baden: Nomos, 2010).

Tetzlaff, Rainer, *Die Weltbank: Machtinstrument der USA oder Hilfe für die Entwicklungsländer* (Munich: Weltforum Verlag, 1980).

(ed.), *Menschenrechte und Entwicklung* (Bonn: Stiftung Entwicklung und Frieden, 1993).

Weltbank und Währungsfonds: Gestalter der Bretton-Woods-Ära (Opladen: Leske und Budrich, 1996).

Teubner, Gunther, "Altera Pars Audiatur: Law in the Collision of Discourses," in R. Rawlings (ed.), *Law, Society, and Economy: Centenary Essays for the London School of Economics and Political Science, 1895–1995* (Oxford University Press, 1997), pp. 149–76.

Theobald, Christian, "Die Weltbank: Good Governance und die Neue Institutionenökonomik," *Verwaltungsarchiv*, 89 (1998), 467–87.

Thieme, Werner, *Verwaltungslehre*, 4th edn (Cologne: Heymann, 1984).

Thomas, Chantal and Trachtman, Joel P. (eds.), *Developing Countries in the WTO Legal System* (Oxford University Press, 2009).

Thürer, Daniel and Burri, Thomas, "Self-Determination," in R. Wolfrum (ed.), *Max Planck Encyclopedia of Public International Law* [online edition] (Oxford

University Press, 2008–). Available at www.mpepil.com (last visited April 2013).
Thym, Daniel, "Auswärtige Gewalt," in A. von Bogdandy and J. Bast (eds.), *Europäisches Verfassungsrecht*, 2nd edn (Heidelberg: Springer, 2009), pp. 441–88.
Tietje, Christian, *Internationalisiertes Verwaltungshandeln* (Berlin: Duncker & Humblot, 2001).
"Internationales Wirtschaftsrecht und Recht auf Entwicklung als Elemente einer konstitutionalisierten globalen Friedensordnung," in K. Dicke, S. Hobe, K.-U. Meyn, A. Peters, E. Riedel, H.-J. Schütz and C. Tietje (eds.), *Weltinnenrecht: Liber amicorum Jost Delbrück* (Berlin: Duncker & Humblot, 2005), pp. 783–813.
Todaro, Michael P. and Smith, Stephen C., *Economic Development*, 10th edn (Harlow: Addison Wesley, 2009).
Tomasevski, Katarina, *Development Aid and Human Rights* (London: Pinter, 1989).
Tomuschat, Christian, "Die Charta der wirtschaftlichen Rechte und Pflichten der Staaten: Zur Gestaltungskraft von Deklarationen der UN-Generalversammlung," *Heidelberg Journal of International Law*, 36 (1976), 444–90.
"Das Recht auf Entwicklung," *German Yearbook of International Law*, 25 (1982), 85–112.
"Neuformulierung der Grundregeln des Völkerrechts durch die Vereinten Nationen: Bewegung, Stillstand oder Rückschritt?" *Europa-Archiv*, 38 (1983), 729–38.
"§172: Die staatsrechtliche Entscheidung für die internationale Offenheit," in J. Isensee and P. Kirchhof (eds.), *Normativität und Schutz der Verfassung – Internationale Beziehungen*, Handbuch des Staatsrechts der Bundesrepublik Deutschland (Heidelberg: C.F. Müller, 1992), vol. VII, pp. 483–523.
(ed.), *Modern Law of Self-Determination* (Dordrecht: Nijhoff, 1993).
"Ensuring the Survival of Mankind on the Eve of a New Century," *Recueil des Cours*, 281 (1999), 9–438.
"Art. 281 EGV," in H. von der Groeben and J. Schwarze (eds.), *Vertrag über die Europäische Union und Vertrag über die Gründung der Europäischen Gemeinschaft*. Kommentar, 6th edn, IV (Baden-Baden: Nomos, 2003).
Toye, John, *Dilemmas of Development: Reflections on the Counter-Revolution in Development Theory and Policy* (Oxford: Basil Blackwell, 1987).
Tran, Mark, *China Pulls out of Aid Partnership*, The *Guardian*, November 29, 2011. Available at www.guardian.co.uk/world/2011/nov/29/china-pulls-out-aid-partnership-busan (last visited July 2013).
Trebilcock, Michael J. and Daniels, Ronald J., *Rule of Law Reform and Development: Charting the Fragile Path of Progress* (Cheltenham: Edward Elgar, 2008).
Trubek, David, "The 'Rule of Law' in Development Assistance: Past, Present and Future," in D. Trubek and A. Santos (eds.), *The New Law and Economic*

Development: A Critical Appraisal (Cambridge, New York: Cambridge University Press, 2006), pp. 74–94.

"Toward a Social Theory of Law: An Essay on the Study of Law and Development," *Yale Law Journal*, 82 (1972), 1–50.

Trubek, David and Galanter, Marc, "Scholars in Self-Estrangement: Some Reflections on the Crisis in Law and Development Studies in the United States," *Wisconsin Law Review*, 55 (1974), 1062–101.

Trubek, David and Santos, Alvaros (eds.), *The New Law and Economic Development: A Critical Appraisal* (Cambridge University Press, 2006).

Trute, Hans-Heinrich, Denkhaus, Wolfgang and Kühlers, Doris, "Governance in der Verwaltungsrechtswissenschaft," *Die Verwaltung*, 37 (2004), 451–73.

Trute, Hans-Heinrich, Groß, Thomas, Möllers, Christoph and Röhl, Hans Christian (eds.), *Allgemeines Verwaltungsrecht – zur Tragfähigkeit eines Konzepts*, Festschrift für Eberhard Schmidt-Aßmann (Tübingen: Mohr Siebeck, 2008).

Tsai, Mary C., "Globalization and Conditionality: Two Sides of the Sovereignty Coin," *Law and Policy in International Business*, 31 (2000), 1317–29.

Tudyka, Kurt, *Gesellschaftliche Interessen und Auswärtige Beziehungen* (Katholieke Universiteit Nijmegen, 1978).

Tulloch, Peter, *The Seven Outside: Commonwealth's Asia Trade With The Enlarged EEC* (London: Overseas Development Institute, 1973).

Twining, William, "The Diffusion of Law," *Journal of Comparative Law*, 1 (2006), 237–60.

Twomey, Patrick, "Human Rights-Based Approaches to Development," in M. A. Baderin and R. McCorquodale (eds.), *Economic, Social and Cultural Rights in Action* (Oxford University Press, 2007), pp. 45–70.

Uerpmann-Wittzack, Robert, "Völkerrechtliche Verfassungselemente," in A. von Bogdandy and J. Bast (eds.), *Europäisches Verfassungsrecht*, 2nd edn (Heidelberg: Springer, 2009), pp. 177–226.

United Nations, *The Human Rights Based Approach to Development Co-operation: Towards a Common Understanding Among UN Agencies*. Available at www.undg.org/archive_docs/6959The_Human_Rights_Based_Approach_to_Development_Cooperation_Towards_a_Common_Understanding_among_UN.pdf (last visited July 2013).

United Nations Development Programme, *Human Development Report 2010: The Real Wealth of Nations – Pathways to Human Development*. (New York: Palgrave Macmillan).

Human Development Report 1990 (New York: Oxford University Press, 1990).

Uvin, Peter, *Human Rights and Development* (Bloomfield: Kumarian, 2004).

van de Walle, Nicolas, "Aid's Crisis of Legitimacy: Current Proposals and Future Prospects," *African Affairs*, 98 (1999), 337–52.

African Economies and the Politics of Permanent Crisis (Cambridge University Press, 2001).

van Waeyenberge, Elisa, "Accountability at the World Bank," *Development and Change*, 43 (2012), 615–21.

Vanhoonacker, Sophie and Reslow, Natasja, "The European External Action Service: Living Forwards by Understanding Backwards," *European Foreign Affairs Review*, 15 (2010), 1–18.

Vaughn, Robert, "Transparency in the Administration of Laws: The Relationship Between Differing Justifications for Transparency and Differing Views of Administrative Law," *American University International Law Review*, 26 (2011), 969–82.

Verdirame, Guglielmo, "The Definition of Developing Countries under GATT and Other International Law," *German Yearbook of International Law*, 39 (1996), 164–97.

Virally, Michel, (ed.), *Le droit international en devenir: Un Instrument de la Coopération Technique Multilatérale* (Paris: Presses universitaires de France, 1990).

"La Notion de Programme," in M. Virally (ed.), *Le droit international en devenir: Un Instrument de la Coopération Technique Multilatérale* (Paris: Presses universitaires de France, 1990), pp. 427–46.

"Vers un droit international du développement," *Annuaires français de droit international*, 11 (1965), 3–12.

Voigt, Stefan, *Institutionenökonomik* (Munich: W. Fink Verlag, 2002).

Wadrzyk, Marc, "Is It Appropriate for the World Bank to Promote Democratic Standards in a Borrowing Country?" *Wisconsin International Law Journal*, 17 (1999), 553–77.

Wahl, Rainer, *Rechtsfragen der Landesplanung und Landesentwicklung, Band I* (Berlin: Duncker & Humblot, 1978).

Walker, Neil (ed.), *Sovereignty in Transition* (Oxford: Hart Publishing, 2003).

Waller, Peter P., "Aid and Conditionality," in O. Stokke (ed.), *Aid and Political Conditionality*, EADI Studies in Development (London, Portland: Frank Cass, 1995), vol. XVI, pp. 110–28.

Walz, Julie and Ramachandran, Vijaya, *Brave New World: A Literature Review of Emerging Donors and the Changing Nature of Foreign Assistance*, Center for Global Development, Working Paper 273 (2011). Available at www.cgdev.org/files/1425691_file_Walz_Ramachandran_Brave_New_World_FINAL.pdf (last visited July 2013).

Walzer, Michael, *Spheres of Justice: A Defense of Pluralism and Equality* (New York: Basic Books, 1983).

(ed.), *Toward a Global Civil Society* (New York, Oxford: Berghahn Books, 1995).

Warbrick, Colin, "The Principle of Sovereign Equality," in V. Lowe and C. Warbrick (eds.), *The United Nations and the Principles of International Law: Essays in Memory of Michael Akehurst* (London, New York: Routledge, 1994), pp. 204–29.

Watal, Jayashree, *Intellectual Property Rights in the WTO and Developing Countries* (London, The Hague, Boston: Kluwer Law International, 2001).

Weber, Hermann, "Der Anspruch auf Entwicklungshilfe und die Veränderungen des internationalen Wirtschaftsrechts," *Verfassung und Recht in Übersee*, 11 (1978), 5–25.

Weber, Steven, "Origins of the European Bank for Reconstruction and Development," *International Organization*, 48 (1994), 1–38.

Weiland, Heribert, Wehr, Ingrid and Seifert, Matthias (eds.), *Good Governance in der Sackgasse?* (Baden-Baden: Nomos, 2009).

Weiner, Myron E. (ed.), *Modernization: The Dynamics of Growth* (New York: Basic Books, 1966).

Weiß, Norman, *Kompetenzlehre Internationaler Organisationen* (Heidelberg: Springer, 2009).

Weiss, Stefani and Schmierer, Joscha (eds.), *Prekäre Staatlichkeit und internationale Ordnung* (Wiesbaden: Verlag für Sozialwissenschaften, 2007).

Wet, Erika de, "Holding International Institutions Accountable: The Complementary Role of Non-Judicial Oversight Mechanisms and Judicial Review," in A. von Bogdandy, R. Wolfrum, J. von Bernstorff, P. Dann and M. Goldmann (eds.), *The Exercise of Public Authority by International Institutions: Advancing International Institutional Law* (Heidelberg: Springer, 2010), pp. 855–82.

White, John, *German Aid: A Survey of Sources, Policy and Structures of German Aid* (London: Overseas Development Institute, 1965).

Whitfield, Lindsay (ed.), *The Politics of Aid: African Strategies for Dealing with Donors* (Oxford University Press, 2009).

Whitfield, Lindsay and Fraser, Alastair, "Introduction: Aid and Sovereignty," in L. Whitfield (ed.), *The Politics of Aid: African Strategies for Dealing with Donors* (Oxford University Press, 2009), pp. 1–26.

Whittle, Dennis and Kuraishi, Mari, "Competing with Central Planning," in W. Easterly (ed.), *Reinventing Foreign Aid* (Cambridge: MIT Press, 2008), pp. 461–84.

Wiegand, Gerd, *Organisatorische Aspekte der internationalen Verwaltung von Entwicklungshilfe: Ein Beitrag zur Organisationsanalyse internationaler Organisationen am Beispiel des UNDP und der Weltbank* (Berlin: Duncker & Humblot, 1978).

Wiemann Jürgen, *Die Neuausrichtung der Entwicklungspolitik der Bundesländer vor dem Hintergrund der veränderten internationalen Rahmenbedingungen*, Discussion Paper No. 20. Available at www.die-gdi.de/CMS-Homepage/openwebcms3.nsf/%28ynDK_contentByKey%29/ANES-7KQGGC/$FILE/DP%2020.2008.%20Wiemann.pdf (last visited July 2013).

Williams, David, "Aid and Sovereignty: Quasi-States and the International Financial Institutions," *Review of International Studies*, 26 (2000), 557–73.

Williamson, John, *What Washington Means by Policy Reform in Latin American Adjustment* (Washington, DC: Institute for International Economics, 1990).

Williamson, Oliver E., "The Economics of Governance: Framework and Implications," *Zeitschrift für die gesamte Staatswissenschaft*, 140 (1984), 195–223.

Williamson, Tim, "General Budget Support and Public Financial Management Reform," in S. Koeberle, Z. Stavreski and J. Walliser (eds.), *Budget Support As More Effective Aid?* (Washington, DC: World Bank Publications, 2006), pp. 139–53.

Wischmeyer, Thomas, "Europäische Entwicklungszusammenarbeit und evolutionärer Kompetenzbegriff: Urteilsbesprechung von EuGH C-91/05 und C-403/05," *Verfassung und Recht in Übersee*, 41 (2008), 407–12.

Wolfrum, Rüdiger, "Neue Elemente im Willensbildungsprozeß internationaler Wirtschaftsorganisationen," *Vereinte Nationen*, 29 (1981), 50–6.

"Means of Ensuring Compliance with and Enforcement of International Environmental Law," *Recueil des Cours*, 272 (1998 (1999)), 9–154.

"The Protection of Indigenous People in International Law," *Heidelberg Journal of International Law*, 59 (1999), 369–83.

"Solidarity Amongst States: An Emerging Structural Principle of International Law," in P.-M. Dupuy (ed.), *Völkerrecht als Wertordnung*. Festschrift für Christian Tomuschat (Kehl: Norbert P. Engel, 2006), pp. 1087–101.

(ed.), *Max Planck Encyclopedia of Public International Law* [online edition] (Oxford University Press, 2008–). Available at www.mpepil.com (last visited April 2013).

Wolfrum, Rüdiger and Kojima, Chie (eds.), *Solidarity: A Structural Principle of International Law* (Heidelberg: Springer, 2010).

Woods, Ngaire, "Making the IMF and the World Bank More Accountable," *International Affairs*, 77 (2001), 83–101.

"The Shifting Politics of Foreign Aid," *International Affairs*, 81 (2005), 393–409.

The Globalizers: The IMF, the World Bank, and Their Borrowers (Ithaca: Cornell University Press, 2006).

"Whose Aid?: Whose Influence? China, Emerging Donors and the Silent Revolution in Development Assistance," *International Affairs*, 84 (2008), 1205–21.

World Bank, *2011 World Development Report: Conflict, Security and Development* (Washington, DC, 2011).

Doing Business: Making a Difference for Entrepreneurs (Washington, DC: World Bank Publications, 2011).

A Guide to the World Bank (Washington, DC: World Bank Publications, 2003).

Making Sustainable Commitments: An Environment Strategy for the World Bank (Washington, DC: World Bank Publications, 2001).

Pollution Prevention and Abatement Handbook: Toward Cleaner Production (Washington, DC: World Bank Publications, 1998).

Sub-Saharan Africa: From Crisis to Sustainable Growth (Washington, DC: World Bank Publications, 1989).

Towards Greater Transparency Through Access to Information: The World Bank's Disclosure Policy (Washington, DC: World Bank Publications, 2009).

The World Bank Policy on Access to Information (Washington, DC: World Bank Publications, 2010).

Xu, Jiajun, *The Anatomy of China's Influence on the International Development Finance System*, RCCPB Working Paper No. 28 (2012).

Yee, Sienho and Morin, Jacques-Yvan (eds.), *Multiculturalism and International Law: Essays in honour of Edward McWhinney* (Leiden, Boston: Martinus Nijhoff Publishers, 2009).

Yokota, Yozo, "Non-Political Character of the World Bank," *Japanese Annual International Law*, 2 (1976), 39–64.

Young, Robert James Craig, *Postcolonialism: A Very Short Introduction* (Oxford University Press, 2003).

Zacher, Hans F., "Horizontaler und vertikaler Sozialrechtsvergleich," in B. von Baron Maydell and E. Eichenhofer (eds.), *Abhandlungen zum Sozialrecht* (Heidelberg: C.F. Müller, 1993), pp. 377–430.

Zakaria, Fareed, "The Rise of the Rest," *Daily Beast*, May 3, 2008 (2008). Available at www.thedailybeast.com/newsweek/2008/05/03/the-rise-of-the-rest.html (last visited July 2013).

Zammit Cutajar, Michael (ed.), *UNCTAD and the North-South-Dialogue* (Oxford: Pergamon Press, 1985).

Zemanek, Karl and Ginther, Konrad (eds.), *Völkerrecht zwischen normativem Anspruch und politischer Realität: Festschrift für Karl Zemanek zum 65. Geburtstag* (Berlin: Duncker & Humblot, 1994).

Ziai, Aram, "The Ambivalence of Post-Development: Between Reactionary Populism and Radical Democracy," *Third World Quarterly*, 25 (2004), 1045–61.

Exploring Post-Development: Theory and Practice, Problems and Perspectives (London: Routledge, 2007).

Zilla, Claudia and Harig, Christoph, *Brasilien als "Emerging Donor": Politische Distanz und operative Nähe zu den traditionallen Gebern*, German Institute for International and Security Affairs – SWP-Studie S 07/2012 (2012). Available at www.swp-berlin.org/fileadmin/contents/products/studien/2012_S07_zll_harig.pdf (last visited July 2013).

Zimmermann, Andreas, "Art. 179 EGV," in H. von der Groeben and J. Schwarze (eds.), *Vertrag über die Europäische Union und Vertrag über die Gründung der Europäischen Gemeinschaft*. Kommentar, 6th edn, IV (Baden-Baden: Nomos, 2003).

Zimmermann, Felix and Smith, Kimberley, "More Actors, More Money, More Ideas for International Development Cooperation," *Journal of International Development*, 23 (2011), 722–38.

INDEX

For EU product safety concerns, contact us at Calle de José Abascal, 56–1°,
28003 Madrid, Spain or eugpsr@cambridge.org.

www.ingramcontent.com/pod-product-compliance
Lightning Source LLC
LaVergne TN
LVHW012024041026
849558LV00003B/143

* 9 7 8 1 1 0 7 0 2 0 2 9 0 *